Advances in Crowdfunding

Rotem Shneor • Liang Zhao
Bjørn-Tore Flåten
Editors

Advances in Crowdfunding

Research and Practice

palgrave
macmillan

Editors
Rotem Shneor
School of Business and Law
University of Agder
Kristiansand, Norway

Liang Zhao
School of Business and Law
University of Agder
Kristiansand, Norway

Bjørn-Tore Flåten
School of Business and Law
University of Agder
Kristiansand, Norway

ISBN 978-3-030-46308-3 ISBN 978-3-030-46309-0 (eBook)
https://doi.org/10.1007/978-3-030-46309-0

This Palgrave Macmillan imprint is published by the registered company Springer Nature Switzerland AG.
The registered company address is: Gewerbestrasse 11, 6330 Cham, Switzerland

In loving memory of Prof. Andreas Wyller Falkenberg, an inspirational friend, colleague, and mentor.

Acknowledgements

The authors are grateful for the support of the University of Agder's Library grant for Open Access Publications, as well as the management of the University of Agder's School of Business and Law for their unequivocal and generous support in making this book project a reality.

Contents

Notes on Contributors

Prince Baah-Peprah is a doctoral research fellow at the University of Agder's (UiA) School of Business and Law and a member of the Crowdfunding Research Centre at UiA. He holds a master's degree in International Management from UiA. His research interests lie in marketing strategies in crowdfunding while examining regional and contextual heterogeneities. He currently focuses on how the involvement of experts in the development stage of crowdfunding campaigns reduces risk and enhance project success. Based on his background in management, accounting and finance, he has previously researched entrepreneurial financing and private equity investment in emerging markets.

Daniel Berliner is a doctoral research fellow at the Crowdfunding Research Centre at the University of Agder, Norway. His research interests include investor decisions, crowdfunding and alternative financing, especially in the context of high-technology new ventures. His PhD research focuses on entrepreneurship and alternative financing models. Previous to his PhD studies, he acquired extensive experience working with various high-technology Israeli ventures in the field of branding and strategy.

Wanxiang Cai is a doctoral research fellow at Utrecht University School of Economics (U.S.E.). He holds an MSc in Business Administration from Chongqing University (CQU), School of Economics and Business Administration. In his research Wanxiang analyses to what extent and how social capital and formal institutions affect individual crowdfunding campaigns, transaction volumes on platforms and the development of the financial crowdfunding market. Wanxiang is also affiliated with the European Centre for Alternative Finance. His work has been presented at leading conferences in the field of entrepreneurial finance.

Emmanuel James Chao is currently a senior lecturer and a head of resource and incubation centre at Mzumbe University-Tanzania. Further, he is the founder and chair of the annual International Conference of Business and Management in Emerging Markets (ICBMEM) and an associate researcher at the Centre for Crowdfunding Research at the University of Agder. He holds a PhD in International Management and MSc in International Business from the University of Agder in Norway. He has published in a wide variety of international outlets such as *International Business Research*, *Journal of Global Marketing*, *Journal of Business to Business Relations*, *Journal of Knowledge Management and Practice* among others.

Natalia Drozdova is a doctoral research fellow at NHH, Norwegian School of Economics, where she earlier graduated with a master's degree in International Business. Natalia's research interests include crowdfunding, sharing economy, collaborative consumption and online movements.

Kalanit Efrat is Senior Lecturer of International Business, Marketing and Entrepreneurship at the Ruppin Academic Centre, Israel. Her research interests include international small and medium enterprises (SMEs), collaborative strategies, information and knowledge-based capabilities and crowdfunding. Her articles were published in the *Journal of World Business*, *Technovation*, *International Marketing Review*, *International Business Review* and *Journal of Business Research* among others.

Bjørn-Tore Flåten is an associate professor at the University of Agder School of Business and Law. He holds a PhD in International Management from UiA and an MSc from the Norwegian School of Economics. His research interests revolve around strategic management of knowledge work and entrepreneurship, with focus on knowledge sharing and internet-enabled collaboration within and beyond the boundaries of the firm. Flåten has contributed with book chapters to research-focused edited books, as well as published in journals such as *Information and Organization*, *Journal of e-Business* and the *Norwegian Journal of Geography*. Currently, Flåten is serving as the head of Department of Management and as the Vice Dean of the School of Business and Law. Flåten is also heading the university's Centre for Entrepreneurship. Through the centre, Flåten has also launched UiA Innovation, whose objective is commercialization of research from faculty and students.

Shaked Gilboa is a Senior Lecturer of Customer Experience, Organizational Development and Human Resource Management at the Ruppin Academic Centre, Israel. Her research interests include customer experience among mall shoppers, small businesses' customers, city residents and crowdfunding's creators and backers. Her articles were published in the *European Journal of Marketing*, *Journal of Retailing and Consumer Services*, *Cities* and *International Business Review* among others.

Paul Griffiths is the academic director of postgrads in Banking and Fintech at the EM Normandie Business School. Prior to becoming a full-time academic, Paul spent many years in leadership positions at global management consulting firms, serving boards of blue-chip companies, particularly in the financial services sector. He specializes in management of intangible assets such as intellectual capital and related technologies such as artificial intelligence and Fintech. Having lived and worked in multiple countries, he defines himself as multicultural. Paul brings to his lectures the hands-on experience of having started up from scratch consulting firms in eight countries. His interests in research bridge across the fields of Fintech and knowledge management and the development of knowledge networks, particularly in banking. He holds a master's degree in engineering, has been a Humphrey Fellow (Fulbright Commission) at the University of Minnesota and holds a doctorate in business administration. He is a prolific writer in professional and academic publications and a renowned speaker at conferences and seminars.

Aki Kallio holds LLM degree from the University of Helsinki and currently serves as the Managing Compliance Officer (Corporates &

Institutions, C&I) at the Danske Bank A/S Finland Branch. Kallio is a member of Extended Group Compliance, C&I Compliance and C&I Finland Management Teams. Previously Kallio worked as a Ministerial Adviser in the Financial Markets Department of the Ministry of Finance of Finland (being responsible, among others, for drafting and entering into force the Finnish Crowdfunding Act and acting as a co-head of the Financial Market Department's Fintech—expert group). In addition, he acted as a Finnish representative of the European Commission's informal expert group—"European Crowdfunding Stakeholder Forum (ECSF)". He is also a co-author of first published book on crowdfunding and fintech in Finland (in Finnish: *Joukkorahoitus*,). Prior to joining the Ministry of Finance of Finland he worked for two leading Finnish law firms and as a corporate counsel.

Yuanqing Li is Assistant Professor of Entrepreneurship at Dominican University. She graduated with a Doctor of Philosophy in Business Administration (Entrepreneurship Focus) from the University of Texas Rio Grande Valley (UTRGV). Her undergraduate degree in English Education (Henan Normal University, 2010) and master's degrees in both Teaching Chinese to Speakers of Other Languages (Minzu University of China, 2012) and Management (MBA UTRGV, 2015) have prepared her to teach and conduct research in diverse interests (including entrepreneurship especially in crowdfunding, cross-cultural communication and organizational behaviour).

Anna Lukkarinen is a postdoctoral researcher at Aalto University School of Science in Finland. Her research interests lie in equity crowdfunding, entrepreneurial finance and new ventures. She currently focuses on developing an improved understanding of investor behaviour and decision making in equity crowdfunding, which she does in close collaboration with crowdfunding practitioners. With work background in management consulting at McKinsey & Company and investment banking at Citigroup, she strongly believes in the mutual benefit potential of fostering linkages between academia and the industry.

Natalia Maehle is an associate professor at the Western Norway University of Applied Sciences, Mohn Centre for Innovation and

Regional Development. She holds a PhD from NHH, Norwegian School of Economics. Maehle's research interests include digital business models, innovation, consumer behaviour and branding. She is currently leading a Norwegian part of the international research project supported by the Horizon 2020 ERA-net Cofund SUSFOOD2. Maehle also leads several work packages in an international research project on crowdfunding. She has an excellent track record of publications in the highly ranked international peer-reviewed journals.

Ziaul Haque Munim is Associate Professor of Maritime Logistics at the University of South-Eastern Norway. His research interests include maritime economics and logistics, supply chain management and international business. He holds a PhD in International Management from the University of Agder and an MSc in Supply Chain Management from the Vienna University of Economics and Business. His publications have appeared in leading journals such as the *Journal of Business Research, Asia Pacific Journal of Management, Resources, Conservation & Recycling* and others. He received the Best Paper Award at the IAME 2016 conference and the Young Researcher Best Paper Award at the IAME 2018 conference.

Ana Odorović is a PhD research fellow in the Graduate School in Law and Economics at the University of Hamburg in Germany. Her thesis deals with the question of overcoming asymmetric information in the crowdfunding market from a law and economics perspective. She is also a research affiliate at the Cambridge Centre for Alternative Finance. In 2018, she was a visiting researcher at the University of Oxford. She holds an LLM degree in business law from the Panthéon-Assas University (Paris 2) and a master's degree in economics from the University of Belgrade, where she also teaches economics at the Law school.

Pia Piroschka Otte is a senior researcher at Ruralis, Institute for Rural and Regional Research. In addition, she works as a researcher at NTNU Sustainability within the climate change cluster. Pia has an interdisciplinary background with a PhD in Political Science and a master's degree in Development Studies from NTNU. Her work focuses on social science research addressing energy transitions, climate change and rural/urban development. She is currently leading an international research project that tests the feasibility of offsetting CO_2 emissions from transport through crowdfunding of climate-friendly technologies on local farms.

Stine Øyna is an associate professor at The School of Business and Law, University of Agder, Norway. She holds a PhD in International Business from the same university. Her research interests lie in the intersection between international business and entrepreneurship, with a current focus on born globals, internationalizing SMEs and entrepreneurship education. She has publications in journals such as *International Business Review* and *International Studies of Management and Organization*. She received the Lazaridis Institute SMEs & International Entrepreneurship Best Paper Prize at the EIBA 2018 conference.

Friedemann Polzin is an assistant professor at Utrecht University School of Economics (U.S.E.), Sustainable Finance Lab (SFL) and European Centre for Alternative Finance (ECAF). He holds a PhD from EBS Business School and an MSc in Business Administration from the University of Jena. Friedemann investigates the financing of innovation and entrepreneurship as well as corresponding sources such as banking, venture capital or crowdfunding. Another part of his research looks at the policy environment required for a transition towards a green economy. His work has been published in major innovation, entrepreneurship and sustainability journals.

Anders Rykkja is a doctoral research fellow at the Inland Norway University of Applied Sciences. He holds an MA in Music Business Management from the University of Westminster. Anders currently works on his doctoral thesis, which is on the emergence, adoption and usage of cultural crowdfunding as a supplemental financing mechanism in the cultural and creative industries. Over the last few years as a team member of Knowledge Works, the Norwegian knowledge centre for the cultural and creative industries, he has published reports on a variety of topics, including music industry export, festivals and cultural policy intervention schemes.

Sunghan Ryu is an assistant professor in USC-SJTU Institute of Cultural and Creative Industry at Shanghai Jiao Tong University. He holds a PhD in IT management from the College of Business, KAIST. His research interests include IT innovations in cultural and creative domains and effective information systems applications in the entrepreneurial context. His current research interests revolve around crowdfunding and other alternative finance practices. His works appeared in academic journals including *Journal of Strategic Information Systems*, *Electronic Markets* and *Electronic Commerce Research & Applications* and were presented at prestigious conferences such as ICIS and HICSS.

Priscilla Serwaah is a doctoral research fellow at the School of Business and Law, University of Agder. She previously worked as a teaching assistant at the Kwame Nkrumah University of Science and Technology (KNUST), Ghana. During her master's at the University of Agder, she worked as a consultant for Mechatronics Innovation Laboratory (MIL), located in Grimstad. Her research focuses on entrepreneurial/alternative finance and gender dynamics in crowdfunding.

Rotem Shneor is an associate professor at the University of Agder's School of Business and Law and serves as the academic director of the university's Centre of Entrepreneurship, as well as the founder and head of the university's Crowdfunding Research Centre. He holds a PhD in International Management from UiA and a master's degree from the Norwegian School of Economics (NHH). He established the Nordic Crowdfunding Alliance of platforms, co-founded and currently serves on the board of the Norwegian Crowdfunding Association. In addition, he is serving as an affiliate researcher at the Cambridge University Centre for Alternative Finance and is a co-author to its annual reports. His research covers crowdfunding success, behaviour and motivations, internet marketing and cognitive aspects of entrepreneurship. He has a record of fifteen years in teaching, researching and supporting entrepreneurship. He has published in academic journals (including *JBR*, *ERD*, *IJOEM*, *CCM*, *BJM*, *JPBM*, *EEP*, and *JPM*), trade magazines, as well as contributed several chapters to research-focused edited books and textbooks.

Erik Stam is Professor of Strategy, Organization & Entrepreneurship at Utrecht University School of Economics (U.S.E.). He holds a PhD and MSc from Utrecht University. His research lies in the intersection of economics, geography and government policy and is one of the world's leading scholars in entrepreneurship. Erik has co-authored more than 50 academic articles, edited and contributed to numerous books. He is affiliated with several universities around the global and he also regularly consults governments and entrepreneurship organizations.

Krishnamurthy Suresh is an academic associate at the Indian Institute of Management (IIM), Bangalore, India. He is also a research associate at the Cambridge Centre for Alternative Finance (CCAF), University of Cambridge Judge Business School. He has authored three alternative finance industry reports with CCAF. His research interests lie in the areas of small and medium enterprise (SME) financing, crowdfunding, new and alternative financing models for start-ups and SMEs, as well as regulatory frameworks. He is currently pursuing his PhD from India and was a visiting fellow (Pavate) at the University of Cambridge Judge Business School (CJBS).

Stina Torjesen is an associate professor at the University of Agder's School of Business and Law, where she teaches courses in Business Ethics. Stina holds an MPhil and DPhil in International Relations from the University of Oxford. She served previously as a senior research fellow at the Norwegian Institute of International Affairs and worked for the United Nations in Kazakhstan. She has also worked as a project manager in the sustainability consultancy SIGLA. Her publications include contributions to edited books volumes and articles in academic journals (e.g. *IJSD*, *CSD*, *CAS*, etc.).

Lasse Vuola holds LLM from the University of Lapland and California, Berkeley, and MSc from the University of Jyväskylä. He is serving as CEO and co-founder of the Finnish loan-based crowdfunding platform Fundu Ltd, which employs approximately 20 people in Finland. He is also a co-author of the first published book on crowdfunding and fintech in Finland (in Finnish: *Joukkorahoitus*). Vuola has also worked as a lawyer for many years in Finland's largest business law firm, most recently employed by a law firm Castrén & Snellman Oy. In addition, he has invested in several start-up companies and implemented many cooperation projects with start-up and growth companies, providing him with comprehensive understanding of practical corporate finance bottlenecks.

Karsten Wenzlaff is a PhD research fellow and lecturer in Crowdfunding and Alternative Finance in the Chair for Digital Markets at the University of Hamburg in Germany. He is the co-author of the Alternative Finance Benchmarking Report of the Centre for Alternative Finance at the University of Cambridge and a research affiliate in the European Centre for Alternative Finance at the University of Utrecht. His research focus is alternative finance, corporate crowdfunding and civic crowdfunding, self-regulation of FinTechs and Fintech ecosystems. Karsten has been an expert to the Committee on the Digital Agenda of the German Parliament.

Bryan Zheng Zhang is the co-founder and executive director of the Cambridge Centre for Alternative Finance at the Judge Business School, University of Cambridge. His research examines the accumulation and allocation of capital for start-ups and SMEs through alternative circuits of finance in a geographical and comparative context. Since 2013, Bryan has led and co-authored some of the most influential industry reports on the state of alternative finance both at national and international levels. He has advised and collaborated with numerous institutions and organizations including the Financial Conduct Authority, the British Business Bank, the Department of International Development, the European Commission, the World Bank, Oxfam and Unilever. He is also a research fellow in Finance at Cambridge Judge Business School and a senior fellow at the Financial Innovation Lab. Bryan was trained in economic geography and public policy at Cambridge and Oxford Universities.

Liang Zhao is a postdoc research fellow at the University of Agder's School of Business and Law. He is also a research fellow in China's Public Sector Economy Research Centre (CPSERC) and China-Israel Entrepreneurship and Innovation Centre (CIEIC) at Jilin University in China. In addition, he was an affiliate researcher at the Cambridge University Centre for Alternative Finance. Dr. Liang studies innovation and entrepreneurship, with a special emphasis on reward-based crowdfunding. His research interests include the interactive mechanism of crowdfunding platforms, backers and entrepreneurs; e-trust and backer behaviour; crowdfunding community formation and marketing of crowdfunding campaigns. His research output includes journal articles, book chapters and industry reports. Besides, He also writes popular articles for global FinTech web media such as Crowdfund Insider and Techfoliance. He received his PhD from Amsterdam Business School at the University of Amsterdam in the Netherlands and his cum laude bachelor and master's degrees from Jilin University in China.

Tania Ziegler is the lead in Global Benchmarking at the Cambridge Centre for Alternative Finance (CCAF) and manages the centre's alternative finance benchmarking programme which spans Europe, the Americas, Asia Pacific and the Middle East and Africa. She has authored more than a dozen industry reports since joining the CCAF. She is an expert in SME finance and leads the Centre's work on SME Access to Finance in Latin America. She holds an MSc from the London School of Economics (LSE) and a BA from Loyola College in Maryland. Tania is a 2010 Fulbright Scholar and has spent a period at the International University of Business and Economics in Beijing, China.

List of Figures

List of Tables

1

Introduction: From Fundamentals to Advances in Crowdfunding Research and Practice

Rotem Shneor, Liang Zhao, and Bjørn-Tore Flåten

Crowdfunding is a method to obtain money from large audiences, where each individual provides a small amount, instead of raising large sums from a small group of sophisticated investors (Belleflamme et al. 2014). Such pooling of contributions from multiple backers (Short et al. 2017) is done via the Internet, and often without standard financial intermediaries (Mollick 2014). This phenomenon finds its origin in the application of crowdsourcing principles to the practices of fundraising while creating new community-enabled financing channels (Schwienbacher and Larralde 2012) for a wide variety of projects including commercial, cultural, humanitarian, social, political, environmental, and technological projects to name a few.

What started initially as sporadic independent fundraising initiatives, has transferred into a proliferation of crowdfunding-dedicated platforms, which served as market makers bringing fundraisers and funders to interact via a common trusted system. Indeed, research on the state of the

R. Shneor (✉) • L. Zhao • B.-T. Flåten
School of Business and Law, University of Agder, Kristiansand, Norway
e-mail: rotem.shneor@uia.no; liang.zhao@uia.no; bjorn-tore.flaten@uia.no

R. Shneor et al. (eds.), *Advances in Crowdfunding*,
https://doi.org/10.1007/978-3-030-46309-0_1

global industry, based on data collected from over a thousand platforms, shows that in 2017 global alternative finance volumes (covering all crowdfunding models) reached USD 371 billion, growing by 42% from 2016 volumes (Ziegler et al. 2019). Furthermore, when excluding the unique context of China, global volumes have grown by 28% from USD 47 billion in 2016 to USD 60 billion in 2017, growing by a further 48% to USD 89 billion in 2018 (Ziegler et al. 2020).

However, the term "crowdfunding" is an umbrella term reflecting a wide variety of fundraising models. At the most basic of levels, these models can be distinguished by their underlying logic either intermediating investments or non-investment financing. Thus far, research and practice have distinguished between four core models, including crowd-lending, equity, reward, and donation crowdfunding (Mollick 2014; Belleflamme et al. 2014). The first two capture the dominant investment types of models, and the latter the dominant non-investment types of models. Later in the book, we provide a detailed overview of crowdfunding models in use, their characteristics and unique aspects.

However, for introductory purposes one can highlight the four core models by building on the definitions provided by the Cambridge University Centre for Alternative Finance (hereafter "CCAF") in its annual reports (e.g. Ziegler et al. 2019): (1) *Crowd-lending* is when individual or institutional backers provide loans to borrowers while expecting the repayment of the principle and a set interest within a predefined timeframe. (2) *Equity crowdfunding* refers to backers buying an ownership stake in an organization. (3) *Reward crowdfunding* means that backers provide funding in exchange for non-monetary rewards, most frequently in the form of pre-purchased products or services. And, (4) *donation crowdfunding* is a provision of funding based on philanthropic or civic motivations without expectation of material rewards.

In this chapter, we introduce the fundamental concepts and dynamics of crowdfunding, which will serve as a common understanding for the discussions in the remaining chapters of this book. Here we present the key stakeholders in crowdfunding engagements, as well as the crowdfunding process and stages. This is followed by a brief introduction to each of the book's chapters while highlighting their main insights and contributions.

Crowdfunding Stakeholders

At the core of crowdfunding practice lies an expectation for a "win-win" game, where all parties enjoy various benefits from their involvement in the process, as highlighted in Fig. 1.1. The three main parties to crowdfunding transactions include the fundraiser, the backer, and the platform. Accordingly, in the context of crowdfunding, a *Fundraiser* can be defined as any individual or organization that makes a public call for the financing of project(s) with particular purpose(s). Literature has referred to them as either "fundraisers" (e.g. Wang et al. 2018), "creators" (e.g. Ryu and Kim 2018), or "campaigners" (e.g. Hobbs et al. 2016). Successful fundraisers may reap benefits from the money received, as well as from market validation outcomes that arise from wide public acceptance and support, establishing relations with prospective customers, engaging in cost-efficient marketing promotions, as well as collecting feedback that may inform further product development efforts (Frydrych et al. 2014; Thürridl and Kamleitner 2016; Wald et al. 2019).

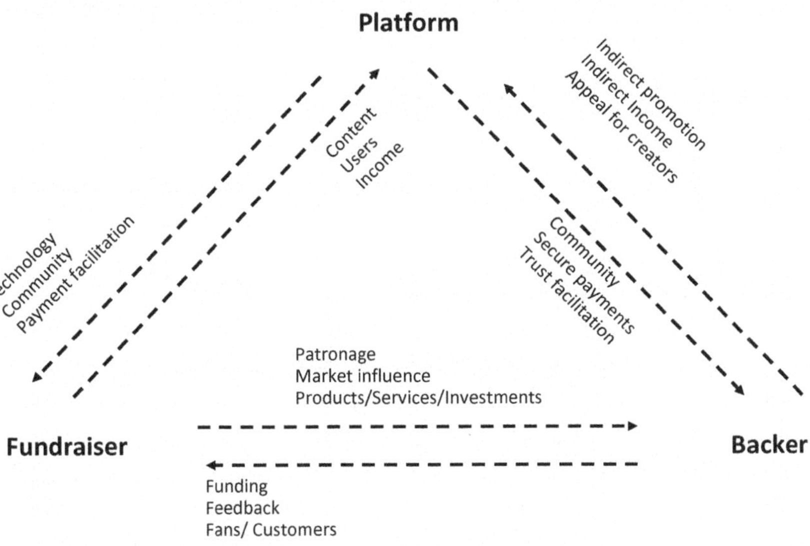

Fig. 1.1 Win-win dynamics in crowdfunding

Similarly, in the context of crowdfunding, a *Backer* can be defined as any individual or organization that provides finance while answering a public call for the financing of project(s) with particular purpose(s). Literature has labelled this group inconsistently as either "backers" (e.g. Shneor and Munim 2019), "funders" (e.g. Kang et al. 2016), "supporters" (e.g. Gerber and Hui 2013), as well as "donors" in donation crowdfunding (e.g. Carvajal et al. 2012), "sponsors" in reward crowdfunding (e.g. Ryu and Kim 2016), "investors" in equity and lending crowdfunding (e.g. Dorfleitner et al. 2018), as well as "lenders" in crowd-lending (e.g. Chemin and de Laat 2013). In terms of benefits from crowdfunding engagements, backers enhance their levels of customer empowerment by influencing the design of future market products, as well as their own future consumption opportunities, while strengthening their sense of belonging to certain groups and communities (Chaney 2019; Gerber et al. 2012; Steigenberger 2017).

A crowdfunding platform is defined as an Internet application linking fundraisers and their potential backers while facilitating the exchanges between them in accordance with pre-specified conditions (Shneor and Flåten 2015). Such intermediaries make their income in forms of campaign success fees and payments for supporting services (Belleflamme et al. 2015). However, at the same time, with each successful campaign completed, their own reputation is enhanced while making them more attractive facilitators for future fundraising initiatives and contribution behaviour. Furthermore, each campaign helps the platform build its own user base (Thies et al. 2018), both in terms of attracting new fundraisers, as well as expanding the value of new users that registered for the purpose of supporting a specific campaign, and converting them into prospective funders of future campaigns as well.

An additional stakeholder, namely the public authorities, while not directly involved in each transaction, do carry great influence on the way the industry develops, and how each party to the crowdfunding transaction interacts with the other. More specifically, regulation sets the rules under which different models of crowdfunding may be practiced by defining compliance requirements primarily aimed at consumer and investor protection. However, at the same time, authorities also have vested interests in supporting new channels for the financing of small and medium sized businesses in their jurisdictions (as job creators and tax payers), as well as enabling greater public contributions to civic, cultural, educational, and environmental initiatives that may align with government policies and agenda. Research here has both theorized about (Kshetri 2015) and empirically showed a clear positive association between perceived adequacy of national crowdfunding regulation and crowdfunding volumes per capita both globally and regionally (Ziegler et al. 2019, 2020).

The Crowdfunding Process

Crowdfunding is not a quick or short-term activity and involves a process with multiple stages, requiring different activities and focus. One earlier conceptualization of this process has identified two stages relevant for backers, including pre-investment and post-investment (Macht and Weatherston 2015). Pre-investment involves due-diligence efforts and investment decision making based on relevant motivations. The post-investment stage relates to additional involvement of backers in a project at later stages either in value adding activities, or additional investments. From a fundraiser perspective, earlier conceptualization referred to three stages simply defined as before, during, and after the campaign (Gerber and Hui 2013).

Taking into consideration additional insights that have emerged in recent years, we propose a more detailed process model including seven distinct stages that while corresponding with earlier conceptualization, do provide some additional clarity. Figure 1.2 presents the three core stages and their sub-stages, while listing related activities fundraisers should engage in during these stages. In this respect, the suggested model represents both descriptive and normative aspects of best practice that fundraisers are encouraged to follow for enhancing the likelihood of their success.

First, before the campaign is formally published and open for money collection, fundraisers usually should engage in (1) *campaign planning*. During this stage, the objectives and goals of the campaign are defined, different platforms are evaluated, one is chosen, campaign materials such

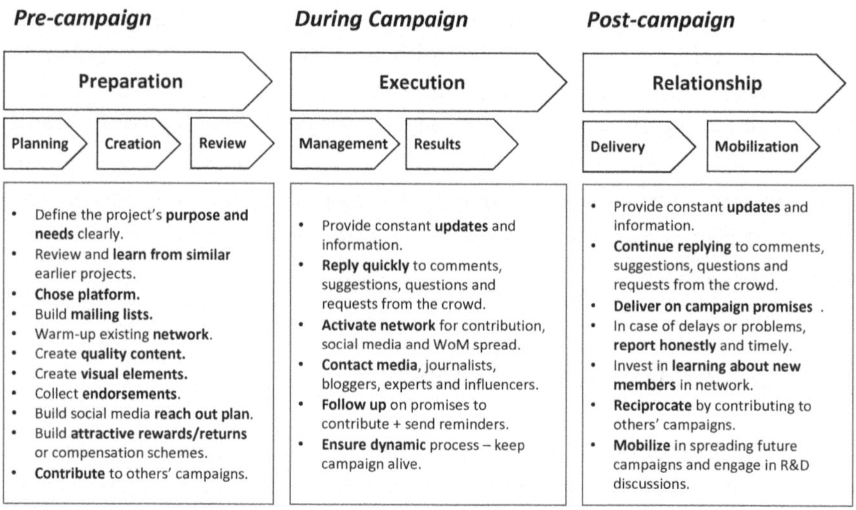

Fig. 1.2 The crowdfunding campaign process

as texts and visual media elements are prepared, promotional strategies are devised, and an execution plan with action points and deadlines can be outlined. Next, fundraisers engage in (2) *campaign creation*—where materials are uploaded to the selected platform, presence in social media is established (e.g. Facebook page, Instagram page, Twitter account, etc.), and initial feedback is collected from first pilot viewers. Lastly, the (3) *campaign review* takes place when the submitted materials are reviewed by platform operators, which ensures compliance with regulation, verification of fundraiser identity, and in some cases quality of the materials provided. When meeting requirements, the platform then approves the campaign for publication, its information is made publicly available, and the collection of funding is enabled.

Second, once approved, the campaign is live and during a set period defined for the campaign, fundraisers engage in (4) *campaign management* which includes promotional efforts both offline and online, and especially via social media platforms, mobilization of network relations takes place, and new information and updates are gradually provided to fans and followers. At this stage, fundraisers need to focus on availability and responsiveness to comments, suggestions, and questions from the crowd for signalling trustworthiness as well as avoiding the loss of prospective contributors. In this sense, during this stage, the backers' decision-making process is both triggered and supported.

This phase ends when the campaign reaches its end date, and (5) *campaign results* are finalized. The results may vary by the scheme under which the campaign was run (Cumming et al. 2019). Campaigns which ran under the "all-or-nothing" schemes are paid out to fundraisers after deduction of platform fees only if they met the minimum stated sum goal. If this goal was not met, payments made are returned to the backers that made them. Campaigns which ran under "keep-it-all" schemes are paid out to fundraisers after deduction of platform fees regardless of whether they have met their minimum stated goals or not. While the former models are relevant for non-investment crowdfunding models, in the case of investment models only the "all-or-nothing" scheme is available. However, some platforms allow campaigns to publish a range rather than a specific sum goal, but in such cases the sum which defines the minimum threshold of the range applies as the basis for "all-or-nothing" pay-out to campaigners.

Finally, once the campaign is finished, a post-campaign stage unfolds. During this period fundraisers must first (6) *deliver on campaign promises* in sending promised products, services, or information, pay back loans with stated interest, or inform investors about firm growth and finances in case of equity investments. In case changes occur to original plans that were specified in campaigns, and informed financial contribution decisions by backers, fundraisers need to honestly inform their backers about such changes and their implications in terms of delays or when surpassing expectations by meeting goals earlier than planned. Furthermore, the backers constitute a network of supporters the fundraisers can and should (7) *develop further relations* with. Such backers are assets that can be mobilized and tapped into in future activities, may they be additional rounds of fundraising or business development activities such as spreading promotional campaigns, or engagement in product development initiatives. In this context, research indeed shows that fundraiser track record and experience can lead to the creation of social capital that supports additional successful fundraising in following campaigns, however it does have its limitations and depreciates over time if excessively used (Butticè et al. 2017).

Towards Advances in Crowdfunding Research and Practice

During the past decade interest in crowdfunding among academic scholars has increased dramatically. Indeed, research has been identified as one of the key pillars that can support both industry development and policy making (De Buysere et al. 2012). An initial mapping of core themes in early crowdfunding research (Moritz and Block 2016) has identified several streams of inquiry including: analyses of fundraisers' motivations to adopt crowdfunding, the determinants of successful crowdfunding campaigns, legal compliance, and challenges primarily with respect to investment crowdfunding models, factors impacting backer behaviour, the role of social networks in crowdfunding, applications of signalling theory in crowdfunding, as well as typologies of crowdfunding models. Here, while initial strides have been made, various authors have suggested that a gap between the available research on crowdfunding (Short et al. 2017) and the increasing academic and public interest in it (Martínez-Climent et al. 2018) remains wide. Lists outlining relevant directions for future research opportunities have been outlined in several literature reviews (e.g. McKenny et al. 2017; Moritz and Block 2016; Shneor and Vik 2020).

Accordingly, in this book, we aim to contribute to improved understanding of crowdfunding by both taking stock of existing knowledge, as well as presenting new aspects and insights that help us advance it. The book includes contributions from a wide range of influential authors and thought leaders from across the globe, representing a range of significant research institutions. In the remainder of this chapter we provide a brief overview of each of the chapters to follow while highlighting their main contributions.

In the first chapter, *Shneor* unravels the diversity of models through which crowdfunding manifests itself. He does so by laying a detailed review of the characteristics of the different crowdfunding models currently in use, as well as the key premises for the use of each. Furthermore, he suggests some of the first frameworks developed for guiding prospective fundraisers in choosing between models. Each of the frameworks is designed for a different type of fundraisers may they be organizations or consumers. In this respect, he provides a useful tool for guiding relevant decision making by practitioners, and at the same time presents a framework that can be tested and fine-tuned in research about such decision making.

In Chap. 2, *Ziegler and colleagues* take a macro level view on crowdfunding market development dynamics and present insights from research on the factors impacting such development trajectories highlighting the roles of economic development, adequate regulation, and IT infrastructure, among others. They present facts and figures from national and regional markets in a comparative manner, while accounting for the diversity of crowdfunding models, growth trajectories, and geographical variations. The chapter shows that crowdfunding is no longer a fringe activity but gradually moving mainstream with substantial volumes recorded nationally, regionally, and globally. Furthermore, it illustrates the dominance of crowd-lending models across regions, as well as their sub-model variations within regions.

The following four chapters examine each of the core models in greater detail. Chapter 3 picks up from the previous chapter and delves deeper into the understanding of the crowd-lending variant of crowdfunding. Here, *Ziegler & Shneor* present the brief history of crowdlending, its diversity of models, the current state of the industry, as well as the underlying mechanisms and principles guiding platform operations including risk assessment and the matching of borrowers and lenders. These discussions are supported with evidence from recent research and highlights the benefits and risks for both lenders and borrowers while assessing the industry development vis-à-vis earlier practices via traditional financial institutions.

In Chap. 4, *Lukkarinen* provides a review of research on equity crowdfunding. She describes the typical equity crowdfunding process, investor characteristics, and investor motivations. Recognizing the limited due diligence efforts of the crowd, Lukkarinen refers to the role of platforms in evaluating and preselecting target ventures. She highlights the importance of rapidly observable campaign features and signals of venture quality in investor decision making, while also emphasizing the relevance of experienced investors and the herding tendency of crowd investors. These discussions are supplemented by a comparison of equity crowdfunding investors with traditional providers of early-stage equity financing enhancing our understanding of the commonalities and differences among these groups of investors.

In Chap. 5, *Zhao & Ryu* present the reward-based crowdfunding model and its unique aspects. This discussion is based on a four-dimensional framework of the crowdfunding process accounting for the fundraisers, the backers, the campaigns, and the platforms. In addition, the development of reward-based crowdfunding is reviewed in a comparative manner across different global regions, highlighting regional variances in terms of developing trends, R&D priorities, female participation, internationalization of platforms, and risks involved. This is supplemented by a literature review of the academic research with a focus on the two main research streams of campaign success drivers, as well as consumer behaviour in reward crowdfunding.

Next, in Chap. 6, *Zhao & Shneor* address the current state and particularities of donation-based crowdfunding, as primarily driven by philanthropic motivations without expectation of monetary or material rewards. In this model intrinsic motivations dominate, and a form of impure altruism characterizes backers that seek satisfaction, joy, and sense of belonging to be achieved with their donations. They suggest that despite accounting for only a marginal share of global crowdfunding volumes, donation crowdfunding is a unique model for supporting a wide range of prosocial and charitable causes, while allowing fundraisers to leverage benefits afforded by ICT solutions for more effective and efficient fundraising. The chapter provides an overview of the limited research available in the context of donation crowdfunding while highlighting donor motivations and behaviour, as well as drivers of success in donation campaigns.

Once the various models are outlined in detail, and the state of both research and practice concerning each are presented, the two chapters that follow shift towards the normative view of crowdfunding. Here, in Chap. 7, *Shneor & Torjesen* present one of the first discussions of ethical issues in crowdfunding practice from multiple stakeholders' perspective. Here, the authors draw on ethical principles outlined in both classical and business-specific approaches and discuss whether crowdfunding presents an ethical solution or a source of ethical problems. To further anchor the discussion, a framework classifying potential ethical dilemmas and pitfalls in crowdfunding practice, as well as potential means for addressing them, is developed for each relevant stakeholder. This framework may both guide practitioner's practice, as well as serve as a theoretical basis for research on ethical practices in crowdfunding.

Furthermore, in Chap. 8, *Cai and colleagues* acknowledge that since financial crowdfunding involves a range of risks, it requires comprehensive governance mechanisms. In this chapter, the authors build a three-level stylized model to explain how legal institutions and social capital at the macro, meso, and micro levels affect the performance of crowdfunding campaigns and the development of the financial crowdfunding market. Such discussion results in highlighting the critical roles of platforms in enforcing laws and building social capital at both the meso and micro levels are highlighted.

In the second part of the book, readers are encouraged to take a step back in order to look forward with two chapters reviewing crowdfunding in a historical perspective. Chapter 9 examines crowdfunding development in the context of the financial industry. Here, *Kallio & Vuola* build on the view that the history of financial markets is marked by continuous fluctuations between economic cycles, which are often caused by structures that enable opportunism and moral hazards. Every crisis contains the seeds of change, but also risks for regulative overreactions. Accordingly, crowdfunding as a form of financing is part of this series of innovations in financial markets. Hence, this chapter gives a historical overview of crowdfunding as part of the history of the ever-changing modern financial markets.

A different perspective, more anchored in the historical evolution of technology, places crowdfunding in the context of Financial Technology (FinTech). Such narrative is outlined in Chap. 10, where *Griffiths* gives an overview of how the financial services sector, especially banking, was a driver for ICT development in the last quarter of the twentieth century, and early years of this century. The chapter examines the conditions that have led banks to "get their eyes off the ball" and open the window for a whole new industrial sector to emerge, namely—Fintech. Furthermore, a framework consisting of a double-entry table where one dimension is financial services functionality and the other technological applications, is suggested for helping readers understand the diversity within the industrial organization of the sector. More specifically, crowdfunding occupies two positions on the functional dimension of this framework: Alternative Finance, and Investment Opportunities.

In the third part of the book, a series of chapters geographically contextualize the crowdfunding industry development while considering relevant drivers, barriers, and growth trajectories, as well as highlighting context particularities. In Chap. 11, *Zhao & Li* discuss the unique conditions and development trends of crowdfunding in China, the world's largest crowdfunding market by far. The authors discuss crowdfunding in China from the perspectives of different stakeholders (platforms, fundraisers, funders, and regulators) and crowdfunding models (reward-based, equity-based, loan-based, and donation-based). Overall, they suggest that while the Chinese crowdfunding market has developed rapidly such development is contrasted with a reality of a relatively underdeveloped regulatory system and availability of personal credit, which are likely to limit further growth. Accordingly, some solutions for addressing these challenges are proposed in this chapter.

Chapter 12 examines crowdfunding market development in the Indian subcontinent, which represents somewhat of a contrast to rapid dynamics that characterized the Chinese crowdfunding market development. Here, *Suresh and colleagues* explore the history, ongoing activity, and future prospects of crowdfunding in the new emerging markets of India and Bangladesh. Overall, they observe that India is largely dominating the crowdfunding activity in the South Asian region, which is otherwise limited in its neighbouring countries. Such discussion highlights the social, cultural, and regulatory conditions influencing such developments.

Chapter 13 veers further afield to the African continent. Here, *Chao and colleagues* present the current state of crowdfunding research and practice in Africa while outlining opportunities and challenges associated with them. The authors suggest that the growing popularity of digital and mobile finance, low penetration of traditional financial institutions, and a long cultural heritage of communal support may enhance crowdfunding uptake in this region. On the other hand, conditions of unclear regulation, relatively low levels of Internet access, and societies characterized by low social trust may all hinder such uptake. Accordingly, African crowdfunding is at its infancy and involves transitory hybrid practices of early adoption, often involving reliance on foreign contributors via donations and pro-social lending platforms.

In Chap. 14, *Efrat and colleagues* present the crowdfunding market in Israel, representing a unique national context that despite adversities has emerged as a regional leader, as well as one of the global leaders, in terms of both general entrepreneurial finance market, and crowdfunding market in particular. The authors argue that crowdfunding has its roots deep in the Israeli entrepreneurship ecosystem. The characteristics of which include collective individualism combined with flat hierarchies, low degree of separation, mandatory army service that enforces innovative thinking and improvisation, Chutzpah, and finally high tolerance for failure, all provide fertile ground for entrepreneurship and facilitate innovative approaches to entrepreneurship funding such as crowdfunding.

Chapter 15 ventures further north and reviews the crowdfunding market in Europe, while highlighting the various facets of its fragmented nature. Here, *Wenzlaff and colleagues* present current market conditions and argue that fragmentation is mostly caused by differences in national regulations, which represent an obstacle to industry growth. At the same time, the European Union has recently introduced the European Crowdfunding Service Provider (ECSP) regime aiming towards harmonized regulations. This regime is expected to facilitate platform growth via easier cross-border transactions and international expansion of platforms operating under the business lending and equity investment models.

In part four of the book, three chapters provide insights into unique aspects of crowdfunding applications for concrete types of campaign objectives. Chapter 16 focused on using crowdfunding for financing sustainable projects, that is projects aiming to extend their goal beyond market success and provide benefit to the larger part of society. Here, *Maehle and colleagues* discuss the definition and dimensions of sustainable development and entrepreneurship. The chapter provides an overview of the existing literature on crowdfunding of sustainable projects. The authors also review four European sustainability-oriented crowdfunding platforms representing different crowdfunding models. This review reveals that sustainable projects have rather high success rates in crowdfunding and may address important dimensions of sustainable development. And while the environmental dimension gets the most attention, pro-social crowdlending seems to have the highest success rates. Hence, the focus on a certain sustainability dimension may influence the choice of the crowdfunding model employed.

Chapter 17 discussed crowdfunding applications in the cultural industries. In this chapter, *Rykkja and colleagues* trace the early adoption of crowdfunding by cultural industries to a comprehensive value chain reconfiguration in the cultural sector, which were triggered by the advent of digitalization on the one hand and the downsizing in public funds in many countries on the other. The authors highlight the importance of studying crowdfunding in the cultural sector, as it presses creators to strike a balance between the commercial and the non-commercial, the economic and the cultural outcomes, as well as the authentic and independent versus the mass dictated and dependent. Accordingly, they review earlier research on cultural crowdfunding, identify core themes that attracted research attention, and outline an agenda for future research.

In Chap. 18, *Wenzlaff* discusses civic crowdfunding, as when crowdfunding campaigns are used for funding the creation or provision of a semi-public good. Unlike other crowdfunding practices, civic crowdfunding creates benefits for people outside of the group of supporters as well. Such a situation creates unique dilemmas as well as motivations for participation. This chapter analyses the literature on civic crowdfunding and proposes to view this through four perspectives: the project, the supporter, the project owner, and the platform. The chapter argues that the platform is central to understanding the self-positioning of projects, supporters, and project owners within civic crowdfunding.

Finally, the concluding fifth part of the book includes two chapters addressing future considerations for crowdfunding research and practice. Chapter 19 highlights the importance of education about crowdfunding highlighting both its benefits and advantages, as well as its risks and challenges. Here, *Shneor & Flåten* argue on the need for crowdfunding education, and present a concrete program developed at the University of Agder as a credit awarding course named the "UiA Crowdfunding Lab". This chapter outlines course objectives, content, pedagogy, and assessment issues, while presenting opportunities for further development.

The book concludes with Chap. 20 which is dedicated to a critical reflection on current crowdfunding research and practice. Here, *Shneor and colleagues* present eight dilemmas that are expected to influence and shape the future of crowdfunding. Each of which is critically discussed and followed by suggestions for future research. These dilemmas include (1) the need to strike a balance between idealism and pragmatism; (2) the extent to which crowdfunding platforms should cooperate with traditional financial institutions; (3) how should we measure crowdfunding success and performance in both financial and socio-economic terms; (4) the need to strike a balance between quantity and quality in campaigns approved for publication on platforms; (5) understanding the conditions and implications of domestic versus international growth of crowdfunding platforms; (6) the responsibility of manoeuvring between facilitation of collective decisions as crowd wisdom while avoiding crowd madness, as well as intentional and unintentional harmful crowd behaviour; (7) whether should platforms focus their technological development on efficiency gains versus community support; as well as (8) how to best inform the public through educational efforts without constraining our understanding of the crowdfunding phenomenon too early.

At this stage, we wish to express our gratitude to all contributors, and invite readers to explore the rest of the book in greater detail.

References

Belleflamme, P., Lambert, T., & Schwienbacher, A. (2014). Crowdfunding: Tapping the Right Crowd. *Journal of Business Venturing, 29*(5), 585–609.

Belleflamme, P., Omrani, N., & Peitz, M. (2015). The Economics of Crowdfunding Platforms. *Information Economics and Policy, 33*, 11–28.

Butticè, V., Colombo, M. G., & Wright, M. (2017). Serial Crowdfunding, Social Capital, and Project Success. *Entrepreneurship Theory and Practice, 41*(2), 183–207.

Carvajal, M., García-Avilés, J. A., & González, J. L. (2012). Crowdfunding and Non-profit Media. *Journalism Practice, 6*(5-6), 638–647.

Chaney, D. (2019). A Principal–Agent Perspective on Consumer Co-production: Crowdfunding and the Redefinition of Consumer Power. *Technological Forecasting and Social Change, 141*, 74–84.

Chemin, M., & de Laat, J. (2013). Can Warm Glow Alleviate Credit Market Failures? Evidence from Online Peer-to-Peer Lenders. *Economic Development and Cultural Change, 61*(4), 825–858.

Cumming, D. J., Leboeuf, G., & Schwienbacher, A. (2019). Crowdfunding Models: Keep-It-All vs. All-Or-Nothing. *Financial Management,* https://doi.org/10.1111/fima.12262

De Buysere, K., Gajda, O., Kleverlaan, R., et al. (2012). A Framework for European Crowdfunding. Retrieved from https://www.fundraisingschool.it/wp-content/uploads/2013/02/European-Crowdfunding-Framework-Oct-2012.pdf.

Dorfleitner, G., Hornuf, L., & Weber, M. (2018). Dynamics of Investor Communication in Equity Crowdfunding. *Electronic Markets, 28*(4), 523–540.

Frydrych, D., Bock, A. J., Kinder, T., et al. (2014). Exploring Entrepreneurial Legitimacy in Reward-Based Crowdfunding. *Venture Capital, 16*(3), 247–269.

Gerber, E. M., & Hui, J. (2013). Crowdfunding: Motivations and Deterrents for Participation. *ACM Transactions on Computer-Human Interaction, 20*(6), 1–32.

Gerber, E. M., Hui, J. S., & Kuo, P.-Y. (2012). Crowdfunding: Why People Are Motivated to Post and Fund Projects on Crowdfunding Platforms. Retrieved from http://www.juliehui.org/wp-content/uploads/2013/04/CSCW_Crowdfunding_Final.pdf.

Hobbs, J., Grigore, G., & Molesworth, M. (2016). Success in the Management of Crowdfunding Projects in the Creative Industries. *Internet Research, 26*(1), 146–166.

Kang, M., Gao, Y., Wang, T., et al. (2016). Understanding the Determinants of Funders' Investment Intentions on Crowdfunding Platforms: A Trust-Based Perspective. *Industrial Management & Data Systems, 116*(8), 1800–1819.

Kshetri, N. (2015). Success of Crowd-Based Online Technology in Fundraising: An Institutional Perspective. *Journal of International Management, 21*(2), 100–116.

Macht, S. A., & Weatherston, J. (2015). Academic Research on Crowdfunders: What's Been Done and What's to Come? *Strategic Change, 24*(2), 191–205.

Martínez-Climent, C., Zorio-Grima, A., & Ribeiro-Soriano, D. (2018). Financial Return Crowdfunding: Literature Review and Bibliometric Analysis. *International Entrepreneurship and Management Journal, 14*(3), 527–553.

McKenny, A. F., Allison, T. H., Ketchen, D. J., et al. (2017). How Should Crowdfunding Research Evolve? A Survey of the Entrepreneurship Theory and Practice Editorial Board. *Entrepreneurship Theory and Practice, 41*(2), 291–304.

Mollick, E. (2014). The Dynamics of Crowdfunding: An Exploratory Study. *Journal of Business Venturing, 29*(1), 1–16.

Moritz, A., & Block, J. H. (2016). Crowdfunding: A Literature Review and Research Directions. In D. Bruntje & O. Gajda (Eds.), *Crowdfunding in Europe: State of the Art in Theory and Practice*. London: Springer.

Ryu, S., & Kim, Y.-G. (2016). A Typology of Crowdfunding Sponsors: Birds of a Feather Flock Together? *Electronic Commerce Research and Applications, 16*, 43–54.

Ryu, S., & Kim, Y.-G. (2018). Money Is Not Everything: A Typology of Crowdfunding Project Creators. *The Journal of Strategic Information Systems, 27*(4), 350–368.

Schwienbacher, A., & Larralde, B. (2012). Crowdfunding of Small Entrepreneurial Ventures. In D. Cumming (Ed.), *The Oxford Handbook of Entrepreneurial Finance*. New York, NY: Oxford University Press.

Shneor, R., & Flåten, B.-T. (2015). Opportunities for Entrepreneurial Development and Growth Through Online Communities, Collaboration, and Value Creating and Co-creating Activities. In H. R. Kaufmann & S. M. R. Shams (Eds.), *Entrepreneurial Challenges in the 21st Century*. Basingstoke: Palgrave Macmillan.

Shneor, R., & Munim, Z. H. (2019). Reward Crowdfunding Contribution as Planned Behaviour: An Extended Framework. *Journal of Business Research, 103*, 56–70.

Shneor, R., & Vik, A. A. (2020). Crowdfunding Success: A Systematic Literature Review 2010–2017. *Baltic Journal of Management, 15*(2), 149–182.

Short, J. C., Ketchen, D. J., McKenny, A. F., Allison, T. H., & Ireland, R. D. (2017). Research on Crowdfunding: Reviewing the (Very Recent) Past and Celebrating the Present. *Entrepreneurship Theory and Practice, 41*(2), 149–160.

Steigenberger, N. (2017). Why Supporters Contribute to Reward-Based Crowdfunding. *International Journal of Entrepreneurial Behavior & Research, 23*(2), 336–353.

Thies, F., Wessel, M., & Benlian, A. (2018). Network Effects on Crowdfunding Platforms: Exploring the Implications of Relaxing Input Control. *Information Systems Journal, 28*(6), 1239–1262.

Thürridl, C., & Kamleitner, B. (2016). What Goes Around Comes Around? Rewards as Startegic Assets in Crowdfunding. *California Management Review, 58*(2), 88–110.

Wald, A., Holmesland, M., & Efrat, K. (2019). It Is Not All About Money: Obtaining Additional Benefits Through Equity Crowdfunding. *The Journal of Entrepreneurship, 28*(2), 270–294.

Wang, T., Liu, X., Kang, M., et al. (2018). Exploring the Determinants of Fundraisers' Voluntary Information Disclosure on Crowdfunding Platforms: A Risk-Perception Perspective. *Online Information Review, 42*(3), 324–342.

Ziegler, T., Shneor, R., Wenzlaff, K., et al. (2019). *Shifting Paradigms—The 4th European Alternative Finance Benchmarking Report.* Cambridge: Cambridge Centre for Alternative Finance.

Ziegler, T., Shneor, R., Wenzlaff, K., et al. (2020). *The Global Alternative Finance Benchmarking Report.* Cambridge, UK: Cambridge Centre for Alternative Finance.

Part I

The Current State of Crowdfunding

2

Crowdfunding Models, Strategies, and Choices Between Them

Rotem Shneor

Introduction

During the last decade, the emergence and growing popularity of crowdfunding were manifested and promoted through the proliferation of thousands of online crowdfunding platforms worldwide. A crowdfunding platform is "an internet application bringing together project owners and their potential backers, as well as facilitating exchanges between them, according to a variety of business models" (Shneor and Flåten 2015, p. 188). According to Méric et al. (2016) most platforms have the following characteristics in common: first, providing fundraisers with campaign presentation formats for their project, which is accessible to all online users; second, allowing small to medium sized financial transactions that enable widespread participation while keeping risks within reasonable limit; and, third, provide relevant financial information about

R. Shneor (✉)
School of Business and Law, University of Agder, Kristiansand, Norway
e-mail: rotem.shneor@uia.no

R. Shneor et al. (eds.), *Advances in Crowdfunding*,
https://doi.org/10.1007/978-3-030-46309-0_2

the campaign and its progress, as well as communication tools for interaction between prospective backers and fundraisers. In addition, some platforms also provide advice, social media PR functionalities, as well as referrals to other supporting services (ibid.).

The operation of platforms is overseen by regulation in each national jurisdiction (Gajda 2017). In addition, self-regulation is also evident through codes of conduct developed by industry associations for their member platforms (Wenzlaff and Odorovic 2020), as well as in rules and procedures developed by platforms themselves for own campaign approval and user verification. Nevertheless, dependency on legal compliance often results in a more constrained scope of operation both in geographical and functional terms. Here, while some platforms have developed into global giants (i.e. Kickstarter, Indiegogo, Gofundme, etc.) or regional actors (i.e. Latvia-based Mintos covering Eastern Europe, Finland-based Investor covering the Nordic countries, etc.), thus far, most platforms remain local and have a domestic focus or very limited international scope of activities (regulatory and international aspects of platform operations will be covered in greater detail in later chapters).

At this stage, it is also worth noting that in addition to platforms, crowdfunding activity also exists in the form of 'individual crowdfunding campaigns' (Belleflamme et al. 2013), which are individual- or organization-specific fundraising efforts carried outside formal platform control and oversight. However, due to the latter's sporadic nature, non-systematic approach, and limited scope within private networks, most research documents crowdfunding with respect to platform activities and not with respect to individual campaigning efforts.

In the current chapter we present crowdfunding model types and their different characteristics. This will be followed by a discussion of how fundraisers may choose the best crowdfunding model for their own project's fundraising needs. The chapter will then conclude by highlighting its main contributions, limitations, as well as implications for research and practice.

Crowdfunding Models: A Typology

Earlier studies have suggested a number of typologies for capturing the differing value propositions, practice patterns, funder motivations, risks and legal compliance needs of crowdfunding platforms (i.e. Haas et al. 2014; De Buysere et al. 2012; Méric et al. 2016; Belleflamme and Lambert 2016). We build on these earlier references but use the most-comprehensive typology currently employed by the Cambridge Centre for Alternative Finance (CCAF) in its annual industry reports (Ziegler et al. 2018b, b, d, 2019; Zhang et al. 2018) and further elaborate on it. This typology is outlined in Table 2.1.

The first model of online crowdfunding to emerge was debt-based, in what is known as peer-to-peer (P2P) or marketplace lending, with the establishment of platforms like Zopa in the UK and Prosper in the USA in 2005. In the CCAF typology, debt-based models include non-deposit taking platforms that facilitate online credit (both in the form of a secured and unsecured loan) to individuals or business borrowers from individuals or institutional investors. In this respect, the platform functions as an intermediary. In some cases, known as balance sheet lending, one can observe a departure from original conceptualization of debt-based crowdfunding, where the platform serves as the loan-provider, drawing upon funds in a dedicated platform balance-sheet. In this respect, the platform goes beyond the role of intermediary facilitating exchanges between lenders and borrowers, and actively funds and services the loan.

A unique sub-set of lending included in the above is what is referred to as 'pro-social lending', which may, but not necessarily, take the form of micro-finance. Here, pro-social lending happens when lenders evaluate prospective borrowers on both traditional financial lending criteria and prosocial, charitable criteria (Allison et al. 2015). Prosocial loans relate to either consumer or business loans and may involve high as well as low sums, while catering projects with social welfare, human development, or environmental well-being and sustainability objectives. Thus, micro-finance can be considered as a sub-set of prosocial loans specifically when loans involve small sums catering to economically disadvantaged and

Table 2.1 An extended CCAF global crowdfunding typology

Generic model		Specific model	Definition
Investment	Debt	P2P / Marketplace Consumer Lending	Individuals or institutional funders provide a loan to a consumer borrower.
		Balance Sheet Consumer Lending	The platform entity provides a loan directly to a consumer borrower.
		P2P / Marketplace Business Lending	Individuals or institutional funders provide a loan to a business borrower.
		Balance Sheet Business Lending	The platform entity provides a loan directly to a business borrower.
		P2P / Marketplace Property Lending	Individuals or institutional funders provide a loan secured against a property to a consumer or business borrower
		Balance Sheet Property Lending	The platform entity provides a loan secured against a property to a consumer or business borrower
		Micro-Finance	Individuals or institutional funders provide a low sum loan to entrepreneurs who are often economically disadvantaged and marginalized.
	Invoice trading	Invoice Trading	Individuals or institutional funders purchase invoices or receivable notes from a business at a discount.
	Equity	Equity Crowdfunding	Individuals or institutional funders purchase registered securities or equity from a business, mostly early stage firms.
		Real Estate Crowdfunding	Direct investment into a property by individuals or institutional funders, usually through the sale of a registered security or subordinated-debt financing through a special purpose vehicle (SPV).
		Debt-based Securities	Individuals or institutional funders purchase debt-based securities (typically a bond or debenture) at a fixed interest rate. Lenders receive full repayment plus interest paid at full maturity.
		Mini Bonds	Individuals or institutions purchase securities from companies in the form of unsecured retail bonds.

		Profit-sharing Crowdfunding	Individuals or institutions purchase securities from a company, such as shares or bonds, and share in the profits or royalties of the business.
		Community Shares	Individuals purchase a withdrawable share capital in cooperative and community benefit societies.
Non-investment	Reward	Reward Crowdfunding	Backers provide funding to individuals, projects or companies in exchange for non-monetary rewards or products. Most commonly in the form of pre-purchase of products prior to their production.
	Donation	Donation Crowdfunding	Donors provide funding to individuals, projects or companies based on philanthropic or civic motivations with no expectation of monetary or material benefit.
		Patronage	Donors make subscription-like payments to individuals to fund an ongoing occupation or career. Most commonly used by artists.

financially marginalized individuals aiming "to improve the well-being of the poor through better access to savings services and loans" (Schreiner 2001).

Equity-based models, including equity crowdfunding, relate to activities where individuals or institutions invest in unlisted shares or debt-based securities issued by a business, typically an SME. Here, entrepreneurs make an open call to sell a specified amount of equity or bond-like shares via the internet in the hope of attracting a large number of investors (Ahlers et al. 2015). As equity-based models have advanced, more diversified applications have emerged beyond venture funding. Here, subsets of the model like Real Estate and Property-based crowdfunding have flourished, with investors able to acquire ownership of a property asset via the purchase of property shares.

Another interesting variant of the equity model relates to community shares, also referred to as the cooperative model. Under this model, funders' investments are collected to support a community project. And while some revenue-generating community projects have the potential of repaying backers wishing to cash-in their shares, most funders are motivated by investing in their local community rather than in financial returns (Gray and Zhang 2017).

A more recent addition to the crowdfunding models has been invoice trading, which is considered as a "fast and easy way in which small and medium sized enterprises (SMEs) can raise short-term debt by pre-financing their outstanding invoices through individual or institutional investors" (Dorfleitner et al. 2017, p. 56.). Such a short-term supply of financing, in which companies sell their accounts receivables at a discount in exchange for immediate cash, helps in alleviating cash-flow challenges that often affect SMEs. Hence, unlike other crowdfunding models, this specific model is less about fundraising per se, and more about cash-flow management that is financed through crowd investments.

Finally, the reward and donation crowdfunding models, are arguably the models most commonly recognized by the public. In the case of these two models, individuals provide funding to a project, an individual, or a business without expectations of monetary returns for the funds raised. Here, while reward models often represent pre-sales of products and services, which funders expect to receive within a certain time frame, in donation, there are no tangible rewards, and funders are likely to have a sense of satisfaction from contributing to something they deem important and are passionate about. One interesting variant of donation crowdfunding captured above is patronage, which involves subscription-like payments (rather than a one-time donation) to individuals to fund an ongoing occupation or career and is of particular relevance for artists (Swords 2017), despite being relatively marginal in the overall crowdfunding sphere thus far.

While the above list of models presents a clear distinction between them, it is important to acknowledge that some platforms offer combinations of models, either as experiment or extensions of their services. These have been labelled as 'Hybrid Models' (De Buysere et al. 2012), and while not representing main stream practice, may offer extra benefits to funders and fundraisers alike. One example here may be a combination of equity and rewards campaign, where an equity investment may also incorporate special benefits for investors as consumers of the products produced by the firm that they are investing in.

In an attempt to simplify matters, and at the most basic of levels, Belleflamme and Lambert (2016) suggest a distinction between 'investment models' and 'non-investment models' defined based on the nature of compensation promised to, and expected by, funders. Accordingly, non-investment models include reward and donation crowdfunding, while investment models include lending and equity models (including royalty models such as profit or income sharing). In addition, one should add the relatively newer model of invoice trading to investment models of crowdfunding.

An additional, simple distinction between platforms is that distinguishing between two types of fundraising strategies. One, labelled as the 'all or nothing' (AON) approach, where fundraisers receive the funds raised only if the campaign has reached its stated minimum goal, otherwise funds are either returned or not charged from backers. The second, labelled as the 'take it all' (TIA) approach, where fundraisers receive the funds raised regardless of whether the campaign reached its stated minimum sum goal or not. The prevailing approach across models is the former, as it may signal greater levels of commitment and seriousness. Nevertheless, the latter is a popular approach in donation and pro-social lending, where some welfare improvement is preferable to none.

Interestingly, research examining the two approaches in the specific context of reward crowdfunding has shown that AON forces fundraisers to bear greater risk but serves as a signal of commitment, which in turn yields higher quality campaigns and greater success rates (Cumming et al. 2019b).

A different typology suggested by Haas et al. (2014), identifies three archetypes of crowdfunding intermediaries by their different value propositions—Hedonism, Altruism, and For-Profit. *Hedonism* platforms are those where backers pledge for innovative or creative products or projects with consumption in mind, all while addressing individuals' interests and sense of joy. These are mostly associated with the Reward crowdfunding model. *Altruism* platforms are those where backers pledge for a 'greater good' or 'enhanced welfare' and are mostly associated with donation or pro-social lending platforms but can also relate to community shares. *For-profit* platforms are those where backers pledge for a profit-oriented return and are associated with equity, royalty (profit sharing), and lending platforms to which one can also add invoice trading.

Nevertheless, the most popular generic classification of crowdfunding models has thus far included—equity, lending, reward and donation (Méric et al. 2016). We suggest adding invoice trading to this generic classification, as it presents a unique new model that only in recent years became significant in volumes in multiple markets, accounting for 22% of the 2017 annual crowdfunding volumes in Latin America (Ziegler et al. 2018b), 18% in the UK (Zhang et al. 2018), and 16% in mainland Europe (Ziegler et al. 2019).

Crowdfunding Models: Key Characteristics

Once the models have been defined, it is important to establish an understanding of their characteristics. Table 2.2 summarizes the key characteristics of each model while providing illustrative figures whenever available from earlier research and industry reports.

Equity models are associated with the highest levels of funds raised, while involving projects with a long time horizon and some of the highest levels of risk, although the latter remains uncertain as available data capture ventures that have entered the equity crowdfunding market at its

Table 2.2 Main crowdfunding model characteristics

	Equity	Lending	Invoice trading	Reward	Donation
Sum raised	Relatively high	Varies among sub-models	Medium	Medium	Low
Europe 2016 figures[a] (value of average campaign)	Equity CF: € 302K Real Estate: € 453K Profit Sharing: € 94K	Debt-based securities: € 275K P2P Property: € 119K P2P Business: € 111K P2P Consumer: € 6.3K	€ 27K	€ 15K	€ 4.6K
Risk	High	Low-Medium	Medium-Low	Medium	Medium
(Default rates in loans, non-delivery rates in reward)	CrowdCube (UK)—10%[b]	Lending Club (USA)—4.6%[c]; Kiva (USA/Global)—1.22%[d]; Yooly (China)—9.95%[e]; Unspecified (China)—11.56%[f]	MarketInvoice (UK)—2%[g]	Kickstarter (USA/Global)—9% Non-delivery and 75.1% delayed delivery[h] 3% Non-delivery, Fraud—0.01%[i]	N/A
Fulfillment time-horizon	Multiple years	Few months to few years	Few months to few weeks	Multiple months	Immediate/short-term
Funder benefits	Ownership of a share in firm or future revenue/profit streams Sense of patronage	Interest payment on loans Sense of patronage	Profit margins between invoice purchase sum and claim value	Consumption Sense of joy Sense of patronage	Sense of joy Sense of mission fulfilment Sense of patronage
Fundraiser benefits	Funding Market validation promotion	Funding Cash-flow remedies Market validation in business loans	Cash-flow remedies	Funding Market validation, Initial sales Initial customers Promotion	Funding Alleviating hardships Improving welfare

(*continued*)

Table 2.2 (continued)

	Equity	Lending	Invoice trading	Reward	Donation
Onboarding rates Europe 2017 figures[j] (value of average campaign)	Very Low (less than 10%)	Low in P2P Consumer, P2P business, and debt-based securities (ca. 17%-22%)	High (ca. 61%)	Medium (ca. 47%)	Very High (ca. 74%)
Successful funding Europe 2017 figures[k] (value of average campaign)	High (ca. 81%)	Low in consumer (ca. 29%) High in business (ca. 83%) Very High in debt-based securities (ca. 95%)	High (ca. 88%)	Medium (ca. 66%)	Medium (ca. 69%)

[a]Ziegler et al. (2018c)
[b]Signori and Vismara (2016)
[c]Emekter et al. (2015)
[d]Dorfleitner and Oswald (2016)
[e]Lin et al. (2017)
[f]Wang et al. (2018)
[g]Dorfleitner et al. (2017)
[h]Mollick (2015a)
[i]Cumming et al. (2019a)
[j]Ziegler et al. (2019)
[k]Ibid.

very early stages. Well-reflective of the risk levels involved, as well as strict regulations governing this model, platforms employ high levels of filtering efforts, with only a small minority of suggested projects being approved for publication and live campaigning (otherwise known as onboarding rate). However, as a result, equity models also present some of the highest success rates among campaigns approved for publication across all models.

The characteristics of lending models are more diverse based on the model employed and the target audience served. Debt-based securities involve the highest volumes raised on average per campaign, low onboarding rates, and very high success rates. On the other hand, P2P consumer lending involves relatively low sums, and despite low onboarding rates, has some of the lowest success rates across all models, as well as some of the highest recorded default rates. An exception here are micro-finance loans exhibiting some of the lowest default rates among all lending models.

Invoice trading is characterized by low default rates, relatively high onboarding, and very high success rates. This may be related to the relative novelty of the model, where platforms need to achieve legitimacy in the market, as well as the fact that transactions tend to involve relatively modest sums in a grander business financing context.

Reward crowdfunding, however, involves more modest sums and is associated with medium onboarding rates and levels of success. Here, while outright fraud is extremely rare, and non-delivery levels remain low, late delivery is a major aspect of fulfilment on reward crowdfunding campaign promises. Delays were frequently associated with either very small sums or very large sums raised (Mollick 2015b). In the former, entrepreneurs are likely to face higher costs than expected, which may delay production and delivery. And in the latter, entrepreneurs may face overfunding and high demands which generate complexities requiring more time to overcome by relatively small businesses (Hainz 2018).

Finally, donation crowdfunding is associated with the lowest sums raised per campaign on average, and is characterized by relatively high onboarding rates, and medium success rates in comparison to other models. However, being one of the least studied crowdfunding models and offering no tangible benefit in return for funds raised, it is more difficult to assess the extent of non-delivery or fraudulent activities under this model.

Fundraiser Model Choice

Once the models have been defined and outlined, and their characteristics presented, prospective fundraisers need to choose the best fitting model for their respective projects. In the current section decision-making frameworks are suggested to guide fundraisers through key considerations when making such choices, based on establishing a good fit between funding needs and each model's characteristics. In total, three frameworks are presented. Figure 2.1 presents the 'Generic Organizational Fundraiser Model Choice Framework'. Figure 2.2 presents its more elaborate version labelled as the 'Extended Organizational Fundraiser Model Choice Framework'. Here, the extended framework incorporates the generic framework. The former is provided for simplification purposes as it covers the most familiar crowdfunding models, while the latter also incorporates newer or less familiar models. In any case, the focus here is on organizations without limitations on size (from micro-entrepreneurs to large businesses) or sectoral affiliation. In addition, Fig. 2.3 presents the "Consumer Fundraiser Model Choice Framework", reflecting individuals with fundraising for non-business private consumption needs.

First, from the perspective of the organizational fundraiser, both the generic and the extended frameworks present relevant guidelines. Here,

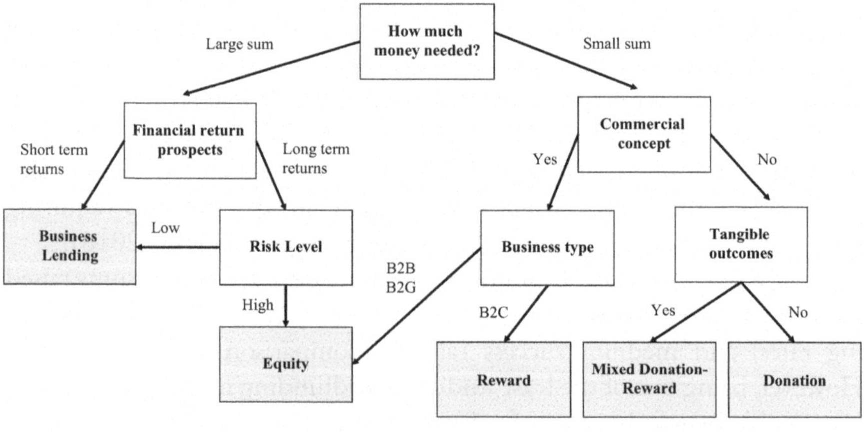

Fig. 2.1 Generic organizational fundraiser model choice framework

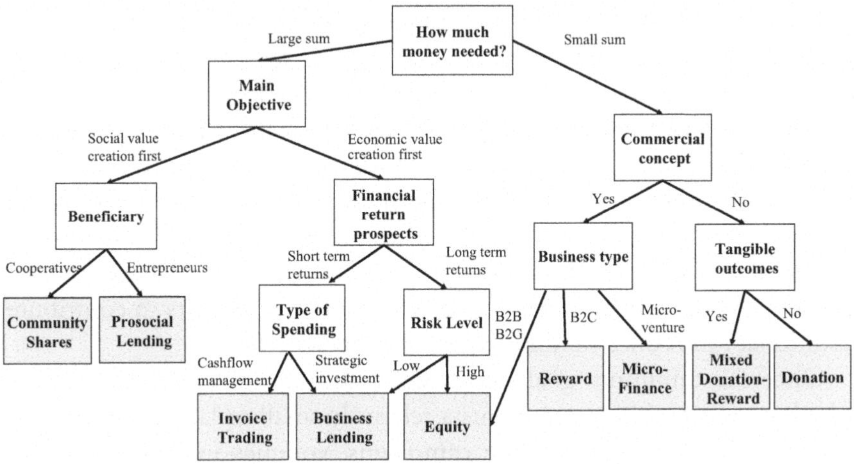

Fig. 2.2 Extended organizational fundraiser model choice framework

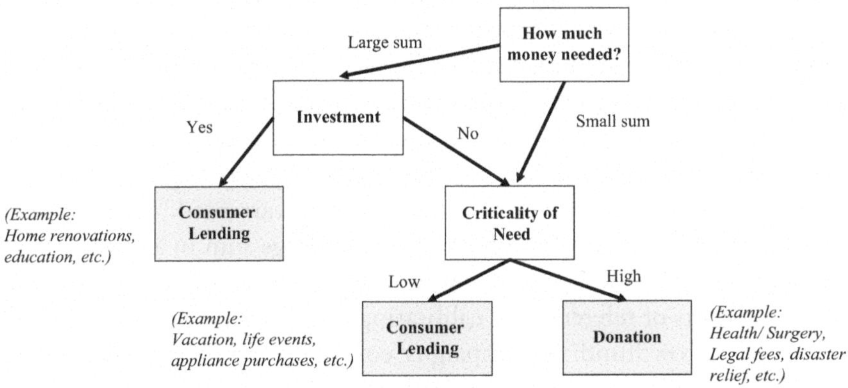

Fig. 2.3 Consumer fundraiser model choice framework

the first issue that requires addressing is an understanding of the sum needed to be raised in the campaign. Establishing such a sum should be based on a detailed project plan and budget that includes all costs expected for the execution of the project itself, the crowdfunding campaigning efforts, and a necessary buffer margin for unexpected costs. Prospective fundraisers should also consider all sources of finances necessary for project execution and the relative share of crowdfunding among these.

Furthermore, how to use the funds raised should be meticulously planned, so that it would be easier to convey what is expected to be achieved by a successful campaign in concrete terms (i.e. number of units produced, number of employees recruited, IPR protections achieved, number of people helped, etc.). Once this is clarified, fundraisers should consider defining both their minimum goals for the fundraising efforts without which the project will not be executed, as well as some 'stretch goals' referring to what can be achieved, beyond minimum goals should the project get overfunded. Specifying stretch goals helps encouraging potential backers to contribute additional funds once minimum goals have been achieved.

Once the minimum goal sum is defined, fundraisers should evaluate whether their ambition represents a relatively small or large sum in comparison to other crowdfunding campaigns' volumes in their respective national market. Such thresholds are imprecise, vary by country, and continue to change annually as the industry develops. Hence, to best understand current local dynamics, fundraisers are encouraged to both consult experts and do some research bench-marking their own goal against earlier campaigns in the same industrial sector and country during the last few years. In very rough terms, and in most countries during 2017–2018, the threshold was between $25K and $50K, where sums below this range can be regarded as relatively small, and above it as relatively large.

In this respect, some words of caution are warranted. First, understanding what constitutes relatively small and large sum in a certain context and point in time should not be considered as solid barriers, but rather as points of reference for calibrating expectations about likelihood of success. Crowdfunding campaigns constantly set new records, and higher sums under various models are being achieved. However, the more ambitious a campaign is, the riskier it is and the more likely it is to require additional campaigning efforts and resources.

Small Sum Campaigns

If the minimum goal sum that was set by the fundraiser falls within the range of relatively small sums, the next consideration is the very nature of the project to be funded. If the project is of a commercial nature, where, simply put, someone is expected to earn financially from, it is considered a business campaign. If the project is non-commercially oriented, and no one is expected to earn financially from its execution, it can be considered as a non-profit project.

Next, if the project is of a non-profit nature, the question becomes whether backers are offered tangible outcomes or benefits in the form of rewards, products or services. If no such benefits are offered, the campaigner should consider using the donation crowdfunding model. If tangible benefits are offered in a non-profit context, the fundraiser may consider a mixed reward and donation model. In such cases, funding is primarily oriented for some 'greater good' but may offer backers tangible benefits in the form of promotional goodies (e.g. caps, cups, or t-shirts promoting the project for attracting further support and funding), or products created by the individuals benefiting from the project being funded (e.g. handcraft, consumer goods, or food and drink experiences created by members of disadvantaged or marginalized social groups whose training, livelihood, or employment is created via funds raised).

However, if the project is business-oriented, the question becomes what type of products and services it is offering to produce or provide. If the products or services cater to certain segments of private consumers, in most cases the reward crowdfunding model will be recommended. Here, the fundraisers can pre-sell their products or services before incurring the costs in their actual production. Such pre-sales, through the offering of different rewards, may also help identify consumer preferences in advance in terms of design, feature inclusion, and pricing. An exception here is when the fundraiser is from an economically disadvantaged and financially marginalized background, and when the project involves a modest micro-venture with limited capacities for delivery of rewards long-distance. In such cases, online micro-finance may be the preferred crowdfunding model, and instead of products supporters can receive modest or no financial returns (which in most cases they reinvest in similar cases).

If the project is business-oriented and the products and services being crowdfunded cater to business or government customers, fundraisers should consider equity campaigning. Since industrial and institutional buyers are concerned with bulk purchases rather than individual rewards, as well as in economic viability encouraging them to contribute via equity crowdfunding may be more relevant than reward crowdfunding. Here, such buyers may enjoy both preferential rates in procurement, as well as potentially earning money indirectly from their own consumption of these products and services via holding an ownership stake in the supplier company.

Large Sum Campaigns

If the minimum goal sum that was set by the fundraiser falls within the range of relatively large sums, the next consideration is the very nature of the project to be funded. If the project funded is primarily expected to generate non-financial returns, it is considered as offering social returns. 'Social returns' is used here as an umbrella term for social, humanitarian and environmental benefits. If the project funded is primarily aimed at generating financial returns, it is considered as offering an investment opportunity.

When projects primarily offer social returns, the question becomes who the main beneficiary of such benefits is. If the project is likely to benefit a group of people with a common social mission and need (for example—village installing windmills or solar panels for resident electricity consumption), they may organize themselves as a cooperative society, while selling ownership shares in the cooperative to its prospective members. However, if the project is likely to benefit entrepreneurs creating social ventures that are primarily concerned with social returns, and financial returns represent secondary concerns, such fundraisers may consider various formats of pro-social lending (e.g. start-up for plastic collecting and recycling that employs unemployed people while cleaning up natural reserves and waterbodies).

When projects primarily offer financial returns from a pure commercial activity, the question becomes what the expected time horizon until backers receive such benefits is likely to be. If the project entails long-term investments, the question again becomes what level of risk is involved. If risks are relatively low, and sufficient cashflows from the project are highly likely, the fundraising venture should consider using a business lending model. However, if risks are relatively high, and cashflow timing and volumes are more uncertain, fundraisers should consider using an equity crowdfunding model by selling ownership stakes in the venture.

Alternatively, if the project entails short-term investments for potential backers, the question becomes how the funding raised will be spent. If funding is used for a strategic investment towards firm enhanced capacities and growth, fundraisers should consider using a business lending model. However, if the funding is used for managing healthier cash-flows, and the firm already has sales, fundraisers should consider using invoice trading.

Consumption-Oriented Campaigns

In addition to organizational fundraisers, a large proportion of crowdfunding volumes is associated with financing consumers. In this context, the model options are more limited, but the volumes are substantial, as shown in the CCAF reports (Ziegler et al. 2018a, b, 2019; Zhang et al. 2018) throughout recent years. However, it is worth noting that while a large portion of such loans is indeed associated with consumption, some of it also camouflages early-stage venturing by single entrepreneurs taking consumer loans to fund their business startup activities.

Here, again, the first aspect to be considered is the amount of money sought. Consumers need to plan for costs associated with the consumption activity they are planning to engage in, as well as the costs associated with the crowdfunding activity. Once such costs are clarified in advanced, a minimum goal sum for a campaign may be set. Once such a sum is defined, fundraisers should evaluate whether their ambition represents a relatively small or large sum in comparison to other consumer crowdfunding campaigns' volumes in their respective national market. As in organizational crowdfunding, such thresholds are imprecise, vary by country, and continue to change annually as the industry develops. Here as well, fundraisers are encouraged to both consult experts and do some research bench-marking their own goal against earlier campaigns with similar goals, which took place in the same country and during the last few years. In very rough terms, and in most countries during 2017–2018, the threshold was between $5K and $10K, where sums below this range can be regarded as relatively small, and above it as relatively large.

If the minimum goal sum that was set by the fundraiser falls within the range of relatively small sums, the next consideration is how critical the funding is to the well-being of the fundraiser. If the funding is very critical for the well-being of the fundraisers (e.g. health or surgery emergencies, payment of legal fees, disaster relief), they should consider a donation crowdfunding model. However, if the funding is not critical to the well-being of the fundraiser as in the cases of regular consumption (e.g. life events such as weddings or birthdays, purchase of home appliances, home renovations and upgrades), fundraisers should consider consumer lending models.

If the minimum goal sum that was set by the fundraiser falls within the range of relatively large sums, the next consideration is how would the funds raised be used. If the funding will be used for investment in physical or human capital (e.g. home renovations and upgrades, education procurement), fundraisers should consider using a consumer lending model. If large sums will be used for consumption rather than investment, the concern for the criticality of funding for the fundraiser's well-being emerges again, and the choice of models follows that described earlier.

Conclusion

In the current chapter all crowdfunding models that have been employed in recent years have been defined and their characteristics outlined. Furthermore, the chapter presents novel frameworks guiding both organizations (including those involving one-man operations) and consumers through a decision-making process towards choosing the model that best fits their funding needs and characteristics. In this sense, the chapter's main contributions are in both presenting one of the most elaborate, up-to-date, and detailed typologies for crowdfunding models currently in use, and in being the first to suggest frameworks for systematic choice-making between models by fundraisers.

Nevertheless, the current chapter has some limitations that also present opportunities for further research. First, the characterization of models that were presented in terms of success rates, onboarding rates, and risk levels capture current dynamics, understanding, and knowledge.

However, since the industry is young and dynamic, and since some evidence for regional differences does exist, these should be revisited and tested empirically in future studies capturing the state of the market at more advanced levels of maturation, and across national and regional markets. Second, the suggested frameworks that were outlined follow a prescriptive and normative nature based on the accumulated experience of working with the industry from its early days til now. However, as such, it represents a certain set of heuristics that may guide prospective fundraisers, but it is not the only relevant set of such heuristics. Accordingly, future studies may seek to both empirically validate the decision process outlined, as well as further develop and amend it in a systematic data collection and analysis efforts (both qualitatively and quantitatively). Third, the organizational model choice frameworks suggested do not differentiate between different kinds of organizations in terms of size, age, or popular awareness. Accordingly, it may be interesting for future researchers to investigate whether model choice heuristics differs by such organizational characteristics.

Finally, the information and frameworks presented in this chapter also have several implications for practice. In this context, prospective fundraisers may consult the typology, model characteristics, and the outlined model choice frameworks and use them in their own fundraising decision making efforts. Furthermore, these may also be used by educators and trainers that wish to introduce crowdfunding to both students and practitioners as roadmaps for navigating through the multiple models available, while providing initial guidance into choosing between them for different project purposes.

References

Ahlers, G. K. C., Cumming, D., Günther, C., et al. (2015). Signaling in Equity Crowdfunding. *Entrepreneurship Theory and Practice, 39*(4), 955–980.

Allison, T. H., Davis, B. C., Short, J. C., et al. (2015). Crowdfunding in a Prosocial Microlending Environment: Examining the Role of Intrinsic Versus Extrinsic Cues. *Entrepreneurship Theory and Practice, 39*(1), 53–73.

Belleflamme, P., & Lambert, T. (2016). An Industrial Organization Framework to Understand the Strategies of Crowdfunding Platforms. In J. Méric, I. Maque, & J. Brabet (Eds.), *International Perspectives on Crowdfunding: Positive, Normative, and Critical Theory*. Bingley: Emerald Group Publishing Limited.

Belleflamme, P., Lambert, T., & Schwienbacher, A. (2013). Individual Crowdfunding Practices. *Venture Capital, 15*(4), 313–333.

Cumming, D. J., Leboeuf, G., & Schwienbacher, A. (2019a). Crowdfunding Models: Keep-It-All vs All-Or-Nothing. *Financial Management*, https://onlinelibrary.wiley.com/doi/abs/10.1111/fima.12262.

Cumming, D. J., Hornuf, L., Karami, M., et al. (2019b). Disentangling Crowdfunding from Fraud Funding, May 16, 2019. Retrieved from https://onlinelibrary.wiley.com/doi/abs/10.1111/fima.12262.

De Buysere, K., Gajda, O., Kleverlaan, R., et al. (2012). A Framework for European Crowdfunding. Retrieved from https://www.fundraisingschool.it/wp-content/uploads/2013/02/European-Crowdfunding-Framework-Oct-2012.pdf.

Dorfleitner, G., & Oswald, E.-M. (2016). Repayment Behavior in Peer-to-Peer Microfinancing: Empirical Evidence from Kiva. *Review of Financial Economics, 30*, 45–59.

Dorfleitner, G., Rad, J., & Weber, M. (2017). Pricing in the Online Invoice Trading Market: First Empirical Evidence. *Economics Letters, 161*, 56–61.

Emekter, R., Tu, Y., Jirasakuldech, B., et al. (2015). Evaluating Credit Risk and Loan Performance in Online Peer-to-Peer (P2P) Lending. *Applied Economics, 47*(1), 54–70.

Gajda, O. (Ed.). (2017). *Review of Crowdfunding Regulation: Interpretations of Existing Regulation Concerning Crowdfunding in Europe North America and Israel*. Brussels: European Crowdfunding Network AISBL.

Gray, M., & Zhang, B. (2017). Crowdfunding: Understanding Diversity. In R. Martin & J. Pollard (Eds.), *Handbook on the Geographies of Money and Finance*. Cheltenham: Edward Elgar Publishing.

Haas, P., Blohm, I., & Leimeister, J. M. (2014). An Empirical Taxonomy of Crowdfunding Intermediaries. In *International Conferences of Information Systems 2014*, Auckland, New Zealand.

Hainz, C. (2018). Fraudulent Behavior by Entrepreneurs and Borrowers. In D. Cumming & L. Hornuf (Eds.), *The Economics of Crowdfunding: Startups, Portals and Investor Behavior*. Cham: Springer International Publishing.

Lin, X., Li, X., & Zheng, Z. (2017). Evaluating Borrower's Default Risk in Peer-to-Peer Lending: Evidence from a Lending Platform in China. *Applied Economics, 49*(35), 3538–3545.

Méric, J., Maque, I., & Brabet, J. (2016). A Cartography of the Academic Literature on Crowdfunding. In J. Méric, I. Maque, & J. Brabet (Eds.), *International Perspectives on Crowdfunding: Positive, Normative and Critical Theory*. Bingley: Emerald Group Publishing Limited.

Mollick, E. (2015a). Delivery Rates on Kickstarter, December 4, 2015. Retrieved from https://ssrn.com/abstract=2699251.

Mollick, E. (2015b). *The Kickstarter Fulfillment Report* [Online]. Kickstarter.com. Retrieved April 30, 2019, from https://www.kickstarter.com/fulfillment.

Schreiner, M. (2001). Informal Finance and the Design of Microfinance. *Development in Practice, 11*(5), 637–640.

Shneor, R., & Flåten, B.-T. (2015). Opportunities for Entrepreneurial Development and Growth Through Online Communities, Collaboration, and Value Creating and Co-creating Activities. In H. R. Kaufmann & S. M. R. Shams (Eds.), *Entrepreneurial Challenges in the 21st Century*. Basingstoke: Palgrave Macmillan.

Signori, A., & Vismara, S. (2016). Returns on Investments in Equity Crowdfunding, April 10, 2016. Retrieved from https://ssrn.com/abstract=2765488.

Swords, J. (2017). Crowd-Patronage—Intermediaries, Geographies and Relationships in Patronage Networks. *Poetics, 64*, 63–73.

Wang, Z., Jiang, C., Ding, Y., et al. (2018). A Novel Behavioral Scoring Model for Estimating Probability of Default Over Time in Peer-to-Peer Lending. *Electronic Commerce Research and Applications, 27*, 74–82.

Wenzlaff, K. & Odorović, A. (2020). Joint Production of Confidence—Self-Regulation in European Crowdfunding Markets. *Baltic Journal of Management, 15*(2), https://doi.org/10.1108/BJM-04-2019-0119.

Zhang, B., Ziegler, T., Mammadova, L., et al. (2018). *The 5th UK Alternative Finance Industry Report*. Cambridge: Cambridge Centre for Alternative Finance.

Ziegler, T., Johanson, D., Zhang, B., et al. (2018a). *The 3rd Asia Pacific Region Alternative Finance Industry Report*. Cambridge: Cambridge Centre for Alternative Finance.

Ziegler, T., Johanson, D., King, M., et al. (2018b). *Reaching New Heights: The 3rd Americas Alternative Finance Industry Report*. Cambridge: Cambridge Centre for Alternative Finance.

Ziegler, T., Shneor, R., Garvey, K., et al. (2018c). *Expanding Horizons: The 3rd European Alternative Finance Industry Report*. Cambridge: Cambridge Centre for Alternative Finance.
Ziegler, T., Suresh, K., Garvey, K., et al. (2018d). *The 2nd Annual Middle East & Africa Alternative Finance Industry Report*. Cambridge: Cambridge Center for Alternative Finance.
Ziegler, T., Shneor, R., Wenzlaff, K., et al. (2019). *Shifting Paradigms—The 4th European Alternative Finance Benchmarking Report*. Cambridge: Cambridge Centre for Alternative Finance.

3

The Global Status of the Crowdfunding Industry

Tania Ziegler, Rotem Shneor, and Bryan Zheng Zhang

Introduction

The advancing pace of technology-enabled innovation is rapidly transforming the financial services industry (Kotarva 2016; Zavolokina et al. 2016). Across the world, developments in financial technology (FinTech) are revolutionizing the way people interact with financial services—allowing faster payments, more secure transactions, user-friendly interfaces, and reducing costs. Crowdfunding represents one category of FinTech developments, addressing needs in capital raising through innovative and digital solutions (Haddad and Hornuf 2019). Specifically,

T. Ziegler (✉) • B. Z. Zhang
Cambridge Centre for Alternative Finance, Judge Business School, University of Cambridge, Cambridge, UK
e-mail: t.ziegler@jbs.cam.ac.uk; b.zhang@jbs.cam.ac.uk

R. Shneor
School of Business and Law, University of Agder, Kristiansand, Norway
e-mail: rotem.shneor@uia.no

R. Shneor et al. (eds.), *Advances in Crowdfunding*,
https://doi.org/10.1007/978-3-030-46309-0_3

fund- and capital-raising crowdfunding, and its related activities, can potentially enable and widen financial access in previously underserved or unserved areas and populations, as well as offer new solutions in areas currently served by traditional financial institutions (Bruton et al. 2015; Lehner 2013).

This chapter will discuss several key international trends as related to crowdfunding market development, as well as provide some insights into the limited research done to date at the macro level attempting to explain such developments. Specifically, the facts and figures presented throughout the chapter are drawn from the research efforts undertaken by the Cambridge Centre for Alternative Finance (CCAF) and its partners culminating in a series of annual industry bench-marking reports. Hence, for full disclosure and avoidance of repetitive referencing, all statistics presented in the current chapter are adopted from the CCAF's recent reports covering the Americas (Ziegler et al. 2018a), the Asia-Pacific (Ziegler et al. 2018b), Europe (Ziegler et al. 2019), the UK (Zhang et al. 2018), and the Middle East and Africa (Ziegler et al. 2018c), unless otherwise indicated.

In the next sections we first present global trends, total volumes, as well as volumes by model. These findings are linked to some explanations that have been suggested in the limited research that has sought to explain macro-level developments. We then present market status at regional level for highlighting commonalities and differences across regions. Finally, we conclude with some implications for research and practice.

A Global Snapshot: Market Volumes and Growth

The global alternative finance market volume is estimated based upon platform data collected from over 3000 unique platforms in 161 countries during the period 2015–2017. A crowdfunding platform is "an internet application bringing together project owners and their potential backers, as well as facilitating exchanges between them, according to a variety of business models" (Shneor and Flåten 2015, p. 188). All platforms are restricted to online, peer-to-peer or crowd-led marketplaces that are open, at least partially, to individual backers and retail investors (the "crowd"). As such, it does not include what are known as 'individual crowdfunding' initiatives (Belleflamme et al. 2013), which are individual- or organization-specific fundraising campaigns carried outside the control and oversight by a formal crowdfunding platform.

The total global alternative finance volume has grown from $11.06 billion in 2013 to $418.52 billion in 2017. Overall, while growth rates are gradually slowing down on an annual basis, total volumes have increased substantially. The slowing of growth rates may signal maturation, at least among early adopters of crowdfunding services, but is more likely to be associated with a growth trajectory that started with a very low absolute base and reached substantial volume in just five years. Figure 3.1 illustrates that despite the slowing of year-on-year growth rate, between 2016 and 2017 global crowdfunding market volume grew by 44% from $290 billion to reach $418 billion. The extent of future growth remains uncertain, but given the head room for growth in more advanced markets, as well as the fact that many developing and emerging markets are still considerably underdeveloped in terms of online capital raising, the global industry is likely to maintain momentum in coming years.

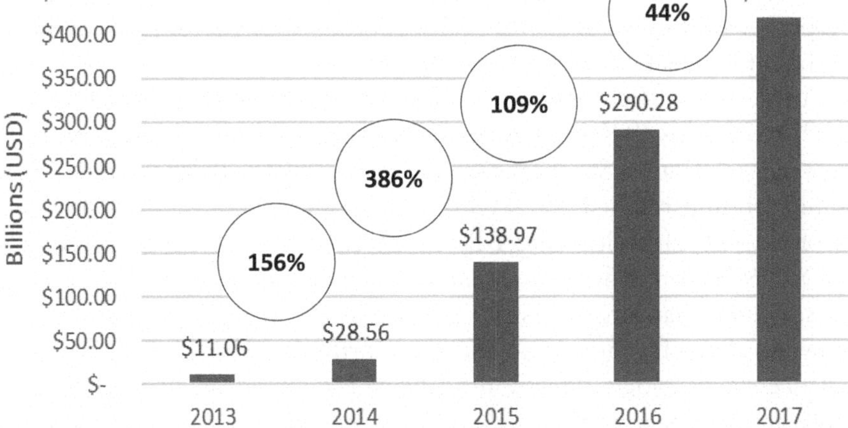

Fig. 3.1 Global volumes 2013–2017 (USD)

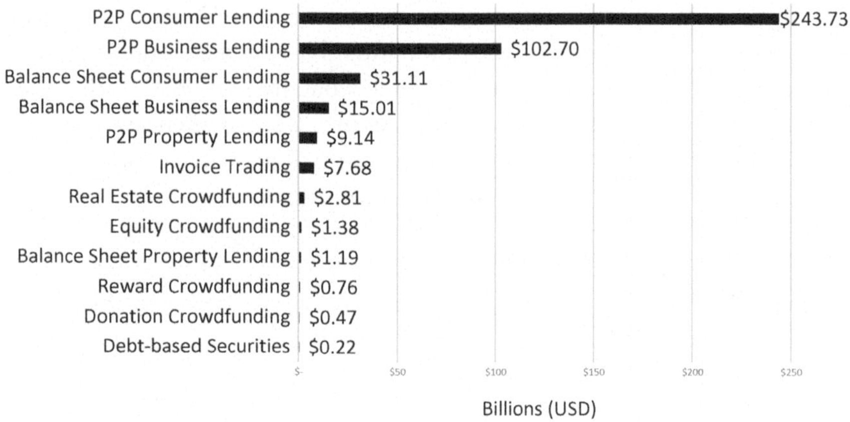

Fig. 3.2 Global volumes by top models 2017 (USD)

When breaking overall volumes into the various crowdfunding models, substantial differences emerge among the models. Figure 3.2 presents the 2017 global volumes by model. In 2017, peer-to-peer (P2P) consumer lending emerged as the leading model with a volume of $243.73 billion, accounting for 58% of global alternative finance volumes. This was closely followed by P2P business lending with $102.7 billion. Indeed, since 2013, these two models have continued to rank first and second every year. Overall, when adding the $9.14 billion associated with P2P property lending, the share of all P2P-lending models accounted for 85% of the total global crowdfunding volumes.

Furthermore, the popularity and pervasiveness of crowd lending are not limited to the P2P models. Since 2016, data shows increasing market activities in Balance Sheet lending models. In 2017, Balance Sheet consumer lending reached $31.11 billion, Balance Sheet business lending recorded $15.01 billion, and Balance Sheet property lending accounted for $1.19 billion. These demonstrate considerable growth especially in jurisdictions that largely restrict investment from retail individuals for crowdfunding. In contrast to the more orthodox P2P-lending models, balance sheet lenders directly fund loans originated on their platforms and therefore assume the credit risk associated. They operate with an intermediation model that is more akin to bank lending, by financing loans with equity and debt on their own balance sheet and, also like banks, periodically refinancing by securitizing pools of the loans they have funded. Unlike regulated bank lenders, however, these balance sheet lenders do not have access to deposits to fund their lending activity. When brought together, all P2P and Balance Sheet models jointly accounted for 96% of global crowdfunding volume in 2017, demonstrating that lending-based models dominate the global crowdfunding landscape.

The remaining volumes were accounted for by other investment models including invoice trading (1.8% of total volumes), real-estate investment crowdfunding (0.6% of total volumes), and equity crowdfunding (0.3% of total volumes). All investment crowdfunding models accounted for 99.8% of global volume. This stands in stark contrast to popular belief often associating crowdfunding with non-investment models such as reward and donation crowdfunding, which collectively only registered a little over $1 billion, representing just 0.2% of total global crowdfunding volume (Fig. 3.3).

Great differences are also observed when breaking global volumes down geographically both at regional and country levels. Here, while volumes of crowdfunding transactions are recorded in some 161 countries, three countries dominated the scene by accounting for 97% of the

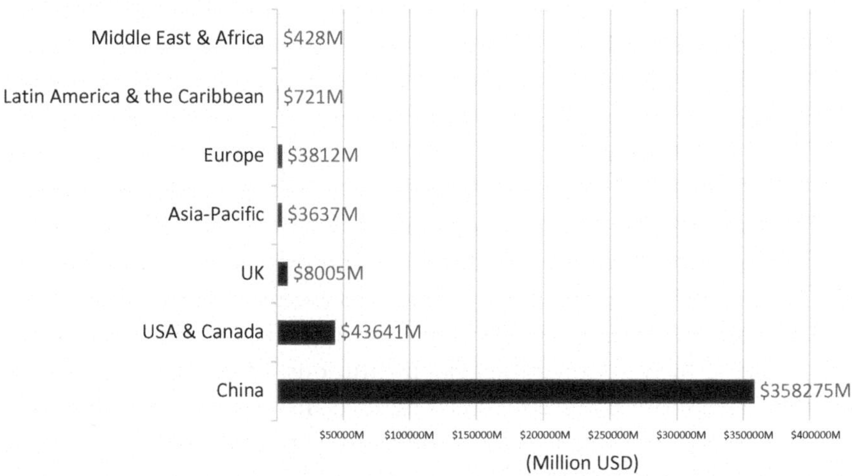

Fig. 3.3 Total 2017 volumes by region (million USD). (Source: Ziegler et al. 2020)

entire global crowdfunding volumes. These three countries are China, the United States, and the UK, representing the regional leaders for the Asia-Pacific region, the Americas and Europe respectively. China is the single largest contributor across all years observed. In 2017, China generated $358.275 billion, representing 86% of the 2017 global figure. The United States and Canada accounted for $43.641 billion (or 10%), and the United Kingdom $8.01 billion (2%) of the 2017 global crowdfunding volume respectively.

In addition to the three global leaders, other important markets are identified and ranked by their respective 2017 volumes as listed in Table 3.1. When we exclude the top three performers, this group includes 14 jurisdictions from Europe, 8 from the Asia-Pacific region, 4 from the Americas, and only 1 from the Middle East and Africa region among the global top 30. This includes both developed (e.g. Canada, Australia, Germany, Netherlands, and Japan) and emerging economies (e.g. India, Brazil, and Indonesia), G8 countries (e.g. France, and Italy) and smaller economies (e.g. Estonia, Latvia, and Georgia), countries that have pioneered the concept of online crowdfunding (e.g. the UK and the United States) as well as relative newcomers to the crowdfunding scene (e.g. Poland and Chile).

However, when examining the 2017 volumes per capita, one can identify a strong correlation between economic development (represented by GDP per capita) and crowdfunding market volumes per capita, indicating that the greater levels of economic development tend to be associated with larger per capita crowdfunding volumes. Figure 3.4 presents this significant correlation among the leading markets (excluding China as a considerable outlier). Such analysis identifies strong market performers such as Estonia, Latvia and Georgia that may represent small open economies that have endorsed crowdfunding and other forms of alternative finance as part of wider market liberalization and economic digitization efforts, and where such services may meet capital needs in markets not fully fulfilled by traditional financial institutions. Other strong performers that have more mature financial markets are countries such as New Zealand, Australia, Finland, Israel, and South Korea. The list also includes countries such as Switzerland, Germany, and Japan which all have well developed financial markets, as well as emerging markets such as India,

Table 3.1 Top thirty national markets by volume in 2017

Rank	Region	Country	Total volume (in USD)	Volumes per Capita (in USD)
1	China (Asia)	China	$358,275,377,038.89	$258.08
2	Americas	United States	$42,773,174,202.50	$131.02
3	UK (Europe)	United Kingdom	$8,004,783,637.55	$122.19
4	Asia	Australia	$1,148,515,565.00	$46.61
5	Asia	South Korea	$1,129,918,098.00	$22.28
6	Americas	Canada	$867,577,549.42	$23.69
7	Europe	France	$747,274,513.52	$11.51
8	Europe	Germany	$672,751,878.90	$8.34
9	Asia	Japan	$348,650,302.00	$2.77
10	Europe	Netherlands	$316,287,611.90	$18.57
11	Middle East	Israel	$295,455,044.29	$35.50
12	Europe	Italy	$271,919,936.14	$4.55
13	Asia	India	$268,579,820.00	$0.20
14	Asia	New Zealand	$261,621,933.00	$56.81
15	Europe	Finland	$222,314,696.19	$38.92
16	Europe	Sweden	$221,890,190.29	$22.37
17	Americas	Brazil	$216,357,244.21	$1.02
18	Europe	Georgia	$195,784,289.95	$49.28
19	Asia	Singapore	$190,821,714.00	$32.99
20	Europe	Spain	$181,620,894.27	$3.94
21	Europe	Poland	$160,967,488.70	$4.17
22	Americas	Mexico	$153,756,417.15	$1.18
23	Americas	Chile	$150,695,263.44	$8.23
24	Europe	Ireland	$120,666,518.06	$25.41
25	Europe	Latvia	$108,236,669.08	$55.66
26	Asia	Taiwan	$103,502,237.00	$4.42
27	Europe	Belgium	$102,704,518.28	$8.97
28	Europe	Estonia	$91,794,107.14	$70.30
29	Europe	Switzerland	$87,114,373.27	$10.30
30	Asia	Indonesia	$80,114,824.00	$0.30

Indonesia, Mexico, and Brazil, where crowdfunding and other forms of online alternative finance are expected to grow more substantively given that financing gaps in these jurisdictions are not well served by incumbents.

Why are some countries more developed in crowdfunding than others?—The limited research to date has pointed to several influential factors. Dushnitsky et al. (2016) found that levels of new crowdfunding

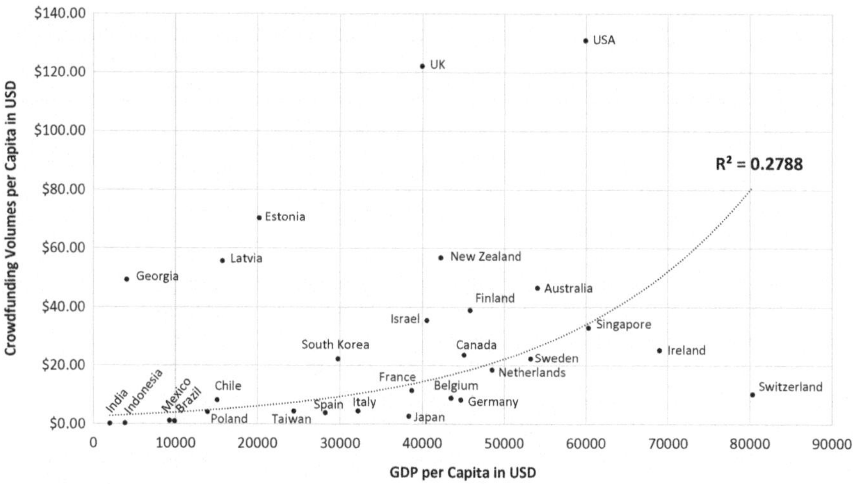

Fig. 3.4 Crowdfunding per capita volumes by GDP per capita 2017—Lead markets

platform creation in the early days of the industry in Europe were positively associated with population size. It was also positively associated with new business ownership levels and the share of platforms operated by a financial operator, but only in the case of reward, donation, and equity platforms (not with respect to creation of lending platforms). The strength of legal rights in terms of borrower and lender protection was found to be positively associated with lending platform formation, but negatively associated with donation and equity platform formation. Economic development was only positively associated with the formation of reward platforms.

Hadded and Hornuf's (2019) analysis of FinTech start-up formation level by country, using the Crunchbase database, showed that it is positively associated with economic development, availability of venture capital, ease of access to loans, availability of labour, good IT infrastructure as captured by number of secure servers, and mobile infrastructure as represented by mobile subscription numbers. In addition, specifically with respect to start-up formation in the financing category (e.g. crowdfunding), the study also finds a positive association with severity of in-country impact from the global financial crisis, less stringent financial regulation, and the strength of legal rights (as represented by the extent of borrower and lender protection).

Finally, a study by Rau (2019), using the CCAF database, shows that national volumes of crowdfunding are positively associated with the rule of law in the country, its quality of regulation, control of corruption, presence of explicit or bespoke crowdfunding regulations, ease of setting up business, and financial profitability of existing financial intermediaries (e.g. the banking sector). Interestingly, neither levels of social trust in strangers nor the adventure seeking tendency of the populace were significantly associated with national crowdfunding volumes.

The following section presents trends in the main national and regional markets. First, since the top three national markets, namely—China, the United States, and the UK, jointly represent 97% of the global market volumes, they are analysed separately. This is followed by a presentation of regional-trends in the three major regions, namely—the Asia-Pacific region, Europe and Latin Americas.

China

China is by far the global market leader, alone accounting for 85% of the 2017 global volumes. It is dominated by P2P consumer-lending activities, responsible for 63% of the total national market volume, and when the Balance Sheet consumer-lending activities are included, the consumer-lending proportion grows to 67% of China's total volume in 2017. Business-lending platforms also play a significant role in the Chinese crowdfunding ecosystem. All consumer and business-lending activities across models (both P2P and Balance Sheet) accounted for 98% of the entire national market volume. In this sense, there is a considerable lack of model diversity in China, with the remaining volume heavily concentrated in property lending or equity crowdfunding.

The prominence of crowd-lending activities in China may stem from continued uncertainty and lagged implementation of Chinese crowdfunding regulation. At present, there is no clear regulatory body at national level responsible for regulating an supervising equity crowdfunding activities (BOP Consulting 2017). Regulatory clarity and framework were lacking for the P2P-lending sector, which has witnessed increasing scrutiny and challenges in recent years. Late in 2016, the China Banking Regulatory Commission issued interim rules for regulating the P2P lending industry, in an effort to curtail credit risk (Chorzempa 2018). Unlike the orthodox P2P-lending model, where the platform serves as an informed intermediary, in many instances across China platforms were acting more like deposit takers with creation of a 'capital pool', with retail investors effectively lending to the platform rather than funding specific loans or loan-parts.

In an effort to properly regulate this sector, Chinese regulators created a '1+3 system' (e.g. one method, three guidelines') to monitor, manage and mitigate industry risks (Ziegler et al. 2018b). As a result of strengthened oversight, the Chinese P2P industry has begun to grapple with liquidity problems, credit risk issues and reconciling new best-practices. Additionally, as regulation has developed, the Chinese marketplace lenders have started to collaborate with traditional banks to a greater extent through partnerships, with 28% having a fund depository relationship with a bank by the end of 2017 (BOP Consulting 2017). Accordingly, it is likely that the 2018 market data will reflect the changing dynamics in China, where volumes are likely to temporarily decline with increasing regulatory oversight.

Unites States of America

In the United States, Balance Sheet consumer lending and P2P consumer lending garnered first and second places respectively in 2017, which together made up 70% of the US market volume. Despite the significant concentration in these two models, the remaining 30% of the market share is far more diversified when compared to China. In the United States, a greater diversity within the crowdfunding industry is manifested by significant volumes of business-lending models, real estate and property-focused activities, equity crowdfunding, and non-investment activities such as reward crowdfunding. Indeed, all fourteen models included in the CCAF reports' taxonomy were present in the United States.

The crowdfunding industry ecosystem in the United States has been shaped significantly by its regulatory frameworks. Specifically, US firms are heavily reliant upon institutional investment, with strict guidelines on marketing and promotions towards retail (unaccredited/accredited) investors. The Jobs Act, the over-arching regulation dictating this landscape, was very much geared towards a broker/intermediary model (Ziegler et al. 2017). As a result, it is not surprising that models which rely upon institutional investment make up a greater proportion of this alternative finance landscape, while models which are more suited towards retail investors (such as Equity Crowdfunding) have seen slower paced growth.

Similarly, a major trend entrenched in the United States, but also evident globally, is the increasing proportion of volume funded by institutional investors via alternative financing platforms. Institutional investors include but are not limited to banks, pension funds, mutual funds, asset management firms, family offices and VC/PE firms. In the United States, 88% of market volume originated from institutional investors—a total of $37.6 billion in 2017. Though the dominance of institutional investment varies by model type, it was most prominent in P2P consumer lending ($14.21 billion, or 97% of the model's total volume), Balance Sheet consumer lending (88% or $11.98 billion) and P2P business lending (76% or $1.1 billion) (Ziegler et al. 2018a).

United Kingdom

The crowdfunding landscape in the United Kingdom is markedly different in composition when compared to China and the United States. P2P business lending is the dominant model in the UK, closely followed by P2P consumer lending. Unlike the United States, Balance Sheet lending activities were significantly lower, and are often blended with other activities on a platform. Typically, a firm can operate a predominantly P2P model with a component that relies upon balance sheet funding.

The UK P2P-lending arena has seen an increase in institutionalization in recent years, though not to the same degree as in the United States. While retail investment remained the main driving force of alternative finance volumes in 2017, 40% of the P2P business-lending volume came from institutional investors, a sharp increase from the 28% in 2016. The corresponding figure for P2P consumer lending was 39%.

Furthermore, the UK also exemplifies a diverse ecosystem, with strong market activities for each of the models within the CCAF reports' taxonomy. Specifically, it is worth noting that in 2017 the UK had the highest volume of equity crowdfunding of any other country in the world valued at $430 million.

The UK has been the pioneering country in Europe venturing into crowdfunding with the establishment of the world's first P2P-lending platform Zopa in 2005. Since then, it has led the European countries in crowdfunding activities and the advancement of regulatory reform in crowdfunding regulations (Gajda 2017). However, like many other aspects of the British economy, future development of the crowdfunding industry is likely to suffer from uncertainties related to the BREXIT process and pending agreement with the European Union, especially with respect to cross-border flows and international operations of platforms (ibid.).

Asia-Pacific, Europe, and the Americas

When excluding the top three performing countries (i.e. China, the United States, and the UK), the annual market volume of Europe and the Asia-Pacific (APAC) region, were quite similar, while those of Latin America and the Caribbean (LAC) were much smaller in 2017. The APAC region grew by 81% in 2017 against the previous year, while Europe saw a 63% annual increase. Growth in the APAC was driven predominantly by two key countries, Australia ($1.15 billion) and South Korea ($1.13 billion), both of which crossed the $1 billion thresholds in 2017. In contrast, there is no single mainland European country that has yet crossed the $1 billion mark. For a fifth year in a row, France ($747.27 million), Germany ($672.75 million), and the Netherlands ($316.28 million) ranked amongst the top three performing European countries. Though smaller, the LAC market has grown rapidly in a relatively short period of time, while achieving 111% year-on-year growth rate between 2016 and 2017. Here, the key national markets include Brazil ($216.36

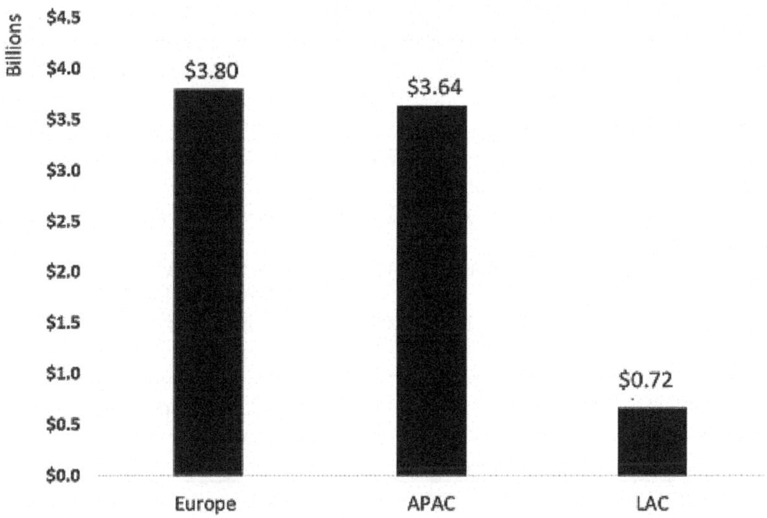

Fig. 3.5 Regional volumes—Europe, Asia-Pacific, and Latin America & the Caribbean (USD). (Source: Ziegler et al. 2020)

million), Mexico ($153.76 million) and Chile ($150.70 million) (Fig. 3.5).

When reviewing the leading six crowdfunding models for each region, making up 90% or more of their respective markets, more regional dissimilarities are evident than similarities, as presented in Table 3.2. In all three regions, P2P Consumer lending is the top-ranking model, but that is where most similarities end.

Though retail investors still contributed the majority of total funding, the APAC region has seen a higher level of institutionalization in 2017 than previous years. Specifically, 98% of Balance Sheet business lending, 43% of the P2P consumer lending and 42% of the Invoice Trading model are driven by institutional investment. With respect to countries with the most active institutional investors, the Indian market took the lead with 74% of its annual funding coming from institutional investors in 2017, followed by Australia (65%) and Indonesia (61%). The pattern of institutionalization correlates heavily with markets that have strong Balance Sheet and P2P/Marketplace-lending sectors.

Table 3.2 Top crowdfunding models by region

Europe		Asia Pacific		Latin America and Caribbean	
Model	Share (%)	Model	Share (%)	Model	Share (%)
P2P Consumer	41	P2P Consumer	23	P2P Consumer	25
Invoice Trading	16	BS Business	19	Invoice Trading	22
P2P Business	14	P2P Property	19	Balance Sheet Consumer lending	17
Real Estate CF	8	P2P Business	17	P2P Business	10
Equity CF	6	Real Estate CF	10	Balance Sheet Business lending	5
Reward CF	5	Invoice Trading	5	Donation CF	4

The European landscape is far more varied, with the representation of debt, equity and non-investment models among the six top ranked market segments. Far more retail investor-oriented, institutionalization has not yet taken root in Europe to the same degree that it has in Asia, or most other regions. P2P consumer lending, the largest single market segment in Europe, only saw 12% of its volume financed by institutional investors. Although the proportion of institutional investment is slightly higher for invoice trading (46%) and P2P business lending (24%), by and large most models were financed by retail investors. This is likely because regulations in most European countries include permissions related to solicitation of retail investors, however, marketing and promotions to retail investors are normally restricted by wealth and previous investment experience.

Following the global trend, in LAC, P2P consumer lending is the largest model within the region and accounted for nearly a quarter of the regional market. Considerable number of platforms operate both P2P and Balance Sheet consumer-lending models. In Mexico, Balance Sheet consumer lending accounted for nearly 45% of the country's overall volume. While consumer lending is the largest model within the region, the overall landscape in LAC is marked by a variety of models, with a focus on business financing activities.

Business-focused funding activities have been viewed as a key priority when considering the usefulness of crowdfunding. Over the past few years, crowdfunding has grown to become a viable funding source for entrepreneurs and small and medium-sized enterprises (SMEs) globally. In 2017, crowdfunding market volume attributed to business financing amounted to $153.2 billion globally, while showing an average annual growth rate of 155% since 2013. China, the United States and the UK provided the bulk of business funding, contributing 32%, 2%, and 1% respectively.

Though in absolute terms business volumes in LAC are dwarfed by comparable figures elsewhere, the dominance of alternative business funding is a key characteristic of the region. In LAC, $565.7 million can be attributed to business-specific fundraises, accounting for nearly 80% of total volume across the region. The top three contributing countries towards business finance were Chile ($150.6 million), Mexico ($73 million), and Brazil ($57 million). Not surprisingly, the majority of business-based alternative finance derived from debt models (92%), such as P2P business lending, invoice trading, etc. Interestingly, a significant proportion of consumer-driven volumes were attributed to business-borrowers too, typically in the form of sole-traders utilizing personal credit to fund their business (Ziegler et al. 2018a). Equity-driven models, such as equity crowdfunding, real-estate crowdfunding and profit-sharing accounted for 7% of all LAC business financing.

When considering the role of institutional investment, 51% of the regional volume was financed by institutional investors ($330.9 million), with the highest levels of institutional investment recorded with respect to Balance Sheet consumer lending (75%, or $84.36 million), invoice trading (73%, or $112.70 million) and P2P consumer lending (47% or $75.95 million).

Conclusion

This chapter has provided a review of the recent status of the global crowdfunding industry while presenting key international trends, as well as presenting some insights from the limited research done at the macro level explaining such developments.

Overall, one can conclude that crowdfunding is no longer a 'fringe' activity but instead has moved into the mainstream. On a global level, growth while slowing down, still represents fast-paced development in comparison to most other industries and financial sectors. At the same time, this slowing of year-on-year growth may indicate initial signs towards market stabilization and consolidation. As incumbent firms begin to consolidate their positions within their respective markets, crowdfunding is gradually maturing, at least among early market movers and adopters.

Furthermore, the market dynamics presented earlier illustrated that crowd-lending models are the most popular form of crowdfunding across the globe. This is closely linked to growing efficiencies thanks to digitization driving greater access to finance and investment opportunities to an ever-larger pool of both lenders and borrowers. The combination of new online credit channels, easy-to-use interfaces and widened access, in parallel with continued scepticism towards traditional financial institutions and their ability and/or willingness to serve all segments of the business community, has created a market opportunity that has been seized by online platforms through a variety of crowd-lending models.

Finally, our review also shows that a thriving crowdfunding market may emerge in both developed economies and emerging markets, regardless of the size of the economy or history of crowdfunding adoption. Limited empirical research also suggests that appropriate regulations, good levels of IT infrastructure, and a generally well-functioning economy may present favourable conditions for the development of crowdfunding industry.

Accordingly, in terms of implications for practice, our findings suggest that countries can benefit from the diversification of financing channels. To achieve this, industry actors and government agencies should work closely together in developing responsible, appropriate, and proportionate regulatory frameworks and policies that both support industry growth, as well as ensure consumer and investor protection, may they be fundraisers (i.e. investees, borrowers, sellers, donation collectors, etc.) or funders (i.e. investors, lenders, backers, buyers, donors, etc.).

When considering implications for research, it becomes clear that opportunities are abundant. There are very few earlier studies that aimed to capture and explain the macro-level growth of the crowdfunding industry, and those that are available mostly capture the industry's early days. Similar studies are necessary for capturing current market dynamics and reflect more mature market conditions. Researchers are encouraged to explore further which factors may impact the trajectory of market development in various settings and given different socio-economic conditions. Such studies may compare emerging and developed markets, as well as markets characterized by high levels of e-readiness and larger scale of digital economy versus those with more modest levels of both.

Future studies may also focus more on the role played by regulations and policies in market development. Insights from such studies can further enhance our understanding about necessary policy components that need to be in place in order to support technology-enabled financial innovation. Research may also expand our understanding of market dynamics by delving deeper into its specific market characteristics, including the extent of institutionalization, international scope of activity and dependencies, as well as default and failure rates at more granular levels.

Finally, as the industry matures, it becomes even more valuable to study the medium- to long-term impacts of crowdfunding activity on real economies. For instance, it would be particularly helpful to capture and measure the impact of the crowdfunding industry on economic development, innovation levels, employment, entrepreneurial venture activity and growth, as well as social impact in terms of access to finance for underserved or unserved social groups and geographical areas in various countries. Such insights are much needed for a better assessment of the crowdfunding industry and its socio-economic impact.

References

Belleflamme, P., Lambert, T., & Schwienbacher, A. (2013). Individual Crowdfunding Practices. *Venture Capital, 15*(4), 313–333.

BOP Consulting. (2017). China UK Equity Crowdfunding Regulatory and Market Comparison Study. Retrieved from http://bop.co.uk/assets/others/China_UK_Crowdfunding_Regulatory_and_Market_Report_Final_24072017.pdf.

Bruton, G., Khavul, S., Siegel, D., et al. (2015). New Financial Alternatives in Seeding Entrepreneurship: Microfinance, Crowdfunding, and Peer-to-Peer Innovations. *Entrepreneurship Theory and Practice, 39*(1), 9–26.

Chorzempa, M. (2018). Massive P2P Failures in China: Underground Banks Going Under. *China Economic Watch* [Online]. Retrieved from https://www.piie.com/blogs/china-economic-watch/massive-p2p-failures-china-underground-banks-going-under2019.

Dushnitsky, G., Guerini, M., Piva, E., et al. (2016). Crowdfunding in Europe: Determinants of Platform Creation Across Countries. *California Management Review, 58*(2), 44–71.

Gajda, O. (Ed.). (2017). *Review of Crowdfunding Regulation: Interpretations of Existing Regulation Concerning Crowdfunding in Europe North America and Israel.* Brussels: European Crowdfunding Network AISBL.

Haddad, C., & Hornuf, L. (2019). The Emergence of the Global Fintech Market: Economic and Technological Determinants. *Small Business Economics, 53*(1), 81–105.

Kotarva, M. (2016). New Factors Including Changes in the Retail Banking Customer Relationship Management (CRM) and Their Exploration by the Fintech Industry. *Foundations of Management, 9*, 69–78.

Lehner, O. M. (2013). Crowdfunding Social Ventures: A Model and Research Agenda. *Venture Capital, 15*(4), 289–311.

Rau, R. (2019). Law, Trust, and the Development of Crowdfunding, 31 May 2019. Retrieved from https://ssrn.com/abstract=2989056.

Shneor, R., & Flåten, B.-T. (2015). Opportunities for Entrepreneurial Development and Growth Through Online Communities, Collaboration, and Value Creating and Co-creating Activities. In H. R. Kaufmann & S. M. R. Shams (Eds.), *Entrepreneurial Challenges in the 21st Century*. Basingstoke: Palgrave Macmillan.

Zavolokina, L., Dolata, M., & Schwabe, G. (2016). The FinTech Phenomenon: Antecedents of Financial Innovation Perceived by the Popular Press. *Financial Innovation, 2*(1), 16.

Zhang, B., Ziegler, T., Mammadova, L., et al. (2018). *The 5th UK Alternative Finance Industry Report*. Cambridge: Cambridge Centre for Alternative Finance.
Ziegler, T., Johanson, D., King, M., et al. (2018a). *Reaching New Heights: The 3rd Americas Alternative Finance Industry Report*. Cambridge: Cambridge Centre for Alternative Finance.
Ziegler, T., Johanson, D., Zhang, B., et al. (2018b). *The 3rd Asia Pacific Region Alternative Finance Industry Report*. Cambridge: Cambridge Centre for Alternative Finance.
Ziegler, T., Suresh, K., Garvey, K., et al. (2018c). *The 2nd Annual Middle East & Africa Alternative Finance Industry Report*. Cambridge: Cambridge Center for Alternative Finance.
Ziegler, T., Reedy, E. J., Le, A., et al. (2017). *The 2nd Americas Alternative Finance Industry Report*. Cambridge: Cambridge Centre for Alternative Finance.
Ziegler, T., Shneor, R., Wenzlaff, K., et al. (2019). *Shifting Paradigms—The 4th European Alternative Finance Benchmarking Report*. Cambridge: Cambridge Centre for Alternative Finance.
Ziegler, T., Shneor, R., Wenzlaff, K., et al. (2020). *The Global Alternative Finance Benchmarking Report*. Cambridge, UK: Cambridge Centre for Alternative Finance.

4

Lending Crowdfunding: Principles and Market Development

Tania Ziegler and Rotem Shneor

Introduction

The crowdfunding phenomenon has entered the world stage with the advent of lending-based crowdfunding in the mid-2000s as two new platforms emerged from both sides of the Atlantic. Zopa was established in the UK in 2005, and briefly afterwards Prosper was established in the United States in 2006. Both broke grounds by mediating between private

T. Ziegler (✉)
Cambridge Centre for Alternative Finance, Judge Business School, University of Cambridge, Cambridge, UK
e-mail: t.ziegler@jbs.cam.ac.uk

R. Shneor (✉)
School of Business and Law, University of Agder, Kristiansand, Norway
e-mail: rotem.shneor@uia.no

R. Shneor et al. (eds.), *Advances in Crowdfunding*,
https://doi.org/10.1007/978-3-030-46309-0_4

lenders and borrowers via dedicated websites, which bypassed traditional financial institutions while benefiting from fees on successful transactions (Bachmann et al. 2011).

The new phenomenon was labelled as Peer-to-Peer (hereafter 'P2P') Lending. Since its emergence, P2P lending has offered good returns to investors and lower cost of capital to borrowers (Hollas 2013). Such model allowed borrowers to receive a loan without a financial institution involvement and a possibility of receiving better conditions than those offered by traditional credit providers (Bachmann et al. 2011). For lenders, the new model presented a new investment and portfolio diversification opportunities, where risk was coupled with credit ratings of loans, and which offered better returns than some of the existing products (ibid.).

The phenomenon received a further push following the global financial crisis as a consequence of the drying up of traditional financing (Bruton et al. 2015). Such development was part of a wider Financial Technology (FinTech) industry development in which technological changes enabled new practices and business models disrupting traditional financial services while building on a degree of user distrust towards traditional institutions following the financial crisis (Haddad and Hornuf 2019). Furthermore, alternative finance models carried the potential to unlock access to finance for individual and business borrowers who might have previously been excluded or marginalised by traditional lending practices (Serrano-Cinca et al. 2015). For both borrowers and investors, the crowdlending space offers unprecedented access, as the barrier to entry is often low, with some platforms offering a minimum investment as little as $1, while the minimum and maximum loan amounts on platforms range from a few dollars, to several million dollars. Hence, overall, crowdlending can offer more diverse sources of funding for the real economy in countries that have previously over-relied on bank lending for growth.

During the last decade, the industry has seen a proliferation of debt-based crowdfunding models from P2P lending to Balance Sheet lending, Invoice Trading, and Debt-based Securities, jointly referred to from now onwards as 'Crowdlending'. Such models have dominated the crowdfunding industry throughout its brief history, with crowdlending almost doubling in size every year. In 2018, crowdlending models accounted for 97% of the USD 300 billion global crowdfunding industry, while exhibiting an average year-on-year growth rate of 93% since 2014 (Ziegler et al. 2020).

Unsurprisingly, in light of this impressive growth, and thanks to its related efficiency gains, some began suggesting that crowdlending represents a real challenge to traditional finance (Hollas 2013; Kotarba 2016). However, others suggest that FinTech solutions may both complement existing financing channels as well as fill market needs from which traditional institutions have withdrawn (Haddad and Hornuf 2019). Indeed, recent empirical evidence clearly shows that traditional financial institutions actively participate in crowdlending and represent an important portion of related volumes (Ziegler et al. 2020).

In this chapter we review the current state of crowdlending. First, we present important milestones in its brief history followed by a detailed classification of the crowdlending model types that have emerged in this period. Next, we present facts and figures reflecting the current state of crowdlending both at global and regional levels. This is followed by a brief review of the mechanisms underlying crowdlending platform operations, supported by insights from current knowledge and existing research. Our chapter then concludes with suggestions for future research, as well as some implications for practice.

A Brief History of Crowd Lending

Crowdlending originated from the emergence of P2P Lending with the launching of ZOPA (Bachmann et al. 2011). Being the first P2P lending platform, ZOPA began its operation in 2005, while originating personal loans to British consumers through funds provided by retail investors. In this respect, individual investors would be matched to borrowers as related to their own lending criteria and appetite, bypassing conventional lending processes. Nearly 15 years on, Zopa was set to become the first 'Unicorn' of the Digital Lending era (Armstrong 2018).

Within a year, the US-based platform Prosper was launched and closely followed up by Lending Club, both focusing on the consumer lending market as well as on refinancing of student loans. P2P lending activities in the United States have some critical contextual differences that should be highlighted. The first relates to how the industry self-identifies. In the United States, firms have broadly adopted the moniker of 'marketplace' instead of 'peer-to-peer' largely to reflect the difference of stakeholders that utilise their services. The United States tends to rely heavily on sale of full or partial loans to institutional or professional investors, rather than focusing on matching retail individuals to borrowers (Milne and Parboteeah 2016). In this respect, the firms act more in a syndicate manner, creating a mechanism for matching loan-notes to interested investors.

As this marketplace began to grow quickly within the United States, concerns over how to best regulate it also emerged. By 2008, the Securities and Exchange Commission of the United States began to require P2P Lending firms (marketplace lenders) to register the loans executed on their platform as a security (Barry 2019). Specifically, investors would be purchasing non-recourse notes representing fractional interests in specific underlying consumer loans (Popescu 2016). Though this was the first example of regulating the P2P Lending industry, regulation of alternative finance activities in the United States is arguably still in flux. Notably, the JOBS Act was not signed into law until 2012, with a slow roll-out of legislation and regulatory guidance that persists in the United States as of today.

By 2010, examples of P2P Lending FinTech firms began to emerge worldwide, with some of the first examples of P2P lending focused on the Small and Medium-sized Enterprises (hereafter 'SME') or Business borrower space. Since their launch in 2010, Funding Circle became one of the first FinTech firms to apply the P2P lending model specifically to business loans (Milne and Parboteeah 2016). Though the consumer lending model remains the single largest iteration of P2P Lending, the asset class has expanded significantly, with firms now offering business loans, property loans, mortgages, and an array of other debt-facilities.

In 2011, the first P2P Lending-focused trade-body emerged in the form of the UK's "Peer-to-Peer Finance Association". Though this trade-body has since ceased its activities, its emergence came at a critical point for the advancement of the landscape in the UK (Nixon 2020). This association implemented a code of conduct, effectively creating rules for 'self-regulation' in advance of formal regulation of the industry. By 2013, the UK's Financial Conduct Authority launched its first consultation on Crowdfunding, which included digital lending activities referred to as 'loan-based crowdfunding'. Since 2014, the P2P lending market in the UK has fallen under the remit of the FCA. By 2016, examples of proposed or existing regulation of P2P/Marketplace activities was apparent globally.

By the end of the decade, crowdlending has become a global and mainstream activity, with platforms operating in nearly every country in the world. However, nowhere as prominently as in China, which grew to be the world's largest crowdlending market, estimated at USD 356 billion in 2017 (Ziegler et al. 2018). More specifically, China presents an interesting evolution path in a unique context characterized by relatively undeveloped regulatory environment, where loans are riskier than in the United States or the United Kingdom, the credit referencing system is not fully developed, and where loans are financed primarily by households (Milne and Parboteeah 2016).

However, recent years have seen growing concerns with fraud in the Chinese crowdlending space, especially following the collapse of platforms such as Ezubao, which was found to be operating as a "Ponzy scheme" (Zhang and Miller 2017). Late in 2016, the China Banking Regulatory Commission issued interim rules for regulating the P2P lending industry, in an effort to limit credit risk (Chorzempa 2018). This was necessary to address problems where Chinese platforms were acting more like deposit takers with creation of a 'capital pool', with retail investors effectively lending to the platform rather than funding specific loans or loan-parts intermediated by the platforms, as elsewhere. This crackdown has led to a course correction, with the Chinese crowdlending market seeing a 34% decline in market volume between 2017 and 2018 (Ziegler et al. 2020). Following regulatory crackdown and the exit of platforms suspected of questionable practices, it is expected that the market may gradually recover in the future, but it remains unclear how quickly and to what extent such recovery will occur. Despite this decline, China remains the largest crowdlending market in the world with a volume of close to USD 215 billion in 2018 (ibid.).

A Continually Evolving Classification of Models

While the concept of private individuals lending money without mediation is not new or revolutionary, what makes crowdlending a new phenomenon is the conduct of such transactions over the Internet while using online platforms (Bachmann et al. 2011). Most importantly, these are non-deposit taking platforms that facilitate online credit (through either secured or unsecured loans) to individuals or business borrowers, with capital lent by individuals or institutional investors. These platforms, and the models they represent, have evolved as a response to the gaps in the traditional credit market dominated by banks, and live outside of the incumbent or traditional debt ecosystem.

Crowdlending, also referred to as 'FinTech Credit', can be defined as all credit activity facilitated by platforms that match borrowers with lenders (investors) and includes activities referred to as "P2P lending", "loan-based crowdfunding" or "marketplace lending" and also may include platforms that use their own balance sheet to intermediate between borrowers and lenders (Bank for International Settlements and Financial Stability Board 2017).

This chapter will adopt the classification used and developed by the Cambridge Centre for Alternative Finance (CCAF) in its annual industry bench-marking reports (e.g. Ziegler et al. 2020). This classification includes a variety of alternative finance lending models that fall under the broader scope of FinTech Credit. In the text that follows, definitions and terms provided are adopted from the CCAF reports, unless stated otherwise.

First, *Peer-to-peer (P2P) Lending*—is a model in which a group of individual or institutional investors provide a loan (secured or unsecured) to a consumer or business borrower. In its most orthodox form, the P2P lending platform acts as a marketplace that connects the borrower and investor(s) such that the risk of financial loss if the loan is not repaid is with the investor and not with the platform. Depending upon the jurisdiction, this model may be referred to as Loan-based Crowdfunding, Marketplace Lending, or Collaborative Financing.

The mechanics, as graphically presented in Fig. 4.1, are as follows. The P2P lending firm provides potential borrowers with an easily accessible

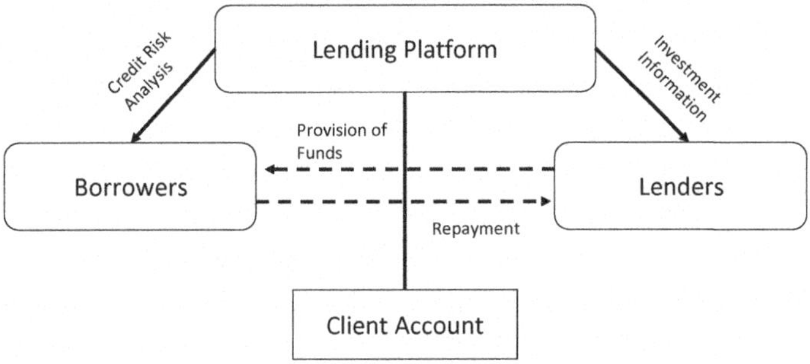

Fig. 4.1 Traditional P2P lending model. (Source: Bank for International Settlements and Financial Stability Board (2017). Market structure, business models and financial stability implications Bank for International Settlements. The full publication is available on the BIS website free of charge: www.bis.org)

and low-cost loan application, which is processed on an online platform. In most cases, the P2P lending firm will rely upon traditional credit scoring facilities and borrower-provided financial information in order to assess the borrower's affordability, loan price, and rating, while verifying the information provided within the loan application. Nevertheless, in-house methodologies used for platforms' own loan risk assessment are difficult to ascertain, as these are proprietary and disclosure is limited (Bank for International Settlements and Financial Stability Board 2017). With the advent of Open Banking, APIs to connect to individualized financial data is on the rise, but this is largely occurring within the constraints of the European Union.

In the early days of P2P lending, investors would review individual loan applications and make the decision to lend their funds against their own assessment. In this respect, the P2P Lending firm would function only as an intermediary, executing the loan once self-matched by lenders. As the model has developed, it is now far more common for the lending platform to automatically match individual lenders against pre-selected loan criteria. Regardless, the platform is typically responsible for communicating appropriate credit grades, setting a pre-fixed interest rate (a shift away from auction models that were more popular at the inception of P2P lending) and servicing the loan once it has been originated.

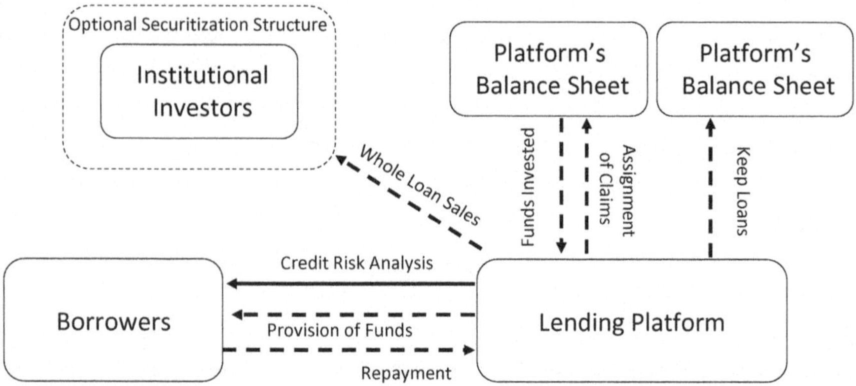

Fig. 4.2 Balance sheet lending model. (Source: Bank for International Settlements and Financial Stability Board (2017). Market structure, business models and financial stability implications Bank for International Settlements. The full publication is available on the BIS website free of charge: www.bis.org)

Second, *Balance Sheet Lending*—refers to a model in which a digital lending platform directly retains consumer or business loans (either whole loans or partial loans), using funds from the platform operator's balance sheet. These platforms therefore function as more than just intermediaries, originating and actively funding loans, so the risk of financial loss if the loan is not repaid is with the platform operator. In this respect, the platform operator looks more like a non-bank credit intermediary (Bank for International Settlements and Financial Stability Board 2017). The mechanics of this model are described in Fig. 4.2.

While the above represent the largest share of crowdlending volumes, as well as the most common practice. Recent years have seen the emergence of additional models such Invoice Trading, Debt-based Securities and Mini Bonds. Here, *Invoice Trading*, one of the fastest growing models, refers to an online marketplace where businesses can sell partial or whole receivables (invoices) at a discount. Individual lenders or institutional investors may serve as the counterparty in the sale transaction, again opening a new investment opportunity to a wider public of investors. This model is of particular importance for SMEs for raising short-term debt by pre-financing their outstanding invoices through individual or institutional investors (Dorfleitner et al. 2017).

Debt-based Securities are models where individuals or institutional funders purchase securities, typically a bond or debenture, at a fixed interest rate. And *Mini Bonds* refer to a model in which individuals or institutions purchase securities from companies in the form of an unsecured bond which is 'mini' because the issue size is much smaller than the minimum issue amount needed for a bond issued in institutional capital markets. Furthermore, Mini Bonds are not always transferable, either because the issue size is too small to provide secondary market liquidity or because prospectus exemptions require investors to hold the bond until maturity. Other terms can be very similar to traditional corporate bonds, such as being subject to early call provisions allowing the issuer to repay prior to maturity if its prospects improve.

Extended Services and Functionalities

As FinTech credit markets mature and the number of players increases, extended services and functionalities emerge. One type of such extensions may be identified in the emergence of aggregator platforms, which are tools that compile data from a range of platforms to allow borrowers to find suitable loan products from several crowdlending platforms in a centralised location. Aggregators offer an opportunity for lenders to compare loan products efficiently across platforms and better understand their different financing options. Aggregators may also act as brokers and potentially receive commission on referred business.

A second type of extension is associated with the establishment of secondary markets. In response to the largely illiquid nature of loan parts or traches held by investors, some platforms (or third-parties) have established secondary markets. In crowdlending, a secondary market acts as a marketplace that allows lenders to sell their loan parts before the loan reaches maturity. Here, the purchaser may be another lender or even the platform itself (in balance sheet lending). Loans may be sold at—a discount or premium, or they might be sold at par, assuming the loan is amortizing or repaid in accordance with the loan schedule. Where secondary markets are highly automated and the platform has discretion to buy and sell on behalf of investors, it is common for a standard valuation algorithm to assign values to each loan in real time, so that the platform can ensure it is swapping one loan for another of equivalent value. However, secondary markets for P2P loans are a relatively new development, not all platforms offer secondary markets, and many secondary markets are highly illiquid.

The State of the Crowdlending Market

In the current section we present the most up-to-date market data from the 2019 CCAF Global Alternative Finance Report (Ziegler et al. 2020). In 2018, the global alternative finance volumes amounted to just over $300 billion, 97% of which derived from models that would fall under lending activities.

Since starting to track the alternative finance industry, the P2P Consumer Lending model has remained the single largest volume driver, accounting for 66% of all alternative lending volumes. This was followed by P2P Business Lending (17%) and Balance Sheet Business Lending (7%). Individual borrowers, or consumers, are the largest group of borrowers as illustrated in Fig. 4.3, driving Fintech Credit activities globally. Consumers are individuals, typically receiving an unsecured loan. Although loan size varies significantly by jurisdiction, individuals tend to borrow between USD $2,500–30,000, with annual percentage rates ranging typically between 7% and 20%. Borrowers use these loans to consolidate their debt or refinance credit on their credit cards; to purchase a vehicle, repay a student loan, pay utility bills or wedding expenses, or to cover the costs associated with illness or unexpected hardship. More specifically, it should be noted that research conducted by the CCAF suggests that borrowers using P2P or Balance Sheet Consumer Lending are increasingly seeking loans to support their business (sole-traders, micro-business, early stage capital).

Table 4.1 presents the annual development in crowdlending volumes. While the industry has experienced a dramatic growth year-on-year since 2013 (when data was first collected), a notable drop can be observed in five of the eight applicable models between 2017 and 2018. This drop can be explained by market dynamics in China, while the rest of the world has seen continued healthy growth.

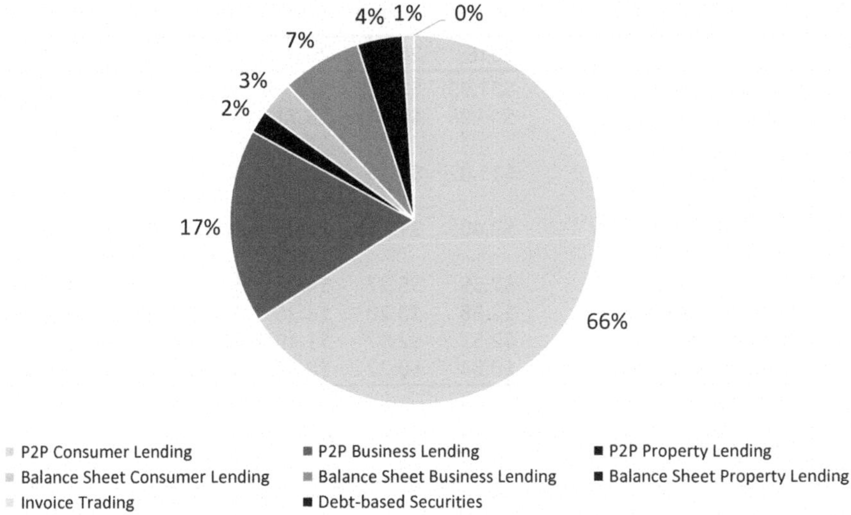

Fig. 4.3 Proportion of global volume from key crowdlending models

Table 4.1 Global alternative lending in USD billion (inclusive of China figures)

	2018	2017	2016	2015	2014	2013
P2P Consumer Lending	$195.29	$243.80	$157.60	$73.09	$21.78	$6.62
P2P Business Lending	$50.33	$103.59	$61.59	$43.70	$10.50	$2.20
Balance Sheet Business Lending	$21.08	$16.02	$33.99	$2.97	$1.30	$0.51
Balance Sheet Property Lending	$11.02	$1.19	$0.57	$0.00	$0.00	$0.00
Balance Sheet Consumer Lending	$9.78	$31.17	$12.43	$3.21	$0.72	$0.09
P2P Property Lending	$5.73	$9.14	$11.40	$7.12	$1.62	$0.26
Invoice Trading	$3.22	$7.68	$3.38	$2.20	$0.75	$0.18
Debt-based Securities	$0.85	$0.22	$0.47	$0.03	$0.02	$0.01

As mentioned earlier, despite China remaining as the global market leader in alternative lending, wide-spread closures of P2P and balance sheet lending platforms have occurred due to the implementation of increasingly strict regulations. Since July 2018, the absolute number of firms, as well as the trading volume of China's P2P lending platforms, have shown a continuing downward trend month by month. According

Table 4.2 Global alternative lending in USD billion (exclusive of China figures)

	2018	2017	2016	2015	2014	2013
P2P Consumer Lending	$31.99	$19.30	$24.40	$27.77	$9.44	$3.49
Balance Sheet Business Lending	$14.95	$8.14	$6.71	$2.40	$1.16	$0.50
Balance Sheet Property Lending	$11.02	$1.19	$0.57	$0.00	$0.00	$0.00
Balance Sheet Consumer Lending	$9.40	$15.34	$3.05	$3.09	$0.69	$0.09
P2P Business Lending	$7.59	$5.27	$4.93	$4.60	$2.46	$0.77
P2P Property Lending	$3.88	$3.20	$4.36	$1.56	$0.14	$0.02
Invoice Trading	$2.53	$2.07	$1.10	$0.74	$0.48	$0.15
Debt-based Securities	$0.84	$0.22	$0.22	$0.03	$0.02	$0.01

to the data from WDZJ (P2P online loan industry portal in China), as of November 30, 2019, the number of operating marketplace lending platforms in China was 456, a decrease of 87.24% compared to 3574 (historical peaks) in December 2015; the monthly trading volume in November 2019 dropped to 50.623 billion, having fallen by almost 80% compared to its peak in 2017.

When we remove China from the alternative finance equation (Table 4.2), we see considerable annual growth across seven of the eight applicable alternative finance models. As expected, P2P Consumer Lending is the largest model even when China's activity is removed, and we note a 66% annual growth from $19.3 billion in 2017 to $31.99 billion in 2018. Balance Sheet Business Lending ($14.95 billion) and Balance Sheet Property Lending ($11.02 billion) became the second and third largest models, respectively. 2018 was marked by considerable rapid growth of balance sheet models, though it is important to note that more than half of the FinTech firms operated according to the P2P lending model as well. This suggests that there is increasing emphasis on firms to take on origination risk, moving away from exclusively matching models.

Regional Variances

Regional volumes of crowdlending are summarized in Table 4.3. When we consider where crowdlending activities are geographically concentrated (while excluding China), the United States (cumulative lending

Table 4.3 Crowdlending models 2018 by model and region (in USD billion)

	P2P Consumer Lending	P2P Business Lending	P2P Property Lending	Balance Sheet Consumer Lending	Balance Sheet Business Lending	Balance Sheet Property Lending	Invoice Trading	Debt-based Securities
Africa	$0.11	$0.02	$0.00	$0.00	$0.05		$0.00	$0.01
APAC (excl. China)	$0.98	$1.77	$0.66	$0.88	$0.92	$0.02	$0.09	$0.00
Canada	$0.03	$0.05	$0.06	$0.12	$0.39	$0.01	$0.05	
Europe	$2.89	$1.00	$0.14	$0.10	$0.08	$1.38	$0.80	$0.17
LAC	$0.43	$0.13	$0.05	$0.14	$0.26	$0.01	$0.55	$0.13
Middle East	$0.10	$0.05	$0.56		$0.01		$0.04	
UK	$2.06	$2.54	$1.76	$0.64	$0.86	$0.07	$0.85	$0.53
US	$25.39	$2.03	$0.66	$7.52	$12.39	$9.53	$0.14	$0.01

$57.7 billion) ranks first, followed by the United Kingdom ($9.3 billion), the Asia-Pacific ($5.3 billion) and Europe ($6.6 billion). Moreover, if we look at the breakdown of lending activity by model type, we see that certain regions have greater emphasises on P2P lending activities versus balance-sheet lending activities. In Europe and the United Kingdom, for instance, there is a greater emphasis on P2P lending models, while in the United States and Canada, a greater emphasis is placed on balance sheet lending models.

As has been mentioned on a few occasions, the largest volume driving model is P2P Consumer Lending. However, it is worth mentioning that when we consider lending that was directed to business borrowers, nearly $28 billion dollars went to start-ups, SMEs and business entities. Interestingly, a large proportion of business borrowers came from P2P Consumer Lending platforms, receiving a consumer loan in order to support their business funding needs.

Businesses, particularly SMEs, are using various Digital Lending products to meet their working or expansion capital needs. To illustrate the importance of these channels for SME financing, we provide insights from the United Kingdom, which earned a reputation as a leader in P2P Business Lending, as well as an environment in which SME finance is recorded systematically.

Sources of UK SME Finance are presented in Fig. 4.4. The Bank of England estimates that £57.7 billion was lent to SMEs by national banks in 2018, which represents a slight increase compared to last year's figure of £57 billion (UK Finance 2018). By comparing the UK P2P Business Lending volume against that of the UK Finance annual estimate of new loans to SMEs, it has shown that business crowdlending has increased its share of total lending steadily from just 0.3% in 2012 to 14.55% in 2018.

Assuming that the vast majority of borrowers in peer-to-peer business lending are, in fact, small businesses with an annual turnover of less than £2 million, the chart below shows that the volume of P2P Business Lending in the United Kingdom is estimated to be equivalent to 34.8% of all bank lending to small businesses in 2018, almost 20% increase against the previous year. Therefore, P2P Business Lending is becoming an increasingly important contributor to overall SME financing in the United Kingdom in comparison to bank lending channels.

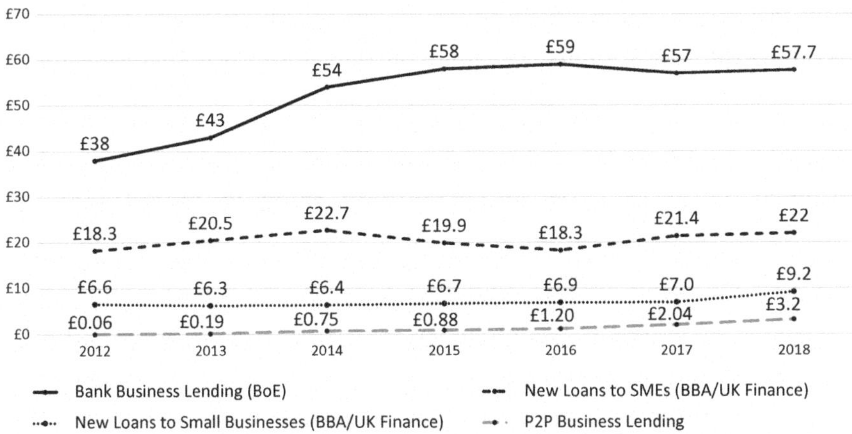

Fig. 4.4 Sources of UK SME finance 2012–2018 (in billion GBP)

Risk Assessment in Crowdlending

A fundamental problem underlying crowdlending is that of asymmetrical information (Leboeuf and Schwienbacher 2018), especially as it relates to mitigating potential risks presented when evaluating potential borrowers. Bachmann et al. (2011) refer to several key determinants that P2P Lending firms must evaluate in order to combat principal-agent problems and provide an overview of the financial characteristics of the borrower as the main indicator of creditworthiness.

Individuals seeking to lend via a P2P lending platform will not always have the requisite tools or skill set to comprehensively assess risk. Therefore, the platform often conducts an analysis of potential borrowers, assigning appropriate risk bands before offering credit. Whilst individual investors must still assess and determine the levels of risk they are willing to take, the risks associated with certain borrowers are often determined by the platform itself.

While in-house methodologies used by platforms for loan risk assessment are difficult to ascertain, as these are proprietary and disclosure is limited (Bank for International Settlements and Financial Stability Board 2017), they usually assess a borrower based on a number of set indicators.

Such indicators include the borrower's existing credit (using traditional credit scoring), any capital or collateral that may exist, the capacity to repay the loan (debt-to-income ratio), and the conditions which the borrower is willing to adhere to. In some cases, platforms may employ an alternative underwriting process using algorithmic-based approaches to credit scoring and non-traditional data, alongside more traditional methods, to determine if the loan is of an acceptable risk level.

When underwriting an *SME borrower*, the credit assessment requirements are usually more robust than in the case of individual borrowing. In such cases, a platform will typically restrict lending to firms with less than three years of credit history and will require recent filed company accounts and information on company management. In some cases, the platform may also restrict lending to firms with a certain level of annual turnover (for example—requiring more than USD $50,000 in annual turnover at minimum). Furthermore, in the case of underwriting a *property loan*, the platform should ideally assess the underlying asset, its location and sector, as well as procure independent valuations on the property and reassure itself that appropriate permission has been granted for any planned development. The platform should also assess the proposed exit strategy (sale, refinance etc.) for the property.

Alternative Credit Analytics

Crowdlending platforms may employ more varied and sophisticated credit assessment practices than traditional financiers. FinTech credit platforms may access a range of potential borrowers' data, which may not be typically sourced and analysed by banks. However, some 'mainstream' credit providers are also incorporating alternative credit analytics into the credit approval process. The types of data, include location-based information, social networking information, hardware data, online shopping and other online behaviour, but also more diffused data on educational attainment and performance, as well as labour market profile and performance (Hale 2019). The lender feeds available data into their algorithm to establish creditworthiness. As algorithms are generally proprietary, it is difficult to ascertain which data points are used and how they are weighted, when determining a credit rating. As a rule, however, there appears to be more evidence of previously excluded borrowers being accepted than of previously accepted borrowers being rejected based on alternative data (ibid.). In this context, machine learning can also be used to analyse data captured during the credit analysis phase. It can also be used to gather data on borrowers with a thin credit file.

While most platforms do not yet offer instantaneous, automated credit approval, some platforms can provide loan approval and disbursement within a few hours (for example, via mobile money). Others are working to bring approval times down to a few minutes. Alternative credit analytics reduces the need for case-by-case manual approval thus increasing the efficiency of the loan approval process.

Pricing

As crowdlending fundamentally occurs online, it reduces operating costs for credit intermediaries by removing the need for physical branches while allowing heavy (or full) automation of loan application, credit risk assessment and pricing processes (Bank for International Settlements and Financial Stability Board 2017). They are also not reliant on legacy infrastructure as banks may be and as a result, pricing will not be impacted by normal pricing considerations of traditional bank lenders. In addition, platforms may fall outside of certain licensing or other regimes, thus reducing regulatory or compliance costs. A study by Autonomous Research (2016) found that the ratio of operating expenses to total costs was less than 2% for Lending Club, a consumer and business P2P lending platform in the United States, and 6% for the largest traditional lenders.

For these reasons FinTech lending platforms may offer lower interest rates for borrowers and/or higher returns to investors (Bank for International Settlements and Financial Stability Board 2017). Research has shown varied outcomes, however, with some studies showing little difference in borrower interest rates and investor rate of return given a similar risk profile (De Roure et al. 2016). It is sometimes difficult to compare the two rates due to a lack of equivalent loans.

Ethical Considerations in Crowdlending

Taking into consideration recent experiences with irresponsible lending leading to high levels of personal lending via credit cards (Richards et al. 2008), which was further exacerbated by the subprime lending upheaval (Gilbert 2011), have all left their mark, and were part of the reasons for the emergence of alternative crowdlending channels. However, these problems were created by individuals who failed in their moral duties when making decisions that later led to significant harmful consequences from default and bankruptcy and all the way to suicide (Gilbert 2011; Richards et al. 2008).

Such moral pitfalls are also relevant for operators of crowdlending platforms, which must strike a delicate balance between business survival and growth and the intermediation of responsible lending. Furthermore, at a macro level, it remains to be seen to what extent does crowdlending reduces or increases long-term indebtedness of borrowers overall, as well as its relative burden on their economies. Research on these aspects of crowdlending are virtually absent and require further attention due to the importance of ethical practice for the well-being of all stakeholders involved.

Loan Defaults & Provision Funds

Some loan defaults are inevitable. Platforms therefore recommend that investors diversify their portfolio on-platform to offset some of the negative effects of default. For example—Funding Circle, a UK-based P2P business platform, recommends a minimum investment of £2000 split across at least 200 loans (McCorquodale 2018). Platforms can sometimes offer provision funds to protect investors from default—a small proportion of monthly loan repayments are placed into a segregated fund. In the event of a default, the provision fund may be utilised on a discretionary basis to ensure that investor repayment occurs as expected. The level of protection and the breadth of coverage depends upon the policy of the platform, as well as the characteristics of different loan cohorts.

While diversification across a large number of borrowers already provides lenders with substantial protection against default and loss (Milne and Parboteeah 2016), defaults do occur. In such cases, platforms attempt to extract as much of the value of the loans from the borrower as is possible within their responsible lending obligations. This involves a combination of soft interventions as well as legal ones carried out according to contract or to insolvency law. For example, the platform may, in acting for investors/creditors, appoint an administrator or receiver, and coordinate with other creditors. Or they might enforce against the security pledged by the borrower. In practice, recoveries are rarely a core competence of the platform operator and thus are often outsourced to debt collection agencies (Bank for International Settlements and Financial Stability Board 2017).

In this context, several academic studies have sought to identify key determinants of crowdlending defaults. Here, a study by Serrano-Cinca et al. (2015) analysing data from Lending Club, has showed that default was associated with borrowers with lower annual income, higher levels of indebtedness, shorter credit histories, and loan purpose where small business and education exhibiting highest likelihood of default. A different study by Lin et al. (2017) was conducted in the context of a Chinese crowdlending platform and showed that higher default rates were recorded among men vs. women, younger vs. older, divorced vs. married, low vs. highly educated individuals, short vs. long working experience, those working for small companies vs. those working for large companies, those who have high debt to income ration vs. those with low debt to income ratio, and those who have a delinquency history vs. those that don't have such history. Furthermore, the higher the amount of monthly repayments the higher likelihood of default. Overall, studies suggest that platforms capture many of the risks in their assessments, and the credit or risk ratings they present are good predictors of default likelihood (Serrano-Cinca et al. 2015; Emekter et al. 2015).

In addition, an interesting insight has been highlighted in a study by Ge et al. (2017), which tapped into the unique context of Chinese crowdlending, where social media is tightly intertwined with platform profiles. Their analysis found a significant decrease in loan default rate and increase in default repayment probability, when such information was shared by the platform on the borrower's social media accounts. This indicates that borrowers are deterred by potential social stigma, and that social information can be used both for credit scoring and default reduction and repayments.

Lender Characteristics

Both Individual or retail lenders/investors are non-professional individuals, that typically fall into one of three categories: (1) certified high net-worth or sophisticated investors; (2) ordinary investors who receive regulated advice (e.g. from a financial advisor); or (3) ordinary investors who self-certify and invest within a regulated prescribed cap (e.g. cap on the amount invested by an individual at a defined percentage of wealth or income, or a cap on the amount that can be invested in a single loan product).

Individual lenders may also be accredited or unaccredited, depending upon the jurisdiction. In many countries there are restrictions that allow only for accredited individuals to participate in digital lending. Accreditation permits individuals to purchase securities that are not registered with financial authorities or are public.

For example, the CCAF has produced an extensive investor-profiling for the UK FinTech credit market (Zhang et al. 2017). The results reveal that P2P Lending investors in the United Kingdom tend to be predominantly males aged over 55, with undergraduate degrees and earning above the average (~£26,500) per annum. They also tend to have some experience in investment or finance. Elsewhere in Europe, Oxera (2015) showed that awareness of P2P lending was associated with higher education and higher income.

The CCAF's research into the risk perceptions of United Kingdom alternative finance investors (Zhang et al. 2017) found that investors in P2P consumer loans see the asset class as similar to managed funds in terms of risk profile and should thus expect similar returns. P2P business loans, on the other hand, are seen as riskier, and of comparable risk level to listed equities. Property P2P is ranked somewhere in between the two.

Institutionalization of Investment in Crowdlending

Institutionalization refers to the proportion of volume which can be attributed to institutional investors, such as pension funds, mutual funds, asset management firms and banks in what is otherwise labelled as 'the crowd'. This excludes individual investors, such as accredited or unaccredited investors. However, the influx of institutional funding from traditional financial institutions, coupled with the increasing involvement of high net worth investors, is also blurring and pushing the boundaries of original conceptualization of the P2P Lending model.

To a certain degree, the involvement of institutional investors in crowd finance may be controversial. There is some evidence that they might have historically derived better returns on platforms than those platforms' individual investors (Mohammadi and Shafi 2017). Here, when institutions are able to self-select loan parts on a more granular basis than individuals, and if they get first pick of the loans on offer, then not only will they derive higher returns, but also make it very difficult for individual investors' portfolios to be optimised.

Figure 4.5 presents the share of institutional versus retail investors in crowdlending. Though retail investment remains the main driving force

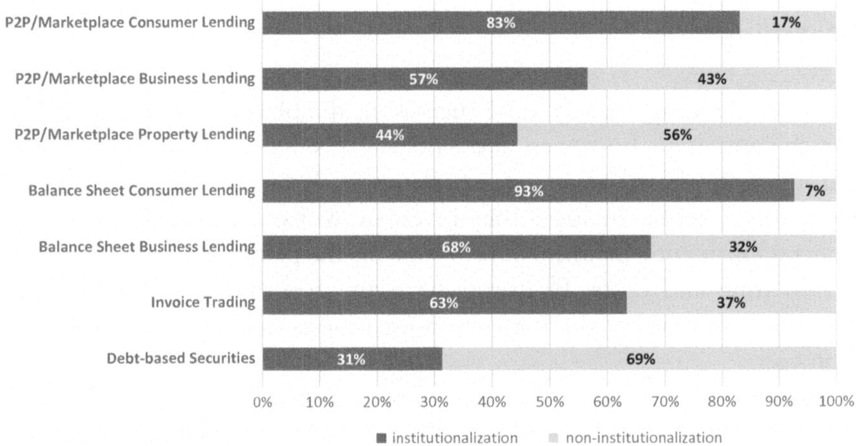

Fig. 4.5 Institutional vs. retail investors in crowdlending (globally) in 2018

of alternative finance volumes, institutional investors also contributed significant sums. The sources of institutional funding vary significantly between models, although P2P lending models tend to attract investment from traditional banks, pension funds, hedge funds and asset management firms. Public and governmental funders, such as local authorities, also actively lend through such channels. In the United Kingdom, during 2017 (Zhang et al. 2018), 40% (£815 million) of the P2P Business Lending volume came from institutional investors, a sharp increase from 28% in 2016. The corresponding figure for P2P Consumer Lending was 39% (£554 million) in 2017.

According to CCAF Global Report (2020), certain lending models lend themselves to greater institutionalization. In 2018, on a global basis, models of consumer lending are heavily influenced by institutional engagement, with balance sheet activities also having considerable influence from institutions. Regionally, the United States is heavily driven by institutional investors with 85% of funding originating from institutional investors. Africa and the Middle East, on the other hand represent regions with lowest proportion of institutional investments, with 17% and 12% respectively. In all other regions (Asia Pacific, Canada, Europe, Latin America, and the UK), institutional investors account for close to 50% of funding.

Matching

For crowdlending models to be successful, the platform must efficiently match compatible borrowers and lenders. This may be done manually or automatically, based on investor preferences. Retail investors may prefer to manually select the loans they invest in, whilst institutional investors may establish auto-investment criteria with the platform to reduce transaction time and costs. Platforms have an incentive to automate loan selection, to simplify the loan selection process and to reduce transaction costs.

Investors have numerous ways of participating in a digital lending platform. Early P2P Lending models allowed individuals to select the specific loans they wanted to participate in, and, on some platforms, bidding for loan parts in an auction at a price of their choice. However, what are commonly referred to as 'self-select' and 'auction' options are becoming increasingly rare. Instead, automated loan selection has become popular practice. In such process, lenders selecting 'investment criteria', which the platform uses to 'auto-invest' the lender's money in loans meeting that criteria.

The most common practice in automation is known as '*Automated Lender Diversification*'. Such approach implies that the lender is a passive investor, being matched against available loan parts/tranches that adhere to his or her predetermined preferences in terms of duration, risk appetite, amount, interest rate, etc. The platform will diversify exposure to new loans within the loan book that meet the investors pre-set selections. In this context, an approach growing in popularity, especially in the United States and the United Kingdom, is the '*Managed Portfolio Approach*'. In this case, lenders may select from two or three 'managed' lending options, where they are no longer selecting their desired duration or a specific interest rate. Rather, they will be joining a portfolio that offers a range of acceptable return, and the platform diversifies lender funds by exposing them across the loan book that fits the lender's 'managed option' (e.g. Zopa Cor & Zopa Plus). To ensure investors receive a consistent product, the platform will continuously move loans into and out of their portfolio so that the portfolio as a whole has the promised attributes.

Such automated assignment mechanisms are likely to attract increased scrutiny from regulators, as they could be construed as constituting investment advice, portfolio management, collective investment, or multilateral trading facilities. This may restrict platforms from offering the service or increase licensing requirements.

Success in Crowdlending

Success in crowdlending is associated with fulfilment of loans, indicating that target sums for a loan were successfully raised from prospective investors. A recent literature review by Shneor and Vik (2020) has identified nine persistent variables which were associated with successful loan fulfilment across multiple studies. First, with respect to borrowers, various signals of risk have been associated with success. Indeed, earlier studies show a positive association of credit scores and success (e.g. Kuwabara et al. 2017; Pope and Sydnor 2011), a negative association between debt to income ratio and success (e.g. Larrimore et al. 2011; Pope and Sydnor 2011), and positive association between previous successful loan raising and success in later loan raising (e.g. Barasinska and Schäfer 2014; Chen et al. 2017). In addition, studies suggest that female borrowers are more successful than men (e.g. Chen et al. 2017; Pope and Sydnor 2011), and this has sometimes been related to asking relatively smaller loans.

Second, certain loan terms were associated with greater success. Unsurprisingly, studies show that successful loans were associated with lower sums (e.g. Kuwabara et al. 2017; Yum et al. 2012), shorter time-horizons (e.g. Galak et al. 2011; Lee and Lee 2012), and higher interest rates (e.g. Feng et al. 2015; Larrimore et al. 2011). Furthermore, success was also positively associated with longer stated duration of campaigns (e.g. Larrimore et al. 2011; Lee and Lee 2012), and higher levels of on-site crowd interactions with borrowers via comments and Q&A (e.g. Lee and Lee 2012; Yum et al. 2012).

Conclusion

Crowdlending emerged as the leading model of crowdfunding in both scope and scale in every region. It is considered as both a challenge and supplement to traditional credit service providers by opening opportunities for investment and borrowing for wider groups of people. For lenders, it offers new investment opportunities, often involving better returns than some alternative investment channels, as well as opening to incorporate new small-scale investors that have not enjoyed such opportunities before. For borrowers, it offers new channels to access credit, often either offered at better terms or by including groups that have previously been marginalized and underserved by traditional credit service providers.

In the current chapter we present the brief history of crowdlending, its diversity of models, the current state or the industry, as well as the underlying mechanisms and principles guiding platform operations including risk assessment and the matching of borrowers and lenders. The discussion is supported by a review of related research, while highlighting trajectories of industry development trends.

Implications for Research

While receiving some attention, opportunities for research into crowdlending realities remain abundant. First, while most research focuses on P2P consumer lending, more research is needed into the particularities of business and property lending in the P2P model, as well as research examining alternative models to P2P including Balance Sheet lending, Invoice Trading, and Debt-based Securities. Here, with respect to all models, scholars are encouraged to examine the motivations for borrowers to use such channels vs. traditional ones, as well as the motivation of lenders to invest via such channels versus alternative investment channels. Furthermore, enhancing our knowledge about drivers of success in filling loans outside of the P2P consumer lending context may be valuable for would be borrowers and platforms that use such models. Alternatively, new research into success drivers in the P2P consumer lending space may also be conducted but should cover new national and cultural contexts beyond the United States and China, which represent most studies published thus far.

Second, of special importance are studies that may examine the impact of crowdlending in broad terms examining to which extent has it delivered on its promises. Here, studies should explore whether indeed access to credit has been improved in various contexts and social groups. Moreover, studies should examine whether crowdlending is used as a supplement or as an alternative to traditional credit services, and whether the conditions offered for such loans are indeed better than those offered elsewhere. Finally, in this context, future research may also examine the impact of crowdlending on indebtedness of individuals and organizations in different socio-economic contexts, studying whether debt burdens have increased, decreased, or remained unchanged following the use of crowdlending.

Implications for Practice

Practical implications are evident with respect to borrowers, lenders, platforms, and regulators. First, individuals and organizations interested in borrowing should examine and educate themselves about opportunities being provided by crowdlending platforms, while comparing them to other channels of credit. Once they decide to use such services, in order to improve their chances of receiving the loan, they should provide reliable information that may reduce the risk associated with their loan requests. At the same time, research suggested that they should aim for shorter term loans and be actively engaged with prospective lenders via social and platform communication tools.

Second, in terms of lenders, would be investors should educate themselves about the services offered by various crowdlending platforms, the different investment products available, and the risks associated with them. While research shows that platform risk assessments and ratings are good predictors of loan default, investors should examine a variety of risk indicators that can better inform their decision. Furthermore, in jurisdictions where automatic assignment of loans is allowed by law, investors should consider using such options for diversification and risk spreading across a portfolio of loans that match their preferences.

Third, platforms should engage in continuous learning about service developments in the industry with focus on process automation and streamlining, as well as the adoption of advanced machine learning in risk assessment and default prediction. This would enhance crowdlending FinTech platforms to fully tap into the cost efficiencies their mode of operations was set to achieve. Furthermore, despite temptation to onboard as many loans as possible, platforms should be wary of risky loans that may tarnish their reputation among prospective investors, as well as trigger regulatory crackdown that may limit industry development beyond the required risk management.

Finally, regulators should follow the industry and engage in active dialogue with its players towards developing regulatory frameworks that balance investor and borrower protection and industry growth, or support increase of access to credit while ensuring responsible use of it. Furthermore, public authorities should be concerned with informing the public about both the opportunities and risks associated with crowdlending engagements through encouraging and/or requiring training for individuals and organizations that use such services to a greater scale and frequency than others.

References

Armstrong, P. (2018). Here Are The U.K. Companies That Will Be Unicorns In 2019. Retrieved January 17, 2020, from https://www.forbes.com/sites/paularmstrongtech/2018/08/13/here-are-the-uk-companies-that-will-be-unicorns-in-2019/#308da7547c81.

Autonomous Research. (2016). Digital Lending: The 100 Billion Dollar Question. Retrieved January 19, 2020, from https://next.autonomous.com/digital-marketplace-lenders.

Bachmann, A., Becker, A., Buerckner, D., et al. (2011). Online Peer-to-Peer Lending – A Literature Review. *Journal of Internet Banking and Commerce, 16*(2), 1–18.

Bank for International Settlements & Financial Stability Board. (2017). Market Structure, Business Models and Financial Stability Implications Bank for International Settlements.

Barasinska, N., & Schäfer, D. (2014). Is Crowdfunding Different? Evidence on the Relation Between Gender and Funding Success from a German Peer-to-Peer Lending Platform. *German Economic Review, 15*(4), 436–452.

Barry, E. (2019). The History of US Peer-to-Peer Lending. Retrieved January 17, 2020, from https://www.finder.com/p2p-lending-usa.

Bruton, G., Khavul, S., Siegel, D., et al. (2015). New Financial Alternatives in Seeding Entrepreneurship: Microfinance, Crowdfunding, and Peer-to-Peer Innovations. *Entrepreneurship Theory and Practice, 39*(1), 9–26.

Chen, D., Li, X., & Lai, F. (2017). Gender Discrimination in Online Peer-to-Peer Credit Lending: Evidence from a Lending Platform in China. *Electronic Commerce Research, 17*(4), 553–583.

Chorzempa, M. (2018). Massive P2P Failures in China: Underground Banks Going Under. *China Economic Watch* [Online]. Retrieved from https://www.piie.com/blogs/china-economic-watch/massive-p2p-failures-china-underground-banks-going-under.

De Roure, C., Pelizzon, L., & Tasca, P. (2016). *How Does P2P Lending Fit into the Consumer Credit Market?* Deutsche Bundesbank Discussion Papers. Deutsche Bundesbank.

Dorfleitner, G., Rad, J., & Weber, M. (2017). Pricing in the Online Invoice Trading Market: First Empirical Evidence. *Economics Letters, 161*, 56–61.

Emekter, R., Tu, Y., Jirasakuldech, B., et al. (2015). Evaluating Credit Risk and Loan Performance in Online Peer-to-Peer (P2P) Lending. *Applied Economics, 47*(1), 54–70.

Feng, Y., Fan, X., & Yoon, Y. (2015). Lenders and Borrowers' Strategies in Online Peer-to-Peer Lending Market: An Empirical Analysis of ppdai.com. *Journal of Electronic Commerce Research, 16*(3), 242–260.

Galak, J., Small, D., & Stephen, A. T. (2011). Microfinance Decision Making: A Field Study of Prosocial Lending. *Journal of Marketing Research, 48*(SPL), S130–S137.

Ge, R., Feng, J., Gu, B., et al. (2017). Predicting and Deterring Default with Social Media Information in Peer-to-Peer Lending. *Journal of Management Information Systems, 34*(2), 401–424.

Gilbert, J. (2011). Moral Duties in Business and Their Societal Impacts: The Case of the Subprime Lending Mess. *Business and Society Review, 116*(1), 87–107.

Haddad, C., & Hornuf, L. (2019). The Emergence of the Global Fintech Market: Economic and Technological Determinants. *Small Business Economics, 53*(1), 81–105.

Hale, T. (2019). How Big Data Really Fits into Lending. Retrieved January 19, 2020, from https://ftalphaville.ft.com/2019/03/13/1552488421000/How-big-data-really-fits-into-lending/.

Hollas, J. (2013). Is Crowdfunding Now A Threat to Traditional Finance? *Corporate Finance Review, 18*(1), 27–31.

Kotarba, M. (2016). New Factors Including Changes in the Retail Banking Bustomer Relationship Management (CRM) and Their Exploration by the Fintech Industry. *Foundations of Management, 9*, 69–78.

Kuwabara, K., Anthony, D., & Horne, C. (2017). In the Shade of a Forest Status, Reputation, and Ambiguity in an Online Microcredit Market. *Social Science Research, 64*, 96–118.

Larrimore, L., Jiang, L., Larrimore, J., et al. (2011). Peer to Peer Lending: The Relationship Between Language Features, Trustworthiness, and Persuasion Success. *Journal of Applied Communication Research, 39*(1), 19–37.

Leboeuf, G., & Schwienbacher, A. (2018). Crowdfunding as a New Financing Tool. In D. Cumming & L. Hornuf (Eds.), *The Economics of Crowdfunding: Startups, Portals and Investor Behavior*. Cham: Springer International Publishing.

Lee, E., & Lee, B. (2012). Herding Behavior in Online P2P Lending: An Empirical Investigation. *Electronic Commerce Research and Applications, 11*(5), 495–503.

Lin, X., Li, X., & Zheng, Z. (2017). Evaluating Borrower's Default Risk in Peer-to-Peer Lending: Evidence from a Lending Platform in China. *Applied Economics, 49*(35), 3538–3545.

McCorquodale, R. (2018). How to Earn a More Stable Return with Diversification. Retrieved January 19, 2020, from https://www.fundingcircle.com/blog/2018/06/earn-stable-return-diversification/.

Milne, A., & Parboteeah, P. (2016). *The Business Models and Economics of Peer-to-Peer Lending*. Brussels: European Credit Research Institute.

Mohammadi, A., & Shafi, K. (2017, March). How Wise Are Crowd? A Comparative Study of Crowd and Institutions in Peer-to-Business Online Lending Markets. https://static.sys.kth.se/itm/wp/cesis/cesiswp450.pdf.

Nixon, G. (2020). Peer-to-Peer Trade Body Is Axed as Lenders such as Funding Circle, RateSetter and Zopa Join a Wider Fintech Group. Retrieved January 17, 2020, from https://www.thisismoney.co.uk/money/investing/article-7881555/Peer-peer-platforms-shut-independent-trade-body.html.

Oxera. (2015). Crowdfunding from an Investor Perspective. Retrieved January 19, 2020, from https://ec.europa.eu/info/sites/info/files/file_import/160503-study-crowdfunding-investor-perspective_en_0.pdf.

Pope, D. G., & Sydnor, J. R. (2011). What's in a Picture?: Evidence of Discrimination from Prosper.com. *Journal of Human Resources, 46*(1), 53–92.

Popescu, G. (2016). The Complete Guide to Regulation of Marketplace Lending. Retrieved January 17, 2020, from https://lending-times.com/2016/04/21/the-complete-guide-to-regulation-of-marketplace-lending/.

Richards, M., Palmer, P., & Bogdanova, M. (2008). Irresponsible Lending? A Case Study of a U.K. Credit Industry Reform Initiative. *Journal of Business Ethics, 81*(3), 499–512.

Serrano-Cinca, C., Gutiérrez-Nieto, B., & López-Palacios, L. (2015). Determinants of Default in P2P Lending. *PLOS ONE, 10*(10), e0139427.

Shneor, R., & Vik, A. A. (2020). Crowdfunding Success: A Systematic Literature Review 2010–2017. *Baltic Journal of Management, 5*(2), 149–182.

UK Finance. (2018). SME Finance in the UK: Past, Present and Future. Retrieved from https://www.ukfinance.org.uk/system/files/UK-Finance-SME-Finance-in-UK-AW-web.pdf.

Yum, H., Lee, B., & Chae, M. (2012). From the Wisdom of Crowds to My Own Judgment in Microfinance Through Online Peer-to-Peer Lending Platforms. *Electronic Commerce Research and Applications, 11*(5), 469–483.

Zhang, S., & Miller, M. (2017). China's New Illegal Fundraising Topped $36 billion Last Year. Retrieved April 30, 2019, from https://www.reuters.com/article/us-china-fraud-crackdown/chinas-new-illegal-fundraising-topped-36-billion-last-year-idUSKBN17R11X.

Zhang, B., Ziegler, T., Garvey, K., et al. (2017). *Entrenching Innovation: The 4th UK Alternative Finance Industry Report*. Cambridge, UK: Cambridge Centre for Alternative Finance.

Zhang, B., Ziegler, T., Mammadova, L., et al. (2018). *The 5th UK Alternative Finance Industry Report*. Cambridge, UK: Cambridge Centre for Alternative Finance.

Ziegler, T., Johanson, D., Zhang, B., et al. (2018). *The 3rd Asia Pacific Region Alternative Finance Industry Report*. Cambridge, UK: Cambridge Centre for Alternative Finance.

Ziegler, T., Shneor, R., Wenzlaff, K., et al. (2020). *The Global Alternative Finance Benchmarking Report*. Cambridge, UK: Cambridge Centre for Alternative Finance.

5

Equity Crowdfunding: Principles and Investor Behaviour

Anna Lukkarinen

Introduction

Since the first online equity crowdfunding platform was established in France in 2008, equity crowdfunding has rapidly gained foothold across the world as an equity financing mechanism for early-stage entrepreneurial ventures. It allows ventures to gather funds for growth and expansion, and some ventures have indeed reached strong growth after their equity crowdfunding campaign, although many others have failed (Schwienbacher 2019). The investor base is composed of unaccredited as well as accredited investors, and increasingly also professional investors such as angel investors and venture capital funds (Wang et al. 2019).

The equity crowdfunding market grew strongly in the early 2010s across the world. From 2016 onwards, volumes in some regions have

Parts of the content of this chapter have been extracted from the overview chapter of the Aalto University Doctoral Dissertation referred to as — Lukkarinen (2019) and are provided here with the author's permission.

A. Lukkarinen (✉)
School of Science, Aalto University, Espoo, Finland
e-mail: anna.lukkarinen@aalto.fi

R. Shneor et al. (eds.), *Advances in Crowdfunding*,
https://doi.org/10.1007/978-3-030-46309-0_5

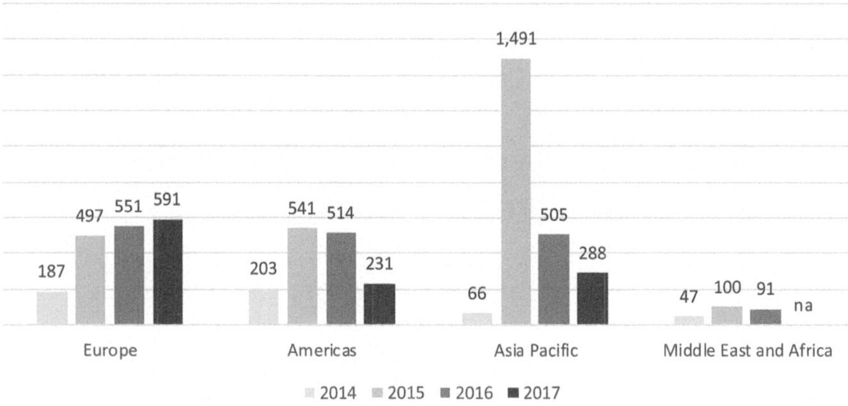

Fig. 5.1 Equity crowdfunding volumes (million EUR). (Source: Based on figures reported in Garvey et al. 2017; Zhang et al. 2018; Ziegler et al. 2018a, b, c, d, 2019)

experienced declines driven by regulatory uncertainty and constraints (Garvey et al. 2017; Ziegler et al. 2018a). The largest individual countries for equity crowdfunding are the United Kingdom (EUR 378 million in 2017) and the United States (EUR 209 million in 2017) (Ziegler et al. 2018a, 2019). Figure 5.1 presents yearly equity crowdfunding volumes by region.

Equity Crowdfunding Principles

While various different practices and conventions exist in equity crowdfunding across platforms and countries, certain principles have become widely established. Figure 5.2 presents a typical equity crowdfunding process.

The first contact between ventures and platforms is commonly inbound: interested ventures contact the platform. However, contact may also be established through outbound origination whereby the platform approaches attractive ventures, or through third-party referrals. Platforms vet and filter the ventures interested in conducting a campaign, with the extent of legal and financial due diligence varying by platform (Löher 2017; Schwienbacher 2019). If the outcome of the assessment is favourable, the venture proceeds to prepare and implement the

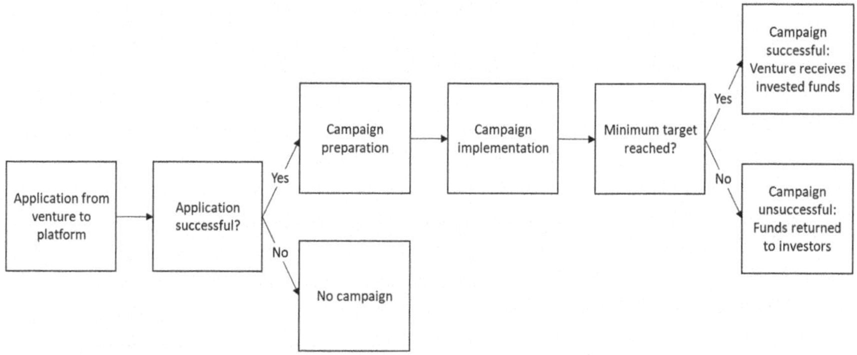

Fig. 5.2 Typical equity crowdfunding process under the all-or-nothing model. (Source: Modified from Lukkarinen et al. 2016)

crowdfunding campaign. The preselection funnel of platforms is often highly selective. In Europe, 6% of applicant ventures were deemed qualified by platforms and were thus onboarded to conduct a campaign in 2017 (Ziegler et al. 2019). Most equity crowdfunding platforms operate under the all-or-nothing model, in which the campaign must reach its pre-set minimum funding target in order to become successful and for the venture to receive the invested funds. If the minimum target is not reached, the funds are returned to investors (Tuomi and Harrison 2017).

The revenue model of platforms typically relies mostly on success fees or listing fees from fundraisers (Barbi and Mattioli 2019; Hornuf and Schwienbacher 2016; Shafi 2019). Compared with traditional forms of early-stage equity investing, the standardized online nature of the equity crowdfunding investment process allows for very low transaction costs. Indeed, low investor-side transaction costs, along with low minimum investment thresholds, are key factors enabling the participation of large crowds in equity crowdfunding (Kim and Viswanathan 2019). Accordingly, the bargaining power of individual crowd investors both pre- and post-investment is usually low. As fundraisers and platforms define the campaign details beforehand, prospective investors cannot influence transaction terms or covenants (Hornuf and Schmitt 2017). General shareholder rights vary by country and by platform. While some platforms call for the use of the same share class for equity crowdfunding investors as for other equity investors (Vismara 2018), others offer shareholders' agreements in which the shares offered via crowdfunding form a separate class with no voting rights (Frydrych et al. 2014; Hornuf and Neuenkirch 2017; Tuomi and Harrison 2017; Walthoff-Borm et al. 2018).

Investor Characteristics and Motivations

Investor Characteristics

Equity crowdfunding investors are a very diverse group of individuals with varying levels of professional and educational backgrounds (Lukkarinen et al. 2017) and investor professionalism (Guenther et al. 2018). Thus far, the majority of equity crowdfunding investments have been made by individuals who have no professional affiliation with investing. However, platforms are also attracting angel investors and venture capitalists who are seeking portfolio diversification and the convenience of standardized online investment processes (Bessière et al. 2019; Wang et al. 2019). For instance, in the Australia-based sample of Guenther et al. (2018), 10% of equity crowdfunding investors were accredited or professional investors.

Equity crowdfunding investors are predominantly male, although the share of female investors has been growing (Ziegler et al. 2018a, d, 2019). Investor age varies but averages at around 40, and investors' experience with other forms of investing ranges from none to extensive (Baeck et al. 2014; Guenther et al. 2014; Hornuf and Neuenkirch 2017; Lukkarinen et al. 2017; Mohammadi and Shafi 2018).

Heterogeneous Motivations

Investors' motivations for investing in equity crowdfunding are very heterogeneous, and they vary both between investors and between campaigns (Goethner et al. 2018; Lukkarinen et al. 2017). Accordingly, research has suggested that investments would be motivated mainly by an aim to earn financial returns (Baeck et al. 2014; Cholakova and Clarysse

2015; Kim and Viswanathan 2019), mainly by intrinsic reasons such as obtaining personal satisfaction (Schwienbacher and Larralde 2012), or by a combination of both (Collins and Pierrakis 2012; Daskalakis and Yue 2017). Survey results by Bretschneider and Leimeister (2017) indicate that equity crowdfunding investors are motivated by several factors, such as the ability to receive recognition, to influence campaign outcomes, to create an online image, and to receive returns or rewards, but not by altruistic motives. Vismara (2019), on the other hand, suggests that some equity crowdfunding investors may invest out of a wish to support sustainable development in the world. As such, no consensus exists as of yet about investor motivations in equity crowdfunding, perhaps due to their inherent heterogeneity and the rapid evolution of the industry.

Investors' Relationship with Fundraisers

While part of the investments in equity crowdfunding come from the family, friends, and other social connections of the entrepreneurs, the majority of investment activity is driven by the "true crowd" (Ahlers et al. 2015; Vismara 2018). According to a survey conducted by Guenther et al. (2014), 4% of equity crowdfunding investors are family members or friends of the fund seekers. Similarly, a survey by Lukkarinen et al. (2017) indicates that personal knowledge of the entrepreneur or the team was on average not considered an important decision criterion by equity crowdfunding investors. Furthermore, a dataset sourced from the database of an Australian equity crowdfunding platform indicates that 3% of equity crowdfunding investors are somehow connected to the venture (Guenther et al. 2018).

Thus, while some equity crowdfunding investments originate through the connections and marketing activities of fundraising ventures, platforms have a central role in attracting prospective investors to the campaign websites (Baeck et al. 2014). Consequently, rather than relying solely on their existing networks, entrepreneurs who conduct equity crowdfunding campaigns make an effort to build new ties and to expand their networks by attracting new investors via the platform (Brown et al. 2019).

Investing Behaviour

Investors' Limited Due Diligence

Although the equity crowdfunding market has been growing in size and relevance, with possibly significant implications for fundraising ventures (White and Dumay 2017), equity crowdfunding has limited centrality from the point of view of individual investors. It is usually a sporadic activity, with most investors having invested in only one or few equity crowdfunding campaigns on any focal platform (Baeck et al. 2014; Bapna 2019; Mohammadi and Shafi 2018), and with the median or average sums invested running relatively low, typically in the low thousands of euros (Bapna 2019; Block et al. 2018; Mahmood et al. 2019). Indeed, most investors describe the sums they invest via equity crowdfunding as "small" and as representing a small part of their overall investment portfolios (Estrin et al. 2018).

Accordingly, and in line with bounded rationality theory (Simon 1991), the investment target evaluation process of equity crowdfunding investors tends to be very limited. A survey of equity crowdfunding investors by Guenther et al. (2014) found that, on average, investors spend less than an hour to study the business plan, less than an hour on the campaign page, and less than an hour to study the venture's home page. Equity crowdfunding platforms, on the other hand, usually dedicate significant time and effort to evaluate each venture before deciding on its suitability for fundraising, thereby providing investors with a certain level of quality assurance for the campaigns that become available on platforms (Cumming et al. 2018; Guenther et al. 2018; Lukkarinen et al. 2016).

Investing time and effort in one-on-one communications between small-sum investors and fundraisers makes little economic sense in equity crowdfunding (Moritz et al. 2015). Accordingly, the majority of equity crowdfunding investors do not communicate directly with the entrepreneur (Guenther et al. 2014; Moritz et al. 2015). However, entrepreneurs and investors utilize digital pseudo-personal communications, such as videos, online investor relations channels, and social media, which enable investors to form a view of the venture and its management (Moritz et al. 2015).

Information asymmetries in the equity crowdfunding setting are high, as prospective investors possess considerably less knowledge about the fundraising venture than do the entrepreneurs (Piva and Rossi-Lamastra 2018). While investors do not usually conduct lengthy target evaluation processes or engage in personal communications to mitigate the hindering effect of information asymmetries, they do tend to take into account rapidly observable campaign features (Lukkarinen et al. 2016). These include the presence (Li et al. 2016) and length (Vismara et al. 2017) of videos, the minimum allowed investment (Hornuf and Schwienbacher 2018a; Lukkarinen et al. 2016), and visual cues such as logos (Mahmood et al. 2019). Investment decision criteria that equity crowdfunding investors have highlighted as important in investor surveys include the perceived informativeness of the campaign page and materials, clarity and uniqueness of the business idea and products, characteristics of the entrepreneur and the team, the explanation for the planned used of funds, perceived openness and trustworthiness, and the presence of a credible lead investor (Bapna 2019; Kang et al. 2016; Lukkarinen et al. 2017; Moritz et al. 2015; Ordanini et al. 2011).

Ventures can signal the attractiveness of the investment opportunity and the underlying venture quality to prospective investors in a variety of ways (Ahlers et al. 2015). The share of equity retained by the entrepreneurs in the equity offering signals the entrepreneurs' belief in the future prospects of the venture and influences investor interest (Ahlers et al. 2015; Vismara 2016). Entrepreneurs' human capital, as measured by business education and entrepreneurial experience, serves as a low-ambiguity signal of venture quality and thereby drives investments (Piva and Rossi-Lamastra 2018). A venture's intellectual capital can signal innovation capabilities, managerial skills, and overall venture quality (Ralcheva and Roosenboom 2016) while also creating entry barriers to competitors (Piva and Rossi-Lamastra 2018), although findings about the effect of the possession of intellectual property rights on campaign success remain mixed (Ahlers et al. 2015; Kleinert et al. 2020). As business failure can signal a lack of entrepreneurial skill, prospective equity crowdfunding investors discount entrepreneurs who have previously experienced a business failure, unless the investors receive evidence that the failure was due to bad luck rather than a lack of entrepreneurial skill (Zunino et al. 2017). Furthermore, investors prefer taking the high risks inherent in equity crowdfunding (Kleinert et al. 2020) when the entrepreneurs seek to reduce uncertainty by offering detailed financial information (Ahlers et al. 2015).

Updates posted by entrepreneurs on the campaign site during the campaign have a positive impact on fundraising performance, as they can convey messages about venture value to prospective investors in a trustworthy and easily observable manner (Hornuf and Schwienbacher 2018b; Li et al. 2016). Update content matters, with updates about developments that have taken place during the campaign considered most relevant by investors (Block et al. 2018).

Angel and venture capital investors typically conduct extensive, or at least moderate, due diligence on their investment targets (Fried and Hisrich 1994; Van Osnabrugge 2000). Ventures that have already secured Angel or venture capital investors are thus more likely to successfully raise funding in equity crowdfunding campaigns, as the presence of professional investors helps mitigate the adverse effect of information asymmetries (Kleinert et al. 2020; Mamonov and Malaga 2018).

Importance of Other Investors' Actions

Most equity crowdfunding platforms allow for digital visibility, with all prospective investors usually able to see in real-time the total amount already invested, the number of investors or investments already committed to a campaign, and investment-related comments written by other users (Ahlers et al. 2015; Hornuf and Schwienbacher 2018b; Kim and Viswanathan 2019; Lukkarinen et al. 2016). This contrasts the funding dynamics of initial public offerings, in which investors do not know the amount of money already invested by others at the time of subscription (Vismara 2016). Accordingly, when making investment decisions, equity crowdfunding investors consider not only the available venture information and predetermined campaign characteristics, but also the within-campaign funding dynamics, thereby at least partially relying on the behaviour of others.

In particular, later investors have the opportunity to take the behaviour of previous investors into account in their decision making (Vismara 2018). Campaigns with a larger number of early investors are more likely to become successful, possibly because early investments send a signal of trust and confidence to prospective later investors and because early investors may contribute to the word-of-mouth around a campaign (Lukkarinen et al. 2016; Vulkan et al. 2016). Experienced early investors, in particular, have a strong influence on the investment decisions of prospective later investors (Kim and Viswanathan 2019; Vismara 2018), and especially on the decisions of small crowdinvestors (Cumming et al. 2019).

Furthermore, the size of previous investments positively predicts subsequent investment activity at campaign level, as large investments may send a signal of the respective investor possessing knowledge that others do not have (Åstebro et al. 2018; Hornuf and Schwienbacher 2018b; Vulkan et al. 2016). Similarly, the amount of time that has passed since the most recent investment in a campaign has a negative effect on the likelihood and size of subsequent investments, as an absence of investments can be indicative of a lack of investors who would possess positive private signals of the campaign (Åstebro et al. 2018). Such herding behaviour can increase the likelihood of investors investing in low-quality ventures in which they might not invest without the cues observed from the crowd. Consequently, Stevenson et al. (2019) introduce the term *crowd bias* to refer to "an individual's tendency to follow the opinions of the crowd despite the presence of contrary objective quality indicators" (p. 348).

Most platforms host discussion boards on which users can pose questions to the entrepreneurs and discuss the investment opportunity with other users. Discussions tend to have a positive effect on investment activity, although the effect depends on the discussion topic (Kleinert and Volkmann 2019). Positive comments by previous investors, in particular, have a positive effect, as they may contain positive information about the attractiveness of the venture (Hornuf and Schwienbacher 2018b).

Local Bias

Much like investors in other forms of investing (e.g., Grinblatt and Keloharju 2001), equity crowdfunding investors are locally biased. Suggested reasons for equity crowdfunding investors' tendency to invest in ventures located geographically close to them include access to better and more tangible information and an ability to better monitor the venture (Guenther et al. 2018; Hornuf and Schmitt 2017). The local bias effect is weaker for financially more literate investors, perhaps because they are more likely to pursue risk reduction through portfolio diversification (Hornuf and Schmitt 2017).

A distinct aspect of local bias is investors' tendency to invest domestically. This preference stems from the benefits of geographic proximity, difficulties caused by differences in legal frameworks, and the burden and risks associated with foreign currency investments (Niemand et al. 2018). Interestingly, while investors are indeed sensitive to geographic distance when investing domestically, distance is not relevant in cross-border investments, perhaps because of the difficulty of leveraging local knowledge in any cross-border investment, regardless of distance (Guenther et al. 2018; Maula and Lukkarinen 2019).

The share of cross-border investments has been growing, however, along with platforms' increasing internationalization efforts. While the United States is still strongly domestically focused (Ziegler et al. 2018a), cross-border investments represented 9% of funding outflows and 16% of funding inflows among European platforms (Ziegler et al. 2019) and 31% and 22% of outflows and inflows, respectively, among Asia Pacific platforms (Ziegler et al. 2018d) in 2017.[1] The Australia-based sample of Guenther et al. (2018) portrayed a 9% share of cross-border investors, whereas the Finland-based sample of Maula and Lukkarinen (2019) and the Germany-based sample of Hornuf and Schmitt (2017) featured 8% and 9% cross-border investments, respectively. As cross-border investing opens up a large multiple of investment opportunities compared to domestic investing, the attention that cross-border investors pay to foreign campaigns becomes an important driver of investors' investment choices (Maula and Lukkarinen 2019).

Comparison of Early-Stage Equity Financing Forms

Equity crowdfunding addresses partly the same market as traditional forms of entrepreneurial finance, most notably angel investors, venture capitalists, and micro funders.[2] Partly, however, it serves to fund such ventures that might otherwise be left unfunded (Harrison and Mason 2019). Table 5.1 presents a comparative summary of different forms of early-stage equity financing. Salient similarities between neighbouring forms are highlighted in italic.

In several respects, equity crowdfunding investors bear resemblance to traditional micro funders. Both make relatively small high-risk investments using their own money, with the investing activity not being their main occupation. While some of their investments are motivated by returns, both can also invest out of a willingness to support the target venture. They both expend very limited effort to evaluate the target, although the decision making of equity crowdfunding investors may also partly rely on their knowledge of the platform having already pre-evaluated the target (Tuomi and Harrison 2017).

A key differentiator between equity crowdfunding and more traditional forms of early-stage equity financing is the digital nature of online crowdfunding, which renders it possible for ventures to gather investments from large numbers of people without personal entrepreneur-investor interactions and with a high degree of visibility towards investors (Horvát et al. 2018; Kim and Viswanathan 2019).

It is worth noting in this context that, from the viewpoint of an entrepreneurial venture, the different forms of financing need not be mutually exclusive, nor is their sequential order invariable. Entrepreneurial ventures can use different sources of funding at different lifecycle stages. Ventures that have successfully secured financing through equity crowdfunding have been shown to be more likely to attract investments from angel investors or venture capitalists in follow-up funding rounds (Hornuf et al. 2018), whereas ventures with unsuccessful equity crowdfunding campaigns may fail with no opportunities for follow-up funding (Walthoff-Borm et al. 2018). In addition, ventures can use several forms

Table 5.1 Comparison of different forms of early-stage equity financing

Features	Equity crowdfunding investors	Micro funders	Angel Investors	Venture capitalists
Funder characteristics				
Typical funder background	Often high education, many with no entrepreneurial background (Lukkarinen et al. 2017)	Often high education, many with entrepreneurial background (Avdeitchikova 2008)	High education, previous experience from entrepreneurship, consulting, and industry (Politis and Landström 2002)	Previous experience from finance, consulting, and industry (Wilson and Testoni 2014)
Heterogeneity of funder space	Very high: crowd composed of many different types of investors (Block et al. 2018; Moritz et al. 2015)	High: varying demographic backgrounds, investment amounts, and skills (Maula et al. 2005; Szerb et al. 2007)	Relatively high: diversity in competence, motivations, and investment activity (Sullivan and Miller 1996)	Low (although categories exist): firms unified by an aim to earn profits and efforts to hire suitable staff (MacMillan et al. 1985)
Source of funds	*Investor's own money* (Wilson and Testoni 2014)	*Investor's own money* (De Clercq et al. 2012)	*Investor's own* (Mason and Harrison 2008)	Others' money pooled into venture capital fund (Sahlman 1990)
Centrality of investing activity for funder	*Not central; limited contributions of time and money* (Estrin et al. 2018)	*Not central; limited contributions of time and money* (Szerb et al. 2007)	Often central (Mason and Harrison 2008; Politis and Landström 2002)	Very central; key purpose of venture capital firm (Tyebjee and Bruno 1984)
Venture characteristics				
Risk level	*Very high risk* (Signori and Vismara 2018; Walthoff-Borm et al. 2018)	*Very high risk* (De Clercq et al. 2012)	High risk (Avdeitchikova 2008; Landström 1993)	Rather high risk (De Clercq et al. 2012; Van Osnabrugge 2000)

Lifecycle stage	Very early-stage, early-stage, or advanced early-stage (Cumming and Vismara 2017; Rossi 2014)	Very early-stage; earlier than angel investors (Avdeitchikova 2008)	Early-stage; earlier than venture capital (Mason and Harrison 2008)	Advanced early-stage; later than angel investors (Mason and Harrison 2008)
Investment decision process				
Motivations for investing	*Various; including intrinsic and extrinsic* (Harrison and Mason 2019; Lukkarinen et al. 2017)	*Various; including intrinsic and extrinsic* (De Clercq et al. 2012; Maula et al. 2005)	Financial returns important, but also intrinsic motivations (Van Osnabrugge 2000)	Financial returns highly important (Sudek 2006; Wilson and Testoni 2014)
Extent of target evaluation	Limited (conducted by individual)/medium (conducted by platform) (Ahlers et al. 2015; Guenther et al. 2018)	Limited; conducted by individual (Maula et al. 2005)	Medium; conducted by individual, possibly with support from angel network (EBAN 2014; Wiltbank 2009)	Extensive; involves staff and often external advisors (Fried and Hisrich 1994; Wilson and Testoni 2014)
Key investment criteria	Rapid-to-observe venture and campaign features (Block et al. 2018; Lukkarinen et al. 2016)	Financial, social, and environmental venture and team features (De Clercq et al. 2012; Estapé-Dubreuil et al. 2016)	*Entrepreneur, team, product, market, business plan, exit opportunities* (Prowse 1998; Sudek 2006; Van Osnabrugge 2000)	*Product, market, entrepreneur, team, expected returns, exit opportunities* (MacMillan et al. 1985; Streletzki and Schulte 2013)
Funding mechanism characteristics				

(*continued*)

Table 5.1 (continued)

Features	Equity crowdfunding investors	Micro funders	Business angels	Venture capitalists
Role of digitalization	Central; all or most activity via online platform, allowing for high volumes and visibility (Horvát et al. 2018; Kim and Viswanathan 2019)	*Limited; in-person interactions via personal connections or organizations* (Estapé-Dubreuil et al. 2016; Maula et al. 2005)	*Limited but emerging; face-to-face contacts important, some are starting to use platforms* (Brown et al. 2019; Van Osnabrugge 2000)	*Limited; social networks, direct contacts and proactive outreach important* (Tyebjee and Bruno 1984)
Transaction costs	Very low due to standardized and automated processes and the online nature of communications (Hornuf and Schmitt 2017; Löher 2017)	Low; close pre-investment connections contribute to low screening and monitoring requirements (De Clercq et al. 2012)	Relatively low; administration costs are small (Landström 1993)	High; costs include advisory fees (Van Osnabrugge 2000)
Bargaining power of individual investors	Very low; deal terms pre-determined by venture (Hornuf and Schmitt 2017)	Medium; small investments but opportunity to make information requests (De Clercq et al. 2012)	Relatively high; personal negotiations before deal (Van Osnabrugge 2000)	Very high; formal contract formulation processes, high equity stakes, time devoted for negotiations (Tyebjee and Bruno 1984; Van Osnabrugge 2000)

Connections between funders and the venture				
Pre-investment relationship	Often no relationship (Guenther et al. 2018; Vismara 2018)	Rather often a pre-existing family or friendship relationship (De Clercq et al. 2012; Maula et al. 2005)	Often a relationship or prior knowledge of the entrepreneur (Avdeitchikova 2008)	Only occasionally prior knowledge of the entrepreneur (Fried and Hisrich 1994; Tyebjee and Bruno 1984)
Communication during investment process	Usually no personal communication (Guenther et al. 2014; Moritz et al. 2015)	Varying levels of social connection (De Clercq et al. 2012)	*Active, including face-to-face meetings* (Van Osnabrugge 2000)	*Very active, including many face-to-face meetings* (Fried and Hisrich 1994; Van Osnabrugge 2000)
Post-funding involvement of funders	Very limited, passive (Brown et al. 2019; Walthoff-Borm et al. 2018; Wilson and Testoni 2014)	Varied but often limited and light, sometimes passive (Avdeitchikova 2008; Estapé-Dubreuil et al. 2016)	*Often active via board position or advisory roles* (Mason and Harrison 2008)	*Active via board position or advisory roles; control* (Tyebjee and Bruno 1984; Van Osnabrugge 2000)

Source: Lukkarinen (2019)

simultaneously. Complementarities, such as a possibility of co-investing in deals, have been previously identified between venture capital funds and angel investors (Harrison and Mason 2000). Similarly, equity crowdfunding campaigns have begun attracting investments from angel investors and venture capital funds, with angel investors making use of the digital screening and investing opportunities offered by equity crowdfunding platforms, and with venture capitalists acting as lead investors in high-volume deals (Brown et al. 2019; Itenbert and Smith 2017).

Discussion

Since its inception in 2008, online equity crowdfunding has experienced strong market growth. Consequently, equity crowdfunding has gathered wide research interest, and it has come to justify its existence as a standalone research target.

The investor base in equity crowdfunding is diverse, with some investors originating from the close social networks of the entrepreneurs, but with much activity also being driven by the "true crowd". In addition, angel and venture capital investors are increasingly making use of the opportunities offered by equity crowdfunding platforms. While investors' motivations for investing are heterogeneous, a wish for financial returns is important. In accordance with the limited centrality of equity crowdfunding from the investor's point of view, crowdinvestors spend very limited time evaluating target ventures. They focus on rapidly observable campaign features, signals of venture quality, and the actions of other investors when making investment decisions. Equity crowdfunding complements the spectrum of traditional venture financing mechanisms. While it bears certain resemblance to other forms of early-stage equity financing, equity crowdfunding is clearly distinguishable by its special features stemming from its digital nature, in particular its high degree of investor-side visibility into campaign funding dynamics and the low contributions of time and money required for making an investment.

Implications for Research

Research on equity crowdfunding can anchor itself in the wider context of not only crowdsourcing or crowdfunding, but also that of early-stage equity investing or even public stock investing (Cummings et al. 2019). As findings can differ by investor type and by venture type, research on equity crowdfunding can benefit from taking into account the heterogeneity of investors' motivations, decision criteria, and characteristics, on the one hand, and the diversity of fundraisers, on the other hand. Furthermore, as investors and platforms are increasingly active across country borders, cross-country and cross-platform research identifying similarities and differences across country and platform contexts is increasingly needed. Finally, although research about campaign success factors and investor features in equity crowdfunding is already abundant (Mochkabadi and Volkmann 2020), it dates empirically back to the early stages of industry development. As industry characteristics and dynamics vary across lifecycle stages, further research on equity crowdfunding at platform, investor, and investment level becomes necessary as the industry matures. Furthermore, the maturing state of the industry makes it increasingly possible to assess post-campaign outcomes for investors and for fundraisers.

Implications for Practice

The present research findings on equity crowdfunding investors have also practical implications. An awareness of investors' limited due diligence and investors' reliance on non-traditional decision criteria when making equity crowdfunding investments can support policymakers in their pursuit of the optimal level of regulation. The heterogeneity of the funder space offers platforms opportunities to differentiate their services at platform level and at investor level. Platforms can accommodate the existence of different investor segments by focusing explicitly on certain segments and selecting fundraisers in accordance with segment preferences, or by targeting and serving different segments in different ways. As certain demographic segments, notably women, remain a minority, platforms and fundraisers may consider adopting approaches to increasingly attract such presently underserved segments. Platforms' increased targeting efforts can improve their ability to match investors and ventures and thus enhance ventures' ability to gather funding.

Conclusion

The key challenges presently faced by the equity crowdfunding industry relate to investor returns, share liquidity, and platform profitability (Schwienbacher 2019). Although the long-term term outcome of the industry is yet to be seen, equity crowdfunding carries potential to offer a positive impact on new venture financing and development (Brown et al. 2019; Mochkabadi and Volkmann 2020) and even on the wider society and environment (Testa et al. 2019; Vismara 2019). To entrepreneurial ventures, equity crowdfunding offers an alternative form of equity financing that they may turn to out of choice or out of necessity (Walthoff-Borm et al. 2018). To investors, it offers an opportunity to diversify their investment portfolios across company lifecycle stages, financial instruments, and, increasingly, across geographies.

Acknowledgement The author gratefully acknowledges that this work was supported by a grant from the Finnish Foundation for Share Promotion.

Notes

1. Funding inflows represent investments made into fundraisers located in the platform country by investors located outside that country. Funding outflows represent investments made into fundraisers located outside the platform country by investors located in the platform country (definitions as used in the survey by Ziegler et al. 2019).
2. Micro funders, or micro angels, can be defined as informal early-stage investors who contribute limited amounts of their personal financial and human capital resources to purchase equity in entrepreneurial ventures that are majority owned by others. They can include family, friends, as well as more distant "foolhardy" investors (Avdeitchikova 2008; De Clercq et al. 2012; Maula et al. 2005; Szerb et al. 2007). The concept dates back to the time before online crowdfunding.

References

Ahlers, G. K., Cumming, D., Günther, C., & Schweizer, D. (2015). Signaling in Equity Crowdfunding. *Entrepreneurship Theory and Practice, 39*(4), 955–980.

Åstebro, T., Fernández, M., Lovo, S., & Vulkan, N. (2018). Herding in Equity Crowdfunding. Retrieved May 26, 2019, from https://ssrn.com/abstract=3084140.

Avdeitchikova, S. (2008). On the Structure of the Informal Venture Capital Market in Sweden: Developing Investment Roles. *Venture Capital, 10*(1), 55–85.

Baeck, P., Collins, L., & Zhang, Z. (2014). *Understanding Alternative Finance: The UK Alternative Finance Industry Report*. Cambridge, UK: University of Cambridge.

Bapna, S. (2019). Complementarity of Signals in Early-stage Equity Investment Decisions: Evidence from a Randomized Field Experiment. *Management Science, 65*(2), 933–952.

Barbi, M., & Mattioli, S. (2019). Human Capital, Investor Trust, and Equity Crowdfunding. *Research in International Business and Finance, 49*, 1–12.

Bessière, V., Stéphany, E., & Wirtz, P. (2019). Crowdfunding, Business Angels, and Venture Capital: An Exploratory Study of the Concept of the Funding Trajectory. *Venture Capital*, forthcoming.

Block, J., Hornuf, L., & Moritz, A. (2018). Which Updates During an Equity Crowdfunding Campaign Increase Crowd Participation? *Small Business Economics, 50*(1), 3–27.

Bretschneider, U., & Leimeister, J. M. (2017). Not Just an Ego-trip: Exploring Backers' Motivation for Funding in Incentive-based Crowdfunding. *Journal of Strategic Information Systems, 26*(4), 246–260.

Brown, R., Mawson, S., & Rowe, A. (2019). Start-ups, Entrepreneurial Networks and Equity Crowdfunding: A Processual Perspective. *Industrial Marketing Management, 80*, 115–125.

Cholakova, M., & Clarysse, B. (2015). Does the Possibility to Make Equity Investments in Crowdfunding Projects Crowd Out Rewards-based Investments? *Entrepreneurship Theory and Practice, 39*(1), 145–172.

Collins, L., & Pierrakis, Y. (2012). *The Venture Crowd: Crowdfunding Equity Investment into Business*. London, UK: Nesta. Retrieved May 26, 2019, from http://www.nesta.org.uk/publications/venture-crowd.

Cumming, D. J., & Vismara, S. (2017). De-segmenting Research in Entrepreneurial Finance. *Venture Capital, 19*(1–2), 17–27.

Cumming, D., Hervé, F., Manthé, E., & Schwienbacher, A. (2018). Hypothetical Bias in Equity Crowdfunding. Retrieved May 26, 2019, from https://ssrn.com/abstract=3114526.

Cumming, D., Meoli, M., & Vismara, S. (2019). Investors' Choices Between Cash and Voting Rights: Evidence from Dual-class Equity Crowdfunding. *Research Policy, 48*(8), 103740.

Cummings, M. E., Rawhouser, H., Vismara, S., & Hamilton, E. L. (2019). An Equity Crowdfunding Research Agenda: Evidence from Stakeholder Participation in the Rulemaking Process. *Small Business Economics*, forthcoming.

Daskalakis, N., & Yue, W. (2017). User's Perceptions of Motivations and Risks in Crowdfunding with Financial Returns. Retrieved May 26, 2019, from https://ssrn.com/abstract=2968912.

De Clercq, D., Meuleman, M., & Wright, M. (2012). A Cross-country Investigation of Micro-angel Investment Activity: The Roles of New Business Opportunities and Institutions. *International Business Review, 21*(2), 117–129.

EBAN. (2014). Investment Principles and Guidelines. European Business Angel Network. Retrieved May 26, 2019, from http://www.eban.org/knowledge-center/.

Estapé-Dubreuil, G., Ashta, A., & Hédou, J.-P. (2016). Micro-equity for Sustainable Development: Selection, Monitoring and Exit Strategies of Micro-angels. *Ecological Economics, 130*, 117–129.

Estrin, S., Daniel Gozman, D., & Khavul, S. (2018). The Evolution and Adoption of Equity Crowdfunding: Entrepreneur and Investor Entry into a New Market. *Small Business Economics, 51*(2), 425–439.

Fried, V. H., & Hisrich, R. D. (1994). Toward a Model of Venture Capital Investment Decision Making. *Financial Management, 23*(3), 28–37.

Frydrych, D., Bock, A. J., Kinder, T., & Koeck, B. (2014). Exploring Entrepreneurial Legitimacy in Reward-based Crowdfunding. *Venture Capital, 16*(3), 247–269.

Garvey, K., Chen, H.-Y., Zhang, B., Buckingham, E., Ralston, D., Katiforis, Y., et al. (2017). *Cultivating Growth: The 2nd Asia Pacific Region Alternative Finance Industry Report*. Cambridge, UK: Cambridge Center for Alternative Finance.

Goethner, M., Luettig, S., & Regner, T. (2018). *Crowdinvesting in Entrepreneurial Projects: Disentangling Patterns of Investor Behavior*. Jena Economic Research Papers 2018-018. Friedrich-Schiller-University Jena.

Grinblatt, M., & Keloharju, M. (2001). How Distance, Language, and Culture Influence Stockholdings and Trades. *Journal of Finance, 56*(3), 1053–1073.
Guenther, C., Hienerth, C., & Riar, F. (2014). *The Due Diligence of Crowdinvestors: Thorough Evaluation or Gut Feeling Only?* Paper Presented at the 12th International Open and User Innovation Conference, Boston, Massachusetts, July 28–30.
Guenther, C., Johan, S., & Schweizer, D. (2018). Is the Crowd Sensitive to Distance? How Investment Decisions Differ by Investor Type. *Small Business Economics, 50*(2), 289–305.
Harrison, R. T., & Mason, C. M. (2000). Venture Capital Market Complementarities: The Links Between Business Angels and Venture Capital Funds in the United Kingdom. *Venture Capital, 2*(3), 223–242.
Harrison, R. T., & Mason, C. M. (2019). Venture Capital 20 Years On: Reflections on the Evolution of a Field. *Venture Capital, 21*(1), 1–34.
Hornuf, L., & Neuenkirch, M. (2017). Pricing Shares in Equity Crowdfunding. *Small Business Economics, 48*(4), 795–811.
Hornuf, L., & Schmitt, M. (2017). *Does a Local Bias Exist in Equity Crowdfunding?* Max Planck Institute for Innovation & Competition Research Paper No. 16-07. Retrieved May 26, 2019, from https://ssrn.com/abstract=2801170.
Hornuf, L., & Schwienbacher, A. (2016). Crowdinvesting: Angel Investing for the Masses? In H. Landström & C. Mason (Eds.), *Handbook of Research on Business Angels* (pp. 381–397). Cheltenham: Edward Elgar.
Hornuf, L., & Schwienbacher, A. (2018a). Internet-based Entrepreneurial Finance: Lessons from Germany. *California Management Review, 60*(2), 150–175.
Hornuf, L., & Schwienbacher, A. (2018b). Market Mechanisms and Funding Dynamics in Equity Crowdfunding. *Journal of Corporate Finance, 50*, 556–574.
Hornuf, L., Schmitt, M., & Stenzhorn, E. (2018). *Equity Crowdfunding in Germany and the UK: Follow-up Funding and Firm Failure*. Max Planck Institute for Innovation and Competition Research Paper No. 17–09.
Horvát, E.-Á., Wachs, J., Wang, R., & Hannák, A. (2018). *The Role of Novelty in Securing Investors for Equity Crowdfunding Campaigns*. Paper Presented at the 6th AAAI Conference on Human Computation and Crowdsourcing HCOMP 2018, Zurich, Switzerland, July 5–8.
Itenbert, O., & Smith, E. E. (2017). Syndicated Equity Crowdfunding: The Trade-off Between Deal Access and Conflicts of Interest. Retrieved May 26, 2019, from https://ssrn.com/abstract=2933822.
Kang, M., Gao, Y., Wang, T., & Zheng, H. (2016). Understanding the Determinants of Funders' Investment Intentions on Crowdfunding Platforms. *Industrial Management Data Systems, 116*(8), 1800–1819.

Kim, K., & Viswanathan, S. (2019). The Experts in the Crowd: The Role of Experienced Investors in a Crowdfunding Market. *MIS Quarterly, 43*(2), 347–372.

Kleinert, S., & Volkmann, C. (2019). Equity Crowdfunding and the Role of Investor Discussion Boards. *Venture Capital, 21*(4), 327–352.

Kleinert, S., Volkmann, C., & Grünhagen, M. (2020). Third-party Signals in Equity Crowdfunding: The Role of Prior Financing. *Small Business Economics, 54*(1), 341–365.

Landström, H. (1993). Informal Risk Capital in Sweden and Some International Comparisons. *Journal of Business Venturing, 8*(6), 525–540.

Li, X., Tang, Y., Yang, N., Ren, R., Zheng, H., & Zhou, H. (2016). The Value of Information Disclosure and Lead Investor in Equity-based Crowdfunding: An Exploratory Empirical Study. *Nankai Business Review International, 7*(3), 301–321.

Löher, J. (2017). The Interaction of Equity Crowdfunding Platforms and Ventures: An Analysis of the Preselection Process. *Venture Capital, 19*(1–2), 51–74.

Lukkarinen, A. (2019). *Drivers of Investment Activity in Equity Crowdfunding.* Doctoral dissertation, Aalto University School of Business. 190 pages. Aalto University publication series DOCTORAL DISSERTATIONS, 40/2019. ISBN 978-952-60-8444-2 (electronic). 978-952-60-8443-5 (printed) http://urn.fi/URN:ISBN:978-952-60-8444-2.

Lukkarinen, A., Teich, J. E., Wallenius, H., & Wallenius, J. (2016). Success Drivers of Online Equity Crowdfunding Campaigns. *Decision Support Systems, 87*, 26–38.

Lukkarinen, A., Seppälä, T., & Wallenius, J. (2017). Investor Motivations and Decision Criteria in Equity Crowdfunding. Retrieved May 26, 2019, from https://ssrn.com/abstract=3263434.

MacMillan, I. C., Siegel, R., & Narasimha, P. N. S. (1985). Criteria Used by Venture Capitalists to Evaluate New Venture Proposals. *Journal of Business Venturing, 1*(1), 119–128.

Mahmood, A., Luffarelli, J., & Mukesh, M. (2019). What's in a Logo? The Impact of Complex Visual Cues in Equity Crowdfunding. *Journal of Business Venturing, 34*(1), 41–62.

Mamonov, S., & Malaga, R. (2018). Success Factors in Title III Equity Crowdfunding in the United States. *Electronic Commerce and Research Applications, 27*, 65–73.

Mason, C. M., & Harrison, R. T. (2008). Measuring Business Angel Investment Activity in the United Kingdom: A Review of Potential Data Sources. *Venture Capital, 10*(4), 309–330.
Maula, M., & Lukkarinen, A. (2019). Attention Across Borders: Investor Attention as a Driver of Investment Choices in Cross-Border Equity Crowdfunding. Retrieved November 21, 2019, from https://papers.ssrn.com/sol3/papers.cfm?abstract_id=3487467.
Maula, M., Autio, E., & Arenius, P. (2005). What Drives Micro-angel Investments? *Small Business Economics, 25*(5), 459–475.
Mochkabadi, K., & Volkmann, C. K. (2020). Equity Crowdfunding: A Systematic Review of the Literature. *Small Business Economics, 54*(1), 75–118.
Mohammadi, A., & Shafi, K. (2018). Gender Differences in the Contribution Patterns of Equity-crowdfunding Investors. *Small Business Economics, 50*(2), 275–287.
Moritz, A., Block, J., & Lutz, E. (2015). Investor Communication in Equity-based Crowdfunding: A Qualitative-empirical Study. *Qualitative Research in Financial Markets, 7*(3), 309–342.
Niemand, T., Angerer, M., Thies, F., Kraus, S., & Hebenstreit, R. (2018). Equity Crowdfunding Across Borders: A Conjoint Experiment. *International Journal of Entrepreneurial Behavior and Research, 24*(4), 911–932.
Ordanini, A., Miceli, L., Pizzetti, M., & Parasuraman, A. (2011). Crowd-funding: Transforming Customers into Investors Through Innovative Service Platforms. *Journal of Service Management, 22*(4), 443–470.
Piva, E., & Rossi-Lamastra, C. (2018). Human Capital Signals and Entrepreneurs' Success in Equity Crowdfunding. *Small Business Economics, 51*(3), 667–686.
Politis, D., & Landström, H. (2002). Informal Investors as Entrepreneurs: The Development of an Entrepreneurial Career. *Venture Capital, 4*(2), 78–101.
Prowse, S. (1998). Angel Investors and the Market for Angel Investments. *Journal of Banking and Finance, 22*(6-8), 785–792.
Ralcheva, A., & Roosenboom, P. (2016). On the Road to Success in Equity Crowdfunding. Retrieved May 26, 2019, from https://ssrn.com/abstract=2727742.
Rossi, M. (2014). The New Ways to Raise Capital: An Exploratory Study of Crowdfunding. *International Journal of Financial Research, 5*(2), 8–18.
Sahlman, W. A. (1990). The Structure and Governance of Venture-capital Organizations. *Journal of Financial Economics, 27*(2), 473–521.
Schwienbacher, A. (2019). Equity Crowdfunding: Anything to Celebrate? *Venture Capital, 21*(1), 65–74.

Schwienbacher, A., & Larralde, B. (2012). Crowdfunding of Entrepreneurial Ventures. In D. Cumming (Ed.), *The Oxford Handbook of Entrepreneurial Finance* (pp. 369–391). Oxford, UK: Oxford University Press.
Shafi, K. (2019). Investors' Evaluation Criteria in Equity Crowdfunding. *Small Business Economics*, forthcoming.
Signori, A., & Vismara, S. (2018). Does Success Bring Success? The Post-offering Lives of Equity-Crowdfunded Firms. *Journal of Corporate Finance, 50*, 575–591.
Simon, H. A. (1991). Bounded Rationality and Organizational Learning. *Organization Science, 2*(1), 125–134.
Stevenson, R. M., Ciuchta, M. P., Letwin, C., Dinger, J. M., & Vancouver, J. B. (2019). Out of Control or Right on the Money? Funder Self-efficacy and Crowd Bias in Equity Crowdfunding. *Journal of Business Venturing, 34*(2), 348–367.
Streletzki, J.-G., & Schulte, R. (2013). Which Venture Capital Selection Criteria Distinguish High-flyer Investments? *Venture Capital, 15*(1), 29–52.
Sudek, R. (2006). Angel Investment Criteria. *Journal of Small Business Strategy, 17*(2), 89–103.
Sullivan, M. K., & Miller, A. (1996). Segmenting the Informal Venture Capital Market: Economic, Hedonistic, and Altruistic Investors. *Journal of Business Research, 36*(1), 25–35.
Szerb, L., Rappai, G., Makra, Z., & Terjesen, S. (2007). Informal Investment in Transition Economies: Individual Characteristics and Clusters. *Small Business Economics, 28*(2), 257–271.
Testa, S., Roed Nielsen, K., Bogers, M., & Cincotti, S. (2019). The Role of Crowdfunding in Moving Towards a Sustainable Society. *Technological Forecasting and Social Change, 141*, 66–73.
Tuomi, K., & Harrison, R. T. (2017). A Comparison of Equity Crowdfunding in Four Countries: Implications for Business Angels. *Strategic Change, 26*(6), 609–615.
Tyebjee, T. T., & Bruno, A. V. (1984). A Model of Venture Capitalist Investment Activity. *Management Science, 30*(9), 1051–1066.
Van Osnabrugge, M. (2000). A Comparison of Business Angel and Venture Capitalist Investment Procedures: An Agency Theory-based Analysis. *Venture Capital, 2*(2), 91–109.

Vismara, S. (2016). Equity Retention and Social Network Theory in Equity Crowdfunding. *Small Business Economics, 46*(4), 579–590.
Vismara, S. (2018). Information Cascades Among Investors in Equity Crowdfunding. *Entrepreneurship Theory and Practice, 42*(3), 467–497.
Vismara, S. (2019). Sustainability in Equity Crowdfunding. *Technological Forecasting and Social Change, 141*, 98–106.
Vismara, S., Benaroio, D., & Carne, F. (2017). Gender in Entrepreneurial Finance: Matching Investors and Entrepreneurs in Equity Crowdfunding. In A. N. Link (Ed.), *Gender and Entrepreneurial Activity* (pp. 271–288). Cheltenham: Edward Elgar.
Vulkan, N., Åstebro, T., & Sierra, M. F. (2016). Equity Crowdfunding: A New Phenomena. *Journal of Business Venturing Insights, 5*, 37–49.
Walthoff-Borm, X., Schwienbacher, A., & Vanacker, T. (2018). Equity Crowdfunding: First Resort or Last Resort? *Journal of Business Venturing, 33*(4), 513–533.
Wang, W., Mahmood, A., Sismeiro, C., & Vulkan, N. (2019). The Evolution of Equity Crowdfunding: Insights from Co-investments of Angels and the Crowd. *Research Policy, 48*(8), 103727.
White, B. A., & Dumay, J. (2017). Business Angels: A Research Review and New Agenda. *Venture Capital, 19*(3), 183–216.
Wilson, K. E., & Testoni, M. (2014). Improving the Role of Equity Crowdfunding in Europe's Capital Markets. Retrieved May 26, 2019, from http://ssrn.com/abstract=2502280.
Wiltbank, R. E. (2009). Siding with the Angels: Business Angel Investing – Promising Outcomes and Effective Strategies. London, UK: Nesta. Retrieved May 26, 2019, from https://www.effectuation.org/wp-content/uploads/2016/06/wiltbank-business-angel-investing-1.pdf.
Zhang, B., Ziegler, T., Mammadova, L., Johanson, D., Gray, M., & Yerolemou, N. (2018). *The 5th UK Alternative Finance Industry Report*. Cambridge, UK: Cambridge Center for Alternative Finance.
Ziegler, T., Johanson, D., King, M., Zhang, B., Mammadova, L., Ferri, F., et al. (2018a). *Reaching New Heights: The 3rd Americas Alternative Finance Industry Report*. Cambridge, UK: Cambridge Center for Alternative Finance.
Ziegler, T., Shneor, R., Garvey, K., Wenzlaff, K., Yerolemou, N., Hao, R., et al. (2018b). *Expanding Horizons: The 3rd European Alternative Finance Industry Report*. Cambridge, UK: Cambridge Center for Alternative Finance.

Ziegler, T., Suresh, K., Garvey, K., Rowan, P., Zhang, B., Obijiaku, A., et al. (2018c). *The 2nd Annual Middle East & Africa Alternative Finance Industry Report*. Cambridge, UK: Cambridge Center for Alternative Finance.
Ziegler, T., Suresh, K., Johanson, D., Zhang, B., Shenglin, B., Luo, D., et al. (2018d). *The 3rd Asia Pacific Region Alternative Finance Industry Report*. Cambridge, UK: Cambridge Center for Alternative Finance.
Ziegler, T., Shneor, R., Wenzlaff, K., Odorović, A., Johanson, D., Hao, R., et al. (2019). *Shifting Paradigms: The 4th European Alternative Finance Benchmarking Report*. Cambridge, UK: Cambridge Center for Alternative Finance.
Zunino, D., van Praag, M., & Dushnitsky, G. (2017). *Badge of Honor or Scarlet Letter? Unpacking Investors' Judgment of Entrepreneurs' Past Failure*. Tinbergen Institute Discussion Paper; No. 2017-085/VII. Amsterdam, The Netherlands: Tinbergen Institute.

6

Reward-Based Crowdfunding Research and Practice

Liang Zhao and Sunghan Ryu

Introduction

In the last decade, fundraising has dramatically changed by the emerging of crowdfunding (Mollick 2014). As an extension of crowdsourcing (Schwienbacher and Larralde 2012), crowdfunding is defined as "a collective effort by individuals who network and pool their money together, usually via the Internet, to invest in or support the efforts of others" (Ordanini et al. 2011). Via crowdfunding, individuals can contribute to different kinds of projects ranging from entrepreneurial to prosocial projects (Roma et al. 2017). Moreover, some have also suggested that as an

L. Zhao (✉)
School of Business and Law, University of Agder, Kristiansand, Norway
e-mail: liang.zhao@uia.no

S. Ryu
USC-SJTU Institute of Cultural and Creative Industry,
Shanghai Jiao Tong University, Shanghai, China
e-mail: shryu@sjtu.edu.cn

R. Shneor et al. (eds.), *Advances in Crowdfunding*,
https://doi.org/10.1007/978-3-030-46309-0_6

online fundraising method, in reward crowdfunding, the geographical barrier of traditional fundraising channels may be eliminated to a certain degree (Agrawal et al. 2015).

In this chapter, we focus on the reward-based crowdfunding model. Through reward-based crowdfunding supporters can provide funding to individuals, projects, or organizations in exchange for non-monetary rewards such as products or services, while accepting a certain degree of risk of non-delivery on campaign promises (Shneor and Munim 2019). Like other crowdfunding models, besides being a fundraising channel, reward-based crowdfunding can also work as a marketing tool (Brown et al. 2017) and a base of co-creation (Xu et al. 2016). Specifically, through the pre-ordering mechanism, entrepreneurs can boost their sales at the early stage market entry of new products. It can also be used to test the market potential of new products in order to diminish market uncertainty. Besides, entrepreneurs can improve products which may better match consumers' needs by engaging customers to take part in the developing process of new products (Messeni Petruzzelli et al. 2019).

The purpose of the current chapter is thus to review the fundamentals of reward-based crowdfunding, especially with respect to its potential influences on entrepreneurial financing and start-up incubation. Accordingly, we first discuss the definition, mechanisms, and unique aspects of reward-based crowdfunding. Next, the regional characteristics of reward-based crowdfunding development are presented. Then, through an extensive literature review, two main research streams of reward-based crowdfunding (success drivers and contributor behaviour) are summarized. Finally, this chapter highlights the implications for practice and research, as well as mentions potential contributions and limitations.

Definition, Mechanisms, and Unique Aspects

Reward-based crowdfunding can be considered as the most publicly familiar crowdfunding model, where backers contribute to projects without any monetary returns (Mollick 2014). Instead, they expect to receive material compensations (e.g. real products) as well as immaterial compensations (e.g. thank-you letter) in return of their contributions (Gerber et al. 2012).

The rewards commonly used in reward-based crowdfunding campaigns fall into three categories (Colombo et al. 2015; Thürridl and Kamleitner 2016): pre-orders, services, and recognition. Particularly, campaign creators offer their products in a pre-order mechanism through which backers have early access to the products. As part of the process, contributors also evaluate the products and may offer creators useful suggestion on how to make the products better at satisfying their needs. Recognition and services are examples of immaterial rewards. Recognition as a reward applies to the entry-level backers (backers contributing a small amount of money). Here, creators may write thank-you letters to such backers or display their names on the website in order to acknowledge their contribution. Creators may also provide special services, instead of physical products, as rewards for backers. Examples of these may include private performances and screenings, training and educational experiences, free usage of commercial services being developed, and so on.

Reward-based crowdfunding is a two-sided market (Tomczak and Brem 2013). Specifically, the supply side of the market consists of a group of backers who are willing to contribute to crowdfunding campaigns for achieving material or immaterial compensations. The demand side of the market consists of a group of campaign creators who design their campaigns in order to get projects they are developing funded. This two-sided market is in most cases operated through an online intermediary (crowdfunding platform) such as Kickstarter.

In this chapter, a framework (Fig. 6.1) is applied to explain the mechanism of reward-based crowdfunding. It consists of four essential elements (campaigns, creators, backers, and platforms) of the whole reward-based crowdfunding process (Ordanini et al. 2011). The three elements (creators, backers, and platforms) will be discussed separately at the different phases of the crowdfunding process namely—the preparation phase, the crowdfunding phase, and the outcome phase. Specifically, the preparation phase refers to the period before launching campaigns. The crowdfunding phase refers to the active fundraising period of campaigns, and

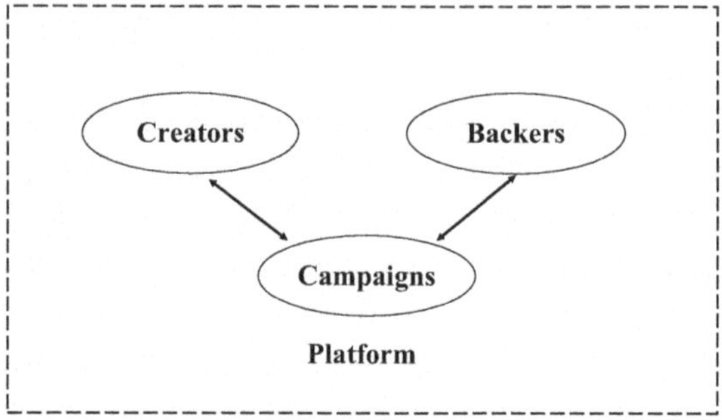

Fig. 6.1 The four-dimension framework of reward-based crowdfunding

the outcome phase refers to the consequences of crowdfunding campaigns, once they are closed and the fundraising period is over.

Campaigns

The process of decision-making and strategic thinking of the crowdfunding participants is mainly based on what is presented in the crowdfunding campaigns (Messeni Petruzzelli et al. 2019). Therefore, the campaign is the core of the framework. Here, project creators design their crowdfunding campaigns following guidelines of crowdfunding platforms and other sources of advice, often stressing the importance of information disclosure for crowdfunding success.

First, project creators need to set up the funding targets of their campaigns, as covering all related costs for fulfilling the projects' objectives. Here, funding "targets" mean the amount of money they aim to collect through the crowdfunding process. Next, in order to present their projects to the potential backers, project creators are required to describe their projects in comprehensive ways by providing adequate and truthful information in the forms of texts, images, and/or videos (Ahlers et al. 2015). The provided information relates to the project and its rewards, the background of the creator(s) and the perceived risks of surrounding the future project execution process. In addition, the rewards also play vital roles. Before launching their projects, project creators need to design their own reward schemes. In the reward schemes, creators are required to clarify the benefits to the backers based on the different levels of contributions. Usually, a reward scheme should include several reward tiers with different prices associated with each. These often come in the forms of different number of units of the products, different versions of same products, opportunities for creative collaborations of various kinds, creative experiences and creative mementoes depending on different contribution levels (Kuppuswamy and Bayus 2017).

As the campaigns are designed and officially launched online, backers should find out which campaigns are worth contributing to and how much to contribute based on the provided information. In the meanwhile, crowdfunding platforms provide the technical infrastructure for information presentation, payment facilitation, and interaction around campaigns in order to facilitate a smooth crowdfunding process.

Creators

Creators are individuals or organizations with a project that requires funding, are the source of information about the project, and are responsible for delivering on the campaign promises once the campaign is finished.

Preparation Phase: Before launching campaigns, creators should clearly define their business idea by answering the following questions: what the final product/service is, what the overall scope is, what the overall vision is, and what the final target is. Once all the answers to the above are known, creators can start to design their campaigns. Designing a crowdfunding campaign must follow according to the requirements of the crowdfunding platform and will often include multiple media elements and a textual description answering critical issues about the concept, the people behind it, and the project execution plan. Information related to legal issues, launch date, and duration should be taken into consideration when designing crowdfunding campaigns (Mollick 2014).

Crowdfunding Phase: Once the business idea is determined and the campaign is designed, the crowdfunding phase starts when a campaign is officially launched online. The campaign ends at the stated end date of the campaign's fundraising duration. From the creator's perspective, the crowdfunding phase is critical as it is closely related to the crowdfunding efforts' results. Therefore, creators should spend time and effort to establish and maintain the relationship with potential backers and niche groups in order to promote the awareness about their campaigns. In addition, to facilitate fundraising, creators should also provide extra information related to the campaigns through interaction with backers, social media promotional efforts, sharing of updates, and campaign improvements.

Outcome Phase: The outcome phase starts when the crowdfunding phase is finished. For platforms adopting the "all-or-nothing" mechanism, the entire amount of the fundraising will only be transferred to the creator if the campaign is successful (the final fundraising amount is equal or exceeds the fundraising target). A commission fee should be deducted from the total collected amount by the platform before funds are transferred to the creator. Alternatively, for platforms using the "keep-it-all" mechanism, the sum of contributions raised will be transferred to creators (after deducting the commission fee for platform services) irrespective of whether the campaigns' fundraising targets have been achieved or not. Regardless of fundraising model, creators have the responsibilities to execute the projects and deliver the promised rewards within the timeframe stated in the campaign, after they receive the funds raised.

Backers

Backers are individuals or organizations who provide financial contributions for the crowdfunding campaign in return for a promised reward.

Preparation Phase: Before contributing to crowdfunding campaigns, backers should be familiarized with the concept of reward-based crowdfunding and make sure they understand how it works, as week as its related risks and benefits.

Crowdfunding Phase: During the crowdfunding phase, backers should decide whether and how much to contribute to a campaign based on their evaluation of the provided campaign information and the perceived risk level of the campaign. In addition, backers may also be interested in acting as co-creators of the supported campaigns (Mollick 2014). They may interact with campaign creators by asking campaign-related questions on the crowdfunding platform or by writing comments concerning campaign updates in order to help the creators improve their products/services (Steigenberger 2017). In addition, with the embedding of social media, backers can easily spread campaign information and make their favourite campaigns go viral through their online social networking as social media exposure is positively associated with campaign success (Gerber et al. 2012). Indeed, research by Shneor and Munim (2019) has shown that both information-sharing intention and financial contribution intentions lead to actual financial contribution behaviour.

Outcome Phase: For campaigns run on platforms using the "all-or-nothing" mechanism, backers can only receive their rewards if a campaign is successful (the final fundraising amount equalizes or exceeds the fundraising target). However, if a campaign is failed, the contributions will be refunded to the backers. In terms of the "keep-it-all" platforms, backers will receive their rewards, regardless of the outcome of a campaign. Nevertheless, in most cases, backers don't receive rewards immediately but within pre-stated periods of time required for completing product development, manufacturing, and shipment.

Platforms

Paraphrasing Shneor and Flåten's (2015) definition of crowdfunding platforms into the reward crowdfunding context, a reward crowdfunding platform can be defined as an internet application bringing together project creators and their potential backers, as well as facilitating exchanges between them according to the reward crowdfunding conventions presented earlier.

Preparation Phase: In the preparation phase, as information intermediaries, platforms should host educational sessions about crowdfunding to the public in order to introduce crowdfunding to the general public. Such efforts are likely to help support the development of a crowdfunding community, which may consist of future backers and creators. In terms of backers, contributing to crowdfunding campaigns might be risky. As a novel fundraising channel, crowdfunding is tangled with market uncertainty and information asymmetry (Roma et al. 2017). To decrease perceived risks, crowdfunding platforms should set up an extensive campaign review process to verify whether a campaign has satisfied the basic requirements for launching online in terms of information disclosure and fundraiser identity verifications. In that way, platforms may ensure avoiding the publication of illegal and immoral campaigns, such as campaigns related to fraudulent activities, money laundering, criminal, and terrorist funding. For creators, platforms should give suggestions on defining, developing, and presenting creators' business ideas, as well as guide them in designing attractive crowdfunding campaigns. Besides, all fees related to the campaign process should also be disclosed to creators in advance for proper campaign budget planning.

Crowdfunding Phase: During the crowdfunding phase, crowdfunding platforms may help creators and backers to exchange information through different channels. For example, platforms are encouraged to integrate instant messaging tools, third-party social network websites and microblog links on campaigns' webpages to facilitate extensive interaction between creators and backers (Zheng et al. 2014). In addition, platforms can also support the promotion of campaigns through online marketing. Platforms may also selectively promote certain campaigns as part of "staff picks" recommendations, or in direct promotions to special interest groups among their users. Lastly, legal and ethical compliance should also be taken into consideration in the crowdfunding phase. Platforms should apply identity verification of backers to ensure ethical contributing practices.

Outcome Phase: In the final phase, depending on the different mechanisms ("all-or-nothing" or "keep-it-all"), platforms will transfer the total fundraising to the creators after deducting the commission fee for their services. Creators have the obligations to complete their projects and fulfil rewards once the money is received. However, given the uncertainty underlying the post-crowdfunding process, reward-based crowdfunding platforms may warn backers if they notice that some projects may not go as planned. For example, some campaigns may suffer from delivery delays or no delivery (Mollick 2014). However, platforms do not carry legal precautions about such problems as it is backers' responsibilities to understand the risks and their consumer rights by law before participating in crowdfunding activities. Nevertheless, a platform's long-term survival depends on the positive experience of users, and its engagement in follow-up on campaign promise delivery is linked to its own interest in long term success. In such cases, platforms may follow up on creators to ensure they meet their obligations. In addition, possible refunds or alternative options to complete the projects may also be offered to the backers. Finally, the platform should maintain relations with new users brought by with the campaign and continue informing them about future campaigns that they may find interesting, based on them opting to receive such information.

Regional Variances

Reward-based crowdfunding as a global phenomenon may not operate in the same way in different regions. Because some factors such as financial infrastructures, regulatory environments, and technological advancements may vary by region. Hence, consideration and discussion at the regional level is also warranted. In this section, we report the situation in different regions around the world in order to provide a better understanding of reward-based crowdfunding from a global perspective by taking regional features into consideration.

China

According to the 3rd Asia Pacific Region Alternative Finance Industry Report (Ziegler et al. 2018b), reward-based crowdfunding is a popular crowdfunding model in China in terms of the number of participants. Although reward-based crowdfunding works similar all over the world, there are still some special features in the Chinese reward-based crowdfunding market. Generally, reward-based crowdfunding market in China is still growing. However, the number of reward-based crowdfunding platforms in China is decreasing. It means the reward-based crowdfunding market in China is highly concentrated. For instance, the fundraising of several large reward-based platforms (e.g. JD, Taobao) account for approximately 90% of the total market fundraising volume. Almost all the reward-based crowdfunding platforms in China operate domestically. Most platforms do not have global websites and global brands. Reward-based crowdfunding platforms in China usually do not accept contributions out of China. Therefore, cross-border inflows and outflows in Chinese reward-based crowdfunding market are rare. Defaults, regulatory changes, and fraud are perceived as the main obstacles of reward-based crowdfunding development in China.

Asia-Pacific (APAC)

According to the same report (Ziegler et al. 2018b), the reward-based crowdfunding market is still growing in Asia-Pacific (APAC) areas (excluding China). Here, 96% of reward-based crowdfunding platforms place "media and promotion" as their key focus of R&D. Approximately 81% of all the reward-based crowdfunding platforms in APAC (excluding China) have been actively pursuing customer verification, payment processing, and e-learning. Around 69% of the reward-based crowdfunding platforms have pursued R&D into "community management". However, only 29% of the reward-based crowdfunding platforms in APAC refer gamification as their key R&D focus and for customer relationship management (CRM) the rate is 36%. With respect to female participation in the APAC region, 18% of all the reward-based crowdfunding fundraisers (e.g. campaign creators) are female, and female backers accounted for 27% of the total backers. Some 17% of the backers in APAC have supported campaigns abroad. Approximately 15% of reward-based platforms in the region are having both a global website and a global brand, but only 1% of the total fundraising of reward-based crowdfunding is contributed by backers out of APAC. Fraud and cyber-security breach are perceived as the main risks of reward-based crowdfunding in the APAC area.

UK

According to the 5th UK Alternative Finance Industry Report (Zhang et al. 2018), reward-based crowdfunding is experiencing a decline in volume in the UK, which is likely related to the result of 63% of reward-based platforms reported slightly alternating their business model in 2017. Specifically, 14% of the operating costs of crowdfunding platforms account for the R&D mostly invested towards customer support tools for social media promotions. Moreover, approximately 75% of all the reward-based crowdfunding platforms in the UK choose to invest in e-learning, customer verification and payment processing as their R&D focuses. Half of the reward-based platforms in the UK have also pursued R&D into artificial intelligence, community management and performance enhancement features. In terms of female participation, in the UK, 56% of all the reward-based crowdfunding fundraisers are female and female backers accounted for 38% of total backers. Reward-based crowdfunding is the most international crowdfunding model in the UK with approximately 75% of platforms having both global websites and global brands and with approximately half of the inflow transactions made cross-border. In terms of risks, concerns about possible collapse of a platform due to malpractice is perceived as the main risk of reward-based crowdfunding industry in the UK.

Middle East and Africa

According to the 2nd Annual Middle East and Africa Alternative Finance Industry Report (Ziegler et al. 2018c), non-financial crowdfunding models (reward-based crowdfunding and donation-based crowdfunding) account for the majority proportion of the alternative finance market in the Middle East and Africa (MEA) region. It is the key feature distinguishing the alternative finance market in the MEA region from other alternative finance markets. Due to the low economic and infrastructural development level, all the reward-based crowdfunding activities in the Middle East and Africa areas remain domestic activities with no cross-border transactions, internationalization and R&D investment. In terms of female participation, 27% of the reward-based crowdfunding fundraisers are female and female backers account for 33% of the total backers. Reward-based crowdfunding development in the Middle East and Africa are exposed to various risks. For instance, fraud is perceived as the most serious risk in African reward-based crowdfunding market followed by collapse due to malpractice, defaults and changes to regulation. In the Middle East areas, defaults are placed as the greatest risk followed by changes to regulation, collapse due to malpractice and fraud.

Europe

According to the 4th Annual European Alternative Finance Report (Ziegler et al. 2019), 67% of reward-based crowdfunding platforms have placed community management as the key focus of R&D investment in European areas. This is closely followed by 66% of platforms that have pursued R&D into social media and promotional tools. Customer Relationship Management (CRM) is chosen by 48% of the reward-based platforms as their main R&D focus and process streamlining have been chosen as priority R&D focus by 37% of the European reward-based crowdfunding platforms. Referring to female participation, 49% of the reward-based crowdfunding fundraisers are female and female backers accounted for 54% of the total backers. About 27% of reward-based crowdfunding platforms in Europe only focus on the local markets with no global websites and brands. However, 58% of reward-based crowdfunding platforms have both global websites and global brands. About 6% of reward-based crowdfunding platforms in Europe choose to utilize a global brand name but localize the websites and contents for certain markets. Compared to other crowdfunding models in Europe, reward-based crowdfunding model has the lowest level of cross-border funding flows. Specifically, cross-border funding outflows account for 9% of the total market volume and 21% of the transactions are made by cross-border funding inflows. Finally, in terms of risks, cyber-security breach is perceived as the most significant risk factor followed by changes to regulation and campaign fraud in the European reward-based crowdfunding market.

The Americas

According to the 3rd Americas Alternative Finance Industry Report (Ziegler et al. 2018a), reward-based crowdfunding reported a decline in 2017 in the US and Canada. However, in Latin American and Caribbean (LAC) areas, reward-based crowdfunding has continued to grow with newly established alternative finance ecosystems. Regarding R&D, 88% of reward-based crowdfunding platforms in the Americas have emphasized customer support tools for social media promotion as their priority R&D focus. Some 63% of the platforms mention payment processing and e-learning as two important R&D focuses. Furthermore, half of the platforms have pursued R&D into community management features. In terms of internationalization, 80% of reward-based crowdfunding platforms in the US have both global websites and global brands. In the LAC areas, the rate is 87%. For cross-border inflow and outflow, 11% of transactions were associated with cross-border inflows, and 18% of transaction were associated with cross-border outflows in the US reward-based crowdfunding market in 2017. Regarding female participation, 50% of the reward-based crowdfunding fundraisers are female and female backers account for 32% of the total backers. Specifically, in the US, 47% and 53% of fundraisers and funders are female respectively. In the LAC area, 47% and 56% of fundraisers and funders are female respectively. In the reward-based crowdfunding market of the Americas, cybersecurity breach is perceived as the most significant risk factor followed by collapse due to malpractice and campaign fraud.

Literature Review

After presenting the stakeholders and the current status of reward-based crowdfunding globally, in the followings section we review the literature on reward crowdfunding in different disciplines, including management, entrepreneurship, and information systems. Based on database searches employing the terms "crowdfunding" and "reward-based" as the keywords, we collected and analysed 30 studies published in influential journals in each discipline. Based on the analysis, we identified two main research streams: (1) success drivers of crowdfunding campaigns and (2) factors affecting individual contributors' behaviour.

Success Drivers

A strand of literature on reward crowdfunding highlights factors critical for determining the success of a crowdfunding project. First, a stream of research found that effective dissemination of information regarding the project and creator via the crowdfunding platform is important to crowdfunding success (Mollick 2014). Information on project quality (e.g. a competition-winning business plan) and social information (e.g. other potential contributors' willingness to invest) serve as effective cues for potential contributors (Ciuchta et al. 2016). In relation to this, the characteristics of the creators play a significant role in attracting and retaining the attention of contributors and thereby in determining a campaign's success. For example, creators' social information and educational backgrounds have all been shown to affect the success of a campaign (Mollick 2014). Similarly, Boeuf et al. (2014) found that disclosure of personal information about project creators has positive influence on crowdfunding success because it helps obtain a higher level of trust from potential contributors. In the same vein, Frydrych et al. (2014) argue that information on the creator adds legitimacy to the project, attracting more contributors as a result. Ryu and Kim (2018) found that reward value and societal contribution of a campaign are influential campaign characteristics affecting crowdfunding success.

Second, information on project progress posted on the project page is another influential factor. Investor participation in early project stages is essential for signalling project quality and subsequently attracting more investors (Agrawal et al. 2015; Burtch et al. 2013; Colombo et al. 2015). The success of a campaign is fully mediated by the funds collected in the campaign's early days (Colombo et al. 2015). Kim and Viswanathan (2019) showed that information about early contributors with expertise has a distinct influence on later investors. Regarding communication between the creators and their contributors, Antonenko et al. (2014)

pointed out that intensive communication, such as reacting promptly to questions and providing frequent status updates, positively influences crowdfunding success.

Third, it has been found that different types of creator and contributor networks act as key influencers of crowdfunding success. For example, based on the social capital theory, Zheng et al. (2014) examined how project creators' social network ties, experience in funding other projects, and the shared meaning between creators and investors impact crowdfunding success. Particularly, internal social capital developed inside a crowdfunding community contributes significantly towards triggering "a self-reinforcing mechanism" of a crowdfunding project (Colombo et al. 2015). Social capital accumulated from the contributors' social networking site (SNS) is also positively associated with the success of the project (Kang et al. 2017).

Finally, campaign attributes are important. Belleflamme et al. (2014) find that the types of campaigns that are part of non-profit organizations are more successful than those of other organizational forms. Several design components, such as duration, goal, and inclusion of a video on a campaign site, are all associated with success (Mollick 2014). More specifically, Mollick (2014) argues that potential contributors are more likely to select realistic funding goals, as campaign goals that are too high or too low are not likely to lead to a successful campaign. Relatedly, Zhao and Vinig (2017) found that the application of lottery as a reward for a crowdfunding campaign has a positive influence on crowdfunding success. Linguistic styles and texts used in campaign descriptions also influence the success of crowdfunding campaigns (Parhankangas and Renko 2017; Allison et al. 2017). Linguistic styles that make a campaign more understandable and relatable to potential contributors enhance the success of social campaigns but hardly matter for commercial campaigns (Parhankangas and Renko 2017). Relatedly, based on the Elaboration Likelihood Model, Allison et al. (2017) found logically persuasive messages (cognitive) and emotionally persuasive cues (affective) influence crowdfunding campaign success.

Contributor Behaviour

A second stream of research on reward crowdfunding has documented various factors affecting contributors' behaviour. First, some studies show that different social influences drive the demand for crowdfunding. For example, Skirnevskiy et al. (2017) identified the significant role of peer effects in crowdfunding. The physical distance between creators and contributors are also found to have significant effects on contributor behaviours (Agrawal et al. 2015; Kang et al. 2017). Local contributors are more likely to pledge at the early stages of the funding period than distant contributors, and they are less sensitive to peer effects. They are also less sensitive to information about the cumulative amount of funding (Lin and Viswanathan 2015). In similar vein, contributors are more likely to contribute to "culturally similar and geographically proximate" creators' projects (Burtch et al. 2014). Relatedly, recognizing the importance of contributions at the early stages, a small set of studies has attempted to show why and who are more likely to make earlier contributions. For example, Kuppuswamy and Bayus (2017) showed the importance of goal proximity in explaining fund timing. Specifically, they found that people are more likely to contribute when a project approaches its funding goal, where they can make an impact on the ultimate success of fundraising, than when the funding goal has been reached. Also, research shows that contributors who are experts (Kim and Viswanathan 2019) or local (Kang et al. 2017; Agrawal et al. 2015; Giudici et al. 2018) tend to participate in crowdfunding earlier.

Second, beyond social influence, some research has investigated how the available information or format of crowdfunding affect funders' decisions. For example, Davis et al. (2017) found that contributors' decision to pledge is positively influenced by perceived product creativity and the influence of perceived product creativity is promoted when contributors perceive the creator as passionate. From the perspective of platform design, permission to control the disclosure of funding information was found to increase the number of contributions and simultaneously to decrease the amount of each contribution (Burtch et al. 2015).

Finally, an additional group of studies focused on psychosocial factors such as individual contributors' motivation. For example, Zheng et al. (2018) examined the positive effects of contributors' psychological ownership towards a campaign on their decision to contribute. Contributors also engage in crowdfunding campaigns with different intentions (Gerber et al. 2012). Contributors often seek rewards from the campaigns, in the form of tangible products or intangible rewards. Contributors would also support creators and their campaigns for upholding values. Some contributors may join crowdfunding to engage in a community where they are willing to be a part of. Shneor and Munim (2019) apply the "theory of planned behaviour" (TPB) for addressing the relationship between contribution intentions, behaviour, and their antecedents. They found that both financial contribution intentions and information-sharing intentions are positively related to actual contribution behaviour. Relatedly, Ryu and Kim (2016), with surveys and matched transaction data from platforms, identified four types of contributors based on their motivations to participate in crowdfunding. The four types of contributors are angelic backers, reward hunters, avid fans, and tasteful hermits. Angelic backers are similar in many aspects to charitable donors while reward hunters are similar to traditional investors. Avid fans are the most enthusiastic contributor group and similar to members of a brand community. Tasteful hermits fully support the crowdfunding campaigns but are less concerned with relational aspects of crowdfunding behaviour.

Implications

Implications for Research

Given the differences between reward-based crowdfunding and traditional funding channels, the drivers of crowdfunding campaign success, and the factors impacting individual contribution behaviour have both been extensively examined in the crowdfunding literature. The literature supports the view that reward-based crowdfunding possesses both common aspects as a funding channel and distinguished aspects as a new type of channel. That is, reward-based crowdfunding can be considered as a riskier form of online commerce, where people pre-order products before the products are fully developed and produced, while accepting a degree of risk of non-delivery or deviations from campaign promises. Reward-based crowdfunding is similar in some respects to the traditional funding sources in that potential contributors make a decision based on information they are exposed to and/or collect. This is important because creators in the reward-based crowdfunding context are still expected to present their resources and capabilities to potential contributors. The differences are that they may leverage different types of information. Social information and progress of a campaign may be more critical factors in the context of reward crowdfunding.

Although previous literature found some implicative mechanisms of reward-based crowdfunding, the current body of literature has several limitations, which indicate our future research directions. First of all, while the literature validated the factors influencing campaign success and individual contributors' behaviours, detailed theoretical mechanism of how a specific factor affects the campaign performance or contributor behaviour has not been well addressed. Future research can find more theoretical evidence for the findings so far, or develop new theories explaining the underlying dynamics in the specific context of reward-based crowdfunding.

Second, the main research streams on reward-based crowdfunding have focused on explicit factors related to creators and their projects as affecting the success of a crowdfunding campaign, but less attention has been paid to the motivation of players on both sides. Creators and contributors join crowdfunding for different motivations (Gerber et al. 2012; Ryu and Kim 2016, 2018). As discussed, a few pioneering studies dealt with motivations in the reward-based crowdfunding context, but the literature has not established how those motivations interact with other factors, such as campaign characteristics. To fill this gap, future research can delve deep into how different motivations interrelate with crowdfunding success and contributor behaviours. Specifically, because motivations are psychological factors, examining how motivations interact with other attributes such as demographics, campaign, or platform characteristics could be an important consideration.

Third, in consideration of the risks embedded in the context of reward-based crowdfunding, researchers are expected to deal with these risk factors. Reward-based crowdfunding is not free from drawbacks such as delays in fulfilment and potential fraud (Mollick 2014). Future research could identify that specific types of campaigns may be more prone to certain risks, compared to other campaigns. More importantly, examining the effectiveness of the current coping mechanisms of reward-based crowdfunding in mitigating such risks could be a promising research domain.

Finally, the extant literature on crowdfunding has myopically focused on the success of campaigns "inside" crowdfunding platforms. Recently, the perspective is expanding to post-campaign phenomena by examining the effects of crowdfunding success on follow-on performance of start-ups (Roma et al. 2017). Nevertheless, we still know little about how crowdfunding can influence entrepreneurial organizations' long-term performance and thus survival. Regarding this gap between the findings from previous literature and expected role of crowdfunding in longer term, future research can identify how crowdfunding affects subsequent performance.

Implications for Practice

The current body of literature on reward-based crowdfunding also provides practical implications, especially into the launch of crowdfunding campaigns and the management of platforms. For potential creators, the literature provides some guidance. Most of all, different aspects of information quality and effective communication of that information are critical for a reward-based crowdfunding campaign. A strand of research identified specific attribute or characteristics of campaigns and their creators that boost individual contributors' behaviour and thus crowdfunding success. Those results can provide practical aid in this regard. More importantly, in addition to polishing the campaign itself, understanding the social aspects of reward-based crowdfunding is critical to reaching the goal amount. Creators must understand the importance of earlier pledges and momentum throughout the campaign process. They are expected to develop a strategy to collect a group of earlier contributors according to the nature of the campaign. Strong social capital of a creator from inside and outside of the crowdfunding platform should help the creator initiate this momentum towards crowdfunding success.

For platform operators, the current literature provides implications related to building up a sustainable platform. Platform operators should not only try to expand their platforms but also understand the existence of different types of creators and contributors on their platforms. Based on this understanding, they can offer the most suitable benefits based on their distinct characteristics. For example, social campaigns and commercial campaigns may draw different types of (potential) contributors and thus need different formulas for crowdfunding success. If they can provide more customized guidance for novice creators, their platforms can enjoy higher rates of crowdfunding success and thus enhance their sustainability. Finally, in order to build up sustainable platforms, they are required to understand the combinative characteristics of reward-based crowdfunding, providing both commercial and communal values to both creators and contributors (Ryu and Kim 2018).

Conclusion

As an innovative entrepreneurial fundraising channel, crowdfunding has gained increasing popularity in the last few years (Mollick 2014). Specifically, reward-based crowdfunding, the best-known crowdfunding model, has attracted increasing attention from the public. It has offered feasible opportunities for entrepreneurs to test new business ideas, conduct market research, and access early-stage financing. Despite the growing popularity of reward-based crowdfunding research, as well as the increasing relevance of employing reward-based crowdfunding for entrepreneurial financing, relatively little literature has systematically investigated it as a unique phenomenon separated from other crowdfunding models.

To mitigate this gap, we have highlighted the reward-based crowdfunding model and the unique aspects of it. In this chapter, we have comprehensively discussed the reward-based crowdfunding phenomenon based on a four-dimension framework which includes the main players engaged in the crowdfunding process: the creators, the backers, the campaigns, and the platforms. In addition, an evidence-based introduction to the reward-based crowdfunding development across different regions is also provided. We have highlighted the regional variances by including the facts of developing trends, R&D priority, female participation, internationalization, cross-border transaction and risk in different reward-based crowdfunding markets. A literature review of the academic research on reward-based crowdfunding was also provided in this chapter by focusing on two main research aspects: success drivers and consumer behaviour. Based on the findings of the literature review, the practical and theoretical implications of what we know about reward-based crowdfunding were discussed.

References

Agrawal, A., Catalini, C., & Goldfarb, A. (2015). Crowdfunding: Geography, Social Networks, and the Timing of Investment Decisions. *Journal of Economics & Management Strategy, 24*(2), 253–274.

Ahlers, G. K. C., Cumming, D., Günther, C., & Schweizer, D. (2015). Signalling in Equity Crowdfunding. *Entrepreneurship Theory and Practice, 39*(4), 955–980.

Allison, T. H., Davis, B. C., Webb, J. W., & Short, J. C. (2017). Persuasion in Crowdfunding: An Elaboration Likelihood Model of Crowdfunding Performance. *Journal of Business Venturing, 39*(1), 53–73.

Antonenko, P. D., Lee, B. R., & Kleinheksel, A. J. (2014). Trends in the Crowdfunding of Educational Technology Startups. *TechTrends, 58*(6), 36–41.

Belleflamme, P., Lambert, T., & Schwienbacher, A. (2014). Crowdfunding: Tapping the Right Crowd. *Journal of Business Venturing, 29*(5), 585–609.

Boeuf, B., Darveau, J., & Legoux, R. (2014). Financing Creativity: Crowdfunding as a New Approach for Theatre Projects. *International Journal of Arts Management, 16*(3), 33–48.

Brown, T. E., Boon, E., & Pitt, L. F. (2017). Seeking Funding in Order to Sell: Crowdfunding as a Marketing Tool. *Business Horizons, 60(2), 189–195.*

Burtch, G., Ghose, A., & Wattal, S. (2013). An Empirical Examination of the Antecedents and Consequences of Contribution Patterns in Crowd-Funded Markets. *Information Systems Research, 24*(3), 499–519.

Burtch, G., Ghose, A., & Wattal, S. (2014). Cultural Differences and Geography as Determinants of Online Prosocial Lending. *MIS Quarterly, 38*(3), 773–794.

Burtch, G., Ghose, A., & Wattal, S. (2015). The Hidden Cost of Accommodating Crowdfunder Privacy Preferences: A Randomized Field Experiment. *Management Science, 61*(5), 949–962.

Ciuchta, M. P., Letwin, C., Stevenson, R. M., & McMahon, S. R. (2016). Regulatory Focus and Information Cues in a Crowdfunding Context. *Journal of Applied Psychology, 65*(3), 490–514.

Colombo, M. G., Franzoni, C., & Rossi-Lamastra, C. (2015). Internal Social Capital and the Attraction of Early Contributions in Crowdfunding. *Entrepreneurship Theory and Practice, 39*(1), 75–100.

Davis, B. C., Hmieleski, K. M., Webb, J. W., & Coombs, J. E. (2017). Funders' Positive Affective Reactions to Entrepreneurs' Crowdfunding Pitches: The Influence of Perceived Product Creativity and Entrepreneurial Passion. *Journal of Business Venturing, 32*(1), 90–106.

Frydrych, D., Bock, A. J., Kinder, T., & Koeck, B. (2014). Exploring Entrepreneurial Legitimacy in Reward-based Crowdfunding. *Venture Capital, 16*(3), 247–269.

Gerber, E. M., Hui, J. S., & Kuo, P. (2012). *Crowdfunding: Why People Are Motivated to Post and Fund Projects on Crowdfunding Platforms*. Paper presented at the International Workshop on Design, Influence, and Social Technologies: Techniques, Impacts and Ethics.

Giudici, G., Guerini, M., & Rossi-Lamastra, C. (2018). Reward-based Crowdfunding of Entrepreneurial Projects: The Effect of Local Altruism and Localized Social Capital on Proponents' Success. *Small Business Economics, 50*(2), 307–324.

Kang, L., Jiang, W., & Tan, C.-H. (2017). Remarkable Advocates: An Investigation of Geographic Distance and Social Capital for Crowdfunding. *Information & Management, 54*(3), 336–348.

Kim, K., & Viswanathan, S. (2019). The 'Experts' in the Crowd: The Role of Experienced Investors in a Crowdfunding Market. *MIS Quarterly, 43*(2), 347–372.

Kuppuswamy, V., & Bayus, B. L. (2017). Does My Contribution to Your Crowdfunding Project Matter? *Journal of Business Venturing, 32*(1), 72–89.

Lin, M., & Viswanathan, S. (2015). Home Bias in Online Investments: An Empirical Study of an Online Crowdfunding Market. *Management Science, 62*(5), 1393–1414.

Messeni Petruzzelli, A., Natalicchio, A., Panniello, U., & Roma, P. (2019). Understanding the Crowdfunding Phenomenon and Its Implications for Sustainability. *Technological Forecasting and Social Change, 141*, 138–148.

Mollick, E. (2014). The Dynamics of Crowdfunding: An Exploratory Study. *Journal of Business Venturing, 29*(1), 1–16.

Ordanini, A., Miceli, L., Pizzetti, M., & Parasuraman, A. (2011). Crowdfunding: Transforming Customers into Investors Through Innovative Service Platforms. *Journal of Service Management, 22*(4), 443–470.

Parhankangas, A., & Renko, M. (2017). Linguistic Style and Crowdfunding Success Among Social and Commercial Entrepreneurs. *Journal of Business Venturing, 32*(2), 215–236.

Roma, P., Petruzzelli, A. M., & Perrone, G. (2017). From the Crowd to the Market: The Role of Reward-based Crowdfunding Performance in Attracting Professional Investors. *Research Policy, 46*(9), 1606–1628.

Ryu, S., & Kim, Y.-G. (2016). A Typology of Crowdfunding Sponsors: Birds of a Feather Flock Together? *Electronic Commerce Research and Applications, 16*, 43–54.

Ryu, S., & Kim, Y.-G. (2018). Money Is Not Everything: A Typology of Crowdfunding Project Creators. *Journal of Strategic Information Systems, 27*(4), 350–368.

Schwienbacher, A., & Larralde, B. (2012). Alternative Types of Entrepreneurial Finance. In *The Oxford Handbook of Entrepreneurial Finance*. New York, NY: Oxford University Press.

Shneor, R., & Flåten, B.-T. (2015). Opportunities for Entrepreneurial Development and Growth through Online Communities, Collaboration, and Value Creating and Co-Creating Activities. In H. R. Kaufmann & S. M. R. Shams (Eds.), *Entrepreneurial Challenges in the 21st Century* (pp. 178–199). Basingstoke: Palgrave Macmillan.

Shneor, R., & Munim, Z. H. (2019). Reward Crowdfunding Contribution as Planned Behaviour: An Extended Framework. *Journal of Business Research, 103*, 56–70.

Skirnevskiy, V., Bendig, D., & Brettel, M. (2017). The Influence of Internal Social Capital on Serial Creators' Success in Crowdfunding. *Entrepreneurship Theory & Practice, 41*(2), 209–236.

Steigenberger, N. (2017). Why Supporters Contribute to Reward-Based Crowdfunding. *International Journal of Entrepreneurial Behaviour & Research, 23*(2), 336–353.

Thürridl, C., & Kamleitner, B. (2016). What Goes Around Comes Around? Rewards as Strategic Assets in Crowdfunding. *California Management Review, 58*(2), 88–110.

Tomczak, A., & Brem, A. (2013). A Conceptualized Investment Model of Crowdfunding. *Venture Capital, 15*(4), 335–359.

Xu, B., Zheng, H., Xu, Y., & Wang, T. (2016). Configurational Paths to Sponsor Satisfaction in Crowdfunding. *Journal of Business Research, 69(2), 915–927.*

Zhang, B., Ziegler, T., Mammadova, L., Johanson, D., Gray, M., & Yerolemou, N. (2018). *The 5th UK Alternative Finance Industry Report.* Cambridge: The Cambridge Centre for Alternative Finance.

Zhao, L., & Vinig, T. (2017). Hedonic Value and Crowdfunding Project Performance: A Propensity Score Matching-based Analysis. *Review of Behavioral Finance, 9*(2), 169–186.

Zheng, H., Li, D., Wu, J., & Xu, Y. (2014). The Role of Multidimensional Social Capital in Crowdfunding: A Comparative Study in China And US. *Information & Management, 51*(4), 488–496.

Zheng, H., Xu, B., Zhang, M., & Wang, T. (2018). Sponsor's Cocreation and Psychological Ownership in Reward-based Crowdfunding. *Information Systems Journal, 28*(6), 1213–1238.

Ziegler, T., Johanson, D., King, M., Zhang, B., Mammadova, L., Ferri, F., Trappe, R., et al. (2018a). *Reaching New Heights: The 3rd Americas Alternative Finance Industry Report.* Cambridge: The Cambridge Centre for Alternative Finance.

Ziegler, T., Johanson, D., Zhang, B., Ben, S., Wang, W., Mammadova, L., Hao, R., et al. (2018b). *The 3rd Asia Pacific Region Alternative Finance Industry Report.* Cambridge: The Cambridge Centre for Alternative Finance.

Ziegler, T., Suresh, K., Garvey, K., Rowan, P., Zhang, B., Obijiaku, A., Hao, R., & Alqahtani, F. (2018c). *The 2nd Annual Middle East and Africa Alternative Finance Industry Report.* Cambridge: The Cambridge Centre for Alternative Finance.

Ziegler, T., Shneor, R., Wenzlaff, K., Odorović, A., Johanson, D., Hao, R., & Ryll, L. (2019). *Shifting Paradigms: The 4th Annual European Alternative Finance Report.* Cambridge: The Cambridge Centre for Alternative Finance.

7

Donation Crowdfunding: Principles and Donor Behaviour

Liang Zhao and Rotem Shneor

Introduction

Crowdfunding, as an innovative fundraising channel, aims to exploit the power of the crowd for supporting various kinds of projects which may not easily get funded through traditional ways of fundraising (Lambert and Schwienbacher 2010). In the realm of donation funding, crowdfunding has simplified the process of fundraising for prosocial purposes by integrating information collection, donation transaction, and interactive communication into one standardized process (Belleflamme et al. 2013). This has led some to claim that donation-based crowdfunding has redefined the way of charitable giving is done, as it fuses traditional charitable giving and IT-enabled crowdfunding together (Gleasure and Feller 2016).

Compared with traditional charitable fundraising strategies, donation-based crowdfunding provides a way for potential donors to reach people/

L. Zhao (✉) • R. Shneor
School of Business and Law, University of Agder, Kristiansand, Norway
e-mail: liang.zhao@uia.no; rotem.shneor@uia.no

R. Shneor et al. (eds.), *Advances in Crowdfunding*,
https://doi.org/10.1007/978-3-030-46309-0_7

groups in need of help without the constraints of physical distance (Tanaka and Voida 2016). Furthermore, from a fundraiser perspective, donation crowdfunding allows for greater efficiencies in terms of geographical reach (Agrawal et al. 2015), reduced transaction and coordination costs (Choy and Schlagwein 2016), as well as richer and more frequent interactions with prospective donors. Accordingly, donation crowdfunding has been employed in a variety of contexts beyond pure charity causes (Gleasure and Feller 2016), and have been applied to support independent journalism (Jian and Shin 2015), indie documentary film productions (Sørensen 2012), cultural heritage projects (Oomen and Aroyo 2011), supporting educational work (Meer 2014), and scientific research (Wheat et al. 2013).

When compared to other crowdfunding models, donations represent one of the smallest models by volume in most regions. In 2017, donation crowdfunding volumes were estimated at, USD 290 million in the Americas (Ziegler et al. 2018a), USD 113 million in Europe including (EUR 53 million in mainland Europe and GBP 41 million in the UK) (Zhang et al. 2018; Ziegler et al. 2019), USD 63 million in the Middle East and Africa (Ziegler et al. 2018c), and USD 53 million in the Asia-Pacific region (Ziegler et al. 2018b). Except for the Middle East and Africa, where donations account for 17% of total the crowdfunding volume, in all other regions this model only represents 1% or less. Accordingly, the share of donation crowdfunding in the total global crowdfunding volume represents only 0.1%.

These more modest volumes may be associated with the fact that, unlike other crowdfunding models, donation-based crowdfunding does not include offering the backers material or monetary rewards for their contributions, hence implying different motivations driving related behaviour, as well as relations between fundraisers and backers. More specifically, supporters of donation-based crowdfunding campaigns are said to be motivated by altruism, peer recognition, respect, or esteem rather than by tangible and monetary rewards (Benkler 2011). Hence, to better understand donor behaviour in this context, as well as to boost success of donation campaigns, it is important to understand the working mechanisms of donation-based crowdfunding.

The purpose of this chapter is thus to review current knowledge about donation-based crowdfunding, while examining its core features, and factors driving donor behaviour in this context. Accordingly, we first discuss the current state and characteristics of donation-based crowdfunding, while highlighting its unique aspects. Next, the success factors of donation-based crowdfunding campaigns are summarized based on a review of earlier studies examining them. This is followed by a literature review and discussion concerning the factors impacting donor behaviour. Finally, we conclude by suggesting implications for practice and research.

Characteristics of Donation Crowdfunding

Donation-based crowdfunding has become a new channel to provide monetary support for non-profit, prosocial, and other "do good" initiatives. It is a type of philanthropy (Gerber and Hui 2013) reflecting an emerging and innovative online charity paradigm (Gerber et al. 2012). Similar to other crowdfunding models, the donation-based crowdfunding model is composed of three elements: the campaign initiators/fundraisers, the donors/backers, and the online platforms.

The donation-based crowdfunding platforms offer opportunities for fundraisers to launch campaigns as an open call over the internet for donations to charitable purposes within fixed time durations (Shneor and Munim 2019; Mollick 2014; Belleflamme et al. 2014; Gerber et al. 2012). Compared to the traditional charitable giving, with the help of information technology, donation-based crowdfunding is said to reduce the coordination and transaction costs associated with donation collections in a significant way (Choy and Schlagwein 2016). Besides, donation-based crowdfunding tends to collect small amounts from large crowds instead of seeking large amounts from a small group of affluent donors (Lu et al. 2014). With the involvement of the social network sites (SNS), donation-based crowdfunding initiators can easily broadcast their campaigns to a wider range of potential donors and establish social relationships with such crowds (Liang and Turban 2011).

While traditional charitable giving and donation crowdfunding share many commonalities, they may also differ to varying degrees with respect to several aspects. Here, internet-based crowdfunding platforms and social network sites (SNS), allow for greater real-time interaction (e.g. updates, comments, live streams, etc.) between donors and project initiators throughout the fundraising process (Kuppuswamy and Bayus 2017), as well as afterwards. Incorporating dedicated promotional efforts via SNS, help spread information to the public in new and effective ways (Lambert and Schwienbacher 2010), as in targeted advertising, which increase the probability of successful fundraising.

Other benefits reflect greater process efficiency. First, donation crowdfunding provides opportunities for wider geographical reach, where contributions may be collected from non-local donors with no previous connections to the fundraisers (Agrawal et al. 2015) in a manner that would have been a lot more expensive to achieve otherwise. Second, coordination and transaction costs associated with fundraising may be significantly reduced by the applications of advanced ICT tools (e.g. timely online interactions, digital and mobile payment systems, etc.) (Choy and Schlagwein 2016). And, third, donation crowdfunding also present opportunities to tap into more active donors who may be actively seeking opportunities to contribute to causes on crowdfunding platforms instead of passively waiting for opportunities (Gleasure and Feller 2016), as well as enabling a lower threshold for their involvement and activism, requiring supporters to simply share the campaign with their own networks often through a single-button click.

Success Factors of Donation Crowdfunding Campaigns

Since donation-based crowdfunding is a special type of charitable giving (Gerber and Hui 2013), some factors identified as influencing successful fundraising in traditional charitable giving may also be relevant in donation-based crowdfunding. Research on donor's willingness to donate in the context of traditional charitable giving is usually associated with altruistic orientation and tendencies (Choy and Schlagwein 2015). Donors are encouraged to donate by their sense of empathy towards specific charitable purposes (Gerber et al. 2012), while representing the emotional state of the individuals (Hoffman et al. 1999).

A recent literature review by Shneor and Vik (2020) has identified seven persistent variables which were found to impact successful donation crowdfunding across multiple studies. First, the target sum set for fundraising is positively associated with success, suggesting that the higher the target the greater the likelihood of success in donation crowdfunding. Second, inclusion of a video in the campaign materials is associated with greater success in comparison to donation campaigns that do not include a video. This finding was linked to lowering the cognitive efforts required for processing campaign information, which is effective at facilitating donations Third, donors react more positively to campaigns closer to them geographically or ideologically. Fourth, female campaign creators are associated with higher success than male campaign creators, which may be related to both more modest funding requirements and better social mobilization capacities of women as driven by empathy and relational focus. Fifth, availability of fundraisers' social capital as reflected by social network size, is also positively associated with success. Sixth, campaigns aiming at educational projects are more likely to receive donations for other purposes. And, finally, the level of maturity of the platform on which campaigns are published is also positively associated with success, suggesting that campaigning on more mature platforms is likely to enhance chances of funding success.

Nevertheless, these still represent slim pickings, as research of success drivers in donation crowdfunding remains limited and mostly explorative (Mollick 2014; Shneor and Vik 2020). Parallel to studies examining the impact of factors related to either the campaign, fundraiser, or platform, an additional line of inquiry into donor behaviour has gradually emerged. We review studies examining donor behaviour in the following sections.

Donor Behaviour in Donation Crowdfunding

Why individuals should contribute to donation-based crowdfunding campaigns has been identified as an interesting and important research question (Gerber and Hui 2013). It is interesting because contribution in the donation-based crowdfunding context may differ from that in other crowdfunding models. This is primarily because, while other crowdfunding models, offer individuals material or monetary rewards for their contribution (Zvilichovsky et al. 2015; Gerber and Hui 2013), donation crowdfunding does not offer such rewards (Gleasure and Feller 2016). Accordingly, the research into donor behaviour in the context of donation crowdfunding has referred to impure altruistic behaviour involving intangible rewards, which may satisfy both certain extrinsic and intrinsic motivations.

Altruism and Charitable Giving

Altruism is often used to explain individuals' charitable behaviour, and describes a situation where individuals try to help others, even if it comes at some personal cost (Khalil 2004). It is the motivation to increase another person's welfare, which is contrasted with egoism, the motivation to increase one's own welfare (Batson and Powell 2003). According, to Khalil (2004), altruism can be explained through two different dimensions: the interactional and the self-actional dimensions. On the one hand, the interactional dimension of altruism suggests that individuals' altruistic behaviour can be rationally explained. Such approach argues that altruistic behaviour tends to be triggered by delayed external rewards such as reciprocity (Cox 2004), vicarious enjoyment (Kahneman and Miller 1986), and natural-selection-based consequence (Haidt 2007). On the other hand, the self-actional dimension of altruism is normatively anchored. Hence, the self-actional dimension is not based on delayed external rewards but on the attributes of altruistic behaviour such as norms, mind structures, and culture (Khalil 2004).

When examining research conserving altruism in the context of donation crowdfunding, most references seem to rely on the self-actional dimension of altruistic behaviour. According to Andreoni (1990), the self-actional dimension of altruism includes pure altruism, warm glow, and impure altruism. Here, pure altruism describes the situation when individuals donate because it can improve the difficult situation of the recipients. External rewards such as hedonic benefits and warm-glow effects may not explain pure altruism donors' behaviour (Loewenstein and Small 2007; Andreoni 1990). Pure altruism donors are outcome-based and are primarily concerned with the extent to which a cause deserves support (Carpenter et al. 2008).

The warm-glow effect (Andreoni 1990) refers to the situation where individuals experience pleasure and satisfaction from helping others. Such senses of mental pleasure and satisfaction help to boost individuals' self-esteem (Fehr and Gächter 2000) and it also explains why individuals with the warm-glow mindset continue to conduct altruistic actions when they can otherwise "free-ride" and wait for others to help (Andreoni 1990). Warm glow is empathy-based. Donors are psychosocially connected with the receivers through the donor–receiver interaction (Park 2000), which is a process in which empathy tends to amplify the positive feelings from helping others or feelings of guilt when refusing to help (Andreoni et al. 2017). In such case, donors may feel compassion (Hoffman et al. 1999) towards certain causes, which may be described in donation crowdfunding campaigns while stimulating donation behaviour that enhance their sense of satisfaction and joy about supporting these causes (Gerber and Hui 2013; Gerber et al. 2012).

Though, the outcome-based pure altruism and empathy-dependent warm glow have provided valuable insights for understanding personal charitable behaviour, some argue that altruistic giving is always triggered by the impure altruism (Andreoni 1990). Impure altruism implies a situation where a combination of both pure altruism and warm glow will influence individuals' behaviour (Crumpler and Grossman 2008). And when examining the limited literature on donor motivation and behaviour specifically in the donation-based crowdfunding context, it appears that authors often explain donor behaviour by impure altruism (Gerber and Hui 2013; Burtch et al. 2013; Choy and Schlagwein 2015).

Motivation in Charitable Giving

Motivation directs and stimulates human behaviour (Murray 1964). It is viewed as the engine for satisfying physiological needs (Vallerand 1997) while capturing the degree to which a person is moved to perform a particular action (Deci et al. 1991). According to theory, motivations may be classified as either intrinsic or extrinsic (Deci et al. 1991), as well as either individually driven or socially driven (Alam and Campbell 2012; Kaufmann et al. 2011).

One of the prominent motivation theories is the "self-determination theory" (SDT), which explores the individual's self-motivated or self-determined behaviour (Ryan and Deci 2000). As such, it offers a detailed framework to differentiate between intrinsic and extrinsic motivations, while acknowledging that their mutually reinforcing nature also affects individuals' behavioural intentions (ibid.). Intrinsic motivation is derived from individual's inherent enjoyment of doing something, and extrinsic motivation stems from the separable outcome of doing something (ibid.). Thanks to its wide appeal and acceptance, this classification has also been employed in earlier crowdfunding literature (e.g. Gerber and Hui 2013; Wang et al. 2019; Zhang and Chen 2019).

Some studies have suggested that charitable giving can be caused by extrinsic motivations such as the satisfaction of personal heroism (Piliavin and Charng 1990) and personal atonement of sins (Schwartz 1973). However, evidence with respect to donation-based crowdfunding, mainly suggests that intrinsic motivations dominate such behaviour (Zhao and Sun 2020; Gleasure and Feller 2016; Bretschneider et al. 2014; Gerber and Hui 2013).

Specifically, individuals were found to contribute to donation-based crowdfunding in order to help others, support causes, or be part of a community (Gerber and Hui 2013). These may be triggered by a sense of empathy, sympathy, nostalgia, reciprocity, or commemoration (Andreoni 1990; Eisenberg and Miller 1987; Sargeant 1999), which may enhance positive feelings with contribution behaviour. Such positive feelings may represent intangible rewards in the form of a sense of enjoyment, competence, and autonomy (Deci and Ryan 1985; Oliver 1980). Such intrinsic motivations may explain donor behaviour, which does not involve material compensation. Furthermore, an earlier study by Zhao and Sun (2020) has shown that providing extrinsic rewards in prosocial campaigns will diminish donors' intrinsic motivations to donate in the donation-based crowdfunding context.

An alternative approach to the differentiation between intrinsic and extrinsic motivations, as suggested by the SDT (Ryan and Deci 2000), emphasizes that motivation is more than a personal concept and has social attributes (Akerlof 2006). Accordingly, classifying motivations as either individually driven or socially driven may also provide valuable insights to investigations of contribution behaviour in the crowd economy in general (Alam and Campbell 2012; Kaufmann et al. 2011), and donation crowdfunding in particular.

Individual motivation is generated by the desire of individuals regardless of the existence of a social group (Cohen et al. 2005). In contrast, social motivation stems from the presence of a social group and individual actions are triggered by the social group (Akerlof 2006). Furthermore, when combining the intrinsic vs. extrinsic dimensions (Deci et al. 1991) with the individual vs. social dimensions of motivation, four subcategories emerge: individual-extrinsic motivation, individual-intrinsic motivation, social-extrinsic motivation, and social-intrinsic motivation (Choy and Schlagwein 2015). At the individual level, the extrinsic motivation refers to the desire to achieve a specific result by doing something and the intrinsic motivation relates to the individual's personal satisfaction of doing something. At the social level, an individuals' social-extrinsic motivation related to signalling compliance with group expectations in terms of action beyond words, and social-intrinsic motivation relates to achieving a sense of belonging to a collective of like-minded people.

In terms of donation-based crowdfunding, donors' motivations such as helping others and supporting causes are typically individual (Gerber and Hui 2013). For example, individuals may donate to donation-based campaigns because they feel passionate about the campaigns (Choy and Schlagwein 2015). In addition, some donors are socially motived (Akerlof 2006). They donate to achieve social belonging and peer recognition (Alam and Campbell 2012; Bretschneider et al. 2014; Kaufmann et al. 2011). Here, donors donate because they want to be parts of the charity crowdfunding community and they enjoy engaging and collaborating with the community (Gerber et al. 2012).

Conclusion

Despite representing a small share of global crowdfunding volumes, donation crowdfunding is a unique model for supporting a wide range of prosocial and charitable causes, while allowing fundraisers to leverage benefits afforded by ICT solutions for more effective and efficient fundraising efforts than traditional methods and channels. This chapter has taken stock of the knowledge emerging from the limited research available in the donation crowdfunding context. We have highlighted the motivations of contributors to donate funding to such campaigns as driven by impure altruism, while acknowledging that most work has stressed intrinsic motivations both at the individual and at the social level. Furthermore, the success drivers of donation crowdfunding campaigns have been presented with respect to factors at the fundraiser, campaign, and platform levels. Nevertheless, donation crowdfunding remains an understudied context with much room for further exploration. Some ideas in this direction are presented below.

Implications for Research

While preliminary insights on factors impacting donation crowdfunding success factors are available, they tend to follow recipes adopted from studies conducted in commercial and investment-oriented models. Hence, it is recommended that future studies should devote more attention to examining factors unique to the donation context. Here, research should embark on capturing what successfully triggers aspects associated with donor behaviour, and how do campaign features support the necessary emotive reactions of joy, satisfaction, warm glow, as well as a sense of group belonging and compliance with social expectations. Such approach would require a departure from reliance on platform data, and a shift towards primary data collection through surveying and/interviewing of users. This would help bridge the gap between campaign success and donor behaviour and provide valuable insights how the two hang-together in a theoretically sound manner.

An additional venue for future research may include comparative studies of donation crowdfunding versus traditional donation fundraising practices, crowdfunding dynamics across models, as well as across social, cultural, and sectoral groups. First, studies that will compare crowdfunding versus traditional donation collection channels, may provide evidence and insights about the added value or costs associated with the practice of each, and will be go beyond the speculative suggestions that have been outlined in research thus far. Second, a comparative study across crowdfunding models, can better clarify what are the common drivers and aspects of crowdfunding in general, while highlighting the unique aspects associated with donation crowdfunding beyond the clear differentiation between tangible and intangible rewards and benefits. Finally, studies comparing donation crowdfunding across differing contexts, may help identify sectors, social and cultural groups that may be more receptive to donation crowdfunding than others, as well as different strategies employed in different contexts to encourage donor engagements and contributions.

Implications for Practice

Insights from our review of the current state of donation crowdfunding research and practice may inform platforms in designing their products and services, as well as inform fundraisers interested in running a donation crowdfunding campaign. In this context, platforms should develop features that may enhance donors' sense of satisfaction and joy from giving. Such features may include interactive visualizations of impact such as progression bars, number of people affected, improved conditions (e.g. gas emission reductions, quantity of water cleansed, etc.), number of equipment units provided to needy, and so on. In addition, platforms may invest in community management features that will allow members to join certain interest groups, while receiving symbolic acknowledgement for their contributions to these groups (e.g. virtual badges, status levels, and public endorsements).

From the fundraiser perspective, fundraisers need to invest in creating a sense of ideological proximity with their prospective donors, employing emotional cues to trigger empathy in their messaging, as well as proactively engage with targeted groups via social media. In addition, since donors do not receive material rewards for their contributions, fundraisers should ensure smooth and ongoing communication with donors about project progress, execution, and impact during and after the campaign. This is both to enable a sense of satisfaction about donation at different points in time and to strategically establish long-term relations with fans, who are prospective future donors as well.

References

Agrawal, A., Catalini, C., & Goldfarb, A. (2015). Crowdfunding: Geography, Social Networks, and the Timing of Investment Decisions. *Journal of Economics & Management Strategy, 24*(2), 253–274.

Akerlof, R. J. (2006). A Theory of Social Motivation. Unpublished manuscript, Cambridge, MA.

Alam, S. L., & Campbell, J. (2012). *Crowdsourcing Motivations in a Not-for-Profit GLAM Context: The Australian Newspapers Digitisation Program.* Australasian Conference on Information Systems.

Andreoni, J. (1990). Impure Altruism and Donations to Public Goods: A Theory of Warm-Glow Giving. *The Economic Journal, 100*(401), 464–477.

Andreoni, J., Rao, J. M., & Trachtman, H. (2017). Avoiding the Ask: A Field Experiment on Altruism, Empathy, and Charitable Giving. *Journal of Political Economy, 125*(3), 625–653.

Batson, C. D., & Powell, A. A. (2003). Altruism and Prosocial Behavior. In I. B. Weiner (Ed.), *Handbook of Psychology* (pp. 463–484). John Wiley & Sons, Inc.

Belleflamme, P., Lambert, T., & Schwienbacher, A. (2013). Individual Crowdfunding Practices. *Venture Capital, 15*(4), 313–333.

Belleflamme, P., Lambert, T., & Schwienbacher, A. (2014). Crowdfunding: Tapping the Right Crowd. *Journal of Business Venturing, 29*(5), 585–609.

Benkler, Y. (2011). The Unselfish Gene. *Harvard Business Review, 89*(7–8), 76–85.

Bretschneider, U., Knaub, K., & Wieck, E. (2014). *Motivations for Crowdfunding: What Drives the Crowd to Invest in Start-ups?* European Conference on Information Systems, Tel Aviv, Association for Information Systems.

Burtch, G., Ghose, A., & Wattal, S. (2013). An Empirical Examination of the Antecedents and Consequences of Contribution Patterns in Crowd-Funded Markets. *Information Systems Research, 24*(3), 499–519.

Carpenter, J., Connolly, C., & Myers, C. K. (2008). Altruistic Behavior in a Representative Dictator Experiment. *Experimental Economics, 11*(3), 282–298.

Choy, K., & Schlagwein, D. (2015, May). *IT Affordances and Donor Motivations in Charitable Crowdfunding: The "Earthship Kapita" Case*. ECIS.

Choy, K., & Schlagwein, D. (2016). Crowdsourcing for a Better World: On the Relation Between IT Affordances and Donor Motivations in Charitable Crowdfunding. *Information Technology & People, 29*(1), 221–247.

Cohen, A. B., Hall, D. E., Koenig, H. G., & Meador, K. G. (2005). Social Versus Individual Motivation: Implications for Normative Definitions of Religious Orientation. *Personality and Social Psychology Review, 9*(1), 48–61.

Cox, J. C. (2004). How to Identify Trust and Reciprocity. *Games and Economic Behavior, 46*(2), 260–281.

Crumpler, H., & Grossman, P. J. (2008). An Experimental Test of Warm Glow Giving. *Journal of Public Economics, 92*(5–6), 1011–1021.

Deci, E. L., & Ryan, R. M. (1985). The General Causality Orientations Scale: Self-Determination in Personality. *Journal of Research in Personality, 19*(2), 109–134.

Deci, E. L., Vallerand, R. J., Pelletier, L. G., & Ryan, R. M. (1991). Motivation and Education: The Self-Determination Perspective. *Educational Psychologist, 26*(3–4), 325–346.

Eisenberg, N., & Miller, P. A. (1987). The Relation of Empathy to Prosocial and Related Behaviors. *Psychological Bulletin, 101*(1), 91.

Fehr, E., & Gächter, S. (2000). Cooperation and Punishment in Public Goods Experiments. *American Economic Review, 90*(4), 980–994.

Gerber, E. M., & Hui, J. (2013). Crowdfunding: Motivations and Deterrents for Participation. *ACM Transactions on Computer-Human Interaction (TOCHI), 20*(6), 34.

Gerber, E. M., Hui, J. S., & Kuo, P. Y. (2012, February). Crowdfunding: Why People Are Motivated to Post and Fund Projects on Crowdfunding Platforms. In *Proceedings of the International Workshop on Design, Influence, and Social Technologies: Techniques, Impacts and Ethics* (Vol. 2, No. 11, p. 10). Evanston, IL: Northwestern University.

Gleasure, R., & Feller, J. (2016). Does Heart or Head Rule Donor Behaviors in Charitable Crowdfunding Markets? *International Journal of Electronic Commerce, 20*(4), 499–524.
Haidt, J. (2007). The New Synthesis in Moral Psychology. *Science, 316*(5827), 998–1002.
Hoffman, D. L., Novak, T. P., & Peralta, M. (1999). Building Consumer Trust Online. *Communications of the ACM, 42*(4), 80–85.
Jian, L., & Shin, J. (2015). Motivations Behind Donors' Contributions to Crowdfunded Journalism. *Mass Communication and Society, 18*(2), 165–185.
Kahneman, D., & Miller, D. T. (1986). Norm theory: Comparing reality to its alternatives. *Psychological review, 93*(2), 136.
Kaufmann, N., Schulze, T., & Veit, D. (2011, August). More than Fun and Money. Worker Motivation in Crowdsourcing-A Study on Mechanical Turk. *AMCIS, 11*(2011), 1–11.
Khalil, E. L. (2004). What Is Altruism? *Journal of Economic Psychology, 25*(1), 97–123.
Kuppuswamy, V., & Bayus, B. L. (2017). Crowdfunding Creative Ideas: The Dynamics of Project Backers in Kickstarter. A Shorter Version of This Paper Is In "*The Economics of Crowdfunding: Startups, Portals, and Investor Behavior*", L. Hornuf & D. Cumming (eds.).
Lambert, T., & Schwienbacher, A. (2010). An Empirical Analysis of Crowdfunding. *Social Science Research Network, 1578175*, 1–23.
Liang, T. P., & Turban, E. (2011). Introduction to the Special Issue Social Commerce: A Research Framework for Social Commerce. *International Journal of Electronic Commerce, 16*(2), 5–14.
Loewenstein, G., & Small, D. A. (2007). The Scarecrow and the Tin Man: The Vicissitudes of Human Sympathy and Caring. *Review of General Psychology, 11*(2), 112–126.
Lu, C. T., Xie, S., Kong, X., & Yu, P. S. (2014, February). Inferring the Impacts of Social Media on Crowdfunding. In *Proceedings of the 7th ACM International Conference on Web Search and Data Mining* (pp. 573–582). ACM.
Meer, J. (2014). Effects of the Price of Charitable Giving: Evidence from an Online Crowdfunding Platform. *Journal of Economic Behavior & Organization, 103*, 113–124.
Mollick, E. (2014). The Dynamics of Crowdfunding: An Exploratory Study. *Journal of Business Venturing, 29*(1), 1–16.
Murray, E. J. (1964). *Motivation and Emotion*. Prentice-Hall.
Oliver, R. L. (1980). A Cognitive Model of the Antecedents and Consequences of Satisfaction Decisions. *Journal of Marketing Research, 17*(4), 460–469.

Oomen, J., & Aroyo, L. (2011, June). Crowdsourcing in the Cultural Heritage Domain: Opportunities and Challenges. In *Proceedings of the 5th International Conference on Communities and Technologies* (pp. 138–149). ACM.

Park, E. S. (2000). Warm-Glow Versus Cold-Prickle: A Further Experimental Study of Framing Effects on Free-Riding. *Journal of Economic Behavior & Organization, 43*(4), 405–421.

Piliavin, J. A., & Charng, H. W. (1990). Altruism: A Review of Recent Theory and Research. *Annual Review of Sociology, 16*(1), 27–65.

Ryan, R. M., & Deci, E. L. (2000). Intrinsic and Extrinsic Motivations: Classic Definitions and New Directions. *Contemporary Educational Psychology, 25*(1), 54–67.

Sargeant, A. (1999). Charitable Giving: Towards a Model of Donor Behaviour. *Journal of Marketing Management, 15*(4), 215–238.

Schwartz, S. H. (1973). Normative Explanations of Helping Behavior: A Critique, Proposal, and Empirical Test. *Journal of Experimental Social Psychology, 9*(4), 349–364.

Shneor, R., & Munim, Z. H. (2019). Reward Crowdfunding Contribution as Planned Behaviour: An Extended Framework. *Journal of Business Research, 103*, 56–70.

Shneor, R., & Vik, A. A. (2020). Crowdfunding Success: A Systematic Literature Review 2010–2017. *Baltic Journal of Management, 15*(2), 149–182.

Sørensen, I. E. (2012). Crowdsourcing and Outsourcing: The Impact of Online Funding and Distribution on the Documentary Film Industry in the UK. *Media, Culture & Society, 34*(6), 726–743.

Tanaka, K. G., & Voida, A. (2016, May). Legitimacy Work: Invisible Work in Philanthropic Crowdfunding. In *Proceedings of the 2016 CHI Conference on Human Factors in Computing Systems* (pp. 4550–4561). ACM.

Vallerand, R. J. (1997). Toward a Hierarchical Model of Intrinsic and Extrinsic Motivation. In *Advances in Experimental Social Psychology* (Vol. 29, pp. 271–360). Academic Press.

Wang, T., et al. (2019). Exploring Individuals' Behavioral Intentions Toward Donation Crowdfunding: Evidence from China. *Industrial Management & Data Systems, 119*(7), 1515–1534.

Wheat, R. E., Wang, Y., Byrnes, J. E., & Ranganathan, J. (2013). Raising Money for Scientific Research Through Crowdfunding. *Trends in Ecology & Evolution, 28*(2), 71–72.

Zhang, H., & Chen, W. (2019). Backer Motivation in Crowdfunding New Product Ideas: Is It about You or Is It about Me? *Journal of Product Innovation Management, 36*(2), 241–262.

Zhang, B., Ziegler, T., Mammadova, L., et al. (2018). *The 5th UK Alternative Finance Industry Report*. Cambridge, UK: Cambridge Centre for Alternative Finance.

Zhao, L., & Sun, Z. (2020). Pure Donation or Hybrid Donation Crowdfunding. *Baltic Journal of Management, 15*(2).

Ziegler, T., Johanson, D., King, M., et al. (2018a). *Reaching New Heights: The 3rd Americas Alternative Finance Industry Report*. Cambridge, UK: Cambridge Centre for Alternative Finance.

Ziegler, T., Johanson, D., Zhang, B., et al. (2018b). *The 3rd Asia Pacific Region Alternative Finance Industry Report*. Cambridge, UK: Cambridge Centre for Alternative Finance.

Ziegler, T., Suresh, K., Garvey, K., et al. (2018c). *The 2nd Annual Middle East & Africa Alternative Finance Industry Report*. Cambridge, UK: Cambridge Center for Alternative Finance.

Ziegler, T., Shneor, R., Wenzlaff, K., et al. (2019). *Shifting Paradigms – The 4th European Alternative Finance Benchmarking Report*. Cambridge, UK: Cambridge Centre for Alternative Finance.

Zvilichovsky, D., Inbar, Y., & Barzilay, O. (2015). *Playing Both Sides of the Market: Success and Reciprocity on Crowdfunding Platforms*. Available at SSRN 2304101.

8

Ethical Considerations in Crowdfunding

Rotem Shneor and Stina Torjesen

Introduction

Parallel to the impressive growth of crowdfunding in recent years, we are also witnessing a growing concern with ethical aspects of crowdfunding practice. Here, while not representing mainstream developments, stories about platforms and campaigns suspected of fraud have attracted both public and media attention. For example, at the platform-level, investigation into misappropriation of funds, as in the case of Sweden-based crowdlending platform TrustBuddy, ended up with it filing for bankruptcy in 2015 with substantial losses for its lenders (Palmer 2016). In China, the Ezubao crowdlending platform, succumbed to government crackdown on illegal fundraising, revealing its operations as a 'Ponzy scheme' (Zhang and Miller 2017). Moreover, at the campaign level, and within the reward-crowdfunding context, an independent study (Mollick 2015) showed that 9% of campaigns failed to deliver on promised

R. Shneor (✉) • S. Torjesen
School of Business and Law, University of Agder, Kristiansand, Norway
e-mail: rotem.shneor@uia.no; stina.torjesen@uia.no

R. Shneor et al. (eds.), *Advances in Crowdfunding*,
https://doi.org/10.1007/978-3-030-46309-0_8

rewards, 8% of dollars pledged went to failed projects, and 7% of backers failed to receive their chosen reward. Such cases include non-delivery on commercial concepts like iBackPack, which raised USD 720K on Indiegogo for its urban backpack concept, and Central Standard Timing, which raised more than USD 1 million on Kickstarter for the 'world's thinnest watch', to name just two (Carpenter 2017). Other cases are more sinister, including the GoFundMe donation campaigns by US citizen Jennifer Flynn Cataldo, requesting help in paying medical bills associated with cancer she did not have, raising more than USD 38K, before being convicted of fraud (ibid.).

The above examples can serve as triggers for a discussion of ethical issues in crowdfunding practice, which, surprisingly, has largely been absent in earlier research. An exception here has been a short communication by Snyder et al. (2016), who called for ethics-focused research on medical crowdfunding in particular, as it raises concerns with exposure to fraudulent campaigns, loss of privacy, and fairness in how medical crowdfunding funds are distributed. Other related studies have taken a legalistic rather than ethical perspective, while addressing legal anchoring of investor protection in crowdfunding (e.g. Heminway 2014; Pierce-Wright 2016). Indeed, ethical aspects in finance have been obscured by the preoccupation with legalization, under the incorrect assumption that what is legal is also ethical, versus how ethics serve as the foundation for regulation (Boatright 2010).

The current study will address this gap by mapping and classifying ethical considerations in crowdfunding practice, while relating them to the different stakeholders who are parties to the development of the crowdfunding activities, including—fundraisers (entities that raise capital for a project), platforms (web applications facilitating the fundraising), funders (actual and potential funding providers to crowdfunding campaigns), and regulators (public authorities overseeing the law-making related to crowdfunding practice). Furthermore, crowdfunding can be viewed as a phenomenon at the intersection between the disciplines of finance, entrepreneurship, marketing, e-commerce, and social networking. Hence, since, to the best knowledge of the authors, no earlier study has addressed ethical considerations specifically in the context of crowdfunding, we draw on principles discussed in studies of ethics in finance

(Boatright 2010), entrepreneurial finance (Fassin and Drover 2017), entrepreneurship (Bucar and Hisrich 2001), marketing (Dunfee et al. 1999), e-commerce (Roman 2007), and online social networking (Light and McGrath 2010).

In the following sections, we first address classical approaches to business ethics, and we then delve deeper into the context of crowdfunding, while exploring related dilemmas from a multiple stakeholder perspective. We then suggest a framework outlining potential ethical pitfalls in crowdfunding practice, as well as some mechanism for addressing them. Finally, we conclude by highlighting the contributions, limitations, and implications of the current study.

Classical Approaches to Ethical Decision Making in Business

Simply put, business ethics deals with what people in business *ought* to do. In business ethics neither do we merely describe business practices, nor do we attempt to predict what will happen on, say, the stock market, or with company sales following a distinct type of marketing campaign (Sandbu 2011; DesJardins 2009). Instead we ask, in a given business situation, what is the *right* thing to do (Sandbu 2011). More specifically we identify moral reasons for or against different courses of action and weight them against each other (ibid., p. 12). These reasons may often correspond to our moral instincts, or gut feelings of what is right or wrong, but they are not derived from our intuition. Instead, in business ethics we search for moral claims, or underlying principles of what may, from a given perspective, constitute good behaviour and we attempt to logically and consistently apply these when we make decisions.

There are several 'schools' in business ethics and these offer different sets of ethical reasons or principles that can guide decision making. The three main schools are 'Kantian deontology', utilitarianism, and virtue ethics.

'Kantian deontology' derives from the works of the philosopher Immanuel Kant (1785/1991). In Kantian approaches business managers are advised to search for a general principle that can offer guidance when faced with a specific ethical challenge. A key test to whether a principle can be seen as morally robust is to ask if the manager could get all other mangers to follow the same principle in all similar situations (Kant's categorical imperative in Donaldson and Dunfee 1994). In crowdfunding this 'do unto other as you would have them do unto you' approach would manifest itself if a fundraiser was tempted to over-exaggerate the benefits of a product being developed. Would it be rational for the funder to operate in a market where all suppliers, competitors, and customers over-exaggerated their products' performance or customers over-exaggerated their willingness to pay? The likely answer here is no. In Kantian business ethics this means the fundraiser must reason that he or she has a duty not to over-exaggerate and that suppliers, competitors, and customers have a right to be given truthful information by the manager.

In Kantian business ethics we deliberate the reasons for why an action is the right thing and we seek to fulfil our duties and uphold the rights of others as best we can. Utilitarianism (Mill 2016), by contrast, is less concerned with prior reasoning and individual rights, but focus instead on the overall consequences of our actions. When faced with alternative courses of action a manager should choose the action that will maximize the future welfare, wellbeing or happiness of the most people (Donaldson and Dunfee 1994; Mill 2016). In this context, and in line with Veenhoven (1991), happiness can be considered as incorporating both a sense of contentment when comparing life-as-it-is to perceptions about how-life-should-be, and how one feels affectively in terms of gratification of basic bio-psychological needs.

Accordingly, crowdfunding fits the spirit of utilitarianism well. Many products and initiatives either leave well-being at the same level or increase it for a large number of people. Few initiatives would, when all consequences are calculated, produce a total sum of happiness that is lower than when the campaign commenced. Utilitarian ethics encourages fundraisers to develop campaigns, products, or initiatives where the positive consequences for the largest number of people is maximized. This resonates well with campaigns where social entrepreneurship is at the core, but commercial and profit-seeking campaigns may also fit the utilitarian logic.

In both utilitarianism and Kantian business ethics we have dictums which we can attempt to logically and consistently apply, that is, 'greatest sum of happiness to the greatest number of people' and 'do unto others as you would have them do unto you'. In the third school 'virtue ethics' it is harder to distil unified principles. Instead, when searching for guidance on actions and decision making, we are prompted to ask ourselves, 'What would a virtuous person do?' Aristoteles and his book *Nicomachean Ethics* serves as a centre piece in virtue ethics. Aristoteles advices us to develop our moral wisdom through a combination of knowledge and life experience (practical wisdom). We are on a journey of personal development where we increasingly come to understand and experience what virtue is. A virtue often resides on the 'golden mean' between two excesses. For example, if we develop the virtue temperance, we are increasingly avoiding greed as well as unnecessary abstinence. Similarly, as many initiators of crowdfunding platforms or fundraiser will likely develop a keen understanding of, when launching a campaign, you can neither be cowardly nor foolhardy, but must demonstrate the virtue courage (DesJardins 2009).

Donaldson and Dunfee (1994) note that while these three ethical schools of thought provide useful overall guidance to decision making, they fail to reflect and assist with often complex and very context specific challenges facing business managers. In crowdfunding we also have the added problem that platforms and campaigns may attract interest and support from across countries and even continents. Donaldson and Dunfee's "integrative social contract theory" addresses these challenges by laying out some general ('macrocontract') principles, and then, within the confines of these principles, encourages business managers to elucidate the informal ('microcontract') 'rules of the game' in the transactions they engage in. The latter includes the understanding and adhering to local expectations for ethical behaviour. Some of the general principles that can and should constrain managers regardless of location can be 'core human rights, including those to personal freedom, physical security and well-being, political participation, informed consent, the ownership of property, the right to subsistence, and the obligation to respect the dignity of each human person (ibid., p. 267).

Finally, it bears stressing that the way business ethics is studied and taught has been challenged in recent years by Mary Gentile and the movement 'Giving Voice to Values' (GVV) (Gentile 2010). Gentile argues that teachers and scholars of business ethics spend too much time debating abstract questions of right and wrong, when the real struggles of employees and managers is not to understand that practices they may be observing or form part of are wrong, but rather to find the strength to voice their concerns. 'Giving Voice to Value' urges business schools to alter teachings from primarily debating moral philosophical problems and prioritize building confidence and the ability to raise concerns. The implications for crowdfunding are that platforms and fundraisers should strive to create a culture where employees and managers are deliberately empowered and encouraged to speak up if they encounter dubious business practices.

Crowdfunding: An Ethical Solution or Problem?

Crowdfunding can be considered both as an ethical solution to old problems and as a source for new ethical challenges to be addressed. The very concept of crowdfunding, at its core, represents a solution to traditional barriers of access to finance, which resonates well with the utilitarian ethos of reform and social improvement. Similarly, crowdfunding presents an answer to growing scepticism towards, and disillusionment with, traditional financial institutions, which have triggered and overseen cycles of economic booms and busts in recent decades. In this view, anyone with access to internet can potentially raise funds for a project of their choice from anyone else with access to internet. This implies greater democratization in the use and allocation of financial resources, as well as greater say of the public in its choices of future consumption, provisioning of public goods, and the free promotion of ideas.

First, building on the principles of the democratization of finance (Erturk et al. 2007), crowdfunding practice implies that: (1) the exclusive (if not monopolistic) control of traditional financial institutions and their criteria for allocating financial resources to individuals, organizations, or projects is weakened through competitive offerings from the crowd; (2) more individuals, organizations, and projects can be financed overall, and especially those from environments where discrimination based on gender, sexuality, ethnicity, and religiosity are rampant; (3) more individuals and organizations can influence product and service development efforts towards fulfilling needs of their future consumption, while somewhat weakening the power of manufacturers, wholesalers, and retailers in making such choices for them; (4) individuals and organizations can have more opportunities for investment in general, and for high- and medium-risk investments in particular; and (5) through greater access to finance and investment opportunities, inequalities in society can be minimized in the longer term.

Second, in terms of provisioning of public goods, crowdfunding may be especially relevant where existing institutions fail to provide them. Such projects can include the financing of health care services and equipment for needy individuals (e.g. Berliner and Kenworthy 2017), education services and equipment for needy individuals (e.g. Meer 2014), research work and equipment (e.g. Byrnes et al. 2014), communal purchases of renewable energy solutions for electricity consumption (e.g. Lam and Law 2016), funding of communal cultural activities and institutions, as well as their restoration/renovation and maintenance (e.g. Josefy et al. 2017), etc.

And, third, crowdfunding can serve as a platform for free and democratic distribution and exchange of ideas through financially supporting social, political, religious, and environmental activism. Here, funds can be raised for financing civic and social initiatives, political parties, public legal actions, production and distribution of ideologically infused media (i.e. books, magazines, videos, etc.), and so forth.

Overall, these ethical advantages, seem to relate closely to notions of what has been referred to as the 'collective level of consumer empowerment', where alternative modes of social organization around consumption are constructed and emerge from collaboration with others (Papaoikonomou and Alarcón 2015). Here, traditional information asymmetries are destabilized and may be remedied via alternative and more democratic fundraising channels, which may also serve as social aggregation platforms around causes of interest that may go beyond consumption.

On the other hand, some also view crowdfunding as a source of new ethical problems. Such view challenges the assumption that the 'wisdom of the crowd' is coming up with optimal solutions. Here some critics warn about the 'madness of the crowd', the 'tyranny of the majority', and unintentional legitimization of institutional failures. First, the concerns with the madness of the crowd, involve situations where groups of people can be collectively misguided and even illogical and delusional (Mackay 2006). Such situations are exacerbated by herding behaviours and information cascades, where later decision making is based on inferences from earlier decision making by others (Shiller 2015). Hence, when a critical mass of individuals makes a decision based on incomplete information or outright misinformation, risk assessment based on others' behaviour can be heavily misguided. Such situations represent a far cry from Kantian business ethics suggesting that managers should continuously consider their rights and duties in relation to others, including vulnerable individuals. Here, while these concerns are mostly associated with investor protection and related disclosure requirements (Heminway 2014), they are also relevant for non-investment campaigning in terms of consumer and donor protection.

Second, concerns with the tyranny of the majority (Guinier 1995), as adopted from political science, relates to situations where decisions made by a majority groups do not account for the needs of minorities, or comes at the expense and even directly hurting minority groups. The very definition of crowdfunding is based on public funding of small sums from a large group of people, but what about small groups of people who are unable to raise large sums from the crowd, or when a large group raises funding for an initiative that implies an oppression of a minority.

And, third, by replacing failing public institutions in funding of public goods (i.e. health care, education, environmental protection, etc.), the crowd indirectly legitimizes these institutional shortcomings. Here, while some failure to finance public goods is a result of objective lack of funding, some of it may also be a result of mismanagement of public funds and even corruption in certain cases (Dorotinsky and Pradhan 2007). Hence, funding of public goods via crowdfunding reduces the pressure on, and responsibility of, public institutions and may indirectly legitimize cases of their mismanagement. While this may lead to considerable improvement in well-being in the short-term, utilitarian principles of achieving greatest happiness for the greatest number of people may be violated in the long-term.

In the following section we delve deeper and outline potential ethical pitfalls for the stakeholders involved in crowdfunding practice, as well as some mechanisms for addressing such challenges and dilemmas.

Mapping Ethical Considerations in Crowdfunding

Since crowdfunding practice involves multiple stakeholders, the current section will outline ethical dilemmas and pitfalls with respect to each of the four key stakeholders involved, including—platform, fundraiser, funder, and regulator. This review will follow the approach of Waters and Bird (1989), highlighting that unethical practice can be both 'against' the firm (e.g. false costs reporting for personal gain) and 'for' the firm (e.g. paying bribes for closing deals or getting licences). Accordingly, we address ethical considerations that relate to actions both for and against the relevant stakeholder. Now, while all stakeholders may be subjected to ethical dilemmas common to practice outside the context of crowdfunding, our review will focus on the dilemmas most relevant specifically to the context of crowdfunding.

Crowdfunding Platforms

A crowdfunding platform is 'an internet application bringing together project owners and their potential backers, as well as facilitating exchanges between them, according to a variety of business models' (Shneor and Flåten 2015, p. 188). Platforms operate in accordance with crowdfunding models that include both investment (i.e. peer-to-peer lending, equity CF, revenue sharing, etc.) and non-investment models (i.e. reward and donation CF). Due to the young nature of the industry, most platforms represent relatively young start-ups with limited resources and a survivalist modus operandi. As such, they are subjected to pressures and

Table 8.1 Ethical pitfalls for platforms

Ethical pitfalls		Options for addressing
For platform success	Against platform success	
• Misappropriation of crowd funds for covering platform expenses • Misuse of user data and privacy violation • Hidden and unclearly specified pricing • Misrepresentation of campaign results and dynamics • Approve publication of unethical/untrustworthy campaigns • Cutting corners in quality and security • Operating outside existing legal frames	• Ideological biases in campaign approval • Provide ill advice to fundraisers (not experts in everything)	• State regulation of platform operations and published content • Self-regulation by industry organizations • Self-regulation by industry and users • Accounting reviews • Periodic external audits on ethical practices • Platform-level ethical concern reporting and communication lines • Ethics training of employees

dilemmas common to other entrepreneurial ventures (Hannafey 2003; Harris et al. 2009), primarily including the liability of newness and decision making under conditions of resource scarcity.

Table 8.1 outlines key ethical pitfalls platforms may fall into when attempting to deal with the pressures of liability of newness and resource scarcity. Such pitfalls include intentional and non-intentional instances of abuse of power, compromise on quality and security, as well as misinformation. All of which may be characterized as violations of ethical intent, means, or ends captured in the third basic perspective of ethical marketing (Laczniak and Murphy 2006). Abuse of power can come in the forms of misappropriating crowd funds for covering platform expenses (in jurisdictions where platforms can manage crowd funds), the misuse of user data while violating privacy or harvesting commercial value from such data without consent and/or knowledge of the users. Alternatively, abuse of power may also be evident in unfair exclusion of otherwise ethical campaigns based on ideological biases of platform managers, and the provision of ill advice on areas outside the specialization of platform employees. A different challenge relates to compromise on quality that may be manifested in approving publication of ethically questionable projects, as well as cutting corners in quality checks of campaigns, quality of service, and data security. In addition, instances of misinformation may include hidden and unclearly specified pricing, and the misrepresentation of campaign results and dynamics all to attract more fundraisers and funders to the platform.

In addition, since generally innovation comes before regulation, some crowdfunding platforms may be faced with dilemmas of operating in national jurisdictions completely lacking relevant regulations, or where existing regulation results in less ethical solutions for the public. In the former, platforms operating without clear regulatory guidelines and under heavy resource constraints, may be tempted to adopt more relaxed interpretations of user validation procedures, campaign quality filtering needs, investor and customer protection requirements, as well as limitations on the use of funders' monetary contributions. In such cases, self-regulation via platform management, industry associations, as well as via critic media and public opinion may replace national regulation in the short term, but stakeholders should engage authorities towards establishing relevant legal frameworks in the long run.

Alternatively, examples of the latter cases can be related to excessive costs associated with entry barriers and compliance requirements for loan facilitators, which enshrine monopolies of large credit providers offering loans with higher interest rates and under worse conditions than those offered via crowd lending platforms; limitation of platforms abilities to manage portfolio investments for funders resulting in higher rather than lower risks for users; limitations on distribution of equity campaign information in the age of social media networking and free information flows online; as well as long and expensive permit procedures for donation fundraising projects, to name a few. In such situations, while regulatory amendment can be encouraged via public debates and lobbying, platforms are faced with the options of either exiting the market until regulatory changes are implemented or walking the fine lines of civil disobedience (Falkenberg and Falkenberg 2009) with tight legal support and often under special permission and under supervision of financial authorities.

Some of the mechanisms that may help ensure the ethical practice of crowdfunding platforms include adherence to and work on advancing crowdfunding-related state regulations. In addition to state regulation, which may require long political negotiation cycles, self-regulation through industry associations' codes of conduct, as well as self-regulation by users in flagging out ethically questionable campaigns and practices can also prove useful. Hence, ethical platforms need to ensure that both they and the fundraisers using them achieve a behavioural standard in excess of obligations specified in existing laws, a requirement corresponding with Laczniak and Murphy's (2006) second basic perspective of ethical marketing.

Furthermore, and regardless of formal legal requirements, platforms can be required to engage in periodic financial auditing, as well as ethical auditing (Laczniak and Murphy 2006), possibly by third-party organizations. Finally, other mechanisms for ensuring ethical practices at the platform level, may include ethical training to employees (ibid.), as well as establishment of communication and reporting procedures for ethical concerns of both employees and the public. The latter providing the crowd with an opportunity to exercise its own responsibility in demanding ethical campaigns and campaigning.

Fundraisers

A fundraiser, in the context of crowdfunding, can be defined as an individual or organization actively raising funds from the crowd for a specified purpose outlined in a fully or partially publicly available campaign or loan request. In earlier research, and often pending on the crowdfunding model involved, fundraisers are also referred to as 'campaign creators' or 'creators' in most models of crowdfunding, 'loan takers' or 'borrower' specifically in the peer-to-peer lending, and 'donation collectors' in context of donation crowdfunding. Here, it is important to stress that our understanding of fundraising goes well beyond charitable gift giving with which the concept has been most frequently associated earlier (e.g. Anderson 1996). Hence, fundraising in crowdfunding can be associated with sales and investment, as well as donation. And accordingly, ethical

Table 8.2 Ethical pitfalls for fundraisers

Ethical pitfalls		Options for addressing
For fundraiser success	Against fundraiser success	
• Overselling and provision of misleading info • Share personal sensitive information • Fundraising for projects with unethical objectives • Fundraising for projects with unethical outcomes • Misrepresentation of campaign results and dynamics	• Misuse of funds raised (from bad choices to criminal use) • Delivering substandard products and services to funders • No or misinformation after campaign end in case of delays or failure	• Quality checks and verifications by platform • Regulating eligibility to run campaigns + rights and obligations • Guidelines for ethical fundraising • Require supportive materials for critical fundraiser claims • Ethical concern reporting and communication lines

considerations for salespeople (i.e. Valentine and Barnett 2002), entrepreneurs (i.e. Hannafey 2003; Harris et al. 2009), and charity collectors (i.e. Anderson 1996) may apply.

Table 8.2 outlines key ethical pitfalls fundraisers may fall into when attempting to deal with the pressures to perform, succeed, and avoid failure. Here, paraphrasing Laczniak and Murphy's (2006) first basic perspective of ethical marketing, fundraisers should never view funders (and other supporters) as merely a means to a profitable end, but should place people first and ensure that their projects achieve real social benefit beyond satisfying a narrow customer segment need.

Relevant pitfalls here include intentional and non-intentional instances of abuse of power, compromise on quality, misinformation, as well as directly or indirectly hurting humans, animals, or the environment. Cases of abuse of power may be manifested in failing to deliver on campaign promises by misusing of funds raised for other purposes than the ones stated in campaign. A different situation can also involve in using personal information of investors without their consent or knowledge. Instances of compromise on quality may be in the delivery of substandard products and services, or those produced under ethically questionable conditions for saving costs, while deviating from specifications and promises outlined in campaign. Cases of misinformation can include situations in which fundraisers engage in 'overselling' while providing misleading and partial information, misrepresenting campaign results and dynamics as the campaign develops, or misinforming, or even failing to inform funders in case of delivery delays or project failure once campaign is finished. Finally, fundraisers may engage in projects with unethical objectives and/or outcomes that can hurt humans (i.e. actions against minority groups, fraudulent activities, criminal activities, etc.), animals (i.e. involving animal cruelty and abuse, etc.), or the environment (i.e. production and/or consumption damaging environment, etc.).

Various mechanisms may help ensure the ethical practice of fundraisers in crowdfunding which include adherence to crowdfunding-related state regulations. In addition to requirements specified in law, platforms can issue ethical guidelines for fundraisers with a checklist fundraises can go through before submitting campaigns. Other actions by platforms can include systematic quality checks and verifications activities both as specified by law and as not specified by law but required for ethical practice. More specifically, requirements for proper disclosure of information about critical aspects of the campaign, risks involved in fulfilment of its promises, as well as the identity of the fundraisers should be closely observed and enforced by platforms. Finally, platforms may provide a dedicated communication line for flagging concerns about unethical practice by fundraisers, and when needed leading to the freezing of a running campaign until ethical concerns are removed. Such option provides an outlet for the crowd to exercise its own responsibility to demand ethical campaigns and campaigning.

Funders

A Funder, in the context of crowdfunding, can be defined as an individual or organization providing financial resources in response to a concrete call for funding in the form of a crowdfunding campaign or peer-to-peer loan application/request, and based on pre-specified conditions stated in such calls. Funders have also been referred to as 'backers', 'contributors', and

Table 8.3 Ethical pitfalls for funders

Ethical pitfalls		Options for addressing
For funder success	Against funder success	
• Bully/Pressure others into support • Funding projects with unethical objectives • Funding projects with unethical outcomes • Learning about opportunity on platform but closing deals without platforms	• Public harassment or shaming of fundraisers, causes, or other funders • Public misinformation about campaigners, causes, or other funders	• Platform sanctions against funders and campaigners • Guidelines for ethical CF support • Ethical concern reporting and communication lines • Regulating funder rights and obligations

'supporters' in all crowdfunding models; 'investors' in the various investment models of crowdfunding; 'loan givers' or 'lenders' specifically in peer-to-peer lending; and 'donors' in donation crowdfunding. Accordingly, ethical considerations of funders in the context of crowdfunding may relate to those relevant to investors (Drover et al. 2014), lenders (e.g.—in case of institutional lenders—Cowton 2002), customers, and donors (e.g. as in ethics as value sought by consumers—Smith 1996).

Table 8.3 outlines key ethical pitfalls funders may fall into when being concerned with the success of crowdfunding campaigns they have or have not supported, as well as considering the ethical value proposition of such campaigns. Relevant pitfalls here include intentional and non-intentional instances of abuse of power, misinformation, as well as directly or indirectly hurting humans, animals, or the environment. Abuse of power may be evident in instances of bullying and unfair pressure of others to financially support campaigns through actual or implied harassment and/or public shaming on social media. Alternatively, wealthy supporters may force fundraisers to close deals they have learned about on platforms outside the platform and without its involvement, at the expense of platform income and public profit. In terms of misinformation, here situations may involve the public spreading and sharing misleading and/or inaccurate information (not originating from the fundraiser) about campaigns and the fundraisers behind them for enhancing either the success or the failure of a campaign. And, in terms of potentially hurting humans, animals, and the environment, funders may fail to assess negative ethical implications of projects with clear or hidden unethical objectives and/or outcomes.

Here, again, some mechanisms may help ensure the ethical practice of funders in crowdfunding which include adherence to crowdfunding-related state regulations. In addition to requirements specified in law, platforms can issue ethical guidelines for funders about engagement with other prospective funders about campaigns. Other actions by platforms may include a dedicated communication line for flagging concerns about unethical practice by funders, and when needed leading to the freezing of relevant accounts until ethical concerns are removed, and even informing users about false information being shared about the relevant campaign and/or fundraiser. And, finally, platforms can also include an incentive or sanctions scheme for funders based on the extent to which they behave ethically.

Regulators

A regulator, for the purpose of our discussion, refers to the governmental authority/body responsible for formulation, amendment, and entry of laws into the national law books that control practices related to crowdfunding. Such authorities include national legislators/parliaments, which rely on input provided by institutions including (but not limited to) ministries of finance and economy, financial regulatory authorities, national consumer protection agencies, and so on. Indeed, earlier theorizing effort building on institutional theory, has highlighted the importance of regulators for crowdfunding success (Kshetri 2015) and investor protection (Heminway 2014). Others have reported a significant association between perceived adequacy of crowdfunding regulation (by platforms) and its volumes per capita in European countries (Ziegler et al. 2019), as well as globally (Ziegler et al. 2020).

Accordingly, the very process in which the regulator defines boundaries for the crowdfunding industry may also include ethical considerations of its own, primarily addressing ethical objectives of regulation, ethical regulation process, and ethical outcomes of regulation. Table 8.4 presents

Table 8.4 Ethical pitfall for regulators

Ethical pitfalls		Options for addressing
For public protection	Against public protection	
• Enforce new laws that are excessive and reduce ethical outcomes (lower access to finance with worse conditions) • Enforce new laws that are too permissive reducing ethical outcomes (encouraging irresponsible and risky behaviour)	• Avoid amendments to law while enforcing existing laws that provide less ethical outcomes (lower access to finance with worse conditions) • Protection of traditional financial monopolies • Not providing opportunities for public hearings on ethical implications of laws	• Parliamentary hearings about ethical implications of existing regulation • Sandbox regulatory processes for involving stakeholders in regulation review • Setting national ethical concern reporting and communication lines • Commission expert assessments of ethical aspects in current regulation

potential ethical pitfalls in this context. First, in terms of ethical objectives of regulation, regulators must avoid reluctance to review ethical implications of existing regulation under changing technological and social conditions. Such situations may include intentional and non-intentional bureaucratic avoidance of law amendments that may enhance ethical objectives. Second, regulation processes should follow ethical procedures, as when not providing opportunities for public hearings on the ethical implications of existing laws, or avoidance of sandbox processes where both industry players and regulators interact in formulating laws that fit new technological and social conditions. And third, failing to address negative ethical implications of existing or proposed laws. In case of existing laws, regulators should consider whether they provide unnecessary protection for monopolistic powers reducing overall public welfare. And in the case of new proposed laws, regulators should strike a balance between over- and under-regulation, which may result in excessive or too permissive laws that will lead to differing ethically questionable outcomes.

Certain actions and practices may help ensure the ethical outcomes of regulatory work in the context of crowdfunding. First, regulators may commission expert assessments as well as hold parliamentary hearings on the ethical implications of current regulation in face of new technological and social conditions. Second, regulators can closely engage with industry players in a sandbox process for both mapping potential ethical pitfalls in crowdfunding practice and developing legal remedies for them. And, third, regulators can establish a formal unit or function where members of the public can report and flag unethical practices that can serve as input for future regulation, or as basis for suspending operations of relevant actors when relevant.

Conclusion

The current discussion is one of the first to address ethical considerations in crowdfunding practice. It does so from the perspectives of multiple stakeholders including platforms, fundraisers, funders and the regulator, and outlines concrete potential ethical pitfalls and mechanisms for addressing them. Overall, we suggest that while crowdfunding practice can serve as a solution to earlier ethical challenges in the financial sector, it also presents some new ethical challenges that need to be addressed by stakeholders with relevant policy and action.

From a practical perspective, our mapping of ethical pitfalls and mechanisms for addressing them can serve as prescriptive guidelines for the various stakeholders in their efforts to ensure, enhance, and improve ethical practice in crowdfunding. Here, crowdfunding platforms can formulate ethical guidelines for fundraisers and funders, introduce incentive and sanction schemes for ethical practice by both, train its employees, and develop codes of conduct for them to follow. In addition, regulators can engage in activities that enable evaluation of the ethical implications of existing regulation under new technological and social conditions of the internet economy and social media age, as well as engage in ethical procedures of regulatory amendments towards better ethical outcomes of new laws.

Finally, in terms of research, due to the absence of earlier research on ethics in the context of crowdfunding, opportunities for relevant discoveries are abundant. Accordingly, we hereby outline several such opportunities. First, future studies may identify and analyse the implications and effects of ethical practices of platforms in various crowdfunding models, as well as national, sectoral, and segment contexts. Second, researchers may examine the role played by ethical considerations in the decision of funders to financially support campaigns, as well as share information about them. Third, researchers can assess the impact of ethical cues in campaign content and materials on the success of such campaigns. And, fourth, other studies may attempt to assess the ethical implications of existing regulatory frameworks in different countries, while examining whether they correlate with better market results overall, and ethical outcomes in particular.

References

Anderson, A. (1996). *Ethics for Fundraisers*. Bloomington, IN: Indiana University Press.

Berliner, L. S., & Kenworthy, N. J. (2017). Producing a Worthy Illness: Personal Crowdfunding Amidst Financial Crisis. *Social Science and Medicine, 187*, 233–242.

Boatright, J. R. (2010). Ethics in Finance. In J. R. Boatright (Ed.), *Finance Ethics: Critical Issues in Theory and Practice*. Hoboken, NJ: John Wiley & Sons Inc..

Bucar, B., & Hisrich, R. D. (2001). Ethics of Business Managers vs. Entrepreneurs. *Journal of Developmental Entrepreneurship, 6*(1), 59–82.

Byrnes, J. E. K., Ranganathan, J., Walker, B. L. E., et al. (2014). To Crowdfund Research, Scientists Must Build an Audience for Their Work. *PLoS One, 9*(12), 1–29.

Carpenter, N. (2017). The 5 Biggest Crowdfunding Failures of All Time. Retrieved April 30, 2019, from https://www.digitaltrends.com/cool-tech/biggest-kickstarter-and-indiegogo-scams/.

Cowton, C. J. (2002). Integrity, Responsibility and Affinity: Three Aspects of Ethics in Banking. *Business Ethics: A European Review, 11*(4), 393–400.

DesJardins, J. R. (2009). *An Introduction to Business Ethics*. New York, NY: McGraw-Hill Higher Education.

Donaldson, T., & Dunfee, T. W. (1994). Toward a Unified Conception of Business Ethics: Integrative Social Contracts Theory. *Academy of Management Review, 19*(2), 252–284.

Dorotinsky, W., & Pradhan, S. (2007). Exploring Corruption in Public Financial Management. In E. J. Campos & S. Pradhan (Eds.), *The Many Faces of Corruption: Tracking Vulnerabilities at the Sector Level*. Washington, DC: The World Bank.

Drover, W., Wood, M. S., & Fassin, Y. (2014). Take the Money or Run? Investors' Ethical Reputation and Entrepreneurs' Willingness to Partner. *Journal of Business Venturing, 29*(6), 723–740.

Dunfee, T. W., Smith, N. C., & Ross, W. T. (1999). Social Contracts and Marketing Ethics. *Journal of Marketing, 63*(3), 14–32.

Erturk, I., Froud, J., Johal, S., et al. (2007). The Democratization of Finance? Promises, Outcomes and Conditions. *Review of International Political Economy, 14*(4), 553–575.

Falkenberg, A. W., & Falkenberg, J. (2009). Ethics in International Value Chain Networks: The Case of Telenor in Bangladesh. *Journal of Business Ethics, 90*(3), 355–369.

Fassin, Y., & Drover, W. (2017). Ethics in Entrepreneurial Finance: Exploring Problems in Venture Partner Entry and Exit. *Journal of Business Ethics, 140*(4), 649–672.

Gentile, M. C. (2010). *Giving Voice to Values: How to Speak Your Mind When You Know What's Right*. New Haven: Yale University Press.

Guinier, L. (1995). *Tyranny of the Majority: Fundamental Fairness in Representative Democracy*. New York, NY: The Free Press.

Hannafey, F. T. (2003). Entrepreneurship and Ethics: A Literature Review. *Journal of Business Ethics, 46*(2), 99–110.

Harris, J. D., Sapienza, H. J., & Bowie, N. E. (2009). Ethics and Entrepreneurship. *Journal of Business Venturing, 24*(5), 407–418.

Heminway, J. M. (2014). Investor and Market Protection in the Crowdfunding Era: Disclosing to and for the 'Crowd'. *Vermont Law Review, 38*, 827–847.

Josefy, M., Dean, T. J., Albert, L. S., et al. (2017). The Role of Community in Crowdfunding Success: Evidence on Cultural Attributes in Funding Campaigns to 'Save the Local Theater'. *Entrepreneurship Theory and Practice, 41*(2), 161–182.

Kant, I. (1785/1991). *'Perpetual Peace: A Philosophical Sketch'. Kant: Political Writings*. Cambridge: Cambridge University Press.

Kshetri, N. (2015). Success of Crowd-Based Online Technology in Fundraising: An Institutional Perspective. *Journal of International Management, 21*(2), 100–116.

Laczniak, G. R., & Murphy, P. E. (2006). Normative Perspectives for Ethical and Socially Responsible Marketing. *Journal of Macromarketing, 26*(2), 154–177.

Lam, P. T. I., & Law, A. O. K. (2016). Crowdfunding for Renewable and Sustainable Energy Projects: An Exploratory Case Study Approach. *Renewable and Sustainable Energy Reviews, 60*, 11–20.

Light, B., & McGrath, K. (2010). Ethics and Social Networking Sites: A Disclosive Analysis of Facebook. *Information Technology & People, 23*(4), 290–311.

Mackay, C. (2006). *Extraordinary Popular Delusions and the Madness of Crowds*. Petersfield, Hampshire: Harriman House.

Meer, J. (2014). Effects of the Price of Charitable Giving: Evidence from an Online Crowdfunding Platform. *Journal of Economic Behavior & Organization, 103*, 113–124.

Mill, J. S. (2016). Utilitarianism. In S. M. Cahn (Ed.), *Seven Masterpieces of Philosophy*. New York, NY: Routledge.

Mollick, E. (2015). *The Kickstarter Fulfillment Report* [Online]. Kickstarter.com. Retrieved April 30, 2019, from https://www.kickstarter.com/fulfillment.

Palmer, K. (2016). Peer-to-Peer Firm Tells Lenders They Will Lose a Quarter of Their Cash. Retrieved April 30, 2019, from https://www.telegraph.co.uk/finance/newsbysector/banksandfinance/12109898/Peer-to-peer-firm-tells-lenders-they-will-lose-a-quarter-of-their-cash.html.

Papaoikonomou, E., & Alarcón, A. (2015). Revisiting Consumer Empowerment: An Exploration of Ethical Consumption Communities. *Journal of Macromarketing, 37*(1), 40–56.

Pierce-Wright, C. H. (2016). State Equity Crowdfunding and Investor Protection. *Washington Law Review, 91*(2), 847–886.

Roman, S. (2007). The Ethics of Online Retailing: A Scale Development and Validation from the Consumers' Perspective. *Journal of Business Ethics, 72*(2), 131–148.

Sandbu, M. E. (2011). *Just Business: Arguments in Business Ethics*. Upper Saddle River, NJ: Prentice Hall.

Shiller, R. J. (2015). *Irrational Exuberance: Revised and Expanded* (3rd ed.). Princeton, NJ: Princeton University Press.

Shneor, R., & Flåten, B.-T. (2015). Opportunities for Entrepreneurial Development and Growth Through Online Communities, Collaboration, and Value Creating and Co-creating Activities. In H. R. Kaufmann & S. M. R. Shams (Eds.), *Entrepreneurial Challenges in the 21st Century*. Basingstoke: Palgrave Macmillan.

Smith, C. N. (1996). Ethics and the Typology of Customer Value. In K. P. Corfman & J. G. J. Lynch (Eds.), *Advances in Consumer Research*. Provo, UT: Association for Consumer Research.

Snyder, J., Mathers, A., & Crooks, V. A. (2016). Fund My Treatment!: A Call for Ethics-Focused Social Science Research into the Use of Crowdfunding for Medical Care. *Social Science & Medicine, 169*, 27–30.

Valentine, S., & Barnett, T. (2002). Ethics Codes and Sales Professionals' Perceptions of Their Organizations' Ethical Values. *Journal of Business Ethics, 40*(3), 191–200.

Veenhoven, R. (1991). Is Happiness Relative? *Social Indicators Research, 24*(1), 1–34.

Waters, J. A., & Bird, F. (1989). Attending to Ethics in Management. *Journal of Business Ethics, 8*(6), 493–497.

Zhang, S., & Miller, M. (2017). China's New Illegal Fundraising Topped $36 Billion Last Year. Retrieved April 30, 2019, from https://www.reuters.com/article/us-china-fraud-crackdown/chinas-new-illegal-fundraising-topped-36-billion-last-year-idUSKBN17R11X.

Ziegler, T., Shneor, R., Wenzlaff, K., et al. (2019). *Shifting Paradigms – The 4th European Alternative Finance Benchmarking Report*. Cambridge, UK: Cambridge Centre for Alternative Finance.

Ziegler, T., Shneor, R., Wenzlaff, K., et al. (2020). *The Global Alternative Finance Market Benchmarking Report*. Cambridge, UK: Cambridge Centre for Alternative Finance.

9

Legal Institutions, Social Capital, and Financial Crowdfunding: A Multilevel Perspective

Wanxiang Cai, Friedemann Polzin, and Erik Stam

Introduction

The recent emergence of financial investment crowdfunding (i.e., equity and lending crowdfunding) has attracted substantial attention from policy makers and academic researchers alike. Crowdfunding exhibits tremendous potential to support entrepreneurial activities. The market size of equity crowdfunding is expected to reach \$36 billion by 2020, exceeding the size of the venture capital market at that time (Cumming et al. Forthcoming). Financial investment crowdfunding (hereafter 'financial crowdfunding') involves a range of risks from an investor's point of view (Kirby and Worner 2014). The great number of 'unsophisticated investors' (defined according to level of income and wealth) in financial crowdfunding makes governance problems more pronounced (Cumming et al. Forthcoming) and thus requires more attention.

Institutions, defined as 'the rules of the game in a society' (North 1991), can mitigate the risks in financial crowdfunding to some extent.

W. Cai (✉) • F. Polzin • E. Stam
Utrecht University School of Economics, Utrecht, Netherlands
e-mail: w.cai@uu.nl; f.h.j.polzin@uu.nl; e.stam@uu.nl

R. Shneor et al. (eds.), *Advances in Crowdfunding*,
https://doi.org/10.1007/978-3-030-46309-0_9

Research on venture capital has shown that legal institutions, measured by government effectiveness, quality of regulatory policies, control of corruption, rule of law, political stability, and voice and accountability, have a positive effect on the development of the venture capital market (Li and Zahra 2012). Social capital can to some degree substitute legal institutions in financial markets when legal institutions are deficient (Peng and Heath 1996). Social capital (e.g., trust, reciprocity, and social norms) punishes individuals whose behaviours deviate from social norms (Bowles and Gintis 2002). For instance, in group lending, social capital enhances an individual's willingness to borrow money via monitoring the loans and punishing defaults in a group liability arrangement (Karlan 2007). Especially in a virtual context, in which members temporarily work together to complete a joint task through digital technologies, trust involves establishing and monitoring standards to improve team performance (Crisp and Jarvenpaa 2013). Thus, in crowdfunding contexts, we expect that social capital will contribute to the group outcome (i.e., campaign success).

Previous research on the relationship between social capital and financial crowdfunding has focused mainly on the micro level, that is, how entrepreneurs' social capital affects the success of crowdfunding campaigns and backers' involvement (Vismara 2016; Colombo et al. 2015; Eiteneyer et al. 2019). Little crowdfunding research has investigated the role of legal institutions and social capital at the macro level. To the best of our knowledge, only one paper has empirically demonstrated that both legal institutions and social capital have a positive effect on national crowdfunding volume (Rau 2017). On the one hand, a standard macro-to-macro research cannot explicitly identify *how* legal institutions and social capital affect the development of crowdfunding markets. On the other hand, it is difficult for research at the micro level to take institutional variation into account. Thus, cross-level research may clarify the role of legal institutions and social capital at the macro level in financial crowdfunding governance. For instance, trust in strangers (relational social capital at the macro level) increases investors' propensity to invest in equity crowdfunding (crowdfunding outcomes at the micro level) (Kshetri 2018), and legal institutions can protect investors' benefits, thereby affecting their funding intentions.

Previous research has suggested that legal institutions at the macro level may not fully explain the heterogeneity in entrepreneurial activities across countries and that the meso level should thus be involved to bridge the research on macro and micro levels (Kim et al. 2016). The effect of legal institutions on financial markets depends not only on the degree to which laws protect investor rights but also on the degree to which those laws are enforced (La Porta et al. 2006).

Crowdfunding involves three main actors: Fundraisers post their project online, crowds observe these projects and decide whether to invest, and platforms function as a bridge to connect fundraisers and investors. A recent study suggested that in crowdfunding campaigns, platforms play the active role of providing due diligence (Cumming and Zhang 2018). To some extent, the due diligence provided by platforms reflects the degree to which platforms enforce legal regulations on crowdfunding, because most regulators require platforms to check the validity of documents provided by issuers before posting their project online. Thus, the protection of investors also relies on platforms' enforcement of regulations on financial crowdfunding. Moreover, social capital embedded in platforms affects the formation of fundraisers' social capital at the micro level. From a micro-to-macro perspective, the number of successful campaigns on platforms and the number of platforms also affect the aggregation of crowdfunding outcomes at the macro level. Thus, we introduce a platform-level analysis that provides a deeper understanding of the relationship among legal institutions, social capital, and crowdfunding performance.

The rest of the chapter is organized as follows: the 'Conceptual Background' section briefly introduces the concepts of legal institutions and social capital, as well as their effect on general financial crowdfunding. 'Crowdfunding and Institutions at Macro and Micro Levels' section clarifies the traditional macro-micro-level model to explain how legal institutions and social capital at both macro and micro levels affect individual crowdfunding campaigns and the development of financial crowdfunding markets. 'Towards a Multilevel Analysis of Financial Crowdfunding and Institutions' section introduces the meso-level analysis. 'Conclusion' section summarizes how legal institutions and social capital affect financial crowdfunding with a three-level model.

Conceptual Background

In this section, we introduce the main conceptual building blocks of our study. Two streams of literature have investigated how risks in financial crowdfunding, and entrepreneurial finance more generally, can be mitigated.

Legal Institutions

Legal institutions play an important role in the governance of financial markets. North (1991) originally highlighted the role of secure property and contractual rights in discouraging investments and specialization. Later research demonstrated that legal institutions are essential in the development of financial markets and entrepreneurial activities. La Porta et al. (1997, 1998) explored the effect of legal protections of investors on financial development. They suggested that countries with legal systems which protect the right of investors, enforce private property rights, and support private contractual arrangements have more flourishing financial markets.

More recent research has also demonstrated a relationship between different legal institutions and the development of entrepreneurial finance. For example, legal institutions (aggregated by government effectiveness, rule of law, political stability, voice and accountability, and quality of regulatory policies, etc.) are positively associated with the volume of venture capital in a country (Li and Zahra 2012). Grilli et al. (2016) created a framework to explain how both formal and informal institutions affect venture capital activities. They divided legal institutions into fiscal policy and other legal regulations: tax rate on capital gains, fiscal regulations on investee companies, and corporate income tax are conducive to the development of venture capital activities; other legal regulations, including the legal system, labour regulations, investor protection regulations, and regulations on protection of property rights, affect venture activities as well.

As a novel channel of entrepreneurial finance, financial crowdfunding has some similarities with venture capital; thus, we expect that legal institutions will also influence the development of the financial crowdfunding market. A second stream of literature has extensively discussed social capital, as a type of informal institution, in relation to crowdfunding (Cai et al. 2019).

Social Capital

Social capital is an informal institution that disciplines individuals' behaviours. Adler and Kwon (2002, p. 23) defined social capital as 'the goodwill available to individuals or groups. Its source lies in the structure and content of the actor's social relations. Its effects flow from the information, influence, and solidarity'. In the field of business and economics, especially in relation to finance, social capital has been discussed mainly at micro and macro levels.

At the micro level, Nahapiet and Ghoshal (2000) divided social capital into three dimensions: structural, relational, and cognitive social capital. Regarding entrepreneurial finance, entrepreneurs' structural social capital is normally measured by their social networks, their relational social capital can be measured by investors' trust in them, and their cognitive social capital comprises the shared values, culture, and goals of fundraisers and investors. The authors developed a framework to elaborate on how different dimensions of social capital create intellectual capital through the exchange and combination of knowledge. Later research demonstrated a positive relationship between different dimensions of social capital and access to different forms of entrepreneurial finance. For example, entrepreneurs rely on their social networks to gain access to venture capital (Batjargal and Liu 2004; Shane and Cable 2002). Business angels make use of their structural, relational, and cognitive social capital to identify and evaluate investment opportunities (Sørheim 2003). In banking, network complementarity can enhance a firm's access to bank loans and reduce the cost of capital (Uzzi 1999). Moreover, the shared culture of borrowers and lenders reduces the default rate in group lending (Karlan 2007).

At the macro level, social capital is viewed as a type of soft territorial capital which contributes to regional development (Camagni 2017; Westlund and Bolton 2003). The interplay of different types of social relationships leads to dense combinations of such relationships, which are dependent on geographic proximity and thus lay the foundation of regional social capital (Malecki 2012). Westlund and Bolton (2003, p. 79) defined regional social capital as 'spatially-defined norms, values, knowledge, preferences, and other social attributes or qualities that are reflected in human relationship. In regional studies, social capital functions as both "glue" and "lubricant"', maintaining cooperation and facilitating the interaction and flows within organizations (Malecki 2012). Social capital has a positive effect on macroeconomic growth (Knack and Keefer 1997), regional innovation, and entrepreneurship (Akçomak and Ter Weel 2009; Feldman and Zoller 2012). Regional social capital also affects the development of financial markets. A previous study suggested that social capital contributes to the development of stock markets in Italy (Guiso et al. 2004). A cross-country study demonstrated a positive relationship between social capital and both financial depth and efficiency (Calderón et al. 2002).

Crowdfunding and Institutions at Macro and Micro Levels

In this section, we analyse previous research and, based on its results, build a two-level model to elaborate on how legal institutions and social capital affect financial crowdfunding at macro and micro levels.

In line with previous studies (Martínez-Climent et al. 2018; Rau 2017), we focus only on the two types of financial return models (lending and equity). Investors in financial crowdfunding are driven mainly by financial returns, and the motivation to support others ranks among the least important factors (Vismara 2018). Financial crowdfunding is closer to other forms of financial investment, such as microlending, business angels, and venture capital, making it more applicable to economic approaches like signalling theory (Ahlers et al. 2015; Bapna 2017; Vismara 2016). Financial crowdfunding involves higher risks compared to nonfinancial crowdfunding. Among the main risks faced by investors are default or nonpayment, fraud, illiquidity by fundraisers, lack of transparency in operations, closing or failure of the platform, and cyber-attacks (Kirby and Worner 2014). This is supported by interviews with fundraisers and investors, who indicate that they regard equity crowdfunding investing as high risk and high return (Estrin et al. 2018). Moreover, most investors in financial crowdfunding are less experienced and face large information asymmetries when evaluating the quality of projects (Ahlers et al. 2015; Bapna 2017).

Macro-Level Dynamics

Some features of financial crowdfunding resemble those of entrepreneurial finance, such as business angels and venture capital (Lukkarinen et al. 2016). For example, in both financial crowdfunding and investment by business angels, investors driven by financial return invest their own funds in projects. In the United Kingdom, angel investors are normally found in equity crowdfunding platforms. In China, on the other hand, most equity crowdfunding platforms adopt the leader–follower model, in which both business angels and venture capitalists do the due diligence for and endorse the projects, thereby attracting subsequent investors. Some research has indicated that equity crowdfunding is more likely to be the complement of business angels (e.g., Hornuf and Schwienbacher 2016). Therefore, we expect that the influence of both legal institutions and social capital on financial crowdfunding will be similar to that on other entrepreneurial financial sources, such as business angels and venture capital.

Rau (2017) investigated the correlation between legal institutions and crowdfunding volume. He focused on the effect of overall legal regimes (the regulations on financial crowdfunding are excluded). He found that overall legal regimes (including control of corruption and the overall financial market development) and social capital (measured by trust in strangers) have a positive effect on national financial crowdfunding volume. Because legal regimes and regulations on financial crowdfunding may have different effects on crowdfunding volume, we discuss them separately.

Regulations on financial crowdfunding protect investors by setting requirements for the minimum income or net assets to enter the market (Hornuf and Schwienbacher 2017). The effect of regulations on crowdfunding might play out differently: On the one hand, the protections of investors encourage them to invest in financial crowdfunding. For example, a recent report found a positive relationship between the platform owners' perceived adequacy of regulation and national crowdfunding volume (Ziegler et al. 2019). On the other hand, excessively strong protections of investors reduce the number of qualified investors and harm the motivation of fundraisers. Hence, regulators need to strike a balance between crowdfunding market promotion and the protection of retail investors.

As for social capital, Rau (2017) quantitatively demonstrated that trust in strangers has a positive effect on national financial crowdfunding volume. Therefore, we suggest that social capital at the macro level may have a positive impact on the development of financial crowdfunding markets.

Micro-Level Dynamics

At the micro level, we discuss only the role of social capital. Previous research on crowdfunding has examined the determinants of crowdfunding success mainly at the micro level and has demonstrated that structural, relational, and cognitive dimensions of social capital affect the success of crowdfunding campaigns at the micro level (Cai et al. 2019).

Previous research on structural social capital in financial crowdfunding has suggested that entrepreneurs can make use of their private social networks (i.e., family and friends) to raise money (Lukkarinen et al. 2016). The size of entrepreneurs' social networks is perceived as reflecting the quality of the project and thereby attracts more investors to support the campaign (Vismara 2016). Such investor networks can trigger herding, which increases the chance of campaign success (Liu et al. 2015).

Regarding relational social capital, investors' trust in fundraisers plays an important role in their decision-making. In lending crowdfunding, lenders' economic status, including credit grades, verified bank accounts, and debt-to-income ratio, reflects their ability to pay the interest on time, thereby exerting a positive influence on crowdfunding success (Greiner and Wang 2010). Previous successful campaigns are also positively associated with fundraisers' trustworthiness (Yum et al. 2012). Other measurements of trust in fundraisers include third-party endorsements (Greiner and Wang 2010; Chen et al. 2016), entrepreneur–sponsor interactions (Xu and Chau 2018), and the disclosure of personal information (Ge et al. 2017). All of these studies demonstrated that investors' trust in fundraisers encourages them to invest in the projects.

Cognitive social capital has received less attention in financial crowdfunding research. Only one paper has investigated lending crowdfunding. Burtch et al. (2014) found that the cultural distance between borrowers and lenders has a negative influence on lending actions.

Interactions Between Financial Crowdfunding and Institutions at Macro and Micro Levels

Above, we show that both legal institutions and social capital at the macro level affect individual behaviours at the micro level, thereby affecting the performance of individual crowdfunding campaigns (*macro-micro mechanism*). This mechanism is depicted in Fig. 9.1.

Legal institutions at the macro level affect individual crowdfunding campaigns directly and through the mediation effect of social capital. First, mandatory information disclosure requires firms to post certain information on the platform, which can send signals reflecting the quality of the projects to potential investors (Ahlers et al. 2015). Such signals can reduce the information asymmetry between investors and entrepreneurs, helping them evaluate the true value of the projects. Moreover, legal protections of investors encourage them to invest in the project without worrying about potential defaults in crowdfunding.

Legal institutions are positively associated with trust (Berggren and Jordahl 2006). The enormous risks associated with financial crowdfunding discourage investors to support campaigns. Stronger legal protections of investors can increase their trust in both the project and fundraisers: First, comprehensive registration requirements allow only high-quality projects to be listed on the platform (Cumming and Zhang 2018),

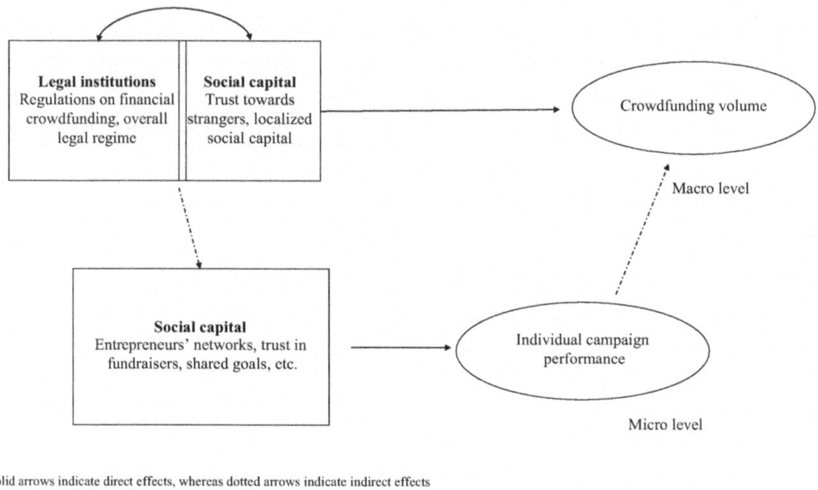

Fig. 9.1 Interactions between financial crowdfunding and institutions at macro and micro levels

increasing investors' trust in the campaign. Stricter legal regulations prevent fundraisers from intentionally deceiving investors, thereby enhancing investors' trust that fundraisers are listing projects in good faith. Thus, the legal institutions affect individual crowdfunding campaigns by increasing investors' trust in the projects. Based on these arguments, we put forward our first proposition:

Proposition 1 Social capital at the micro level can mediate the effect of legal institutions on the success of individual crowdfunding campaigns.

Social capital at the macro level also has an impact on individual crowdfunding campaigns. Giudici et al. (2018) measured localized relational social capital by the number of nonprofit organizations, recycling, voter turnout, and satisfaction with relationships with friends. They found that social capital at the macro level affects the performance of reward-based crowdfunding campaigns by enhancing the effect of local altruism on the contributions from local investors. In a qualitative study of equity crowdfunding, Kshetri (2018) argued that investors' trust in strangers increases their tendency to invest in the projects. Therefore, social capital at the macro level has a positive effect on the performance of crowdfunding campaigns.

The aggregation of crowdfunding success at the micro level affects the crowdfunding volume at the macro level. In line with prior findings that excessively strong legal protection of crowdfunders may reduce the number of crowdfunding campaigns in a country, stronger legal institutions may not lead to higher regional crowdfunding volume. Thus, higher individual crowdfunding performance does not entail higher regional crowdfunding volume. In fact, before 2015, the United States allowed only sophisticated investors to enter crowdfunding markets, but the country subsequently lowered the requirement in an effort to attract more funding from small investors.

Entrepreneurship research has suggested that social capital plays a more important role when legal institutions are weaker. For instance, in emerging economies, venture capitalists rely on social relationships and their networks to screen potential investment opportunities and monitor investees (Ahlstrom and Bruton 2006). Moreover, the effect of trust on financial development is less important when the legal system is more efficient (Guiso et al. 2004). A comparative study indicated that the effect of fundraisers' social capital on campaign success in China is higher than that in the United States (Zheng et al. 2014). Although the authors attributed this finding to cultural differences between the two countries, it still indicates that in a developing market, investors rely on social sanctions to protect their benefits. Therefore, we believe that entrepreneurs' social capital, as well as social capital at the macro level, can replace legal institutions in financial crowdfunding; that is, when the legal institutions are weaker, fundraisers' social capital has a stronger effect on crowdfunding success. Thus, we arrive at our second proposition:

Proposition 2 Legal institutions moderate the relationship between social capital (at both macro and micro levels) and individual crowdfunding success.

Towards a Multilevel Analysis of Financial Crowdfunding and Institutions

The Role of Platforms in Crowdfunding

Crowdfunding platforms are an active intermediary between entrepreneurs and investors. First, they enforce the regulations on financial crowdfunding to supervise transactions between investors and fundraisers. Second, they establish specific rules to reduce potential risks in crowdfunding. Finally, they provide some value-added services for projects.

On financial crowdfunding platforms, inexperienced investors face abundant risks. Regulators require fundraisers to publish a prospectus and platforms to ensure the validity of information disclosed by fundraisers. Therefore, platforms conduct due diligence for fundraisers to mitigate the information asymmetry between fundraisers and investors. They aim at sorting out both lower-quality projects and lower-quality investors. The degree of due diligence varies across platforms. Fierce competition among platforms may result in allowing unsecured fundraisers to enter the market (Yoon et al. 2019). In fact, some regulators (e.g., the Financial Conduct Authority in the United Kingdom) did not establish specific requirements for information disclosure, allowing crowdfunding platforms to follow their own standards for due diligence. Further, to attract more funding, some platforms did not check the qualifications of investors. A popular article attributed the increasing default rates of Chinese P2P lending projects partly to platforms' practice of pooling funds illegally from investors (Liu 2018). Moreover, UK platforms are obligated to educate investors about the risks involved in financial crowdfunding. Apparently, the degree to which investors are educated varies: Some platforms list only the potential risks for investors, whereas others require investors to pass a test during the registration process.

Second, platforms create their own rules for running campaigns, which affect the behaviours of both entrepreneurs and crowdfunders. There are two main types of business models for crowdfunding: 'all-or-nothing' and 'keep-it-all'. In the all-or-nothing model, only successful campaigns can collect money from investors, making entrepreneurs more likely to disclose information about the projects to ensure the success of the crowdfunding project (Cumming and Zhang 2018). Platforms also establish different rules for investors' decision-making. For instance, in some platforms, all investors have to make decisions together (e.g., investors in AngelList have to join a syndicate and follow a leader to invest in certain projects), whereas in most other platforms, investors can make decisions independently. In some P2P lending platforms, borrowers must disclose their economic status (e.g., debt-to-income ratio, credit grades, verified bank accounts), which reflect their ability to the money (Greiner and Wang 2010). Recently, some platforms (e.g., Zopa and Lending Club) have adopted artificial intelligence to create credit scores for borrowers. In Chinese P2P lending markets, platforms have adopted various methods of reducing potential risks involved in investing, including risk reserves funding, third-party endorsements, and fund custodian mechanisms (Yoon et al. 2019). The fee structure also influences platform-specific rules. Platforms which charge fees only for successful projects are more willing to conduct due diligence, whereas those that receive fees from all projects may devote less effort to due diligence (Cumming and Zhang 2018).

Overall, platforms provide a series of additional services for fundraisers to pursue crowdfunding success and even future funding successes, including promotion services, business planning, financial analysis, strategic guidance, exist assistance, and advisory services for future funding (Cumming and Zhang 2018; Rossi and Vismara 2018). Both theoretical and empirical research have investigated how these services affect individual crowdfunding success. For instance, Wu et al. (2018) built a theoretical model to examine how the quality and matching services provided by platforms affect their performance. They suggested that excluding low-quality projects is profitable if investors' preference for project quality is substantial enough. Rossi and Vismara (2018) tested the relationship between platform services and the number of successful campaigns. They found that only post campaign services offered by platforms (e.g., exit assistance, second market, advisory services for future funding, etc.) positively affect the number of successful campaigns.

Platforms as the Meso Level

As discussed above, a simple macro-micro-level research design may face two analytical shortcomings: the ecological fallacy and disaggregation bias (Kim et al. 2016). In our case, the ecological fallacy means that the inferences of macro-to-micro research may be misleading if they are attributed to a lower level of analysis. Thus, it might be arbitrary to attribute the negative effect of excessively strong protection of investors on crowdfunding volume to the damage of entrepreneurial initiatives. Disaggregation bias describes situations in which the results of micro-level research may not be transferable to the macro level. Therefore, we cannot simply conclude that the results at the micro level can be replicated at the macro level or vice versa. A recent study suggested that the factors that contribute to crowdfunding success vary across platforms (Dushnitsky and Fitza 2018), which indicates that crowdfunding research should take into consideration the nature of the platform.

For two reasons, we follow Kim et al. (2016) by introducing the platform as a meso-level factor in the multilevel analysis of institutions and financial crowdfunding. First, both social capital and legal institutions exist at the meso level. Through interactions among participants, trust, networks and shared goals can be developed on crowdfunding platforms (Cai et al. 2019), while platforms create their own rules and business models, which to some extent can be seen as regulations at the meso level (e.g., establishing specific information-disclosure requirements, designing mechanisms to reduce potential risks, educating investors, and using specific fee structures).

Second, platforms are essential in creating social capital and enforcing legal institutions in crowdfunding activities. The term 'crowdfunding community' has been used widely in crowdfunding research (e.g., Belleflamme et al. 2014; Agrawal et al. 2014). Even in financial crowdfunding, investors can also benefit from 'community benefits', such as investment experience (Belleflamme et al. 2014). Thus, investors rely to some extent on interactions with others to alleviate information asymmetry in financial crowdfunding (Liu et al. 2015; Wang et al. 2019). In addition, platforms conduct due diligence as well as put forward platform policies, which not only enforce the legal institutions at the macro level but also strengthen trust among investors. This forms the basis for our third proposition:

Proposition 3 Crowdfunding platforms at the meso level mediate the effect of legal institutions and social capital on crowdfunding success.

Social capital and legal institutions are associated with social capital and legal institutions at other levels. For example, trust can penetrate to other levels; that is, the higher the trust towards strangers (macro level), the higher the trust towards platforms and fundraisers will be. In addition, legal institutions at the macro level affect crowdfunding campaigns through the enforcement of regulations. Furthermore, legal institutions also affect trust at different levels (this phenomenon is discussed further in the next section). Thus, we suggest that platforms constitute the meso level in a multilevel model, which can mitigate both the ecological fallacy and the disaggregation bias.

Although social capital is a multidimensional concept, we focus only on trust—the most frequently discussed dimension in social-capital-based research on financial crowdfunding—in our three-level model. This approach can clearly explain how social capital and legal institutions across different levels jointly affect financial crowdfunding.

Three-Level Model of Institutions and Financial Crowdfunding

Legal institutions and social capital at the macro level can directly and indirectly (via social capital) affect crowdfunding campaigns. The direct effect can be seen in the two-level model proposed above. The meso level plays an important role in the indirect effect. The degree to which legal institutions protect investors also depends on the enforcement of regulations by crowdfunding platforms. Only strong enforcement of regulations on financial crowdfunding by platforms enhances the protection of investors, affecting their decision-making. Moreover, platforms may follow their own standards in information disclosure, which can affect the number and the content of signals sent by projects' information, which can in turn mitigate the information asymmetry between investors and fundraisers. Second, platforms must educate and select investors. If platforms allow only qualified investors to enter the markets and inform them of potential risks, investors have a greater chance of identifying high-quality campaigns.

Legal institutions also affect social capital on both meso and micro levels. Regulations on financial crowdfunding affect the quality of platforms, because they can operate only after being approved by the financial authority. Only high-quality platforms are allowed to operate, which enhances investors' trust that platforms are a reliable venue on which to invest and can protect their interests. Second, regulations on financial crowdfunding may clarify platforms' responsibility for conducting due diligence. For instance, in the United Kingdom, platforms must ensure that the information disclosure of the project is fair, clear, and not misleading (FCA n.d.). Thus, platforms which conduct adequate due diligence receive higher trust from investors, because such due diligence enables investors to screen low-quality projects (Cumming and Zhang 2018).

Trust at macro and meso levels increases the trust in fundraisers, thereby enhancing their funding intentions. Trust at the macro level (trust in strangers) reflects people's willingness to be vulnerable to others' actions (Mayer et al. 1995). In financial crowdfunding, investors risk losing their money. Higher trust at the macro level may increase investors' trust in platforms and fundraisers, because they are more willing to take the risks involved in crowdfunding investments. Moreover, investors' trust at the meso level increases their trust in fundraisers, because platforms enforce rules for the listed projects. Empirical research has demonstrated that trust in platforms (meso level) is positively associated with trust in fundraisers (micro level) (Chen et al. 2014).

We suggest that the relationship between crowdfunding outcomes at micro and macro levels requires further elaboration, especially regarding the role of platforms. First, legal institutions affect the creation of platforms. For instance, Dushnitsky et al. (2016) found that the strength of legal rights in a country's credit market has a positive effect on the creation of lending crowdfunding platforms and a negative influence on

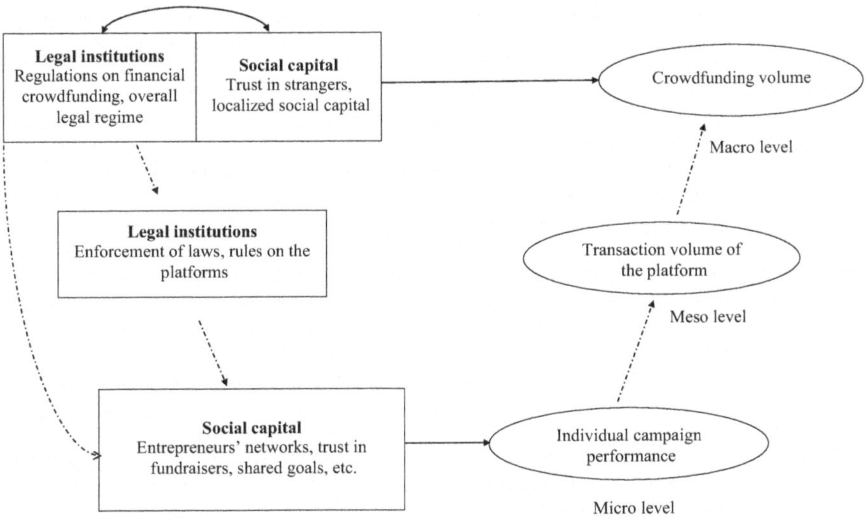

Fig. 9.2 Interactions between financial crowdfunding and institutions at macro, meso, and micro levels

equity crowdfunding platforms. Second, the services of platforms also affect the number of successful campaigns conducted on them. For instance, post campaign services increase the number of successful campaigns on a platform (Rossi and Vismara 2018). Therefore, taking platforms into account may provide a deep understanding of how the aggregation of successful crowdfunding campaigns affects regional crowdfunding volume. Figure 9.2 illustrates the overall framework of the three-level model.

Conclusion

Using a two-level model, this chapter explains how legal institutions and social capital at macro and micro levels affect crowdfunding performance across micro and macro levels. We suggest that legal institutions and social capital (at both macro and micro levels) affect crowdfunding campaigns and that the role of social capital may replace that of legal institutions in financial investment crowdfunding.

To enhance the explanatory power of the two-level model, we introduce crowdfunding platforms as a meso level. We explain the role of platforms in the crowdfunding market and then elaborate on the mechanism by which the meso level bridges macro- and micro-level analyses. Platforms moderate the effect of regulations on financial crowdfunding and increase investors' trust in fundraisers by due diligence. The number of successful campaigns of platforms and the total number of platforms in turn affects the aggregation of crowdfunding outcomes at the macro level. These mechanisms improve our understanding of the role of platforms in the development of financial crowdfunding markets.

This chapter suggests directions for future crowdfunding research. Compared to micro-level research, macro- and meso-level crowdfunding studies are rare. To determine whether the empirical results of micro-level research can be replicated at meso and macro levels, more empirical evidence is required. Furthermore, the interactions between legal institutions and social capital across different levels require more exploration. This chapter provides a framework for conducting such research (e.g., analysing the moderation of due diligence on the relationship between legal institutions at the macro level and individual crowdfunding campaigns).

This chapter also has practical implications for both policy makers and platform owners. On the one hand, policy makers should consider the enforcement of regulations by crowdfunding platforms. Although most regulators demand that platforms ensure the validity of information disclosed by fundraisers, supervision of platforms is lacking. Only if platforms follow relevant regulations on crowdfunding can these regulations effectively regulate the crowdfunding market. On the other hand, platform owners should recognize the role of platform rules in platform performance. By adopting suitable rules and a suitable business model, owners can improve their business performance.

References

Adler, P. S., & Kwon, S.-W. (2002). Social Capital: Prospects for a New Concept. *Academy of Management Review, 27*(1), 17–40.

Agrawal, A., Catalini, C., & Goldfarb, A. (2014). Some Simple Economics of Crowdfunding. *Innovation Policy and the Economy, 14*(1), 63–97.

Ahlers, G. K. C., Cumming, D., Günther, C., & Schweizer, D. (2015). Signaling in Equity Crowdfunding. *Entrepreneurship Theory and Practice, 39*(4), 955–980.

Ahlstrom, D., & Bruton, G. D. (2006). Venture Capital in Emerging Economies: Networks and Institutional Change. *Entrepreneurship Theory and Practice, 30*(2), 299–320.

Akçomak, İ. S., & ter Weel, B. (2009). Social Capital, Innovation and Growth: Evidence from Europe. *European Economic Review, 53*(5), 544–567.

Bapna, S. (2017). Complementarity of Signals in Early-Stage Equity Investment Decisions: Evidence from a Randomized Field Experiment. *Management Science, 65*(2), 933–952.

Batjargal, B., & Liu, M. (2004). Entrepreneurs' Access to Private Equity in China: The Role of Social Capital. *Organization Science, 15*(2), 159–172.

Belleflamme, P., Lambert, T., & Schwienbacher, A. (2014). Crowdfunding: Tapping the Right Crowd. *Journal of Business Venturing, 29*(5), 585–609.

Berggren, N., & Jordahl, H. (2006). Free to Trust: Economic Freedom and Social Capital. *Kyklos, 59*(2), 141–169.

Bowles, S., & Gintis, H. (2002). Social Capital and Community Governance. *The Economic Journal, 112*(483), F419–F436.

Burtch, G., Ghose, A., & Wattal, S. (2014). Cultural Differences and Geography as Determinants of Prosocial Lending. *MIS Quarterly, 38*(3), 773–794.

Cai, W., Polzin, F., & Stam, E. (2019). *Crowdfunding and Social Capital: A Systematic Literature Review*. SSRN Scholarly Paper ID 3361748. Rochester, NY: Social Science Research Network. Retrieved from https://papers.ssrn.com/abstract=3361748.

Calderón, C., Chong, A., & Galindo, A. (2002). Development and Efficiency of the Financial Sector and Links with Trust: Cross-Country Evidence. *Economic Development and Cultural Change, 51*(1), 189–204.

Camagni, R. (2017). Regional Competitiveness: Towards a Concept of Territorial Capital. In R. Capello (Ed.), *Seminal Studies in Regional and Urban Economics: Contributions from an Impressive Mind* (pp. 115–131). Cham: Springer International Publishing.

Chen, D., Lai, F., & Lin, Z. (2014). A Trust Model for Online Peer-to-Peer Lending: A Lender's Perspective. *Information Technology and Management, 15*(4), 239–254.

Chen, X., Zhou, L., & Wan, D. (2016). Group Social Capital and Lending Outcomes in the Financial Credit Market: An Empirical Study of Online Peer-to-Peer Lending. *Electronic Commerce Research and Applications, 15*, 1–13.

Colombo, M. G., Franzoni, C., & Rossi-Lamastra, C. (2015). Internal Social Capital and the Attraction of Early Contributions in Crowdfunding. *Entrepreneurship Theory and Practice, 39*(1), 75–100.

Crisp, C. B., & Jarvenpaa, S. L. (2013). Swift Trust in Global Virtual Teams: Trusting Beliefs and Normative Actions. *Journal of Personnel Psychology, 12*(1), 45–56.

Cumming, D. J., & Zhang, Y. (2018). *Are Crowdfunding Platforms Active and Effective Intermediaries?* SSRN Scholarly Paper ID 2882026. Rochester, NY: Social Science Research Network. Retrieved from https://papers.ssrn.com/abstract=2882026.

Cumming, D. J., Vanacker, T., & Zahra, S. A. (Forthcoming). Equity Crowdfunding and Governance: Toward an Integrative Model and Research Agenda. *Academy of Management Perspectives*.

Dushnitsky, G., & Fitza, M. A. (2018). Are We Missing the Platforms for the Crowd? Comparing Investment Drivers Across Multiple Crowdfunding Platforms. *Journal of Business Venturing Insights, 10*, e00100.

Dushnitsky, G., Guerini, M., Piva, E., et al. (2016). Crowdfunding in Europe: Determinants of Platform Creation Across Countries. *California Management Review, 58*(2), 44–71.

Eiteneyer, N., Bendig, D., & Brettel, M. (2019). Social Capital and the Digital Crowd: Involving Backers to Promote New Product Innovativeness. *Research Policy, 48*(8), 103744.

Estrin, S., Gozman, D., & Khavul, S. (2018). The Evolution and Adoption of Equity Crowdfunding: Entrepreneur and Investor Entry into a New Market. *Small Business Economics, 51*(2), 425–439.

Feldman, M., & Zoller, T. D. (2012). Dealmakers in Place: Social Capital Connections in Regional Entrepreneurial Economies. *Regional Studies, 46*(1), 23–37.

Financial Conduct Authority. (n.d.). *FCA Handbook*. Retrieved May 21, 2019, from https://www.handbook.fca.org.uk/handbook/COBS/.

Ge, R., Feng, J., Gu, B., et al. (2017). Predicting and Deterring Default with Social Media Information in Peer-to-Peer Lending. *Journal of Management Information Systems, 34*(2), 401–424.

Giudici, G., Guerini, M., & Rossi-Lamastra, C. (2018). Reward-Based Crowdfunding of Entrepreneurial Projects: The Effect of Local Altruism and Localized Social Capital on Proponents' Success. *Small Business Economics, 50*(2), 307–324.

Greiner, M. E., & Wang, H. (2010). Building Consumer-to-Consumer Trust in E-Finance Marketplaces: An Empirical Analysis. *International Journal of Electronic Commerce, 15*(2), 105–136.

Grilli, L., Latifi, G., & Mrkajic, B. (2016). *Institutional Determinants of Venture Capital Activity: A Survey of the Literature and a Research Agenda*. SSRN Scholarly Paper ID 3105441. Rochester, NY: Social Science Research Network. Retrieved from https://papers.ssrn.com/abstract=3105441.

Guiso, L., Sapienza, P., & Zingales, L. (2004). The Role of Social Capital in Financial Development. *American Economic Review, 94*(3), 526–556.

Hornuf, L., & Schwienbacher, A. (2016). Crowdinvesting: Angel Investing for the Masses? In H. Landström & C. Mason (Eds.), *Handbook of Research on Business Angels* (pp. 381–398). Cheltenham: Edward Elgar.

Hornuf, L., & Schwienbacher, A. (2017). Should Securities Regulation Promote Equity Crowdfunding? *Small Business Economics, 49*(3), 579–593.

Karlan, D. S. (2007). Social Connections and Group Banking. *The Economic Journal, 117*(517), F52–F84.

Kim, P. H., Wennberg, K., & Croidieu, G. (2016). Untapped Riches of Meso-Level Applications in Multilevel Entrepreneurship Mechanisms. *Academy of Management Perspectives, 30*(3), 273–291.

Kirby, E., & Worner, S. (2014). *Crowd-Funding: An Infant Industry Growing Fast*. Staff Working Papers. IOSCO Research Department.

Knack, S., & Keefer, P. (1997). Does Social Capital Have an Economic Payoff? A Cross-Country Investigation. *The Quarterly Journal of Economics, 112*(4), 1251–1288.

Kshetri, N. (2018). Informal Institutions and Internet-Based Equity Crowdfunding. *Journal of International Management, 24*(1), 33–51.

La Porta, R., Lopez-de-Silanes, F., Shleifer, A., & Vishny, R. W. (1997). Legal Determinants of External Finance. *The Journal of Finance, 52*(3), 1131–1150.

La Porta, R., Lopez-de-Silanes, F., & Shleifer, A. (2006). What Works in Securities Laws? *The Journal of Finance, 61*(1), 1–32.

Li, Y., & Zahra, S. A. (2012). Formal Institutions, Culture, and Venture Capital Activity: A Cross-Country Analysis. *Journal of Business Venturing, 27*(1), 95–111.

Liu, J. (2018). The Dramatic Rise and Fall of Online P2P Lending in China. *TechCrunch* (blog). Retrieved May 24, 2019, from http://social.techcrunch.com/2018/08/01/the-dramatic-rise-and-fall-of-online-p2p-lending-in-china/.

Liu, D., Brass, D. J., Lu, Y., et al. (2015). Friendships in Online Peer-to-Peer Lending: Pipes, Prisms, and Relational Herding. *MIS Quarterly, 39*(3), 729–7A4.

Lukkarinen, A., Teich, J. E., Wallenius, H., et al. (2016). Success Drivers of Online Equity Crowdfunding Campaigns. *Decision Support Systems, 87*, 26–38.

Malecki, E. J. (2012). Regional Social Capital: Why It Matters. *Regional Studies, 46*(8), 1023–1039.

Martínez-Climent, C., Zorio-Grima, A., & Ribeiro-Soriano, D. (2018). Financial Return Crowdfunding: Literature Review and Bibliometric Analysis. *International Entrepreneurship and Management Journal, 14*(3), 527–553.

Mayer, R. C., Davis, J. H., & Schoorman, D. F. (1995). An Integrative Model of Organizational Trust. *Academy of Management Review, 20*(3), 709–734.

Nahapiet, J., & Ghoshal, S. (2000). Social Capital, Intellectual Capital, and the Organizational Advantage. In *Knowledge and Social Capital* (pp. 119–157). Boston: Butterworth-Heinemann.

North, D. C. (1991). Institutions. *Journal of Economic Perspectives, 5*(1), 97–112.

Peng, M. W., & Heath, P. S. (1996). The Growth of the Firm in Planned Economies in Transition: Institutions, Organizations, and Strategic Choice. *Academy of Management Review, 21*(2), 492–528.

Porta, R., Lopez-de-Silanes, F., Shleifer, A., & Vishny, R. W. (1998). Law and Finance. *Journal of Political Economy, 106*(6), 1113–1155.

Rau, P. R. (2017). *Law, Trust, and the Development of Crowdfunding. Cambridge Centre for Alternative Finance Conference*. Cambridge, UK.

Rossi, A., & Vismara, S. (2018). What Do Crowdfunding Platforms Do? A Comparison Between Investment-Based Platforms in Europe. *Eurasian Business Review, 8*(1), 93–118.

Shane, S., & Cable, D. (2002). Network Ties, Reputation, and the Financing of New Ventures. *Management Science, 48*(3), 364–381.

Sørheim, R. (2003). The Pre-Investment Behaviour of Business Angels: A Social Capital Approach. *Venture Capital, 5*(4), 337–364.

Uzzi, B. (1999). Embeddedness in the Making of Financial Capital: How Social Relations and Networks Benefit Firms Seeking Financing. *American Sociological Review, 54*(4), 481–505.

Vismara, S. (2016). Equity Retention and Social Network Theory in Equity Crowdfunding. *Small Business Economics, 46*(4), 579–590.

Vismara, S. (2018). Information Cascades Among Investors in Equity Crowdfunding. *Entrepreneurship Theory and Practice, 42*(3), 467–497.

Wang, W., Mahmood, A., Sismeiro, C., et al. (2019). The Evolution of Equity Crowdfunding: Insights from Co-investments of Angels and the Crowd. *Research Policy, 48*(8), 103727.

Westlund, H., & Bolton, R. (2003). Local Social Capital and Entrepreneurship. *Small Business Economics, 21*(2), 77–113.

Wu, W., Huang, X., Li, Y., et al. (2018). Optimal Quality Strategy and Matching Service on Crowdfunding Platforms. *Sustainability, 10*(4), 1–17.

Xu, J. J., & Chau, M. (2018). Cheap Talk? The Impact of Lender-Borrower Communication on Peer-to-Peer Lending Outcomes. *Journal of Management Information Systems, 35*(1), 53–85.

Yoon, Y., Li, Y., & Feng, Y. (2019). Factors Affecting Platform Default Risk in Online Peer-to-Peer (P2P) Lending Business: An Empirical Study Using Chinese Online P2P Platform Data. *Electronic Commerce Research, 19*(1), 131–158.

Yum, H., Lee, B., & Chae, M. (2012). From the Wisdom of Crowds to My Own Judgment in Microfinance Through Online Peer-to-Peer Lending Platforms. *Electronic Commerce Research and Applications, 11*(5), 469–483.

Zheng, H., Li, D., Wu, J., et al. (2014). The Role of Multidimensional Social Capital in Crowdfunding: A Comparative Study in China and US. *Information & Management, 51*(4), 488–496.

Ziegler, T., Shneor, R., Wenzlaff, K., Odorovic, A., Johanson, D., Hao, R., & Ryll, L. (2019). *Shifting Paradigms: The 4th European Alternative Finance Benchmarking Report.* Cambridge, UK: Cambridge Centre for Alternative Finance.

Part II

Crowdfunding in Historical Context

10

History of Crowdfunding in the Context of Ever-Changing Modern Financial Markets

Aki Kallio and Lasse Vuola

Introduction

Crowdfunding is a means of raising finance for projects from the crowd often through an internet-based platform where project owners pitch their idea to potential backers, who are typically not professional investors, although increasing activity by institutional investors has been recorded. Crowdfunding takes many forms and sometimes without any potential for a financial return. Crowdfunding in its current context is relatively young and business models are evolving at a fast pace. Crowdfunding platforms have emerged recently since internet technology evolved in such a way as to allow easy and simple two-way

A. Kallio (✉)
Danske Bank A/S Finland Branch, Helsinki, Finland
e-mail: aki.kallio@danskebank.fi

L. Vuola
Fundu Ltd., Helsinki, Finland
e-mail: lasse.vuola@fundu.fi

R. Shneor et al. (eds.), *Advances in Crowdfunding*,
https://doi.org/10.1007/978-3-030-46309-0_10

communication. This enables interaction between the members of the crowd of investors, as well as between the crowd and the project owners pitching their specific projects (European Securities and Markets Authority 2014).

In 2017, alternative finance volumes from across Europe grew by 36%, from 7.67 billion euros to 10.44 billion euros (Ziegler et al. 2019). Overall, the major share of European volume still originates from the UK (68%). However, excluding the UK, the European online alternative finance market grew at nearly double the UK's year-on-year growth rate—63% in comparison to 35% in 2017. While this growth was not as strong as in 2016 (101%), there was visible growth in each sub-region of continental Europe. As a whole, the market grew by just over 1.3 billion euros to 3.369 billion euros in 2017 (Ziegler et al. 2019). While there was an overall growth, the rate of growth seems to have cooled in some more mature markets even though it is continuing (Ziegler et al. 2019).

The growth of crowdfunding as a new complementary and alternative form of financing is indisputable, and its importance to businesses both domestically and internationally is already remarkable (Ziegler et al. 2019). With the ever-increasing advent of digitalization combined with tightening regulation for banks, alternative finance has become an important part of the present financial markets. The alternative of today may turn out to be the mainstream of tomorrow. It is therefore important to evaluate the role of crowdfunding as part of the history of the financial markets. This is particularly relevant in the context of what is currently happening in financial markets via the transformation brought about by digitalization and ever-increasing regulatory burden imposed especially towards banks while restricting their ability to finance small and medium-sized enterprises (SMEs). Crowdfunding, at least for the time being, can be considered one of the most viable examples of the gradual transformation of financial markets caused by emergence of financial technology (fintech). Thus, crowdfunding joins an important group of innovations, which have changed, formed, and developed the financial markets through time like credit cards, stocks, mutual funds, and online banking, all of which have been influential innovations and disruptors of their time (Atack and Neal 2009).

However, as a phenomenon, there is nothing new in crowdfunding and similar ways to access finance have been utilized in the past. Currently crowdfunding is increasingly establishing itself as an integral part of the finance industry especially for start-ups and early phase companies that have traditionally been funded by "family, friends, and fools" in order to develop and gradually attract more interest (by direct investments and/or other collaboration) from sophisticated investors and venture capital funds (Kallio and Vuola 2018; Ziegler et al. 2019). This chapter focuses on those forms of crowdfunding, which have the most relevance to the financial markets, namely debt- and investment-based crowdfunding, and aims to give an analysis why, what, and how crowdfunding has become the phenomenon we are witnessing today and at the same time contextualize it as one of the continuous innovations in the history of ever-changing modern financial markets.

Fundamentals of the Financial System

The financial system is a complex environment comprising of different markets that use various financial instruments, such as equities and bond markets, and includes a number of different institutions such as pension funds, banks, insurance companies, funds, large companies, and retail investors (Drake and Fabozzi 2010). The purpose and functioning of financial markets from an economical perspective is based on a fairly simple point of view: markets channel money from surplus sectors to deficit sectors. This mechanism leads, in theory, to the allocation of capital in a most efficient and profitable way for the economy as a whole. Well-functioning financial markets and financial system in general are a prerequisite for the economic activity and growth we are familiar with. In market driven economies, general welfare is strongly connected to efficiency of the markets (Drake and Fabozzi 2010; Kallio and Vuola 2018).

Main functions of the financial markets are (i) providing information to and between market participants, which at best makes the market work transparently and allows the information available to be immediately, equally, and correctly reflected in the prices of the financial instruments; (ii) enabling efficient allocation of funds from the surplus sector to the deficit sector often through intermediaries such as banks so that funding for necessary investments can be acquired at the lowest possible cost and without delay; (iii) risk management aimed at proportionate spread of the risk inherently built into financial markets to be divided among different investments quantitatively over time; and (iv) providing liquidity, the purpose of which is to enable an investment acquired from the financial markets to be cheaply, easily, and quickly liquidated to cash (Atack and Neal 2009; Drake and Fabozzi 2010).

The usual cause of acquiring financing is rooted in a situation where a company's (or private person's) own capital is not sufficient to carry out the necessary or targeted investments, cover running costs, or overcome unexpected costs. In these cases, equity or debt financing become the most viable option. Financing is a way to mobilize resources quicker compared to collection of such resources by cash flow, which would take a considerable amount of time. The leverage function of new capital enables faster growth, but it involves a cost. In practice, the company is always forced to pay compensation for the use of the capital it has acquired. Equity financing is in practice direct equity investments into the company in which the investor receives an ownership share equalling the value of his investment in the company. The return on equity investment consists of the profit distributed by the company as well as profits re-invested into the company. These may increase at par if the valuation of the holding in the company increases, so the return on equity investment is theoretically unlimited. Similarly, the risk is at most equal to the invested equity (not more, not less) (Ferran 2008; Drake and Fabozzi 2010).

Debt financing is both short term (i.e. for a period of less than one year), such as trade payables and overdrafts, and long term (i.e. over a period of one year or more), such as bonds and bank loans. Debt financing is always external financing, and, as such, there is always an underlined obligation to repay on fixed terms compared to equity. On the other hand, debtor also carries the credit risk and the risk of the company having sufficient cash flow, which the lender must carefully consider when making a financing decision in addition with the evaluation of potential collaterals. The risk of an unsecured debt investment is at most equal to the borrowed capital and overdue, accrued and unpaid interest related thereto (Ferran 2008). Often an investor seeks to secure his position contractually, but also by using various collateral arrangements that secure status of the creditor in the event of a serious default and ultimately in the event of insolvency of the company (Ferran 2008). Debt financing takes precedence in the ranking of the payment order in case of an insolvency of the company compared to equity financing (Ferran 2008). Since profit is a reward for risk taken in business, the lower rank of equity means more risk compared to debt. Therefore, the profit expectancy in equity is generally higher than in debt (Drake and Fabozzi 2010).

The board and the management of a company have a fiduciary duty towards the owners. Rational companies aim to optimize their financing seeking for the best available capital structure. With debt financing the company can, from the owners' perspective, often lower the total cost of capital because investors usually require higher risk premium in relation to equity investments than for debt investments (Drake and Fabozzi 2010). In general, owners of the company try to protect themselves against dilution of ownership making debt finance often a lucrative way to grow through leverage (Ferran 2008). In addition, liability to pay interest in relation to debt financing might provide opportunities to optimize corporate taxation of the company in some jurisdictions (Drake and Fabozzi 2010). With the current stagnating low interest rate era, high leverage ratio may well seem lucrative from owners' perspective.

Setting the Scene

The history of financial markets and finance are united by continuous fluctuations between economic cycles from bull markets to bear markets or bubbles to recessions as well as crises usually caused by structures that enable opportunism and moral gambling. Every crisis contains the seeds of a change, but also risks for regulative overreactions, as well as drastic market reactions. One example is the Great Depression of the US in

1929, which was caused by virtually free speculative trading of stocks and derivatives to the general public and the loss of trust through separation of ownership, as explained by Berle & Means in *The Modern Corporation and Private Property* in 1932. Another and more modern example is the subprime crisis that began in 2007, which was caused by securitization of speculative mortgages and secondary markets related thereto, which at first stage caused widespread credibility gap between banks (i.e. credit crunch), and then later spread across the financial markets as a whole. This latter crisis gradually grew into a worldwide financial crisis eventually leading to the European sovereign debt crisis when several European countries experienced the collapse of major financial institutions, bankrupts of numerous of the countries' biggest companies, high government debt, and rapidly rising bond yield spreads in government securities (Bradley 2013; Chambers and Dimson 2016).

The European sovereign debt crisis also heavily influenced later changes to functioning of and initiatives taken by the European Central Bank (ECB) such as (i) the long-term refinancing operation (LTRO), which is an enhanced credit support measure to support bank lending and liquidity in the euro area announced in 2011, (ii) the targeted longer-term refinancing operations (TLTROs), which are euro system operations that provide financing to credit institutions announced 2014, 2016, and 2019, respectively, and (iii) the asset purchase programme (APP), which is part of a package of non-standard monetary policy measures that also includes targeted longer-term refinancing operations initiated in mid-2014 including corporate sector purchase programme (CSPP), public sector purchase programme (PSPP), asset-backed securities purchase programme (ABSPP), and third covered bond purchase programme (CBPP3). The aim of the ECB with abovementioned programmes was on the one hand to offer banks long-term funding at attractive conditions in order to preserve favourable borrowing conditions for banks and stimulate bank lending to the real economy and on the other to support the monetary policy transmission mechanism and provide the amount of policy accommodation needed to ensure price stability (European Central Bank 2020). In addition, the crisis acted as a catalyst to a still persisting zero-level (or even negative) interest rate environment in Europe.

The former (i.e. Great Depression) led to the implementation of two important acts in the US. First, the Banking Act (i.e. the Glass–Steagall Act), which prohibited any one bank from both accepting deposits and underwriting securities, in order to ensure that if a bank made significant losses underwriting securities, deposits would not be adversely affected. And, second, the extremely tight Securities Act of 1933, representing the first major federal legislation to regulate the offer and sale of securities in the US in order to ensure that buyers of securities receive complete and accurate information before they invest in securities, which is still in force in the US with only some relief from the original statute (Cassis 2017; Mitchener 2005). Both Acts restricted banks' business opportunities largely for the benefit of the general public and society as a whole.

The latter caused tightening of bank regulation, such as risk-weighted capital requirements, market condition, and investor protection, in the global financial markets (especially in the US and Europe) (Chambers and Dimson 2016, pp. 193–194). The enactment of the Dodd–Frank Act in the US was a response to the subprime crisis and brought about the most significant changes to financial regulation in the US since the 1930s preventing the US government from bailing out failing banks with taxpayers' money and imposing short-selling restrictions. In Europe, similar legislative changes were implemented and, with enactments of, among others, the Capital Requirements Directive IV (CRD IV) and the Markets in Financial Instruments Directive II (MIFID II), many restrictions were imposed on banks' businesses. Actions taken both in the US and Europe have heavily impaired banks' business opportunities, by way of, among others, tying their capital to much higher ratios than before the crisis, preventing or even restricting the use and leverage of their balance sheets as well as increasing regulatory compliance and wider conduct requirements (Zestos 2016).

This restrictive trend, as described, has been particularly strong in Europe, with the result that especially the financing of small and medium-sized enterprises (SMEs) has become more challenging. This has been counterbalanced by large-scale EU-wide financing and guarantee arrangements, whose long-term effects are still unknown. In future, we shall learn whether this partial "socialization" of credit risk to the taxpayers was an effective means to counterbalance the tightening regulation. Examples of these approaches, include a corporate bond purchase programmes started by the ECB (as referred above) and the setting up the European Fund for Strategic Investments, which is an EU budget guarantee that provides a shield for the European Investment Bank covering most risky part of the projects it has funded. In authors' view, once these instruments have been introduced to the markets, it may be hard to withdraw them even in the bull market leading into a long-term partial socialization of SME credit risk to taxpayers.

Like other forms of financing, crowdfunding always works within a particular jurisdiction. The provisions laid down in the regulation, in particular the mandatory ones, must be taken into account when utilizing all forms of financing. Besides understanding the history and functioning of global financial markets, it is always necessary to place the activity within the given operating environment and regulations related thereto (Drake and Fabozzi 2010). At the same time social institutions, such as governments, central banks, market supervisors, and supranational institutions, strive to promote trading to maintain economic growth while contrary to this goal also control the markets and operations therein in order to prevent the emergence and spread of systemic risks. Financial law includes acts, which in many cases point to opposite ways aiming at enabling efficient exchange to support investment, economic growth, and employment, and, at the same time, to prevent actions threatening the basic operation of national economies through avoiding emergence of systemic crises. The goal of financial market legislation is simple: trying to optimize the functioning of the financial market. Efficiency in the financial markets does not mean extreme liberalism. On the contrary, the financial market regulation should be limited to what is necessary so that overall confidence in the financial system remains (Drake and Fabozzi 2010).

Every statute increases complexity of the legal system in a non-linear manner. New regulation may lead to artificial market practices and efficiency losses for all market players. Hence, regulation should, from a market liberal economic perspective, focus on ensuring the functioning of key market mechanisms with minimal interruption. In *Confusion de Confusiones* Joseph de la Vega well stated in 1688 that financial system is at the same time "the fairest and most deceitful business ... the noblest and the most infamous in the world, the finest and most vulgar on earth".

Things have not changed so much after de la Vega. The aim for the regulator is to incentivize the fairness and nobleness and de-incentivize the deceitfulness and vulgarness.

Efforts to maximize the interests of different stakeholders in the financial markets, and competition among them, create incentives for moral gambling, which lawmakers seek to counter by creating and imposing counter-incentives as well as effective control and enforcement systems. Financial market regulation always affects competitiveness of stakeholders in the financial markets, and regulation that is too burdensome can be seen detrimental to the whole financial market system. On the other hand, legislation can also help speed up market disruption (PWC 2017). Delays are a challenge for the legislator: decision delay, legislative delay, and implementation delay cause problems for effective and well-functioning legislation. The longer the delays the legislator is facing are, the easier it is for crises to emerge and the deeper they can become.

Similarly, the faster the new forms of financing, innovations, and practices are emerging in the financial markets, the more challenging is the role of the financial market supervisor and the legislator. However, as the legislator and market supervisor seek to control systemic risk by observing and regulating existing phenomena, new forms or models and other financial innovations are evolving at an ever-increasing pace in the financial markets. Of these, crowdfunding is an illustrative example. A considerable amount of new financial regulation has come into effect during the last years affecting those operating in the financial markets by increased costs and complexity. This emphasises the ongoing struggle between the stakeholders operating in the financial markets and the broad, ever-increasing, and multi-level regulation shaping the fundaments of financial ecosystem (Kallio and Vuola 2018).

The Brief History of the Modern Financial System

The development of the international financial system is in every respect a historical, economic, and political process. Because of this, it is essential to briefly outline the past, in addition to the present, in order to be able to assess potential future developments and guidelines of the financial markets. The beginning of the international financial system as we know it today dates back to the 1970s, but, more broadly speaking, a global financial system has existed much longer. This further stresses the importance to understand events, notions and wider developments described in the written financial history, which provides the means to comprehend functioning of modern financial markets. In *On the Genealogy of Morals* Friedrich Nietzsche noted in 1887 that the whole idea of duty and personal obligation is rooted in the oldest and the most primitive relationship there is, the relationship between creditor and debtor. This statement continues to quite accurately describe fundamental relationships in the modern financial markets.

The financial markets tend to operate in cycles, which differ depending on the subject matter (volatility, share prices, etc.) under consideration. For example, it is possible to assess the business cycle or the stock market cycle, which largely differ from each other due to differences in relation to the underlying subject matter in question. Although history may not be said to repeat itself, the cyclicity of the financial markets has largely been scientifically proven (Marmer 2016; Chambers and Dimson 2016; Atack and Neal 2009) although the timing of different cycles cannot be determined with any precision.[1] Therefore, it is not surprising that the financial markets witness both highs and lows, of which the former can in the worst case create a financial bubble[2] and the latter a recession meaning a deeper and longer lasting economic downturn.[3] Previous major changes in the financial markets may be categorized in many ways (Atack and Neal 2009). They can be approached through economic bubbles in relation to their impact on the real economy.

One way to outline the most important financial market development stages is to divide them into five phases. In the first phase in the nineteenth century, the leading European industrialized countries and the colonized non-European regions they ruled moved to a gold-denominated currency system that collapsed during World War I. There were sincere efforts to return the gold-denominated currency system in the 1920s, but they failed. This can be considered the second phase of the financial markets' development. In the third phase, the Great Depression of the US, followed by significant tightening of the US financial market regulation and eventually World War II caused international financial markets to shut down almost completely. The fourth stage of the international financial system began after World War II based on gradual dismantling of the post-war regulated economy and opening of the international financial markets, which lasted up to the oil crisis of the 1970s. After the 1970s, we have more or less lived in the current historical era comprising building of the global financial system based on neoclassical theoretical approach and characterized by ever-increasing globalization. This can be called the fifth stage, which we are still in (Kari 2016). The end of the 2010s has been marked by a certain degree of inward turning tendency, during which even many influential parties have openly denied functioning of the open and global financial system. The future will show whether we are in the middle of changing paradigm and living the beginning of the new sixth stage in which the international financial system is being gradually overtaken by separate national and inward-looking systems such as we are currently, at least to some degree, witnessing in the US, Brazil, and Russia to a greater extent. Recent outbreak of COVID-19 virus might further accelerate such inward-looking tendencies on a global level.

Understanding of historical changes of both the financial market and the financial system as a whole will help to put new financial innovations, such as crowdfunding and, more broadly, fintech into perspective (Chambers and Dimson 2016). The change in the financial markets is an extremely wide and complex matter influenced by technological advances and digitalization. Also, the current political, economic, and ideological conditions affect the financial system as a whole. While international development seems to be moving towards an increasingly global financial market (despite some inward-looking tendencies), diverse corporate cultures, differences in politics, as well as legislation between countries remain prevalent.

The Modern Emergence of Crowdfunding

There is nothing new in sourcing money from the crowds. However, crowdfunding, as a concept, is a modern financial service enabled by advanced digitalization. The underlying technology of which has the potential to help investors to find ventures and projects, which need financing and, accordingly, allows the ventures or projects to find investors and backers to finance their growth and development (Dresner 2014, p. 3). Based on one definition "crowdfunding" refers to the ability of pooling small amounts of capital from a potentially large pool of interested funders and supporters (Short et al. 2017). This definition, however, is close to the definition of an initial public offering (IPO). The ability of pooling in IPO is mainly based on the marketing efforts of investment banks acting as "underwriters" whereas in crowdfunding it is based on the digital online platform and its functionalities. In recent years, we have witnessed hybrid models where IPOs have also been executed through crowdfunding platforms.

A crowdfunding platform is "an internet application bringing together project owners and their potential backers, as well as facilitating exchanges between them, according to a variety of business models" (Shneor and Flåten 2015, p. 188). The crowdfunding platforms act as intermediaries between investors and companies (or other projects) and facilitate opportunities for investors to find and support the projects they are interested in (Spacetec 2014). The platform's core value proposition is in taking down the transaction costs and lowering the bar to start a fundraising campaign effort. Just a decade ago, it was basically impossible for an early stage venture to reach out to tens of thousands of potential investors in a cost-efficient way.

Thus far, crowdfunding has been gaining ground very rapidly (European Commission 2016). Major contributing factors to this growth and spread of crowdfunding are both the international crisis in the financial markets in 2008 that has led, inter alia, tightening the capital adequacy and solvency requirements for credit institutions, and the explosion of internet usage and usability, which together have made it possible to reach large crowds of potential funders in a cost-effective manner (IOSCO 2015).

In the near future, crowdfunding may become an increasingly important source of non-bank financing. Worldwide crowdfunding market has been estimated to reach 371 billion euros in 2017 and based on market data strong growth in recent years has been continued (Ziegler et al. 2019), although the rate of growth seems to have cooled in some more mature markets (Ziegler et al. 2019). Crowdfunding is increasingly establishing itself as an integral part of the finance industry especially for start-ups and early phase companies that have traditionally been funded by "family, friends, and fools". Furthermore, crowdfunding provides a feasible alternative to unsecured bank loans that have, for the time being, been one of the most important sources of external financing for SMEs in some jurisdictions, while being almost non-existent in others (European Commission 2018b).

A Brief History of Crowdfunding

Crowdfunding as a form of financing is not a new phenomenon (Spacetec 2014). A similar approach has been used to manage investment risks before internet time (Dresner 2014). For example, in shipping, one of the oldest forms of risk management are guarantee agreements between traders and shipping companies, in which upon the event of loss of cargo all pay part of such loss, but when cargo arrives safely, all parties to the contract (i.e. the guarantors) will receive their proportional share of the profits. This approach has provided the necessary financing to carry out high-risk projects and at the same time enabled successful diversification of the risk associated with the project between the parties.

The basic principles of the crowdfunding business go back to the early eighteenth-century Ireland, where "forefather of microcredits" Jonathan Swift[4] founded the Irish Loan Fund. The Fund offered small loans to low-income rural families who did not have the collateral required by large banks or proper credit history. By the nineteenth century, more than 300 schemes were implemented in Ireland in all of which small amounts were lent by private investors to individuals who needed a loan for short periods.

One of the early contemporary crowdfunding campaigns was carried out in the US in 1885 when the project of the Statue of Liberty on Liberty Island off New York had run into severe financial difficulties. When other means had proven ineffective, Joseph Pulitzer decided to launch a fundraising campaign to fund the erection of a pedestal for the Statue of Liberty in his own newspaper, *The New York World*. In exchange for a donation, he promised to publish the names of all donors in his magazine regardless of the amount. Over 160,000 donors in about five months had donated more than US $100,000 to erect the pedestal. Most of the donations were quite small—from a few cents to one dollar (Dresner 2014). However, while possibly the most famous and most often cited, the Statue of Liberty project was not the first crowdfunding campaign.

Even earlier examples of crowdfunding are evident. One example is when poet Alexander Pope set out to translate Greek poetry into English in 1713, an effort that included the translation of Homer's epic poem, "The Iliad", and asked donors to pledge two gold guineas to support his work in exchange for having the donors' names published in the acknowledgements of an early edition of the book. Another example is that in the end of the eighteenth century, the famous composer Mozart took a similar path. He wanted to perform three piano concertos in a concert hall in Vienna and published an invitation to prospective backers offering manuscripts to those who agreed to donate funds for this purpose. This approach mirrors the way in which Kickstarter operates today, where campaigners offer backers the first chance to get access to new products offered in campaigns. However, while Mozart failed to reach his funding goal on his first attempt, he succeeded a year later in a second attempt, where 176 backers donated enough funds to bring his concerto tour alive and they were all mentioned in his concertos' manuscript.

Muhammad Yunus further developed Jonathan Swift's idea on micro-credits and microfinance by founding the Grameen Bank in 1976 (being authorized in 1983 by national legislation to operate as an independent bank in Bangladesh). The goal was to grant loans for entrepreneurs too poor to qualify for traditional bank loans. The bank's funding has come from different sources, and the main contributors have shifted during times from bulk agencies to central bank of Bangladesh. Grameen Bank is founded on the principle that loans are better than charity to interrupt poverty: they offer people the opportunity to take initiatives in business or agriculture, which provide earnings and enable them to pay off the debt and start a social climb. The Bank has offered credit to classes of people formerly outscoped: the poor, women, illiterate, and unemployed people. Access to credit is based on reasonable terms, such as the group lending system and weekly instalment payments, with reasonably long terms of loans, enabling the poor to build on their existing skills to earn better income in each cycle of loans. He and Grameen Bank were jointly awarded the Nobel Peace Prize in 2006 for their efforts through micro-credit to create economic and social development from below (Grameen Bank 2006).

Between 1996 and 1997, the British rock band Marillion funded its tour in the US by collecting US $60,000 from its fans via the internet. This project and other successful fan-based funding rounds that followed gave a boost to the increasing popularity of contemporary crowdfunding from the beginning of twenty-first century. Wider utilization of the form of financing and the spread thereof was made possible by the ever-increasing accessibility to the internet and its growing use by both businesses and households, which in turn made it possible to cost-effectively reach a large crowd at the same time. ArtistShare was one of the first modern crowdfunding services when it was released in the US in 2003. Through its service the artists had, and still have, the opportunity to seek funding to cover their recording costs from a wide audience such as their own supporters and fans. Here, supporters making financial contributions receive the right to download the artist's album (or song) once it is completed. The success of ArtistShare has also attracted other players to the market, of which perhaps the best known and most successful are reward-based platforms Indiegogo since 2008 and Kickstarter from 2009.

When donation and reward-based crowdfunding started to become widespread successes, it was relatively clear that a similar approach would also be used in the capital markets to raise investment-oriented finance. During the last decade, the market started to see platforms seeking to enable capital raising from investors by utilizing opportunities offered by the internet to collect and share investment information in an easier and faster manner, while simplifying the process and using standard terms. Here, the goal was to simplify, to the extent possible, the acquisition of finance from previously heavy and burdensome processes by using modern technology. In the past, acquisition of finance from angel investors lasted at least a number of months, but by using the internet the same funding could be secured within days or at most within a few weeks. One of the most successful pioneers in the industry are the US-based peer-to-peer and business-to-business lending platform—Lending Club, founded

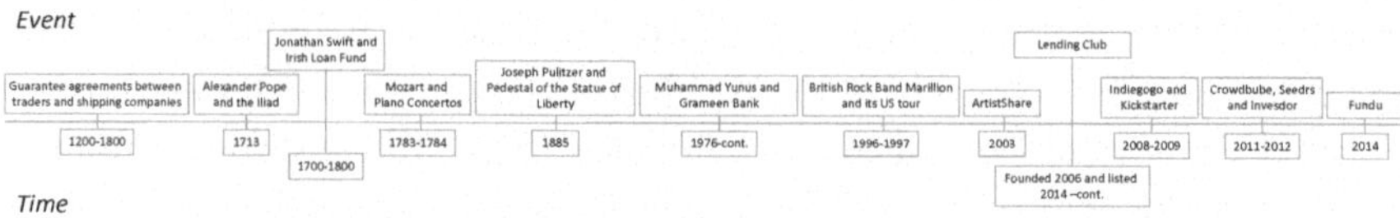

Fig. 10.1 Timeline—Brief history of crowdfunding

in 2006 in San Francisco and listed in December 2014 on the New York Stock Exchange (Freedman and Nutting 2015), and UK-based Zopa, which was launched in 2005 (Kupp and Anderson 2007) as well as Finnish-based equity platform Invesdor, which was founded in 2012, and being the first MIFID II licensed crowdfunding platform to operate cross-border in Europe (Fig. 10.1).

Crowdfunding and Its Significance in the Modern Era

Starting in 2007 from the overheated housing market in the US, and reaching full speed in 2008, the financial crisis has significantly changed the functioning of international financial markets. Increased regulation, and in particular the tightening of capital requirements for banks, has contributed to the need to find new sources of finance for businesses. Tighter regulation, especially the risk-weighted capital requirements has limited the number of companies that banks could provide debt finance for, and, in turn, led to increased borrowing costs. Therefore, it can be argued that at least to a certain extent, the changes described here have reduced the capacity of credit institutions to meet the financing needs of companies. In addition, a weak and precarious economic situation, which has only recently turned for better, has increased the risk of credit losses and thereby reduced banks' risk appetite (European Commission 2013). The situation has had a particularly strong impact on European SMEs, which have, due to historical reasons, been dependent on bank financing and, hence, resorted to alternative sources of financing (European Commission 2013, 2015). This is expected to affect the diversification of financial markets in the future. In particular, changes in the regulation of financial institutions can be seen as a limiting factor on the effective functioning of financial markets for entrepreneurial finance and growth companies.

The financial position and access to finance for growth companies and SMEs have weakened to some extent globally. As a result, companies have not always been able to meet the funding needs for their projects from existing sources of finance, which has in certain situations led to a financing gap (European Commission 2018b). Of course, not all the companies are fundable by any means of finance. However, statistics published by European Central Bank have shown evidence of a decline in access to finance for growth companies and SMEs especially in Europe in the aftermath of financial crisis even though situation has gradually improved in recent years. Based on surveys, also covenants (i.e. special conditions) as well as the security requirements of corporate loans have been tightened and interest for corporates, but especially SMEs risen (European Central Bank 2019). Although the situation in Europe is relatively good in comparison to other continents, it has developed for the worse since the financial crisis. Structural deficiencies, overcapacity, low/negative interest rates, and the absence of a pan-European banking regulatory agency have all likely contributed to European banks experiencing persistent profitability challenges (Deloitte 2019).[5] In Europe, the proportion of SMEs that mention access to finance as one of their main problems, and hence feel that they are not able to drive all potentially profitable projects, has grown (European Central Bank 2019). These findings may well be proof that the EU and national level SME guarantee facilities have not had the expected outcome. In addition, it is uncertain how socialization of credit risk affects the economy as a whole in zero (or even negative) central bank interest environment.

Low interest rates weaken banks' profitability and reduce the transparency of the actual price paid by the customer, which depends on not only each customer's financial status and profitability of the business but also the banks' current fundraising costs and the pursued level of profitability. Based on business and investor surveys (such as European Central Bank

2019) growth companies experience slower growth and higher growth thresholds. Hence, businesses, as they continue to grow, are often lacking access to finance and ability to entice new owners through listings. Low availability of alternative sources of funding, lack of expertise, and the relatively high cost of the listing process, as well as negative attitudes of owners, slow down the growth path of companies.

Therefore, from the perspective of growth-oriented companies, funding opportunities that are complementary or alternative to bank financing, such as risk and equity finance (i.e. bond markets, crowdfunding, venture capital) have increased their importance. Equity crowdfunding is especially important to finance the growth of technology-intensive businesses and innovative companies in general. This is even more relevant when a company is looking for new markets or planning to develop new products. Palmer has concluded in his study that the price of the (crowd) funding (i.e. associated costs) is not the main reason why some companies decide to use crowdfunding instead of traditional sources of finance. The main reason for companies to avoid bank-based financing is, according to Palmer, to avoid the heavy bureaucracy involved in dealing with banks in the first place (Palmer 2016).

The prevailing (zero or even negative interest) market conditions have also forced investors to look into new channels for investments providing high yields with higher risks, which have not been available from traditional sources of finance, such as banks balance sheet financing or capital markets in general. Both loan and investment-based crowdfunding include many opportunities for investors looking for investments with different return-to-risk ratios. From the investors' perspective, crowdfunding also offers a new way to diversify investments and seek higher than average profits with a higher risk profile compared to more general investment products available in the market. However, the several hundred years old banking institution is unlikely to vanish any time soon. On the contrary, there is strong indication that some leading business banks have established successful partnerships with crowdfunding platforms and other fintech companies (Nordea 2018; BBVA 2019; Deloitte 2019).

What Next?

The Fourth Industrial Revolution is underway. According to Statista—a German online portal for statistics, which makes data collected by market and opinion research institutes and data derived from the economic sector and official statistics available—there were about 26 billion devices connected to the internet around the world in 2019. The total installed base of internet connected devices is projected to amount to 75.44 billion worldwide by 2025, a fivefold increase in ten years. The internet of things, enabled by the already ubiquitous internet technology, seems to be the next major step in delivering internet's promise of making the world a connected place (Statista 2019). Currently it seems that artificial intelligence, machine learning, and the internet of things will have the most effect on the financial sector (Deloitte 2019). Digitalization is currently shaping the financial market sector with a force that has not been experienced in this scale before (Chambers and Dimson 2016). The disruption we are currently witnessing means a development during which many existing policies might be abandoned, and new ones adopted within a relatively short term. This has become even more evident after the outbreak of COVID-19 virus and how it has forced governments, institutions and companies to adopt to new and digitalized ways of working.

The financial market has, throughout its history, experienced tremendous economic and functional breakthroughs and changes, but basic operating models have remained largely unchanged, unlike, for example in industrial and service sectors (Atack and Neal 2009; Chambers and Dimson 2016). However, digitalization and technological advancement have significantly changed people's behaviour since the beginning of the twenty-first century. The virtual world has entered into all aspects of human life, and modern devices (such as tablets, mobile phones, smart watches, etc.) and applications (such as Facebook, Instagram, WhatsApp, WeChat, Skype, different e-mail applications, etc.) allow people to be continuously reached and contacted. This has given people many new opportunities to improve their living conditions and use of time, but, at the same time, mixed and overlapped time between work and leisure.

In parallel, social interaction is increasingly moving into the internet and its complex social media networks (Joinson et al. 2009; Kallio and Vuola 2018).

Not surprisingly, in the same context, people's expectations towards (financial) service providers have changed. This naturally influences financial markets, which are not a separate fort from the rest of society. People's expectations as consumers require ongoing development work from the financial markets so that financial market participants are better equipped to meet people's ever-growing expectations. Nascent technology creates numerous new business opportunities in all business sectors.[6] In the financial markets of the near future, it is likely that besides existing incumbent market operators, such as banks, also big technology companies like Amazon, Facebook (especially with its proposed cryptocurrency project Libra), Apple, Google, Tencent, or Alibaba, who are already integrating payment services on a large scale to their own services, will take a big share of the markets (Deloitte 2019).

Advances in technology seem to ensure that internet, and other sharing networks, will become more significant and take a larger part of our living environment, which will also inevitably change the financial markets as well, while enabling new service concepts and forms of financing (Morel et al. 2018). This poses challenges for current financial market participants, especially for banks (Deloitte 2019) but also creates a correspondingly high potential to newcomers (disruptors), investors, and companies seeking finance. Lawmakers and market supervisors are facing challenging times, though it is essential to keep in mind that the biggest and often most amazing things happen in a period of big breakthroughs or changes that can at this stage only be expected to accelerate through technological development. With these developments, the role of central banks may be changing rapidly. For instance, ECB is examining whether to develop a digital currency as an alternative to cash (Financial Times 2019). To further support and derive from the project, a body of six central banks (the Bank of England, Bank of Canada, BOE, the Bank of Japan, the European Central Bank, the Riksbank, and the Swiss National Bank, along with the Bank for International Settlements) have been set in order to "share experience as they assess the potential cases for central bank digital currency in their home jurisdictions" (Bloomberg 2020).

Fintech refers to those technological innovations in the field of financial services that may lead to new business models, applications, processes, or products and have a significant ancillary effect on financial markets and institutions in the way financial services are provided. The history of the financial market is full of financial innovations, but the importance of these innovations has grown and market transformation accelerated by technological advances (European Commission 2018a). Accordingly, the market is, at an accelerating pace, deploying various fintech solutions that leverage digital identification, mobile applications, cloud services, big data analysis, artificial intelligence, blockchain, and distributed ledger technologies. New technologies are changing the financial industry and the way consumers and businesses buy services. This creates opportunities for fintech-based solutions that improve access to finance and financial inclusion of digitally networked consumers (PWC 2017).

Today, crowdfunding is used to finance business growth at an accelerated pace. Until recently, it has generally been considered to be appropriate during the seed and growth stages for start-ups and especially small businesses (Spacetec 2014) involving financing from non-professional investors often reaching sums between ten thousand euros to a few million euros. In the financial markets, crowdfunding is typically seen as a high-risk mezzanine as well as debt or equity financing. However, the paradigm might be shifting. The crowdfunding market has already seen institutional interest, which may further accelerate growth of this form of financing (Ziegler et al. 2019). This trend is partly supported by regulation making crowdfunding part of regulated financial markets, as well as governments' continuous will to impose ever-stricter regulation to existing financial market players.

There may well be an underlying risk that the crowds will be pushed back in the most successful platforms, which are able to show long-term track record especially in debt crowdfunding. If this happens, the credit rating models of platforms would have been battle-tested by the non-professional crowds, but eventually the professional investors will come and harvest the fruit. In addition, deepening deflation in the financial markets seems to push more and more institutional investors to alternative finance in order to pursue profits, which are less available from traditional sources. However, recent research has shown that institutionalization across all crowdfunding model types has actually decreased between 2016 and 2017. This includes funding from pension funds, mutual funds, asset management firms, and banks (Ziegler et al. 2019).

Conclusion

The size of the crowdfunding market, and hence the importance of this form of financing, has grown rapidly (European Commission 2016) and continues to grow based on recent studies (Ziegler et al. 2019). Crowdfunding transactions taking place digitally on different technological platforms via the internet is a concrete demonstration of how digitalization and business models applying new technological solutions can influence access to finance. Subsequently, such solutions also channel and allocate the limited resources of society to benefit a larger pool of companies, investors, and consumers, and hence supporting the society as a whole.

Nevertheless, crowdfunding is not immune to risks, immorality, opportunism, and moral hazard, which have been witnessed in the financial sector from the start. Here, although the systemic risk may be quite low for the economy as a whole, it is for the benefit of all stakeholders in crowdfunding that some level of governmental control is being exercised. So far, it may be fair to argue that there are no crowdfunding platforms that are "too big to fail". The business model of crowdfunding involves the ability to seek instant profits from and at the expense of investors, for example, by loosening the service platform's customer selection. Here, it may be argued that less-informed investors may take risks which better informed investors may not. This risk is highlighted by a fact that crowdfunding platform operators are often start-ups themselves struggling with adequate cash flows and may be pressed to onboard campaigns and investors less selectively. This argument defends reasonable minimum capital requirements.

In the end, the markets naturally repair themselves when investors start to avoid those crowdfunding platforms, which price the risks of their projects and operations poorly or indifferently. For a young and developing industry, the market-based correction mechanism may not necessarily be sufficient, because the industry's overall reputation can significantly weaken already from one bigger moral gambling case. This is true especially in the current situation where advanced self-regulation of the industry has not yet formed, but competition on market shares and customers has constantly been growing and tightening. The biggest risk for crowdfunding industry and its long-term success would seem to be the industry itself if it does not take these signs of danger seriously enough.

The history of the financial markets is full of innovations, starting from the invention of money and using it as a medium of exchange, the exit from the gold-denominated currency system, and all the way to the increasing popularity of online payment systems. Crowdfunding as a form of financing is part of this series of innovations in the general history of financial markets. Crowdfunding has in quite short period acquired a small but significant position in the international financial markets making it important and accessible funding channel especially for start-ups and SMEs. It can also be stated that crowdfunding has democratized the process of commercialization and financing by making investing in start-ups more widespread and easier to access for all people, instead of being accessible to only high-net-worth individuals, business angels, or venture funds (Ziegler et al. 2019). This has also given new opportunities for companies seeking financing and diversified the functioning of existing financial markets.

The evolution of financial markets or corporate finance naturally will not end in crowdfunding. For example, blockchain technology can, if sufficiently advanced, enable completely new business models that can challenge, when scaled adequately enough, traditional corporate finance as well as crowdfunding as we know it today. Blockchain technology, like other fintech innovations, can have a significant impact on the development of financial markets in the future (Deloitte 2019). This also relates to cyber security and data privacy in general, which are issues that need to be addressed globally in order to capitalize on the benefits of digitalization not just for the good of financial markets, but for the society as a whole (European Commission 2018a). The big challenge for the regulators in this rapidly changing financial environment is to maintain an attitude of "mend it, don't end it".

In the future, it is necessary for researchers to further study the historical evolution and development of crowdfunding markets in the wider context of financial markets. The relevance of crowdfunding as a new form of financing to market participants (i.e. investors, companies, and established operators like banks) would be worthwhile researching. This is especially true in the current exceptional financial market environment, which is characterized by zero or even negative interest rates, as well as continuous liquidity injections by central banks and government-led projects or initiatives (especially in Europe), such as the European Fund for Strategic Investments and its local counterparts. An alternative historical approach may be comparisons between the development of crowdfunding and other innovations in financial markets, highlighting common and different drivers and barriers to such developments, and the actors behind them. There is also a need for more (historical) study on both the positive and negative implications of financial innovations (including crowdfunding), the determinants of risk taking by institutional and individual investors, the governance problems (including conflict of interest between different stakeholders), and the causes of volatility in financial markets in relation to emergence of fintech. All these issues have practical implications to the success and implementation speed of new financial innovations to practice and everyday service offering and use by individual banks, companies, and households.

Also increasing regulatory burden, which has mostly fallen on the shoulders of established financial institutions like banks, might distort the functioning of financial markets even further and create more concerns among investors and in the public, which can have unprecedented effects to the financial markets of today. Big shifts in current paradigm in the financial markets can make crowdfunding more attractive to institutional investors in the future. The relationship between institutional investors and crowdfunding platforms is a particularly interesting research opportunity, as it may have profound effects on industry development, and the extent to which it will remain loyal to its grass-root ideals.

Further, more research is needed on the effects on and implications of the crowdfunding industry on systemic risk especially if the growth of the industry continues as strong as it has to date. It will also be interesting to follow how quickly and agile crowdfunding platforms will adapt innovations of fintech (blockchain, AI, cloud computing, etc.) into their everyday operations compared to, for example, banks, as well as what effects will that have on the future position and service portfolios of platforms and banks respectively. In growing markets, there also seems to be an increasing pressure for consolidation of the crowdfunding platforms as well as expansion of their current product lines and ability to adapt to new and more scalable business models (e.g. setting up alternative investment funds in order to ensure steadier cash flow as well as expanding from solely lending-based crowdfunding to cover other crowdfunding forms). In addition, it is interesting to study the increasing syndication and cooperation activities between traditional banks and crowdfunding platforms.

In conclusion, we are living in interesting times of constantly evolving financial markets. In order to be able to predict future trends and directions, we must understand the past and derive from the teachings of history; and in this particular case-financial history. In order to understand history, it is essential not to highlight only similarities between historical episodes such as the Great Depression of 1929 and the subprime crisis of 2007 but also differences.[7] Such an approach shows us that history does not always have such a conclusive predictive power than we would probably like it to have (Chambers and Dimson 2016). However, history has always provided invaluable guidance to those willing to learn from events, and especially mistakes, of the past. At the finalizing phase of this chapter we are witnessing an outbreak of COVID-19 virus that hammers the global economy at forces rarely seen before. The outcomes of such crises are hard to predict. We might be entering into a beginning of a new era of disintegration in EU and rising levels of nationalisation. On the other hand, the solidarity may even strenghten among EU states, and the level of global co-operation and transparency might increase and improve.

From practical standpoint, it is useful to contextualize crowdfunding—a modern and digitalized form of financing—as part of financial markets, its rules, and mechanics. In order to achieve such a goal, it is essential to understand fluctuations between economic cycles driven by historical, economic, and political processes. Crowdfunding and fintech in general will definitely offer many interesting research topics for researchers in the financial markets for years to come.

Notes

1. Although the economic history of the past 300 years has shown many instances of financial crises and bank failures, their effects on asset values and on the real economy have been quite varied. Much depends on how the authorities react to these events. Although we understand from history the factors that lead to and exacerbate crises, the attempts to make such crises less frequent and less virulent have been largely misguided (Chambers and Dimson 2016, p. xvi).
2. "Economic bubble" means a situation in the economy where a price of a trading object (e.g. a stock or other commodity) differs from the balanced price defined by the fundamentals of the market (based on availability, valuation, supply, etc.). The bubble may form, for example, to the prices of stocks or house prices (Chambers and Dimson 2016, pp. 149–168 and 174–175). One of the traditional and frequently used examples of "economic bubble" is the so-called tulip mania, which was an investment bubble in the Netherlands between 1634 and 1637, where prices of tulip bulbs entering the markets most recently rose to record levels and eventually collapsed. The highest price of tulips was in 1637. Tulip mania is considered one of the first economic bubbles in the modern financial markets.
3. Economic cycles affect, among others, (i) the number of loan transactions, (ii) the size of the loan facilities, (iii) pricing for the loans, (iv) default rates, and (v) institutional demand for secondary trading. A buoyant economy with low default rates encourages lenders to commit to large loans and more frequently, whereas a contracting economy usually results in a more cautious approach in the number of transactions and the terms on which the loans are made. A deteriorating economy with high default rates spurs the secondary market in distressed loans (Mugasha 2007, p. 6).
4. Jonathan Swift is better known as an author of a well-known prose satire; Gulliver's Travels, or Travels into Several Remote Nations of the World. In Four Parts. By Lemuel Gulliver, First a Surgeon, and then a Captain of Several Ships.

5. US banks, compared to their European counterparts, are ahead on multiple measures. Aggressive policy interventions and forceful regulations helped propel US banks to health more quickly. And more recently, favourable GDP growth, tax cuts, and rising rates have further bolstered the state of the industry. Total assets in the US reached a peak of $17.5 trillion. Capital levels are up as well, with average tier 1 capital ratio standing at 13.14%. Return on equity (ROE) for the industry is at a post-crisis high of 11.83%. Efficiency ratios also are at their best. Similarly, on other metrics, such as non-performing loans and number of failed institutions, the US banking industry is robust (Deloitte 2019, p. 1).
6. For example: (i) video rentals (Blockbusters) have gone online (Netflix, Viaplay, HBO), (ii) instead of CDs, music is listened online via web streaming services (Spotify), (iii) instead of travel agencies, most trips and accommodations are booked directly through internet platforms (e-aggregators) (Trivago, Ebookers), and (iv) instead of visiting branches, banking is handled through online banking channels or, increasingly, via banking applications on mobile phones.
7. For example, complex and highly automatized/digitalized structured financial products—non-existent during crisis of the 1930s—were vastly used in global financial markets prior to the subprime crisis. The use of as well as lack of understanding related to these products has been identified as one of the major contributing factors to the subprime crisis (Chambers and Dimson 2016, pp. 272–276).

References

Atack, J., & Neal, L. (2009). *The Origins and Development of Financial Markets and Institutions—From the Seventeenth Century to the Present.* Cambridge: Cambridge University Press.

BBVA. (2019). *BBVA-backed Holvi Announces Plan to Expand in Europe.* Press Release, May 16. Retrieved December 1, 2019, from https://www.bbva.com/en/bbva-backed-holvi-announces-plan-to-expand-in-europe/.

Berle, A., & Means, G. (1932). *The Modern Corporation and Private Property.* New York: The Macmillan Company.

Bloomberg. (2020). *Central Banks Team Up to Study Case for Digital Currencies.* Retrieved January 1, 2020, from https://www.bloomberg.com/news/articles/2020-01-21/central-banks-team-up-to-study-case-for-digital-currencies.

Bradley, C. M. (2013). From Global Financial Crisis to Sovereign Debt Crisis and Beyond: What Lies Ahead for the European Monetary Union? *Transnational Law and Contemporary Problems, 22*(9), 9–39.

Cassis, Y. (2017). *Regulatory Responses to the Financial Crises of the Great Depression: Britain, France and the United States*. Retrieved December 1, 2019, from https://archive.kenan.ethics.duke.edu/wp-content/blogs.dir/2/files/2013/10/Regulatory-responses_cassis.pdf.

Chambers, D., & Dimson, E. (2016). *Financial Market History—Reflections on the Past for Investors of Today*. Cambridge: Cambridge University Press.

de la Vega, J. (1688). *Confusion de Confusiones: Portions Descriptive of the Amsterdam Stock Exchange* (H. Kellenbenz, Trans., Harvard University, 1957). Retrieved December 1, 2019, from https://www.gwern.net/docs/economics/1688-delavega-confusionofconfusions.pdf

Deloitte Touche Tohmatsu Limited. (2019). *Banking and Capital Markets Outlook—Reimagining Transformation*. Retrieved December 1, 2019, from https://www2.deloitte.com/cy/en/pages/financial-services/articles/gx-banking-industry-outlook.html.

Drake, P. P., & Fabozzi, F. J. (2010). *The Basics of Finance: An Introduction to Financial Markets, Business Finance, and Portfolio Management* (Vol. 192). John Wiley & Sons.

Dresner, S. (2014). *A Guide to Raising Capital on the Internet*. Hoboken, New Jersey: John Wiley & Sons.

European Central Bank. (2019). *Survey on the Access to Finance of Enterprises—April to September 2019*. Retrieved December 1, 2019, from https://www.ecb.europa.eu/stats/ecb_surveys/safe/html/index.en.html

European Central Bank. (2020). *Asset Purchase Programmes*. Retrieved January 1, 2020, from https://www.ecb.europa.eu/mopo/implement/omt/html/index.en.html

European Commission. (2013). Green Paper: Long-Term Financing of the European Economy. *COM,* 150. Brussels, March 25. Retrieved December 1, 2019, from https://eur-lex.europa.eu/legal-content/EN/TXT/PDF/?uri=CELEX:52013DC0150&from=EN

European Commission. (2015). Green Paper: Building a Capital Markets Union. *COM*, 63. Brussels, February 18. Retrieved December 1, 2019, from https://eur-lex.europa.eu/legal-content/EN/TXT/PDF/?uri=CELEX:52015DC0063&from=EN.

European Commission. (2016). Commission Staff Working Document: Crowdfunding in the EU Capital Markets Union. *SWD*, 154. Brussels, May 3. Retrieved December 1, 2019, from https://ec.europa.eu/transparency/regdoc/rep/10102/2016/EN/10102-2016-154-EN-F1-1.PDF.

European Commission. (2018a). Communication from the Commission to the European Parliament, the Council, the European Central Bank, the European Economic and Social Committee and the Committee of the Regions on FinTech Action Plan: For a More Competitive and Innovative European Financial Sector. *COM*, 109. Brussels, March 8. Retrieved December 1, 2019, from https://eur-lex.europa.eu/resource.html?uri=cellar:6793c578-22e6-11e8-ac73-01aa75ed71a1.0001.02/DOC_1&format=PDF

European Commission. (2018b). Proposal for a Regulation of the European Parliament and of the Council on European Crowdfunding Service Providers (ECSP) for Business. *COM*, 113. Brussels, March 8. Retrieved December 1, 2019, from https://eur-lex.europa.eu/resource.html?uri=cellar:0ea638be-22cb-11e8-ac73-01aa75ed71a1.0003.02/DOC_2&format=PDF.

European Securities and Markets Authority. (2014). Opinion. Investment-based Crowdfunding. ESMA/2014/1378, December 18. Retrieved December 1, 2019, from https://www.esma.europa.eu/sites/default/files/library/2015/11/2014-1378_opinion_on_investment-based_crowdfunding.pdf.

Ferran, E. (2008). *Principles of Corporate Finance Law*. Oxford: Oxford University Press.

Financial Times. (2019). *ECB Explores Development of a Digital Currency*. Retrieved December 1, 2019, from https://www.ft.com/content/56db1f62-104b-11ea-a7e6-62bf4f9e548a.

Freedman, D., & Nutting, M. R. (2015). *A Brief History of Crowdfunding Including Rewards, Donation, Debt, and Equity Platforms in the USA*, Updated November 5. Retrieved December 1, 2019, from https://www.freedman-chicago.com/ec4i/History-of-Crowdfunding.pdf

Grameen Bank. (2006). *The Nobel Peace Prize 2006*. Retrieved December 1, 2019, from http://www.grameen.com/the-nobel-peace-prize-2006/.

International Organization of Securities Commissions. (2015). *Crowdfunding*. Survey Responses Report. FR29/2015, December 12. Retrieved December 1, 2019, from https://www.iosco.org/library/pubdocs/pdf/IOSCOPD520.pdf.

Joinson, A., McKenna, K., Postmes, T., & Reips, U. D. (Eds.). (2009). *Oxford Handbook of Internet Psychology*. Oxford: OUP.

Kallio, A., & Vuola, L. (2018). *Joukkorahoitus*. Liettua (in Finnish—Abstract in English).

Kari, M. (2016). *Suomen rahoitusmarkkinoiden murros 1980-luvulla*. Oikeushistoriallinen tutkimus (in Finnish—*Transformation of the Finnish financial markets in the 1980s*).

Kupp, M., & Anderson, J. (2007). Zopa: Web 2.0 Meets Retail Banking. *Business Strategy Review., 18*(3), 11–17.

Marmer, Harry S. (2016). *Lessons from Capital Market History—Popular Beliefs and Stylized Facts*. Retrieved December 1, 2019, from https://www.cfainstitute.org/en/research/cfa-magazine/2016/lessons-from-capital-market-history-expanded.

Mitchener, K. J. (2005). Bank Supervision, Regulation, and Instability During the Great Depression. *Journal of Economic History, 65*(1), 152–185.

Morel, P., Teschner, C., Paoli, P., Vialaron, F., Bertali, V., Mikroulis, K., & Lavrov, B. (2018). *Fintech in Capital Markets 2018: Boosting Productivity Through Technology Innovation*. The Boston Consulting Group. Retrieved December 1, 2019, from http://image-src.bcg.com/Images/BCG_2018_Capital_Markets_Fintech_White_Paper_March_16_tcm108-187378.pdf.

Mugasha, A. (2007). *The Law of Multi-Bank Financing—Syndicated Loans and the Secondary Loan Market*. Oxford: Oxford University Press.

Nietzsche, F. (1887). *On the Genealogy of Morality Friedrich—A Polemic*.

Nordea Bank Abp. (2018). *Nordea and Invesdor to Initiate Collaboration in Digital Financing for Finnish Growth Companies*. Press Release, May 30. Retrieved December 1, 2019, from https://www.nordea.com/fi/media/uutiset-ja-lehdistotiedotteet/press-releases/2018/05-30-07h00-nordea-and-invesdor-to-initiate-collaboration-in-digital-financing-for-finnish-growth-companies.html

Palmer, A. (2016). *Smart Money. How High-Stakes Financial Innovation is Reshaping Our World for the Better*. New York: Basic Books.

PWC. (2017). *Global Fintech Report 2017: Redrawing the Lines: FinTech's Growing Influence on Financial Services*. Retrieved December 1, 2019, from https://www.pwc.com/gx/en/industries/financial-services/assets/pwc-global-fintech-report-2017.pdf

Shneor, R., & Flåten, B.-T. (2015). Opportunities for Entrepreneurial Development and Growth through Online Communities, Collaboration, and Value Creating and Co-Creating Activities. In H. R. Kaufmann & S. M. R. Shams (Eds.), *Entrepreneurial Challenges in the 21st Century*. Basingstoke: Palgrave Macmillan.

Short, J. C., Ketchen, D. J., McKenny, A. F., et al. (2017). Research on Crowdfunding: Reviewing the (Very Recent) Past and Celebrating the Present. *Entrepreneurship Theory and Practice, 41*(2), 149–160.

SpaceTec Capital Partners GmbH. (2014). *Crowdfunding Innovative Ventures in Europe—The Financial Ecosystem and Regulatory Landscape*. Brussels: European Commission, Directorate-General of Communications Networks, Content & Technology.

Statista. (2019). *Internet of Things (IoT) Connected Devices Installed Base Worldwide from 2015 to 2025*. Statista Research Department, November 14. Retrieved December 1, 2019, from https://www.statista.com/statistics/471264/iot-number-of-connected-devices-worldwide/

Zestos, G. K. (2016). *The Global Financial Crisis—from US Subprime Mortgages to European Sovereign Debt*. London: Routledge.

Ziegler, T., Shneor, R., Wenzlaff, K., et al. (2019). *Shifting Paradigms—The 4th European Alternative Finance Benchmarking Report*. Cambridge, UK: Cambridge Centre for Alternative Finance.

11

The FinTech Industry: Crowdfunding in Context

Paul Griffiths

Introduction

The last three decades of the twentieth century witnessed the adoption of information and communications technology (ICT) by business corporations at an increasing rate and banks were leaders and trendsetters in this process. However, this leadership role of banking in the development of corporate ICT was lost in the second half of the first decade of this millennium. This chapter intends to shed light on the process that led to this. In so doing, it addresses the questions: Why did FinTech emerge as an industrial sector, independent of banking?

The author is strongly connected to the world of ICT transformation and of banking as an information intensive industry. He entered the business world as a young graduate during the mainframe-based, bespoke systems age; he then oriented his career towards management consulting, where he carried out and led technology-enabled business transformation

P. Griffiths (✉)
EM Normandie Business School, Métis Lab, Oxford, UK
e-mail: pgriffiths@em-normandie.co.uk

R. Shneor et al. (eds.), *Advances in Crowdfunding*,
https://doi.org/10.1007/978-3-030-46309-0_11

projects in the enterprise resource planning (ERP) era and the customer relationship management (CRM) and e-commerce solutions era; he replaced legacy core-banking systems by more modern client-server platform ones. On the academic side, he went back to university and enrolled on a doctoral programme that he researched into strategy-technology alignment in banks from which he graduated in 2005. He then became a full time academic and for the last three years has been researching the industrial organization of the FinTech sector. So, it is from this broad background that bridges across the practitioner and academic worlds in banking and technology that he sets out to address the above questions.

The rest of this chapter is organized in the following way. Section "Twentieth Century: ICT Emerging and Evolution" will give an overview, based on the author's professional experience, of the evolution of ICT in the last three decades of the twentieth century. From the specific perspective of banks, it will show that the financial sector in general, and banking in particular, was a driver of the ICT evolution during that period, until the mid-2000s. Section "Advent of the Tipping Point: Why Did Banks Lose Control?" will, based on current literature, identify three root-causes for banks to have lost control over the ICT agenda in the financial sector. In having lost control of the evolution of ICT, Section "A New Industrial Sector: The Emerging of FinTech" will give a framework to understand how the FinTech sector is structured based on a classification of the players according to the functional services they offer and the types of technology they apply. It will emphasize the role of crowdfunding in this landscape. Section "Discussion" will offer a discussion on the findings, and Section "Conclusions" will draw some conclusions.

Twentieth Century: ICT Emerging and Evolution

The last three decades of the twentieth century witnessed the adoption of information and communications technology (ICT) by business corporations at an increasing rate. During the 1970s and 1980s it was large systems developed and running on mainframe computers, with bespoke applications of narrow functional scope and weak integration with other functional applications. ICT was essentially about number-crunching large volumes of flat files, initially fed in by perforated cards and later in the period by magnetic tapes and discs. It was a domain restricted to the largest corporations, prominent amongst them the big banks, government institutions and universities. Systems were all corporate and managed by large IT departments with battalions of in-house programmers, analysts and systems engineers complemented by professional staff belonging to the large systems companies (that later called themselves 'integrators') such as IBM, Honeywell-Bull, ICL, Unysis. The technology platforms on which these corporate applications were developed were proprietary, with no convertibility from one vendor's platform to another vendor's: Client lock-in was the name of the game.

Democratization of ICT and its access to the smaller corporations and companies came in the mid-to-late 1980s and early 1990s with the advent of the mini-computer, the table-top personal computer, local area networks, handheld devices and, very importantly, the relational database. Democratization turned into revolution with the access to, and popularization of, the Internet.

The until then reigning mainframe computer and its centralized architecture ceded part of its domain to the distributed client-server architecture. The mainframe did not completely go away as those organizations who had them tended to keep the mainframe as database server due to its low cost per transaction for large volumes of transactions.

In parallel with client-server a significant change in the 1990s was the advent of the enterprise resource planning (ERP) systems with a new key player that with time became the dominant player in the corporate applications world, breaking the until then hegemony of the Anglo-Saxon companies: SAP from Waldorf, Germany. Being the four founders of SAP ex-IBM engineers, the first versions of their ERP ran on mainframes, but they really took off with their first client-server version that they called R/3. There were competing providers such as Oracle (with its Financials), JDEdwards, and PeopleSoft. This wave responded to a significant change in philosophy and the name of the game now had two dimensions: (a) it was all about packaged solutions, that is solutions that did not need code developed from scratch for each corporation, but that would be standard with the possibility of configuring parameters for limited adaptation to each company; and (b) integration was dominant over best-of-breed solutions, that is that now it was more important to have integration across functional applications than to have the best individual and isolated application.

Integrated packaged solutions brought with them another significant change: the concept of 'leading practices' in business processes. While the bespoke systems of the mainframe era were modelled in line with the processes of each company, in the ERP era the company would adapt its processes to the leading practices in-built in the solution. The implications of this is that the implementation of an ERP system would lead to significant changes in processes that, in turn, radically changed people's jobs. Thus, change management became an important component of implementation projects, with a focus on stakeholder management and training of people in entire processes, not just their specific task in a large process as was the case before.

Another change that came with the ERP wave is how projects were organized. The configuration of a systems project team was no longer a team of highly technical analysts and programmers, but people who were versed in business processes. The bulk of the work was not in coding but in parameter configuration and change management activities. So, the project teams were integrated mainly by non-technical systems people. ERP projects were not referred to as systems or technology projects anymore, but as business transformation projects enabled by technology.

Ripples of ERP in 1991–1993 became waves in 1994–1998 and turned into tsunamis approaching 2000 and the generalized policy of implementing 'vanilla' ERPs to sort the Y2K problem (this term was coined by Gartner Group and refers to the fact that the early mainframe systems had only two-digits for the year in dates, so it was suspected that they would all fail with the advent of the new millennium). With the advent and establishment of ERPs, came the reduction in the size of the IT departments in corporations. In effect, what adopting and implementing ERP meant was that the development of new functionalities to adapt to changes in the legal and tax environment, or to the need for new functionalities, was outsourced to the ERP vendors.

Of course, ERP were not the panacea that appears at first sight. Significant amount of coding to ensure integration with legacy systems or vertical industry-specific applications were still necessary. Although 'big bang' projects were highly promoted, common sense and risk management led to many projects being piloted and phased in, which meant that temporary interfaces had to be developed. And although the ERP vendors did produce their solutions with specific flavours for different industries, this was still not enough and corporations demanded having some of their vertical functionality developed outside of the ERP. For example, SAP achieved a highly competent footprint in the consumer packaged goods (CPG) and in the utilities industries, but never managed to produce convincing solutions for the core-banking functionalities despite having invested heavily in its solution for that sector. In other words, coding and development effort for integration did not entirely go away.

After the ERP binge running up to Y2K came the hangover in the form of a relative slowdown in the ERP market, but that did not stop the corporate-systems business as a whole. At around the time that ERP slowed down e-commerce and client relationship management (CRM) solutions emerged with force. E-commerce was the hottest product but it was severely impacted by 9/11 and the implosion of dot.com, recovering afterwards but growing at a more moderate pace.

With the slowdown of the ERP market and of the global economy after 9/11, came a consolidation within the corporate ICT solutions industry. SAP expanded its functionality into CRM, e-commerce and business intelligence through internal developments but later broke this tradition by entering the acquisitions path. Oracle, on the other hand, acquired PeopleSoft, Siebel (the leading CRM provider), JDEdwards, and many others, with significant pains in converting all these independent applications into a coherent, seamless offering to its clients. Oracle also moved into the hardware space by acquiring SUN Microsystems and SAP moved into Oracle's traditional realm, the database layer, through acquisition, too. Oracle articulated the concept of 'stack', from hardware to enterprise application, through operating systems, databases, integration layers and others. Oracle publicized itself as being able to offer the whole stack or just some of the layers.

The strong narrative of ERP vendors in terms of the importance of integration started weakening with the advent of intelligent middleware communications platforms that made unnecessary the dreaded point-to-point, or one-to-one, interface development. The nightmarish spaghetti-style interfaces that haunted CIOs and kept them awake at night, could now be substituted by simpler to understand middleware layers into which applications could easily be plugged in. Another highly significant concept that was materializing and coming of age at the turn of the century was the API (application programming interface—term that was coined decades before by Cotton and Greatorex 1968), a set of subroutine definitions, communications protocols and tools for building software. As will be seen in Section "Discussion", APIs would play an important role in the FinTech world.

The prior paragraphs give an overview of how corporate ICT in general developed from the 1970s to the early 2000s. The effect on business transformation of the adoption of ICT was highly significant, but nowhere more than in banking. Banking is an information-intensive industry, by which it is meant that differentiation comes exclusively from their intellectual capital and information or, in other words, their people, processes, relationships, and technology (Clayton and Waldron 2003; Griffiths 2003, 2005; McKeen and Smith 1996; OECD 2003, pp. 65–66).[1]

Driven by this dependence on information, banks played very much of a leading role in adoption and development of ICT, and the trajectory they followed differed from the mainstream CPG, retail, industrial products, and utilities corporations. Banks were clearly ahead of the pack in the early phase of that period, that of the bespoke systems running on mainframe computers. They were so heavily vested in those technologies and had such high numbers of transactions compared to the other industries, that they could not make the business case for moving to client-server. This, together with the fact that banking processes and applications had become highly sophisticated and business critical at an extreme, disincentivized the ERP vendors to develop vertical solutions for banking in the early days of ERP. Eventually SAP did propose a banking-solution, but its adoption was disappointingly slow and hardly ever with an end-to-end footprint but limited to fragmented pieces of the business.

Essentially, the largest banks are trapped, to this day, in their legacy systems.

Indeed, banks have adopted standard packaged solutions in many parts of their business, particularly the highly technical middle office, but the back office remains on the legacy systems. That is not to say that there have not been any client-server solutions for banks, but the more successful ones have been developed by specialized companies and not the leading ERP vendors. For example, Citi co-developed a client-server core banking system with a company called i-Flex in India, to implement in its smaller operations around the world (it later divested from i-Flex and a few years later i-Flex was absorbed by Oracle). So, essentially, banks did not participate in the ERP part of the prior narrative.

Notwithstanding their attachment to the legacy mainframe systems, banks did make some memorable breakthroughs, of which the ATM is a notable example. The generalization of ATMs in the 1980s enabled banks to give 24 × 7 service and significantly lower their banking transaction costs. This led the self-service kiosk technology that is still in the process of being adopted by other corporations in most other industries and government.

The ATM was followed by the waves of phone banking, home banking, and Internet banking. They all had in common pushing their clients out of the branch office and lowering further the costs of banking transactions and brought with them the need for omni-channel, that is the need to show the same face to the client independently of what channel the client chose to interact with her bank. So, the big banks that had departed from mainstream in the ERP age, took leadership again in the CRM phase. With this came the transformation of the banking branch office, that until the 1990s was a mini-bank in its own right with all functionalities in the branch. From the turn of the century banks took all the back-office and middle-office functionalities (e.g., bookkeeping and accounting, credit scoring, loan origination) from the branch to the head office, and most of the transactional activity out of the branch to remote channels. The branch office became far smaller and focused on value-added client services.

This narrative brings us to the mid-2000s when a tipping-point with several fronts was reached in the ICT world as will be developed in later sections. As has briefly been outlined in this section, ICT in business and government went from a rarity in the 1970s to complete infiltration and dissemination in the early 2000s. What this story is telling us is that during this period of study the world, or at least what we generally refer to as the Western world, almost unperceptively migrated from an industrial economy of predominantly tangible assets, to a knowledge one where intangible ones overwhelmingly predominate over the tangible. This is a new era where the application of ICT radically changed, and where banks lost their grip on its development.

The importance that ICT took on in the business world in general, but especially so in such an information-intensive sector as is banking, makes the research question stated in Section "Introduction" of the utmost relevance both to the practitioner and to the academic world. The process through which this happened is described in the next section.

Advent of the Tipping Point: Why Did Banks Lose Control?

Overview

A thorough review of the literature on the emerging of the FinTech sector was carried out—the emphasis was put on academic papers from 2012 onwards, as it is thought that before then would be too close to the events for clarity and that it has been found by Zavolokina et al. (2016, p. 9, fig. 1) that article publication numbers started growing that year. Based on that search this section identifies three root-causes that, although unrelated to each other, happened to coincide in time and lead banks to have lost control over the ICT agenda in the financial sector. The narrative in Section "Twentieth Century: ICT Emerging and Evolution" brings us to the mid-2000s and it announces that around that time several major events happened in the banking, the ICT world and society in general that led to the emerging of a new industrial sector that we nowadays call FinTech as a contraction of financial technology. The Basel Committee on Banking Supervision (BCBS) defines FinTech quite broadly as

> *[t]echnologically enabled financial innovation that could result in new business models, applications, processes or products with an associated material effect on financial markets and institutions and the provision of financial services.* (Claessens et al. 2018; Palazzeschi 2018)

So for BCBS FinTech is a form of innovation, but a very broad one at that, as it includes business models, applications, processes, or products. Dorfleitner et al. (2017) while admitting that there is no universally accepted definition of FinTech, take a more cautious approach and refrain from proposing a definition based on that while accepting that most companies in the FinTech sector share certain features, there are always enough exceptions to render them inadequate for producing a general definition. They opt to give a summary description of the different service domains of FinTechs, that they group in four: (a) financing, (b) asset management, (c) payments (in which they include cryptocurrencies), and (d) other FinTechs. The latter includes a hotchpotch of things such as insurance; search engines and comparison sites; technology, IT and infrastructure; plus 'other FinTechs'. Both approaches have limitation: BCBS stay at a conceptual level, and Dorfleitner et al. (2017) are far too broad and encompassing, which unsurprisingly gives place to so many exceptions.

In this chapter we will overcome those problems and propose and adopt a definition. We will overcome the BCBS limitation by defining FinTech as a company/organization, and we will narrow the service offering domain. We will limit the services to banking services, that is services where the core competence is managing credit risk, market risk, or banking operational risk. So, by FinTech in this chapter we understand *not the technology itself, but a digital technology-enabled entrepreneurial initiative that offers services to clients that would traditionally be considered within the domain of banks; or that are an innovative service in the natural business domain of banks; or that help banks develop their back-office processes.*

So, returning to the research question—*Why did FinTech emerge as an industrial sector, independent of banking?*—and to focus the mind we will address it by responding to four subquestions:

- What caused banks to lose leadership in the development of corporate ICT systems?
- What enabled the FinTech sector to emerge with such vitality in a business dominated by behemoths?
- What encouraged entrepreneurs to move into the service domain traditionally served by banks?
- How is the FinTech industry organized and where does crowdfunding fit in?

Arner et al. (2017) divide the co-evolution of finance and technology into three stages, namely:

(a) The *analogous age* prior to the late twentieth century,
(b) the *digitalization era* that goes from the late twentieth century until 2008, and
(c) the *diverging era* with the advent of new financial providers based on advanced technologies.

As is mostly the case, there is not a single cause for the advent of the tipping point that moved the evolution of finance and technology into the *diverging era*. This research identifies three unrelated causes that happened in the 2007–2008 point in time; it is quite probable that none of these causes alone would have caused such a disruption, but their coincidence in time enabled them to feed into each other and cause havoc in the banking industry. The first is the global financial crisis known as the Great Recession that is generally accepted as having been caused by the banking system and its greed in the mortgage segment. The second is several nearly simultaneous major breakthroughs in the technology sector that led to a drastic drop in entry barriers to the banking services sector. And finally, significant social changes with the coming of age of the millennial generation and their growing role in the business world and in relationship to banking. The rest of this section will flesh out these three causes.

The Effect of the Great Recession

The 2007–2008 recession put banks in the US, the UK, and several countries on the European continent at the brink of collapse leading to systemic failure which, in turn, led banking authorities in those markets to bail them out with public funds. Subsequent investigation into the events detected that banks accelerated their growth by taking on excessive risk that they partially transferred to other organizations through financial engineering devises concocted by their investment banking arms. In conjunction with this, the population became extremely critical of banks and there was general distrust in these institutions. These three factors led national authorities to react, and in many cases over-react, with the result of far more stringent banking regulations that caused great regulatory challenges to the banks (European Central Bank 2016; Haddad and Hornuf 2019; Kotarba 2016). These more stringent regulations worked in two directions (see Fig. 11.1).

The first was in the sense of demanding banks to significantly increase their regulatory capital so that never again would they need to be rescued with public money. Because as a result of the crisis capital was costly to acquire by banks, they reacted by reducing the denominator of the capital adequacy ratio, that is by reducing their exposure to risk. They did this by pruning those clients of higher-risk profile, and by letting go the less

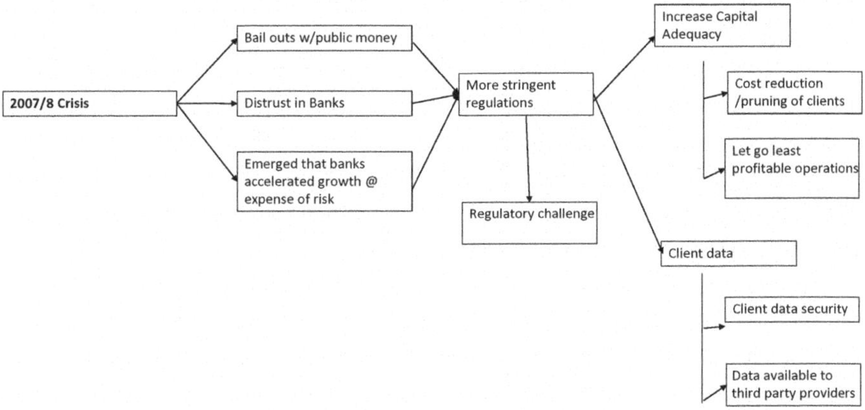

Fig. 11.1 The effect of the 2007–2008 crisis

profitable operations (e.g., certain products and geographic markets). The resulting reduction in scale in turn led them to embark on cost reduction initiatives (European Central Bank 2016; Kotarba 2016).

The other way in which more stringent regulations worked was related to client data. On the one hand the authorities put emphasis on client data security, and on the other hand bank regulators demanded that client data be made available to third-party providers in order to break the oligopoly of incumbent banks and increase competition in banking service (European Commission 2014, 2015; Tammas-Hastings 2017).

The Effect of Major Technological Breakthroughs

At the time the banks focused all their senses inside to cope with the regulatory changes that came because of the crisis, three key technology phenomena were happening. The first is incremental and refers to the continuing of Moore's law that translated into lower prices and thus giving more and more people access to devices (Lundstrom 2003; Waldrop 2016).

The second was the swift coming of age of Cloud computing with a change in mind-frame in the business community in the sense that moving from on-premise applications to cloud ones did not bring extra risks in terms of data security, and that adopting an on-demand model for technology appropriation had significant operational and balance sheet advantages (Ambrust et al. 2010; Rimal et al. 2009).

The third phenomenon was surely disruptive and is the advent of the first i-Phone and from there all the forms of smartphones that came after it. Moreover, the smartphone had the effect of enabling the development of social networks and, thus, the side effect of the advent of the data tsunami usually understated as Big Data (Barkhuus and Polichar 2011; Lee and Shin 2018; Smolan and Erwitt 2012).

These three phenomena had effect on what was to be the emerging FinTech sector, and on incumbent banks. The effects on these two groups initially developed quite independently of each other, but as will be seen opportunities for cross-fertilization emerged in later stages (EY 2018, p. 28; Gai et al. 2018; Lee and Shin 2018).

Looking at the FinTech sector first, it is found that the conjunction of the three technological phenomena had the effect of both lowering entry barriers for small new players to offer components of financial services and giving many more people access to devices and thus become potential clients for these new entrants to the financial services market offering. As opposed to entrepreneurial technology-based start-ups in other sectors, in general these new players in the FinTech sector did not have cash to burn at outrageous rates, so they developed two characteristics. On the one hand they are limited in the scope of their service, and on the other they take incremental opportunities in relatively mature markets that offer them quick cash-flow. These two characteristics translate into them focusing on niche but profitable parts of the incumbent banks' business, causing strong reaction from the banks who denounce them as avoiding regulations to take the icing of their cake (Lacasse et al. 2016).

The conjunction of taking the more profitable pieces of the banks' business and being able to serve many more people who were then possessing digital devices, converted into great opportunities for the emerging FinTechs. But their increasing visibility and the protests of the incumbent bankers led banking regulators to observe this new sector and extend at least part of the regulations to them.

From the perspective of incumbent banks, these three technological phenomena and their derivations (i.e., social networks and Big Data) had a significant impact on their own operations. Bank clients were demanding new channels such as mobile and generating massive data flows that offered significant potential if properly exploited. However, they also posed unsurmountable challenges in terms of cybersecurity, of data analytics issues and of data visualization complexities to incumbent banks that were constrained by their legacy systems as described above. This led the banks to start seeing FinTechs as potential enablers for their own processes in this new era of financial services (EY 2018; Gai et al. 2018).

Particularly on continental Europe where FinTechs were being funded more by banks than venture capital (Lee and Shin 2018), risk management challenges emerged quickly and were addressed by regulators which erected barriers for FinTechs to operate as independent client-facing service providers, but opened opportunities in the banks that were funding them. So, in general, the antagonistic atmosphere between incumbent

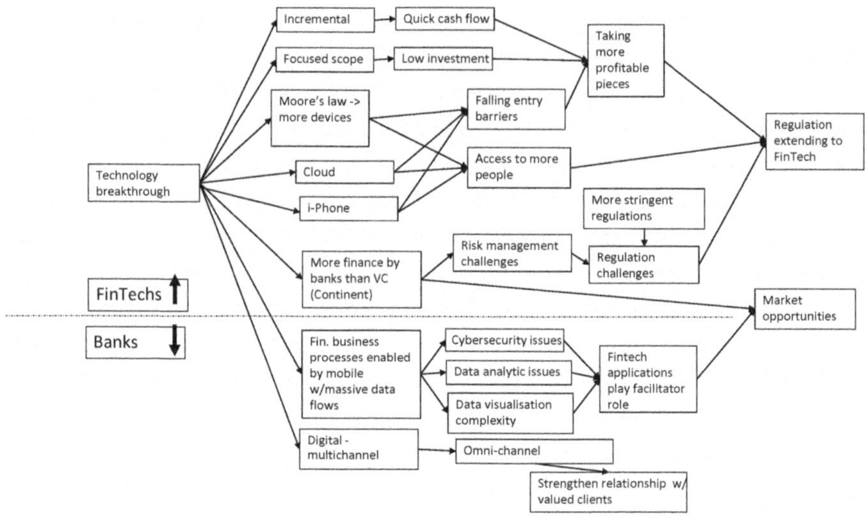

Fig. 11.2 The effect of major technological breakthroughs on FinTech and banks

banks and FinTechs that prevailed in the early post-2008 years gave way to a more collaborative spirit between both sectors. This effect of the technological breakthroughs is depicted graphically in Fig. 11.2.

The Effect of Social Changes

At the time of the financial crisis and the advent of the technological phenomena described above, the business world was going through major social transformations in terms of power as depicted by Naim (2013), of the changes in mindset that came with Generation Y taking a growing role in the workforce and of the advent of social entrepreneurs and entrepreneurship.

The Generation Y are avid adopters of mobile banking as long as it is easy to use and it poses no excessive risks in terms of data security. Both these conditions were hard to meet for incumbent bankers due to their legacy platforms, but straight forward for the FinTechs. On the other hand, due to the capital constraints mentioned above banks put effort into developing CRM processes and solutions that enabled them to strengthen their relationship with their 'valued' (i.e., the older more affluent) customers, and let go their less profitable and higher risk ones, as the Generation Y were seen to be. This opened a segment of great potential to the FinTechs (Boonsiritomachai and Pitchayadejanant 2017; Lee and Shin 2018).

In parallel with the above and especially in the Anglo-Saxon world, there emerged a new breed of what were to be called social entrepreneurs whose projects did not pursue a predominantly financial objective and thus were unfit to be assessed in terms of the banks' traditional credit scoring criteria. This new breed of entrepreneurs resort to alternative finance sources such as crowdfunding so became another market opportunity for FinTechs (Kotarba 2016).

On continental Europe it was found that while people do not trust banks much more than in the Anglo-Saxon world, they have less incentive to leave their banks and trust FinTechs even less than banks. So that becomes a barrier for FinTechs on the continent.

The effects of social changes are depicted and summarized in Fig. 11.3.

As a result of these three external forces (i.e., the Great Recession and subsequent regulatory changes, the technology breakthroughs, and the social changes) acting nearly simultaneously, banks lost control of the

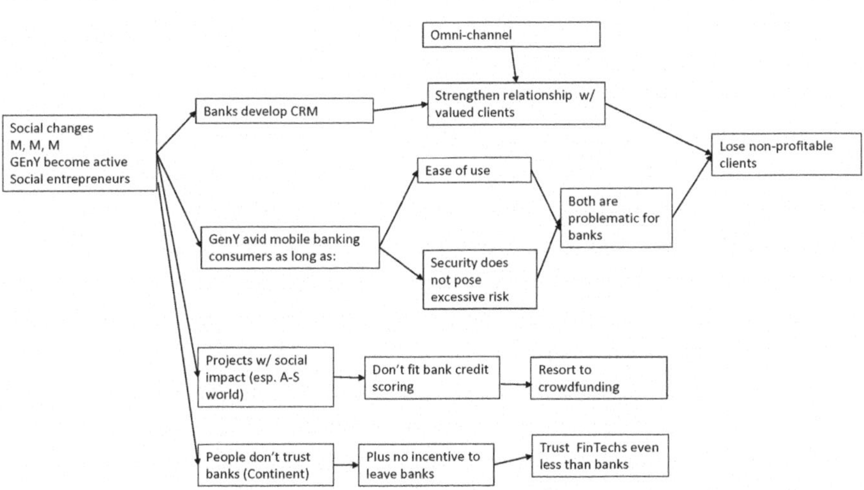

Fig. 11.3 Effects of social changes on banks and FinTech

evolution of ICT and left the door wide open for technology entrepreneurs to set up independently and eat away at the icing of their cake. The next section gives an overview of the industrial organization of this new sector.

A New Industrial Sector: The Emerging of FinTech

As mentioned above the FinTech sector is quite different from other technology-driven entrepreneurial or start-up sectors in the sense that it did not access massive funding and therefore its companies had to be focused in terms of service scope, and it did not produce great new markets but rather served extant markets that were until then poorly or underserved by banks. While, due to the latter, initially the relationship between traditional banks and FinTechs was notoriously antagonistic, with the passage of time banks realized that their constraints from legacy systems would obstruct them entering the digital era, so started to see FinTechs as possible collaborators to help overcome those barriers. This is particularly so in the data-oriented, security and privacy, and compliance spaces (Duan and Da 2012; Gai et al. 2018; Roumani et al. 2016).

Growth of the FinTech sector in terms of investment is literally exponential, going from $1.8 billion in 2010 to $19 billion in 2015 according to some sources (Citi 2016 cited by Leong et al. 2017) or from $1.5 billion in 2010 to $22 billion in 2015 according to others (Shuttlewood et al. 2016) and there are indications of steep growth in 2016 (Lee and Shin 2018). Within this context, seven banking-service areas emerge as the domains where FinTechs carry out their offering. These are: alternative finance, transactions, investment markets, banking back office, financial inclusion, cryptocurrencies, and business partner integration.

Alternative finance refers to services that supersede the traditional lending function of banks. They include personal finance, consumer finance, small and medium enterprise lending, and prominent in this category is *crowdfunding* in its four formats: reward-based, donation-based, equity-based and loan-based. Examples of reward-based crowdfunding companies include Kickstarter, Indiegogo, CrowdFunder, and RocketHub; of donation-based are GoFundMe, GiveForward, and FirstGiving; of equity-based crowdfunding companies are AngelList, Early Shares, and Crowdcube; finally, of loan-based crowdfunding companies are Funding Circle and Cumplo (Lee and Shin 2018; Shneor and Munim 2019 citing Ziegler et al. 2018).

Transactions refers to one of the most active areas of FinTech as are payments and remittances. These two areas were traditionally controlled by banks but are now giving way—in the case of payments by offering layers of service overlaying those of traditional banks and biting away at parts of the fees that banks charge in this space. In the case of remittances, it is about offering channels that circumvent bank services and fees altogether (Lee and Shin 2018).

Investment markets include services such as equity financing, retail investment, institutional investment, fund management and crowdfunding as an opportunity for investing (Lee and Shin 2018; Shneor and Munim 2019).

Banking back office is about FinTechs supplying banks agile services such as banking infrastructure, financial security services, identity verification, compliance, business tools, financial research, and energy efficiency in regard to achieving green finance. Prominent amongst these are RegTech, a flavour of FinTech aimed at helping banks comply with the demands of regulators and assist banking supervisors in keeping track of the banks under their watch (Gai et al. 2018; Puschmann 2017; Tammas-Hastings 2017).

Financial inclusion means reaching out to the unbanked and offering financial services at an extremely low cost and fill a gap that banks have never tackled, with well thought through and low-cost service offerings; micro-finance is prominent amongst this category (Lacasse et al. 2016).

Cryptocurrencies emerged as an initiative to circumvent banks altogether in the payments space but have not materialized as such; up to now they have served more as investment than payment instruments, and with doubtful outcomes at that. However, the distributed ledger technology that underlies them could be of application in many other areas such as trading and 'smart contracts' (Chen 2018; Hawlitschek et al. 2018).

Business partner integration is about FinTech offering services that bridge across the traditional offerings of banks and of other sectors with large business-to-consumer operations, such as telecommunications, retailers and airlines (Kumar et al. 2006; Rosingh et al. 2001; Schmitt and Gautam 2016).

To deliver these services FinTechs will apply one or multiple emerging technologies such as the DANCE acronym (Data, Algorithm, Networks, Cloud, Exponential) proposed by McAfee and Brynjolfsson (2017) and others including mobile, distributed ledgers, bioinformatics and behavioural biometrics, robots, all-in-one smartcards, and others.

It is helpful to understand the industry to present this in the form of a double entry table and map the FinTech companies onto the cells of this matrix (see Table 11.1).

The rest of the chapters in this book will develop the contents that will fit into the columns under alternative finance and investment markets of this framework. Those are the two service domains in the FinTech I/O framework where crowdfunding plays a key role. In the first case in its funding role, and in the second in its investment opportunities role. Just as an example of how this works, Table 11.2 reproduces the contents of one cell in this framework: The cell corresponding to Alternative Finance as a service domain, and data analytics and the exploiting of Big Data as a predominant enabling technology for those services.

It should be noted that in the Table 11.2 there are the four kinds of crowdfunding companies described above, but there are also other companies such as Touch Bank, which is a retail bank, or Retail Capital, which lends through partnership with banks, and do not conform to the crowdfunding principles but nevertheless are FinTechs in the alternative finance space.

With all this information in mind, the next section will extract some insights into how the FinTech sector emerged and evolved, and it will address the research question.

Discussion

Many interesting insights emerge from this analysis of the FinTech sector, of which four will be mentioned in this section. The first is that technological breakthroughs are all important but are only a necessary but not a sufficient condition for the advent of FinTech. Cultural-based influences

Table 11.1 The FinTech I/O framework

	Alternative Finance: Profitable Finance; Consumer banking; SME lending; Crowd-funding	*Transactions*: Payments; Remittances	*Investment Markets*: Equity financing; Retail investment Institutes. Investment; Crowd-funding	*Back Office*: Banking Infrastructure: Fin. Security; Business tools; Financial research; Regtech	*Financial Inclusion*: Reaching out: Fees and Profitability; Micro-finance	*Cryptocurrencies*: Payment or investment instrument? ICO.	*Business Partner integration*: Telcos, Retail, Airlines
<u>D</u>ata: Exploiting 'Big Data'							
<u>A</u>lgorithms: AI and Cognitive Computing							
<u>N</u>etworks: 5G, faster data accumulation							
<u>C</u>loud: Lower entry barriers; local vs central computation							
<u>E</u>xponential improvement in digital h/w; Moore's law effect							
Mobile							
Robotics							
Bioinformatics & behavioural biometrics							
Distributed Ledgers							
All-in-One smartcards							
VR, interactive & AR							

Table 11.2 Sample from the repository of FinTechs

Company's name	Country	Activity	Notes	Website
Lendingkart	India	Business loan for small business	Co-lending with banks	www.lendingkart.com
KredX	India	Business loan for small- and medium-sized businesses	Investors/applied for an Non-Banking Financial Company (NBFC) licence	www.kredx.com
Wefinance	USA	Lending to particular by funding from particulars		www.wefinance.com
Upstart	USA	Bring together high-potential borrowers and investors	Calculate credit score based on borrower's background	www.upstart.com
SoFi	USA	P2P lending for students		www.sofi.com
Rocket Mortgage	USA	Loans and mortgages	Focus on millennials	www.rocketmortgage.com
C2fo	UK	Short-term loans		C2fo.com
Zopa	UK	P2P lending	Founded in 2005, one of the first sites directly bringing together borrowers and savers, cutting out financial institutions from the lending process (NYT)	www.zopa.com
Touch bank	Russia	Retail banking	Online credits, loans, card, account management without paperwork, saving management	www.touchbank.com

(continued)

Table 11.2 (continued)

Company's name	Country	Activity	Notes	Website
Smart asset	USA	Advices throughout database (find best credit, loan solution among all propositions in the market	Tax, retirement, bank, account comparison tool	Smartasset.com
Simple finance	Russia	Micro lending	Asset-based loans, unsecure loans	www.ewdn.com

have also been essential and probably the most important was the Millennium generation taking their place in the labour and consumer markets. The incumbent bankers disregarded them to focus on more affluent baby-boomers, particularly in asset management services. What the banks did not anticipate is that Millennials are not individually affluent yet but that they are on the way to being the largest demographic group and as a group they hold over $1 trillion in wealth (Pitchbook).[2] This group is not interested in investing in active management funds and having costly financial advisors; they want passive management funds that can be monitored through their mobile phone. What is even of more impact is that the older generations learn to trust technologies that are embraced by the Millennials, so disregarding this generation exposes them to losing their senior relations.

A second insight is that according to some sources of the seven service categories of FinTechs, the most highly funded (Venture Scanner 2019) are lending to consumers and to businesses, (meaning small- and medium-sized enterprises, SMEs). Most of this is based on the peer-to-peer business model thus constructing links between borrowers and investors. Some of the FinTechs in this space are co-lending with banks and loan criteria vary across companies, but most want to avoid the classic credit scoring criterion in favour of seeking the highest potential borrowers and the most interesting personal projects. Based on keeping a low operating cost, these FinTechs can offer lower rates to borrowers and higher returns to lenders or investors. This insight is saying that crowdfunding is in a highly relevant position within FinTechs.

The third insight, as anticipated, is that banks have departed from their original antagonistic view of FinTechs to start finding potential in them as start-up venture opportunities and, more importantly, as resources for internal projects to make their operation more responsive, secure, compliant and efficient (EY 2018; Lee and Shin 2018). Typically, they look at FinTechs to help them reduce operational costs, provide more personalized services through data, and respond to customer behaviour changes. As a result of this, FinTechs have extended their role from retail customer facing to the back office or middle office of banks. Although it is mentioned above that alternative lending is the most funded domain, this can be contested based on the massive resources that are increasingly going into security and privacy initiatives (Gai et al. (2018), citing Gartner, says that the cybersecurity market reached $75 billion in 2015 and is projected to reach $170 billion by 2020; a significant share of this will go to financial services).

Finally, it has been said that in the UK, following the 2007–2008 financial crisis and the tarnished image with which established banks came out of it, the regulators proactively promoted FinTechs in the hope that challenger banks would emerge from them. And in effect this did happen as several challenger banks have emerged (e.g., Monzo, Metro) but their real impact on the market concentration has been marginal with the five big banks still firmly in control. What is even more disappointing is that some of these challenger banks have had to have their business models closely scrutinized by the banking supervisors under suspicion of adopting aggressive lending practices and even manipulating of balance sheets to avoid increased demand for fresh regulatory capital (FT 2019). It is hoped that the implementation of open banking supported by regulations such as Payment Services Directive 2 (PSD2) will enable FinTechs and the most agile and forward-looking mainstream banks to offer more API-enabled services and thus change the oligopolistic structure of the banking business. Traditional banks will not go away but they will most likely become a component of a more fragmented industry in the form of a network of hyperspecialists (Malone et al. 2011).

This evolution of the evolving relationship of banks and FinTechs is summarized in Fig. 11.4.

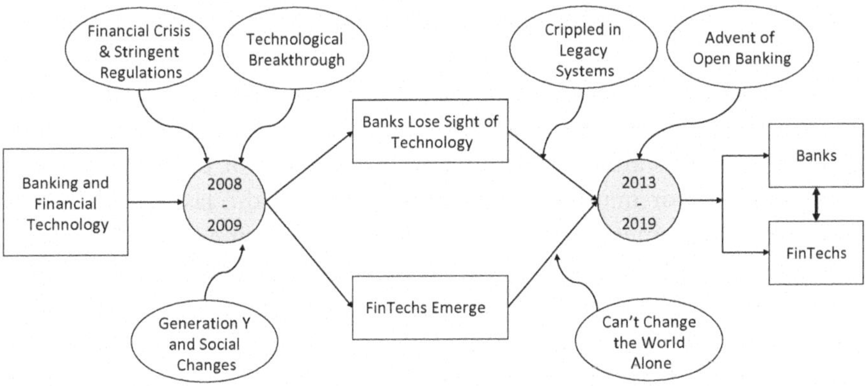

Fig. 11.4 Evolution of the relationship between banks and FinTechs

So, returning to the research question, *Why did FinTechs emerge as an industrial sector, independent of banking?* A combination of factors happening nearly simultaneously led banks to get distracted from the transformations that were happening around them. Just as the banks were looking inside their own organization to deal with the severe regulatory changes being imposed upon them as a result of the Great Recession, bankers did not perceive the importance that new technologies such as the smartphone were having, nor did they understand the cultural changes that were starting to happen with the coming of age of Gen-Y.

The effect of the smartphone and thus accessibility to devices of a mass market of relatively low income individuals, combined with the lowering of barriers to entry into the banking business of agile entrepreneurs that came with the maturing of cloud computing, enabled FinTech companies to roar into activity.

What encouraged entrepreneurs to move into the multiple banking services domains was the fact that they could detect a great number of underserved banking customers, with a young mindset, to whom they could approach with a narrow service offering driven by technology. That the offering was narrow meant that investment in developing application was relatively low; and the fact that the market was already there meant that cash flow would start coming in quickly. The combination of these two factors meant that the amount of working capital required was relatively low.

The fact that the FinTech companies developed relatively focused service offerings within a far reaching service industry as is banking, and that their services are enabled by a large spectrum of technologies that either emerged or matured in the second half of the last decade when this sector was emerging, has led the FinTech sector to encompass a large number of companies with quite different configurations. The framework presented in Table 11.1 as a double-entry table, with seven service-offering domains in one dimension, and over ten technology categories in the other, helps to understand how the sector is organized and where each company plays.

Conclusions

In summary this research has found that, distracted by the 2007–2008 crisis and its immediate regulatory changes, the banking industry lost sight of the technological breakthroughs and social changes that were happening around it. As a result, after decades of having been a driver and leader for technological change, the industry left windows wide open for nimble companies based on ground-breaking technologies to emerge and 'eat its lunch'.

It is extraordinary that in such a closely regulated industry as banking, these FinTech entrepreneurs could have found gaps in regulations to eat away at some of the most profitable icing on the banking industry's cake. It is also extraordinary that in such a short period of time FinTechs could open into so many different business domains, enabled by the emerging of such an unprecedented number of different game-changing technologies.

The FinTechs managed this feat with little capital in comparison with the deep pockets of the institutions they were outpacing. They achieved this precisely by focusing on niches where the market was already there and waiting for a solution. So, in a way, it was more a pull by social changes than a push by the FinTechs (this is quite different from other areas of technology-based entrepreneurship where the pioneers created a market). However, FinTechs should not become complacent as regulation is creeping in. Approximately one-third of the FinTech business in the Eurozone is not regulated, but going forward, FinTechs should count on the fact that banking regulations will move further into their space.

Crowdfunding and other forms of alternative finance occupy a position of relevance within the FinTech sector and together have the greatest fraction of investment as compared to the other six business domains included in the FinTech industrial organization framework. Clearly banks have great difficulty in financing the SME segment, where its traditional credit scoring techniques are not appropriate. There is, thus, a promising opportunity for crowdfunding to grow in this space.

Banks have found it hard to keep up as selecting a new technology that will drive its processes is no minor decision for a bank and in times when so many technologies are emerging, it is hard to predict which will be the winning ones. This is not a level field: Clearly banks as incumbents have far more to lose than FinTechs so the question we need to ask ourselves is this: Do extant strategy-technology alignment models apply to banks in times of so much disruption? Banks need to address this issue.

This review of the FinTech sector as a framework to give context to the theme of crowdfunding that is the focus of the rest of this book, is necessarily generic and bridges across the different markets. But clearly the process of emerging of the FinTech sector and the evolution of its relationship to banks, as synthesized in the process described in Fig. 11.4, will change from market to market. As a result of the stage of economic development, the regulatory environment, the quality of the technological infrastructure, the different attitudes towards the financial sector, and many others, the FinTech sector has evolved differently in each market. There is scope to do comparative analyses of this evolution between markets and thus arrive at a more granular knowledge on its evolution.

Finally, another question for future research is why, despite the advent of the FinTech sector with all its diverse set of players, has the market structure in terms of market control by a small number of traditional players, remained essentially unchanged. Will open banking be the answer to this problem?

Notes

1. OECD (2003, pp. 65–66) finds that financial intermediation organizations '*are intensive users of information and thus have the greatest scope to benefit from ICT*'.
2. https://pitchbook.com/news/articles/blend-becomes-latest-fintech-startup-to-bank-a-mega-round-in-2019

References

Ambrust, M., Fox, A., Griffith, R., Joseph, A. D., Katz, R., Konwinski, A., Lee, G., Patterson, D., Rabkin, A., Stoica, I., & Zaharia, M. (2010, April). A View of Cloud Computing. *Communications of the ACM, 53*(4), 50–58. https://doi.org/10.1145/1721654.1721672.

Arner, D. W., Barberis, J., & Buckley, R. P. (2017). FinTech, RegTech, and the Reconceptualization of Financial Regulation. *Northwestern Journal of International Law and Business, 37*(3), 371–382.

Barkhuus, L., & Polichar, V. E. (2011, August). Empowering Through Seamfulness: Smart Phones in Everyday Life. *Journal Personal and Ubiquitous Computing, 15*(6), 629–639. https://doi.org/10.1007/s00779-010-0342-4.

Boonsiritomachai, W., & Pitchayadejanant, K. (2017). Determinants Affecting Mobile Banking Adoption by Generation Y Based on the UTAUTM Modified by the TAM Concept. *Kasetsart Journal of Social Science*. https://doi.org/10.1016/j.kjss.2017.10.005.

Chen, Y. (2018). Blockchain Tokens and the Potential Democratization of Entrepreneurship and Innovation. *Business Horizons, 61*(4), 567–575.

Claessens, S., Frost, J., Turner, G., & Zhu, F. (2018). Fintech Credit Markets Around the World: Size, Drivers and Policy Issues. *BIS Quarterly Review,* September, pp. 29–49.

Clayton, T., & Waldron, K. (2003). *E-Commerce Adoption and Business Impact, A Progress Report, in Economic Trends, ICT and Economic Growth: Evidence from OECD Countries, Industries and Firms*. OECD Publications.

Cotton, I. W., & Greatorex, F. S. (1968). Data Structures and Techniques for Remote Computer Graphics. *Proceedings of the AFIPS '68 (Fall, Part I) Joint Computer Conference*, December 9–11, San Francisco, California, pp. 533–544. https://doi.org/10.1145/1476589.1476661.

Dorfleitner, G., Hornuf, L., Schmtt, M., et al. (2017). Definition of FinTech and Description of the FinTech Industry. In G. Dorfleitner, L. Hornuf, M. Schmitt, & M. Weber (Eds.), *FinTech in Germany*. Cham: Springer International Publishing.

Duan, L., & Da, X. (2012). Business Intelligence for Enterprise Systems: A Survey. *IEEE Transactions on Industrial Informatics Information, 8*(3), 679–687.

European Central Bank. (2016). *ECB Banking Supervision: SSM Priorities 2016* [online]. Retrieved from https://www.bankingsupervision.europa.eu/ecb/pub/pdf/publication_supervisory_priorities_2016.en.pdf?024a0072fe923441556e5bba7251dd6d.

European Commission. (2014). Investment Services and Regulated Markets (MiFID 1 & MiFID 2). Retrieved June 2, 2019, from https://ec.europa.eu/info/law/markets-financial-instruments-mifid-ii-directive-2014-65-eu_en.

European Commission. (2015). Payment Services (PSD 2)—Directive (EU) 2015/2366. Retrieved June 2, 2019, from https://ec.europa.eu/info/law/payment-services-psd-2-directive-eu-2015-2366_en.

EY. (2018). *ASEAN FinTech Census 2018*. Retrieved June 19, 2019, from https://www.ey.com/Publication/vwLUAssets/EY-asean-fintech-census-2018/$FILE/EY-asean-fintech-census-2018.pdf.

Financial Times. (2019). *BoE Raises Alert Over 'Aggressive' New Lenders,* June 16.

Gai, K., Qiu, M., & Sun, X. (2018). A Survey on Fintech. *Journal of Network and Computer Applications, 103*, 262–273.

Griffiths, P. D. R. (2003). *A Literature Review: Converting Information Technology Investments into Shareholder Value in Financial Services Organisations*. Henley Working Papers, HWP 0315, ISBN. 1861811780.

Griffiths, P. D. R. (2005). *The Application of Market Power Theory as a Value Driver for Information Technology Investment Decisions: A Study of Six Chilean Banks*. Doctoral thesis, Henley Management College/Brunel University.

Haddad, C., & Hornuf, L. (2019). The Emergence of the Global Fintech Market: Economic and Technological Determinants. *Small Business Economics, 53*(1), 81–105.

Hawlitschek, F., Notheisen, B., & Teubner, T. (2018). The Limits of Trust-Free Systems: A Literature Review on Blockchain Technology and Trust in the Sharing Economy. *Electronic Commerce Research and Applications, 29*, 50–63.

Kotarba, M. (2016). New Factors Inducing Changes in the Retail Banking Customer Relationship Management (CRM) and Their Exploration by the Fintech Industry. *Foundations of Management, 8*. ISSN 2080-7279. https://doi.org/10.1515/fman-2016-0006.

Kumar, A., Nair, A., Parsons, A., & Urdapiletta, E. (2006). *Expanding Bank Outreach through Retail Partnerships: Correspondent Banks in Brazil.* World Bank Working Papers, https://doi.org/10.1596/978-0-8213-6702-5

Lacasse, R. M., Lambert, B. A., Osmani, E., Couture, C., Roy, N., Sylvain, J., & Nadeau, F. (2016). A Digital Tsunami: Fintech and Crowdfunding. *Proceedings of International Scientific Conference on Digital Intelligence*, April 4–6, UQAR, Quebec, Canada.

Lee, I., & Shin, Y. J. (2018). Fintech: Models, Investment Decisions, and Challenges. *Business Horizons, 61*, 35–46. https://doi.org/10.1016/j.bushor.2017.09.003.

Leong, C., Tan, B., Xiao, X., Tan, F. T. C., & Sun, Y. (2017). Nurturing a Fintech Ecosystem: The Case of a Youth Microloan Startup in China. *International Journal of Information Management, 37*, 92–97.

Lundstrom, M. (2003). Moore's Law Forever? *Science, 299*(5604), 210–211. https://doi.org/10.1126/science.1079567.

Malone, T. W., Laubacher, R., & Johns, T. (2011). The Age of Hyperspecialisation. *Harvard Business Review, 89*, 56–65.

McAfee, A., & Brynjolfsson, E. (2017). *Machine Platform Crowd: Harnessing our Digital Future.* New York: Norton.

McKeen, J. D., & Smith, H. A. (1996). *Assessing the Value of Information Technology: A Focus on Banking and Insurance.* Working Paper #94-27, Queens University.

Naim, M. (2013). *The End of Power.* New York: Basic Books.

OECD. (2003). *ICT and Economic Growth: Evidence from OECD Countries, Industries and Firms.* OECD Publications.

Palazzeschi, E. (2018) *Fintech: Why and What Is in the Regulatory Pipe.* Presentation at Fintech Conference, EM-Normandie & Oxford Fintech & Smart Law Society, March 15.

Puschmann, T. (2017). Fintech. *Business & Information Systems Engineering, 59*(1), 69–76. https://doi.org/10.1007/s12599-017-0464-6.

Rimal, B. P., Choi, E., & Lumb, I. (2009). A Taxonomy and Survey of Cloud Computing Systems. *Proceedings of the 2009 Fifth International Joint Conference on INC, IMS and IDC*, August 25–27, Seoul. https://doi.org/10.1109/NCM.2009.218.

Rosingh, W., Seale, A., & Osborn, D. (2001). *Why Banks and Telecoms Must Merge to Surge.* Strategy+Business (Technical & Innovation, Q2 2001, Issue 23). Retrieved June 22, 2019, from https://www.strategy-business.com/article/17163?gko=4cda6.

Roumani, Y., Nwankpa, J., & Roumani, Y. (2016). Examining the Relationship Between Firm's Financial Records and Security Vulnerabilities. *International Journal of Information Management, 36*(6), 987–994.

Schmitt, M. G., & Gautam, T. (2016). Transformation of Banking Institutions: Comparing Germany and India. In H. Ellermann, P. Kreutter, & W. Messner (Eds.), *The Palgrave Handbook of Managing Continuous Business Transformation*, (pp. 151–171). Palgrave-Macmillan.

Shneor, R., & Munim, Z. H. (2019). Reward Crowdfunding Contribution as Planned Behavior: An Extended Framework. *Journal of Business Research, 103*, 56–70.

Shuttlewood, P., Volin, M., & Wozniak, L. (2016). Global fintech investment growth continues in 2016 driven by Europe and Asia, accenture study finds. https://newsroom.accenture.com/news/global-fintech-investment-growth-continues-in2016-driven-by-europe-and-asia-accenture-study-finds.htm.

Smolan, R., & Erwitt, J. (2012). *The Human Face of Big Data*. Sausalito, CA: Against All Odds Productions.

Tammas-Hastings, D. (2017) The Exploding Popularity of RegTech. *LSE Review*. Retrieved December 12, 2018, from http://blogs.lse.ac.uk/business-review/2017/07/07/the-exploding-popularity-of-regtech/.

Venture Scanner. (2019). Fintech Q1 Update [Online]. Retrieved June 3, 2019, from http://insights.venturescanner.com/category/financial-technology/.

Waldrop, M. M. (2016). The Chips Are Down for Moore's Law: The Semiconductor Industry Will Soon Abandon Its Pursuit of Moore's Law. *Nature, 530*, 144–147. https://doi.org/10.1038/530144a.

Zavolokina, L., Dolata, M., & Schwabe, G. (2016). The FinTech Phenomenon: Antecedents of Financial Innovation Perceived by the Popular Press. *Financial Innovation, 2*(1), 1–16.

Ziegler, T., Shneor, R., Garvey, K., Wenzlaff, K., Yerolemou, N., Zhang, B., & Hao, R. (2018). *Expanding Horizons: The 3rd European Alternative Finance Industry Report*. Cambridge: Cambridge Centre for Alternative Finance.

Part III

Crowdfunding in Geographic Context

12

Crowdfunding in China: Turmoil of Global Leadership

Liang Zhao and Yuanqing Li

Introduction

Crowdfunding is the practice of funding a project or venture by raising small amounts of money from the public via the Internet. Since the establishment of the first crowdfunding platform ("Demohour") in China in 2011, crowdfunding has gained substantial popularity in the country. However, the growth of crowdfunding in China is still at early stage compared to other markets and overall market potential.

The development of crowdfunding in China can be divided into three stages. First, a "Rudimentary stage" (2011–2013), when the number of platforms and the scale of fundraising was small, and the number of

L. Zhao (✉)
School of Business and Law, University of Agder, Kristiansand, Norway
e-mail: liang.zhao@uia.no

Y. Li
Brennan School of Business, Dominican University, River Forest, IL, USA
e-mail: yli@dom.edu

R. Shneor et al. (eds.), *Advances in Crowdfunding*,
https://doi.org/10.1007/978-3-030-46309-0_12

crowdfunding platforms grew slowly. Second, a "Hyper-growth stage" (2014–2015), when the number of platforms and the scale of fundraising began to increase rapidly, and when the scale of transactions expanded rapidly. And, most recently, a third "Cautious development stage" (2016–present), where due to the stricter supervision of alternative finance, the number of platforms has decreased and so did the volumes of funds raised. Most of the crowdfunding platforms were waiting for the official regulatory policy before restarting/expanding their business. Accordingly, the growth rate of the crowdfunding industry has been slowed down.

Based on past developments, the Chinese crowdfunding market has carried out some favourable explorations in crowdfunding practice. Specifically, crowdfunding project initiators have found out the power of social network interaction in boosting crowdfunding success. Some integrated crowdfunding platforms have been transferred into vertical platforms in order to strengthen competitive advantages. For example, some comprehensive crowdfunding platforms have transformed into specialized crowdfunding platforms. And, furthermore, Chinese crowdfunding practitioners have started to explore ways to educate the public and potential investors.

In term of market size and market balance, despite being the largest in the world (Ziegler et al. 2019), the Chinese crowdfunding industry exhibits slower growth rates. The slower growth rate is mainly subject to the following problems: Firstly, the policy and legal environment of crowdfunding in China are still immature and under development, and there are still some frictions between the crowdfunding innovation and profit models and the current laws and regulations (e.g. Lin 2017; You 2017). Secondly, the Chinese-style crowdfunding credit system lacks a degree of credibility. Thirdly, intellectual property in crowdfunding projects is insufficiently protected. Lastly, Chinese society in general has limited understanding of crowdfunding and there are many misunderstandings about its use and associated risks and benefits. Accordingly, if the above problems can be solved, the Chinese crowdfunding industry is expected to achieve and regain rapid development in a standardized, regulated, and healthy way.

The purpose of the current chapter is thus to review the landscape of the crowdfunding industry in China, with a focus on providing meaningful insights from this unique and important market. We first provide extensive descriptions of different crowdfunding models in China. Based on that, we then generate context insights in different models respectively. Next, the current regulations of different crowdfunding models in China is presented and discussed. Then, through an extensive literature review, main crowdfunding research related to the Chinese market are exhibited and summarized. Finally, this chapter highlights the implications for practice and research, as well as mentioning potential future research directions.

Volumes by Models and Context Insights

As crowdfunding has different operating models, it is necessary to take all the main crowdfunding models into consideration in order to properly capture the comprehensive crowdfunding landscape in China. In this section, we report data and analysis for the four main crowdfunding models (reward-based, equity-based, loan-based, and donation-based) in China and then provide special insights of each model respectively.

Reward-Based Crowdfunding

Reward-based crowdfunding is identified as individuals contributing comparatively small amounts of money to crowdfunding projects in return for different kinds of non-monetary reward (e.g. physical products, services), while accepting a certain degree of risk of non-delivery on campaign promises (Shneor and Munim 2019). Reward-based crowdfunding is the best-known crowdfunding model in China.

According to the China Crowdfunding Industry Development Research (Yuan and Chen 2018), there were 90 operating reward-based crowdfunding platforms in mainland China. Geographically, these reward-based crowdfunding platforms are operating in 20 provincial-level administrative regions across the country. Most of the platforms are established in the coastal areas which have better financial conditions and entrepreneurial culture. Compared to the coastal areas, only a few platforms are established in the northeast, northwest, and southwest of

China. Specifically, there are 26 reward-based crowdfunding platforms in Beijing followed by Guangdong (12), Zhejiang (11), Jiangsu (7), Shandong (7), and Shanghai (6). The platforms in the coastal area capture 77% of all reward-based crowdfunding platforms in mainland China.

In 2017, 18,209 reward-based crowdfunding projects were successfully online. Among the online projects, 13,927 projects got successfully funded by the end of their fundraising periods. The success rate is 76.48%. The sum of the fundraising targets of all successful projects is RMB 2.09 billion (approx. USD 0.3 billion). Eventually, the successful projects have raised RMB 9.743 billion (approx. USD 1.38 billion) in total, which is approximately 4.5 times higher than the expected funding amount. The total backer number of successful projects is approximately 23 million (Yuan and Chen 2018).

Among the successful projects, 4144 projects got funded in the range of RMB 50,000–100,000 (approx. USD 7106–14,211) followed by RMB 10,000–50,000 (approx. USD 1421–7106) (3967 projects), RMB 1000–10,000 (approx. USD 142–1421) (2600 projects) and less than RMB 1000 (approx. USD 142) (647 projects). The projects within the top four fundraising ranges are 11,358 which account for 81.57% of all the successful projects. There were only 208 projects that were successfully funded with an amount of more than RMB 1 million (approx. USD 0.14 million).

Reward-based crowdfunding projects in mainland China can be classified into seven main categories: technology, film, and television, agriculture, tourism, music, publishing and games. Technology, agriculture, and music are the top three categories for reward-based crowdfunding in China by number of campaigns. Technology ranked first with 3558 online projects, followed by agriculture with 3351 online projects, and music ranked third with 806 online projects. Projects from the top three categories account for 42% of the total number of online projects.

Insights on Reward-Based Crowdfunding

As the best-known crowdfunding model, reward-based crowdfunding in China has some unique characteristics. First, Chinese reward-based crowdfunding supporters are more "realistic" compared with the supporter in other mature crowdfunding markets (e.g. the U.S. crowdfunding market). Most of the Chinese backers invest their money in the projects in order to buy future products. Besides that, they tend to be less interested in participating in co-creation processes (Yuan and Chen 2018). In this sense, they behave more like consumers than like supporters. Accordingly, reward-based crowdfunding can be considered as equal to pure product pre-selling in China.

In addition, reward-based crowdfunding has been used as an online marketing/market testing channel by Chinese e-commerce giants (e.g. Alibaba, JD). These corporations' participation in crowdfunding is not for fundraising but for launching their own products, increasing product awareness, and finding potential consumers.

Lastly, different from other reward-based crowdfunding markets, no commission fees are charged by most Chinese reward-based crowdfunding platforms. Instead, platforms get their income and profits from online marketing and advertising services.

Equity-Based Crowdfunding

In terms of equity-based crowdfunding, individuals invest money in purchasing offerings of private company securities with an expectation of receiving monetary rewards in the future. Equity-based crowdfunding is a game of capital markets. Therefore, it is subjected to financial regulations (Ahlers et al. 2015).

By the end of 2017, there were 89 equity-based crowdfunding platforms operating in mainland China. Geographically, among the 34 provincial-level administrative regions, equity-based crowdfunding platforms only cover 13 regions. Like the distribution of reward-based crowdfunding, most equity-based platforms are located in economically developed areas, while few platforms are established in the northeast, northwest, and southwest part of China. Specifically, 29 equity-based crowdfunding platforms are based in Beijing followed by Guangdong (24), Shanghai (15), Zhejiang (8), and Sichuan (4). The platforms in the above area capture 90% of all equity-based crowdfunding platforms in mainland China.

According to the China Crowdfunding Industry Development Research (Yuan and Chen 2018), 1053 equity-based crowdfunding projects were successfully online in 2017. Among the online projects, 745 projects got successfully funded by the end of their fundraising periods. The success rate is 70.75%. The successful projects have raised RMB 3.361 billion (approx. USD 0.48 billion) in total. In terms of categories, equity-based crowdfunding projects in mainland China can be classified into eight main categories: technology, physical stores, film and television, agriculture, tourism, music, publishing, and games. Projects from the eight main categories account for 77% of the total number of online projects. Among the eight categories, physical store, technology, and film and television are the top three categories by the number of projects. The physical store ranked top with 562 online projects, followed by technology with 137 online projects and film and television ranked third with 85 online projects.

In 2017, the total number of successful projects' backers was 41,900. Most of the successful projects are with a small number of investors. Specifically, 63% of all the successful projects had less than 60 investors. 93% of all the successful projects had less than 160 investors. Relatively few projects had many investors. Here, only 44 projects had more than 160 investors, which account for 7% of all the successful projects. In terms of total fundraising amount, 42% of all the successful projects had a total fundraising amount of less than RMB 1 million (approx. USD 0.14 million); 91% of all the successful projects had a total fundraising amount of less than RMB 10 million (approx. USD 1.4 million), while only 69 projects have successfully raised more than RMB 10 million (approx. USD 1.4 million) through equity crowdfunding, which account for 9% of all successful projects.

Insights on Equity-Based Crowdfunding

Equity-based crowdfunding has not yet been legalized in China. Equity-based crowdfunding in China refers to "Internet non-public equity financing". As public offering in China is under extremely strong supervision by the government, equity-based crowdfunding in China can only be executed in the form of private offering (Hu and Yang 2014). As a private offering, "equity-based crowdfunding" in China is strictly controlled and supervised by the China Securities Regulatory Commission (CSRC), China Banking Regulatory Commission (CBRC), China Insurance Regulatory Commission (CIRC), and the People's Bank of China (Huang et.al. 2018).

The development of equity-based crowdfunding in China suffers from perceived uncertainty, void of legalization, and strict investor threshold. Therefore, in terms of investor numbers, equity-based crowdfunding is the least popular crowdfunding model when compared to the other models (reward-based, loan-based, and donation-based).

Loan-Based Crowdfunding

Loan-based crowdfunding is also known as online Peer to Peer (P2P) lending. P2P lending is the practice of lending money to individuals or businesses through online platforms while matching lenders with borrowers, which is repaid with interest added (Mamonov and Malaga 2018). For lenders, loan-based crowdfunding platforms usually offer better interest rates than standard commercial banks.

According to an annual P2P lending report (WDZJ 2018), by the end of 2017, there were 1931 P2P lending platforms operating in mainland China. Geographically, 410 P2P lending platforms were based in Guangdong followed by Beijing (376), Shanghai (261), and Zhejiang (233). The P2P lending platforms in the top four areas capture 66% of all P2P platforms in mainland China. The total volume of transactions of P2P lending in mainland China has reached RMB 2805 billion (approx. USD 400.33 billion) in 2017 with an overall profit ratio of 9.45%. The number of investors and borrowers in the P2P industry in 2017 were approximately 17 million and 23 million respectively. The average lending period was 9.16 months in 2017.

The loan balance (e.g. remaining amount to be paid) of P2P loans is also increasing. By the end of 2017, the overall loan balance of the P2P lending industry in mainland China has reached RMB 1225 billion (approx. USD 160.56 billion). Geographically, Beijing, Shanghai, and Guangdong ranked the top three regions in terms of loan balance with the total volume of RMB 439 billion (approx. USD 62.39 billion), RMB 325 billion (approx. USD 46.19 billion), and RMB 227 billion (approx. USD 32.26 billion) respectively. The top three regions accounted for 81% of the total loan balance volume in 2017. Zhejiang, Jiangsu, and Sichuan ranked third to sixth with the loan balances of RMB 106 billion (approx. USD 15.06 billion), RMB 38 billion (approx. USD 5.4 billion), and RMB 13 billion (approx. USD 1.85 billion) respectively (WDZJ 2018).

In China, loan-based crowdfunding is the only model which has institutional participation. Institutional investors engage and collaborate with P2P lending platforms. By the end of 2017, 212 P2P lending platforms received investment from state-owned companies. 153 P2P lending platforms received investments from venture capital. 126 P2P platforms received investment from publicly listed companies and 15 P2P lending platforms received funds from banks (WDZJ 2018).

Insights on Loan-Based Crowdfunding

Loan-based crowdfunding (online P2P lending) in China has its unique characteristics. First, providing supply chain financial service through loan-based crowdfunding has been a new trend in the loan-based crowdfunding market of China. The Supply chain financial service connects various parties (buyer, seller, and financing institution) in a transaction organically to lower financing costs and improve business efficiency. There were 118 online P2P lending platforms providing supply chain financial services in 2017 (WDZJ 2018).

Second, mergers and acquisitions among platforms are popular in the loan-based crowdfunding market of China. It makes the market more and more concentrated. For large platforms, the concentration process can further consolidate the platforms' business capabilities and increase their competitiveness. For small and medium-sized platforms, the market concentration strategy gives them a way to survive under conditions of fierce competition.

Last, to expand influence, some Chinese P2P lending platforms (e.g. China Rapid Finance, Hexindai, PPdai) choose to get on overseas listings in the U.S. Some mature Chinese P2P lending platforms (e.g. Dianrong, Lufax) have opened overseas branches to offer P2P lending services in southeast Asia to increase scale and profits.

Donation-Based Crowdfunding

Donation-based crowdfunding is usually used for funding social causes, NGOs, and charity projects. Through donation-based crowdfunding, individuals donate money to support social causes, charitable projects, or persons with no expectation of receiving tangible rewards in return, while enjoying intangible benefits such as the feeling of self-fulfilment and mental satisfaction.

Specifically, there were 12 donation-based crowdfunding platforms operating in mainland China by the end of 2017 and 9513 donation-based projects were successfully launched on these platforms. Different from other crowdfunding models, donation-based crowdfunding in China follows the "keep it all" principle. This means that there will be no unsuccessful projects (unless no funds are raised at all). Here, fundraisers set funding goals and keep the entire amount raised regardless of whether they meet their goals or not (Tomczak and Brem 2013). In 2017, total fundraising target was expected to be about RMB 1.90 billion (approx. USD 0.27 billion) and the actual total fundraising amount was about RMB 401 million (approx. USD 56.99 million). Among all related projects, 6467 have raised less than RMB 10,000 (approx. USD 1421) and 1711 projects have raised amounts in the range of RMB 10,000–50,000 (approx. USD 1421–7105). In other words, 86% of all the donation-based projects (8178) have raised less than RMB 50,000 (approx. USD 7105) and only 1335 projects got funded with more than RMB 50,000 (approx. USD 7105) (Yuan and Chen 2018).

In 2017, the total backer number of all the projects was 15.98 million. Specifically, 3839 projects had between 100 and 500 supporters, 1689 projects had between 50 and 100 supporters, and 1538 projects had less than 50 supporters. Overall 74% of all the donation-based projects (7066) had less than 500 supporters (Yuan and Chen 2018).

Insights on Donation-Based Crowdfunding

Donation-based crowdfunding industry in China is still in its initial stage of development. Specifically, in terms of platform numbers, there were only 12 donation-based crowdfunding platforms in mainland China, which is substantially a lower number of platforms when compared with the total number of platforms operating in all crowdfunding models. In 2017, the total fundraising amount of donation-based crowdfunding in China was RMB 401 million (approx. USD 56.99 million). This sum was far from enough to mitigate the huge supply gap of public welfare (Yuan and Chen 2018).

In addition, donation-based crowdfunding platforms in China are not charitable organizations but private-owned companies. Therefore, they need to pay their own daily expenses by charging commission fees or advertising fees. Because of the charity nature of donation-based crowdfunding, whether charging fees can be applied as the revenue source of donation-based crowdfunding in China is questionable.

Lastly, donation-based crowdfunding in China is usually used to solve individual cases/help individuals rather than to organizational initiatives. This means that offering help to needed groups through donation-based crowdfunding is still under exploration and development in China.

Regardless of crowdfunding model operated, as elsewhere, platforms are subjected to differing regulatory requirements. In the following section we explore the current state of crowdfunding regulation in China.

Current Regulation

Because of the lack of specific regulations for supervising crowdfunding, the Chinese crowdfunding market has grown rapidly since its emergence in 2011. However, perceived substantial risks challenge all crowdfunding participants (investors, project initiators, and crowdfunding platforms) in China (Zhu and Hu 2019). To promote a more secure environment for developing the crowdfunding industry, the Chinese crowdfunding market supervision is based on two core principles: separate supervision and information disclosure.

In term of separate supervision, the equity-based crowdfunding is mainly regulated by the China Securities Regulation Commission (CSRC). The loan-based crowdfunding must be carried out under the supervision of the China Banking and Insurance Regulatory Commission (CBRC) and the People's Bank of China. In opposite, the donation-based crowdfunding and the reward-based crowdfunding are not included in the financial supervision system because they are not providing financial products and services. In addition, the Ministry of Industry and Information Technology (MIIT), the National Development and Reform Commission (NDRC), and other related ministries and commissions are required to participate in the supervision of cybersecurity and credit information system (Yuan and Chen 2018).

The crowdfunding platform is the main body for crowdfunding practices. The supervision of crowdfunding platforms is based on information disclosure. Since the crowdfunding platform is an intermediary between investors and project initiators it is required to establish a systematic and institutionalized information disclosure system in order to mitigate information asymmetry between these parties. Based on the two core principles, the central government of China has issued a series of policy announcements to regulate the operations of different crowdfunding models.

Reward-Based Crowdfunding Regulation in China

Reward-based crowdfunding is considered as product pre-selling in China. Under this viewpoint, the supporters of reward-based crowdfunding are the "consumers" and the project developers of reward-based crowdfunding are the "sellers". The reward-based crowdfunding platform acts like an online trading intermediary. The regulation of reward-based crowdfunding should be the same as the ones used to supervise online

B2C marketplaces. In general, it is subject to the supervision of the "State Administration for Industry and Commerce of the People's Republic of China". The "Law of the People's Republic of China on the Protection of Consumer Rights and Interests" and the "Administrative Measures for Online Trading" are applied to the regulating process of reward-based crowdfunding.

Specifically, as "consumers", the rights of reward-based crowdfunding supporters are under the protection of the "Law of the People's Republic of China on the Protection of Consumer Rights and Interests" and the "Administrative Measures for Online Trading". As "sellers", project developers should take related legal obligations. As "online trading intermediaries", crowdfunding platforms should take legal responsibilities related to the infringement of consumer rights caused by the products or services provided on the platforms. In addition, the "State Administration for Industry and Commerce of the People's Republic of China" may impose administrative penalties in cases of misconduct by platforms.

However, reward-based crowdfunding cannot be equally treated as general online consumption according to the concept at its core, as backers also accept a certain degree of risk of non-delivery on campaign promises (Shneor and Munim 2019). This leads some to suggest that it should be regarded as investing behaviour rather than pure consumption. Therefore, supervision may also be different. The backers of crowdfunding projects should have self-awareness of the risks and share the risks with project developers in order to achieve their mutual ambitions in a relatively high information asymmetry environment. If crowdfunding participants' rights and interests are infringed, they should be able to take legal action to defend their rights. Therefore, reward-based crowdfunding platforms should only serve as information intermediaries and not as credit intermediaries, and under such conditions they will also not assume any responsibility.

To sum up, based on different understandings of reward-based crowdfunding, there is still controversy on how to protect the rights and interests of reward-based crowdfunding participants in China.

Equity-Based Crowdfunding Regulation in China

Among the four models of crowdfunding, the regulation of equity crowdfunding is the most complicated. Due to current legislation void, genuine equity crowdfunding has not been officially accepted and carried out in China. The Chinese government has announced a series of legal provisions to manage the equity crowdfunding market in a quasi-regulated manner. The legislation remains unfinished and the ongoing legislation progress is as follows:

- On December 18, 2014, the Securities Association of China (SAC) issued the "Private Equity Crowdfunding Administrative Measures (Trial Version)". This is the first officially issued equity crowdfunding regulation. However, this trial version has no legal effect.
- On July 18, 2015, the People's Bank of China and other nine ministries issued the "Guiding Opinions on Promoting the Healthy Development of Internet Finance (Guiding Opinion)". In this "Guiding Opinion", equity crowdfunding is officially defined as the activities of public small-amount equity financing through the Internet. Publicity and small amount are two basic principles of equity crowdfunding. The equity crowdfunding platform is an information intermediary rather than a credit intermediary and equity crowdfunding is officially supervised by China Securities Regulation Commission (CSRC).
- On August 7, 2015, the CSRC issued the "Notice of the General Office of the China Securities Regulatory Commission on Conducting Special Inspections of Institutions Engaging in Equity Financing via the Internet". According to this notice, no organization or individual may carry out equity crowdfunding activities in China without the approval of the CSRC. In addition, it is stipulated that "equity crowdfunding" refers specifically to "public equity crowdfunding", while the existing "private equity crowdfunding" will be replaced by "private equity financing", and the maximum number of investors that can participate in an equity crowdfunding project is 200.

- On August 10, 2015, the SAC issued the "Measures for the Administration of Over-the-Counter Securities Business Recordation". In accordance with the measures, equity crowdfunding in China has been officially divided into two categories: "public offering (equity crowdfunding)" and "private offering (online non-public equity financing)".
- On August 17, 2016, the CSRC issued the "Interim Measures for the Administration of the Business Activities of Online Lending Information Intermediary Institutions". It is stipulated that the P2P platforms cannot be engaged in equity crowdfunding business.
- On April 14, 2016, the CSRC issued the "Implementation Plan for Special Rectification on Risks in Equity Crowdfunding" in order to get prepared to rectify the existing problems in Chinese equity crowdfunding market.
- On December 1, 2018, Li Zhibin, director of the SFC's Office for Combating Illegal Securities Futures, revealed that the CSRC is currently developing and improving the "Measures for the Pilot Administration of Equity Crowdfunding" at the third China New Financial Summit Forum.

Loan-Based Crowdfunding Regulation in China

China has the world's largest P2P lending market. However, this immature market is still suffering from some inherent risks such as the lack of credit and risk controls, the lack of industry standards, and regulation challenges.

At the national regulatory level, China Banking Regulatory Commission (CBRC), and other related departments have officially established a "1 + 3 supervision system" to monitor, manage, and mitigate inherent risks in Chinese P2P market (Huang 2018). Specifically, the "1 + 3 supervision system" refers to "one method plus three guidelines" which is mainly composed of the following regulatory documents:

- "Interim Measures for the Administration of Online Lending Intermediary Institutions' Business Activities" (Issued by the CBRC on 17 August 2016)
- "Guideline on the Administration of Recordation and Registration of Online Lending Intermediary Institutions" (Issued by the CBRC, Ministry of Industry and Information Technology and State Administration of Industry and Commerce on 28 November 2016)
- "Guideline on the Custodian Business for Online Lending Funds" (Issued by the CBRC on 22 February 2017)
- "Guideline on Information Disclosure of Online Lending Intermediary Institutions' Business Activities" (Issued by the CBRC on 24 August 2017)

Besides, the National Internet Finance Association (NIFA) has also issued several rules and standards on the information disclosures and self-regulation of Chinese P2P market in 2016.

At the local regulatory level, being supplements, some developed regions (e.g. Beijing, Shanghai) have begun to develop self-regulatory frameworks and associations by taking regional variations into consideration. Self-regulation is effective in reducing the regulatory burden and cost, eliminating the information asymmetry between the market and the regulatory authority and improving market standardization.

Donation-Based Crowdfunding Regulation in China

In China, public fundraising for charitable purposes is mainly related to the "Charity Law of the People's Republic of China". According to this law, there are clear regulations on charitable organizations using the Internet and other platforms to conduct public fundraising. Organizations or individuals that do not have the qualification for public fundraising may not use public fundraising.

Most donation-based crowdfunding projects in China are created by individuals who are facing difficulties. These troubled individuals use crowdfunding as the channel to seek help from the greater society. Fundraising activities for certain troubled individuals are guided by self-interest. Therefore, donation-based crowdfunding in China is not charitable fundraising but social assistance and may not apply to the "Charity Law of the People's Republic of China".

On July 20, 2017, the Ministry of Civil Affairs announced the "Basic Specifications for the Internet-based Public Fundraising Platform for Charity Organizations" and the "Basic Management Regulations for the Internet-based Public Fundraising Platform for Charity Organizations" to manage donation-based crowdfunding market. Donation-based crowdfunding is officially distinguished from charity fundraising.

According to the specifications and regulations, project developers should take full responsibilities of the authenticity of the provided information. Donation-based crowdfunding platform should strengthen project information review and disclosure, inform potential donors on the potential risks of the projects, and clarify the traceability of responsibility. In addition, donation-based crowdfunding platforms should disclose platform operation information to the public at least every six months.

Review of Key Research Done in China

Though the first Chinese crowdfunding platform "Demohour" went online in 2011, most Chinese crowdfunding platforms were launched after 2014 (Yuan and Chen 2018). Since then, the crowdfunding concept has been recognized in China in both research and practice with researchers starting to investigate this phenomenon within the Chinese market. In order to summarize the findings of such research, we conducted a literature review. Generally, we found out that the crowdfunding research focused on the Chinese market is still limited in scope compared to the ones based on Western market data. Specifically, our main findings are summarized as follows:

First, most of the existing Chinese crowdfunding studies are focused on investigating the success factors of crowdfunding. These mostly rely on the signalling theory and Elaboration Likelihood Model (e.g. Zheng et al. 2016; Bi et al. 2017), which were frequently adopted as the main theoretical foundations. Based on the data collected from the key players of Chinese crowdfunding market (e.g. JD Crowdfunding; Demohour;

Zhongchou), Chinese crowdfunding literature reveals that social capital (Shahab et al. 2019; Kang et al. 2017; Chen et al. 2018), trust and commitment (Zheng et al. 2016; Zhao et al. 2017; Liang et al. 2019), campaign characteristics (Du and Wang 2016; Du et al. 2019; Zhao and Vinig 2017), campaign quality (Xu et al. 2016; Yuan et al. 2016; Shahab et al. 2019; Chen et al. 2018; Zhang et al. 2017; Bi et al. 2017), as well as backer and initiator interaction (Wang et al. 2018; Xie et al. 2019) are positively associated with crowdfunding success in China.

Second, many studies explore the current status of crowdfunding in China compared to the one in other countries. In general, the degree of development of crowdfunding markets in developed countries is higher than that of developing countries (Rau 2018). However, as an emerging market, the volume of the Chinese crowdfunding market grows rapidly and has become the largest crowdfunding market in the world (Ziegler et al. 2018). Compared with the Western crowdfunding markets, the Chinese crowdfunding market has its unique characteristics. Specifically, in terms of reward-based crowdfunding, the Chinese contributors are more realistic compared to the ones in Western markets. Specifically, their motivations to contribute are mainly generated by receiving the rewards but not by helping to further develop the business ideas (Yuan and Chen 2018). In addition, the Chinese crowdfunding market is controlled by several key players (Yuan and Chen 2018). The performance of the key players (e.g. Taobao Crowdfunding, JD Crowdfunding) counts for most of the market share in China (Huang et al. 2018). As a latecomer of the crowdfunding market, the legal framework related to the regulation of the Chinese crowdfunding market is immature which hinders its further development (Yuan and Chen 2018). Specifically, this immature legal framework has brought problems such as fraud, illegal fundraising, and money laundering (Huang et al. 2018). As a result, the growth rate of the Chinese crowdfunding market has been slowed down as legal frameworks are being revisited (Chirisa and Mukarwi 2018).

Third, crowdfunding has proved to be a feasible tool in supporting creative industries and sustainable projects in China (Sun and Meng 2015). Two-thirds of the reward-based crowdfunding projects in the Chinese market are related to creative industries such as film, music, publication, animation, design, and games (Sun and Meng 2015). Besides, crowdfunding is also used to support sustainable campaigns in China (Lam and Law 2016). The success of sustainable crowdfunding projects is closely associated with public opinion and brand effect in the Chinse market (Chen et al. 2018).

Implications for Research and Practice

Theoretical Implications

Based on the review of the key Chinese crowdfunding literature, we found that existing research has provided valuable insights for understanding the Chinese crowdfunding market. However, the limitations of the current literature indicate several future research directions as well.

First, most of the existing Chinese crowdfunding literature are replicative studies. These replicate previous crowdfunding studies by using the Chinese data in order to test the validation of previous findings in non-Chinese crowdfunding market (e.g. Zheng et al. 2017). Future research could generate more special outputs by taking unique Chinese cultural factors and market characteristics into consideration. For instance, "Guanxi" is a special element of Chinese culture, which has been embedded in the daily practices of the Chinese business community (Chung and Hamilton 2001). It should be beneficial to enrich the Chinese crowdfunding literature by investigating the impact of "Guanxi" on Chinese crowdfunding practices (Zhao and Vinig 2019). Besides, the Chinese crowdfunding market has strong connections to several Chinese Internet giants (e.g. Alibaba, JD, and Tencent) (Yang and Zhang 2016). It would be interesting to explore the influences of these Internet giants on the formation and development of the Chinese crowdfunding market, and their relations with crowdfunding platforms.

Second, in terms of research perspectives, most of the existing literature aims to explore the success factors of crowdfunding in the Chinese market by analysing real market data from the platforms. The signalling theory and Elaboration Likelihood Model are mostly adopted by Chinese crowdfunding literature (e.g. Zheng et al. 2016; Bi et al. 2017). Besides, the total amount of research related to equity crowdfunding and loan-based crowdfunding is smaller compared to the research associated with reward-based and donation-based crowdfunding. To generate more meaningful insights, future research could try to analyse the Chinese crowdfunding market from other perspectives by applying alternative theoretical frames (Huang et al. 2018). In addition, more research on equity-based crowdfunding and loan-based crowdfunding should be generated.

Practical Implications

This chapter also provides several practical implications for Chinese crowdfunding practitioners, contributors, and regulators.

First, Chinese investors tend to rely on personal relationships to help make investment decisions as the Chinese business is relation-based. The personal relationship is used as substitutes for formal institutional support (Xin and Pearce 1996). In terms of the Chinese crowdfunding market, project initiators' social capital levels should be closely associated with crowdfunding success (Shahab et al. 2019). Therefore, Chinese crowdfunding practitioners should pay attention to their social capital accumulation by interacting with potential contributors to create personal trust and take full advantage of the power of social capital to promote projects within their target audiences.

Second, Chinese crowdfunding contributors are more pragmatic compared to the ones in the Western markets (Yuan and Chen 2018). Specifically, they contribute for getting the rewards, rather than being parts of the process of the project "co-creation" (Yuan and Chen 2018). Therefore, it is beneficial for Chinese crowdfunding campaign initiators to pay more attention to the design and delivery of the crowdfunding rewards. For instance, compared with the other campaigns, the campaigns with clear descriptions, well-designed reward prototypes, and determined delivery time are expected to have higher probabilities to get successful fundraising.

Third, it is of great importance for the regulators to strengthen the regulative framework to guarantee the healthy development of the equity-based and loan-based crowdfunding models in China. The regulative framework should be designed within the existing Chinese legislation system and cultural background (Hu and Yang 2014). Under the established framework, specific principles and regulations need to be promulgated to provide adequate supervision of the whole crowdfunding market and offer timely information disclosures to market participants. In addition, the development of Chinese loan-based crowdfunding market has been greatly impeded by fraud caused by the lack of nationwide credit rating systems (Wei 2015). Therefore, a comprehensive credit rating system should be established to support the development of the Chinese loan-based crowdfunding market.

Lastly, for promoting crowdfunding industry in China, it is also important to create a close integration between social media sites, digital payment systems, and crowdfunding platforms to create a seamless, convenient, and efficient process for information sharing and transactions.

Conclusion

In conclusion, given the uniqueness of culture, regulation, and social systems in China, the concept of Chinese crowdfunding could be considered as a combination of Chinese unique characteristics and general crowdfunding principles (Funk 2019). In this chapter, we introduce and discuss the crowdfunding phenomena in China concretely from the perspectives of different stakeholders (platforms, fundraisers, funders, and regulators) and crowdfunding models (reward-based, equity-based, loan-based, and donation-based). Generally, the Chinese crowdfunding market has developed rapidly and has become the world's largest crowdfunding market (Ziegler et al. 2018). However, we also find out that there are some problems in the Chinese crowdfunding market, such as underdeveloped regulatory system and personal credit system (Chirisa and Mukarwi 2018). These problems will limit the further development of the Chinese crowdfunding market. To solve these problems, specific solutions have been proposed in this chapter. Practically, this chapter can be used as prescriptive guidelines for Chinese crowdfunding stakeholders to enhance and improve market performance. In addition, we also point out some meaningful research topics for researchers to explore the Chinese crowdfunding phenomena further.

References

Ahlers, G. K. C., Cumming, D., Günther, C., et al. (2015). Signaling in Equity Crowdfunding. *Entrepreneurship Theory and Practice, 39*(4), 955–980.

Bi, S., Liu, Z., & Usman, K. (2017). The Influence of Online Information on Investing Decisions of Reward-based Crowdfunding. *Journal of Business Research, 71*, 10–18.

Chen, J., Chen, L., Chen, J., et al. (2018). Mechanism and Policy Combination of Technical Sustainable Entrepreneurship Crowdfunding in China: A System Dynamics Analysis. *Journal of Cleaner Production, 177*, 610–620.

Chirisa, I., & Mukarwi, L. (2018). A Comparative Analysis of Africa and Chinese Crowdfunding Markets. In U. G. Benna & A. U. Benna (Eds.), *Crowdfunding and Sustainable Urban Development in Emerging Economies* (pp. 147–163). Hershey, PA: IGI Global.

Chung, W. K., & Hamilton, G. G. (2001). Social Logic as Business Logic: Guanxi, Trustworthiness, and the Embeddedness of Chinese Business Practices. In R. Appelbaum, W. Felstiner, & V. Gessner (Eds.), *Rules and Networks: The Legal Culture of Global Business Transactions* (Vol. 1, pp. 325–346). Portland, OR: Hart Publishing.

Du, Z., Li, M., & Wang, K. (2019). "The more options, the better?" Investigating the Impact of the Number of Options on Backers' Decisions in Reward-based Crowdfunding Projects. *Information & Management, 56*(3), 429–444.

Du, Z., & Wang, K. (2016). *Choice Schema Design of Crowdfunding Campaigns: An Exploratory Study.* Paper Presented at the 20th Pacific Asia Conference on Information Systems, Chiayi, Taiwan, June 27.

Funk, A. S. (2019). *Crowdfunding in China: A New Institutional Economics Approach* (1st ed.). Cham: Springer International Publishing.

Hu, T. L., & Yang, D. (2014). The People's Funding of China: Legal Developments of Equity Crowdfunding-Progress, Proposals, and Prospects. *University of Cincinnati Law Review, 83*(2), 445–476.

Huang, R. H. (2018). Online P2P Lending and Regulatory Responses in China: Opportunities and Challenges. *European Business Organization Law Review, 19*(1), 63–92.

Huang, Z., Chiu Candy, L., Mo, S., et al. (2018). The Nature of Crowdfunding in China: Initial Evidence. *Asia Pacific Journal of Innovation and Entrepreneurship, 12*(3), 300–322.

Kang, L., Jiang, Q., & Tan, C.-H. (2017). Remarkable Advocates: An Investigation of Geographic Distance and Social Capital for Crowdfunding. *Information & Management, 54*(3), 336–348.

Lam, P. T. I., & Law, A. O. K. (2016). Crowdfunding for Renewable and Sustainable Energy Projects: An Exploratory Case Study Approach. *Renewable and Sustainable Energy Reviews, 60*, 11–20.

Liang, T.-P., Wu, S. P.-J., & Huang, C.-c. (2019). Why Funders Invest in Crowdfunding Projects: Role of Trust from the Dual-process Perspective. *Information & Management, 56*(1), 70–84.

Lin, L. (2017). Managing the Risks of Equity Crowdfunding: Lessons from China. *Journal of Corporate Law Studies, 17*(2), 327–366.

Mamonov, S., & Malaga, R. (2018). Success Factors in Title III Equity Crowdfunding in the United States. *Electronic Commerce Research and Applications, 27*, 65–73.

Rau, P. R. (2018). Law, Trust, and the Development of Crowdfunding. Retrieved June 1, 2019, from https://ssrn.com/abstract=2989056.

Shahab, Y., Ye, Z., Riaz, Y., et al. (2019). Individual's Financial Investment Decision-making in Reward-based Crowdfunding: Evidence from China. *Applied Economics Letters, 26*(4), 261–266.

Shneor, R., & Munim, Z. H. (2019). Reward Crowdfunding Contribution as Planned Behaviour: An Extended Framework. *Journal of Business Research, 103*, 56–70.

Sun, X., & Meng, Q. (2015). Puzzles about the "Crowdfunding" in Cultural Industry and Its Ecological Countermeasures. *Open Journal of Social Sciences, 3*(7), 7–14.

Tomczak, A., & Brem, A. (2013). A Conceptualized Investment Model of Crowdfunding. *Venture Capital, 15*(4), 335–359.

Wang, N., Li, Q., Liang, H., et al. (2018). Understanding the Importance of Interaction Between Creators and Backers in Crowdfunding Success. *Electronic Commerce Research and Applications, 27*, 106–117.

WDZJ. (2018). 2017 Annual Chinese P2P lending Industry Report. Retrieved June 1, 2019, from https://osscdn.wdzj.com/upload/2017wdnb.pdf.

Wei, S. (2015). Internet Lending in China: Status Quo, Potential Risks and Regulatory Options. *Computer Law & Security Review, 31*(6), 793–809.

Xie, K., Liu, Z., Chen, L., et al. (2019). Success Factors and Complex Dynamics of Crowdfunding: An Empirical Research on Taobao Platform in China. *Electronic Markets, 29*(2), 187–199.

Xin, K. K., & Pearce, J. L. (1996). Guanxi: Connections As Substitutes for Formal Institutional Support. *Academy of Management Journal, 39*(6), 1641–1658.

Xu, B., Zheng, H., Xu, Y., et al. (2016). Configurational Paths to Sponsor Satisfaction in Crowdfunding. *Journal of Business Research, 69*(2), 915–927.

Yang, D., & Zhang, X. (2016). Review of the Domestic Crowdfunding Industry Development. *Journal of Service Science and Management, 9*(1), 45–49.

You, C. (2017). Recent Development of FinTech Regulation in China: A Focus on the New Regulatory Regime for the P2P Lending (Loan-based Crowdfunding) Market. *Capital Markets Law Journal, 13*(1), 85–115.

Yuan, H., Lau, R. Y. K., & Xu, W. (2016). The Determinants of Crowdfunding Success: A Semantic Text Analytics Approach. *Decision Support Systems, 91*, 67–76.

Yuan, Y., & Chen, L. (2018). *China Crowdfunding Industry Development Research* (1st ed.). Shang Hai Jiao Tong University Press.

Zhang, W., Yan, X., & Chen, Y. (2017). Configurational Path to Financing Performance of Crowdfunding Projects Using Fuzzy Set Qualitative Comparative Analysis. *Engineering Economics, 28*(1), 25–34.

Zhao, L., & Vinig, T. (2017). Hedonic Value and Crowdfunding Project Performance: A Propensity Score Matching-Based Analysis. *Review of Behavioral Finance, 9*(2), 169–186.

Zhao, L., & Vinig, T. (2019). Guanxi, Trust and Reward-based Crowdfunding Success: A Chinese Case. *Chinese Management Studies*. Forthcoming.

Zhao, Q., Chen, C.-D., Wang, J.-L., et al. (2017). Determinants of Backers' Funding Intention in Crowdfunding: Social Exchange Theory and Regulatory Focus. *Telematics and Informatics, 34*(1), 370–384.

Zheng, H., Hung, J.-L., Qi, Z., et al. (2016). The Role of Trust Management in Reward-based Crowdfunding. *Online Information Review, 40*(1), 97–118.

Zheng, H., Xu, B., Wang, T., et al. (2017). Project Implementation Success in Reward-Based Crowdfunding: An Empirical Study. *International Journal of Electronic Commerce, 21*(3), 424–448.

Zhu, C. C., & Hu, J. (2019). Internet Financial Regulation and Law Analysis of China. In S.-B. Tsai, C.-H. Shen, H. Song, & B. Niu (Eds.), *Green Finance for Sustainable Global Growth* (pp. 173–192). Hershey, PA: IGI Global.

Ziegler, T., Johanson, D., Zhang, B., Ben, S., Wang, W., Mammadova, L., Hao, R., et al. (2018). *The 3rd Asia Pacific Region Alternative Finance Industry Report*. Cambridge: The Cambridge Centre for Alternative Finance.

Ziegler, T., Shneor, R., Wenzlaff, K., Odorović, A., Johanson, D., Hao, R., & Ryll, L. (2019). *Shifting Paradigms: The 4th Annual European Alternative Finance Report*. Cambridge: The Cambridge Centre for Alternative Finance.

13

Crowdfunding Prospects in New Emerging Markets: The Cases of India and Bangladesh

Krishnamurthy Suresh, Stine Øyna, and Ziaul Haque Munim

Introduction

In 2013, the World Bank published a report on crowdfunding's potential in emerging markets, which estimated a market opportunity for South Asia alone of close to USD 5 billion (The World Bank 2013). The South Asia region consists of predominantly collectivist societies (Hofstede Insights 2019)—India, Bangladesh, Sri Lanka, Pakistan, Bhutan, and Nepal—where helping others through donations is an integral part of

K. Suresh (✉)
Indian Institute of Management Bangalore (IIM B), Bangalore, India

S. Øyna
School of Business and Law, University of Agder, Kristiansand, Norway
e-mail: stine.oyna@uia.no

Z. H. Munim
Faculty of Technology, Natural Sciences and Maritime Sciences, University of South-Eastern Norway, Horten, Norway
e-mail: Ziaul.H.Munim@usn.no

R. Shneor et al. (eds.), *Advances in Crowdfunding*,
https://doi.org/10.1007/978-3-030-46309-0_13

prevailing religious obligations and societal norms. Thus, these countries share certain cultural and religious traits that are highly consistent with the principles of crowdfunding. Yet, by 2017, the alternative finance activity in the region amounted to no more than USD 269 million, 96% of which was related to the Indian market (see Table 13.1), indicating a vast untapped potential in the Asian economies.

In the current chapter, we explore the history, ongoing activity, and future prospects of crowdfunding in new emerging markets. Specifically, we look into the cases of India and Bangladesh. Both countries represent interesting crowdfunding markets due to the cultural inclinations described above, combined with their large populations (1.3 billion people in India and 165 million in Bangladesh) and number of people living in extreme poverty (15% of the population in Bangladesh and 21% in India) (The World Bank 2019). India is, by far, the leading market of alternative finance in the South Asia region, and thus provides an interesting case to explore. The alternative finance market in Bangladesh, on the other hand, is still in its infant stage and thus far less developed. Comparing and contrasting the state and types of crowdfunding in these two markets thus allow us to reach new insights.

The remainder of this chapter consists of sections focusing on India and Bangladesh, respectively. Both sections cover the history, including cultural roots of crowdfunding in the given market, prevailing models and platforms, regulatory issues, and future prospects. Given the relatively more developed state of crowdfunding in India versus Bangladesh, the section on India is naturally more comprehensive. The chapter concludes with a few summarizing remarks on the state of crowdfunding in new emerging markets.

Table 13.1 Alternative finance volume in South Asian countries

Country	Volume (USD)[a]	Population (M)[b]	Volume per capita
Bangladesh	10,272	161	0.0001
Bhutan	10,000	0.8	0.0133
Nepal	1,014,850	28	0.0361
India	268,579,820	1352	0.1986
Pakistan	8,571,762	212	0.0404
Sri Lanka	38,926	21	0.0018

[a]Ziegler et al. (2018)
[b]The World Bank database

Crowdfunding in South Asia

Research on crowdfunding in South Asia is still somewhat limited, although a few contributions do exist. Crowdfunding studies in the Indian context examine regulatory issues (Marakkath and Attuel-mendes 2015), business model transformation (Srivastava 2016; Chirputkar et al. 2015; Gupta and Bose 2019), risk factors (Leela 2016), crowdfunding intention (Baber 2019a), and drivers of growth (Pa 2018). Similarly, studies in the Bangladeshi context examine crowdfunding business model (Adhikary and Kutsuna 2016), awareness and drivers of crowdfunding (Adhikary et al. 2018), and the drivers of crowdfunding intention (Hasan et al. 2018; Munim et al. 2020). In sum, these studies build knowledge relating to crowdfunding on the individual (backer), firm, and societal levels.

Until 2014, a few crowdfunding platforms were operational in India, and people believed that family or friends or venture capital firms would determine crowdfunding campaign success (Srivastava 2016). A majority of the early platforms were associated with creative industries like filmmaking, publishing, and design (ibid.). On the contrary, in 2019, the existing Bangladesh crowdfunding platforms are not fully functional but are more dedicated to raising funds for medical treatment or equity (Munim et al. 2020). In both the Indian and Bangladeshi context, the main drivers of crowdfunding are increased demand for alternative finance due to improved socio-economic status, significant increase of internet users, complexity of documentation, and requirement for tangible securities for credit applications in traditional financial institutions such as banks (Srivastava 2016; Adhikary et al. 2018; Marakkath and Attuel-mendes 2015).

In terms of factors influencing crowdfunding intention, findings are similar in the Indian and Bangladeshi contexts. For instance, technological awareness and experience of traditional financial market have a positive influence on a backer's crowdfunding intention (Baber 2019b; Hasan et al. 2018). Meanwhile, in societies like India and Bangladesh which can be "characterized by a low degree of thin trust between strangers, people are less willing to contribute to/invest in fundraising efforts by a stranger" (Kshetri 2015, p. 106). Therefore, the campaign owner being friends and family is positively associated with a backer's crowdfunding intention in the Indian context (Baber 2019a). However, the quality of the campaign and media coverage is more important in the Bangladesh context (Munim et al. 2020).

Crowdfunding in India

History

Crowdfunding or crowdsourcing, in various forms and under various names, has existed in India since ancient times. For instance, 'Chanda' involves people collecting small sums of money from large crowds to finance religious, cultural, and other events like festival celebrations in the local community. Another example of a historic crowdfunding campaign happened in 1962, during the war with China. The then Indian Prime Minister, Jawaharlal Nehru, appealed to the citizens of the country to contribute to the defence fund. Thousands of people, especially women, donated not only money but also their jewellery. The campaign was said to have collected over USD 220,000 in cash and much more in gold. Later, in 1976, a group of 500,000 milk farmers from the Indian state Gujarat contributed to fund the movie 'Manthan,' which was estimated around INR 1.1 million (USD 1 ≈ INR 70). After the inception of modern-day (internet-based) crowdfunding, the Indian online crowdfunding started its operations in 2012 with the launch of Wishberry, Ketto, and Milaap (Impact Guru 2017).

Prevailing Models and Platforms

The four prevailing models of crowdfunding—reward, equity, lending, and donation—are all represented in the case of India, and Fig. 13.1 presents their levels. Loan-based crowdfunding is responsible for the majority of the activity. Since 2016, equity and donation-based crowdfunding have reached similar levels. The volume of reward-based crowdfunding, however, remains low. The different types of crowdfunding in the Indian context are discussed below.

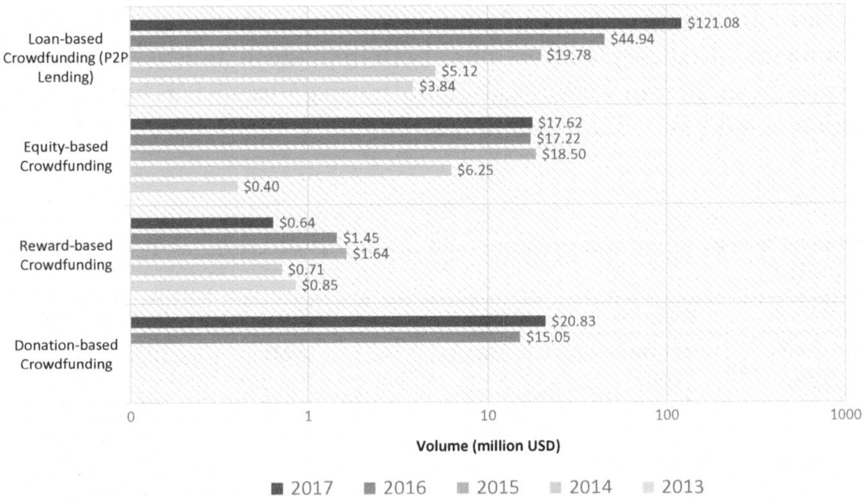

Fig. 13.1 Indian crowdfunding market volumes by model (2013–2017). (∗Based on figures from Ziegler et al. [2018])

Donation-Based Crowdfunding

Philanthropy—including charity and donations—is an integral part of the Indian culture and tradition, visible through its mention in the first Indian scripture—known as Vedas (Bhasin 2019). In India, the word 'donation' or 'giving' has different nomenclature based on religion. The Hindus term it as *daana* (giving) and *dakshina* (alms), Buddhists call it as *Bhiksha* (alms), while it is *zakat* (prescribed offerings) and *sadaqah* in Islam (Viswanath and Dadrawala 2004). As per classical Hinduism, it is considered as the *duty* of an individual to help those who are in need (Bornstein 2009). Donations are usually made for social, religious, cultural, as well as political causes. Earlier, donation was an individual activity. However, the establishment of socio-religious institutions during the nineteenth century gave birth to scientific or institutional philanthropy, which is later dominated by NGOs, trusts, and foundations.

Donation-based crowdfunding is the second-largest model by volume after P2P lending in India. Around USD 21 million were raised in 2017 (see Fig. 13.1), and, as of May 2019, there are more than 25 donation-based (Table 13.2) crowdfunding platforms operating. Campaigns on these platforms allow both individuals and NGOs to raise money in support of various causes under categories such as health, education, community development, and others.

Table 13.2 List of popular donation and reward-based crowdfunding platforms in India

Platform	Website	Model	Foundation	Commission[a]
Desired Wings	desiredwings.com	Reward	2015	10%
Dreamwallets	dreamwallets.com	Reward	2015	5% (9% under Keep What You Get (KWYG) model)
EduDharma	edudharma.com	Donation	2017	5%
Fueladream	fueladream.com	Donation + Reward	2016	Normal campaigns 6% and group campaigns 9%
GiveIndia	giveindia.org	Donation	2000	5–10%
ImpactGuru	impactguru.com	Donation	2014	*Self-driven*: 5% for individuals and social enterprises, 3% for NGOs; *Accelerate*: 12%
Ketto	ketto.org	Donation	2012	5–6%
Milaap	milaap.org	Donation	2010	5%
Wishberry	wishberry.in	Reward	2012	10%
Gocrowdera	gocrowdera.com	Donation + Reward	2014	0%

[a]Fees excluding processing charges, GST, and payment gateway charges. Data compiled from platform websites (as of May 21, 2019)

A popular form of donation-based crowdfunding in India is non-monetary donations, where backers donate products, meals, or medicine to people in need. Donatekart is one such platform that enables backers to donate various products to the NGOs which they wish to support. Another platform, Give India, enables backers to support the delivery of midday meals to poor children across the country through one of their initiatives—*Mission 10 Million Meals*. Finally, in the last two to three years, *medical crowdfunding* has taken off in India, where platforms like Milaap, Ketto, and ImpactGuru assist common people in raising money for expensive medical treatments. Given the population and poverty levels of the country, these forms of non-financial return crowdfunding have the potential to make a substantial socio-economic impact.

Reward-Based Crowdfunding

In the case of reward-based crowdfunding, backers receive a non-financial reward in return for the money contributed: as of May 2019, about nine to ten reward-based platforms were operating in India (including reward + donation, see Table 13.2), the most prominent ones being Wishberry and Fueladream. Noteworthy, some of the campaigns on Fueladream are run by students raising funds for social causes. For example, one such campaign ran by students, aimed at raising funds to help with the education of children from underprivileged homes, has been funded 534 times (Goal: INR 1,080,000). Also, platforms like Desired Wings and Rug Beneath My Feet are exclusive women-centric platforms. As per Ziegler et al. (2018), around USD 5.3 million has been raised by these platforms over the years from 2013 to 2017 (see Fig. 13.1) of which 40% of the fundraising was for business purposes.

Equity-Based Crowdfunding

India has developed into a start-up hub with the third-largest start-up ecosystem in the world, home to more than 20,000 start-ups (KPMG 2018), more than 63 million micro, small, and medium enterprises

(MSMEs) (Government of India 2017) and more than 210 active incubators/accelerators (NASSCOM 2018). Traditionally, start-ups are being funded through angel investors, private equity, or loan arrangements with banks and other financial institutions. However, since the global financial crisis of 2008, financing through traditional means became even more challenging, resulting in a credit gap where nearly 50 million MSMEs have an unmet debt demand of USD 198 billion (PWC 2018). In line with the rapid growth in the number of established start-ups, alternative means of financing these enterprises evolved.

Under equity crowdfunding, the equity shares of the company are issued to the investors in consideration for their investment. There are around 15 such platforms operating in India (as of May 2019), LetsVenture being the most prominent one (see Table 13.3). The platform has more than 4400 angel investors and has funded over 172 deals. By 2016, around 200 companies had been crowdfunded by equity-based platforms, and the total amount raised was over INR 3.5 billion. The average ticket size for small working capital was between INR 5 million and INR 60 million, while average fund-raised ticket size was between INR 30 and 40 million (Menon 2016). However, the regulatory challenges for equity crowdfunding have curbed the growth prospects of the industry. As per Ziegler et al. (2018), around USD 60 million has been raised by these platforms over the years, from 2013 to 2017 (see Fig. 13.1).

Table 13.3 List of popular equity crowdfunding platforms in India

Platform	Website	Foundation
1Crowd	1crowd.co	2015
Ah! Ventures	ahventures.in	2009
ANGLEPaisa	anglepaisa.com	2015
Coseeding	coseeding.com	2016
Enablers	enablersinvestment.com	2014
Grex	grex.in	2014
LetsVenture	letsventure.com	2013
SpicyFunds	spicyfund.com	2011
ientra	ientra.com	2016

Commission information of most of the equity crowdfunding platforms is not publicly available

Lending-Based Crowdfunding (Peer-to-Peer Lending)

Alternative lending is one of the fastest-growing segments in the Indian Fintech space, reflecting the unmet financial needs of Indian consumers and businesses. Over 40% of the population and around 90% of small businesses are not linked to formal financial institutions (EY 2017). Also, nearly 90% of the consumer market is unaddressed by the existing financiers due to insufficient credit scores (ibid.). The failure of banks and other financial institutions to meet the needs of these segments, especially after the global crisis, led to the rise of alternative lending in India. As of 2017, there were more than 225 alternative lending companies in India (ibid.).

Like other emerging economies, the country has multiple informal sources of financing for the unbanked population, like chit funds and microfinance. Chit funds are schemes that combine savings and credit (Kapoor et al. 2012). Chit funds could be registered or unregistered, organized by formal financial institutions or informal groups such as friends and relatives. In India, there are more than 10,000 registered chit funds and around 200,000 unregistered ones. The value of the unregistered chit fund industry is estimated to almost 100 times the registered value, which is about INR 300 billion (Acharya 2013).

In India, though still in a nascent stage, P2P is one of the fastest-growing markets, with current market size of around INR 2 billion, including both consumer and business loans (Saleem 2018). The market is expected to reach over USD 5 billion by 2020 (Deloitte 2017). There are currently between 40 and 50 platforms operating under the P2P model, although only 11 are registered with the Reserve Bank of India, so far. The most prominent P2P platforms are Faircent, Finzy, Lendenclub, and Monexo. The interest rates on these platforms are generally categorized based on the riskiness of loans (i.e. low risk—ultra high risk, and 'unidentified'), range between 14 and 36% (over 40% for unidentified).

In addition to providing an attractive asset class for lenders, the P2P industry acts as an avenue for financial and credit inclusion through addressing underserved people and small businesses. Mostly, the borrowers of the industry are from tier-two and tier-three locations, who would

Table 13.4 List of RBI registered peer-to-peer lending platforms in India

No	Platform	Website	Foundation	Interest rates
1	Cash Kumar	cashkumar.com	2014	18–30% (flat)
2	Monexo	monexo.co/in	2016	12–30% (for salaried loans)
3	Faircent	faircent.com	2013	12–28% (excluding unrated borrowers)
4	Peerlend.in	peerlend.in	2015	14–36%
5	AnyTimeLoan.in	anytimeloan.in	2014	Interest as low as 0.05% per day
6	i2ifunding	ki2ifunding.com	2015	12–36%
7	OMLP2P	omlp2p.com	2016	10.99–36%
8	Finzy	finzy.com/invest	2016	10.99–27.99%
9	PaisaDukan (BigWin Infotech)	bigwininfotech.com	2018	12–24%
10	Lendenclub	lendenclub.com	2015	12–35%
11	Liquiloans	liquiloans.com	2018	>10.99%

Interest rates are per annum (unless specified otherwise) and based on the riskiness of loans. Data compiled from list of NBFC-P2P companies registered with Reserve Bank of India as on March 27, 2019.

otherwise rely on money lenders for credit, paying exorbitant interest rates. Notably, participation from women (as fundraisers and investors) has been increasing in the recent past. From 2013 to 2017, P2P platforms in India included nearly USD 195 million in overall market volume, of which USD 33.19 million were for business purposes (see Fig. 13.1 and Table 13.4).

Regulations

Regulations largely depend on the type of crowdfunding. Like most of the other countries, there are no bespoke regulations for donation and reward-based crowdfunding in India. Since there is no financial return involved in these models, they fall outside the purview of regulators like the securities market and the central bank. However, they come under the ambit of other regulations related to the payment of donations (e.g. Income Tax Act 1961) and campaign content (e.g. Information Technology Act 2000). Both individuals and organizations can run campaigns on these non-financial return crowdfunding platforms. However, only Indian nationals holding an Indian bank account can raise funds. For non-profit entities to receive contributions from abroad, an FCRA (Foreign Contribution Regulation Act) approval is mandatory. Yet with equity and lending-based crowdfunding, the situation is quite different.

All types of money lending are regulated by the central bank of India—the Reserve Bank of India (RBI). Although P2P lending came to India in 2014, there was no specific regulation in place until the latter half of 2017 (Menon 2016). In 2017 RBI issued directions targeting 'Non-Banking Financial Companies' and specifically P2P lending platforms. These directions require all P2P lending platforms to obtain a certificate from RBI, while also limiting the financial services that such platforms can provide and the amount of money they can manage (e.g. maximum INR 5 million per lender and INR 50,000 to the same borrower). Additionally, the regulations do not open for the international flow of funds.

The securities market regulator, SEBI's *Consultation Paper on Crowdfunding in India* (2014), proposed a framework for raising of funds by start-ups and SMEs, through online crowdfunding platforms or websites. The proposed guidelines restrict both who are eligible to become equity crowdfunding platforms (e.g. recognized stock exchanges, SEBI-registered depositories, associations and networks of investors), who can receive funding through these platforms (i.e. early-stage start-ups/SMEs <4 years old) and how much a company can raise (i.e. <INR 100 million/12 months).

Future Prospects

Although the ideology of crowdfunding in India traces back to the Vedic period (1500–1100 BCE), online crowdfunding is still in a somewhat nascent stage. Compared to matured markets like China, USA, UK, and Europe, there is a big gap in terms of awareness, education, acceptance, and usage of crowdfunding. In the 2013–2017 period, the Indian crowdfunding volume reached USD 450 million, which is only a fraction of the potential indicated by the World Bank (The World Bank 2013). However, the industry has seen tremendous growth with a volume of USD 268 million in 2017 alone, and year-on-year growth of 116% (Ziegler et al. 2018).

The significant growth rate can be attributed to socio-economic inequality, financial exclusion, unmet financial demand (credit gap), along with various other factors. The growth of non-financial return or community-based crowdfunding is driven by an increase in charity and philanthropy among people in India, a rise in foreign donations, and support for new and innovative causes. Growth in peer-to-peer lending is related to the credit gap and unbanked population. Finally, growth in equity crowdfunding can be explained by a combination of factors, and partly by the exponential growth in start-ups and SMEs. Yet, there are also several factors hindering the further expansion of the crowdfunding market.

The lack of regulatory guidelines for crowdfunding in general and equity crowdfunding, in particular, is likely hindering the growth and prospects of the industry. The industry needs to be supported by concrete guidelines in order to secure the interests of both platforms and platform users, as well as the society in general. For this purpose, inferences could be drawn from the UK's FCA regulations for investment-based crowdfunding and JOBS Act from the USA. Considering a few companies have already been crowdfunded by equity-based platforms in India, the perspective of these key stakeholders could also be considered in framing the guidelines.

Although crowdfunding in India is already covering a wide array of sectors, there still exists a number of areas that could benefit from the concept. Examples include agriculture, legal, real estate, and politics. Even though real estate and political crowdfunding have taken off recently, lessons could be drawn from developed markets like the Middle East and the USA, for its future prospects. Having one of the largest agricultural markets in the world, India could most likely benefit from agricultural crowdfunding, which is quite popular and successful in Nigeria and other African countries.

Crowdfunding in Bangladesh

History

Bangladesh, similar to India, has a long history of crowdfunding-like approaches to donation and collection of money. Bangladesh is home to Nobel laureate Dr Muhammad Yunus, known for initiating the concept of 'microfinance' which involves lending small amounts of money to a large number of people with the purpose of alleviating poverty (Kickul et al. 2012). Another example is the so-called Somity concept, which refers to an informal co-operative where a group of people (particularly women) save together a portion of their salary or a household income that is later invested in a business (Scheyvens 2002). Somity is identical to the 'Chit Fund' concept in the Indian context. Also, during the two Eid festivals, large sums of money are donated by Muslims in the country to people in need (the concepts of *zakat* and *sadaqah* as mentioned earlier). Today, there exist crowdfunding platforms relying on the concept of Muslim donations (e.g. www.launchgood.com).

There are several examples of informal crowdfunding from Bangladesh. In 2012, when the government of Bangladesh decided to finance the Padma Bridge project (budget USD 6.7 billion, currently under construction) from domestic sources, they invited all the citizens of Bangladesh to contribute financially by donating any amount of money to designated bank accounts (Bdnews24 2012). Another example is the Rohingya refugee crisis in 2017 when a large number of people from all over the world contributed small sums of money to help people fleeing from Myanmar (UNHCR 2017). Also, collecting money from the crowd is a common way to fund medical treatment of people in need, and aid people in rural areas during the annual periods of natural calamities like floods and cyclones. Both individuals and NGOs use these types of collections.

With the help of digitalization, such activities of raising funds are now largely done via the internet, for instance through local Facebook groups such as Mastul Foundation, Donate Bangladesh, and Biddanondo. Some of these Facebook groups are aiming to move their activities to donation-based crowdfunding platforms in the near future. The JAAGO

Foundation, a civil society organization that promotes the education of the deprived children of the country, also uses a dedicated donation webpage (donate.jaago.com.bd) to raise funds. Meanwhile, the first Bangladeshi crowdfunding platform, Projekt.co, was launched in 2015.

Prevailing Models and Platforms

As can be seen in Table 13.1, the crowdfunding scenario is rather limited in Bangladesh compared to other South Asian countries. Only USD 10,272 was reported for Bangladesh in Ziegler et al. (2018), while the number is USD 268,579,820 for neighbouring country India and USD 8,571,762 for Pakistan. Indeed, India is a larger market than Bangladesh, but Pakistan has a similar market size in terms of population. These numbers, together with the history of informal crowdfunding in Bangladesh, indicate a vast untapped potential.

For a country with more than 160 million inhabitants and a long-rooted history of donation and helping others, the possibilities of crowdfunding are still largely underexplored. In an online survey conducted by the authors, among 253 Bangladeshi respondents, 33.20% had never heard about crowdfunding before participating in the survey. Similarly, Adhikary et al. (2018) conducted a physical survey in small Bangladeshi cities and found that only 5% of the 270 small business owners that were surveyed had heard of crowdfunding. Despite the low levels of crowdfunding awareness, people generally show a positive attitude towards using crowdfunding. About 78.6% of 253 respondents in the survey by the authors and 84% of 270 respondents in the survey by Adhikary et al. (2018) indicate that they would like to use a Bangladeshi platform. Consequently, the concept of crowdfunding seems to be poorly diffused in the Bangladeshi context.

The first crowdfunding platform in Bangladesh, Projekt.co, was inaugurated in 2015 as a reward-based platform focusing on the creative industries such as music, arts, and technology. The platform was, however, closed down in 2017 due to the lack of popularity of crowdfunding in Bangladesh. Another platform, donation-based GoRiseMe, was initiated in 2015. GoRiseMe is still in operation and has accommodated 33 campaigns since inception (GoRiseMe 2019), indicating that Bangladeshi people are getting familiar with the concept of crowdfunding. However, they have yet to achieve a successful campaign.

In 2018 two new platforms started their journey—oporajoy.org and fundsme.com.bd. Oporajoy is a donation-based platform and has successfully funded one campaign so far. The campaign raised about USD 150 to help a student pay for admission fees at the University of Dhaka. In total, 38 backers donated to support the campaign. Noteworthy, Oporajoy has been operating informally in Bangladesh for a few years before launching as a formal digital crowdfunding platform. Before 2018, the founder of Oporajoy was posting fund requirements for medical treatment on social media and a simple website. She has been collecting donations via cash, cheque, bank deposit, and mobile banking (e.g. Bkash), in order to support medical patients. This is an example of business model adaptability based on the context. Payment through online gateway has only recently become popular in Bangladesh. Thus, in 2018, Oporajoy transformed its operation to a modern-looking crowdfunding website with online payment gateway accommodating all possible payment mediums in the Bangladeshi context.

Today, a few crowdfunding platforms exist in Bangladesh, although with limited activity and success so far. Fundsme, which is an equity-based platform, is a sister firm of BD Venture Limited—one of two functioning venture capital firms in Bangladesh. The Fundsme project is partially funded by the Department for International Development of the UK. Despite having several published campaigns, Fundsme has not successfully funded any campaigns so far. Currently, there are no peer-to-peer lending platforms in Bangladesh, and no functioning reward-based platform, although Banglafunding.com is expected to launch as a reward-based platform in the near future. Table 13.5 summarizes key information on current and former crowdfunding platforms in Bangladesh.

Table 13.5 Crowdfunding platforms in Bangladesh

Platform	Website	Model	Foundation	Commission
Projekt	projekt.co	Reward	2015	N/A
GoRiseMe	goriseme.com	Donation	2015	3%, for Paypal 3.4% + €0.35 per donation
Fundsme	fundsme.com.bd	Equity	2018	Upfront fee on the funding goal
Oporajoy	oporajoy.org	Donation	2018	5%

While the Bangladeshi crowdfunding platforms have had limited success so far, many Bangladeshi campaigns were successfully funded on international crowdfunding platforms like Kickstarter, IndieGoGo, and GoFundMe. As of May 2019, searching for the word 'Bangladesh' reveals 37 campaigns on Kickstarter, 71 on IndieGoGo, and 1714 on GoFundMe. Many of these campaigns raised 100% of their pledged amount, indicating potentials of crowdfunding in the context of Bangladesh. United Nations Development Programme (UNDP) Bangladesh has also executed several successful crowdfunding campaigns to support multiple causes such as Youth Empowerment through Skills (YES) (UNDP Asia and the Pacific 2016) and farmers' access to international markets (Dhaka Tribune 2017).

Regulation

There are ongoing discussions on the need for a legal framework on crowdfunding in Bangladesh (The Financial Express 2018). Despite the existence of several platforms, no such framework exists so far. Dr Habib, a professor and director of the Bangladesh Institute of Bank Management (BIBM), argued that lack of policy and regulatory framework is making it difficult to explore the potential of crowdfunding in Bangladesh (The Financial Express 2019). Due to extensive bureaucracy, the formation of such legal frameworks typically takes many years in the Bangladeshi context. However, in an informal telephone interview, a founder of a Bangladeshi crowdfunding platform expressed positive signals towards the development of a legal framework in the near future for crowdfunding in Bangladesh.

Meanwhile, similar to the Indian context, donation and reward-based platforms can be operated without any dedicated regulation. Reward-based platforms come under the Information and Communication Technology (ICT) Act 2006, which was enacted to facilitate e-commerce and encourage the growth of information technology. The ICT Act was later amended in 2013 and included provisions for imprisonment and/or fines for cyber-crimes (Export.gov 2018). Equity and peer-to-peer lending platforms, however, require governmental action as soon as possible.

Future Prospects

Based on the trends in the Indian and other South Asian markets, and the culture and history of monetary contributions among the population, crowdfunding appears to be a well-suited funding option for Bangladesh. Yet, among the Bangladeshi crowdfunding platforms, there was only one valid and successful crowdfunding campaign. Also, crowdfunding seems to be relatively unknown among Bangladeshi people, indicating a need for training and awareness in order for crowdfunding to become a viable funding option. In this vein, future research should investigate the barriers of crowdfunding in Bangladesh and how to overcome them.

Lack of regulatory guidance is one of several possible barriers. Assuming some similarity among the Indian and Bangladeshi market, P2P crowdfunding is a particularly relevant model for Bangladeshi alternative finance market (also in line with Adhikary et al. 2018). Given that lending and equity-based crowdfunding are dependent on regulatory interference, Bangladeshi financial authorities are required to act in order to realize the inherent potential of crowdfunding in the country. As no P2P lending platform exists in Bangladesh, establishing such platforms is likely another important enabler for crowdfunding growth in Bangladesh.

Future research should further investigate backers' investment intention in the Bangladeshi context. Hasan et al. (2018) find that technological awareness and subjective norms positively influence backers' crowdfunding intentions. Besides, Munim et al. (2020) find that liking the campaign idea and positive media coverage increases backers' likelihood of investing in a campaign. Thus, crowdfunding platforms should make sure that campaigns published in their website are innovative and appealing. Platforms and campaign owners need to promote their campaigns in media channels such as newspaper, radio, and TV to increase the success rate.

Conclusion

Both India and Bangladesh represent interesting crowdfunding markets due to the compatibility between the principles of crowdfunding and their cultures of giving, combined with their large and relatively poor populations. Although crowdfunding in India is in its infancy compared to developed markets like the USA, UK, and China, India is responsible for 96% of the alternative finance volume in the South Asia region. Indian crowdfunding platforms include all the major types of crowdfunding, with lending-based platforms being responsible for the majority of the volume. Bangladesh, together with Bhutan, is the least developed alternative finance markets in South Asia. So far, there are few platforms, and the ones that exist have limited volume and success. Yet, multiple Bangladeshi campaigns have been successful on international crowdfunding platforms, indicating a positive trend also in Bangladesh. Although at drastically different stages of development, India and Bangladesh share a vast unrealized potential with respect to the opportunities of future crowdfunding industry development.

Regardless of the significant deviation in volume, both Indian and Bangladeshi crowdfunding markets are contextually similar, at the same time, unique in comparison to other parts of the world. For instance, donation-based crowdfunding volume ranks second in India and the most popular in Bangladesh. In contrast, donation-based crowdfunding by volume and popularity ranks much lower in the North American and European contexts. Unlike many other parts of the world, contextually modified dedicated women-centric platforms, chit funds, and e-commerce-based crowdfunding models are visible in both India and Bangladesh. The relatively high share of donation-based crowdfunding activity could be attributed to the collectivist culture, the high degree of religiosity, and the socio-economic situation. These potential explanations could all motivate future research on crowdfunding in South Asia.

For both India and Bangladesh, regulatory issues and sustainability of crowdfunding platforms have been a crucial issue that needs to be studied further. For equity-based crowdfunding, Kshetri (2015) proposes that a "clear regulatory framework that balances the interests of entrepreneurs and investors reduced uncertainty" (p. 106). Local or international professional organizations such as National Crowdfunding Associations (NCFAs), the World Bank, or USAID can provide support to improve the crowdfunding ecosystem (Kshetri 2015; Adhikary et al. 2018). In sum, alternative finance, in general, and crowdfunding activity, in particular, are growing in both countries, although a vast unmet potential remains.

References

Acharya, N. (2013). Unregistered Chit Funds Having a Field Day. *Business Standard*. Retrieved May 22, 2019, from https://www.business-standard.com/article/finance/unregistered-chit-funds-having-a-field-day-110072500020_1.html.

Adhikary, B., & Kutsuna, K. (2016). Small Business Finance in Bangladesh: Can 'Crowdfunding' be an Alternative? *Review of Integrative Business and Economics Research, 4*(4), 1–21.

Adhikary, B., Kutsuna, K., & Hoda, T. (2018). *Crowdfunding: Lessons from Japan's Approach*. Singapore: Springer.

Baber, H. (2019a). Subjective Norms and Intention-A Study of Crowdfunding in India. *Research in World Economy, 10*(3), 136–146.

Baber, H. (2019b). Factors Underlying Attitude Formation Towards Crowdfunding in India. *International Journal of Financial Research, 10*(4), 46–54.

Bdnews24. (2012). Banks to Open Padma Bridge Donation Accounts. Retrieved November 19, 2019, from https://bdnews24.com/business/2012/08/08/banks-to-open-padma-bridge-donation-accounts.

Bhasin, S. (2019). Philanthropy in India Focuses on One's Roots, Progresses to the Community, and Usually Remains Low-Key. *The Economic Times*. Retrieved November 19, 2019, from https://economictimes.indiatimes.com/news/company/corporate-trends/philanthropy-in-india-focuses-on-ones-roots-progresses-to-the-community-and-usually-remains-low-key/articleshow/68161607.cms.

Bornstein, E. (2009). The Impulse of Philanthropy. *Cultural Anthropology, 24*(4), 622–651.

Chirputkar, A. C., Shweta, S., & Tarkas, J. (2015). Crowd Funding as a Tool of Business Transformation to Micro Enterprises in India-A Conceptual Framework. *Indian Journal of Science and Technology, 8*(S4), 115–125.

Deloitte. (2017). Regulatory Sandbox, Making India a Global Fintech Hub. Retrieved May 22, 2019, from https://www2.deloitte.com/content/dam/Deloitte/in/Documents/technology-media-telecommunications/in-tmt-fintech-regulatory-sandbox-web.pdf.

Dhaka Tribune. (2017). UNDP, GCM to Crowd-Fund for Small Farmers in Bangladesh. Retrieved May 30, 2019, from https://www.dhakatribune.com/bangladesh/2017/09/21/undp-start-crowd-funding-small-farmers-bangladesh.

Export.gov. (2018). Bangladesh—ECommerce. Retrieved May 30, 2019, from https://www.export.gov/article?id=Bangladesh-ECommerce.
EY. (2017). The Battle for the Indian Consumer. Retrieved May 10, 2019, from https://www.ey.com/Publication/vwLUAssets/ey-the-battle-for-the-indian-consumer/$File/ey-the-battle-for-the-indian-consumer.pdf.
GoRiseMe. (2019). Retrieved May 30, 2019, from https://goriseme.com/about.
Government of India, Ministry of Micro, Small and Medium Enterprises. (2017). Annual Report 2017–18. Retrieved May 22, 2019, from https://msme.gov.in/sites/default/files/MSME-AR-2017-18-Eng.pdf.
Gupta, G., & Bose, I. (2019). Strategic Learning for Digital Market Pioneering: Examining the Transformation of Wishberry's Crowdfunding Model. *Technological Forecasting and Social Change, 146*, 865–876.
Hasan, M. R., Ahmad, M. S., Rahman, M. S., & Islam, M. T. (2018). Exploring the Prerequisites of Institutionalizing Crowdfunding Process in Bangladesh as an Alternative Financing Option for the Startups. *Global Journal of Management and Business Research, 18*(1), 17–31.
Hofstede Insights. (2019). Retrieved November 18, from https://www.hofstede-insights.com/product/compare-countries/.
Impact Guru. (2017). Key Moments in the History of Crowdfunding (So Far). In *Medium (Blog)*, October 31. Retrieved May 22, 2019, from https://medium.com/@ImpactGuru/12-key-moments-in-the-history-of-crowdfunding-so-far-3f614273d95.
Kapoor, M., Schoar, A., Rao, P., & Buteau, S. (2012). Chit Funds as an Innovative Access to Finance for Low-Income Households. *Review of Market Integration, 3*(3), 287–333.
Kickul, J., Terjesen, S., Bacq, S., & Griffiths, M. (2012). Social Business Education: An Interview with Nobel Laureate Muhammad Yunus. *Academy of Management Learning & Education, 11*(3), 453–462.
KPMG. (2018). Startup Ecosystem in India—Growing or Matured? Retrieved May 22, 2019, from https://assets.kpmg/content/dam/kpmg/in/pdf/2019/01/startup-landscape-ecosystem-growing-mature.pdf.
Kshetri, N. (2015). Success of Crowd-based Online Technology in Fundraising: An Institutional Perspective. *Journal of International Management, 21*(2), 100–116.
Leela, V. (2016). Crowdfunding: A Study of Risk Factors. *South Asian Journal of Management, 23*(3), 170–192.
Marakkath, N., & Attuel-mendes, L. (2015). Can Microfinance Crowdfunding Reduce Financial Exclusion? Regulatory Issues. *International Journal of Bank Marketing, 33*(5), 624–636.

Menon, S. (2016). Crowd Control: Sebi Warns Turns Off Crowdfunding Tap for Startups. *The Economic Times*. Retrieved May 22, 2019, from https://economictimes.indiatimes.com/small-biz/money/crowd-control-sebi-warning-turns-off-crowdfunding-tap-for-startups/articleshow/54202702.cms.

Munim, Z. H., Shneor, R., Adewumi, O., & Shakil, M. H. (2020). *Determinants of Crowdfunding Intention in a Developing Economy Context: Ex-ante Evidence from Bangladesh, International Journal of Emerging Markets.* (forthcoming)

NASSCOM. (2018). Indian Tech Start-up Ecosystem—Approaching Escape Velocity. Retrieved May 22, 2019, from https://www.nasscom.in/knowledge-center/publications/indian-tech-start-ecosystem-2018-approaching-escape-velocity.

Pa, I. A. (2018). Innovations in Financing SMEs: A Study on the Growth of Crowdfunding in India. *Wealth: International Journal of Money, Banking & Finance, 7*(3), 66–75.

PWC. (2018). Fintech Trends Report India—2017. Retrieved May 22, 2019, from https://www.pwc.in/assets/pdfs/publications/2017/fintech-india-report-2017.pdf.

Saleem, S. (2018). Lessons for P2P Lending in India. *Live Mint*, September 12. Retrieved May 22, 2019, from https://www.livemint.com/Money/tuI4wvfqdbVH9nQVYC1M5I/Lessons-for-P2P-lending-in-India.html.

Scheyvens, H. (2002). Power and Poverty: The Shapla Neer Experience. *Asia Pacific Viewpoint, 43*(3), 329–342.

Securities and Exchange Board of India (SEBI). (2014). Consultation Paper on Crowdfunding in India. Retrieved November 19, 2019, from https://www.sebi.gov.in/sebi_data/attachdocs/1403005615257.pdf.

Srivastava, R. (2016). The Investment Model of Crowdfunding for MSME (Micro, Small and Medium Enterprises) in India. In J. Méric, I. Maque, & J. Brabet (Eds.), *International Perspectives on Crowdfunding: Positive, Normative and Critical Theory* (pp. 169–184). Bingley: Emerald Group Publishing Limited.

The Financial Express. (2018). Call to Set Up Legal Framework for Crowdfunding. Retrieved May 29, 2019, from https://thefinancialexpress.com.bd/trade/call-to-set-up-legal-framework-for-crowdfunding-1515647001.

The Financial Express. (2019). Crowdfunding: Developing Policy and Regulatory Framework. Retrieved May 29, 2019, from https://thefinancialexpress.com.bd/views/crowdfunding-developing-policy-and-regulatory-framework-1546440494.

The World Bank. (2013). Crowdfunding's Potential for the Developing World. In infoDev (Ed.), World Bank. Retrieved May 30, 2013, from http://www.infodev.org/infodev-files/wb_crowdfundingreport-v12.pdf.
The World Bank. (2019). Poverty & Equity Data Portal. Retrieved November 18, 2019, from http://povertydata.worldbank.org/poverty/home/.
UNDP Asia and the Pacific. (2016). UNDP Bangladesh Launches YES Crowdfunding Campaign. Retrieved May 30, 2019, from http://www.asia-pacific.undp.org/content/rbap/en/home/blog/2016/11/28/UNDP-Bangladesh-launches-YES-Crowdfunding-Campaign.html.
UNHCR. (2017). Bangladeshis Race to Save Rohingya Refugees in Need. Retrieved November 18, 2019, from https://www.unhcr.org/news/latest/2017/10/59de1bfb4/bangladeshis-race-save-rohingya-refugees-need.html.
Viswanath, P., & Dadrawala, N. (2004). Philanthropy and Equity: The Case of India. *Global Equity Initiative, Harvard University*. Retrieved May 14, 2019, from https://www.cbd.int/financial/charity/india-phequity.pdf.
Ziegler, T., Johanson, D., Zhang, B., Shenglin, B., Wang, W., Mammadova, L., Hao, R., Luo, D., Wang, Z., Chen, H., Alam, N., Ryu, S., Suresh, K., Jenweeranon, P., Yerolemou, N., Ryll, L., Huang, E., & Hao, X. (2018). *The 3rd Asia Pacific Region Alternative Finance Industry Report*. Cambridge: Cambridge Centre for Alternative Finance.

14

Crowdfunding in Africa: Opportunities and Challenges

Emmanuel James Chao, Priscilla Serwaah, Prince Baah-Peprah, and Rotem Shneor

Introduction

The crowdfunding phenomenon in Africa is somewhat lagging other regions and is still at its infancy. Despite the relatively slow adoption of crowdfunding in Africa, it is often regarded as a mechanism with great potential for increasing access to finance for entrepreneurs in developing economies in general and Africa in particular (The World Bank Group 2015). According to the Cambridge Centre for Alternative Finance (hereafter—"CCAF"), African volumes in a variety of crowdfunding models reached US $182 million in 2016, growing 118% from US $83 million in 2015 (Ziegler et al. 2018). From a regional perspective,

E. J. Chao (✉)
Mzumbe University, Mzumbe, Tanzania
e-mail: ejchao@mzumbe.ac.tz

P. Serwaah • P. Baah-Peprah • R. Shneor
School of Business and Law, University of Agder, Kristiansand, Norway
e-mail: priscilla.serwaah@uia.no; prince.baah-peprah@uia.no; rotem.shneor@uia.no

R. Shneor et al. (eds.), *Advances in Crowdfunding*,
https://doi.org/10.1007/978-3-030-46309-0_14

whereas 41% of these volumes have been recorded in West Africa, 28% have been recorded in Southern Africa, 24% in Eastern Africa, and the remaining 7% in North and Central Africa (ibid.).

Despite representing the smallest global region in terms of volumes, Africa exhibits one of the greatest potentials for crowdfunding growth. This potential is based on Africa's global leading position in terms of adopting digital finance and mobile money, the relative low penetration of traditional financial institutions, as well as crowdfunding's cultural fit with traditional funding practices. Evidence shows that digital financial solutions have been expanding access and reach to consumers, especially for the unbanked and under-banked, while significantly lowering costs of such services and making it possible to serve the base of the pyramid in a more profitable way (Rowan et al. 2018). Furthermore, mobile money became an important component in Africa's financial services landscape, as driven by more than 140 mobile money service firms catering to one in every ten African adults (Chironga et al. 2017).

At the same time, low penetration levels of traditional financial institutions, such as banks and funds, are prevalent in many African economies (KPMG 2015). This situation leads to a systematic discrimination of micro and small enterprises in terms of access to finance, as well as often insurmountable guarantees that are required for such financing when access to finance is at least formally available. Efforts have been made to fill this gap through financial solutions provided by microcredit agencies and community institutions (George et al. 2016). However, the extent to which such interventions provide an efficient and sustainable solution remains questionable. In this context, several studies compare crowdfunding to microfinance while suggesting that the advantages of the former can compensate for the inefficiencies in the latter (Wolf 2017; Oruezabala and Peter 2016).

In terms of cultural fit, some of the limited research into crowdfunding in Africa argues that modern crowdfunding can function well in supplying funding for African entrepreneurs as it represents a technological solution for "centuries-old and culturally-rooted sub-Saharan practices of individuals helping each other through communal reciprocity" (Wolf 2017). Some also argue that it can be viewed as a conceptual broadening of the participatory financing system familiar to locals from microfinance institutions (Oruezabala and Peter 2016). Furthermore, the potential for crowdfunding is also linked to contributions through diaspora philanthropy, where social capital embedded in African diaspora connections may translate into diaspora members funding of entrepreneurs in their countries of origin (Flanigan 2017). Here, while African entrepreneurs exhibit limited knowledge of crowdfunding, they also express interest in using it once familiarized with the concept, as shown by a pioneering study made in Rwanda (Berndt and Mbassana 2016).

Overall, the conditions presented above seem to suggest great promise for crowdfunding in answering market needs that are insufficiently met by existing institutions, while simultaneously supporting development, growth, and entrepreneurship. In the current chapter we explore the current state of crowdfunding research and practice in Africa, while highlighting some of the challenges and gaps for further exploration.

The Current State of Crowdfunding in Africa

In reviewing the current state of the crowdfunding industry in Africa, we mostly report findings from the CCAF second annual Middle East and Africa bench-mark report (Ziegler et al. 2018). And, hence, unless otherwise noted, all facts and figures presented in this subsection are referring to findings from the above-named source.

Unlike other regions, where funding is locally driven by indigenous investors and platforms, crowdfunding in Africa has extensively been dominated by backers from outside of Africa. In 2016, African crowdfunding volumes reached $181.27 million, while growing 118% from 2015. However, a substantial part of this amount, capturing 88% of 2016 volumes and 89% of the 2015 volumes, was raised through foreign-based platforms headquartered in Europe and the United States. The growth curve and the dominance of foreign funds signal Africa's unexploited crowdfunding opportunities and the embryonic status of crowdfunding as a financing vehicle in Africa. These indicators may suggest several implications worth highlighting. First, there is a high possibility for the continent to continue to experience exponential growth. Second, a growing share of activities may emerge from within Africa as local platforms sprout, the populace gets better educated about and better familiarized with crowdfunding, and as regulatory institutions build legal frameworks that are more conducive and enabling of a crowdfunding ecosystem. Such developments are likely to increase indigenous backers' and investors' appetite towards crowdfunding local projects.

The African continent includes multiple regional and national markets with diverse development levels, institutional environments, and geographical conditions. Such diversity is also evident when examining the development of crowdfunding in various regions of the continent. Here, in terms of size, between 2013 and 2016, the East African region has emerged as a consistent market leader with an average annual market share of 38%. West Africa comes second with 34%, followed by the South African region with 17%. Central and North Africa are behind with 7% and 4% respectively. While some decline was registered in East and Central Africa in recent years, dramatic growth has been recorded in Southern Africa (824% in 2015 and 116% in 2016) and Western Africa (150% in 2016), which are associated with market development in South Africa and Nigeria respectively. Strong growth was also observed in North Africa growing 80% on average between 2013 and 2016, with most activities in Egypt.

At the national level, Kenya and Uganda dominate the Eastern African region. Nigeria and Cote D'Ivoire account for the major share of the Western African region. South Africa, Rwanda, and Egypt solely dominate the Southern, Central, and the Northern African regions respectively. On a continental basis, Nigeria, South Africa, and Kenya dominate Africa's crowdfunding industry overall. These three countries jointly account for 74–82% of annual African crowdfunding market volumes between 2013 and 2016.

When examining African crowdfunding by model, and like other global regions, evidence shows that a large proportion of crowdfunding volume is associated with investment models, which accounted for 79% of total volumes in 2015 and 63% in 2016. When splitting these volumes further among the various investment models, lending-based models jointly account for the largest share of investment-crowdfunding volumes, capturing 90% of such volumes in 2015 and 56% in 2016. These percentages correspond to volumes equal to $59 million in 2015 and $63 million in 2016. This development is mostly evident with respect to peer-to-peer business lending that grew 46% between 2015 and 2016, while crowd-based pro-social microlending remained stable at $34 million in both 2015 and 2016. Nevertheless, 2016 has seen the introduction of additional crowdfunding investment models in the continent. Here, equity, real estate, and profit-sharing models grew from $6.39 million in 2015 to $51.31 million in 2016, jointly representing an impressive 701% growth. Overall, the emergence of these models jointly represents 28% of total volumes raised in 2016, which explains the shrinking share of crowdlending out of investment model volumes, while the actual amount has increased.

At the same period, non-investment models of crowdfunding accounted for 21% of total volumes raised in 2015 and 37% of volumes in 2016. Here, reward-based crowdfunding experienced a modest increase from $3.17 million in 2015 to $4.17 million in 2016, while accounting for 2.3% of total volumes raised in 2016. Donation-based crowdfunding, on the other hand, exhibits more substantial volumes and growth while mostly relying on funders based outside of Africa. Under this model, $14.26 million were raised in 2015 and $63.11 million were raised in 2016, growing 342% between 2015 and 2016. This implies that donation crowdfunding is the single largest model of crowdfunding in the continent, representing 35% of total volumes raised in Africa during 2016. This stands at a stark contrast to all other regions in the world, where peer-to-peer lending models dominate.

While not yet substantiated in empirical research, one may suggest several explanations for the prominence of donation crowdfunding in the African crowdfunding context. First, one can argue that Africa is just following market development observed elsewhere, where initial crowdfunding activities were associated with non-investment types of crowdfunding that later paved the way towards the proliferation of investment-crowdfunding platforms (Bruton et al. 2015). Indeed, these dynamics have been observed in many countries in Europe, Asia, and the Americas. Second, and closely linked to the previous explanation, is the concern with risk and development of trust. In this sense, non-investment-crowdfunding engagements represent lower risk, involve modest sums, and are characterized by fewer regulatory compliance barriers than investment crowdfunding (Belleflamme and Lambert 2016; Ziegler et al. 2019). As such, non-investment crowdfunding becomes easier to implement and experiment with. Once individuals accumulate positive experiences with these models, they may develop greater willingness to gradually engage in activities that may be considered riskier, involve higher sums, and may carry greater regulatory implications (e.g. investor protection).

As the status of crowdfunding practice is now established, we now turn to examining the status of research on crowdfunding in African contexts while presenting key findings emerging from such academic work.

Emerging Insights from Crowdfunding Research in Africa

Research into crowdfunding in Africa is limited and represents early stages of market development, with most related studies being more conceptual in nature. Here, according to Wolf (2017), the crowdfunding phenomenon is congruent with traditional communal reciprocity culture of sub-Saharan African individuals. This view is also shared by Berndt (2016), who suggests that crowdfunding is a modern form of credit associations in the African context, where individuals invest in the businesses of others. Interestingly, the tradition of credit associations and other forms of microfinancing (delivered in diverse formats) have existed in many African cultures for decades. Credit associations work on the principle of communal reciprocity, where individuals usually contribute money periodically into a communal fund and the collected amount is either shared among the community members or invested on their behalf (ibid.). Notable examples of these credit associations include Susu in Ghana, Mabati in Kenya, Ekub in Ethiopia, Tontine in Mali, and Stokvels in South Africa (Coetzee 2013). Regardless of the form, these schemes thrive on small-scale financing to support group saving methods, and often involved communities are embedded with a culture of mutual supporting for business ideas.

Several studies attempt to compare crowdfunding to microfinance, with authors proposing that the advantages of the former can compensate for the inefficiencies in the latter (Wolf 2017; Oruezabala and Peter 2016). Here, based on a sample of 50 Gabonese small businesses, Oruezabala and Peter (2016) note that 78% of these SMEs derived their funding from personal funds, family, and credit associations. Thus, most of these small businesses are excluded from microfinancing, possibly due to their inability to meet certain requirements. Indeed, the researchers argue that some Microfinance Institutions are moving away from their social mission, a development that opens opportunities for crowdfunding platforms and makes crowdfunding an attractive alternative for small businesses.

Wolf (2017) suggests that the over-reliance of microfinance on subsidies makes it unsustainable thereby limiting its success and impact. Moreover, there have been calls for microfinance to focus not only on poverty reduction but also on social emancipation through creativity (de Haan and Lakwo 2010). In contrast, crowdfunding platforms are known avenues for creative and innovative ventures (Wolf 2017). Thus, although crowdfunding might draw some inspiration from microfinancing (Munyanyi and Mapfumo 2018), it can promote co-creation of innovation between entrepreneurs and funders (Wolf 2017) while strengthening the overall entrepreneurial financing dynamics which already exist in the microfinance industry (Oruezabala and Peter 2016). Accordingly, in their proposed model for crowdfunding penetration and success in Africa, Oruezabala and Peter (ibid.) present crowdfunding platforms as a source of new resources, rather as a new way to tap into old resources.

To these considerations, Flanigan (2017) introduces an additional important consideration by examining how crowdfunding could contribute towards enhancing diaspora philanthropy. For this purpose, she defined diaspora philanthropy as "money, goods, volunteer labor, knowledge and skills, and other assets donated for the social benefit of a community broader than ones' family members, in a country or region where there is a population with whom the donor(s) have ancestral ties" (ibid., p. 498). Here, Flanigan notes that an integration of the literature on the two phenomena shows that crowdfunding technologies could enhance the delivery of diaspora philanthropy—where diaspora philanthropy is seen as a subset of remittance flows into countries.

In the same spirit, online philanthropy may be viewed as the giving of financial and social capital for promoting human welfare through online platforms (Munyanyi and Mapfumo 2018). Hence, through crowdfunding, African migrants can continue supporting entrepreneurial activities by helping family members and friends in their countries of origin via the mediation of crowdfunding platforms. Again, this may be in tandem with remittances which serves as an important source of incoming capital in many African countries. Indeed, remittances sent by African migrants reached nearly $40 billion in 2010, an amount equivalent to 2.6% of Africa's gross domestic product (Mohapatra and Dilip 2011). As noted by Flanigan (2017), strategically capitalizing on the shared characteristics and complementary strengths of crowdfunding and diaspora philanthropy can help diaspora generated 'philanthropic crowdfunding' thrive.

Furthermore, diaspora members offer networks and knowledge that could help offset crowdfunding's vulnerabilities. Indeed, earlier research shows that diaspora networks have significant impact on cross-border investment (Leblang 2010). And that diaspora investments in countries of origin are affected by perceived ethnic advantage (over other investors) and altruistic tendencies, while perceptions of business impediments do not affect such investments (Gillespie et al. 1999). Bringing such insights into the context of crowdfunding, platforms may reduce informational and technical barriers for such investment opportunities and may enhance their likelihood by tapping into diaspora members' sense of ethnic advantage and altruistic orientation towards opportunities in their countries of origin. The latter reflecting beliefs that investors should invest in one's country of origin and not just send donations there (ibid.). One example for such initiative is the French-based LelapaFund platform, which is dedicated to facilitating investments in Africa by tapping onto African diasporas, which, according to one of its co-founders, perceive fewer barriers to such investments while normalizing risk associated with African venturing (Mulligan 2015).

Other authors have explored the factors influencing the plausibility of crowdfunding in Africa. More specifically, Munyanyi and Mapfumo (2018), focusing on Zimbabwe, identified four factors that influence the plausibility of crowdfunding, including strong and active social network, easy and reliable payment system, a passionate audience, and a funding gap. In this context, the identification of crowdfunding success drivers in Africa and how they can be directed towards economic development in the region are extremely important for both entrepreneurs and funders. A good example of such approach can be found in suggestions that crowdfunding may be adapted to solving regional issues such as power shortages, which are usually experienced in most parts of Africa, and by addressing a concrete need affecting people's lives, which will make crowdfunding more attractive for those who live in affected areas (Berndt 2016).

Challenges for the Development of Crowdfunding in Africa

Whereas crowdfunding is considered to present great opportunities towards enhancing access to finance, as well as supporting entrepreneurship, innovation, and development in Africa, it is also important to consider some challenges that may hinder crowdfunding adoption and growth in the continent. This is especially important when taking into considerations that the main vehicles for crowdfunding market development, namely crowdfunding platforms, are mostly entrepreneurial ventures themselves. And while entrepreneurs deal with adversity regardless of context, some challenges reign prominent in African contexts in general (e.g. Alon and Shneor 2017; Belwal and Singh 2008) and the African crowdfunding context in particular.

Regulation

In this context, researchers particularly emphasize that regulatory factors matter (Berndt 2016; Flanigan 2017). This assertion is supported by Munyanyi and Mapfumo (2018) who argue that, despite the viability of crowdfunding in Zimbabwe, there is a lot to be done to set up an enabling regulatory framework in the country. Overall, the health and strength of the SME sector in Africa is often viewed as a policy priority in most countries across the continent. Accordingly, African governments may address crowdfunding regulation as an enabler of domestic innovation and entrepreneurship. One path for such development may be facilitated by learning from the experiences of other countries elsewhere around the world. In this context, earlier research in Europe indeed showed that the more adequate national regulation is perceived to be by platforms operating in the same national market, the higher the overall crowdfunding volumes per capita in the same market (Ziegler et al. 2019).

Thus far, there remains "no bespoke, tailor-made alternative finance regulation regime that has been enacted in Africa as has been the case in other more established markets" (Ziegler et al. 2018, p. 22). And, in the absence of crowdfunding-specific regulation, generic financial services regulation applies to firms seeking to provide services falling within the scope of activities covered in existing laws. Nevertheless, several regulatory initiatives to support financial innovation more generally have been adopted by various African government agencies. These include, but are not limited to, various steps taken towards establishing regulatory sandbox processes for financial technology companies in Kenya, Mauritius, Mozambique, Rwanda, South Africa, and Uganda (Ziegler et al. 2018). In addition, the African Crowdfunding Association was established in 2015 as an industry organization dedicated to lobbying in favour of crowdfunding legislation creation and reforms, increasing public awareness of crowdfunding, and ensuring industry practices that protect investors and democratize access to capital (African Crowdfunding Association 2019).

Information Technology Infrastructure

Since online forms of crowdfunding heavily depend on access to social media and social networking sites, as well as web-based platforms, internet access is paramount to its successful dissemination and uptake. Here, an important challenge for the development of the industry in Africa relates to internet infrastructure and the relative low internet penetration in many regions across the continent. As a whole, internet penetration rate in Africa stood at just 37.3% in May 2019 in comparison to 60.8% in the rest of the world (Miniwatts Marketing Group 2019). Here, again, regional and national variations do exist, and while some countries report relatively high penetration levels such as 83% in Kenya and 80.1% in Liberia, others exhibit much lower rates such as 1.3% in Eritrea and 4.1% in Niger (ibid.). Such conditions limit the ability of African fundraisers to capitalize on the value of network externalities in crowdfunding (Wolf 2017). To overcome such challenges, crowdfunding platforms operating in Africa have leveraged mobile technology while using innovative ways to create and promote projects via SMS, popular mobile apps (e.g. WhatsApp, Messenger, Viber), and use of mobile money to fund projects (Boum 2016).

Social Trust

Furthermore, from a social-normative perspective, African countries are often found to be characterized by a relative low level of social trust (Delhey and Newton 2005). Social trust was defined as "the belief that others will not deliberately or knowingly do us harm, if they can avoid it, and will look after our interests, if this is possible" (ibid., p. 311). While this may seem at odds with traditional crowdfunding practices in Africa, it is explained by the distinction between trust towards in-group members versus strangers. Africans may exhibit trust towards familiar in-group members, while exhibiting lower levels of trust towards strangers outside their immediate circle of acquaintances (Posel and Hinks 2012) than other societies. However, both trust between strangers and trust towards online transaction are required in order to facilitate a thriving crowdfunding market (Kshetri 2015).

Research from other contexts of online transactions shows that satisfactory online customer experience enhances trust in e-retailing/online shopping (Rose et al. 2012) and in e-banking/online banking (Ghane et al. 2011). Taken together, these insights may suggest that trust can also be created with experience, and that adoption may be enhanced by creating opportunities for crowdfunding experience with low entry thresholds. Moreover, the transparency involved in crowdfunding transactions can serve as a trust facilitating mechanism (Spanos 2018). Here, information about delivery and repayment of loans, as well as non-delivery or non-payment on loans, will be publicly available and deter fundraisers from shirking such responsibilities for avoiding a damage to their reputation and self-image. Indeed, research shows that concerns about disclosure, visible failure, and projecting desperation hinder entrepreneurs from using crowdfunding (Gleasure 2015), and by extension may help curtail related moral hazards. In addition to the above, the transparent digital recording of transactions can also help in limiting opportunities for corruption in the financial sector, which represents a concern in various African countries (Hanlon 2002; Demetriades and Fielding 2012).

Finally, as platform survival and growth depend on positive user experiences and successful campaigning, most platforms engage in careful campaign filtration, validation, and selection processes. This is evident in platform onboarding rates, which reflect the percentage of campaigns published out of total campaigns requesting to be published on a given platform. Here, while onboarding rates are not yet available for African platforms, European platforms report average onboarding rates of 49% in reward crowdfunding, 74% in donation crowdfunding, 17–22% in leading crowdlending models, and 6% in equity crowdfunding (Ziegler et al. 2019). In this sense, platforms serve as risk-reducing players in comparison to independent and unverified fundraising initiatives that do not go through the scrutiny of platform validation procedures (e.g. fundraiser identity verifications, background checks).

Early Days of African Crowdfunding: Hybrid Forms of Crowdfunding

As mentioned earlier, African crowdfunding for Africans and by Africans remains at a very early stage. Accordingly, fundraisers in this sphere attempt to tap into crowdfunding's promises of improved access to finance and enhanced transparency, while manoeuvring between existing barriers to adoption at both social and institutional levels. Such efforts can be characterized as hybrid forms of crowdfunding implying combinations of multiple channels for fundraising in addition to crowdfunding platforms. In this section, we present several illustrative examples of such hybrid forms from East African crowdfunding campaigns.

First, a donation campaign created for a Tanzanian member of parliament, who got shot and was severely injured, sought to raise funds for his medical treatments. The campaign was created on the US-based global platform Gofundme by a group of Tanzanian diaspora members in the United States (Kolumbia 2017). However, in parallel, locals in Tanzania used M-Pesa mobile money to support the same campaign where the money was being paid directly to the account of the beneficiary. The local campaign was steered primarily through Word of Mouth. Here, even though most of middle-class Tanzanian citizens had the capacity to make their contribution via the Gofundme platform, they preferred sending their contribution using mobile money and direct bank account transfers. As a result, most online contributors were members of the diaspora.

Second, a different donation campaign was created to raise fund for the development of the Fishmate platform. This platform aims to serve the fishing and aqua-culture industry as a channel for information aggregation and dissemination, as well as a marketplace linking demand and suppliers among fishing communities in Kenya. The campaign was created on the global Dutch-based platform Onepercentclub by the entrepreneur—Mukeli Matai (Raymond 2015). Here, again, support from foreign and diaspora members was collected via the platform, but in addition Mutai needed to build a group of individuals who would form the base of her campaign in Kenya. This group, however, was either unable or reluctant to contribute money through the platform. In response, Mutai formed an offline fundraising campaign effort known locally in its traditional name—"Harambee". Under this effort, a "treasurer" was appointed to collect money from contributors via the M-Pesa mobile payment system or in cash. This treasurer then made a single contribution to the Onepercentclub platform, which then transferred funds to Mutai's bank account. Overall, Fishmate raised €2678 from about 20 family members in Kenya, a sum which was later matched with €6000 from the Cheetah Fund. Here, the matching fund scheme presented is an important incentive for her network to contribute online via the platform and not directly.

Third, in one of the first reward campaigns launched through a new platform being developed in Tanzania under the Dar Technology and Business Incubator, it was reported that individuals collected money from peers offline and then transferred the collected sum to the intended recipient. A major challenge from this method as highlighted by the platform owners is the difficulty in identifying those who contributed through offline groups because it is only possible to track the one who transferred the funds. As money laundering is a concern in most of the countries, it is important to establish the identity of contributors for complying with legal and ethical practices in fundraising. Here, while the platform does request detailed information from contributors of relatively large sums, it remains a challenge to establish the accuracy and trustworthiness of such information.

Overall, the above examples indicate that crowdfunding uptake in Africa requires overcoming challenges associated with trust and technical concerns at early stages of crowdfunding engagement. The cases presented above suggest that campaigners complement campaigns posted in online platforms with traditional or technical payment systems Africans are already well familiar with. Specifically, combinations of online and offline efforts seem to support fundraising activities by tapping into different groups of prospective contributors. Such approach has received support in earlier studies showing that offline activities play an important role in sustaining online communities (Lin 2007).

Indeed, initial steps towards understanding the role of offline activities in crowdfunding have shown several interesting findings in other contexts. Here, a study of civic crowdfunding (when citizens, in collaboration with government, fund projects providing a community service) concluded that integrating online and offline approaches are essential for such campaigns' success (Stiver et al. 2014). And, a different study on crowdlending in the United States showed that when borrowers are registered in same state as the borrowing group leader (used as proxy for likelihood of offline interactions) crowd loans get more bids from prospective lenders but show no effect on the total amount raised (Kuwabara et al. 2017).

Conclusion

In this chapter, the current state of crowdfunding research and practice in Africa has been outlined while highlighting some of the opportunities and challenges associated with them. Overall, we show that African crowdfunding is at its infancy. However, the extent to which crowdfunding may deliver on its promises of improved access to finance and enablement of growth remains to be substantiated empirically as the market grows and the industry matures.

Here, on the one hand, conditions of growing popularity of digital and mobile finance, low penetration of traditional financial institutions, and a long cultural heritage of communal mutual support may enhance crowdfunding uptake. On the other hand, conditions of unclear regulation, relatively low levels of internet access, and societies characterized by low social trust may all hinder crowdfunding uptake. Hence, for wider public adoption of crowdfunding, stakeholders interested in such development may need to engage in relevant policy development, implementation of technological solutions suitable for available ICT and financial infrastructure, raising public awareness through education, reducing user entry barriers, and creating low-risk or risk-free incentives for trial. Such actions can support the shift away from donation collection to investment fundraising, and from reliance on foreign investors towards enabling local micro-investors to build up their own capital base.

Implications for Future Research

Our review clearly shows that research on crowdfunding in the African context remains limited and conceptual. This implies that opportunities for future research are abundant and especially when considering empirical work that can test and challenge insights and findings from elsewhere around the world. Specifically, future research should focus on investigating crowdfunding adoption and its implication for development in Africa. Such efforts will enhance the understanding of how and to what extent does crowdfunding help in unlocking the potential of access to finance and investment opportunities for wider financial inclusiveness, business development, and job creation in Africa. Studies on crowdfunding adoption may explore the applicability of existing theoretical frameworks such as the Technology Acceptance Model (Venkatesh and Davis 2000) and the Theory of Planned Behaviour (Ajzen 1991), as well as highlight needs for their modification in the new realities of digital and mobile finance in development contexts. Studies examining the impact of crowdfunding can help us measure and capture the extent to which crowdfunding contributes to venture creation, survival, and growth, as well as the extent to which crowdfunding enables greater inclusivity and access to finance for groups that traditionally struggle with it such as women (Carter and Rosa 1998; Coleman 2000) and minorities (Ram et al. 2003).

Furthermore, the African context itself may represent a particularly conducive environment to study several important issues. First, research should identify and explore the effectivity of mechanisms and strategies for establishing trust in crowdfunding in societies characterized by low social trust. Second, research can also examine complementarities of offline and online dimensions of crowdfunding in environments characterized by limited ICT infrastructure and e-readiness. Third, research can examine the role played by diaspora in African crowdfunding campaign success in general, as well as facilitators of trust for African crowdfunding campaigns particularly vis-à-vis other international supporters.

Implications for Practice

Our review also shows that the African crowdfunding industry is at its infancy. As a new emergent sector that aims to solve market gaps by both extending and supplementing existing fundraising channels, certain critical elements need to be developed for supporting such efforts. First, regulators should engage with domestic and international industry players, as well as peers in other countries in reviewing and amending legal frameworks towards accommodating a good balance between user and investor protection while enabling the industry's responsible and sustainable growth. In addition, government bodies in collaboration with educational institutions may engage in developing training programmes and dissemination of public information about the risks and benefits of using crowdfunding for fundraising and investment purposes for both individuals and organizations.

In parallel, platforms aiming to establish themselves in African markets need to invest their resources into developing technological solutions that fit development realities and infrastructure conditions in Africa (e.g. integration of mobile payment, social media, and instant messaging functionalities), implementing relevant filtration and validation procedures for quality assurance and avoidance of fraud (e.g. creative solutions for identity verification and documentation), as well as introducing incentive mechanisms to encourage trial by prospective users while reducing entry barriers and risks associated with such trial (e.g. internal insurance funds, gradual increasing sums for fundraising based on historical performance of users).

References

African Crowdfunding Association. (2019). *African Crowdfunding Association: Moving Africa Forward* [Online]. Cape Town, RSA: African Crowdfunding Association. Retrieved June 10, 2019, from https://africancrowd.org/.

Ajzen, I. (1991). The Theory of Planned Behavior. *Organizational Behavior and Human Decision Process, 50*(2), 179–211.

Alon, I., & Shneor, R. (2017). More Than Makeup: How Atsoko Overcame the Challenges of Entrepreneurship in Tanzania. *Global Business and Organizational Excellence, 36*(6), 25–33.

Belleflamme, P., & Lambert, T. (2016). An Industrial Organization Framework to Understand the Strategies of Crowdfunding Platforms. In J. Méric, I. Maque, & J. Brabet (Eds.), *International Perspectives on Crowdfunding: Positive, Normative, and Critical Theory*. Bingley, UK: Emerald Group Publishing Limited.

Belwal, R., & Singh, G. (2008). Entrepreneurship and SMEs in Ethiopia: Evaluating the Role, Prospects and Problems Faced by Women in This Emergent Sector. *Gender in Management: An International Journal, 23*(2), 120–136.

Berndt, A. (2016). Crowdfunding in the African Context: A New Way to Fund Ventures. In L. Achtenhagen & E. Brundin (Eds.), *Entrepreneurship and SME*

Management Across Africa: Context, Challenges, Cases. Singapore: Springer Singapore.

Berndt, A., & Mbassana, M. (2016). *Crowdfunding: The Beliefs of Rwandan Entrepreneurs*. East Africa Research Papers in Business, Entrepreneurship and Management. Jönköping, Sweden: Jönköping University, Jönköping International Business School.

Boum, E. (2016). Crowdfunding in Africa: Fundraising Goes Digital in Africa – The Emergence of Africa-Based Crowdfunding Platforms. Retrieved April 27, 2019, from http://afrikstart.com/report/wp-content/uploads/2016/09/Afrikstart-Crowdfunding-In-Africa-Report.pdf.

Bruton, G., Khavul, S., Siegel, D., et al. (2015). New Financial Alternatives in Seeding Entrepreneurship: Microfinance, Crowdfunding, and Peer-to-Peer Innovations. *Entrepreneurship Theory and Practice, 39*(1), 9–26.

Carter, S., & Rosa, P. (1998). The Financing of Male- and Female-Owned Businesses. *Entrepreneurship & Regional Development, 10*(3), 225–242.

Chironga, M., De Grandis, H., & Zouaoui, Y. (2017). Mobile Financial Services in Africa: Winning the Battle for the Customer. Retrieved from https://www.mckinsey.com/industries/financial-services/our-insights/mobile-financial-services-in-africa-winning-the-battle-for-the-customer.

Coetzee, J. (2013). Africa's Crowdfunding Context: Starting up Startups the African Way. Retrieved April 23, 2019, from https://ventureburn.com/2013/07/africas-crowdfunding-context-starting-up-startups-the-african-way/.

Coleman, S. (2000). Access to Capital and Terms of Credit: A Comparison of Men- and Women-Owned Small Businesses. *Journal of Small Business Management, 38*(3), 37–52.

de Haan, L., & Lakwo, A. (2010). Rethinking the Impact of Microfinance in Africa: 'Business Change' or Social Emancipation. *The European Journal of Development Research, 22*(4), 529–545.

Delhey, J., & Newton, K. (2005). Predicting Cross-National Levels of Social Trust: Global Pattern or Nordic Exceptionalism? *European Sociological Review, 21*(4), 311–327.

Demetriades, P., & Fielding, D. (2012). Information, Institutions, and Banking Sector Development in West Africa. *Economic Inquiry, 50*(3), 739–753.

Flanigan, S. T. (2017). Crowdfunding and Diaspora Philanthropy: An Integration of the Literature and Major Concepts. *VOLUNTAS: International Journal of Voluntary and Nonprofit Organizations, 28*(2), 492–509.

George, G., Kotha, R., Parikh, P., et al. (2016). Social Structure, Reasonable Gain, and Entrepreneurship in Africa. *Strategic Management Journal, 37*(6), 1118–1131.

Ghane, S., Fathian, M., & Gholamian, M. R. (2011). Full Relationship Among e-Satisfaction, e-Trust, e-Service Quality, and e-Loyalty: The Case of Iran e-Banking. *Journal of Theoretical and Applied Information Technology, 33*(1), 1–6.

Gillespie, K., Riddle, L., Sayre, E., et al. (1999). Diaspora Interest in Homeland Investment. *Journal of International Business Studies, 30*(3), 623–634.

Gleasure, R. (2015). Resistance to Crowdfunding Among Entrepreneurs: An Impression Management Perspective. *The Journal of Strategic Information Systems, 24*(4), 219–233.

Hanlon, J. (2002). Bank Corruption Becomes Site of Struggle in Mozambique. *Review of African Political Economy, 29*(91), 53–72.

Kolumbia, L. (2017). Sh14m Raised Through Online Campaign for Lissu's Treatment in the Past Five Days. Retrieved January 14, 2020, from https://www.thecitizen.co.tz/News/1840340-4110142-4f4pplz/index.html.

KPMG. (2015). *Sector Report: Banking in Africa 2015*. Johannesburg, SA: KPMG.

Kshetri, N. (2015). Success of Crowd-Based Online Technology in Fundraising: An Institutional Perspective. *Journal of International Management, 21*(2), 100–116.

Kuwabara, K., Anthony, D., & Horne, C. (2017). In the Shade of a Forest Status, Reputation, and Ambiguity in an Online Microcredit Market. *Social Science Research, 64*, 96–118.

Leblang, D. (2010). Familiarity Breeds Investment: Diaspora Networks and International Investment. *American Political Science Review, 104*(3), 584–600.

Lin, H. F. (2007). The Role of Online and Offline Features in Sustaining Virtual Communities: An Empirical Study. *Internet Research, 17*(2), 119–138.

Miniwatts Marketing Group. (2019). *Internet World Stats* [Online]. Miniwatts Marketing Group. Retrieved June 5, 2019, from https://www.internetworldstats.com/stats1.htm.

Mohapatra, S., & Dilip, R. (2011). Migrant Remittances in Africa: An Overview. In S. Mohapatra & R. Dilip (Eds.), *Remittance Markets in Africa*. Washington, DC: The World Bank.

Mulligan, G. (2015). Africa Discovers the Power of Crowdfunding. Retrieved January 14, 2020, from https://www.bbc.com/news/business-33100535.

Munyanyi, W., & Mapfumo, A. (2018). Factors Influencing Crowdfunding Plausibility in Post Hyperinflationary Zimbabwe. *International Journal of Contemporary Applied Researches, 5*(10), 99–111.

Oruezabala, G., & Peter, S. G. (2016). Equity Crowdfunding in Africa: How Can Investment Micro-Behaviors Make the Crowdfunding Macro-System Work? In J. Méric, I. Maque, & J. Brabet (Eds.), *International Perspectives on Crowdfunding*. Emerald Group Publishing Limited.

Posel, D., & Hinks, T. (2012). Trusting Neighbours or Strangers in a Racially Divided Society: Insights from Survey Data in South Africa. *Journal of African Economies, 22*(1), 136–162.

Ram, M., Smallbone, D., Deakins, D., et al. (2003). Banking on 'Break-Out': Finance and the Development of Ethnic Minority Businesses. *Journal of Ethnic and Migration Studies, 29*(4), 663–681.

Raymond, S. (2015). Six Things You Need to Know About Crowdfunding in Developing Countries. *World Bank Blogs* [Online]. Retrieved December 16, 2019, from http://blogs.worldbank.org/psd/six-things-you-need-know-about-crowdfunding-developing-countries.

Rose, S., Clark, M., Samouel, P., et al. (2012). Online Customer Experience in e-Retailing: An Empirical Model of Antecedents and Outcomes. *Journal of Retailing, 88*(2), 308–322.

Rowan, P., Garvey, K., Zhang, B., et al. (2018). *FinTech in Uganda: Implications for Regulation*. Cambridge, UK: Cambridge Center for Alternative Finance.

Spanos, L. (2018). Complementarity and Interconnection Between CSR and Crowdfunding: A Case Study in Greece. In G. Grigore, A. Stancu, & D. McQueen (Eds.), *Corporate Responsibility and Digital Communities: An International Perspective Towards Sustainability*. Cham: Springer International Publishing.

Stiver, A., Barroca, L., Minocha, S., et al. (2014). Civic Crowdfunding Research: Challenges, Opportunities, and Future Agenda. *New Media & Society, 17*(2), 249–271.

The World Bank Group. (2015). *Crowdfunding in Emerging Markets: Lessons from East African Startups*. Washington, DC: The World Bank Group.

Venkatesh, V., & Davis, F. D. (2000). A Theoretical Extension of the Technology Acceptance Model: Four Longitudinal Field Studies. *Management Science, 46*(2), 186–204.

Wolf, C. (2017). From Harambee to Modern Crowdfunding: The Opportunities and Challenges in Sub-Saharan Africa. In D. T. Redford (Ed.), *Developing Africa's Financial Services: The Importance of High-Impact Entrepreneurship*. Bingley, UK: Emerald Publishing Ltd..

Ziegler, T., Suresh, K., Garvey, K., et al. (2018). *The 2nd Annual Middle East & Africa Alternative Finance Industry Report*. Cambridge, UK: Cambridge Center for Alternative Finance.

Ziegler, T., Shneor, R., Wenzlaff, K., et al. (2019). *Shifting Paradigms – The 4th European Alternative Finance Benchmarking Report*. Cambridge, UK: Cambridge Centre for Alternative Finance.

15

Israeli Crowdfunding: A Reflection of Its Entrepreneurial Culture

Kalanit Efrat, Shaked Gilboa, and Daniel Berliner

An Introduction: The 'Prenumeranten' Phenomenon

The life story of Yisrael Haim of Belgrade illustrates a vivid picture of Jewish life in the eighteenth and nineteenth centuries. He fled to Vienna due to military struggles, where he was associated with the local aristocracy. During that time, he was familiarized with the *prenumeranten* (a term in Yiddish, literally meaning 'prior numbers'). The prenumeranten was a system used by Western European Jews. Back then, book production was costly, and authors were requested to pay one-third of the publishing costs

K. Efrat (✉) • S. Gilboa
School of Economics and Business Administration, Ruppin Academic Centre, Emek Hefer, Israel
e-mail: kalanite@ruppin.ac.il; shakedg@ruppin.ac.il

D. Berliner
School of Business and Law, University of Agder, Kristiansand, Norway
e-mail: daniel.berliner@uia.no

R. Shneor et al. (eds.), *Advances in Crowdfunding*,
https://doi.org/10.1007/978-3-030-46309-0_15

in advance to the publishers. To collect the required amount, they used the prenumeranten scheme in which the author or other individuals on his behalf travelled to various Jewish communities, seeking to persuade people and establishments with a potential interest in the book to support it. These people and establishments were later recognized for their support by having their names printed in the volume's front matter as an acknowledgement in the book's first edition. Yisrael Haim used this system to publish a complete Ladino translation of the Bible (Bunis 1996). Thus, in the nineteenth century, the prenumeranten was a common system for publishing books, and as many as 8750 Jewish communities across Europe and North Africa participated in it (Cohen 1975).

As such, the prenumeranten system can be considered an early version of the modern crowdfunding concept. At the same time, the innovative approach for soliciting funds illustrates the cultural origins of the Jewish entrepreneurial spirit. Indeed, the crowdfunding concept found fertile ground in Israel, facilitated by a growing need for funds to support various types of ventures. These ventures were accompanied by the curiosity and inquisitiveness that is so typical of Israelis, which facilitated a generally welcoming approach to novel things and ideas. In the following section, we discuss the various aspects of the entrepreneurial ecosystem driving crowdfunding in Israel.

We begin by mapping the main components of the Israeli entrepreneurship ecosystem while discussing each in the context of crowdfunding and provide illustrative examples. We then continue by describing the crowdfunding scene in Israel, detailing its various types, and discussing the emerging trends. We conclude with implications and conclusions.

The Israeli Entrepreneurship Ecosystem

The Facets of Entrepreneurship and Innovation in Israel

The drivers of the Israeli crowdfunding are strongly associated with the country's entrepreneurship ecosystem. Israel has been an entrepreneurship leader for most of the last three decades. It is ranked fifth in the 2019

Bloomberg Innovation Index, tracking the most innovative countries (Jamrisko et al. 2019), and fifth among the developed countries in its entrepreneurial level, as reported in the Global Entrepreneurship Monitor (Menipaz and Avrahami 2019). Moreover, the country has been ranked fourth among the developed countries in the Global Entrepreneurial Spirit Index of the Global Entrepreneurship Monitor, indicating the strong entrepreneurial culture in the country (Menipaz and Avrahami 2019). The innovative culture of Israel is manifested in substantial governmental investments in research and development. Israel is the leading country among the OECD nations in gross domestic spending on R&D, with 4.5% of the country's GDP (as of 2017), and 17.4 researchers per 1000 employed (OECD 2018).

Israel is also an acknowledged leader in the tech industries (Engel and del-Palacio 2011), ending 2018 with $6B of funding raised by 645 companies, an increase of 15% from the previous year, and a 140% increase over five years. In line with these funding numbers, the number of active Israeli high-tech companies has grown by 27% since 2014 (Korbet 2019). One manifestation of Israel's entrepreneurial nature is the number of exits among Israeli high-tech firms. During the last five years, 493 companies executed an exit strategy. Whereas these numbers are declining, with more companies preferring to remain private for longer (Korbet 2019), the *exit* term had long established itself in the Israeli culture. Recent studies discussed the duality surrounding the exit strategy, concluding that whereas previous research tends to address it as a failure, about one-third of the US entrepreneurs consider it to be a signal of success (Wennberg and DeTienne 2014). For the Israeli scene, these numbers are higher. For several years already, *exit* connotes success (Noff 2017).

In line with this burgeoning entrepreneurial environment, whereas only about 8% of the population is employed in the high-tech industry, one of every three Israelis testifies that they know someone who is an entrepreneur (Korbet 2019). Sixty-five per cent of Israelis view entrepreneurship as a desirable career choice, and over 80% of them think that it represents a high success status (GEM Team 2018). Indeed, it is common knowledge that whereas in the past, Jewish mothers longed for their sons to become doctors, nowadays they wish them to be entrepreneurs.

To summarize, these numbers primarily represent a strong belief in the Israeli entrepreneurship scene—by both internal and external stakeholders—defining Israel as a cluster of entrepreneurship and innovation (Engel and del-Palacio 2011). This scene provides fertile ground and growing demand for funding to support the vast and diverse initiatives incepting in Israel on a daily base, among which is crowdfunding.

The Israel Defense Forces (IDF) as a Facilitator of an Entrepreneurial Culture

One institution with an important role in facilitating the Israeli entrepreneurial culture is mandatory army service in the IDF. The majority of the Jewish Israelis between the ages of 18 and 21 are required to enlist to the IDF and are then assigned to an army occupation unit congruent with their education, experience, and abilities and in accordance with the army needs. In the IDF, individuals are thus defined by their army occupation, and this dynamic follows them to their civilian life and future occupations. Senor and Singer (2011) cited an Israeli venture capital investor that sums up the ethos of the IDF: "Israeli **soldiers** are not defined by rank; they are defined by what they are good at" (p. 50). As such, army service plays a much more meaningful role in forming the individual's professional identity than any other factors, such as family origins.

Moreover, due to the various threats the country faces, IDF culture is grounded in innovative thinking and quickly learned lessons, joined by expressions of courage (Johnson 2011). This means, for example, that a combat unit should be able to perform multiple tasks, be flexible enough to react to changes and unexpected circumstances in the battle arena, and be empowered to improvise in the course of battle (Senor and Singer 2011). As such, the IDF culture reflects and promotes the Israeli entrepreneurial culture, characterized by delegating responsibilities to lower-ranking soldiers, operational flexibility, courage, and multi-tasking. Many Israeli entrepreneurs were imbued with these values during their army service and managed to apply them in the business world.

The army also serves as an integrative institution in Israeli society. In the army, many youngsters from varying backgrounds, such as new immigrants and people from diverse socioeconomic levels, serve together for two to three years in mandatory service and for an additional 20 years in annual reserve duty (Senor and Singer 2011). This integration, along with intense interaction, sometimes in life-threatening situations, ties army colleagues together. Consequently, high-tech firms are known to recruit soldiers from specific leading army tech units (Yablonko 2019).

In the context of crowdfunding, creators are driven by both a sense of comradeship, which provides assurance, and a feeling of 'all is possible', which allows them to defy convention and dare to pursue their goals and dreams. Many crowdfunding creators base their first wave of recruitment on their IDF buddies. For example, the donations-based campaign of *Together, we will win—Saving Ronen* was aimed towards funding a lifesaving treatment for a brain cancer patient. The campaign marketing stressed Ronen's biography as an officer and commander in an elite commando unit in the IDF, having participated in bold operations. Many of his backers were former members of the unit. The funding goal was about $285K, and it raised around $336K—a success rate of 118%.

A further example is Indorz, a startup specializing in cannabis farming technology. The firm was founded by two graduates of Israel's most renowned IDF tech unit, which serves as a facilitator of many Israeli startups. The firm launched two crowdfunding equity campaigns. In the first round, the company recruited $1.4M in a combined round, comprising 382 investors supporting the company in an open public platform, and three anonymous angels investing through a dedicated platform. This campaign's success rate was 325%. In a second round, the company recruited an additional $556.5K from 656 investors, reflecting a 390% success rate. These successful funding campaigns can be traced, among other reasons, to the IDF unit where its founders served, a fact stressed in all the media coverage, as the unit is known for its graduates' successes.

Crowdfunding as Entrepreneurial Spillover

As can be seen, entrepreneurship is well integrated in Israeli life. It receives substantial exposure in the news, and many academic institutions have incorporated it in one variety or another (technological/social) into their curriculum. This growing attention calls for an examination of the crowdfunding phenomenon as a variation of 'entrepreneurial spillover'. This means that innovation-driven entrepreneurship can spill over to other fields. While entrepreneurial spillover has previously been used to illustrate how entrepreneurship is transferred across countries (Fairlie and Lofstrom 2015), a more recent study discussed this term as describing a diffusion of entrepreneurship between organizations of the same country (García-Cabrera et al. 2017). Based on the 'entrepreneurial spillover' effect, we may presume that by being exposed to entrepreneurship through various channels, crowdfunding stakeholders are 'infected' by it and 'catch the bug'. In the context of crowdfunding, this spillover operates in two distinct ways. First, it generates an abundance of entrepreneurial initiatives that vary in scale and scope, hence allowing for different funding techniques to blossom alongside it. Second, it speeds up the market's learning process, facilitating the adoption of these tested techniques, thus, driving fundraising volume.

The Story of the Beresheet Spacecraft as a Manifestation of the Role of Crowdfunding in the Israeli Entrepreneurial Ecosystem

This innovative culture can be better explained through a recent example: on April 11, 2019, the *Beresheet* (Hebrew for Genesis, a beginning), a spacecraft designed by the SpaceIL project, made a crash landing onto the moon. A day later, Morris Kahn, the leading investor of the project and president of SpaceIL, announced project Beresheet2, the next spacecraft to be sent to the moon (Etzion 2019). The case of Beresheet is a reflection of the story of the Israeli entrepreneurship culture. The Beresheet initiative began with three young engineers who dreamed of participating in the Google Lunar X Prize challenge. Google's call was targeted at private teams, posing the challenge of building an unmanned spacecraft, land it on the moon, move it 500 metres across the lunar surface, and send high-definition pictures and video recordings back to Earth. The founders established the SpaceIL, a non-governmental agency, and launched an Indiegogo campaign in May 2014 to fund their quest. The campaign managed to raise over $250K, exceeding its goal (118%). The awareness created by their inspiring dream and nurtured by the campaign attracted a community around the project numbering 250 volunteers, as well as leading scientists, engineers, opinion leaders, and organizations. Among these stakeholders were several prominent figures and institutions: the head of the Israel Space Agency, the president of the Weizmann Institute, the president of Tel-Aviv University, Israel Aerospace Industries, and Bezeq (Israel's leading communication company). In subsequent years, the founders managed to secure additional funding of $100M from private investors (*angels*). Thus, it evolved into a joint project of SpaceIL and Israel Aerospace Industries (Goichman 2019). On February 22, 2019, the spacecraft began its journey to the moon. It received continual coverage in the Israeli media, and the Israeli public followed Beresheet journey with much pride and excitement, as Israel aspired to be the seventh nation to launch a spacecraft to the moon and the fourth nation to land on it (i24NEWS 2019).

Goichman (2019) sums up the story of the Beresheet endeavour by saying that the spacecraft is another demonstration of Israeli *chutzpah* (audacious and non-conformist behaviour). With leading nations investing billions of dollars in their space projects, Israel managed to reach a symbolic achievement by thinking 'out of the box', applying simple technologies, and flexibly exploiting opportunities. Thus, the story of Beresheet symbolizes the primary qualities that are driving Israel to become an entrepreneurship leader: daring to take risks, challenging conventions, thinking creatively, improvising, and remaining undaunted of failure along the way, along with communal support from the society in general. Beresheet's journey, therefore, is an exemplary manifestation of a crowdfunding campaign drawing on the meaningful elements of the Israeli entrepreneurial culture on its way to success. These elements will be elaborated next.

Elements of Israel's Entrepreneurial Culture and Their Manifestation in Crowdfunding Campaigns

A recent statement from an Israeli scientist sums up the Israeli entrepreneurship culture: "The courage to think, to improvise, the lack of fear to fail, the lack of fear to challenge conventions" (cited in Yair 2019, p. 25). These aspects—those that make Israel a leading entrepreneurship country—will be addressed in the following discussion. We will also demonstrate how these characteristics are manifested in Israeli crowdfunding campaigns.

Several factors contribute to the Israeli entrepreneurial culture. In an effort to provide readers with a comprehensive recipe of what makes Israel the *startup nation*, Senor and Singer (2011) identified several elements. Some of these elements can be linked to Israel's very establishment in 1948 and the immediate demand to absorb unprecedented numbers of immigrants from 100 different countries; other elements may relate to Israel's having to face ongoing military engagement and threats of terror (Rebhun and Waxman 2004). This combination of various challenges contributes to an innovative culture. In the following section, we describe the cultural elements that comprise the Israeli entrepreneurship ecosystem.

Collective Individualism

The roots of the modern State of Israel can be found in social-Zionistic movements established in the second half of the nineteenth century, which advanced values of egalitarian and collective society (Shindler 2013). The original collective nature of Israel can be found in valuing individuals who were committed to society at large and were willing to contribute to their communities unconditionally. Since then, Israel has transformed into a more individualistic culture, likely influenced by the US. However, the culture has evolved into a collective individualism (Weiss 2003). Weiss (2003) explained this amalgam of collective individualism in the country's unique geopolitical features, comprised of being small in size in comparison with neighbouring countries, joined by an ongoing sense of being bounded by hostile countries, and having to face continuous military and terror threats. This combination has led to a strong sense of community, induced by feelings of isolation. The sense of community manifests itself in open social behaviour, including interaction between individuals of different hierarchical positions. For example, many serial entrepreneurs and venture capitalists freely offer their wisdom and experience to new entrepreneurs (Yin 2017), whereas senior professors and their graduate students maintain close informal relationships (Yair 2019). The communal nature of Israeli society is also manifested in 'one degree of separation'. According to Menipaz and Avrahami (2019), about 59% of Israelis know an entrepreneur, putting Israel in second place among the developed countries regarding familiarity with active entrepreneurs. Israelis feel free to contact anyone quickly, even those they do not know (Yin 2017).

An example of the strong collectivism of Israelis can be found in the *Bringing Yehuda Back Home* campaign. Yehuda is an IDF officer who was severely injured during his army service and had become disabled due to his injury. For him to return to reside near his parents' home, he required a custom-built unit designed to accommodate his physical condition. Friends of Yehuda's family launched a campaign aimed at collecting money to fund the construction of the unit. The original funding goal was set at about $171.4K. The funding goal was reached in a matter of 18 hours. By the time the campaign ended, a sum of $447.4K was collected from 8382 backers, a success rate of 261%. Some additional examples of successful donation campaigns from recent years include campaigns raising large sums of money to support families of terror victims (ranging from $285.7K to $571.4K). These examples demonstrate how social solidarity drive Israelis to quickly converge into a community of backers that are committed to support the campaign and continue to be involved in it.

Low Power Distance and Lack of Hierarchy

The egalitarian nature of Israeli society is also manifested in its low power distance (Hofstede 2001). Israel scores 13 out of 100 on Hofstede's power distance index, indicating a very low societal power distance across life stages and organizations. This low power distance is expressed in expectations from employees to be autonomous and from managers to be accessible to their employees. Managers count on the experience of their employees, and employees expect to be consulted. Superiors often allow their subordinates to take the lead, with the latter freely challenging the thoughts and notions of the higher ranks (Yair 2019). Israelis are more likely to judge ideas by their content than by the status of their originator (Yair 2019). The workplace is characterized by an informal atmosphere and direct communication (Hofstede 1985). Israel's low power distance is congruent with Senor and Singer's (2011) assertions regarding Israeli culture as "class-less", and how this element surfaces in day-to-day business operations, with Israelis prone to challenge everything. Hofstede (1985) discussed at length how national and organizational institutions interact based on their value systems, claiming an indisputable link between the two. The low power distance indicator offers a clear example of how features of institutions at the national level merge into the business environment, thus, providing the business environment with a competitive advantage. Indeed, the inclination to continually challenge higher-ups and the lack of hierarchy lead to a sense of chaos that is facilitative of entrepreneurship (Nooteboom 1994). Examples for low power distance can be found on social media interactions between creators and backers, where backers leave questions and even phone numbers on the campaigns' social media pages (especially Facebook), requesting creators to phone them.

Israeli Chutzpah

Israel's egalitarian character, linked with an inclination to improvise and engage in courageous acts, as manifested in the Israel Defense Forces (IDF), can be related to the notion of *chutzpah*. In their book on the startup nation, Senor and Singer (2011) discussed the role of chutzpah at length as a trigger and facilitator of Israeli innovativeness. The term chutzpah is a Yiddish language expression, defined as a "laudable audacity or apparent effrontery that actually conceals a brave and often new approach to a subject or endeavour" (Schultz 2007, p. 209). A recent study by Efrat and Souchon (2016) explored the components of chutzpah, revealing it as a complex attitude encompassing creativity, spontaneity, originality, and boldness, on the one hand, and defiance, bluntness, transgression, and irreverence for conventions, on the other. Overall, these components allow for challenging existing ideas and paradigms, out-of-the-box thinking, and bold actions (Yair 2019).

While only scant academic efforts have addressed chutzpah, the concept is pervasive in popular, non-academic publications, primarily indicating its having been well integrated in businesses' day-to-day operations (Tellez 2015). In the context of entrepreneurship, chutzpah carries a distinguishing mark of guts, risk-taking, and can-do behaviours, the fuel that drives entrepreneurs forward (Morato 2012; Yin 2017). Israelis are courageous and are prepared to try things that other cultures do not (Yair 2019). They are also known for their improvisation habits, enabling them to be undeterred by low budgets and sub-optimal facilities and equipment to reach their goals (Yair 2019). Yin (2017) summarizes, claiming that "When Israelis see an opportunity, they tend to take the plunge and start something 'quick and dirty' to see if it works".

An example of chutzpah manifestation in crowdfunding is the story of *Fashanga*, an Israeli online fashion mall. The company was established by two young Israeli entrepreneurs having no previous knowledge or experience in the local fashion scene. That did not stop them from establishing an online fashion mall company while launching an equity campaign that managed to raise over $120K from eight investors. Following its initial success, the company launched a second equity-based campaign, raising over $200K from 27 investors. According to one of the co-founders, they specialize in spotting opportunities; they noticed that Israel was lacking a local online mall that would enable Israelis to shop locally while enjoying the international experience. *Fashanga*'s co-founders demonstrated boldness, daring, defiance, and creativity, all qualities associated with chutzpah.

Another example is *Just Beyond our Border—Israelis for the Syrian Children* campaign, which reflected irreverence for conventions. The campaign was initiated in 2016 by the Israeli humanitarian organization, 'Israeli Flying Aid', aiming to collect money for purchasing products and equipment for Syrian children. The campaign raised $444.3K from 8227 backers. The campaign reflected Israeli chutzpah in lifting the curtain of secrecy of the humanitarian aid provided by Israel (through a special unit of the IDF established for this purpose) to Syrians who suffered through the ongoing civil war.

High Tolerance for Failure

Chutzpah behaviour is often accompanied by a high tolerance for failure. A recent report published by the Israel Venture Capital (IVC) research centre estimates that only 4 out of 100 startups succeed, and only 4 out of every 500 will survive independently (IVC 2017). Therefore, the likelihood of failure would appear to be considered as a deterrent, inhibiting entrepreneurs from initiating new ventures. Studies on entrepreneurship have reported that tolerance of failure promotes innovation and creativity, enabling the organization to take daring moves (Kowang et al. 2015). In the Israeli context, senior managers in its high-tech industry, as well as senior scientists, treat failure as having positive features, enabling one to derive benefit from the experience, as long as he or she gets back on their feet (Yair 2019; Yin 2017).

An example of high tolerance for failure is the *TLT Board* campaign. The founder launched a campaign to raise money for an electric skateboard before he had a product in his hand. This campaign was a component of the founder's participation in a reality TV show aimed at assisting beginning entrepreneurs in their projects. The founder was very doubtful about the campaign's prospects of success and did not expect much. The campaign funding goal was approximately $2.9K, and it managed to raise around $29.8K from only 40 backers, with a success rate of 1043%. Following the success of the first campaign conducted on the Israeli platform, Headstart, the founder launched an additional campaign at Indiegogo platform a year later that did not reach its funding goal. However, the founder did succeed in launching a company selling the TLT boards.

We end this section with two illustrative cases of successful crowdfunding campaigns that encompass the various aspects of the Israeli entrepreneurial ecosystem components. The first is *InnoCan Pharma's* equity campaign, and the second is a rewards-based campaign of *Chocolate Panda.*

InnoCan Pharma: A Successful Equity Campaign

Innocan Pharma is an early-stage pharmaceutical company, established by an experienced team of serial entrepreneurs and pharmaceutical experts, led by an ex-Teva-Israel CEO. The company was founded with the goal of penetrating the worldwide pharmaceutical industry, exceeding USD 1.2 trillion revenues in 2018 (Mikulic 2019), with an innovative idea of embedding cannabis-based ingredients into dermatological products. The nature of the pharmaceutical industry has several components: it is highly regulated, long time-to-market, high cost of research and development, and is dominated by global enterprises, thus comprising a very high-risk endeavour. Nevertheless, InnoCan decided to penetrate this industry by harnessing innovative technologies into the research and development process of new pharmaceutical products and significantly shortening its Time-to-Market. The team peruse their idea and took a daring move, in establishing the entity, was enabled only by the Israeli entrepreneurial "can-do" culture and its high tolerance for failure behaviour (Kowang et al. 2015). This step was taken along with the perception that "even" failure has its positive aspects and can be seen as an opportunity for future learning (Yair 2019; Yin 2017).

On July 2018, InnoCan launched its crowdfunding campaign on the PipelBiz equity platform, with an initial funding goal of about $285.7K. By mid-August, the company had reached an investment of approximately $857.1K, thus achieving a success rate of 296%. The campaign was supported by 522 individuals, representing the full scope of the Israeli population. The campaign attracted investors from various geographical regions, backgrounds, and financial situations, investing sums ranging from $143 to $2.9K.

The company's CEO characterized the six-week campaign as a perfectly structured and timed operation with the goal of reaching the predefined amount. During these six weeks, the company utilized its Facebook company page to raise awareness and to provide updates on its progress. The presence of an ex-Teva-Israel CEO in the company's management team and the fact that the new company was developing new cannabis-based drugs generated huge interest and coverage in major Israeli online and offline media. The company leveraged its founders' and management's personal connections, experience, and reputation in order to raise awareness and attract the attention and trust of as many people as possible. Hundreds of Israelis, investors-to-be, 'picked up the gauntlet', and felt comfortable directly calling the company CEO's personal phone to learn about the investment opportunity, the company's future plans, and prospects of success. During the six-week campaign, the company's CEO stated that she had placed 25 phone calls every day with potential investors in order to explain the company's strategy and gain their trust. This open social behaviour, illustrated by strangers querying the company's CEO on her personal phone for the sake of engaging in an informal direct communication, is an accurate depiction of Israeli's lack of hierarchy and low power distance culture behaviour.

One of the company's declared goals, during and after the campaign, was to progress in the direction of an initial public offering (IPO) in the Canadian Securities Exchange (CSE). Indeed, on September 2019, the company announced a successful IPO on the CSE under the symbol "Inno", transforming its 522 crowdfunding investors into shareholders in a publicly traded company (Accesswire 2019).

The crowdfunding campaign and the company's business plan to penetrate the highly risky pharmaceutical industry—accelerating from 'zero to a hundred in six seconds'—illustrate the uniqueness of the Israeli entrepreneurship scene: risk-taking, high tolerance for failure, and can-do behaviour.

The InnoCan Pharma campaign was the first successful equity crowdfunding campaign to operate under the new Israeli regulation, enabling both early-stage entrepreneurs and crowd-investors to pursue their dreams. By utilizing this mechanism, the company raised the needed capital for its activity, with the crowd-investors given the opportunity to take part and invest in the establishment of the new entity, in the most democratic form. This campaign is still considered to be the most successful of its kind. Subsequently, many other entrepreneurial ventures have successfully raised funds through equity crowdfunding, supported by thousands of new non-accredited Israeli investors who wanted to be a part of the next big Israeli exit success story. Indeed, Wald et al. (2019) concluded that equity crowdfunding investors are driven by egotistical motivations, seeking the designation of 'entrepreneurship investor' as part of their resume.

Chocolate Panda: An Illustrative Case of a Successful Reward Campaign

Chocolate Panda is a vegan chocolate company. The company was established in 2015 by two vegan youngsters (who become a couple during the process), who decided to raise about $8.5K to launch a home business to produce vegan chocolate. The couple had not intended to launch a company, rather saw it only as a hobby. However, the collective nature of Israeli society was manifested in this campaign through the enthusiasm of Israel's very active vegan community. As a result, the campaign went viral, and within a day, the funding goal was reached. By the end of the campaign, they raised about $57.1K, achieving a remarkable success rate of 689%. The campaign was supported by 2394 backers and included 681 backers' comments.

Following the campaign's success, the creators, having considerable chutzpa, lacking the fear of failure, and having no previous experience in business administration, decided to establish a small boutique factory to produce vegan chocolate to replace their original plan of home production. They then set about producing seven different chocolate products, distributing them throughout the country (Lepler 2016).

After their initial success, the creators kept updating their backers through the Headstart platform as well as on their Facebook page. In 2017, they initiated an additional campaign, this time, for vegan chocolate snacks. The funding goal was about $34.2K, achieving about $89.2K, reflecting a 260% success rate. This second campaign was supported by 2101 backers, who wrote 538 comments. During this campaign, a boutique health food chain that was setting its sights on the vegan market decided to back the Chocolate Panda campaign, investing a considerable sum in return for the rights to launch the product's marketing.

The Chocolate Panda story demonstrates how a product that is associated with social values—in this case, the consumption of vegan food—can draw together an already-existing community of devotees that organized itself to boost its promotion and contribute to the campaign's success.

The Israeli Crowdfunding Scene

Development Over Time

Crowdfunding in Israel has become a viable option that is no longer limited to creators wanting to publish their books or music. Nowadays, many Israelis encounter the phenomenon, whether creators seek to open a new business, establish an interest-based community, or confront a personal challenge (medical or otherwise; Goldenberg 2015). Clear evidence of this can be seen in Israel's 2019 national elections when several parties chose to reach out to their backers by launching crowdfunding campaigns.

Rewards-based and donation-based crowdfunding was established in Israel in 2011 (equity-based was established in 2013), tail-winded by the success stories emanating from the predecessor US platforms—Kickstarter and Indiegogo. The Israeli crowdfunding industry is a market leader in the Middle East region and comprises a significant market in Europe. Between 2013 and 2016, the country raised $363.25 million, with an average 11% annual growth rate. In 2015, Israel was the eighth largest market after the UK, France, Germany, The Netherlands, Finland, Spain, and Italy. During 2016, the total funds raised through crowdfunding platforms in Israel have been estimated at $140M. A per-capita measure (2016) that enables a better understanding of the crowdfunding impact on the country, Israel was ranked 8th ($16M), following the UK, Estonia, Monaco, Georgia, Finland, Ireland, and Denmark. Israel's leading type of crowdfunding by far is the equity, raising almost $94M (68% of the total crowdfunding market). Second, comes Peer-to-Peer (P2P) consumer lending, estimated at $33M (24%). The rewards and donations platforms, estimated at $11.15M (8%), comprise the third-largest crowdfunding type (Ziegler et al. 2018b). Figures 15.1 and 15.2 present Israel's crowdfunding activity for 2015 and 2016 compared with other European countries.

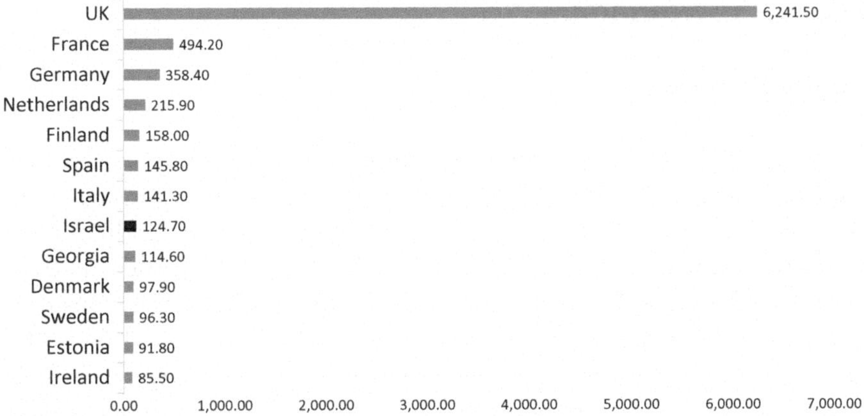

Fig. 15.1 Market volume by country for 2015 (in $ million). (Source: Based on figure from Ziegler et al. 2018a, b)

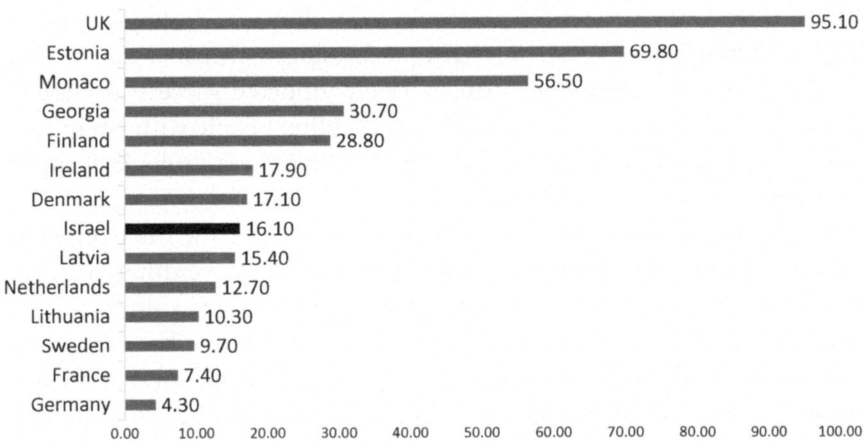

Fig. 15.2 Market volume per capita by country for 2016 (in $ million). (Source: Based on figures from Ziegler et al. 2018a, b; World Bank Data for Israel 2019)

Equity Crowdfunding

Equity Platforms

Between 2013, when Israel's first equity crowdfunding platform was launched, and mid-2017, $875M (IVC 2017) was raised through nine different equity crowdfunding platforms. Equity crowdfunding platforms were launched in Israel, as they were in most of the world, in 2013, after US President Barak Obama signed the Jumpstart Our Business Startups (JOBS) Act, allowing startups to legally raise capital from the crowd by issuing securities and remaining a private company. Since their establishment, equity crowdfunding platforms in Israel have successfully funded approximately 145 Israeli high-tech companies in the fields of internet, IT and software, communication, life science, clean-tech, and semiconductors. Within these companies, 25 have successfully executed an exit strategy, 15 were acquired, and 3 made an initial public offering (IPO). Intel is credited with the most lucrative buy-out deal by acquiring Replay Technologies, a 3-D rendering technology company, for $175M in 2016. Two life science companies have conducted successful Nasdaq IPOs: ReWalk Robotics, an exoskeleton, enabling people with paraplegia to walk, raised $36M in 2014, and UroGen Pharma, a urological cancer treatment developer, raised $58M in 2017.

The Israeli platforms are active under one or more of the three different equity crowdfunding business models, representing three different regulatory paths: (1) the accredited investors-only model, (2) the up-to-35 offerees model, and (3) the offering coordinator model. The regulatory aspects of crowdfunding, according to Israel's Securities Law, will be discussed in the following section. Table 15.1 presents the three models along with the leading platform in each.

The first equity crowdfunding platform was established in Israel in 2013 by OurCrowd and is based solely on accredited, sophisticated, and high-net-worth individual investors willing to invest large amounts of money in high-risk investments. Other than its crowdfunding platform activity, OurCrowd operates as a venture capital fund. By 2019, their joint activity reached $1.2B, with 200 companies and 30,000 registered

Table 15.1 Israel's three equity-based crowdfunding models

Business model	Leading company	Year established	Amounts raised	Number of campaigns
Qualified investors only	OurCrowd[a]	2013	$1.2B[a]	200
Up-to-35 offerees	ExitValley	2015	$27M	64
Offering Coordinator	PipelBiz	Mid-2017	$17M	42

[a]OurCrowd is active as a venture capital fund as well as an equity crowdfunding platform. Data retrieved from the platforms' websites, October 2019

investors in its portfolio, representing an average portfolio size of over $350K. Active in 150 countries worldwide, the company was acknowledged as the third-largest equity crowdfunding company in Europe (OurCrowd 2019).

The second model—the up-to-35-unaccredited investors model—was established in 2015. Under this model, the offer can be revealed to only 35 investors, and thus, it cannot be fully publicized. Several equity crowdfunding platforms are active in the Israeli market under this model. ExitValley is the model's leading platform, raising more than $28M from 15,855 investors, successfully funding 64 campaign in fields such as health, software, food, agriculture, and entertainment.

The third equity crowdfunding model is called Offering Coordinator and was introduced by the ISA to the Israeli audience during 2017. Under this model and its accompanying legislation, a company can publicly promote and advertise the selling of some parts of its equity in return for a predefined price. PipelBiz, the leading platform active under this model, has successfully raised $17M for 42 health, e-commerce, software, entertainment, leisure, and additional campaigns, allowing 7766 individual investors to participate in this most democratic form of crowdfunding.

The three equity crowdfunding models currently operating in Israel represent the development of the Israeli equity crowdfunding market. Started back in 2013 as an exclusive arena limited to high-net-worth investors, equity crowdfunding projects are now available to all Israelis wanting to participate and benefit from this opportunity to finance entrepreneurial ventures. The equity crowdfunding platforms are evolving as well, adjusting themselves and offering new creative programmes to meet the growing interest and competition. For example, ExitValley initiated an internal secondary market programme enabling investors to buy and sell shares from each other. ExitValley intends to launch an internal fund, offering investors a tool to extend and diversify their investment across several companies.

Equity and Regulations in Israel

According to Israel's Securities Law, any offer of securities to the Israeli public needs to be approved by the Israel Securities Authority (ISA). Two key terms require clarification in this regard: 'offer' and 'public'. Whereas the term 'offer' in this context is regarded as any activity, invitation, or intention meant for the convincement to purchase securities, the term 'public' is limited to the Israeli public. Thus, from an international perspective, an offer made to non-Israeli investors is not required to follow the ISA regulations; however, any foreign entity seeking to operate in Israel or approach the Israeli public must comply with the same regulations as the local institutions (ECN Report 2017).

With regard to equity crowdfunding, Israel's Securities Law has three exemptions of offering that are not required to be approved. (1) The offering of securities to no more than 35 individual investors (*up-to-35 offerees model*) on a consecutive period of 12 months. (2) The offering of securities to *sophisticated investors* such as banks, mutual funds, investment managers, investment advisers, underwriters, venture capital funds, and large corporations with equity of at least $14M. (3) The offering of securities to *high-net-worth individuals*, characterized as having $2.2M liquid assets, or having an annual income of $330K in the past two consecutive years, or holding liquid assets valued $1.4M and an annual income of $166K in the past two consecutive years. The three exemptions aforementioned have no restriction on the total investment amount asked by the issuer nor a limit on the maximum amount an individual is allowed to invest.

In 2015, an amendment to Israel's Securities Law was published, allowing companies to raise money through crowdfunding platforms. However, the Crowdfunding Regulations became effective only at the beginning of 2018. Subject to specified terms, these regulations allowed companies to openly offer shares to the Israeli public, and Israeli individuals to make investments in those companies, as long as the activity is taking place on a dedicated and authorized platform (*Offering Coordinator*).

The Crowdfunding Regulations delineate three levels of terms: platform level, issuer level, and investor level. At the platform level, the platform must be registered as an *Offering Coordinator*, pay all fees, report regularly to the ISA, and take reasonable steps to prevent fraud. Moreover, the platform must ensure compliance to the regulations regarding the offer information disclosed to the public. At the issuer level, the regulator restricts the amount that can be raised in a single offering during a period of 12 months to a range of $1.1–1.6M, subject to the involvement of a leading investor, a technology evaluation report from the Israel Innovation Authority, or both. At the investor's level, the regulator limits the maximum investment per individual to $2.8K per campaign and $5.6K per year (ECN Report 2017).

Rewards and Donations Crowdfunding

Rewards and Donations Platforms

The widespread use of crowdfunding in Israel has much to do with the operations of the first rewards-and-donation platform launched in the country—Headstart—launched online in November 2011. Initially, the platform was aimed at equity, but due to regulatory limitations, and in the face of burgeoning international platforms such as Kickstarter and Indiegogo, it began its operations in the rewards and donations domain, entering equity only recently. Headstart's growth to fame can be traced to the success of *Meir Ariel's Memorial Concert* campaign. Meir Ariel was a popular singer and songwriter, who died in 1999. Since Meir Ariel's death, his family launched an annual memorial concert, involving many artists performing his songs. In 2014, the family failed to raise the needed money for the traditional event. They decided to use Headstart, then a newly established crowdfunding platform, to raise about $114.3K, ending with approximately $133.1K, a success rate of 117%. The campaign comprised 1203 backers that supported the campaign in exchange for receiving tickets to the concert (the rewards consisted of various types of ticket deals). A year after the first concert (2015), the campaign for the annual concert raised around $167.4K, supported by 1880 backers, reaching a success rate of 130%.

The Meir Ariel's Memorial Concert Campaign received much attention in the media, contributing to the public's awareness of crowdfunding as an alternative to traditional funding channels. It was the first to demonstrate the power of crowdfunding as an additional way to raise funds among creators who are unable to afford the traditional funding channels.

Headstart had undertaken the challenging task of market education, and thus, its growth paralleled the crowdfunding market growth. The growth pace was primarily dictated by fund-seekers and crowd-funders being persuaded to use crowdfunding. Over the years, several other platforms have been established, all offering similar options for crowdfunding, and not prejudiced towards either rewards or donations campaigns. Whereas the first few years were characterized by hype in the field, recently, the number of funding volumes and platforms have stabilized, resulting in smaller platforms encountering difficulties balancing their business model. This trend signals potential changes in the crowdfunding arena for the near future. Headstart remains Israel's leading platform, capturing about 90% market share for rewards and about 80% for donations. In an October 2019 update in the platform site, Headstart reported that 5258 campaigns achieved their funding goal, raising more than $42.5M, receiving funds from more than 806,500 backers. Indeed, the brand *Headstart* has become a generic name used to refer to any crowdfunding activity. Headstart's two main competitors, Mimoona and Jumpstart, together encompass about 15% of the total Israeli market. The remaining market presence is held by numerous small platforms, mostly specializing in donation-based campaigns. The operating platforms charge fees ranging from 3% to 9%, in addition to VAT (ECN Report 2017).

Figure 15.3 presents Headstart funding volumes over the years, and Fig. 15.4 presents Headstart's success rates. As can be seen from the figures, funding volume reached a peak in 2017, stabilizing in 2018. Success rates also grew over the first few years, stabilizing at around 58% since

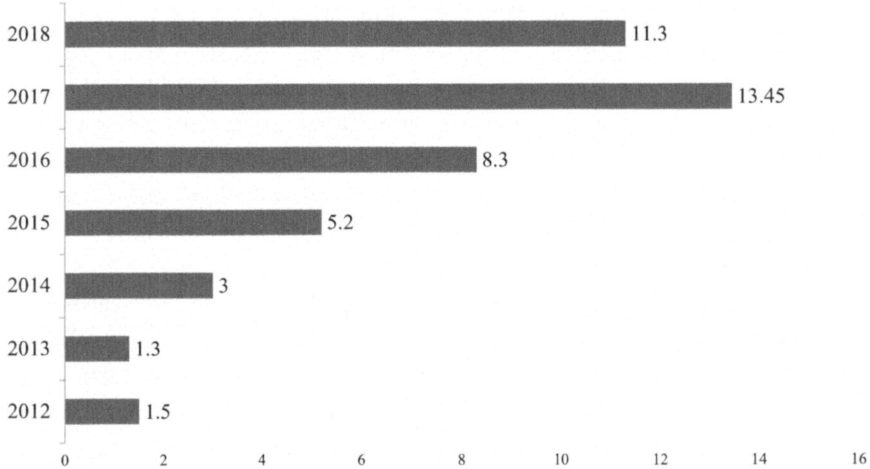

Fig. 15.3 Headstart (rewards and donations campaigns) funding volumes 2012–2018 (in $ million). (Source: Based on data received from the company)

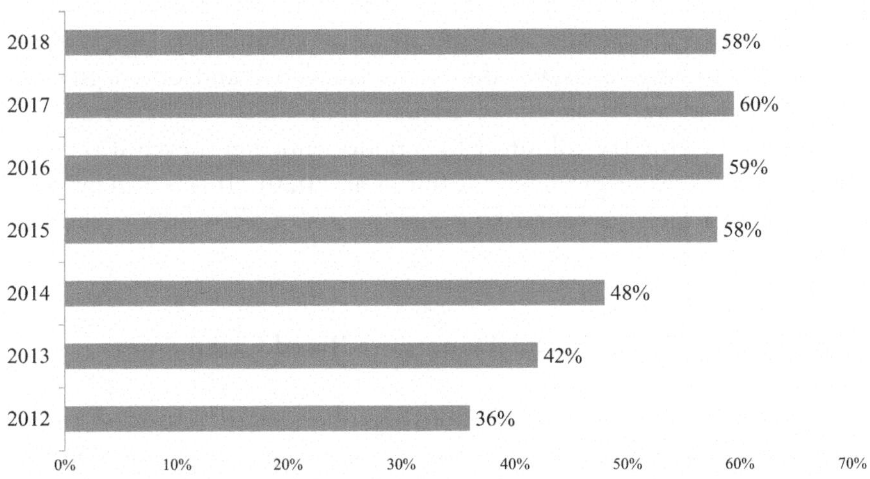

Fig. 15.4 Headstart (rewards and donations campaigns) success rates 2012–2018. (Source: Based on data received from the company)

2015. The company's success rates vary tremendously among the diverse campaign categories. Social campaigns have achieved the highest success rates, reaching 80%, followed by artistic campaigns in fields such as writing, music, comics, and film, as well as campaigns of a well-known annual festival (The Midburn, the Israeli version of Burning Man), reaching 65% success rates. Political campaigns have reached 50% success rates, whereas, surprisingly, tech campaigns have achieved only 22% and lower success rates. Moreover, in rewards campaigns, most creators produce their own products (though often behind schedule). This high rate of successful production seems to be derived from their high commitment to the backers, the majority of whom are friends and family (Samocha 2016).

These success rate statistics indicate that in the formats of rewards and donations, the successful campaigns are those characterized by their domestic nature. For example, support for an individual's medical treatment (social campaigns) or raising money to launch a local band's new album will likely be more successful than launching a campaign for a new tech gadget. For this reason, the non-equity crowdfunding platforms tend not to expand to foreign campaigns and maintain their focus on the domestic Israeli market (Or 2019). Crowdfunding studies report that domestic campaigns have an advantage in reaching their funding goals, as the majority of the backers are from the local community (Josefy et al. 2017). In this respect, Israel, due to its small size and one-degree-of-separation character, behaves like "a small community", in that individuals around the country volunteer to support campaigns, even if they do not know the creator personally (Efrat et al. 2020). This is a manifestation of Israeli society's collective individualism's (Weiss 2003) communal nature.

Regulation in Rewards-and-Donations-Based Campaigns

There are no specific laws or regulations regarding rewards- and donations-based crowdfunding. As the backers do not anticipate any financial profit, return, or non-monetary rewards that are not part of the campaign, no specific regulations, aside from the general consumer protection regulations, are applied (ECN Report 2017).

P2P (Lending) Crowdfunding

Six lending platforms are currently active in Israel; of these, three specialize in loans to small businesses. The total loaned amount was estimated at about $55M in 2018 and a total of $120M since 2013 (year of the first platform's establishment). Out of the total amount, about 25% has been P2P (person-to-person) lending. The leading platform in the field is Tarya. Currently, the estimated amounts represent only a fraction of a per cent of consumers' credit in Israel. The primary reasons for the hesitant development of P2P crowdfunding can be derived from regulation and lack of trust (ECN Report 2017).

Future Trends of Israeli Crowdfunding

Internationalization

As in other Israeli industries, as the equity crowdfunding industry evolves, it becomes international in two key aspects. The first aspect is the growing number of Israeli entrepreneurs looking to launch their campaigns on foreign platforms, mainly the two US giants—Kickstarter and Indiegogo. In facilitating their international presence, both US platforms initiated moves to support an international orientation. Indiegogo has even opened a local office in Israel. The second aspect concerns the entrance of foreign companies as investors in local platforms. These companies primarily provide financing to the local platforms, viewing their investments as strategic moves, and thus, signalling the market's growth potential.

Specialization

Alongside the internationalization of the crowdfunding industry, we note an additional trend in the form of platform specialization. Whereas at the start of Israeli crowdfunding, the local platforms were associated with either equity, P2P, or rewards-and-donation types, these features are now changing. The first and largest rewards-and-donation platform company—Headstart—transformed itself into an umbrella brand through splitting its operations into four separate sub-platforms: one sub-platform retained the original brand—*Headstart*—and serves as a rewards-based platform; the second adopted a new brand—*Giveback*—and houses donations-based campaigns; the third and most recent sub-platform—B*eactive*—focuses on legal struggle campaigns; and the fourth—*Fundit*—specializes mostly on real estate equity crowdfunding. New platforms entering the industry differentiate themselves by adopting a specific niche (e.g., political issues).

Among the equity crowdfunding markets, PipelBiz has announced the opening of the CannaVC, a venture capital fund in partnership with Everest Investment Banking, to support Israel's cannabis technology companies, thus, presenting new, mixed-model investment opportunities. Moreover, OurCrowd, Israel's largest equity crowdfunding platform has recently announced the opening of two new internal funds—one to support medical investments and the second to support environmental impact investments. All these moves represent a trend to specialization, which may be a consequence of the upsurge in the number of competitors.

Conclusions and Implications for Future Research

This chapter sought to shed light on the factors and conditions contributing to the inception and growth of crowdfunding in Israel. Our review of the field identified a set of country-level conditions encompassing the entrepreneurship ecosystem. These conditions include the entrepreneurship and innovation infrastructures, the role of the IDF in facilitating knowledge-based innovation and technologies, and the entrepreneurial spillovers driven by related and supporting organizations. These are complemented by social and cultural aspects, such as Israel's collectivistic and low-power distance society, chutzpah, and a high tolerance of failure.

The crowdfunding field is proliferating across all types, with its primary challenges currently in the form of regulatory barriers. The numbers indicate that crowdfunding is much more than a passing trend, and, with the exception of crowdlending modles, Israel exhibits patterns similar to those in other countries. These developments also apply to future trends.

Alongside the growth in campaigns' numbers and volume, we are witness to the creation of a cumulative body of knowledge, which is used by both platforms and individuals in assisting first-time entrepreneurs. This knowledge facilitates success across crowdfunding types.

Our review carries some practical implications for both platforms and entrepreneurs. Platforms, as they orientate first-time entrepreneurs, should urge them to use their close circle of friends and family as a means to recruit the additional circles based on the one-degree-of-separation phenomenon that characterizes Israeli society. As Israelis value boldness and out-of-the-box thinking, platforms can offer entrepreneurs to launch creative and innovative campaigns. In addition, due to the relatively low fear of failure, they should encourage them to launch additional campaigns, even if the initial campaign did not reach its goal. Regarding equity-based campaigns, both platforms and entrepreneurs can base their campaign advertising on the inclination of many Israelis to take part in the high-tech industry through investing in new startups. Regarding rewards- and donations-based campaign, the most successful campaigns have been those related to social values and social solidarity, a phenomenon consistent with the collectivist nature of Israeli society. Platforms can use these aspects to publicize themselves for potential entrepreneurs in order to appeal to them to use crowdfunding over alternative funding channels.

To advance our current work, we suggest three research endeavours. First, whereas most research to date has focused on the commonalities of crowdfunding across the different types (Macht and Weatherston 2015), we expect that different cultural aspects and dimensions comprise a critical factor (Shneor and Efrat 2014) and, indeed, influence the scale and rate of crowdfunding adoption. This culturally oriented direction of exploration could help advance the understanding of the differences occurring across countries regarding the adoption of crowdfunding and its manifestations (e.g., equity vs non-equity). Second, our chapter frames crowdfunding within the entrepreneurship orientation. However, empirical studies investigating this linkage have mostly focused on the equity forms of crowdfunding (e.g., Estrin et al. 2018). In light of the centrality of such elements to crowdfunding in general, a better understanding of the culturally based entrepreneurial drivers is vital. Hence future research should advance on Efrat's (2014) conclusions concerning the impact of culture on entrepreneurship, and explore the impact of additional macro level aspects (e.g., political and economic) on development and dynamics of non-equity crowdfunding. Third, whereas the crowdfunding phenomenon has attracted significant research attention due to its rapid growth, its role within existing financial frameworks is often overlooked. A valuable research direction could address the linkages, associations, and reciprocity of crowdfunding and additional finance techniques in advancing entrepreneurship.

References

Accesswire. (2019). Innocan Pharma Corporation Announce Closing of Initial Public Offering and Listing on Canadian Securities Exchange Under the Symbol 'Inn'. Retrieved October 23, 2019, from https://www.accesswire.com.

Bunis, D. M. (1996). Yisrael Ḥaim of Belgrade and the History of Judezmo Linguistics. *Histoire Épistémologie Langage, 18*(1), 151–166.

Cohen, B. (1975). *The Haprenumeranten Book* (HebrewBooks). New York: Ryzman Edition.

Efrat, K. (2014). The Direct and Indirect Impact of Culture on Innovation. *Technovation, 34*(1), 12–20.

Efrat, K., & Souchon, A. L. (2016). Chutzpah and Its Linkage to Marketing Innovation, and Performance. In M. W. Obal, N. Krey, & C. Bushardt (Eds.), *Let's Get Engaged! Crossing the Threshold of Marketing's Engagement Era* (Developments in Marketing Science: Proceedings of the Academy of Marketing Science) (p. 165). Cham: Springer.

Efrat, K., Gilboa, S., & Sherman, A. (2020). The Role of Supporter Engagement in Enhancing Crowdfunding Success. *Baltic Journal of Management, 19*(2).

Engel, J. S., & Del-Palacio, I. (2011). Global Clusters of Innovation: The Case of Israel and Silicon Valley. *California Management Review, 53*(2), 27–49.

Estrin, S., Gozman, D., & Khavul, S. (2018). The Evolution and Adoption of Equity Crowdfunding: Entrepreneur and Investor Entry into a New Market. *Small Business Economics, 51*(2), 425–439.

Etzion, U. (2019). The Challenge for Beresheet 2.0: Landing on the Moon and Sticking to the Budget (Hebrew). *Calcalist*. Retrieved April 23, 2019, from www.calcalistech.com (Hebrew).

European Crowdfunding Network (ECN). (2017). Review of Crowdfunding Regulation 2017. Retrieved October 13, 2019, from http://www.eurocrowd.org.

Fairlie, R. W., & Lofstrom, M. (2015). Immigration and Entrepreneurship. In B. R. Chiswick & P. W. Miller (Eds.), *Handbook of the Economics of International Migration* (Vol. 1, pp. 877–911). Amsterdam: Elsevier.

García-Cabrera, A. M., García-Soto, M. G., & Suárez-Ortega, S. M. (2017). Macro-Level Spillovers and Micro-Level Capabilities as Antecedents of Young SMEs' Propensity to Export and to Become a Born Global. *International Entrepreneurship and Management Journal, 13*(4), 1199–1220.

GEM. (2018). *Global Report 2017/18 – Global Entrepreneurship Monitor (GEM)*. Wellesley, MA: GERA.

Goichman, R. (2019). If Beresheet Spacecraft Made It to the Moon – It Will Be in the Most Israeli Way Possible. Retrieved February 24, 2019, from http://www.themarker.com (Hebrew).

Goldenberg, R. (2015). Five Things You Have to Know Before Launching a Crowdfunding Campaign. Retrieved October 26, 2019, from http://www.globes.co.il (Hebrew).

Hofstede, G. (1985). The Interaction Between National and Organizational Value Systems [1]. *Journal of Management Studies, 22*(4), 347–357.

Hofstede, G. (2001). *Culture's Consequences: Comparing Values, Behaviors, Institutions, and Organizations Across Nations* (2nd ed.). Thousand Oaks, CA: Sage Publications.

i24News. (2019). Israel Will Make Second Attempt at Lunar Landing After Beresheet Crash. *i24News*. Retrieved April 23, 2019, from http://www.i24NEWS.tv.

Israel Venture Capital (IVC) Research Center. (2017). Israeli Startup Success Report 1999–2014. Retrieved March 25, 2019, from https://www.ivc-online.com/Research-Center/IVC-Publications/IVC-Surveys/Startup-Report.

Jamrisko, M., Miller, L. J., and Lu, W. (2019). These Are the World's Most Innovative Countries. Retrieved January 22, 2019, from https://www.bloomberg.com/news/articles/2019-01-22/germany-nearly-catches-korea-as-innovation-champ-u-s-rebounds.

Johnson, D. E. (2011). *Hard Fighting: Israel in Lebanon and Gaza*. RAND Arroyo Center. Santa Monica, CA: Rand.

Josefy, M., Dean, T. J., Albert, L. S., et al. (2017). The Role of Community in Crowdfunding Success: Evidence on Cultural Attributes in Funding Campaigns to 'Save the Local Theater'. *Entrepreneurship Theory and Practice, 41*(2), 161–182.

Korbet, R. (2019). Start-up Nation Central: Finder Insights Series – The State of the Israeli Ecosystem in 2018. *Start-up Nation Central*. Retrieved March 22, 2019, from https://www.startupnationcentral.org/.

Kowang, T. O., Long, C. S., & Rasli, A. (2015). Innovation Management and Performance Framework for Research University in Malaysia. *International Education Studies, 8*(6), 32–45.

Lepler, H. (2016). Vegan Chocolate: The Story of 'Panda' (Hebrew). *Ynet*. Retrieved April 10, 2019, from http://www.ynet.co.il.

Macht, S. A., & Weatherston, J. (2015). Academic Research on Crowdfunders: What's Been Done and What's to Come? *Strategic Change, 24*(2), 191–205.

Menipaz, E., & Avrahami, Y. (2019). *Global Entrepreneurship Monitor (GEM) National Report – Israel, 2017/2018*. Beer Sheva, Israel: Ben Gurion University. Retrieved November 5, 2019, from https://www.gemconsortium.org/report/gem-2017-2018-global-report.

Mikulic, M. (2019). Revenue of the Worldwide Pharmaceutical Market from 2001 to 2018 (in Billion U.S. Dollars). Retrieved October 28, 2019, from http://www.statista.com.

Morato, E. A., Jr. (2012). *A Trilogy on Entrepreneurship: Preparing for Entrepreneurship*. EBookIt.com.

Noff, A. (2017). The Next Web: The 10 Israeli Exits That Tell the Story of the Startup Nation. Israel Ministry of Economy and Industry – Foreign Trade Administration. Retrieved March 23, 2019, from https://itrade.gov.il/belgium-english/the-next-web-the-10-israeli-exits-that-tell-the-story-of-the-startup-nation/.

Nooteboom, B. (1994). Innovation and Diffusion in Small Firms: Theory and Evidence. *Small Business Economics, 6*(5), 327–347.

OECD. (2018). OECD Data. Retrieved October 15, 2019, from https://data.oecd.org/israel.htm.

OurCrowd. (2019, March 7). Press Release: OurCrowd Celebrates $1 Billion Raised for 170 Companies, 18 Funds and 29 Exits. Retrieved October 28, 2019, from https://blog.ourcrowd.com/sixyears.

Rebhun, U., & Waxman, C. I. (2004). Introduction. In C. I. Waxman & U. Rebhun (Eds.), *Jews in Israel: Contemporary Social and Cultural Patterns*. Hanover, NH: Brandeis University Press.

Samocha, S. (2016). Big Promises and Flops: The Dark Side of Crowdfunding (Hebrew). *Globes*. Retrieved April 10, 2019, from http://www.globes.co.il.

Schultz, R. (2007). Adjacent Possibilities: Applied Chutzpah. *Emergence: Complexity & Organization, 9*(1/2), 209–210.

Senor, D., & Singer, S. (2011). *Start-Up Nation: The Story of Israel's Economic Miracle*. New York: Random House Digital, Inc..
Shindler, C. (2013). *A History of Modern Israel*. Cambridge: Cambridge University Press.
Shneor, R., & Efrat, K. (2014). Analyzing the Impact of Culture on Average Time Spent on Social Networking Sites. *Journal of Promotion Management, 20*(4), 413–435.
Tellez, O. (2015). Chutzpah Lessons from the Israeli Startup Scene. Retrieved March 21, 2019, from http://www.iati.co.il/news-item/1748/-chutzpah-lessons-from-the-israeli-startup-scene.
Wald, A., Holmesland, M., & Efrat, K. (2019). It Is Not All About Money: Obtaining Additional Benefits Through Equity Crowdfunding. *The Journal of Entrepreneurship, 28*(2), 270–294.
Weiss, M. Z. (2003). The Postmodern State and Collective Individualism: A Comparative Look at Israeli Society and Western Consumer Culture. *The Social Science Journal, 40*(2), 269–281.
Wennberg, K., & DeTienne, D. R. (2014). What Do We Really Mean When We Talk About 'Exit'? A Critical Review of Research on Entrepreneurial Exit. *International Small Business Journal, 32*(1), 4–16.
World Bank. (2019). World Development Indicators. Retrieved October 23, 2019, from http://databank.worldbank.org.
Yablonko, Y. (2019). The Army Against the High-Tech Firms: Beyond the Scene of The War on Talent (Hebrew). *Globes*. Retrieved May 28, 2019, from http://www.globes.co.il.
Yair, G. (2019). Hierarchy Versus Symmetry in German and Israeli Science. *American Journal of Cultural Sociology*. https://doi.org/10.1057/s41290-019-00069-8.
Yin, D. (2017). What Makes Israel's Innovation Ecosystem So Successful. *Forbes Asia*. Retrieved November 5, 2019, from https://www.forbes.com/sites/davidyin/2017/01/09/what-makes-israels-innovation-ecosystem-so-successful/#15b208ef70e4.
Ziegler, T., Shneor, R., Garvey, K., Wenzlaff, K., Yerolemou, N., Hao, R., et al. (2018a). *Expanding Horizons: The 3rd European Alternative Finance Industry Report*. Cambridge, UK: Cambridge Centre for Alternative Finance.
Ziegler, T., Suresh, K., Garvey, K., Rowan, P., Zhang, B., Obijiaku, A., et al. (2018b). *The 2nd Annual Middle East and Africa Alternative Finance Industry Report*. Cambridge, UK: Cambridge Centre for Alternative Finance.

List of Interviews

Aloni, Eyal (July, 2015). Founder of TLT Board.

Peleg, Nitzan (November, 2017). Co-Founder of Fashanga – Online Fashion Mall.

Or, Danny (February, 2019). CEO of Headstart Platform.

Bincovich, Iris (May, 2019). CEO at InnoCan Pharma.

Shiryon, Yaniv (May, 2019). Co-Founder and CEO at ExitValley.

16

Crowdfunding in Europe: Between Fragmentation and Harmonization

Karsten Wenzlaff, Ana Odorović, Tania Ziegler, and Rotem Shneor

Introduction

In recent years, Europe has retained its position as the third largest global market for crowdfunding. Similar to other regional markets, it is dominated by a single country accounting for the majority of related volumes,

K. Wenzlaff (✉)
Faculty of Business, Economics, and Social Sciences, University of Hamburg, Chair Digital Markets, Hamburg, Germany
e-mail: karsten.wenzlaff@uni-hamburg.de

A. Odorović
Faculty of Law, Institute for Law and Economics, University of Hamburg, Hamburg, Germany
e-mail: ana.odorovic@ile-graduateschool.de

T. Ziegler
Cambridge Centre for Alternative Finance, Judge Business School, University of Cambridge, Cambridge, UK
e-mail: t.ziegler@jbs.cam.ac.uk

R. Shneor
School of Business and Law, University of Agder, Kristiansand, Norway
e-mail: rotem.shneor@uia.no

R. Shneor et al. (eds.), *Advances in Crowdfunding*,
https://doi.org/10.1007/978-3-030-46309-0_16

namely the UK. Overall, European crowdfunding volumes were estimated at USD 18 billion in 2018, growing 51% from an estimated volume of 11.9 billion in 2017 (Ziegler et al. 2020). However, the UK accounted for 10.4 billion in 2018, while growing 30% from the USD 8 billion it recorded in 2017. Accordingly, mainland Europe (including 44 countries) has exhibited a dramatic growth of 95% from a total volume of 3.9 billion in 2017 to 7.6 billion in 2018.

Several intriguing features characterize crowdfunding in Europe, which essentially capture different facets of the market fragmentation. First, in global comparison, the UK, as the leading regional market, accounts for a smaller proportion of regional volumes (58% in 2018) than the US does in the Americas (96% in 2018) or China in the Asia Pacific region (97% in 2018). In Europe, a wider distribution of volumes across national markets is evident with the Netherlands, Germany, and France as dominant players. Other countries with large volumes, such as Italy, Spain, or Poland, Sweden, Italy, or Belgium are following closely.

Second, cross-border transactions are limited, and usually associated with non-investment models like reward and donation crowdfunding, where regulatory barriers are minimal. However, Europe has thus far failed to produce a European equivalent to global US-based platforms in these spheres (e.g. Kickstarter, Indiegogo, or GoFundMe) with relevant platforms maintaining local focus and anchoring, while competing with the US-based actors on localized features and services (e.g. language, payment systems, customer support, currency). Moreover, most platforms operating investment models, as in equity-based and debt-based crowdfunding, operate only in one country, partially due to the fragmented regulatory landscape within Europe. However, most European countries represent relatively small domestic markets, where local platforms may struggle to achieve sufficient scale towards profitability without international reach.

Against this backdrop, the European Union has created a unified crowdfunding regulation for equity- and lending-based crowdfunding (European Commission 2018c; European Parliament 2019). The ambition of the European Crowdfunding Service Provider (hereafter 'ECSP') Regime has been to improve access to finance for SMEs across Europe, while paving the way towards fewer limitations on cross-border investment activity within the continent. During the deliberation and negotiation process, the proposal morphed from a so-called opt-in regime to a binding regime for platforms in all member states, constituting a possible source of harmonization and thus reduction of fragmentation in the market starting in 2021, when the regime will come into force.

This chapter's structure is as follows. In the coming section, we first present the current state of crowdfunding markets in Europe, especially with regards to differences between national markets. Next, the principles of the ECSP Regime proposal are presented, and expectations about its impact are outlined. These discussions are supported by insights from research conducted in European countries. We conclude this chapter with a list of suggestions for further research, as well as implications for practitioners in the region.

The Current State of the European Crowdfunding Market

In the current section we present the state of European crowdfunding market. Unless otherwise stated, all data presented are adopted from the Cambridge Centre for Alternative Finance (hereafter 'CCAF') Global Alternative Finance Report (Ziegler et al. 2020) and the Fourth Annual European Alternative Finance Report (Ziegler et al. 2019).

In 2017, 597 European platforms have overseen a market turnover of USD 10.4 billion. In 2018, these figures have grown to 794 platforms overseeing a market volume of USD 18 billion. The majority of platforms are concentrated in the relatively larger Western European economies of the UK (89 platforms), Germany (63 platforms), France (51 platforms), Italy (51 platforms), the Netherlands (45 platforms) and Spain (39 platforms), with a majority of which domestically based. On the other end, Southern and Eastern European countries were served by less than 10 platforms, most of which were foreign-based. Some explanations for this may be found in a study by Dushnitsky et al. (2016), who examined the conditions associated with platform creation at the national level during the early years of the European crowdfunding industry (2008–2014). This study showed that platforms are more likely to be created in countries characterized by larger market sizes (in terms of population), higher entrepreneurship rates (in terms of share of population owning a new business), as well as where traditional financial institutions are involved (in terms of percentage of active platforms operated by established financial organizations) providing the new industry with a degree of legitimacy.

Three European countries have seen volumes surpassing the USD 1 billion mark including the UK (USD 10.4 billion), the Netherlands (USD 1.8 billion), and Germany (USD 1.2 billion), with France closely approaching this threshold with USD 933 million in 2018. Furthermore, from a regional perspective, despite relatively small domestic markets, the Nordic and Baltic States have exhibited strong growth. Here, regional volumes showed that the Nordics (Denmark, Finland, Iceland, Norway, and Sweden) accounted for USD 507 million in 2017 and USD 824 million in 2018, mostly led by Finland (USD 379 million) and Sweden (USD 298 million). The Baltics (Estonia, Latvia, and Lithuania) accounted for USD 265 million in 2017 and USD 539 million in 2018, with Latvia (USD 254 million) taking lead. Other notable regional leaders include Poland in Eastern Europe with USD 333 million and Spain in the Iberian Peninsula with USD 419 million. However, when controlling for market size, highest volumes per capita were recorded in the UK with USD 156, Latvia with USD 132, Estonia USD 121, and the Netherlands with USD 105 in 2018.

The fragmentation of crowdfunding markets in Europe can be grasped by distinguishing several categories of crowdfunding markets: (1) *Market leaders*—countries with a large crowdfunding volume, a few dozen platforms, and high volumes per capita (e.g. UK, Netherlands); (2) *Domestic-growth markets*—countries with a large crowdfunding volume, a few dozen platforms, but low volume per capita mostly driven by domestic transactions (e.g. Germany, France); (3) *International-growth markets*—countries with small crowdfunding volumes, less than 20 platforms but high volume per capita mostly driven by international transactions (e.g. Estonia, Latvia); and (4) *Slow international adapters*—countries with small crowdfunding volumes, less than 20 platforms, and small volume

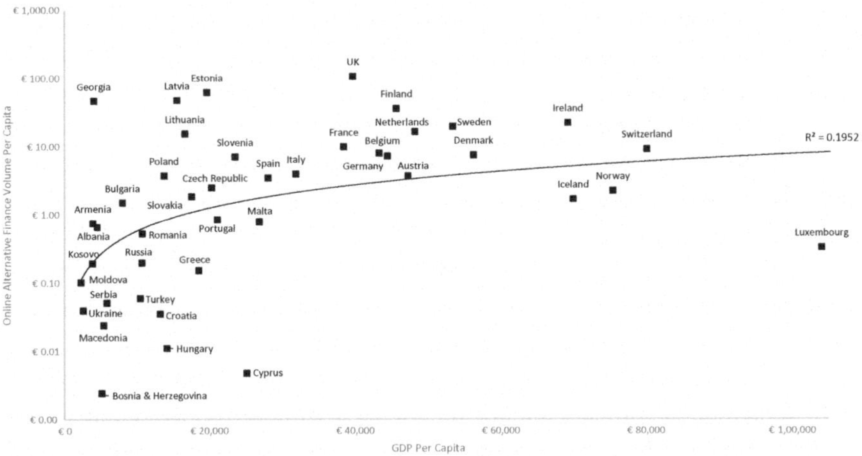

Fig. 16.1 Alternative finance volume per capita versus GDP per capita 2017. (Source: Ziegler et al. 2019)

per capita mostly driven by international transactions (e.g. countries in Central, Southern, and Eastern Europe) (Fig. 16.1).

When plotting per capita volumes against GDP per capita (Fig. 16.1), as indicator of economic development, the results suggest that volumes in countries such as the UK, Estonia, Latvia, Lithuania, and Georgia indicate an efficient utilization of the alternative finance models, whereas countries like Cyprus, Hungary, Bosnia and Herzegovina, and Luxembourg underutilized their alternative finance potential.

High volumes of P2P Consumer and Business Lending activities are associated with higher performance of a country (i.e. UK, Georgia, Latvia, and Estonia), while countries with high volumes of reward-based or donation-based crowdfunding are associated with relative underperformance of a country (i.e. Norway, Iceland, Malta, Greece, Luxembourg). This usually reflects regulatory regimes enabling investment crowdfunding versus regulatory environments in which this is constrained by existing laws, as well as where changes were made very close to data collection period. As a result, the underperformance of countries with large sectors of non-investment crowdfunding is caused by the fact that contributions per project per person are lower in the donation-based and reward-based models of crowdfunding as compared to investment models.

The fragmentation is not only evidenced by the market volumes, but also by their distribution. It is instructive to observe which European countries represent the top three performing markets by volumes according to each crowdfunding model. In 2018, the UK took the top position in 10 of the 13 business models covered by the CCAF report. Germany took the top position in real estate crowdfunding and donation-based crowdfunding, as well as second position in P2P consumer and P2P business lending. And the Netherlands had the largest market for balance sheet property lending, while taking second place in the balance sheet business lending, debt-based securities, as well as the revenue sharing models. Other market leaders include those taking second place, such as Denmark in P2P property lending, Sweden in balance sheet consumer lending, Finland in equity crowdfunding, Italy in invoice trading, and France in reward crowdfunding.

Finally, a different insight into fragmentation in Europe is evident in a recent study by Rossi and Vismara (2018), who analysed services offered by 124 investment crowdfunding platforms from the UK, France, Germany, and Italy. First, they find that platforms offer relatively few services before, during, and after the campaign, and even these vary widely by platforms. The few exceptions offered by a majority of platforms include the facilitation of interaction and period campaign updates. Second, the study also showed that the average annual number of successful campaigns were substantially higher in the UK and France versus those in Germany and Italy. Furthermore, the authors found that platforms offering a higher number of post-campaign services were associated with higher number of successful campaigns, while the number of services offered before and during campaigns were not associated with higher levels of success.

Traditional Financial Institutions in European Crowdfunding Markets

Fragmentation in the European markets is also evident with respect to relations of platforms with institutional investors (e.g. pension funds, asset management firms, banks). In continental Europe in 2017 (i.e.

excluding the UK), USD 511 million (13%) originated from institutional investors, increasing in both relative and absolute size to USD 1.1 billion (14.5%) in 2018. In 2018, these volumes reach USD 4.88 billion (47%). Some markets are heavily dependent on institutional investors, including Italy with 90%, the Benelux region with 88%, and Germany with 64% of the 2018 volumes coming from institutional investors. On the other side of the spectrum, institutional investors were associated with only 2% of volumes in the CIS (Commonwealth of Independent States) and 5% of volumes in Eastern and Baltic European countries in 2018.

Beyond the provision of funding to alternative finance offerings, institutional engagement with platforms is sometimes also evident with respect to organizational relations. Here, platform ownership by institutional partners is evident among 15–20% of platforms operating in Western Europe, but only among 4–8% of platforms operating in Baltic, Central, and South-East Europe in 2017. No platform in Eastern Europe and the CIS was owned by institutional partners in 2017.

International Scope of European Platform Operations

Data collected annually by the CCAF suggests that cross-border transactions and internationalization of platforms is on the rise in Europe. In 2017, 77% of platforms had seen cross-border inflows to local platforms, 44% of platforms saw cross-border outflows. Here, again, fragmentation is evident across Europe, where some regions are home to more internationally oriented platforms, while other regions are characterized by more domestic-facing platforms. In 2017, CIS countries, Georgia, Baltics, and Eastern European countries reported a high level of cross-border flows. Iberia, South-Eastern European countries, Ireland, Central European countries, and the Benelux countries showed a medium level of cross-border flows. Nordic countries, Germany, and France showed relatively low levels of cross-border flows. This is presented in Fig. 16.2.

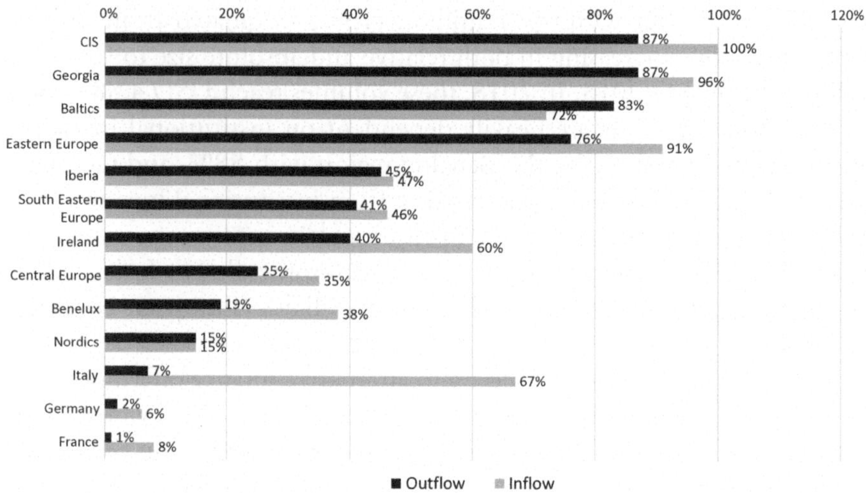

Fig. 16.2 Cross-border flows in European crowdfunding markets 2017. (Source: Ziegler et al. 2019)

These findings are especially relevant for the discussion of the ECSP Regime. According to our market classification suggested above, *Market Leaders* and *Domestic-growth Markets* incorporate a majority of domestic platforms first achieving a degree of scale operations domestically, and then engaging in cautious and limited international expansion. *International-growth Markets* include platforms that emerge from relatively small home markets, leveraging relatively permissive regulatory frameworks, while more aggressively expanding into other country markets for achieving scale, sustainability, and growth. Finally *Slow International Adapters* represent countries, where, despite scale potentialities, growth is constrained by lagging regulatory amendments as well as lower levels of social trust (Delhey and Newton 2005) and suspicion towards digital financial innovations. Here, platforms attempt tapping into international support to achieve legitimacy in the domestic markets, where international funding triggers domestic development and acceptance.

Regulation and European Crowdfunding Market Fragmentation

Thus far, a number of areas in which disparity is evident within the European crowdfunding market have been listed including volumes per country and per capita, number of platforms, model diversity, and extent of dependency on cross-border transactions and flows. In the current section we will explore aspects of fragmentation with respect to regulations and their impact on a European-level market for crowdfunding. Ever since the first report mapping the conditions and prospects of crowdfunding in Europe, regulation was identified as a key pillar that must be addressed (De Buysere et al. 2012), so that appropriate rules and measures are put in place while ensuring the necessary protection of those interested in engaging in crowdfunding (Bruntje and Gajda 2016).

While economic theory suggests that a truly integrated market would reduce disparities considerably, local and regional differences can still occur. In an integrated market, platforms could offer their services across borders, investments would flow to the platform with the best offers, while allowing successful platforms to scale and outperform competitors. However, the motivation of local investors to provide funds to local businesses on local platforms might be higher than investing in businesses residing abroad or platforms abroad, even if both domestic and foreign platforms offer the same or better investment protections and services. Such phenomenon is known from investment research as a home bias (Tesar and Werner 1995), as well as 'not invented here' attitudes towards foreign ideas and technologies (Antons and Piller 2014).

Non-investment crowdfunding models such as those employed by donation- and reward-based platforms are the least constrained in terms of regulation. Platforms like Kickstarter, Indiegogo, Global Giving or GoFundMe, based in the US, have localized the user experience by translating the website into local languages, while operating under their respective international brands (Skotte and Juvik 2019). Donation- and reward-based crowdfunding does not require platforms to be supervised by the financial authorities or comply with investor protection regulation to the extent investment platforms are required to do. Platforms in donation-based and reward-based crowdfunding have to adhere to rules in the area of digital payments, but they partner with a payment provider which ensures regulatory compliance with European laws. There are very few exceptions where donation collection requires special permits such as in Denmark and Finland, but in most other European markets requirements are more flexible. Reward-based crowdfunding platforms have to comply with other European legal frameworks, such as the e-Commerce directive, Consumer rights directive, Copyright directive, or the Platform directive, which is currently under discussion. And although these directives have not been uniformly implemented across the European Union, such regulations haven't prohibited non-investment platforms to scale across Europe.

Most concerns with regulatory fragmentation are associated with investment crowdfunding. Here, the MiFID (2004/39/EC) and MiFID II (2014/65/EU) (Markets in Financial Instruments Directive) (European Commission 2018b) should have provided a unified framework for crowdfunding intermediaries. However, platforms and their industry associations provided evidence in the Impact Assessment of the European Commission that the MiFID-framework is not suitable to their business models. Member states have in the past 'gold-plated' MiFID by adding additional provisions for consumer protection, which made operation of platforms across border an even more demanding, costly, and less efficient process.

A second symptom of a regulatory fragmentation is the different national regimes under which platforms operate. A few member states of the European Union have implemented a bespoke regime for alternative finance service providers (e.g. UK, Finland, France), however, in most European member states a bespoke regime is still lacking, which generates regulatory uncertainty of platforms operating across borders. Furthermore, differences in national regulations across Europe have been argued to not only result in distortions of the market playing fields, but also limit economic growth that can be supported by cross-border offers of crowdfunding (Gajda 2017). In this context the CCAF report showed a clear positive association between crowdfunding volumes per capita and the level to which platforms evaluated local regulations as adequate (Ziegler et al. 2019). Overall, differences in regulatory regimes stem from disparities in licensing requirements, thresholds for prospectus requirements, as well as various consumer and investor protection provisions.

Third, regulatory fragmentation can also be a result of activities of market participants. Platforms have created self-regulation frameworks, which are designed to induce trust in domestic platforms and possibly to establish a market entry barrier for foreign platforms. However, even self-regulation documents as enshrined in codes of conduct and ethics adopted by various industry organization across Europe exhibit significant differences in terms of scope, ambition, and oversight (Odorović and Wenzlaff 2020).

Against this backdrop, the European Union initiated the process towards establishing a pan-European regulatory regime in March 2018. The European Commission's FinTech Action Plan (European Commission 2018a) explicitly envisaged such goal as part of the European Capital Markets Union. More specifically, the ECSP Regime (European Commission 2018c) aimed to close the disparity in national regulations, provide robust investor protection, enable platforms to cater to clients in different countries holding a single licence, and allow small and innovative firms to raise funds across borders more effectively. Under such approach, the need to scale up regulatory compliance left limited room for opt-out provisions and partial harmonization in the case of the ECSP Regime.

The European Commission, in its proposal, suggested a passporting regime, similar to the existing MiFID regime for the offering and trading of equity and debt. The Commission proposal prohibited individual member states from adding regulatory requirements for platforms authorized as European Crowdfunding Service Providers. Such a prohibition would have created a level playing field between platforms operating in different states. It would also have curtailed regulatory arbitrage. However, in order to anticipate objection as a compromise with the Council, the Commission's proposal also allowed for the coexistence of national regulatory regimes. Accordingly, platforms wishing to stay within their respective existing regime, or operate only in one country, could stay within these national regulatory frameworks. The proposal by the Parliament sided with the Proposal by the Commission. The Council proposal went a different way. The Council instead proposed a harmonized regime with minimum standards, with member states having the option to increase the requirements on platforms operating in their countries.

The proposed regulation by the Commission foresaw several unique solutions to the regulatory dilemma of harmonizing without stifling innovation. At the same time, the proposal left a few pertaining issues subject to further debate. The European Commission embraced the view that the regulation should focus more on the status and behaviour of crowdfunding intermediaries rather than fundraising firms. Despite substantially differing risk profiles, the proposal incorporated both lending-based crowdfunding for businesses (known as P2P business lending) and equity-based crowdfunding. The blurry line of distinction between some debt and equity instruments justified equal regulatory treatment. However, P2P consumer lending remained outside the scope of the proposed regulation, although the business model of P2P consumer lending is more similar to P2P business lending than to equity-based crowdfunding, and despite the fact that some entrepreneurs took P2P consumer loans to fund their small business ventures.

The critical aspect of investor protection under the proposed regulation is a high level of transparency at the platform and the project levels. Transparency rules serve to attenuate information asymmetry inherent in all financial markets. Investors have imperfect information about both the quality of projects seeking funding and the quality of platforms' services. Therefore, the regulation sets out distinctive transparency rules for project owners and platforms. Here, instead of costly prospectus requirements, project owners have to provide investors with a simplified key investor information sheet to enable them to make sound and informed investment decisions. In this context, another crucial discussion revolves around what should be the investment threshold that triggers the exemption from prospectus requirements. The European Commission proposed a threshold of 1 million euro per project per year. The European Parliament proposed a threshold of 8 million euro per year. The Council allowed member states to set the threshold between 1 million euro and 8 million euro per year. The negotiation concluded by setting a limit at 5 million euro per year and project.

With respect to prospective investors, the European Commission was concerned that retail investors do not understand the nature of crowdfunding investments and the risks they entail. For this reason, the regulation foresees an 'appropriateness test' (a concept also known under MiFID (II)) to be a part of the investors' onboarding procedure. Such a solution is an attempt to circumvent a more burdensome 'suitability test', which would imply that a platform estimates the financial situation of its clients and their ability to bear losses associated with crowdfunding investments.

Several provisions of the regulation referred to business requirements for platforms to ensure, among others, the impartiality before and continuity of business after the completion of a campaign. Given that platforms do not take any risk on their balance sheet, the European Commission deemed capital requirements redundant in case of crowdfunding, thus, leading to a sizable reduction of costs of market entry. The Council Proposal foresaw minimum operating capital, primarily to provide a continuation of the platform business in case of insolvency. In the end, the negotiation concluded with a minimum capital requirement of 25,000 euro.

At the time of writing this chapter, technical details were still emerging, all supporting the underlying notion that the ECSP will lead to a reduction of fragmentation. As a regulation (not a directive), it will be valid in all European member states 12 months after it is passed by the Council, Parliament, and Commission, with the option for each member state to extend the 12 month grace period to 24 months. It provides a unified definition of investment crowdfunding and of crowdfunding service providers. The ECSP regime sets a unified threshold for prospectus requirements at 5 million euro per year and per project. It also stipulates that member states cannot set forth individual investor thresholds.

The ECSP will be especially relevant for lending platforms, because it prohibits member states from requiring a banking licence from lendees or lenders, which will enable new platforms to merge. The conduct of platforms is regulated uniformly across European Union member states, especially in areas of regulatory uncertainty concerning the management of conflict of interest and relations with investors.

Finally, while of great benefit in reducing disparities with respect to investment crowdfunding across Europe, the ECSP will have little effect on P2P consumer lending, as well as on non-investment crowdfunding models, as they are not covered in the proposed regulation (Hooghiemstra 2019). In addition, a remaining loophole may result in that even in cases of investment crowdfunding for businesses, not all platforms will be covered in situations where member states decide that certain financial instruments are not deemed as securities, which are covered by the ECSP. Moreover, other critical regulatory aspects related to crowdfunding practice are also not covered by this regulation. For example, in terms of taxation, some European countries offer tax incentive schemes to investors and companies using crowdfunding (e.g. UK, France, Italy, Belgium, and Spain), while other countries do not, and even among those offering incentives, such schemes vary widely (Cicchiello et al. 2019).

Outcomes of Crowdfunding in Europe

Due to both sensitivity of information and the relative recency of the phenomenon, only limited evidence from a few studies is available about the outcomes of crowdfunding in European countries. Here, a study examining P2P loans in Lithuania from the Finbee P2P consumer lending platform (Gaigalienė and Česnys 2018) showed a default rate (defined as loan payment more than 90 days late) of 13% in a sample of 6324 loans analysed.

A different study examining 413 equity funded firms in Germany and the UK (Hornuf et al. 2018) found that overall 77 firms (18.8%) successfully raised follow-up funding after the latest equity crowdfunding campaign, and 69 firms (16.7%) went insolvent, were liquidated, or were dissolved. Furthermore, the study showed that, in comparison to UK firms, equity crowdfunded German firms stood a higher chance of raising follow-up funding from business angels or venture capital, but also had a higher likelihood of failure.

Conclusions

This chapter has presented evidence on the fragmented nature of European crowdfunding with respect to volumes, number of platforms, model composition and leadership, involvement of traditional financial institutions, dependency levels on cross-border transactions, and state of national regulation. However, while fragmentation in the European crowdfunding market was high in previous years, such disparities are expected to decrease with harmonized regulation and a boost in cross-border developments.

The new rules laid out by the ECSP Regime hold promise to reduce fragmentation further, benefitting both large and small platforms towards healthier scale up supported by expansion to other European countries. Fragmentation in non-investment crowdfunding will likely continue, because of its exclusion from the ECSP regime, as well as the locally anchored nature of most of the small-scale fundraising initiatives characterizing non-investment models.

Implications for Future Research

While our review presents interesting insights about current realities in the European crowdfunding market, it also opens up opportunities for future research. Most importantly, there is the need for longitudinal study of market development dynamics, attempting to identify whether harmonization of regulation will indeed limit the extent to which the market is fragmented, as well as to what extent it will contribute to the international expansion of crowdfunding platforms across Europe. Other aspects in this context may relate to the study of the impact international platforms may have on local platforms, as international scope of investment may be more appealing to prospective fundraisers.

It will also be interesting to research the impact of clear and harmonized regulation on moves by traditional financial institutions, examining whether this will encourage them to enter the crowdfunding space and under which organizational and ownership formats. In this respect, it remains to be seen whether crowdfunding will deliver on its ideological promises of democratization of finance, or whether it will be overtaken by traditional actors with deeper pockets. This is especially relevant in mainland Europe, which has a long tradition of reliance on the banking system that can be used to enhance the legitimacy and credibility of crowdfunding actors among the general public.

In addition, more research is necessary on the outcomes of crowdfunding in the European context, capturing its short- and long-term effects on businesses, entrepreneurs, and investors. Such research remains rare and anecdotal, but of tremendous value for future platform development, policy making, and investor behaviour.

Implications for Practice

First, investment crowdfunding platforms should follow the entry into force of the ECSP regulation in their respective countries, as well as countries they may wish to expand to, and adjust their operations accordingly. This implies developing strategies both for facing new competitors from neighbouring countries entering the platforms' home markets, as well as market entry strategies for countries they may wish to enter into themselves. Such strategies may include strategic partnerships, joint venturing, as well as platform mergers across Europe.

Second, once the greatest regulatory barriers have been addressed, platforms should focus attention on improving public education and understanding of crowdfunding to support its uptake in the various markets. Regulatory ambiguity may have been detrimental for participation in this market, and with such clarity platforms should engage in more strategic customer relationship management in terms of both retaining existing users, as well as recruiting new ones.

Finally, with greater regulatory clarity, opportunities for collaboration between traditional and alternative finance players are likely to increase. Here, platform operators should strike a delicate balance between being overpowered by deep pocket institutions that may want a stake in this new fast developing market, while remaining loyal to the original driving forces behind the market in terms of expanding access to finance, and greater sharing of profits with the wider public.

References

Antons, D., & Piller, F. T. (2014). Opening the Black Box of "Not Invented Here": Attitudes, Decision Biases, and Behavioral Consequences. *Academy of Management Perspectives, 29*(2), 193–217.

Bruntje, D., & Gajda, O. (2016). *Crowdfunding in Europe: State of the Art in Theory and Practice*. London: Springer International Publishing.

Cicchiello, A. F., Battaglia, F., & Monferrà, S. (2019). Crowdfunding Tax Incentives in Europe: A Comparative Analysis. *The European Journal of Finance, 25*(18), 1856–1882.

De Buysere, K., Gajda, O., Kleverlaan, R., et al. (2012). A Framework for European Crowdfunding. Retrieved from https://www.fundraisingschool.it/wp-content/uploads/2013/02/European-Crowdfunding-Framework-Oct-2012.pdf.

Delhey, J., & Newton, K. (2005). Predicting Cross-national Levels of Social Trust: Global Pattern or Nordic Exceptionalism? *European Sociological Review, 21*(4), 311–327.

Dushnitsky, G., Guerini, M., Piva, E., et al. (2016). Crowdfunding in Europe: Determinants of Platform Creation Across Countries. *California Management Review, 58*(2), 44–71.

European Commission. (2018a). FinTech Action plan: For a More Competitive and Innovative European Financial Sector. European Commission, Brussels. Retrieved from https://eur-lex.europa.eu/legal-content/EN/TXT/?uri=CELEX:52018DC0109.

European Commission. (2018b). Investment Services and Regulated Markets—Markets in Financial Instruments Directive (MiFID). European Commission, Brussels. Retrieved from https://ec.europa.eu/info/business-economy-euro/banking-and-finance/financial-markets/securities-markets/investment-services-and-regulated-markets-markets-financial-instruments-directive-mifid_en.

European Commission. (2018c). Proposal for a Regulation of the European Parliament and the Council on European Crowdfunding Service Providers (ECSP) for Business. European Commission, Brussels. Retrieved from https://eur-lex.europa.eu/resource.html?uri=cellar:0ea638be-22cb-11e8-ac73-01aa75ed71a1.0003.02/DOC_1&format=PDF.

European Parliament. (2019). European Crowdfunding Service Providers (ECSP) for Business. European Parliament, Brussels. Retrieved from https://oeil.secure.europarl.europa.eu/oeil/popups/ficheprocedure.do?lang=en&reference=2018/0048(COD).

Gaigalienė, A., & Česnys, D. (2018). Determinants of Default in Lithuanian Peer-to-Peer Platforms. *Management of Organizations: Systematic Research, 80*(1), 19–36.

Gajda, O. (Ed.). (2017). *Review of Crowdfunding Regulation: Interpretations of Existing Regulation Concerning Crowdfunding in Europe North America and Israel*. Brussels: European Crowdfunding Network AISBL.

Hooghiemstra, S. N. (2019). Will the Proposed European Crowdfunding Regulation Lead to a 'true' European Market for Crowdfunding? July 25. Retrieved from https://papers.ssrn.com/sol3/papers.cfm?abstract_id=3492981. https://doi.org/10.2139/ssrn.3492981.

Hornuf, L., Schmitt, M., & Stenzhorn, E. (2018). Equity Crowdfunding in Germany and the United Kingdom: Follow-up Funding and Firm Failure. *Corporate Governance: An International Review, 26*(5), 331–354.
Odorović, A. & Wenzlaff, K. (2020). Joint Production of Confidence—Self-Regulation in European Crowdfunding Markets. *Baltic Journal of Management, 15*(2). https://doi.org/10.1108/BJM-04-2019-0119.
Rossi, A., & Vismara, S. (2018). What Do Crowdfunding Platforms Do? A Comparison between Investment-based Platforms in Europe. *Eurasian Business Review, 8*(1), 93–118.
Skotte, R., & Juvik, H. (2019). *Localization of Crowdfunding Platforms: The Influencing Role of Culture, Institutions and Geography*. Master's in Business Administration, University of Agder.
Tesar, L. L., & Werner, I. M. (1995). Home Bias and High Turnover. *Journal of International Money and Finance, 14*(4), 467–492.
Ziegler, T., Shneor, R., Wenzlaff, K., et al. (2019). *Shifting Paradigms—The 4th European Alternative Finance Benchmarking Report*. Cambridge, UK: Cambridge Centre for Alternative Finance.
Ziegler, T., Shneor, R., Wenzlaff, K., et al. (2020). *The Global Alternative Finance Benchmarking Report*. Cambridge, UK: Cambridge Centre for Alternative Finance.

Part IV

Crowdfunding in Sectoral Context

17

Crowdfunding Sustainability

Natalia Maehle, Pia Piroschka Otte,
and Natalia Drozdova

Introduction

This chapter focuses on the potential of using crowdfunding for financing sustainable projects, that is projects aiming to extend their goal beyond market success to providing benefits to wider society (Schaltegger and Wagner 2011). Modern societies are facing numerous challenges related to sustainability that are expected to become even more significant in the future. Achieving sustainability therefore represents one of the key objectives on today's agenda, as demonstrated by the recent climate change protests and prominence of the sustainability topic in the public

N. Maehle (✉)
Western Norway University of Applied Sciences, Bergen, Norway
e-mail: Natalia.Mehle@hvl.no

P. P. Otte
Ruralis – Institute for Rural and Regional Research, Trondheim, Norway
e-mail: pia.otte@ruralis.no

N. Drozdova
Norwegian School of Economics, Bergen, Norway
e-mail: natalia.drozdova@nhh.no

R. Shneor et al. (eds.), *Advances in Crowdfunding*,
https://doi.org/10.1007/978-3-030-46309-0_17

debate. As a universal call to action, the UN member states adopted in 2015 the UN Sustainable Development Goals (SDGs) addressing some of the most pressing issues such as global warming, poverty, and migration. Growing focus on sustainability among policymakers and consumers encourages businesses to embrace sustainability as their working practice and strive to develop sustainable innovations. Entrepreneurs represent an important driving force for sustainable transitions by exploiting the opportunities provided by market imperfections and developing innovative business solutions that resolve environmental and societal challenges (Cohen and Winn 2007). The innovative power of entrepreneurship can therefore help move economic systems towards sustainability (Cohen and Winn 2007; Dean and McMullen 2007).

Despite their increasing importance, sustainable entrepreneurs often experience problems getting funding from traditional sources due to the higher complexity of their value propositions (Ortas et al. 2013). By incorporating a triple bottom line approach (including economic, environmental, and societal concerns) sustainable entrepreneurs consider a wide range of stakeholder interests (Bocken et al. 2014; Belz and Binder 2017). However, this can add ambiguity and complexity to the sustainable projects leading to higher risk perceptions among conventional investors. Thus, it is important to find alternative solutions for financing sustainable initiatives. Bocken et al. (2014) identify crowdfunding as an example of a business model that can help develop and scale up sustainable innovations by bringing together like-minded individuals, firms, and investors. Furthermore, Belz and Binder (2017) demonstrate that crowdfunding is an ideal source of funds for sustainable entrepreneurs, as their focus on socially relevant aspects is likely to attract interest from a large number of backers, who are motivated to invest in the social good.

Recent developments in the crowdfunding market support this idea. Several platforms catering only to sustainable projects have been recently established and most mainstream crowdfunding platforms have a considerable proportion of sustainable projects. Crowdfunding for sustainability has also become an emerging research area. Lately, the topic has attracted considerable interest among researchers (Motylska-Kuzma 2018; Testa et al. 2019; Wehnert et al. 2019; Petruzzelli et al. 2019). However, ongoing discussion around success of sustainable crowdfunding campaigns has displayed rather contradictory findings (Hörisch 2015; Calic and Mosakowski 2016) and more research in this field is necessary.

The current chapter aims to address this need. To begin with, we discuss the definition and dimensions of sustainable development and sustainable entrepreneurship. Then we provide an overview of the existing literature on crowdfunding of sustainable projects, with special focus on the peculiarities of sustainable entrepreneurial ventures and success and challenges related to their crowdfunding activities. To illustrate which dimensions of sustainability and SDGs are addressed in crowdfunding and which crowdfunding models can be used for sustainable projects, we review four European sustainability-oriented crowdfunding platforms representing different crowdfunding models. Finally, we discuss our main findings and suggest future research directions for crowdfunding of sustainable projects.

Sustainable Development: Definition and Dimensions

The terms "Sustainable Development" and "Sustainability"—often used interchangeably[1]—emerged from the environmental movement in the late 1960s/early 1970s, a movement rooted in a strong criticism of the traditional economic growth theories that dominated the immediate post-WWII period. Sustainable development was institutionalized in the Brundtland report in 1987 and was followed by the Rio Declaration in 1992 and the 2030 Agenda for Sustainable Development in 2015 (Purvis et al. 2018). The agenda includes 17 goals addressing the different dimensions of sustainable development (e.g. reduction of inequalities, spur economic growth while at the same time tackling environmental challenges like climate change) (UN 2019). The SDGs are universal and thus concern all countries and not only developing countries as the prior Millennium Development Goals did (Halisçelik and Soytas 2019).

Sustainable development is a widely used concept. The most commonly used definition comes from the (Brundtland) report "Our

Common Future". Here sustainable development was defined as the "development that meets the needs of the present without compromising the ability of future generations to meet their own needs" (WCED 1987, p. 51). This definition follows a strong normative, ethical approach by advocating for a kind of social contract between contemporary and future generations (Hansmann et al. 2012). Some scholars have argued for a revision of the definition to further emphasize the environmental relevancy. In this view, sustainable development is defined as "Development that meets the needs of the present while safeguarding Earth's life-support system, on which the welfare of current and future generations depends" (Griggs et al. 2013, p. 306). This view argues for policies that place a value on environmentally friendly choices and costs on environmentally unsustainable actions (Griggs et al. 2013, p. 307).

Sustainable development originally captures three dimensions: economic, social, and environmental sustainability, with the environmental dimension most frequently referred to in research and among practitioners (Soini and Birkeland 2014). Some have expanded the existing framework with an additional institutional (Hosseini and Kaneko 2012; Spangenberg 2004) or cultural dimension (Hawkes 2001; Soini and Birkeland 2014).

In broad terms, the **economic dimension** focuses on maintaining economic growth and encompasses high levels of income (Halisçelik and Soytas 2019) and growing GDP. Economic growth has long been a key concern for nations across the world but has also been highly criticized due to the pressure it places on the environment. Hence, economic sustainability is about changing the current approach to economic growth and finding ways of developing a new economy based on sustainable development (Moldan et al. 2012) that allows for economic growth within our environmental limits.

The **social dimension** is the least defined (Dempsey et al. 2011; Murphy 2012). It tends to address issues related to social justice and social inclusion such as better education and health (Halisçelik and Soytas 2019). Spangenberg (2004) draws a difference between macro (e.g. distribution of income and assets) and micro (e.g. education, training, social contacts) levels of the social dimension. Most approaches focus on the social dimension in terms of achieving national welfare but it is also possible to incorporate an international and intergenerational perspective (Murphy 2012). Murphy (2012, p. 20) suggests a policy framework that connects the social with the environmental dimension. The framework captures 13 policy objectives grouped under 4 conceptual classifications including equity, awareness for sustainability, participation, and social cohesion.

As with the other dimensions, the **environmental dimension** has been defined in many different ways. Overall, it is "based on a notion of eco-system services—both renewable and non-renewable resources and waste absorptive capacity that provide benefits to humans and thus improve their welfare" (Moldan et al. 2012, p. 11). Environmental sustainability involves maintaining these services and, consequently, living within the limitations of the biophysical environment (ibid.). Energy consumption, material flows, and land use are three categories that form the centre of the environmental dimension and are used as indicators for measuring environmental sustainability (Spangenberg 2004). In the academic literature, there has been a strong focus on cleaner production within sustainable development (see, e.g., Jegatheesan et al. 2009; Dovì et al. 2009).

Table 17.1 illustrates how the 17 SDGs relate to the three dimensions of sustainable development and provides examples of the key targets within each SDG. We can see that many of the SDGs address more than one dimension, which illustrates the interconnection between the three dimensions and complexity of sustainable development due to the need to balance different interests (Hansmann et al. 2012). This interconnection is crucial because economic growth alone cannot be considered as a success if it does not lead to a more equal income distribution (Halisçelik and Soytas 2019) or exceeds the planet's ecological limits. Only economic growth that is utilized for public wealth in the form of a welfare state is socially sustainable (Spangenberg 2004).

Sustainable Entrepreneurship

The relationship between entrepreneurship and sustainable development has been addressed by various streams of literature, including the concepts of ecopreneurship (Cohen 2006; Schaltegger 2002), social

Table 17.1 Dimensions of sustainable development (to be achieved by 2030) in relation to SDGs

SDGs	Economic dimension: examples of targets	Social dimension: examples of targets	Environmental dimension: examples of targets
SDG 1: End poverty in all its forms everywhere	Eradicate extreme poverty; reduce at least by half the proportion of living in poverty; ensure equal rights to economic resources	Implement nationally appropriate social protection systems; achieve substantial coverage of the poor and the vulnerable	Build resilience of the poor and those in vulnerable situations, reduce their exposure and vulnerability to climate-related extreme events
SDG 2: Zero hunger	Double the agricultural productivity and incomes of small-scale food producers; increase investments in rural infrastructure	End hunger and ensure access to food by all people; end all forms of malnutrition	Ensure resilient agricultural practices that help maintain ecosystems and strengthen capacity for adaptation to climate change
SDG 3: Good health and well-being	Support the research and development of vaccines and medicines; provide access to affordable essential medicines and vaccines	Reduce the global maternal mortality ratio to less than 70 per 100,000 live births; end preventable deaths of newborns and children	
SDG 4: Quality education	Ensure that all girls and boys complete free, equitable, and quality primary and secondary education	Eliminate gender disparities in education; adults and children achieve literacy and numeracy	

(*continued*)

Table 17.1 (continued)

SDGs	Economic dimension: examples of targets	Social dimension: examples of targets	Environmental dimension: examples of targets
SDG 5: Gender equality	Give women access to ownership and control over land and other forms of property, financial services, and natural resources	End all forms of discrimination against all women and girls everywhere; eliminate all forms of violence against all women and girls	
SDG 6: Clean water and sanitation	Implement integrated water resources management at all levels, including through transboundary cooperation as appropriate	Achieve universal and equitable access to safe and affordable drinking water sanitation and hygiene for all	Improve water quality by reducing pollution; increase water-use efficiency across all sectors; protect and restore water-related ecosystems
SDG7: Affordable and clean energy	Promote investment in energy infrastructure and clean energy technology; upgrade technology for supplying modern and sustainable energy services	Universal access to affordable, reliable, and modern energy services	Increase share of renewable energy

(continued)

Table 17.1 (continued)

SDGs	Economic dimension: examples of targets	Social dimension: examples of targets	Environmental dimension: examples of targets
SDG 8: Decent work and economic growth	Sustain per capita economic growth in accordance with national circumstances; achieve higher levels of economic productivity	Achieve full and productive employment and decent work for all with equal pay; eradicate forced labour and human trafficking	Improve global resource efficiency and endeavour to decouple economic growth from environmental degradation
SDG 9: Industry, innovation, and infrastructure	Develop quality, reliable, sustainable, and resilient infrastructure, including regional and transborder infrastructure, to support economic development and human well-being; increase the access of small-scale industrial and other enterprises		Upgrade infrastructure and retrofit industries to make them sustainable, with greater adoption of clean and environmentally sound technologies and industrial processes
SDG 10: Reduced inequalities	Progressively achieve and sustain income growth of the bottom 40% of the population	Empower and promote the social, economic, and political inclusion of all, irrespective of age, sex, disability, race, ethnicity, origin, religion	
SDG 11: Sustainable cities and communities	Decrease the direct economic losses relative to GDP caused by disasters	Ensure access for all to adequate, safe, and affordable housing; enhance inclusive and sustainable urbanization	Protect and safeguard the world's cultural and natural heritage; reduce the adverse per capita environmental impact of cities

(*continued*)

Table 17.1 (continued)

SDGs	Economic dimension: examples of targets	Social dimension: examples of targets	Environmental dimension: examples of targets
SDG 12: Responsible consumption and production	Rationalize inefficient fossil-fuel subsidies that encourage wasteful consumption by removing market distortions	Support developing countries to strengthen their scientific and technological capacity to move towards more sustainable patterns of consumption and production	Achieve the sustainable management and efficient use of natural resources; halve per capita global food waste at the retail and consumer levels
SDG 13: Climate action	Fully operationalize the Green Climate Fund through its capitalization as soon as possible	Improve education, awareness-raising and human and institutional capacity on climate change mitigation and adaptation	Strengthen resilience and adaptive capacity to climate-related hazards and natural disasters
SDG 14: Life below water	Increase the economic benefits to least developed countries from the sustainable use of marine resources	Increase scientific knowledge, develop research capacity, and transfer marine technology	Prevent and significantly reduce marine pollution of all kinds; effectively regulate harvesting and end overfishing
SDG 15: Life on land	Mobilize and significantly increase financial resources from all sources to conserve and sustainably use biodiversity and ecosystems	Promote fair and equitable sharing of the benefits arising from the utilization of genetic resources and promote appropriate access to such resources	Ensure the conservation, restoration, and sustainable use of terrestrial and inland freshwater ecosystems and their services

(*continued*)

Table 17.1 (continued)

SDGs	Economic dimension: examples of targets	Social dimension: examples of targets	Environmental dimension: examples of targets
SDG 16: Peace, justice, and strong institutions	Significantly reduce illicit financial and arms flows; substantially reduce corruption and bribery of all forms	Significantly reduce all forms of violence and related death rates everywhere; end abuse, exploitation, trafficking, and all forms of violence against and torture of children	
SDG 17: Partnerships	Strengthen domestic resource mobilization, including through international support to developing countries, to improve domestic capacity for tax and other revenue collection	Encourage and promote effective public, public-private, and civil society partnerships, building on the experience and resourcing strategies of partnerships	

entrepreneurship (Nicolls 2006; Ridley-Duff 2008), institutional entrepreneurship (DiMaggio 1988), and sustainable entrepreneurship (Schaltegger and Wagner 2011).

Sustainable entrepreneurship is defined as "the process of discovering, evaluating, and exploiting economic opportunities that are present in market failures which detract from sustainability, including those that are environmentally relevant" (Dean and McMullen 2007, p. 58). Unlike conventional entrepreneurship, sustainable entrepreneurship extends the goal beyond market success to initiating societal change and changing market conditions and regulations. The main goal of sustainable entrepreneurship is to contribute to sustainable development of the market and society as a whole (Schaltegger and Wagner 2011). While pursuing this goal, sustainable entrepreneurship aims at balancing economic, social, and ecological objectives (Cohen et al. 2008; Schaltegger and Wagner 2011; Thompson et al. 2011) by replacing existing production methods, products, market structure, and consumption patterns with products and services with superior environmental and social impacts. Sustainable entrepreneurship includes focusing on sustainability performance (combining social and environmental performance) as a core business goal combined with large market influence and large social or political influence. This distinguishes it from related concepts such as ecopreneurship, institutional entrepreneurship, and traditional social entrepreneurship (Schaltegger 2002; Schaltegger and Wagner 2011).

Research shows that while there are some similarities between conventional and sustainable entrepreneurship, there are also important differences in the mission and performance measurement systems (Austin et al. 2006; Schaltegger and Wagner 2011). While conventional entrepreneurship tends to focus on business success and the economic interests of shareholders, the core motivation of sustainable entrepreneurs is to contribute to solving societal and environmental problems, thus addressing the demands of a larger group of stakeholders (Schaltegger and Wagner 2011). Moreover, as sustainable entrepreneurs address commercial market failures, problems for conventional entrepreneurs may represent opportunities for sustainable entrepreneurs. As for measuring performance, it is challenging to measure the societal and environmental impact of sustainable entrepreneurial ventures, while conventional entrepreneur can rely on relatively tangible and quantifiable measures such as financial indicators, market share, and customer satisfaction (Austin et al. 2006).

However, the distinction between sustainable and conventional entrepreneurship is not dichotomous but can be represented as a continuum ranging from purely sustainable to purely economic (Austin et al. 2006): conventional entrepreneurs also provide benefits to society in the form of new products, services, and jobs, while sustainable entrepreneurs must still create economic value. Therefore, in most cases entrepreneurial ventures include both sustainable and commercial value creation.

Funding and Forming a Sustainable Business

The process of sustainable entrepreneurship consists of six phases: recognizing a social or ecological problem; recognizing a social or ecological opportunity; developing a double bottom line solution (balancing between economic and social or ecological goals); developing a triple bottom line solution (balancing between economic, social, and ecological goals); funding and forming a sustainable enterprise; and creating or entering a sustainable market (Belz and Binder 2017).

Current research on the process of sustainable entrepreneurship is rather limited, with the majority of studies focusing on the first phase of the process, including opportunity recognition, development, and exploitation (Belz and Binder 2017). While funding an entrepreneurial venture is a critical activity in the formation of a new business (Shane 2003), there is little research on the funding of sustainable businesses.

Sustainable entrepreneurs often lack access to adequate funding. Ortas et al. (2013) describe the lack of funding as a central obstacle that hinders sustainable development. The need for sustainable entrepreneurs to balance between economic, social, and ecological goals creates constraints in the early funding phases because investors may perceive those objectives to be not as attractive as purely profit-oriented undertakings. It may also take longer for sustainable projects to become profitable due to the multiplicity of project goals. Moreover, the majority of sustainable entrepreneurs have very limited business experience, which can lead to difficulties in attracting funding from banks or professional investors (Choi and Gray 2008).

Later studies, however, have demonstrated that it is possible for sustainable enterprises to receive various types of seed capital, such as bank loans, crowdfunding, personal assets, and private funding from family and friends, as well as public funding (Belz and Binder 2017). For example, a focus on environmental and societal value creation helps social entrepreneurs to obtain public funding. In addition, venture capitalists are showing more interest in the development of sustainable start-ups as they are balancing financial with social and environmental returns (Bocken 2015).

Success of Sustainable Crowdfunding Campaigns

Crowdfunding liberates access to finance for entrepreneurs and, at the same time, enables consumers to decide which products or services they want to see on the market. In this way, crowdfunding helps to "democratise" innovation as it allows entrepreneurs who would otherwise lack the resources to find funding and markets, to erase geographic, social, and economic boundaries of innovation (Mollick and Robb 2016). Testa et al. (2019) argue that crowdfunding represents a novel socio-technical practice with the potential to upscale and transform financial and (potentially) sustainable regimes.

Recent studies have suggested that non-profits that primarily engage in prosocial activities are more successful at crowdfunding than for-profit entities (Belleflamme et al. 2013). Backers value the social orientations of the projects and are often driven by normative or altruistic motives (Gerber and Hui 2013). Therefore, socially oriented organizations may find it easier to attract money via crowdfunding for initiatives that are of interest to the general public due to their reduced focus on profits. In particular, crowdfunding is an appropriate source of funding for sustainable entrepreneurs who not only focus on the profit-seeking goal but also have to balance between economic, social, and ecological goals (Belz and Binder 2017).

However, empirical studies provide ambiguous results on the appropriateness of crowdfunding for financing sustainable entrepreneurship. For example, Calic and Mosakowski (2016) find that a sustainability orientation positively affects funding success for crowdfunding projects on the Kickstarter platform. In particular, they provide evidence that projects with either social or environmental orientation, relative to commercially oriented projects, are not only more likely to achieve their funding goals but also more likely to receive higher total pledge amounts. A study conducted by Vismara (2019) also provides evidence of the benefits of sustainability-oriented ventures (in equity crowdfunding in particular).

Conversely, Hörisch (2015) did not find any positive correlation between ventures' sustainability orientation and crowdfunding success. The results of this study even suggest that environmental orientation can *negatively* affect the success of crowdfunding projects. Furthermore, Moss et al. (2015) claim that crowd-investors often act like traditional investors and mainly focus on profit-seeking opportunities. Further studies could provide a deeper understanding of the success criteria for crowdfunding as an instrument for financing sustainable ventures.

Challenges Associated with Sustainable Crowdfunding Campaigns

A number of challenges are associated with crowdfunding for sustainable ventures.

First, some studies doubted the success of crowdfunded ventures after the funding process ended. For example, Lambert and Schwienbacher (2010) claim that ventures resorting to crowdfunding might have already failed to receive funding from conventional sources and thus have (potentially) failed to fulfil criteria that are important for long-term entrepreneurial success. This claim, combined with the notion that the majority of sustainable entrepreneurs have very limited business experience (Choi and Gray 2008), illustrates some important challenges for the post-funding stage of crowdfunding for sustainable entrepreneurs, as backers "typically do not look much at collaterals or business plans, but the ideas and core values of the firms" (Lehner 2013, p. 290). Therefore, they may end up funding projects that have few prospects for growth and, eventually, survival.

Second, an empirical investigation of environmental crowdfunding projects shows that many projects failed to disclose information on the actual environmental benefits created (Hörisch 2019). For that reason, backers are often unable to evaluate whether the environmental benefits are actually realized. Interestingly, in a study of 57 environmentally oriented projects, only 2 projects provided quantitative information on the environmental effects, and, based on the disclosed information, both projects had higher energy consumption in the post-funding phase than the target energy consumption established during the crowdfunding campaign (Hörisch 2019). Moreover, this study highlights that project owners are more likely to disclose the financial results rather than environmental effects of the project. Inadequate communication around environmental effects can have several explanations. First, entrepreneurs do not document environmental effects in detail, as neither backers nor platforms (even the environmental ones) require this kind of information. In many cases, it is difficult to measure the environmental impact, and it is a very demanding job to include all sources of emissions. An alternative explanation is that many environmental projects simply have not achieved their claimed goals (Hörisch 2019). Petruzzelli et al. (2019) suggest that, in order to cope with this challenge, owners of sustainability-oriented projects should pay significantly higher attention to communication with backers and the preparation of follow-up activities.

Sustainability-Oriented Platforms

To understand the landscape of sustainability-oriented crowdfunding and which dimensions of sustainable development and SDGs are addressed in the projects seeking crowdfunding, we review four large European sustainability-oriented platforms. As a part of the selection process, we conducted an extensive search among the European platforms based on the following criteria: sustainability orientation and platform size (larger and more established platforms were preferred). The platforms also should have represented different crowdfunding models to provide a comprehensive overview of the sustainability-oriented crowdfunding projects. As a result, we selected four platforms: one loan-based, one reward-based, one donation-based, and one hybrid platform combining various crowdfunding models. The review was conducted in three periods: December 2017, May 2019, and October 2019.

Platform A: Loan-Based

Platform A is a UK-based peer-to-peer lending platform. Since its establishment in 2012, it has been connecting developers of sustainable, eco-friendly energy infrastructure projects with investors interested in long-term income, filling the niche of long-term debt markets under-served by the banks. Platform A acts as an arranger, distributor, and approving authority for debentures—that is, a type of debt instrument that is not secured by physical assets or collateral and instead only backed by the general creditworthiness and reputation of the issuer—issued by the projects hosted on the platform. In addition, Platform A hosts a digital marketplace for debentures of the projects that were successfully funded on the platform, where Platform A's users can trade their investments among themselves.

Due to the strict project selection procedure, only a handful of projects are published annually. On average, five to six projects per annum collect funds, usually with no more than two—three campaigns active at any given moment. Projects on Platform A can be categorized based on the type of renewable energy technology where 52% of projects focus on solar technology, 28% on wind technology, 4% on hydro technology, and 16% on biomass technology. Platform A also divides projects into three categories based on their risk level. Projects classified as established debentures (52%) are associated with the lowest risk as they are issued by businesses that are already operational and whose revenues come from relatively stable and predictable sources. The second category, growth projects (36% of the projects), consists of projects that involve a greater risk, but also higher expected returns. These are the investments into the development of a new generation of sustainable power generation technologies where the revenues are less predictable. Finally, construction projects seek, as the name suggests, funding for construction of new assets (plants, wind turbines, etc.). These projects comprise the smallest category with only 12% of funds. Thus, it seems that during its selection process Platform A gives priority to the established projects associated with the lowest risk.

Table 17.2 Examples of the projects on Platform A

Project	Details	Sustainable development	
		Dimensions	SDGs
Developing waste gasification facilities to divert waste from landfill and generate lower carbon energy	£5.91 M; 10% a year; 4 year 6 month investment	Environmental, economic	7, 9, 13
Supplying sustainable and renewable electricity and heat to small businesses	£4.55 M; 5% IRR; 18 year investment	Environmental, social, economic	7, 8, 9, 13
Building a 2MW floating tidal stream turbine	£7 M; 12% a year; 2 year 6 month investment	Environmental, economic	7, 9, 13
Housing developer building quality social housing and affordable homes	£3.1 M; 7% a year; 1 year 7 month investment	Environmental, social, economic	1, 11, 13
Generating sustainable heat for a group of outdoor adventure centres and other businesses	£780 K; 6% IRR; 17 year investment	Environmental, social, economic	7, 3, 9, 13
Developing pumped storage hydro plants	£1.6 M; 10% a year; 3 year 2 month investment	Environmental, economic	7, 9, 13
Using whisky production residues to make biochemicals and biofuels	£4.38 M; 15% a year; 2 year investment	Environmental, economic	7, 9, 13
Helping homeowners to install rooftop solar panels	£675 K; 7.5% IRR; 15 year investment	Environmental, social, economic	7, 9, 11, 13
Building a geothermal power plant	£4.4 M; 2% a year; 1 year 2 month investment	Environmental, economic	7, 9, 13

The projects on Platform A consider all three dimensions of sustainable development (see Table 17.2 for examples of the projects) but focus on the environmental and economic dimensions. Most of the projects aim to combine the goal of developing sustainable, eco-friendly energy infrastructure with the goal of securing economic growth and providing economic returns to their investors. This combination (and careful project selection procedure) leads to the unprecedented success of the crowdfunding campaigns as all the projects published on the Platform A manage to collect the target amount. As for the SDGs, all the projects focus on sustainable energy, innovation, and climate change mitigation practices and therefore address goals 7, 9, and 13. We find some variations among the projects with a social dimension, which also concentrate on the SDGs related to poverty, health, and sustainable communities.

Platform B: Reward-Based

Platform B, founded in October 2014, is a German reward-based crowdfunding platform exclusively for sustainable projects. A very inclusive platform at its core, Platform B does not cater to a narrow range of sustainable initiatives, but welcomes any project that scores high on two axes—sustainability of inputs and outputs. The definition of sustainable input or output is very broad. Inputs, or resources employed in the realization of the project, have to be one or more of the following: "green", eco-, or fair trade-certified, of local origin, used sparingly, recycled, or renewable. As for the outputs, the project has to benefit climate, environment, flora and fauna, cultural property, natural resources, or people.

Being a reward-based platform, Platform B prohibits its projects from offering rewards with a financial return and most of the rewards are purely symbolic with little to no tangible value, for example, a jute bag with project logo or a visit to an animal shelter. However, some projects offer more tangible rewards (particularly pre-sale type crowdfunding campaigns). Platform B uses a flexible funding model, that is, projects can keep the money even if they have not reached a target amount. Only 24% of projects manage to collect 100% or more of their target amount.

Due to its broad definition of sustainability, the projects on Platform B are characterized by a very high degree of heterogeneity and address all the dimensions of sustainable development (see Table 17.3 for examples of the projects). Most of the projects emphasize environmental sustainability, sometimes in combination with social sustainability. However, some of the projects also address sustainable economic growth. The main SDGs targeted are those related to environmental protection and climate change (12, 13, and 15), sometimes in combination with the SDGs related to the social and economic dimensions.

Table 17.3 Examples of the projects on Platform B

		Sustainable development	
Project	Details	Dimensions	SDGs
Establishing an organic farm	€9672 raised of €11,000 target by 5 backers	Environmental, economic	12, 13, 15
Opening a shop for ecologically and fairly produced products	€3904 raised of €10,000 target by 62 backers	Environmental, social, economic	1, 8, 12, 13, 15
Sustainable educational game on protection of marine environment	€8422 raised of €9000 target by 318 backers	Environmental	4, 13, 14
Beach clean-up for plastics	€687 raised of €686 target by 22 backers	Environmental	13, 14
Company organizing sustainable clothing rental	€1027 raised of €978 target by 32 backers	Environmental, economic	9, 12, 13
Extending a café selling organic produce	€1886 raised of €3000 target by 24 backers	Environmental, economic	12, 13, 15
Production of a magazine about local heroes contributing to more sustainable and fair local community	€6752 raised of €6498 target by 122 backers	Environmental, social	1, 8, 11, 12, 13
Non-profit organization taking care of native and exotic wildlife	€22,646 raised of €30,000 target by 639 backers	Environmental	13, 15

Platform C: Donation-Based

Platform C is a donation-based crowdfunding platform headquartered in the United Kingdom. Platform C serves as a two-sided platform that connects donors to good causes with three types of beneficiaries: charities, corporations, and individuals. A charity can set up a personalized webpage with information about the organization and the good causes it is working on, as well as buttons offering visitors the opportunity to donate to the charity or organize fundraisers in its name. Additionally, charities can set up campaigns to gather funds for specific purposes (e.g.

provision of humanitarian aid to those affected by a natural disaster). A company can similarly create its own branded webpage to showcase charitable efforts by company employees and the amount of funding they raise. Finally, individuals can use Platform C not only for making donations but also for fundraising purposes. They can start their own donation-based crowdfunding campaign (e.g. asking help in financing an operation for a relative) or link their fundraising initiative to one of the charities/causes represented on the platform.

Platform C hosts a variety of projects and campaigns across a wide variety of themes. Major thematic categories include health and medical causes; animals and pets; art and culture; local community; education; sports; disability; and international aid (see Table 17.4 for examples of the projects). There is no special category for environmental initiatives but they are represented as part of other categories (e.g. animals, local community). Charities that focus on health and medical issues are by far the most popular of all the categories and score at least two times the number of "Care" hits compared to the environmental charities. The latter do seem to draw more attention than culture-focused charities, but cannot compete with organizations gathering funds for cancer research or helping children in need of medical assistance. Thus, Platform C mostly addresses the SDGs related to the social dimension of sustainable development; however, the environmental dimension is also present (often in combination with a social one). The economic dimension is underrepresented on this platform.

Platform D: Hybrid

Platform D is a European crowdfunding platform for sustainable projects based in the Netherlands and Germany. One of the main requirements for publication on the platform is that the project has to be focused on sustainability; however, the platform does not provide an exact definition of what is considered to be sustainable. Platform D has a hybrid crowdfunding model, giving project owners the ability to choose between multiple types of crowdfunding: reward-, donation-, lending-, and equity-based models, as well as almost any combination of the four. All

Table 17.4 Examples of the projects on Platform C

Project	Details	Sustainable development	
		Dimensions	SDGs
Supporting a domestic violence refuge for women and young girls	£2160 raised of £1200 target by 63 backers	Social	5, 11
The London Marathon for Prostate Cancer UK	£57,290 raised of £40,000 target by 233 backers	Social	3
Create a home for someone in housing need in the UK	£5763 raised of £6000 target by 18 backers	Social	1, 10
Renovating the community garden to benefit the local community and wildlife within it	£993 raised of £1000 target by 58 backers	Social, environmental	11, 15
Beach clean-up	£1168.00 raised of £1000 target by 44 backers	Environmental	13, 14
Building clean, energy-efficient cook stoves to reduce harmful emissions in India	£1600.00 raised of £1600 target by 8 backers	Social, environmental	9, 11, 13
Fundraising for WWF-UK by running Tough Mudder	£3333.39 raised of £3250 target by 128 backers	Environmental	13, 14, 15
Support children and young people's mental health on World Mental Health Day	£7508.86 raised of £7500 target by 82 backers	Social	3
Raising money for a local children's hospice	£18,204.76 raised of £15,000 target by 43 backers	Social	3

types of campaigns employ all-or-nothing funding logic, meaning that if the funding goal is not reached by the end of the funding period, Platform D will refund all contributions within 14 working days.

Platform D's interpretation of the reward-based campaigns is similar to a pre-sale type of crowdfunding, and a typical reward-based campaign is usually initiated by an up-and-coming entrepreneur who is about to launch a new product. In return for funding for manufacturing the product, entrepreneurs give backers a significant discount off the eventual market price and/or additional services or benefits. Donation-based campaigns may also offer small tangible rewards for backers willing to support them. Lending-based campaigns are tailored to established companies generating turnover that would allow them to repay the debt. Normally, the loan runs for a period of between 12 and 60 months (longer for some energy projects) and offers an interest rate between 4 and 10%. Finally, Platform D offers a twist on the concept of equity crowdfunding with its subordinated convertible loan campaigns. Convertible loans are particularly suitable for young companies whose products are still in development, with very limited turnover and no foreseeable cash flow in the near future. Convertible loans have an average duration of five years and provide backers with the option of converting the outstanding loan balance and interest into share certificates at the company whose campaign they funded, thus becoming a minor shareholder. The backers get the option of converting the loan into shares once a substantial (as determined by Platform D) new investor acquires a part of the company. The optional conversion then follows the same terms as the ones between the company and the new investor, but, as a reward for the risk they took, backers receive a discount off the negotiated share price. Investment by backers that opt to forego conversion into shares is treated as a loan with an interest rate of approximately 4–10%. Platform D also allows project owners to create hybrid campaigns, for example, reward + loan or convertible loan + donation + reward combinations. Only loans and convertible loans are mutually exclusive for self-evident reasons.

The most widely represented group of projects on Platform D is the reward and reward + donation campaigns, which together comprise 56% of the projects hosted on the platform. The next cluster comprises the loan + reward combination (11%), followed by loan (9%), donation (9%), and convertible loan (6%). Finally, various hybrids (e.g. convertible loan + reward, loan + donation) conclude the list, with only 1–3% of campaigns attributed to each of these types.

As for the success rates, pure loan campaigns are the most successful with an impressive success rate of 90%, followed by convertible loan + reward (86%), loan + reward (80%), and loan + donation + reward (80%). Pure convertible loan campaigns have a success rate of 77%. Reward and reward + donation campaigns have an average success rate of approximately 69% (very high for this type of crowdfunding), while pure donation campaigns have a success rate of 74%.

As for the dimensions of sustainable development, projects on Platform D are quite heterogeneous and may represent all the three dimensions (see Table 17.5 for examples of the projects). Most of them however focus on environmental and economic sustainability and address the SDGs related to innovation and environmental protection (9, 12, and 13). There are also differences depending on the crowdfunding model, for example, the projects using a donation model usually have less focus on the economic sustainability.

Discussion

The current study demonstrates that crowdfunding can help sustainable entrepreneurs to handle the lack of finance—a critical issue for sustainable ventures (Ortas et al. 2013). The review of the sustainability-oriented platforms reveals that sustainable projects have rather high success rates in crowdfunding and manage to appeal to a wide backer audience. In this way, we provide additional support to Belz and Binder (2017) who demonstrate that crowdfunding fits well as a funding source for sustainable entrepreneurs. Moreover, several studies suggest that prosocial and sustainable orientations positively affect funding success for crowdfunding projects (Belleflamme et al. 2013; Calic and Mosakowski 2016). However, there is still some disagreement among researchers regarding this issue (Hörisch 2015; Moss et al. 2015), and the literature identifies a number of potential challenges in sustainability-oriented crowdfunding (Hörisch 2019; Petruzzelli et al. 2019). One of the main concerns is measuring and communicating their environmental impact (Hörisch 2019). While reviewing the projects on the sustainability-oriented crowdfunding platforms, we observed a lack of detailed information about projects' environmental and societal effects. Petruzzelli et al. (2019) suggest that communication with backers is essential to address this challenge. We believe that one way to demonstrate the project's impact is to highlight how it addresses sustainability dimensions and fulfils different SDGs (by anecdotal evidence and by numbers). This can help capture additional project's benefits beyond market success and illustrate for backers the positive environmental and societal outcomes. The overview of the projects in Tables 17.2, 17.3, 17.4, and 17.5 demonstrates this approach.

Sustainable entrepreneurs often struggle to balance a triple bottom line of economic, social, and environmental goals (Belz and Binder 2017). Therefore, it is interesting to explore which dimensions of sustainable development (economic, social, or environmental) and SDGs are

Table 17.5 Examples of the projects on Platform D

		Sustainable development	
Project	Details	Dimensions	SDGs
Company developing a circular solution for discarded goods	Convertible loan; €820,250 raised of €750,000 target by 200 backers	Environmental, economic	9, 13
A sustainable travel agency	Convertible loan; €885,650 raised of €750,000 target by 511 backers	Environmental, economic	9, 12, 13
A company producing sustainable rainwear	Loan; €125,000 raised of €100,000 target by 108 backers	Environmental, economic	9, 12, 13
Developing infrared heat cushions that are more energy efficient than ordinary heating	Loan; €250,500 raised of €150,000 target by 170 backers	Environmental, economic	7, 9, 13
Pre-sale of the handmade scarves produced by the seniors	Reward; €1130 raised of €1000 target by 14 backers	Social, economic	3, 8
Pre-sale of a waste separating stackable boxes made from recycled plastics	Reward; €40,730 raised of €40,000 target by 163 backers	Environmental, economic	9, 12, 13
Renting out dresses to address sustainability and poverty	Donation; €5331 raised of €5000 target by 80 backers	Environmental, social, economic	1, 9, 12, 13
Supporting a sailing trip made without the use of fossil fuels	Donation; €8173 raised of €7500 target by 121 backers	Environmental	13, 14

addressed in sustainability-oriented crowdfunding and how entrepreneurs manage to merge these sometimes conflicting goals while organizing their crowdfunding campaigns. As we see from the review of the sustainability-oriented platforms, there is a great heterogeneity among the sustainable projects seeking crowdfunding. They may address all the three dimensions of sustainable development and often combine several dimensions. However, the environmental dimension gets the most attention, which is not surprising due to its appeal to more general backer audience. The social dimension is less represented and is mostly relevant for the projects using donation-based crowdfunding. As for the economic dimension, it is integral to projects using loan- and equity-based crowdfunding as they need to provide economic benefits to their backers. In addition, the projects using reward-based crowdfunding of pre-sale type tend to include the economic dimension.

We can therefore conclude that all the crowdfunding models are relevant for sustainable projects and may be used successfully. However, loan-based crowdfunding seems to have the highest success rate. Moreover, focus on a particular dimension of sustainability may influence the choice of the crowdfunding model, for example, it is necessary to emphasize the potential of economic growth even for sustainable projects if they plan to use loan- or equity-based crowdfunding.

Conclusion

The current chapter provides an overview of the existing literature on crowdfunding of sustainable projects and reviews four European sustainability-oriented crowdfunding platforms. As a result, we illustrate how crowdfunding enables entrepreneurs to address the three dimensions of sustainability and various SDGs. In this way, we demonstrate the role of crowdfunding in moving towards a sustainable society and contribute to the emerging research field of sustainable crowdfunding (Testa et al. 2019). In addition, we add to the literature on sustainable entrepreneurship by contributing to the limited research on funding of sustainable ventures and identifying an alternative solution for their access to adequate funding.

Moreover, the current study has a number of practical implications. Sustainable entrepreneurs may find our findings useful when deciding which crowdfunding model best suits their projects. We also provide suggestions that can help them to solve the critical challenge of communicating the sustainability orientation of their projects to potential backers. In addition, the general overview of the field of sustainable crowdfunding can give valuable insights for crowdfunding platforms seeking to embrace sustainable projects as part of their business portfolio.

Nevertheless, a number of important issues in sustainability-oriented crowdfunding still require further exploration. For example, the role of platforms in sustainability-oriented crowdfunding has remained largely untouched (Testa et al. 2019). Another issue that requires further examination is the success factors that contribute to sustainability-oriented crowdfunding. Existing research has not reached a consensus on whether sustainability orientation increases the probability of crowdfunding success or not (Belleflamme et al. 2013; Calic and Mosakowski 2016; Hörisch 2015; Moss et al. 2015). It may also be interesting to see if there is a relationship between the dimensions of sustainable development addressed by the project and the project's crowdfunding success. Finally, we invite future studies to further investigate how using different models (i.e. donation, reward, loan, equity, or their combinations) influences the crowdfunding success.

Acknowledgement The current chapter is a part of the research project COOLCROWD "Local crowdfunding for a lowemission society: Investigating the concept of local climate crowdfunding for Norway", funded by the Research Council of Norway (project number 268223).

Note

1. Although some authors argue that sustainability departs from people's needs while people's well-being is at the base of sustainable development (Moldan et al. 2012).

References

Austin, J., Stevenson, H., & Wei-Skillern, J. J. (2006). Social and Commercial Entrepreneurship: Same, Different, or Both? *Entrepreneurship Theory and Practice, 30*(1), 1–22.

Belleflamme, P., Lambert, T., & Schwienbacher, A. (2013). Individual Crowdfunding Practices. *Venture Capital, 15*(4), 313–333.

Belz, F. M., & Binder, J. K. (2017). Sustainability Entrepreneurship: A Convergent Process Model. *Business Strategy and the Environment, 26*(1), 1–17.

Bocken, N. M. (2015). Sustainable Venture Capital – Catalyst for Sustainable Start-Up Success? *Journal of Cleaner Production, 108*, 647–658.

Bocken, N. M. P., Samuel W. S., Padmakshi R., & Steve E. (2014). A Literature and Practice Review to Develop Sustainable Business Model Archetypes. *Journal of Cleaner Production, 65*, 42–56.

Calic, G., & Mosakowski, E. (2016). Kicking Off Social Entrepreneurship: How a Sustainability Orientation Influences Crowdfunding Success. *Journal of Management Studies, 53*(5), 738–767.

Choi, D. Y., & Gray, E. R. (2008). The Venture Development Processes of 'Sustainable' Entrepreneurs. *Management Research News, 8*(31), 558–569.

Cohen, B. (2006). Sustainable Valley Entrepreneurial Ecosystems. *Business Strategy and the Environment, 15*(1), 1–14.

Cohen, B., & Winn, M. I. (2007). Market Imperfections, Opportunity and Sustainability Entrepreneurship. *Journal of Business Venturing, 22*(1), 29–49.

Cohen, B., Smith, B., & Mitchell, R. (2008). Towards a Sustainable Conceptualization of Dependent Variables in Entrepreneurship Research. *Business Strategy and the Environment, 17*(2), 107–119.

Dean, T. J., & McMullen, J. S. (2007). Toward a Theory of Sustainability Entrepreneurship: Reducing Environmental Degradation Through Entrepreneurial Action. *Journal of Business Venturing, 22*(1), 50–76.

Dempsey, N., Bramley, G., Powers, S., & Brown, C. (2011). The Social Dimension of Sustainable Development: Defining Urban Social Sustainability. *Sustainable Development, 19*(5), 289–300.

DiMaggio, P. J. (1988). Interest and Agency in Institutional Theory. In L. G. Zucker (Ed.), *Institutional Patterns and Organizations: Culture and Environment* (pp. 3–23). Cambridge: Ballinger.

Dovì, V. G., Friedler, F., Huisingh, D., & Klemeš, J. J. (2009). Cleaner Energy for Sustainable Future. *Journal of Cleaner Production, 17*(10), 889–895.

Gerber, E. M., & Hui, J. (2013). Crowdfunding: Motivations and Deterrents for Participation. *ACM Transactions on Computer-Human Interaction, 20*(6), 1–32.

Griggs, D. J., Smith, M. S., Gaffney, O., Rockström, J., Öhman, M. C., Shyamsundar, P., Steffen, W., Glaser, G., Kanie, N., & Noble, I. (2013). Sustainable Development Goals for People and Planet. *Nature, 495*, 305–307.

Halisçelik, E., & Soytas, M. A. (2019). Sustainable Development from Millennium 2015 to Sustainable Development Goals 2030. *Sustainable Development, 27*(4), 545–572.

Hansmann, R., Mieg, H. A., & Frischknecht, P. (2012). Principal Sustainability Components: Empirical Analysis of Synergies Between the Three Pillars of Sustainability. *International Journal of Sustainable Development & World Ecology, 19*(5), 451–459.

Hawkes, J. (2001). *The Fourth Pillar of Sustainability: Culture's Essential Role in Public Planning*. Melbourne: Common Ground P/L.

Hörisch, J. (2015). Crowdfunding for Environmental Ventures: An Empirical Analysis of the Influence of Environmental Orientation on the Success of Crowdfunding Initiatives. *Journal of Cleaner Production, 107*, 636–645.

Hörisch, J. (2019). Take the Money and Run? Implementation and Disclosure of Environmentally-Oriented Crowdfunding Projects. *Journal of Cleaner Production, 223*, 127–135.

Hosseini, H. M., & Kaneko, S. (2012). Causality Between Pillars of Sustainable Development: Global Stylized Facts or Regional Phenomena? *Ecological Indicators, 14* (1), 197–201.

Jegatheesan, V., Liow, J. L., Shu, L., Kim, S. H., & Visvanathan, C. (2009). The Need for Global Coordination in Sustainable Development. *Journal of Cleaner Production, 17*(7), 637–643.

Lambert, T., & Schwienbacher, A. (2010). An Empirical Analysis of Crowdfunding. Retrieved May 15, 2019, from http://www.crowdsourcing.org/document/an-empirical-analysis-of-crowdfunding-/2458.

Lehner, O. M. (2013). Crowdfunding Social Ventures: A Model and Research Agenda. *Venture Capital, 15*(4), 289–311.

Moldan, B., Janoušková, S., & Hák, T. (2012). How to Understand and Measure Environmental Sustainability: Indicators and Targets. *Ecological Indicators, 17*, 4–13.

Mollick, E., & Robb, A. (2016). Democratizing Innovation and Capital Access: The Role of Crowdfunding. *California Management Review, 58*(2), 72–87.

Moss, T. W., Neubaum, D. O., & Meyskens, M. (2015). The Effect of Virtuous and Entrepreneurial Orientations on Microfinance Lending and Repayment: A Signaling Theory Perspective. *Entrepreneurship Theory and Practice, 39*(1), 27–52.

Motylska-Kuzma, A. (2018). Crowdfunding and Sustainable Development. *Sustainability, 10*(12), 4650.

Murphy, K. (2012). The Social Pillar of Sustainable Development: A Literature Review and Framework for Policy Analysis. *Sustainability: Science, Practice and Policy, 8*(1), 15–29.

Nicolls, A. (2006). *Social Entrepreneurship – New Models of Sustainable Social Change*. Oxford: Oxford University Press.

Ortas, E., Burritt, R. R., & Moneva, J. M. (2013). Socially Responsible Investment and Cleaner Production in the Asia Pacific: Does It Pay to Be Good? *Journal of Cleaner Production, 52*, 272–280.

Petruzzelli, A. M., Natalicchio, A., Panniello, U., et al. (2019). Understanding the Crowdfunding Phenomenon and Its Implications for Sustainability. *Technological Forecasting and Social Change, 141*, 138–148.

Purvis, B., Mao, Y., & Robinson, D. (2018). Three Pillars of Sustainability: In Search of Conceptual Origins. Sustainability Science. Retrieved May 9, 2019, from http://eprints.whiterose.ac.uk/136715/7/Purvis2018_Article_ThreePillarsOfSustainabilityIn.pdf.

Ridley-Duff, R. (2008). Social Enterprise as a Socially Rational Business. *International Journal of Entrepreneurial Behaviour and Research, 14*(5), 291–312.

Schaltegger, S. (2002). A Framework for Ecopreneurship. Leading Bioneers and Environmental Managers to Ecopreneurship. *Greener Management, 38*, 45–58.

Schaltegger, S., & Wagner, M. (2011). Sustainability Entrepreneurship and Sustainability Innovation: Categories and Interactions. *Business Strategy and the Environment, 20*(4), 222–237.

Shane, S. A. (2003). *A General Theory of Entrepreneurship: The Individual–Opportunity Nexus*. Cheltenham, UK: Edward Elgar Publishing.

Soini, K., & Birkeland, I. (2014). Exploring the Scientific Discourse on Cultural Sustainability. *Geoforum, 51*, 213–223.

Spangenberg, J. H. (2004). Reconciling Sustainability and Growth: Criteria, Indicators, Policy. *Sustainable Development, 12*(2), 74–86.

Testa, S., Nielsen, K. R., Bogers, M., et al. (2019). The Role of Crowdfunding in Moving Towards a Sustainable Society. *Technological Forecasting and Social Change, 141*, 66–73.

Thompson, N., Kiefer, K., & York, J. G. (2011). Distinctions Not Dichotomies: Exploring Social, Sustainable, and Environmental Entrepreneurship. *Advances in Entrepreneurship, Firm Emergence and Growth, 13*, 205–233.

UN. (2019). Sustainable Development Goals. Retrieved May 15, 2019, from https://sustainabledevelopment.un.org/?menu=1300.

Vismara, S. (2019). Sustainability in Equity Crowdfunding. *Technological Forecasting and Social Change, 141*, 98–106.

WCED. (1987). *Our Common Future, Report of the World Commission on Environment and Development*. Oxford and New York: Oxford University Press.

Wehnert, P., Christian V. B., & Markus B. (2019). In Crowdfunding We Trust? Investigating Crowdfunding Success as a Signal for Enhancing Trust in Sustainable Product Features. *Technological Forecasting and Social Change, 141*, 128–137.

18

Crowdfunding in the Cultural Industries

Anders Rykkja, Natalia Maehle, Ziaul Haque Munim, and Rotem Shneor

Introduction

Cultural production in general, and music in particular, has stood at the forefront of crowdfunding adoption (Moritz and Block 2016; Agrawal et al. 2014), with ArtistShare active from 2003 as a fan-funding platform for music projects being one of the first platforms ever established (Bannerman 2012). This trend is globally driven by challenges faced by

A. Rykkja (✉)
Inland Norway University of Applied Sciences, Hamar, Norway
e-mail: Anders.Rykkja@inn.no

N. Maehle
Western Norway University of Applied Sciences, Bergen, Norway
e-mail: Natalia.Mehle@hvl.no

Z. H. Munim
Faculty of Technology, Natural Sciences and Maritime Sciences, University of South-Eastern Norway, Horten, Norway
e-mail: Ziaul.H.Munim@usn.no

R. Shneor
School of Business and Law, University of Agder, Kristiansand, Norway
e-mail: rotem.shneor@uia.no

R. Shneor et al. (eds.), *Advances in Crowdfunding*,
https://doi.org/10.1007/978-3-030-46309-0_18

cultural organizations such as the cuts in public funding and increased competition for donors and sponsors (Boeuf et al. 2014; Papadimitriou 2017), as well as the advent of digitalization (Hesmondhalgh 2013; Nordgård 2018; Peltoniemi 2015). Both challenges are profoundly affecting the conditions and framework for creating, producing, distributing, and consuming cultural expressions.

Changes in traditional models for investments in cultural production, as well as structures and value chains, create alternative pathways and circumvention of traditional intermediaries (Peltoniemi 2015). For example, in the music sector, there is a shift away from a label-centred economy to an artist-centred economy (Tschmuck 2016), in which the artist holds more aesthetic freedom, and also bigger economic and management responsibilities. Thus, in times with increasing possibilities for self-production of artistic content, crowdfunding represents a pathway towards a more open and diverse sectoral structure, with the potential for realizing a broad spectre of cultural productions.

While a variety of types of crowdfunding models are available, crowdfunding in the cultural sector is predominantly of the reward-based type, mostly mirroring the presale of a product or service. A recent European report found that 88% of the estimated 75,000 campaigns launched by stakeholders in the cultural sector are reward-based (De Voldere and Zeqo 2017). In addition, crowd patronage (Swords 2017) has also been identified as a model allowing subscription-like payments to individuals to fund their ongoing occupation or career, which is often regarded as of particular relevance for artists in line with historical tradition.

Despite the critical role played by artists as first adopters of crowdfunding, research dedicated to the role and impact of crowdfunding on stakeholders in the cultural sector remains limited. This is surprising as crowdfunding may have critical influence on the balance between the commercial and the non-commercial value, the popular and the alternative artistic expression, aesthetic practices both online and offline, as well as the very structure of cultural funding. Indeed some claim that the significance of crowdfunding is in that it 'shift mindsets and realities around organizational possibility, potentially reinforcing and extending, or even altering, the traditional organization of cultural production' (Bannerman 2012, p. 7).

In this chapter we review earlier research on crowdfunding in the cultural sector, while highlighting key research themes and related studies. Next, we outline opportunities for future research development and suggest some implications for practice.

Cultural Crowdfunding

Cultural production refers to creation, production, distribution, and consumption of cultural products and services (Venkatesh and Meamber 2006). Cultural crowdfunding (hereafter 'CCF') refers to the use of crowdfunding for the financing of production, distribution, and consumption of cultural expressions. The distinctive aspects of CCF are anchored in the unique nature of the projects seeking funding. Such projects involve ideas and artistic expressions, which are often characterized as having higher experiential (Power 2002), symbolic (Throsby 2001), and aesthetic value (Hirsch 1972), as well as non-utilitarian nature (Lawrence and Phillips 2002).

Accordingly, originality may play a greater role in assessing market opportunities than utility, and emotional appeal may have greater impact on patterns of consumption than rational considerations. However, what constitutes originality and emotional appeal may differ significantly between individual consumers (Lampel et al. 2006), as it depends on individual taste, preference, and aesthetic opinions (Bourdieu 1984). Thus, neither the producers nor the consumers know ex-ante if the originality dimension of the cultural expression will be in line with the personal preferences of consumers (Kappel 2009).

Like crowdfunding in other sectors, CCF has multiple objectives and benefits that go beyond funding. A recent large-scale study of crowdfunding in the European cultural and creative sectors (De Voldere and Zeqo 2017) found that 80% of surveyed campaigners experienced their crowdfunding campaigns as serving purposes beyond finance, such as audience development, community engagement, skills development, promotion, and market research. Nevertheless, it can be argued that dependence on fans as well as a long tradition of patronage and subscription-based pre-selling have been important precursors of funding cultural projects well before the digital age, and to a greater extent than in other sectors.

Regardless of the objectives of a crowdfunding campaign, the cultural work itself may have both economic and cultural values to a greater or lesser extent. Hence, in order to define what constitutes a cultural project we use Throsby's concentric circles model of the cultural industries (Throsby 2008). Industries closer to the core have greater cultural than economic value, and the further away a sector is positioned from the core, the heavier is its focus on commercial and economic value. Consequently, in the inner circle, where cultural value is perceived as highest, we find the 'core' creative artistic activities such as literature, music, performing arts, and visual arts. Its surrounding layer includes other 'core' industries such as film, photography, museums, galleries, and libraries. The wider circle of cultural and creative industries includes heritage services, publishing and print media, television and radio, sound recording, as well as video and computer games. Finally, the last layer includes related industries with a heavy cultural component including advertising, architecture, design, and fashion.

Industry figures and statistics specific to CCF are limited. Nevertheless, some findings from a study of the European CCF industry (De Voldere and Zeqo 2017) are illustrative. This study revealed that between 2013 and 2016 there were 75,000 CCF campaigns raising a total of EUR 247 million. When broken into sub-industries, data showed the following distribution of campaigns: Film and Audiovisual (33% of campaigns and 29% of transaction volume), Music (22% of campaigns and 17% of transaction volume), Performing Arts (13% of campaigns and 9% of transaction volume), Design (11% of campaigns and 15% of transaction volume), Visual Arts (10% of campaigns and 6% of transaction volume), Literature and Press (8% of campaigns and 13% of transaction volume), Gaming (2% of campaigns and 5% of transaction volume), Architecture (2% of campaigns and 5% of transaction volume), and Heritage (less than 1% in terms of both number of campaigns and transaction volume).

The numerous campaigns and their public records reflect the complexity of CCF realities. For illustration purposes, one can highlight certain cases that have attracted attention from both academics and practitioners. First, in the music sector, musician, singer, and songwriter *Amanda*

Palmer successfully and wholeheartedly embraced crowdfunding when raising USD 1.2 million on Kickstarter from close to 25,000 backers on Kickstarter in 2012. She continued her success via the Patreon platform grossing an additional USD 1.6 million by 2018 from some 15,000 patrons. The reasons behind this success are Palmer's investment in building a community of loyal fans, as well actively engaging with them both online via social media and offline in the physical world (Williams and Wilson 2016). In this respect, Palmer embraced a relationship with her fans by responding to their messages, empathizing with their stories, and talking about all of it in an authentic way on her own channels (Conditt 2019).

A different example from the music sector is the crowdfunding experience of *Public Enemy*, a highly successful million-selling hip-hop group. In 2009, the group launched their crowdfunding campaign on the platform Sellaband. The initial target of the campaign was USD 250,000, but upon reaching only 28% of the goal after two months, they had to lower the objective to USD 75,000 and relaunch the campaign in 2010. Eventually, by October 2010, they succeeded in raising USD 81,950 from 1453 contributors. In this case, the initial failure, despite the group's prominent position and established fanbase, can be explained by the lack of interaction between the group members and their followers, as well as the misalignment between their commercial interests and their followers' price sensitivity (Williams and Wilson 2016). The latter point can be exemplified by the fact that the group was charging USD 100 for two CDs or USD 250 for two CDs and a T-shirt, which may be perceived as either unfairly priced or outside financial capacities of many potential fans.

Other examples from the film industry present additional interesting insights. The following two successful crowdfunding efforts exhibited masterful mobilization of a fanbase, while resulting in different market outcomes at the end of the process.

On the one hand, there is *Iron Sky*, a Finnish-Austrian-Australian cult sci-fi movie franchise. The first movie *Iron Sky* premiered in 2012, with the follow-up *Iron Sky: The Coming Race* distributed to cinemas in 2019. Production and financing of both films relied on a combination of crowdsourcing, crowdfunding, and crowd investment. *Iron Sky* was partly co-created by a community of 2000 fans covering part of the costs by buying 'war bonds' at 50 euros. The fans also contributed to a variety of production tasks and duties including script and score writing, special effects, subtitling, and acting (Kirsner 2009), and even going to the length of setting up their own 'Wreck-a-movie' platform to facilitate participation (Tryon 2015). The funding of production of the sequel came via four different crowdfunding campaigns. Indiegogo hosted three of them, one for script development and promotion (EUR 166,652 from 3517 patrons), one for production (EUR 600,138 from 9408 patrons), and one for post-production (EUR 34,801 from 415 patrons) between July 2013 and November 2016. The fourth campaign on the equity platform Invesdor raised 268,500 euros from 421 investors, with a target set at 50,000–150,000 euros.

Here despite impressive engagement of followers in co-creative participation and fundraising, the case highlights the fragility of crowdfunding in the face of inability to live up to promises. This leads to an imbalance in the relations between promoter and patrons, as fans may feel that their efforts as prosumers and co-creators are taken for granted. While it is difficult to predict the reception of a cultural production financially ex-ante, *Iron Sky* was well off the mark. The second movie only grossed USD 400,000 out of a production cost of some USD 21 million (IMDB 2019), leading the production company to file for bankruptcy. And while that may have been a possibility all along, inadequate communication with supporters throughout the process might have further tarnished the professional reputation of the people behind the campaign.

On the other hand, the crowdfunding success of the *Veronica Mars* movie initiative was supported by over 90,000 fans of the Veronica Mars TV show, which aired from 2004 to 2007. The fans contributing over USD 5.7 million to make the film a reality, almost tripling the original target amount of USD 2 million (Booth 2015). Despite much controversy based on criticism of fan exploitation for funding rich studios, the people behind the campaign needed the money as a symbol of their fandom to convince Warner Bros. that the movie was viable, and hence get them engaged in its production (Chin et al. 2014). Eventually, the film grossed USD 3.5 million internationally and made an additional USD 5.3 million from Blu-ray and DVD sales in the US (The Numbers 2020).

Parallel to CCF practice, as illustrated above, CCF research has emerged to better understand its antecedents, characteristics, patterns, and success while accounting for related complexities and sub-sectoral particularities.

A Review of Research on Cultural Crowdfunding

Research into crowdfunding in the cultural sector has grown considerably in recent years. A bibliometric analysis conducted by Rykkja et al. (2019) of 84 studies on crowdfunding in a wide variety of cultural industries has identified five core themes. These themes address aspects of value creation, roles of the fan community, drivers of campaign success, journalism-specific insights, and reflections on crowdfunding experiences. In this section we present each theme while providing highlights from its key studies.

First, in terms of value creation, several studies have examined how CCF creates value beyond funding. Most studies in this context focus on aspects of value co-creation (Payne et al. 2008) through interaction between campaign creators and the public of prospective fans and backers. Here, a study by Quero et al. (2017) identifies the following seven forms of value co-creation when analysing cases of CCF in Spain: co-ideation, co-design, co-evaluation of ideas, co-financing, co-testing, co-launch, and co-consumption. Nucciarelli et al. (2017) provide similar insights claiming that co-creative interactions between gamers and developers via crowdfunding platforms may offer new value chain configurations involving the user community. More specifically, in the music industry, evidence suggests that crowdfunding is affecting the major labels in terms of adaptation of their marketing model to become more creative, resilient, and artist-friendly while tapping into opportunities of user-centred innovation (Gamble et al. 2017). In addition, when consumption is intertwined with social missions and ideology, crowdfunding may serve as a tool to accomplish social and political ends such as creating communities of support, attracting media attention, and building a reputation for an independent voice, as demonstrated in the analysis of the use of crowdfunding for production of documentary films in Turkey (Koçer 2015).

Second, another strand of studies focuses on the types and roles of fan communities in supporting CCF. Here, some research identifies the criticality of mobilization of existing fan communities for funding cultural productions of established artists (Booth 2015), as well as the importance of investing in building up fan communities as part of the crowdfunding process for supporting new artists (Galuszka and Brzozowska 2016). Members in such fan communities may either take a patron's stance allowing artists to create 'authentic' rather than 'commercially driven' artistic production (Swords 2017) or a prosumer-investor stance influencing the design and production processes (José Planells 2015). In both cases, the support of both affirmational (non-creatively engaged) and transformational (co-creatively engaged) fans has symbolic value that goes beyond their actual financial contributions, as it boosts the artistic credibility of a creator, while enhancing her perceived economic power and value vis-à-vis industry decision-makers and funders (Navar-Gill 2018).

The third research stream examines the drivers of successful CCF campaigning in particular and can be seen as a sector-specific subset of a wider research stream into crowdfunding success in general (e.g. Shneor and Vik 2020). Here, since the majority of CCF has employed the reward crowdfunding model (De Voldere and Zeqo 2017), related research has mostly identified success indicators that are relevant for reward crowdfunding campaigns. Some of the most prevalent findings across studies seem to suggest that success of CCF campaigns is positively associated with (1) project quality signals captured by campaign text length, as well as media richness in terms of the number of images, videos, and graphics included in the campaign (e.g. Bi et al. 2017; Cha 2017); (2) the mobilization and extension of social capital as evident through different levels of social media interaction and spread of e-word-of-mouth in terms of 'likes', comments, and shares (e.g. Bao and Huang 2017; Bi et al. 2017); and (3) the campaigners' human capital in terms of prior professional experience (e.g. Cha 2017; Steigenberger 2017) and prior crowdfunding experience (e.g. Boeuf et al. 2014).

The fourth theme identified includes a series of articles addressing unique aspects of journalism crowdfunding. Journalism may represent a unique context for crowdfunding for several reasons. First, journalism uses donation rather than reward crowdfunding as its main model of choice, in line with the concept of creating public goods rather than products and services for individual consumption. Second, the reliance on crowdfunding creates unique ethical challenges where journalists need to balance their journalistic work between objectivism and agenda advocacy (Hunter 2015) and setting boundaries to co-creation (Porlezza and Splendore 2016). Such problems are potentially conflated by the fact that donors seem to be more motivated by fun and family relations than by ideals of freedom, altruism, and community engagement (Jian and Shin 2015), and therefore tend to support stories focusing on practical guidance for daily living rather than stories on public affairs such as those covering cultural diversity or government and politics (Jian and Usher 2014; Ladson and Lee 2017).

Finally, the fifth group is a collection of case studies about crowdfunding experiences with respect to two sectoral contexts—film producers and GLAM (Galleries, Libraries, Archives, and Museums) organizations. Common across them is the reflection on failure in addition to success, the importance of tapping the right niche crowds, and the development of communities around projects with a sense of belonging. The studies examining film production reflect on experiences of limited success or outright failure, and criticize the extent to which crowdfunding democratizes cultural productions, as it tends to follow capitalistic considerations of consumer value and demand rather than sociocultural considerations (e.g. Papadimitriou 2017; Sheppard 2017). The studies examining GLAM organizations also reflect on experiences of limited success and failure; however, they conclude with pragmatic advice on strong outreach efforts and constant communication with the community (e.g. Bushong et al. 2018; Riley-Huff et al. 2016).

Beyond these five main thematic clusters, one may identify a few smaller groups of studies around some additional themes of interest. For example, two studies examine to what extent crowd evaluations of campaigns differ from those of experts in the context of the performing arts (Mollick and Nanda 2015) and in the context of the music recording industry (Bernard and Gazel 2018). Both studies find that, overall, the crowd and experts tend to agree on project quality; however, experts may be more supportive of innovative projects, while the crowd tends to support less risky and 'mainstream' campaigns.

Another group of studies investigates the implications of CCF at times of cuts and changes in public funding of the arts. The authors with critical approach perceive crowdfunding either as a solution in which crowd volunteerism makes up for the reduction in traditional funding (Perry and Beale 2015) or as a form of political argumentation for defunding public intervention (Brabham 2016). Others, such as Binimelis (2016), highlight that government agencies along with private finance intermediaries (e.g. banks and companies) are still struggling to adapt their strategies to these market developments and shifts.

Opportunities for Future Research on Cultural Crowdfunding

In addition to the themes discussed above, one can also identify potential new themes that future research may follow. While multiple opportunities exist, in the current section we outline three specific areas for further investigation.

First, few studies have investigated barriers and drivers for artists' use and adoption of crowdfunding. The earlier research in this area is limited and has mostly focused on the barriers. Thorley (2012) suggest that crowdfunding force artists to perform unfamiliar downstream activities such as sales and marketing, and hence may not benefit creators who could make important cultural contributions but have neither the inclination to expose themselves nor an already existing community of admirers (Davidson and Poor 2015). More research is necessary for understanding drivers of crowdfunding adoption. Here, creation of a typology of CCF fundraisers based on their fit with CCF practice requirements may be helpful. Moreover, further studies are invited to address the strategies for mitigating crowdfunding adoption barriers for each type of fundraiser, as well as to evaluate the extent to which current and future platform services cater to their needs.

An additional theme for future research may relate to artists' choice of platforms. The limited available research has focused on the choice between international and local platforms. For example, De Voldere and Zeqo (2017) show that although Europe was home to some 600 crowdfunding platforms, almost half of European CCF campaigns (47%) between 2013 and 2017 were hosted on global US-based platform. In an attempt to explain such choice, a recent study by Rykkja et al. (2020) analysing CCF campaigns from the Nordic countries has found that cultural productions with a higher degree of production complexity and those characterized as incorporating composite motives are more likely to use an international platform, while projects with high degree of cultural affinity opt for using local platforms. Additionally, they show that the higher the funding goal, the more fundraisers are likely to opt for using international platforms rather than local ones. Such work may be replicated in different contexts, as well as extended to the choice among different types of platforms such as generalist (e.g. Kickstarter, Indiegogo) versus sector-specific platforms (e.g. ArtFund, DigVentures, Unbound).

Furthermore, since ample evidence exists that countries differ in terms of geographical spread of cultural activity, cultural sector specializations, consumption patterns, and cultural policies (e.g. Bekhuis et al. 2012; Boix et al. 2014; van Hek and Kraaykamp 2013), as well as in terms of crowdfunding volumes, model composition, and platform availability (Ziegler et al. 2020), it is surprising that cross-country comparisons of CCF remain mostly absent. Future studies are encouraged to examine how national level characteristics such as availability of public funding, availability of public-private match-funding schemes, nationalistic tendencies, agglomeration of cultural sectors, regulatory environment, freedom indicators, as well as cultural dimensions may all impact CCF in different environments. Such efforts may help identify macro-level indicators that support or inhibit the development of CFF in different country contexts, while shifting the focus away from micro-level analyses to macro-level ones.

Conclusions

Digitalization has had a pronounced impact on the cultural industries, from reconfigurations of traditional value chains to the opening of new channels for financing and co-production of cultural projects. Unlike in many other industries, the cultural industries have a long history of project financing via patronage and public fundraising initiatives (Swords 2017). Hence, it is not surprising that cultural production has stood at the forefront of adopting crowdfunding as a modern digital format for financing its projects. Nevertheless, CCF seems to rely heavily on non-investment models of crowdfunding (De Voldere and Zeqo 2017; Rykkja et al. 2020) and has not yet ventured into investment finance. Hence, the use of this channel is expected to further evolve and expand. While CCF represents an emerging source of funding, it does not yet substitute traditional funding sources in most cases (Laycock 2016; Navar-Gill 2018; Papadimitriou 2017).

The study of crowdfunding in the specific context of the cultural industries is of interest, as it challenges project creators to strike a balance between the economic and socio-cultural values, as well as between independent expression and co-creation with others. This chapter contributes to the field by identifying key themes in the earlier research related to value creation, fan communities, campaign success drivers, experiences and failures, as well as journalism-specific insights. Besides, we highlight opportunities for future research such as further investigations of drivers and barriers of crowdfunding adoption by artists, platform choices, and macro-level comparative analyses of market conditions that are more or less conducive to successful CCF development and growth.

Furthermore, this chapter suggests some implications for practitioners. First, insights emerging from the research on success and failure of CCF campaigns may inform future fundraisers in their efforts in campaign development, help platforms design their services for campaigners, as well as provide educational content to consultants and trainers advising prospective fundraisers. Here, some of the most prevalent factors in this regard is the importance of social capital build up and mobilization in the form of fan and follower communities offering members opportunities for enhancing their sense of belonging and co-creation. Also, the use of quality materials in campaign information as well as signalling fund-raiser credibility and experience, are of critical importance for enhancing success.

Second, beyond a general need for more crowdfunding-oriented education, there is a specific need for programmes tailored for artists and individuals working in the cultural industries. Such programmes should cover fundamental crowdfunding themes (e.g. crowdfunding models, campaign development, platform choice) in addition to specialized units for CCF. Here, units should cover themes that enhance the sense of self-efficacy and skills in marketing and sales. In addition, programmes should incorporate reflective discussion on dilemmas involving the balance between commercial and non-commercial value creation, independent creation versus co-creation with others, as well as authenticity versus popular demand.

Acknowledgements The work for this publication was supported by the Norwegian Art Council grant number 17/2254, under its 'Digital kultur, estetiske praksiser' programme.

References

Agrawal, A., Catalini, C., & Goldfarb, A. (2014). Some Simple Economics of Crowdfunding. *NBER Innovation Policy & the Economy (University of Chicago Press), 14*(1), 63–97.

Bannerman, S. (2012). Crowdfunding Culture. *Wi: Journal of Mobile Culture, 6*(4), 1–23.

Bao, Z., & Huang, T. (2017). External Supports in Reward-based Crowdfunding Campaigns: A Comparative Study Focused on Cultural and Creative Projects. *Online Information Review, 41*(5), 626–642.

Bekhuis, H., Meuleman, R., & Lubbers, M. (2012). Globalization and Support for National Cultural Protectionism from a Cross-national Perspective. *European Sociological Review, 29*(5), 1040–1052.

Bernard, A., & Gazel, M. (2018). La place de la foule dans le financementde projets musicaux: les financeurs participatifs et l'industrie financent-ils les mêmes projets ? In F. Moreau & Y. Nicolas (Eds.), *Financement participatif: une voie d'avenir pour la culture ?* Paris: Ministère de la Culture.

Bi, S., Liu, Z., & Usman, K. (2017). The Influence of Online Information on Investing Decisions of Reward-based Crowdfunding. *Journal of Business Research, 71*, 10–18.

Binimelis, M. A. (2016). The Crowdfunding Discourses: Balance and Tensions around Audiovisual Democratisation. *Ic-Revista Cientifica De Informacion Y Comunicacion, 13*, 10–18.

Boeuf, B., Darveau, J., & Legoux, R. (2014). Financing Creativity: Crowdfunding as a New Approach for Theatre Projects. *International Journal of Arts Management, 16*(3), 33–48.

Boix, R., Capone, F., De Propris, L., et al. (2014). Comparing Creative Industries in Europe. *European Urban and Regional Studies, 23*(4), 935–940.

Booth, P. (2015). Crowdfunding: A Spimatic Application of Digital Fandom. *New Media & Society, 17*(2), 149–166.

Bourdieu, P. (1984). *Distinction: A Social Critique of the Judgement of Taste*. Cambridge: MA, Harvard University Press.

Brabham, D. C. (2016). How Crowdfunding Discourse Threatens Public Arts. *New Media & Society, 19*(7), 983–999.

Bushong, S., Cleveland, S., & Cox, C. (2018). Crowdfunding for Academic Libraries: Indiana Jones Meets Polka. *The Journal of Academic Librarianship, 44*(2), 313–318.

Cha, J. (2017). Crowdfunding for Video Games: Factors that Influence the Success of and Capital Pledged for Campaigns. *International Journal on Media Management, 19*(3), 240–259.

Chin, B., Jones, B., McNutt, M., et al. (2014). Veronica Mars Kickstarter and Crowd Funding. Retrieved February 8, 2020, from https://doi.org/10.3983/twc.2014.0519.

Conditt, J. (2019). The Crowdfunded Cult of Amanda Palmer. Retrieved February 8, 2020, from https://www.engadget.com/2019/12/13/amanda-palmer-patreon-kickstarter-social-media/.

Davidson, R., & Poor, N. (2015). The Barriers Facing Artists' Use of Crowdfunding Platforms: Personality, Emotional Labor, and Going to the Well One Too Many Times. *New Media & Society, 17*(2), 289–307.

De Voldere, I., & Zeqo, K. (2017). *Crowdfunding: Reshaping the Crowd's Engagement in Culture*. Brussels: European Commission.

Galuszka, P., & Brzozowska, B. (2016). Early Career Artists and the Exchange of Gifts on a Crowdfunding Platform AU—Galuszka, Patryk. *Continuum, 30*(6), 744–753.

Gamble, J. R., Brennan, M., & McAdam, R. (2017). A Rewarding Experience? Exploring How Crowdfunding is Affecting Music Industry Business Models. *Journal of Business Research, 70*, 25–36.

Hesmondhalgh, D. (2013). *The Cultural Industries*. London: Sage.

Hirsch, P. M. (1972). Processing Fads and Fashions: An Organization-set Analysis of Cultural Industry Systems. *American Journal of Sociology, 77*(4), 639–659.

Hunter, A. (2015). Crowdfunding Independent and Freelance Journalism: Negotiating Journalistic Norms of Autonomy and Objectivity. *New Media & Society, 17*(2), 272–288.

IMDB. (2019). *Iron Sky: The Coming Race (2019)* [Online]. Retrieved February 8, 2020, from https://www.imdb.com/title/tt3038708/.

Jian, L., & Shin, J. (2015). Motivations Behind Donors' Contributions to Crowdfunded Journalism. *Mass Communication and Society, 18*(2), 165–185.

Jian, L., & Usher, N. (2014). Crowd-Funded Journalism. *Journal of Computer-Mediated Communication, 19*(2), 155–170.

José Planells, A. (2015). Video Games and the Crowdfunding Ideology: From the Gamer-buyer to the Prosumer-Investor. *Journal of Consumer Culture, 17*(3), 620–638.

Kappel, T. (2009). Ex ante Crowdfunding and the Recording Industry: A Model for the US 29 Loy. *Loyola of Los Angeles Entertainment Law Review, 29*(3), 375–385.

Kirsner, S. (2009). *Fans, Friends and Followers: Building an Audience and a Creative Career in the Digital Age*. CreateSpace Independent Publishing Platform.

Koçer, S. (2015). Social Business in Online Financing: Crowdfunding Narratives of Independent Documentary Producers in Turkey. *New Media & Society, 17*(2), 231–248.

Ladson, N., & Lee, A. M. (2017). Persuading to Pay: Exploring the What and Why in Crowdfunded Journalism. *International Journal on Media Management, 19*(2), 144–163.

Lampel, J., Shamsie, J., & Lant, T. K. (2006). *The Business of Culture: Strategic Perspectives on Entertainment and Media*. Mahwah, NJ: Lawrence Erlbaum Associates.

Lawrence, T. B., & Phillips, N. (2002). Understanding Cultural Industries. *Journal of Management Inquiry, 11*(4), 430–441.

Laycock, R. A. (2016). The Audience's Worth: Crowdfunding as a Source of Film Finance. *Metro Magazine: Media & Education Magazine, 188*, 112–117.

Mollick, E. & Nanda, R. (2015). Wisdom or Madness? Comparing Crowds with Expert Evaluation in Funding the Arts, August 26. Retrieved from http://papers.ssrn.com/sol3/papers.cfm?abstract_id=2443114.

Moritz, A., & Block, J. H. (2016). Crowdfunding: A Literature Review and Research Directions. In D. Bruntje & O. Gajda (Eds.), *Crowdfunding in Europe: State of the Art in Theory and Practice*. London: Springer.

Navar-Gill, A. (2018). Fandom as Symbolic Patronage: Expanding Understanding of Fan Relationships with Industry through the Veronica Mars Kickstarter Campaign. *Popular Communication, 16*(3), 211–224.

Nordgård, D. (2018). *The Music Business and Digital Impacts: Innovations and Disruptions in the Music Industries*. Switzerland, Springer: Cham.

Nucciarelli, A., Li, F., Fernandes, K. J., et al. (2017). From Value Chains to Technological Platforms: The Effects of Crowdfunding in the Digital Game Industry. *Journal of Business Research, 78*, 341–352.

Papadimitriou, L. (2017). Transitions in the Periphery: Funding Film Production in Greece Since the Financial Crisis. *International Journal on Media Management, 19*(2), 164–181.

Payne, A. F., Storbacka, K., & Frow, P. (2008). Managing the Co-creation of Value. *Journal of the Academy of Marketing Science, 36*(1), 83–96.

Peltoniemi, M. (2015). Cultural Industries: Product–Market Characteristics, Management Challenges and Industry Dynamics. *International Journal of Management Reviews, 17*(1), 41–68.

Perry, S., & Beale, N. (2015). The Social Web and Archaeology's Restructuring: Impact, Exploitation, Disciplinary Change. *Open Archaeology, 1*(1), 153–165.

Porlezza, C., & Splendore, S. (2016). Accountability and Transparency of Entrepreneurial Journalism. *Journalism Practice, 10*(2), 196–216.

Power, D. (2002). "Cultural Industries" in Sweden: An Assessment of their Place in the Swedish Economy. *Economic Geography, 78*(2), 103–127.

Quero, M. J., Ventura, R., & Kelleher, C. (2017). Value-in-Context in Crowdfunding Ecosystems: How Context Frames Value Co-creation. *Service Business, 11*(2), 405–425.

Riley-Huff, D. A., Herrera, K., Ivey, S., et al. (2016). Crowdfunding in Libraries, Archives and Museums. *The Bottom Line, 29*(2), 67–85.

Rykkja, A., Munim, Z. H., & Bonet, L. (2020). Varieties of Cultural Crowdfunding: The Relationship between Cultural Production Types and Platform. *Baltic Journal of Management, 15*(2), from https://doi.org/10.1108/BJM-03-2019-0091

Rykkja, A., Munim, Z. H., Maehle, N., et al. (2019). Cultural Crowdfunding—What Do We Know? In *17th Interdisciplinary European Conference on Entrepreneurship Research (IECER)*, Utrecht, Netherlands.

Sheppard, S. N. (2017). I Love Cinema: Black Film and Speculative Practice in the Era of Online Crowdfunding. *Film Quarterly, 71*(2), 25–31.

Shneor, R., & Vik, A. A. (2020). Crowdfunding Success: A Systematic Literature Review 2010–2017. *Baltic Journal of Management, 15*(2), 149–182.

Steigenberger, N. (2017). Why Supporters Contribute to Reward-based Crowdfunding. *International Journal of Entrepreneurial Behavior & Research, 23*(2), 336–353.

Swords, J. (2017). Crowd-Patronage—Intermediaries, Geographies and Relationships in Patronage Networks. *Poetics, 64*, 63–73.

The Numbers. (2020). *Veronica Mars (2014)* [Online]. Nash Information Services, LLC. Retrieved February 8, 2020, from https://www.the-numbers.com/movie/Veronica-Mars#tab=video-sales.

Thorley, M. (2012). An Audience in the Studio–The Effect of the Artistshare Fan-Funding Platform on Creation, Performance, Recording and Production. Journal on the Art of Record Production, 7, 1–29.

Throsby, D. (2001). *Economics and Culture*. Cambridge: Cambridge University Press.

Throsby, D. (2008). The Concentric Circles Model of the Cultural Industries. *Cultural Trends, 17*(3), 147–164.

Tryon, C. (2015). Iron Sky's War Bonds: Cult SF Cinema and Crowdsourcing. In J. P. Telotte & G. Duchovnay (Eds.), *Science Fiction Double Feature: The Science Fiction Film as Cult Text*. Liverpool: Liverpool University Press.

Tschmuck, P. (2016). From Record Selling to Cultural Entrepreneurship: The Music Economy in the Digital Paradigm Shift. In P. Wikström & R. DeFillippi (Eds.), *Business Innovation and Disruption in the Music Industry*. Cheltenham, UK: Edward Elgar.

van Hek, M., & Kraaykamp, G. (2013). Cultural Consumption Across Countries: A Multi-level Analysis of Social Inequality in Highbrow Culture in Europe. *Poetics, 41*(4), 323–341.

Venkatesh, A., & Meamber, L. A. (2006). Arts and Aesthetics: Marketing and Cultural Production. *Marketing Theory, 6*(1), 11–39.

Williams, J. A., & Wilson, R. (2016). Music and Crowdfunded Websites: Digital Patronage and Artist-fan Interactivity. In S. Whiteley & S. Rambarran (Eds.), *The Oxford Handbook of Music and Virtuality*. Oxford: Oxford University Press.

Ziegler, T., Shneor, R., Wenzlaff, K., et al. (2020). *The Global Alternative Finance Benchmarking Report*. Cambridge, UK: Cambridge Centre for Alternative Finance.

19

Civic Crowdfunding: Four Perspectives on the Definition of Civic Crowdfunding

Karsten Wenzlaff

Introduction

Civic crowdfunding is a subset of crowdfunding practices which is increasingly covered both in academic literature and practitioners' reports. The term 'civic crowdfunding' (civCF) describes the financing of projects dedicated to a 'civic' purpose, initiated by 'civic' initiatives, supported by individuals and organizations with 'civic' intentions, and (often) intermediated on online platforms which dedicate themselves to 'civic' purposes and stakeholders. The term 'civic' itself can refer to the actions of and within cities or municipalities, but also to the actions of citizens towards a common goal (Wenzlaff 2020).

CivCF projects cover a wide range of topics. Financing public bridges and streets, public beaches, gardens, playgrounds, theatres, museums, festivals and events, (non-profit) media, science, health institutions,

K. Wenzlaff (✉)
Faculty of Business, Economics, and Social Sciences, University of Hamburg, Chair Digital Markets, Hamburg, Germany
e-mail: karsten.wenzlaff@uni-hamburg.de

R. Shneor et al. (eds.), *Advances in Crowdfunding*,
https://doi.org/10.1007/978-3-030-46309-0_19

political campaigns, and monuments have been placed on platforms dedicating themselves to civCF or within-'Community' categories on platforms dedicated to broader purposes.

The civCF literature is limited but has been growing in recent years. The aim of this chapter is to shed light on the state of civCF research and to expand the definition of civCF as a contribution to future research. CivCF practices are explained through the perspective of the project, the initiators, the supporters, and the platform. The need to analyse civCF through this fourfold-perspective stems from an inadequate definition based on any one of the perspectives. The literature, as is being discussed in the "Definition and Perspectives of Civic Crowdfunding" section, tends to focus only on the project, only on the supporter, only on the project owner, or only on the platform. The contribution of this chapter is to bring these four perspectives together and show how they complement each other.

The method used in this chapter is a narrative literature review (Onwuegbuzie and Frels 2016), with the aim to reflect upon literature which has advanced the debate on civic crowdfunding, supported by twenty short examples of civic CF projects or platforms. For this purpose, fifty-four academic publications (journal articles, book chapters, working papers) and six non-academic practitioners' guidebooks were analysed, which were identified through searching for 'Civic Crowdfunding' on Google Scholar and Web of Science.

The structure of the chapter is as follows: the "Development of Civic Crowdfunding" section discusses the development of civCF. The "Definition and Perspectives of Civic Crowdfunding" section compares definitions of civCF and develops four perspectives, which are then elaborated in the "Perspective 1: Project", "Perspective 2: Supporter", "Perspective 3: Owner", and "Perspective 4: Platform" sections. These are followed by a research agenda and practical implications in the "Conclusion" section.

Development of Civic Crowdfunding

Civic crowdfunding is an old phenomenon. In the late nineteenth century, cultural institutions in the expanding cities were crowdfunded in the sense that cooperatives financed the building of theatres, parks, and swimming facilities.

The financing of the often-quoted Pedestal of the Statue of Liberty at the end of the nineteenth century in New York can be classified as a civCF campaign since it financed a public memorial. Even earlier examples of civCF are the publication of the newspaper 'Wandsbecker Mercurius' in 1745 which was financed through a pre-purchase subscription model.

With the advent of the internet, civCF campaigns were increasingly hosted on crowdfunding platforms (CFPs). An overview of civCF platforms is given in Table 19.1. The vast majority of civCF campaigns are hosted on donation-based CFPs, for instance, the purchasing of the Tasman Beach by the public in New Zealand was hosted on the donation-based platform GiveALittle (Boyle 2016; Doan and Toledano 2018). Civic crowdfunding campaigns can also be found on reward-based crowdfunding CFPs, with both tangible and non-tangible rewards, such as the campaign to bail out the Greek people during the debt crisis (Indiegogo 2015).

Table 19.1 Overview and typology of civic crowdfunding platforms (selection)

	Donation- and reward-based CFPs	Equity- and lending-based CFPs
All-purpose CFPs with civCF project category	International CFPs: GoFundMe, Kickstarter, Indiegogo Local CFPs: Startnext, Wemakeit, Kisskissbankbank, Produzioni Dal Basso	
Special-purpose CFP dedicated to civCF	International CFPs: Spacehive Local CFPs: Ioby, Voorjebuurt, Place2Help	International CFPs: Ethex, Kiva Local CFPs: CommunityShares.org.uk, LeihDeinerUmweltGeld

Campaigns are also hosted on few equity-based CFPs and lending-based CFPs (Assenmacher 2017; Catapult 2018; Wenzlaff et al. 2015; Old et al. 2019). The civic equity-based crowdfunding platform “Leih-Deiner-Stadt-Geld” (Lend money to your city) is facilitating equity investments in city property, such as an investment into firearms equipment at the city of Oestrich-Winkel (LeihDeinerStadtGeld GmbH 2012).

Civic crowdfunding campaigns can be found on special-purpose CFPs, with Spacehive being the most prominent international example. Italy, France, the Netherlands, the UK, Germany, and many other countries have seen platforms dedicated to civic crowdfunding, with a majority of platforms offering donations and pre-sales of rewards. Almost all major international reward-based platforms (like Kickstarter, Indiegogo, GoFundme) and many local reward-based platforms have introduced project categories focussing on civil purposes (Davies 2014). The German platform ‘startnext’, in its category called ‘Community’, featured projects such as the funding of a fountain in a Berlin Park or the Pacific Garbage Screening Project (Förderkreis des FEZ-Berlin e.V. 2018; PGS-Team 2018). The Italian platform Produzioni Dal Basso is an all-purpose CFP which features the category of ‘Social and Community’, making up 1145 projects (of 5771 projects in total) and EUR 3.6m (of 11.4m in total) and thus constituting the biggest category on the platform.

It is interesting to reflect on the interaction between all-purpose CFPs and special-purpose CFPs. The history of platform-based crowdfunding cannot be summarized in this chapter, but with regard to civCF, it should be noted that the first reward-based platforms were special-purpose CFPs dedicated to music and film (Sellaband, Artistshare) which gave rise to all-purpose platforms (Kickstarter, Indiegogo). The success of platforms like Kickstarter and Indiegogo influenced the founding of special-purpose civCF platforms, which in turn motivated the large all-purpose platforms to introduce civCF categories. In equity-based and lending-based crowdfunding, the special-purpose CFPs developed alongside special-purpose CFPs for start-ups, energy projects, or real estate projects. However, international equity-based crowdfunding platforms like OurCrowd do not have a dedicated category to civCF campaigns.

Analysing the interaction between civCF platforms and civCF categories on all-purpose CFPs merits further research since it would provide a narrative for the self-framing of civCF campaigns, which in turn informs their choice of a platform (Lee et al. 2019). There is anecdotal evidence that all-purpose CFPs dedicated to creative industries introduced civCF campaigns categories because of repeated requests to host civCF campaigns, sometimes by project initiators which used the CFP for projects such as funding games, movies, and music albums, and then aiming to use their existing community on the platform to initiate projects with a civic purpose. For instance, the owners of the sustainable condom factory Einhorn used the crowdfunding platform 'startnext' in Germany for funding their business, then proceeded to use the same platform for financing a 'democracy festival' to combat climate change (Einhörnchen 2015; Olympia 2020).

Civic crowdfunding campaigns are not restricted to platforms, as is being discussed in the "Perspective 4: Platform" section. Some of the significant campaigns which received widespread attention in the literature, such as the Luchtsingel Bridge in Rotterdam (Youngwoo 2019) or the funding of statutes by the Louvre Museum (Izzo 2017), were not hosted on platforms, but on newly created websites for the duration of hosting the campaign.

Definition and Perspectives of Civic Crowdfunding

The definition of civCF is not consistent across the literature. This paper identifies four perspectives which are taken as per the different units of analysis: (1) the project, (2) the supporters, (3) the project owners, and (4) the platform (CFP) which hosts the campaign.

One of the first definitions of civCF was very narrow. Barollo and Castrataro posited that civCF takes place outside of public budgets: civCF is the "collective funding of public works and projects—outside the budget of the interested entity or administration—collected by citizens, organisations and private companies sometimes in match funding with the administrations themselves" (Barollo and Castrataro 2013; Oliva 2018; Colasanti et al. 2018). The dichotomy between campaigns which are contributing towards a public budget and campaigns that function outside of public budgets is seldom explicitly discussed in the literature, but present in the different perspectives discussed below. Since that early definition, the overwhelming majority of academic researchers have argued that civCF is characterized by being neither inside nor outside the public budgets, but interacts positively and negatively with public budgets, for instance, both by supplementing public budgets and by highlighting underfunded public services.

Another very narrow definition of civCF suggests it is "the collaborative funding of public infrastructure" (Wenzlaff et al. 2015; Wenzlaff 2017). This definition restricts civCF to immobile, permanent, and public artefacts and institutions. It excludes campaigns for public events, festivals, or civic activism as not being part of civCF in the narrow sense. In this definition, collaboration distinguishes civic crowdfunding from other forms of public fundraising for infrastructure (such as municipals bonds, social impact bonds), supporters can observe each other's actions on the crowdfunding platform and thus coordinate their behaviour indirectly (Nielsen 2018).

This chapter proposes to move beyond these two dichotomies by identifying similarities of four perspectives in civCF.

The project perspective is taken when defining civCF "as the practice applied to civic projects" (Doan and Toledano 2018). Civic projects are projects related to the duties or activities of people in their town, city, or local area. The supporter and project perspective are combined when defining civCF as "the process of raising funds from a large pool of interested agents […] when applied for the provision of public projects" (Damle et al. 2019).

The perspective of the supporters is found in a definition of civCF which "borrows principles from both private crowdfunding and grassroots community organisation by enabling citizens to develop community projects that are funded by donations through an online platform" (Brent 2017).

The perspective of the project owner is taken when civic crowdfunding is defined as "projects that benefit from government assets, funds and sponsorship for the acquisition and development of future public assets" (Hummel 2016), therefore necessitating the involvement of government in the delivering or implementation of the crowdfunding campaign goal.

The perspective of the platform is used when a civic crowdfunding platform is defined as "a type of platform dedicated to fundraising for issues of public concern" (Desmoulins and Charbit 2017), connecting it to both the government involvement and community projects.

In the following sections, the chapter proceeds to discuss each of the four perspectives of civCF in detail. The project perspective is discussed through its outcome, geographic or demographic scope. The supporter perspective is discussed through the motivation and actions of supporters. The project owner perspective relates to the legal status of the project owner and the associated benefits. The platform perspective discusses the geographic area, type of crowdfunding, functionalities, and constraints within the crowdfunding platform.

Perspective 1: Project

Civic crowdfunding can be seen through the lens of the crowdfunding campaign or the project which is being funded. Academic research uses parks, playgrounds, and gardens as unambiguous examples of civCF (Porter and Veenswijk 2018). Would it suffice to simply allow the projects to decide whether they are part of civCF?

No, because on many all-purpose CFPs the distinction between civCF projects and other, more entrepreneurial projects, is not clear-cut. Three examples are given below.

Indiegogo, one of the largest reward-based CFPs globally, allows projects to be placed in the category "Community Projects—For good neighbors everywhere" (Indiegogo 2019b).

The three most-funded projects in this category are indicative of the diverse field of campaigns labelled with civic crowdfunding. 'Stone Groundbreaking Collaborations' received USD 2.5m to create a new line of craft beer pubs. Its placement in the 'Local Businesses'-subcategory indicates it could also be classified as entrepreneurial reward-based crowdfunding campaign. The second-highest community project is the 'Greek Bailout Fund', which raised EUR 1.9m for supporting the Greek population during the debt crisis in 2015. The all-or-nothing goal set the campaign at EUR 1.6b, thus making the campaign unsuccessful despite support from 108.631 people. The third-highest campaign 'Restore the Shore' raised USD 1m for the restoration of a New Jersey beach. The campaign goal was only reached by 84%; however, since Indiegogo also allows keep-it-all (flexible funding) campaigns, the funds were distributed to the cause (Indiegogo 2012, 2015, 2016).

These three examples are all part of the civCF category on Indiegogo but would not necessarily fall into a project-based definition of civCF.

CivCF campaigns should provide a service to a community, either replacing and enhancing existing service to a community (Davies 2014; Stiver et al. 2015) or initiate a new service to citizens (Miglietta and Parisi 2017).

By improving public services, a civCF project provides a participatory culture and enables citizens to interact with government officials, thus impacting government policies (Bonini and Pais 2017). CivCF can provide better participation in urban planning (Brent 2017; Miglietta and Parisi 2017; Shareable 2018; Brandmeyer 2015; Kukla 2014; van Veelen 2015; Sedlitzky and Franz 2019) by using resources more efficiently due to the participatory planning process, which benefits both the supporters as well as the project owners, if project owners are also public entities. As it is being discussed in the "Perspective 2: Supporter" and "Perspective 3: Owner" sections, a distinguishing element of civCF projects is that the project goals are both in the interest of supporters and project owners.

The provision of a public good is essential to a civic crowdfunding campaign, especially in economic analysis (Davies 2014; Hummel 2016; Brent 2017). A public good (as can be seen in Table 19.2) is characterized

Table 19.2 Typology of goods

	Excludable	Non-Excludable
Rivalrous	Private good	Club good
Non-rivalrous	Commons	Public good

by the fact that users cannot be excluded. Its usage is non-rivalrous—the usage of one user does not reduce the utility for another of that good for another user (Samuelson 1954).

Such a narrow definition would effectively eject many campaigns from the definition of civCF. Davies (2014) notes that goods provided by civCF campaigns can be both semi-rivalrous and semi-excludable. For instance, a public bike service is semi-rivalrous because each bike hired by a user is not available for any other user at that particular time, but the general service is available at other times. A civCF campaign for a health infrastructure is semi-excludable since it would not preclude the operator from charging for his services, but at the same time would provide access to citizens to these services (Zhang et al. 2019).

Even excludable-non-rivalrous goods (termed "club good") can be considered as being inside definition of civCF (Desmoulins and Charbit 2017). Crowdfunding a public museum (without entry) would create a public good (Simeoni and De Crescenzo 2018), crowdfunding a private museum would create a club good. The private museum can set exclusion mechanisms (entry prices, access), the art displayed in the museum is characterized by non-rivalrous usage (until overcrowded museums eventually decrease the utility for each user) (Izzo 2017; Foà 2019). The financing of club goods through civCF has the disadvantage of possibly increasing inequality within a community, since it generates a payment obligation for civic participation, which not all members of the community might be able to afford (Davies 2015; Hummel 2016).

Civic crowdfunding campaigns for goods which are rivalrous but non-excludable (termed "commons") can also be within the definition of civCF. An example of a commons good is an outdoor tipi which was financed on Spacehive (Spacehive 2017; Gooch et al. 2020)—there are no access restrictions, but at the same time the tipi can only be used by a limited number of people. The common resource needs to be managed by a central authority, otherwise exploitation of the resource is possible ('free-rider problem'). Civic crowdfunding campaigns can support creating the management structure of commons (Desmoulins and Charbit 2017; Shareable 2018; Catapult 2018).

CivCF is also discussed in the context of so-called digital commons (Ridgway 2015; Bonini and Pais 2017; Carvajal et al. 2012; Rathemacher

2015), funding access to public non-profit media or public digital archives. However, the term 'commons' is used somewhat misleading in this context, because digital resources are essentially non-rivalrous, as their usage does not reduce the utility for other users. 'Digital commons' might be labelled more precisely 'digital public goods'. Crowdfunding journalism, which is categorized under 'digital commons' projects, often results in semi-excludable goods or club goods. For instance, the German journalism project Krautreporter used civCF to establish an online-community of readers, which only had access through pre-payment—a 'digital club good' (Vogt and Mitchell 2016; Wenzlaff et al. 2012; Wenzlaff et al. 2013).

The provision of a public good can also be a secondary goal of the crowdfunding campaign (Davies 2014). A crowdfunding campaign for a private good might achieve a general goal in society, such as improving the benefits from using a public good (Hummel 2016). Coming back to examples of media crowdfunding projects such as Krautreporter, DeCorrespondent, or Die Republik, which created a 'digital club good', it could be argued that these projects also contributed to a 'pure' public good: freedom of media.

Using public goods as secondary goals of civCF campaigns would allow to group also projects found on platforms which are dedicated to private goods only. This "Friendraising" or "Friendfunding" (Mattauch 2015) refers to platforms like GoFundMe, which allow crowdfunding campaigns for personal goals, such as health expenses or vacations. These campaigns would not be civCF. At the same time, the platform GoFundMe, which is dedicated to friendraising, is increasingly used for civCF campaigns. A recent example is a campaign to raise funds for the Border Wall of US-President Trump. This campaign by a private individual gathered more than USD 23m, and tries to establish a public good (a border wall), where the usage is non-excludable (everybody is affected by the border wall) and non-rivalrous (the use of the border wall does not reduce the utility of someone else using the border wall) (Kolfage 2019).

The Trump-Wall is not a friendraising campaign, but a civCF campaign. Since both GoFundMe and Indiegogo belonged to the same company at the campaign beginning, the platform owners should have moved the campaign to Indiegogo and the specific community section if they wanted to keep friendraising and civCF separate. Community-based campaigns with a non-personal cause are also excluded from GoFundMe by the terms of the platform (Indiegogo 2019a). They chose not to because of the personal motivation of the project owner, which made a better fit on GoFundMe. But as will be discussed in the "Perspective 4: Platform" section, the choice of platform does not provide a good proxy for the classification as a civCF project.

Acknowledging that many civCF campaigns do not deliver 'pure' public goods, it would be opportune to focus on local public goods—essentially public goods which are focussed in their impact on a specific region (Desmoulins and Charbit 2017; Foà 2019; Boyle 2016).The geographic and demographic scope is relevant for the classification as a civCF campaign (Mayer 2019). CivCF campaigns often have a place-based nature, in the sense that they refer to a specific region or city.

The geographic and demographic scope is relevant for the classification as a civCF campaign (Mayer 2019). CivCF campaigns often have a place-based nature, in the sense that they refer to a specific region or city.

Some civCF campaigns have an action-based temporary nature in a specific region (Brent 2017). The regional focus does not stem from the location of the supporter or the platform, but from the activities carried out in a specific location. One example is the civic crowdfunding project '12/06/2020 Olympia' which aims to fund a citizen assembly in the Olympic Stadium of Berlin to discuss climate change proposals. This project has an action-based local focus (the assembly in Berlin) and an international public good (combatting climate change) as the campaign goal (Olympia 2020).

The geographic focus of civic crowdfunding campaigns is a central issue in the discussion of the homogeneity of the supporter groups, in the following section. The above example can be tied to the discussion of participation at the beginning of this section—action-based civCF campaigns often have the goal to increase participation in public decision-making (Davies 2014; Mayer 2019; Niemeyer et al. 2018; Kusumarani and Zo 2019; European Crowdfunding Network and Passeri 2018; Goodspeed 2019; Porter and Veenswijk 2018).

To summarize, the nature of a civCF project, especially when it comes to the good provided by the project, is still in debate. A public good in the strictest sense is undoubtedly in the scope of the definition of civic crowdfunding. Yet researchers broaden the definition by also allowing club goods and commons to be included as a campaign goal in civic crowdfunding, or even include private goods with a secondary public outcome. However, with such a broad definition, almost any crowdfunding campaign can be classified as civCF campaign. Together with the place-based nature of civCF projects and the participatory elements discussed at the beginning of this section, a preliminary definition of civCF through the perspective of the project might be: Civic crowdfunding are campaigns which provide a semi-public good, creating participatory mechanisms with a place-based focus. In the next section, this definition will be enhanced with the perspectives of the supporter.

Perspective 2: Supporter

The second perspective relates to the supporters of the civic crowdfunding campaign. The nature of crowdfunding entails that especially for donation-based and reward-based crowdfunding, very few restrictions exist for the supporters. If a platform has enabled an international payment system, then theoretically anyone in the world can contribute to a crowdfunding campaign.

In practice, however, civCF campaigns are mostly supported by individuals in the geographic vicinity of the campaign (Mayer 2019; Desmoulins and Charbit 2017). Looping back to the conclusion of the previous section, it should be noted that the place-based nature of the civCF projects, the connection to local participatory mechanisms, and the provision of local semi-public goods make the appeal to local or regional crowds more likely.

Whether an increased homogeneity is connected to the success of a project is still subject to debate. Smaller communities may have a higher success in implementing a project funded through the civCF campaigns (Mayer 2019). A more diverse group has a higher impact because it allows for a wider distribution of the crowdfunding campaign (Davies 2014; Dejean 2019).

There are few civCF campaigns which appeal to a global audience (Stiver et al. 2015). One example is the unsuccessful campaign to bail out the Greek citizens, which attracted support from all over the globe (Indiegogo 2015). Global civCF campaigns provide a global public good. These campaigns are more difficult to implement through the classic crowdfunding mechanism, but donation-based CFPs serve those who simply want to donate to global causes (Scataglini and Ventresca 2019). Most global donation-based CFPs offer mechanisms to search for campaigns and causes in the vicinity of potential donors, which once again underscores the placed-based nature of civCF (Justgiving 2020).

The local and regional focus of civCF campaigns supports the theory that the interests of supporter groups are more aligned in civCF campaigns than in other campaigns. The self-interest of other crowdfunding campaigns (to receive rewards, obtain shares of companies, or earn interest payments) is replaced by a self-and-other-interest of the supporters (Hummel 2016; Zoellig 2017).

Unlike other forms of crowdfunding, civCF relies less on digital natives and early adopters, seeking new products and services, but instead is characterized by a more extensive mobilization of offline communities (Stiver et al. 2015; Desmoulins and Charbit 2017).

In order to discuss the motives of civCF supporters, this chapter distinguishes the motives of the supporters through three criteria (Desmoulins and Charbit 2017): (1) outcome, (2) action, and (3) communication.

The outcome was already discussed in the previous section. Supporters of civCF campaigns benefit from the provision of the semi-public good (Davies 2014) which is the campaign goal and which supporters can use after the campaign. CivCF campaigns on reward-based CFPs also provide tangible rewards or even payments of interest (Wenzlaff et al. 2015; Hainzer et al. 2014)

The action to support a campaign can by itself be a motivation. The process of mutual awareness of the actions taken by the supporters creates social connectivity between supporters, thus invigorating a community of enablers (van Dijk 2015; Stiver et al. 2015). The emotional returns of participating in the campaign may outweigh the altruistic motive to generate a particular public good (Davies 2015). If the owners of the civic crowdfunding campaign and the supporters of the campaign are based in the same community, then the expectations to contribute to the campaign can become peer-pressure—this reciprocal visibility might also outweigh the altruistic motive to generate a particular public good (Hummel 2016; Wenzlaff 2017).

Communication is the third category of analysis in supporters' motivation. Supporters might be motivated to communicate something about themselves when participating in the campaign. This is undoubtedly true for supporters who are not just individual citizens. Private non-profit organizations (Davies 2014), private for-profit organizations and corporations, public organizations (Hummel 2016), and public for-profit organizations (Wenzlaff et al. 2015; Wenzlaff 2017) can also be found as contributors to civic crowdfunding campaigns. For corporate sponsors of a civic crowdfunding campaign as well as for public entities participating in a civic crowdfunding campaign as co-funding partners, the need for the communication of support might be higher than the actual benefit of the public good being generated. As an example, if a local company supports a civic crowdfunding campaign for a playground, the rationale might be more to communicate civic engagement and not using that playground itself.

The literature on civCF lists numerous potential benefits for the supporters (see Table 19.3). In many cases, the initiators of a civic crowdfunding campaign can be found among the group of likely supporters of a campaign cause. Other forms of crowdfunding do not require or even facilitate the fact that supporters and project owners have to be part of the same peer group. In lending-based crowdfunding, for instance, lenders and lendees have quite different economic backgrounds: one has the funds to lend, one seeks the fund to lend. In civic crowdfunding, supporters and project owners share goals of the civic crowdfunding campaign.

The nature of like-mindedness between supporters and initiators is a defining characteristic of civCF campaigns. Therefore, in the next section, the motivations of the project owner will be discussed as well, especially if they are public entities. Expanding the definition of civCF, it should be noted that civCF supporters are usually individual citizens living in close vicinity to the semi-public good, which is the outcome of the civCF campaign.

Table 19.3 Benefits of civic crowdfunding for supporters

Benefit for supporters	Similar benefit for project owners (PO)?
More transparency, accountability, control of public projects (Wheat et al. 2013; Stiver et al. 2015; Bone and Baeck 2016)	Yes, if PO are citizens. No, if PO are city officials.
Increased efficiency of public spending (Miglietta and Parisi 2017)	Yes.
Promotes ideals of civic society, combatting political apathy and supporting self-organization (Hollow 2013)	Yes.
Shifts the responsibilities of public spending—it empowers the citizens to become an active actor in a local environment, beyond its role as voter or taxpayer (Desmoulins and Charbit 2017)	Yes, if PO are citizens. No, if PO are city officials.
Signals the preferences of citizens towards the government (Brandmeyer 2015; Zoellig 2017).	Yes.
Initiates a public discourse on matters of discontent among citizens. For instance, discontent can arise from urban planning outcomes which do not match the preferences of the citizens (Brandmeyer 2015; Zoellig 2017; van Veelen 2015; Sedlitzky and Franz 2019; Youngwoo 2019).	Yes, if PO are citizens. No, if PO are city officials.
Allows the transformation of public places (Brandmeyer 2015; Zoellig 2017)	Yes.
Allows the reduction of the free-rider problem when managing common resources (Hummel 2016).	Yes.
Increased self-perception of importance and impact of supporters (Bonini and Pais 2017).	Yes.
Enlists citizens as active promoters of their region or city, by motivating them to share local civic crowdfunding campaigns in their global network (Cucari and Nuhu 2017)	Yes.
Through civic crowdfunding campaigns, self-help groups for supporters can be established (Miglietta and Parisi 2017).	Yes.

Perspective 3: Owner

The third perspective refers to the owners or initiators of a civic crowdfunding campaign. CivCF campaigns are initiated either by citizens or by civic organizations (Hainzer and Stötzer 2013; Davies 2014; Brent 2017; Stiver et al. 2015; Zoellig 2017; Desmoulins and Charbit 2017; Gooch et al. 2020).

In addition to citizens or civil society organizations, subnational governments, national governments (Zoellig 2017; Desmoulins and Charbit 2017), and public financial institutions (Wenzlaff 2017) are listed as initiators of civCF campaigns. The theoretical discussions of civCF project initiators focusses on the distinction between governmental civCF (with the initiator being a public agency) and community civCF (with the initiator being a citizen or a non-profit created by citizens) (Sedlitzky and Franz 2019). Governmental civCF can provide many benefits to public entities, which is discussed below.

Public entities can use private funds generated through crowdfunding campaigns for projects that need additional private spending (Assenmacher 2017) or face budget cuts, thereby circumventing budget constraints or alleviating fiscal stress (Stiver et al. 2015; Hummel 2016; Miglietta and Parisi 2017). The bridging of budget gaps through civCF campaigns faces criticisms because it can lead to a biased form of public spending, considering only the perspectives of the donors, or reduce the spending available to groups which cannot compensate through private co-financing (Davies 2015).

This criticism is met by the claim that public entities can leverage public spending with private spending (Desmoulins and Charbit 2017), thereby increasing the impact of public spending. The counterargument to the alleged bias claims that private spending co-financing public spending does not necessarily have to be only on matters of interest to the private donor, thereby allowing other citizens to profit from the leveraged public spending as well.

Certainly, civCF campaigns allow public entities to provide services in collaboration with private service providers (Desmoulins and Charbit 2017; Mayer 2019) allowing the co-production of services, which might lead to greater efficiency of the provided services.

Public services can also be screened and tested through civCF campaigns (Miglietta and Parisi 2017), gauging the interest and appeal of proposed public projects to the citizen. Through the civCF campaigns, the public entities can identify grass-root initiatives, civic networks, and stakeholders for public-private partnerships (PPPs) (Zoellig 2017).

To share ownership with citizens can increase the commitment of citizens to improve the maintenance of urban commons. As discussed before, this evolving concept of citizenship, whereas the citizen is more than just a taxpayer and voter, is of interest to the supporters, but also of interest to the project owner (Hummel 2016; Desmoulins and Charbit 2017). CivCF can also reduce the Not-In-My-Backyard-Attitude (NIMBY) of citizens being opposed to urban and rural development, by ensuring the "buy-in" of affected citizens (Boyle 2016; Zoellig 2017; Wenzlaff 2017; Goodspeed 2019; Jäckels 2019).

CivCF could simplify decision-making, because the participation in civCF campaigns does not hinge on requirements to be registered to vote or to have formal citizenship status. There is no need to create political parties or non-profit organizations, and civCF campaigns do not stand by definition in juxtaposition to political parties, but it reduces the barriers for the formation of new civic initiatives. The semi-unanimous decision-making in civCF allows spontaneous deliberations of public policy through online platforms, without the efforts and information overload that is connected to participatory budgeting (Hummel 2016; Miglietta and Parisi 2017). At the same time, participatory budget mechanisms in combination with civic crowdfunding might help to make both more attractive for citizens (Lee et al. 2016; Niemeyer et al. 2018).

Civic crowdfunding can support public institutions to achieve a better image, for instance, by promoting efforts to establish an entrepreneurial city (Zoellig 2017) or creating instruments for becoming a Smart City (Miglietta and Parisi 2017; Carè et al. 2018).

Several forms of how public institutions can be involved in civic crowdfunding campaigns have been discussed in the literature (Davies 2014, 2015; Wenzlaff 2017; Bone and Baeck 2016; Bonini and Pais 2017; Passeri 2017; European Crowdfunding Network and Passeri 2018):

- *Owner Model*: Owning and initiating a civic crowdfunding campaign. For instance, the Istituzione Villa Smeraldi Museo della Civiltà Contadina, which is owned by the municipality of San Marino di Bentivoglio near Bologna, initiated the campaign "#IlovePomario" on the Italian Platform Ginger to promote a local museum (Ginger and Istituzione Villa Smeraldi Museo della Civiltà Contadina 2016).
- *Facilitator Model*: Co-Funding civic crowdfunding campaigns by matching grants or loans. On donation-based and reward-based

platforms, the matching grant is given to successful campaigns, matching each contribution from the supporter. On equity-based platforms, this co-funding takes place through guarantees. For example, in the UK, the city of Newcastle partnered with the lending-based platform FundingCircle to provide loans to local entrepreneurs. (Light and Briggs 2017)
- *Selling-Service Model*: Supporting civic crowdfunding campaigns by providing services to a civic crowdfunding campaign, for instance, through due-diligence of projects.
- *Curator Model*: Selecting civic crowdfunding campaigns and promoting them to the communication channels of the public institutions. For instance, the city of Berlin created a meta-platform (City of Berlin 2019), where all projects in Berlin on all platforms were featured. The city also ran a crowdfunding competition which gave prices to the best crowdfunding campaigns in specific branches. The meta-platform also offered consultants the opportunity to present themselves and has an FAQ for crowdfunding supporters. The city did not create its own crowdfunding platform; instead it offered services that supported the development of the regional crowdfunding ecosystem (Beaulieu et al. 2015; Wenzlaff 2019).
- *Platform Model*: Owning a civic crowdfunding platform. Public authorities are using so-called white-label crowdfunding platforms (Scataglini and Ventresca 2019). A crowdfunding provider operates the platform on behalf of the authorities with logo and the appearance connected to a city or region. In Germany, the first platform of this kind was called "Nordstarter" which was operated by the city of Hamburg. Federal states also partnered with a crowdfunding platform, often through the public state-owned banks (Recke 2019).

In the next section, the perspective of the platform, which hosts the civic crowdfunding campaigns, is discussed. This section established that civCF cannot be defined through citizens as project owners only but has to incorporate public entities as project owner as well.

Notably missing from such a definition are private companies as the initiator or owner of a civCF campaign—even though private companies overwhelmingly are the recipients of funds on reward-, equity-, and lending-based CFPs. Bringing back to mind the example of the private brewery ranking first among the list of community campaigns on Indiegogo, it becomes apparent that at least for some platforms, private companies can also run civCF campaigns (Indiegogo 2016).

One of the well-known civCF campaigns initiated by a private company is the LuchtSingel campaign, for funding a bridge in Rotterdam, which was initiated by a private architectural office and raised EUR 4m without using a CFP (Wenzlaff 2017; Jäckels 2019; Youngwoo 2019; Pavia 2017; van Veelen 2015). The LuchtSingel project saw significant support from public institutions and private companies, such as the Port of Rotterdam, and is also a prime example of initiating public discourse within the city. Ejecting it from the definition of civCF would be as if ejecting Mickey Mouse from the definition of Disney cartoon characters.

With this in mind, a definition of civCF needs to include the overwhelming majority of citizens and civic institutions acting as project owners. Both elements do not have enough explanatory power to be the sole determinants of a civCF definition. But in combination with the perspective of the supporters and the project goal, it is clear that public institutions play a more significant role in initiating civCF projects than compared to other forms of crowdfunding.

Perspective 4: Platform

The last perspective to be considered is the functionalities and constraints of the civic crowdfunding platform. The intermediation of platforms is the predominant form of crowdfunding across the globe (Nielsen 2018). Platforms curate and select projects. For instance, the civic crowdfunding platform Voorjebuurt takes up to five working days to verify projects before they are being published on the platform (Voorjebuurt 2019). Platforms also facilitate payments, process withdrawal requests, and complaints (Sedlitzky and Franz 2019), and ensure the compliance with regulation (money laundering, investor protection) (Lehner 2013).

Platforms set the rules for the crowdfunding process, to which the projects and the project owners have to adhere. Platforms set the rules for the minimum and the maximum contribution, which has an impact on the type of participation that the platforms allow. Ensuring that small contributions are also possible has a significant impact on the participatory culture of civic crowdfunding (Bonini and Pais 2017).

Platforms also determine the mechanism of success of crowdfunding. The two popular models are the All-or-Nothing model or the Keep-It-All model. In All-or-Nothing campaigns, funds have to reach a pre-set threshold before transferred to the project owner. This model is associated with many reward-based crowdfunding platforms, such as Kickstarter.

The Keep-It-All model does not require a threshold—funds are transferred to the project owner regardless if the target sum of the campaign is reached or not. The Keep-It-All model is often associated with donation-based crowdfunding platforms (Paredes et al. 2018), such as the German platform Betterplace or the friendraising platform GoFundMe.

Some platforms employ both models for structuring crowdfunding campaigns. The US-based platform Indiegogo allows a Keep-It-All model called flexible funding, but also an All-or-Nothing model called Fixed Funding. Spacehive is a civic crowdfunding platform based in the UK and employs the All-or-Nothing model. Goteo, on the other hand, employs the Keep-It-All model (Goteo 2019b; Spacehive 2019; Indiegogo 2019a).

The model used for civic crowdfunding platforms has an enormous impact on the civic crowdfunding projects. Trust in the platform translates into trust into projects (Moysidou and Hausberg 2019). Out of concerns for their reputation, platforms ensure that the projects are feasible. The All-or-Nothing model forces projects to make a realistic calculation of the target sum. The Keep-It-All model allows civCF campaigns to use the funds contributed by the supporters even if a target goal is not reached, thus eliminating the risk of a failed campaign.

The platform asks projects to provide documents about the feasibility of the campaign goal. This allows them eliminating projects that are deemed as unfeasible or unserious (curation). Platforms also choose how visible individual projects are (Davies 2014) by promoting them through social media or newsletters (promotion).

It would not be prudent to define a civic crowdfunding platform only as a subset of donation-based or reward-based crowdfunding (Sedlitzky and Franz 2019), since equity-based crowdfunding (i.e. investments in renewable energy infrastructure), and lending-based crowdfunding (i.e. loans to municipalities) are increasingly popular (Hainzer et al. 2014; Wenzlaff et al. 2015; Bone and Baeck 2016; Assenmacher 2017; Old et al. 2019).

One obvious criterion to define civCF platforms would be self-labelling. Platforms like Spacehive, Voorjebuurt, Goteo, or Place2Help use the label 'Civic Crowdfunding' actively. Other platforms, such as Startnext, Visionbakery, or Indiegogo, have project categories dedicated to civic projects or community projects.

The second criterion to position a platform within civCF would be functionalities that include the participation of citizens through non-financial contributions, such as volunteering or voting (Wenzlaff 2017; Desmoulins and Charbit 2017). For instance, the civic crowdfunding platform Spacehive allows projects to create so-called Wishlists—crowdfunding campaigns can ask for non-financial contributions (Chant and Spacehive 2019). Platforms that are not active in civCF restrict the platform functionalities to financial contributions and comments.

The third criterion to position a platform within civic crowdfunding can be the nature of its business model and the owner of the platform. Both issues are closely related. Private companies own platforms like Voorjebuurt or Spacehive; private non-profit foundations own platforms like Goteo (Goteo 2019a, b; Chant and Spacehive 2019; Spacehive 2019; Voorjebuurt 2019). In both models, the platforms earn income through fees paid by the project owners, often only in the case of a successful campaign. Several fee models exist, such as fixed-fee models, variable-fee models, or voluntary-fee models. However, there are civCF platforms which do not have any fees, not even for the processing of payments. Often these "free" platforms are maintained and operated by a public entity or a private entity with a public purpose (Wenzlaff 2017).

The platform is critical to define civic crowdfunding. By self-labelling, creating distinct project categories, or developing functionalities to involve citizens, projects are attracted to the platform with a specific purpose. These civic projects are reaching out to supporters with a specific mindset, such as contributing to a campaign which has a civic goal, for instance, by creating a semi-public good within a specific region. By doing so, the platforms create a semi-public good in themselves by providing a 'non-material digital infrastructure' which aligns interests of supporters, project owners, and platform providers. Infrastructure is defined as a public good which expands economics opportunities of individual agents through network effects and economies of scale (Buhr 2003; Kasper 2015; Torrisi 2009). The platform provides a technical infrastructure (hosting projects, processing payments), an organizational infrastructure (turning abstract ideas into concrete projects) and a social infrastructure (initiating public debates around civic purposes) (Davies 2014; Nielsen 2018; Logue and Grimes 2019).

It is crucial to keep in mind that the idea of a social-organizational-technical infrastructure provided by a platform is not unique to civCF or crowdfunding in general. Any 'digital' platform can be analysed through this perspective of 'non-material digital infrastructure'. It helps, however, to understand that the platform is central to connecting the three other perspectives in civCF campaign and creating a narrative around the civCF campaigns (Porter and Veenswijk 2018; Lee et al. 2016).

It is also essential to consider that the social-organizational-technical infrastructure can also be provided through the website of the project initiator themselves. The website then becomes a 'one-project'-platform. The missing opportunities for scaling effects and the missing independence for validation, selection, and curation of projects are counterbalanced by the alignment of interests of supporters and the project initiators.

The fourth perspective of the platform makes it necessary to expand the definition of civCF by considering the central function of the platform, as described above, which will be done in the final section.

Conclusion

The previous sections have discussed four perspectives of civic crowdfunding. The section on the project perspective has shown that civCF projects have three distinguishing features: contribute to political participation, provide a semi-public good, and have a place-based nature. The section on the supporters has shown that the geographic vicinity of supporters creates like-mindedness between supporters and project initiators, which as can be seen in the "Definition and Perspectives of Civic Crowdfunding" section on the project owners makes it attractive for public institutions to become project owners. The diversity of benefits obtained by supporters through civic crowdfunding campaigns are beyond the personal benefits of other types of crowdfunding. The "Perspective 1: Project" section has shown that the platforms have a central role in defining the relationship between supporters and owners and determining the impact of the public good generated by the campaign. The "Perspective 1: Project" section also discussed the notion of the platform being a public good, which is more prevailing in civic crowdfunding than in other types of crowdfunding.

The four perspectives in the previous sections motivate this chapter to revise the classic definition of crowdfunding: "*Crowdfunding is an open call, essentially through the Internet, for the provision of financial resources either in the form of donation or in exchange for some form of reward and/or voting rights in order to support initiatives for specific purposes*" (Belleflamme et al., 2014).

In the context of civic crowdfunding, this chapter rephrases the definition by including the purpose, the interaction between supporters and owners, and the platform: "*Civic crowdfunding is an open call, essentially through the internet, for the provision of financial resources to produce place-based semi-public goods with a collaborative and coordinated response by the financial supporters. The civic crowdfunding platform is defined by its aim to facilitate both collaboration and coordination to maintain or improve the public good aimed at by the civic crowdfunding campaign*".

The argument for a revised definition of civic crowdfunding stems from the belief that crowdfunding is more than just the platform, the projects, the project owners, and the supporters. Like many other technological innovations, the practice of crowdfunding creates an ecosystem of services and products, such as networks of consultants, online tools, education opportunities, evaluation methods (Wenzlaff 2017, 2019).

This chapter argues that research in civic crowdfunding should focus more on the specific role that civCF platforms play in the facilitation of projects and how they interact with public institutions. This analysis entails how public support mechanisms can enhance the provision of well-maintained socio-organizational-technical infrastructure.

A research agenda for civic crowdfunding should start with the interaction between special-purpose civCF CFPs and civCF categories on all-purpose CFPs, proceed with segmenting data from the all-purpose CFPs, and analyse success factors in civCF campaigns, especially how they are different from more commercially-oriented entrepreneurial campaigns. Since platforms play such a central role, it would be instructive to analyse the attitudes of both project owners and supporters towards the platforms, primarily if a public entity maintains the platform. Finally, it would help to analyse the implementation of civCF projects, to understand better whether civCF projects are only short-term responses to funding gaps, or can create long-term organizational structures which continue to provide and manage public goods. This could inform the debate on whether civCF erects new barriers to political participation or creates new avenues for citizens to interact with public authorities.

The depth of civic crowdfunding research is increasing (Wenzlaff 2020), with case studies focussing on non-Anglo-American markets being published. Nevertheless, very few cross-country comparisons exist. Given the place-based nature of civCF, the (implicit) assumption that civCF is similar in each country and region needs to be examined critically.

Such an analysis would allow both platforms and public authorities to develop better mechanisms for aligning public budgets and civic crowdfunding campaigns through support mechanisms. Since civCF campaigns are still small compared to other forms of crowdfunding, the outlined research agenda could provide public decision-makers with information on how to design support mechanism to create campaigns of greater volume and possibly more impact. It could also inform the project owners of civCF campaigns whether to focus their efforts on local, regional, or global audiences. Most importantly, the analysis could help project owners identify the right platform and shape their campaign in such a way that the audience relates to the benefits for themselves as well as the benefits for the wider community, which would result in improved semi-public goods provided by crowdfunding.

Acknowledgements The author would like to thank Prof Dr Sebastian Späth, Prof Dr Ivana Pais, Dr Krystallia Moysidou, Prof Dr Piet Hausberg, Prof Dr Rotem Shneor, and two anonymous reviewers for their valuable feedback.

References

Assenmacher, K. (2017). *Crowdfunding als kommunale Finanzierungsalternative.* Wiesbaden: Springer Gabler.

Barollo, A., & Castrataro, D. (2013). Il Crowdfunding Civico: Una Proposta. Retrieved from https://issuu.com/alessiobarollo/docs/civic-crowdfunding.

Beaulieu, T., Sarker, S., & Sarker, S. (2015). A Conceptual Framework for Understanding Crowdfunding. *Communications of the Association for Information Systems, 37*, 1–31.

Belleflamme, P., Lambert, T., & Schwienbacher, A. (2014). Crowdfunding: Tapping the Right Crowd. *Journal of Business Venturing, 29*(5), 585–609.

Bone, J., & Baeck, P. (2016). Crowdfunding Good Causes. Retrieved from https://www.nesta.org.uk/sites/default/files/crowdfunding_good_causes-2016.pdf.

Bonini, T., & Pais, I. (2017). Hacking Public Service Media Funding: A Scenario for Rethinking the License Fee as a Form of Civic Crowdfunding. *International Journal on Media Management, 19*(2), 123–143.

Boyle, T. M. (2016). *The City and the Crowd: An Exploration of Civic Crowdfunding Disruption to Local Government Led City Planning and the Quest to Co-create Liveability.* Master Thesis. Biddeford, ME: University of New England.

Brandmeyer, O. (2015). *Crowdfunding Urbanism—Schwarmfinanzierung in Der Stadtentwicklung.* Technische Universität Berlin, Institut für Stadt- und Regionalplanung.

Brent, D. A. (2017). *The Geography of Civic Crowdfunding: Implications for Social Inequality and Donor-project Dynamics.* Working Paper 2017-09, Department of Economics Louisiana State University.

Buhr, W. (2003). What is Infrastructure? Volkswirtschaftliche Diskussionsbeiträge. Universität Siegen, Fakultät Wirtschaftswissenschaften, Wirtschaftsinformatik und Wirtschaftsrecht. Retrieved from https://econpapers.repec.org/paper/siesiegen/107-03.htm.

Carè, S., Trotta, A., Carè, R., et al. (2018). Crowdfunding for the Development of Smart Cities. *Business Horizons, 61*(4), 501–509.

Carvajal, M., García-Avilés, J. A., & González, J. L. (2012). Crowdfunding and Non-profit Media. *Journalism Practice, 6*(5–6), 638–647.

Catapult. (2018). Civic Crowdfunding—A Guidebook for Local Authorities. Retrieved from http://futurecities.catapult.org.uk/resource/civic-crowdfunding-guidebook-local-authorities/.

Chant, J., & Spacehive. (2019). FAQs. Retrieved from https://about.spacehive.com/faqs/.

City of Berlin. (2019). Crowdfunding Berlin. Retrieved from https://www.crowdfunding-berlin.com/en/.

Colasanti, N., Frondizi, R., & Meneguzzo, M. (2018). Higher Education and Stakeholders' Donations: Successful Civic Crowdfunding in an Italian University. *Public Money & Management, 38*(4), 281–288.

Cucari, N., & Nuhu, K. (2017). *Co-Creation of Value in Relationships Crowdfunding-territory: An Exploratory Study in the Italian Context.* Paper present at the European Conference on Intangibles and Intellectual Capital, Academic Conferences International Limited, Kidmore End, UK.

Damle, S., Moti, M. H., Chandra, P., & Gujar, S. (2019). Aggregating Citizen Preferences for Public Projects Through Civic Crowdfunding. In *Proceedings of the 18th International Conference on Autonomous Agents and MultiAgent Systems*.

Davies, R. (2014). *Civic Crowdfunding: Participatory Communities, Entrepreneurs and the Political Economy of Place.* Master Thesis, Massachusetts Institute of Technology. Retrieved from https://dspace.mit.edu/bitstream/handle/1721.1/89954/890127961-MIT.pdf?sequence=2.

Davies, R. (2015). Three Provocations for Civic Crowdfunding. *Information, Communication & Society, 18*(3), 342–355.

Dejean, S. (2019). The Role of Distance and Social Networks in the Geography of Crowdfunding: Evidence from France. *Regional Studies, 54*(3), 329–339.

Desmoulins, G., & Charbit, C. (2017). *Civic Crowdfunding: A Collective Option for Local Public.* OECD Regional Development Working Papers 2017/02.

Dijk, C. (2015). How Communities Make Crowdfunding Campaigns More Successful: Research into the Success of Crowdfunding Communities and Considerations Towards a Successful Crowdfunding Campaign. Retrieved from http://dare.uva.nl/document/605860.

Doan, M. A., & Toledano, M. (2018). Beyond Organization-centred Public Relations: Collective Action through a Civic Crowdfunding Campaign. *Public Relations Review, 44*(1), 37–46.

Einhörnchen. (2015). Einhorn. *Startnext.com*. Retrieved from https://www.startnext.com/einhorn.

European Crowdfunding Network. (2018). *Triggering Participation—A Collection of Civic Crowdfunding and Match-funding Experiences in the EU*. Brussels: European Crowdfunding Network.

Foà, C. (2019). Crowdfunding Cultural Projects and Networking the Value Creation: Experience Economy between Global Platforms and Local Communities. *Arts and the Market, 9*(2), 235–254.

Förderkreis des FEZ-Berlin e.V. (2018). FEZ-Berlin Brunnen. *Startnext.com*. Retrieved from https://www.startnext.com/fez-berlin-brunnen.

Ginger. (2016). #ILOVEPOMARIO. Retrieved from https://www.ideaginger.it:443/progetti/ilovepomario.html%27.

Gooch, D., Kelly, R. M., Stiver, A., et al. (2020). The Benefits and Challenges of Using Crowdfunding to Facilitate Community-led projects in the Context of Digital Civics. *International Journal of Human-Computer Studies, 134*, 33–43.

Goteo Fundación. (2019a). Donar. *Goteo.Org*. Retrieved from http://en.goteo.org/donate.

Goteo Fundación. (2019b). Goteo.Org: Crowdfunding the Commons. *Goteo.Org*. Retrieved from http://en.goteo.org/

Hainzer, M., & Stötzer, S. (2013). Crowdfunding Für Nonprofit-Organisationen. *Fachzeitschrift Für Verbands- Und Nonprofit-Management, 39*(2), 38–46.

Hainzer, M., Stötzer, S., & Ellmer, M. (2014). Crowdfunding-Basierte Bürgerkreditmodelle in Kommunen. *Zeitschrift Für Öffentliche Und Gemeinwirtschaftliche Unternehmen, 37*(1–2), 54–72.

Hollow, M. (2013). Crowdfunding and Civic Society in Europe: A Profitable Partnership? Retrieved from https://papers.ssrn.com/sol3/papers.cfm?abstract_id=2333635.

Hummel, D. (2016). Civic Crowd-funding: A Potential Test of the Voluntary Theory of Public Finance For Public Capital Goods. *Journal of Public Budgeting, Accounting & Financial Management, 28*(2), 171–195.

Indiegogo. (2012). Restore the Shore. *Indiegogo*. Retrieved from http://www.indiegogo.com/restore-the-shore.

Indiegogo. (2015). Greek Bailout Fund. *Indiegogo*. Retrieved from https://www.indiegogo.com/projects/1324990.

Indiegogo. (2016). Stone Groundbreaking Collaborations. *Indiegogo*. Retrieved from http://www.indiegogo.com/projects/838279/fblk.

Indiegogo. (2019a). Is My Campaign Allowed on Indiegogo? *Indiegogo Help Center*. Retrieved from http://support.indiegogo.com/hc/en-us/articles/360000574528-Is-My-Campaign-Allowed-on-Indiegogo-.

Indiegogo. (2019b). Support Community Projects at Indiegogo. *Indiegogo*. Retrieved from https://www.indiegogo.com/explore/community-projects?project_type=campaign&project_timing=all&sort=most_funded.

Izzo, M. (2017). Stakeholders and Museum Crowdfunding. *Modern Economy, 8*(4), 518–530.

Jäckels, M. (2019). Civic Crowdfunding. In U. Altrock, D. Kurth, R. Kunze, H. Schmidt, & G. Schmitt (Eds.), *Programmatik der Stadterneuerung: Jahrbuch Stadterneuerung 2019* (pp. 73–95). Wiesbaden: Springer Fachmedien.

Justgiving. (2020). *JustGiving*. Retrieved from https://www.justgiving.com/crowdfunding.

Kasper, R. (2015). *A Definition for Infrastructure—Characteristics and Their Impact on Firms Active in Infrastructure*. Technische Universität München. Retrieved from https://d-nb.info/1071370057/34.

Kolfage, B. (2019). We the People Will Build the Wall. *Gofundme.Com*. Retrieved from https://www.gofundme.com/TheTrumpWall.

Kukla, L. (2014). *Stadt- Und Regionalentwicklung 2.0—Crowdfunding Als Kommunales Förderinstrument*. Universität Eichstätt.

Kusumarani, R., & Zo, H. (2019). Why People Participate in Online Political Crowdfunding: A Civic Voluntarism Perspective. *Telematics and Informatics, 41*, 168–181.

Lee, C. H., Bian, Y., Karaouzene, R., & Suleiman, N. (2019). Examining the role of narratives in civic crowdfunding: linguistic style and message substance. *Industrial Management & Data Systems*, Vol. ahead-of-print No. ahead-of-print. https://doi.org/10.1108/IMDS-08-2018-0370.

Lee, C. H., Zhao, J. L., & Hassna, G. (2016). Government-incentivized Crowdfunding for One-belt, One-road Enterprises: Design and Research Issues. *Financial Innovation, 2*(1), 1–14.

Lehner, O. M. (2013). Crowdfunding Social Ventures: A Model and Research Agenda. *Venture Capital, 15*(4), 289–311.

LeihDeinerStadtGeld GmbH. (2012). Investment Investition in Freiwillige Feuerwehr. Retrieved from https://www.leihdeinerstadtgeld.de/oestrich-winkel.

Light, A., & Briggs, J. (2017). Crowdfunding Platforms and the Design of Paying Publics. In *Proceedings of the 2017 CHI Conference on Human Factors in Computing Systems*. Denver, Colorado, USA: ACM Press, pp. 797–809.

Logue, D., & Grimes, M. (2019). Platforms for the people: Enabling civic crowdfunding through the cultivation of institutional infrastructure. *Strat. Mgmt. J*, 1– 31. https://doi.org/10.1002/smj.3110.

Mattauch, C. (2015). Coole Kohle. *Liberal Magazin*.

Mayer, M. (2019). Examining Community Dynamics of Civic Crowdfunding Participation. *Computer Supported Cooperative Work, 28*(5), 961–975.

Miglietta, A., & Parisi, E. (2017). Civic Crowdfunding: Sharing Economy Financial Opportunity to Smart Cities. In E. R. Sanseverino, R. R. Sanseverino, & V. Vaccaro (Eds.), *Smart Cities Atlas* (pp. 159–172). Cham: Springer International Publishing.

Moysidou, K., & J. Piet Hausberg, J. P. (2020). In crowdfunding we trust: A trust-building model in lending crowdfunding. *Journal of Small Business Management, 58*(3), 511–543. https://doi.org/10.1080/00472778.2019.1661682.

Nielsen, K. R. (2018). Crowdfunding through a Partial Organization Lens—The Co-dependent Organization. *European Management Journal, 36*(6), 695–707.

Niemeyer, C., Teubner, T., Hall, M., et al. (2018). The Impact of Dynamic Feedback and Personal Budgets on Arousal and Funding Behaviour in Participatory Budgeting. *Group Decision and Negotiation, 27*(4), 611–663.

Old, R., Boyle, D., Baeck, P., & Bone, J. (2019). *Taking Ownership: Community Empowerment through Crowdfunded Investment*. London: Nesta. Retrieved from https://media.nesta.org.uk/documents/Taking_ownership_v4.pdf.

Oliva, N. (2018). Crowdfunding and Civic Crowdfunding: Theoretical Features and Future Prospects. In U. Comite (Ed.), *Public Management and Administration* (pp. 115–126). London: IntechOpen.

Olympia. (2020). 12/06/2020—Ermögliche mit uns das größte Demokratie Festival. *Startnext.com*. Retrieved from https://www.startnext.com/12062020.

Onwuegbuzie, A. J., & Frels, R. (2016). *Seven Steps to a Comprehensive Literature Review: A Multimodal & Cultural Approach*. Los Angeles: SAGE.

Paredes, H., Barroso, J., & Bigham, J. P. (2018). *All (of us) Can Help: Inclusive Crowdfunding Research Trends and Future Challenges*. Paper Presented at the IEEE 22nd International Conference on Computer Supported Cooperative Work in Design. Nanjing, China.

Passeri, F. (2017). *The European Dimension of Civic Crowdfunding*. Brussels: European Crowdfunding Network.

Pavia, L. (2017). Dalla Do It Yourself (DIY) alla Do It Together (DIT) Strategy: la campagna di crowdfunding "I Make Rotterdam" per la realizzazione del ponte Luchtsingel a Rotterdam in Olanda. *La città creative*, pp. 187–195.

PGS-Team. (2018). Pacific Garbage Screening. *Startnext.com*. Retrieved from https://www.startnext.com/pgs.

Porter, A. J., & Veenswijk, M. (2018). Narrative "End States" and the Dynamics of Participation in Civic Crowdfunding. *International Journal of Communication, 12*, 2367–2386.

Rathemacher, A. (2015). Crowdfunding Access to Archives. *Library Journal, 140*(2), 43.

Recke, M. P. (2019). *Hamburg's Entrepreneurial Ecosystem and the Next Media Initiative: Public Policy Towards Entrepreneurship*. epubli.

Ridgway, R. (2015). Crowdfunding the Commons? In G. Lovink, N. Tkacz, & P. De Vries (Eds.), *Moneylab reader* (pp. 281–294). Amsterdam: Institute of Network Cultures.

Samuelson, P. A. (1954). The Pure Theory of Public Expenditure. *The Review of Economics and Statistics, 36*(4), 387–389.

Scataglini, M., & Ventresca, M. J. (2019). Funding the UN Sustainable Development Goals: Lessons from Donation-based Crowdfunding Platforms. Saïd Business School WP 2019-03. Retrieved from https://ssrn.com/abstract=3328731.

Sedlitzky, R., & Franz, Y. (2019). What if We All Chip In? Civic Crowdfunding as Alternative Financing for Urban Development Projects. *Built Environment, 45*(1), 26–44.

Shareable. (2018). *Sharing Cities: Activating the Urban Commons*. Tides Center/Shareable.

Simeoni, F., & De Crescenzo, V. (2018). Ecomuseums (on Clean Energy), Cycle Tourism and Civic Crowdfunding: A New Match for Sustainability? *Sustainability, 10*(3), 817.

Spacehive. (2017). Learning Tree Tipi and Super Storage! Retrieved from https://wwww.spacehive.com/learning-tree-tipi-and-super-storage.

Spacehive. (2019). Spacehive—Crowdfunding for Local Projects. Retrieved from https://www.spacehive.com/

Stiver, A., Barroca, L., Petre, M., Richards, M., & Roberts, D. (2015). Civic Crowdfunding: How Do Offline Communities Engage Online? In *Proceedings of the 2015 British HCI Conference*, pp. 37–45.

Torrisi, G. (2009). Public Infrastructure: Definition, Classification and Measurement Issues. *Economics, Management, and Financial Markets, 4*(3), 100–124.

Veelen, T. (2015). Civic Crowdfunding: A Financial Kickstart to Urban Area Development? An Analysis of the Institutional Structure in Which Civic Crowdfunding in Urban Area. Retrieved from http://repository.tudelft.nl/assets/uuid:bf8caf4f-79a8-4257-ac88-948518f5cc36/Thesis_Tim_van_Veelen_FINAL.pdf.

Vogt, N., & Mitchell, A. (2016). Crowdfunded Journalism: A Small but Growing Addition to Publicly Driven Journalism. *Pew Research Center's Journalism Project (blog)*. January 20. Retrieved from http://www.journalism.org/2016/01/20/crowdfunded-journalism/.

Voorjebuurt. (2019). Terms and Conditions. Retrieved from https://voorjebuurt.nl/en/pages/terms-and-conditions.

Wenzlaff, K. (2017). Civic Crowdfunding—Finanzierung von Öffentlichen Gütern. In H. Pechlaner & X. Poppe (Eds.), *Crowd Entrepreneurship: Das Gründungsgeschehen Im Wandel* (pp. 215–230). Wiesbaden: Springer Gabler.

Wenzlaff, K. (2019). Developing a Policy Framework for Emerging Crowdfunding Ecosystems. ORF Policy Briefs, No. 302. New Delhi: Observer Research Foundation.

Wenzlaff, K. (2020). Civic Crowdfunding—Overview of the Literature and Contribution to Academic Debate.

Wenzlaff, K., El Mallouki, J., & Partale, A. (2015). Civic Crowdfunding—Wie Crowdfunding Die Stadt Verändert Und Welche Potenziale Das Neue Finanzierungsinstrument Für Städte Und Regionen Hat. *AWV-Informationen*, No. 2, March/April 2015. Retrieved from http://www.awv-net.de/publikationen/awv-informationen/2015/info-2-2014-kopie.html.

Wenzlaff, K., Hoffmann, A., & Pachali, D. (2012). Freiwillig Bezahlen? Crowdfunding Und Social Payment Im Journalismus. In D. Pachali (Ed.), *Öffentlichkeit Im Wandel: Medien, Internet, Journalismus* (pp. 82–87). Berlin: Heinrich-Böll-Stiftung.

Wenzlaff, K., Kramp, L., Novy, L., & Ballwieser, D. (2013). *Journalismus in Der Digitalen Moderne: Einsichten—Ansichten—Aussichten*. Wiesbaden: Springer VS.

Wheat, R. E., Wang, Y., Byrnes, J. E., et al. (2013). Raising Money for Scientific Research Through Crowdfunding. *Trends in Ecology & Evolution, 28*(2), 71–72.

Youngwoo, J. (2019). Building Your City Through Crowdfunding—Rotterdam's "Luchtsingel". *Social Life*. Retrieved from http://www.social-life.co/blog/post/Crowdfunding/.

Zhang, Q., Li, L., Niu Q., & Yu, Y. (2019). How should Civic Crowdfunding Lead China's Home-Based Care Service for the Elderly out of the Financial Shortage? Environmental Analysis of Four Practical Patterns with the Theory of Funding Ecosystem. *Ekoloji, 28*(107), 4197–4204.

Zoellig, R. (2017). *Die Relevanz von Civic Crowdfunding Als Kommunales Finanzierungs- Sowie Beteiligungsinstrument in Der Deutschen Stadtentwicklung*. Master Thesis. Münster: Westphalia Wilhelms University, Institute of Geography.

Part V

The Future of Crowdfunding

20

Crowdfunding Education: Objectives, Content, Pedagogy, and Assessment

Rotem Shneor and Bjørn-Tore Flåten

Introduction

Despite its rapid growth, the practice of online crowdfunding remains a relatively novel phenomenon. Earlier studies have suggested that for the crowdfunding industry to gain greater traction, as well as develop along healthy and ethical lines, it is necessary to educate the public about its challenges and risks, as well as its merits and benefits (De Buysere et al. 2012). Such efforts are aimed at both raising awareness, as well as developing relevant skillsets towards successful crowdfunding practice (De Voldere and Zeqo 2017).

While much information and advice about crowdfunding are freely available online, often their origins, neutrality, rigour, and comprehensiveness may all be questionable. Thus far, a substantial part of educational efforts has taken the form of support services provided by crowdfunding platforms. Such services include a wide range of approaches

R. Shneor (✉) • B.-T. Flåten
School of Business and Law, University of Agder, Kristiansand, Norway
e-mail: rotem.shneor@uia.no; bjorn-tore.flaten@uia.no

R. Shneor et al. (eds.), *Advances in Crowdfunding*,
https://doi.org/10.1007/978-3-030-46309-0_20

from dedicated training materials to informative Questions and Answers sections on their websites (e.g. The Kickstarter Blog, Indiegogo Help & Support, Prosper Help Center, OurCrowd Knowledge), as well as invited seminars by platform representatives in organizations and industry events.

However, while platforms are encouraged to provide information in order to support the onboarding of users for their long-term sustainability and profitability, crowdfunding education often involves non-platform specific information and skillsets that can be applied when using any platform. Furthermore, taking into consideration that most platforms are young and resource-constrained, platforms have limited incentives to pay for a public good such as crowdfunding education. As a result, information provided by such entities may be partial and biased towards their own commercial interests.

Some efforts to overcome these challenges have manifested in educational support provided by crowdfunding industry associations rather than by individual platforms. However, only a minority of industry associations offer such training services (Jegelevičiūtė and Valančienė 2015). Such interventions, while helpful, are still coloured by industry interests. Other sources include the little and very limited advice published on government websites (e.g. Business.gov.au 2019; Consumer.ftc.gov 2019; European Commission n.d.).

Accordingly, there is a growing need for unbiased and academically sound educational programmes in crowdfunding for prospective campaign creators and backers. Thus far, the practice of crowdfunding education within formal educational institutions has mostly involved incorporating it as an 'exotic' sub-theme under more general courses on entrepreneurship, digital marketing, as well as financial technology (hereafter 'FinTech') and innovations in finance. Very few institutions have developed complete course programmes specifically dedicated to crowdfunding.

Hence, this chapter presents first insights on a dedicated crowdfunding course in higher education. It does so by presenting a case of a credit awarding academic 'Crowdfunding Lab' course (Alois 2018) that was developed at the University of Agder (hereafter 'UiA'). This case serves as an illustrative example of how such programmes can be designed and implemented while outlining course objectives, contents, and pedagogy.

A summary of the feedback from the course evaluation provided by the students will also be included. Later, a discussion highlighting opportunities for its further development will be outlined. This chapter concludes with suggestions for research, as well as implications for educators and trainers.

Why Do We Need Crowdfunding Education?

Crowdfunding has emerged at the intersection of two global trends. First, the growth in popular use of technologies enabling digital communication, commerce, and finance has become more pervasive than ever before. Indeed, digitalization has become a major theme for educational and practical concerns in most occupations, and equipping students with relevant knowledge and skillsets has become the call of the hour (Brocato et al. 2015; Harrigan and Hulbert 2011). While digitization brings many operational benefits and efficiencies, they also involve challenges requiring the development of relevant skills in using them.

At the same time, crowdfunding emerged as an alternative source of project funding following the global financial crisis, when traditional financing dried up (Bruton et al. 2015) and public funding faced major cutbacks in many countries (Boeuf et al. 2014). Hence, the use of new FinTech solutions for fundraising seemed to address both emerging market gaps and opportunities, while strengthening notions of individual empowerment (Chaney 2019) when interacting and transacting with businesses and organizations. In this respect, FinTech solutions both complement existing financing channels and fill market gaps that have been underserved by traditional institutions (Haddad and Hornuf 2019).

Accordingly, education should reflect the current environment for project management, adapt to new realities, and equip graduates with relevant knowledge and skills. Relevance here refers to both preparing students for the tasks of work life, as well as for the general context-neutral cultivation of excellence (Simpson 2013) often manifested in the acquisition of core skills. Crowdfunding represents one development in our ever more digital lives, which may be relevant for a wide range of students across disciplines, as it is applicable for the financing of commercial, cultural, humanitarian, social, civic, legal, political, and technological initiatives and projects. Hence, education on a novel phenomenon like crowdfunding serves as an ideal basis for exposing students to what is referred to as 'twenty-first century skills', such as media and technology literacy, communication, and collaborative problem solving (Griffin and Care 2014).

For this purpose, *Crowdfunding Education* is hereby defined as a collection of teaching schemes that inform, train, and educate anyone interested in the responsible planning and execution of crowdfunding campaigns towards project fundraising and/or in responsibly contributing to them financially or otherwise. Here, it is worth stressing some important aspects of this definition. First, the definition stresses that knowledge and skillsets need to be developed by both parties to a crowdfunding engagement—the fundraiser and the backer. Besides the fact that a fundraiser for one project may be a backer of another, both parties need to develop skills in assessing and interacting with each other throughout a crowdfunding process. Second, it stresses the importance of responsibility in crowdfunding engagement to ensure the ethical and non-harmful practice of crowdfunding.

Designing a Crowdfunding Course Programme

While one may wish to build on existing knowledge when designing a course, research on crowdfunding education is virtually non-existent. Nevertheless, research on education in tangent fields such as entrepreneurship, marketing, and financial education suggests the importance of a programme's objectives, content, pedagogy, and assessment procedures (e.g. Crittenden and Crittenden 2006; Fox et al. 2005; Mwasalwiba 2010). This section addresses these aspects with respect to crowdfunding education, as illustrated by the UiA Crowdfunding Lab case, and will be followed by a discussion highlighting opportunities for its further development.

Case in Focus: The UiA Crowdfunding Lab

The Crowdfunding Lab course at UiA is a master's level elective course offered at the School of Business and Law to Norwegian and international exchange students. The reason for using the term 'Lab' in the course's name is based on the pedagogic approach of exposing the students to a social lab setting, in which they work with real cases and experiment with ideas about directions they should take. The course is taught in English, and participants meeting course requirements receive 7.5 credit points according to the ECTS (European Credit Transfer and Accumulation System). It was launched as a pilot in 2018 in collaboration with and co-sponsorship of Innovation Norway, which is the Norwegian government's main instrument for innovation and development of Norwegian enterprises and industry (Innovation Norway n.d.). In 2019 it entered the list of courses as a regular elective course and became fully funded by the university.

Course Objectives

Learning objectives describe what course participants are expected to learn and the behaviours that will demonstrate such learning (Graeff 1998). Hence, course objectives can be divided between those targeting knowledge acquisition outcomes and those targeting skill development outcomes (Crittenden and Crittenden 2006). Others suggested, based on the context of entrepreneurship education, distinguishing between objectives termed as education 'for' versus education 'through' (Mwasalwiba 2010), where the former suggests education stimulating certain behaviour (e.g. starting a new venture), while the latter suggests using behaviour for the acquisition of understanding and skills (e.g. using new venture creation to acquire business skills).

In the current versions of the UiA Crowdfunding Lab course description and syllabus one can identify both knowledge and skill acquisition outcomes in the specified course objectives. First, in terms of knowledge acquisition objectives, the course aims for students to demonstrate familiarity with (1) crowdfunding principles, types, and models and discuss the differences between them; (2) key actors in crowdfunding markets, including platforms types, functionalities, and business models; (3) the role of context (industry, national, and international issues) in crowdfunding practice and patterns; (4) success and failure factors in crowdfunding campaigns; as well as (5) ethical dilemmas in crowdfunding and possible mechanisms for mitigating them. Second, in terms of skill development, the course aims for students to demonstrate skills in (1) crowdfunding campaign planning, as well as component and process development; (2) crowdfunding campaign budget and financial planning; and (3) crowdfunding campaign marketing and promotional planning.

Accordingly, the above-stated objectives relate more to the education 'through' rather than 'for' types of objectives, where crowdfunding campaign development is used as a setting for the acquisition of understanding and skills related to crowdfunding campaign management. In this sense, expected outcomes do not require participants to fundraise or contribute financially to crowdfunding campaigns after the course, but rather to acquire knowledge and skills that may prove helpful for those who may wish to engage in crowdfunding activities in the future. It is therefore more concerned with developing self-efficacy (Bandura 1986), as in one's perception of his or her own ability to perform a behaviour, which in our context will be an engagement in crowdfunding either as a fundraiser, backer, or both. Nevertheless, according to the Theory of Planned Behaviour (Ajzen 1991), higher levels of self-efficacy will enhance the likelihood of developing intentions to engage in crowdfunding, as well as behaviour in such actual engagements (Shneor and Munim 2019).

A noteworthy exception here is with respect to external organizations that voluntarily sign up as cases for what is often referred to as 'student consultancy projects' (Thomas and Busby 2003). Here, organizations seek assistance from students in developing crowdfunding campaigns for both commercial and non-commercial initiatives. Such participation in the course does come with an unstated expectation of future crowdfunding campaigning by the case organizations, hopefully building partially or fully on the students' work and inputs. Such benefits from collaborations with industry fall under the school's community outreach and regional impact efforts (De Faoite et al. 2003) and do not constitute learning objectives in themselves.

For educators, it is worth noting the effort this kind of involvement with external organizations requires. Here, the lecturers' long-time engagement with the crowdfunding industry made it possible to attract key stakeholders to the course. Moreover, engagement with the local industry (e.g. start-ups and SMBs) makes it possible to attract potential businesses and organizations as real-life cases for the course. The benefits of joining are that they receive a complete campaign and execution plan for it, which they later can launch and follow. Furthermore, case firm representatives gain insight in the theory and practice of crowdfunding, as they have a unique opportunity to interact with the students and learn from their perspectives. All this is clearly communicated to the companies before the course starts, when outlying expectations to prospective case participants. It is imperative that they fully commit to such participation, in terms of communication and meetings with students throughout the course, while allowing them enough freedoms to make their own assessments and strategic choices.

Content

Course content is organized in modules, each representing a list of topics covered in class and the reading lists that accompany them (Brocato et al. 2015; Crittenden and Crittenden 2006). Table 20.1 presents UiA Crowdfunding Lab's course modules and the list of core topics they cover.

The course starts with an introductory module defining crowdfunding, its origins, value propositions, and various models. Such introduction is accompanied by a review of the current state of the crowdfunding industry, as well as the FinTech industry more generally. The two modules that follow present practical considerations for campaign planning and execution including crowdfunding model and platforms choice, campaign budget management, as well as campaign marketing and promotions. The fourth module places crowdfunding in the context of social networking and social capital while explaining the logic and mechanisms

Table 20.1 Crowdfunding course modules and topics

Module	Topics
Introduction to crowdfunding	Crowdfunding definitions, value propositions, and models Crowdfunding process and stages State of the crowdfunding industry locally and internationally Crowdfunding in context of the FinTech industry
Campaign budget and finance	Traditional and alternative sources of finance Fundamentals of project budget management Fundamentals of financial planning Crowdfunding-specific costs
Campaign creation and planning	Considerations for crowdfunding model choice Success factors in crowdfunding campaign Crowdfunding campaign marketing and promotional strategies Meeting creators of successful crowdfunding campaigns
Networks and social capital	Network units, structures, and value Social capital Social networking and word-of-mouth Online communities and social networking sites
Crowdfunding platforms	Platform products, services, and responsibilities Considerations for choosing the right platform Meeting platform representatives
Crowdfunding regulation	Current state of crowdfunding regulation in Norway Current state if crowdfunding regulation in Europe Future developments in crowdfunding regulations
Ethical considerations in crowdfunding	Ethical dilemmas in crowdfunding Potential ethical pitfalls by stakeholder Potential remedies for mitigating moral hazard in crowdfunding
Presentation pitching and video skills	Best practice in project presentation Best practice in amateur video production

of value creation through the build-up and mobilization of social relations.

The remaining modules do not require following in any specific order but should follow the first four. Here, the fifth module presents the roles and responsibilities of crowdfunding platforms, as well as allows students to be familiarized with such concrete service providers, the services they offer, their campaign approval procedures, and their respective systems and web interfaces. The sixth module reviews the current status and dynamic evolution of regulation overseeing the different models of crowdfunding both in Norway and in Europe. The seventh module stresses the importance of responsible industry development via a critical review of ethical dilemmas and potential pitfalls stakeholders may face when engaging in crowdfunding, as well as potential remedies for addressing them. And the eighth module involves concrete advice on how to improve and develop presentation pitching skills including the effective use of multimedia and best practice advice in the creation of such elements.

In the absence of a textbook designed for crowdfunding courses, a reading list has been used including a series of academic articles that were clustered around core themes deemed as both fundamental and accessible in terms of reading difficulty. Course materials incorporated the readings and lecture slides developed by the instructors for this course. Here, it is important to note that the reading list served more as supplementary material rather than instructional material, providing students with the opportunity to expand their understanding, as well as familiarise themselves with some research within the area of crowdfunding. All articles were made available to course participants via the university's digital course management system, and each participant was required to summarize one article and share such summary with other course participants.

Here it is important to note that creating an open and supportive, yet demanding, learning environment is crucial for the success of such a course. The students meet face-to-face for a full day of lectures and lab-work once a week. A flexible lecture room with desks, presentation equipment, and black and/or white boards are used in order to present the key modules and topics. Close to the lecture room, smaller group rooms make it possible for the students to break out in groups and work on their project. The lecturers can then easily walk from group to group and supervise the project work. The students can also learn from each other, as well as from the different companies that regularly communicate with the students and vice versa. The flexibility between the lecture room and the group rooms facilitates the dynamic shifts between lecturing, group work, mentoring, and pitching.

Pedagogy

Teaching methods are classified as either traditional and passive or non-traditional and active (Michel et al. 2009; Wingfield and Black 2005). Passive learning is when students passively receive information from the instructor and internalize it through some form of memorization (Wingfield and Black 2005), while active learning involves instructional strategies where students are doing things and think about the things they are doing (Bonwell and Eison 1991). In active learning the instructor is required to facilitate rather than control the learning process while enabling students' self-discovery (Bennett 2006). In this respect, research shows that both active and passive learning methods lead to similar levels of mastery of a subject, however, active learning can lead to improved cognitive outcomes in class-specific materials (Michel et al. 2009). Furthermore, active learning through student consultancy projects was found to enhance the development of skills in communication, teamwork, problem solving, and research, as well as the personal attributes of self-confidence and leadership (Thomas and Busby 2003).

The UiA Crowdfunding Lab course combines both passive and active learning methods in a complimentary manner. The course is organized as a series of eight full-day face-to-face sessions as described above. There is a split between frontal lectures in which instructors and guest lecturers present relevant information to participants, which is then followed by supervised and guided student consultancy project work, in which students implement what they have learned in the lecture into a real-life case work. This allows participants to both receive and apply knowledge while critically thinking about its applicability in the context of their concrete task at hand. The lectures follow the modules presented in Table 20.1 and are provided mostly by the UiA course instructor(s), while being supplemented by guest lecturers chosen for their expertise (e.g. FinTech industry, legal experts, video production specialists) or as representatives of key stakeholders (e.g. platform representatives and experienced fundraisers).

Student consultancy projects have been growing in popularity in a variety of business courses as they allow students an opportunity to integrate their academic and work experiences in the development of solutions for a client's real-world problems (Heriot et al. 2008). At the UiA Crowdfunding Lab, student project work is organized in groups. The groups are formed by the lecturers, who attempt to ensure heterogeneity in terms of nationalities, backgrounds, and gender, while at the same time accommodate one out of the students' top three project preferences. Each group is assigned to an external organization that signed up to partaking in the course with the objective of creating a crowdfunding campaign for one of their projects.

The group assignment follows a short introduction by the external organizations, based on which each student lists their top three or four preferred projects. This is important for keeping the student's motivation, as well as enhancing their sense of commitment based on their own opt-in. In most cases, diversity of interests ensures good spread of project preferences, especially when considering each student indicates multiple project preferences. Throughout the course, the groups are engaged in a structured process for developing a crowdfunding campaign and the writing-up of an execution plan for such campaign. At the end of the course, the students deliver a complete campaign ready for publication and an execution plan that case organizations can follow should they wish to take it live. The execution plan includes a structured analysis (incorporating both qualitative and quantitative elements) and explanation for critical decisions made about the campaign, as well as guidelines for its actual execution. Each decision corresponds to a relevant module in the course programme (discussed earlier in the chapter under 'content').

To ensure progress, and allow for timely interventions, groups present their achievements vis-à-vis stated expectations at four points in time throughout the course. Each presentation builds on the former, and students are expected to implement feedback received by evaluation panels in each round towards the coming presentation. The first presentation takes place on the second session and requires students to present (1) the case in terms of the product, service, or initiative of focus; (2) the problems the underlying product, service, or initiative aims to address or solve; and (3) the objectives of a prospective crowdfunding campaign in terms of understanding the financial and non-financial needs of the case organization.

The second presentation takes place on the fourth session and requires the students to present the same aspects as before and add the following: (4) the choice of crowdfunding model and platform; (5) a general project budget that includes a dedicated sub-budget specific to the crowdfunding campaign; (6) comparative analysis of similar or related historical campaigns including lessons that can be learned from them; and (7) the identification and characterization of target segments for campaign efforts, including their segment-specific communication channels (e.g. websites, online communities, magazines, forums, events).

The third presentation takes place during the sixth session requiring the updated presentation of all aspects covered earlier, while adding the following: (8) campaign value propositions (e.g. non-tangible benefits in donation crowdfunding, rewards in reward crowdfunding, loan terms in crowdlending, and ownership shares and share prices in equity crowdfunding); (9) campaign promotional plan (where, when, and what); (10) Gantt charts detailing campaign action points and schedule; and (11) campaign materials and visual elements including video, images, and main texts.

Finally, the fourth presentation involves a festive event with the participation of case organization representatives, external guests, and an expert panel in which students present their full campaign and plans. At the end of the process, an external evaluation panel, consisting of industry experts, academics, and public support organizations' representatives, announces a winning presentation that provides members of the winning group with certification and a small sum of money to be used on a joint group experience (e.g. dinner, entertainment). Course grading and assessments are done separately based on submitted materials.

Assessment

According to Biggs (1996), educators are encouraged to achieve alignment between course objectives, teaching activities, and assessments in order to achieve maximum consistency throughout the process. Accordingly, assessment of learning occurs throughout the UiA Crowdfunding Lab course in the group project presentations listed earlier. Such presentations provide lecturers with multiple intervention points ensuring proper implementation of course materials in their project work. These interventions also allow students opportunities for constant improvement as well as a better understanding of their own progress.

The feedback provided for each presentation presents students with a 'reality check' better calibrating students' own assessments of their work with those of their instructors. From an instructor perspective, these interventions need to strike a delicate balance between 'bursting bubbles' and 'building steam' (Piperopoulos and Dimov 2015), providing students with critical feedback while avoiding both excessive praise and excessive criticism. The approach here is that everybody has opportunity to improve, albeit from differing progress levels, and all should be encouraged to achieve the best they can. Achievements should be recognized but opportunities for improvement should always be highlighted.

Actual grading only takes place at the end of the course based on a final presentation and all related submitted materials. Course grades are based on two components: 40%—group delivery of crowdfunding campaign materials + 60%—written group report and execution plan. Campaign materials include campaign texts, video, images, examples of social media posts, and any other supporting materials. The written execution plan includes the complete analyses behind all decisions made as well as a concrete list of action points and schedule for campaign management. The written plan is accompanied by the final presentation, which represents the highlights of the more detailed written report.

Table 20.2 outlines the expectations presented to course participants at the beginning of the course and serves as the template on which they

Table 20.2 Crowdfunding course grading form

Component	Content	Percentage of grade
Need clarification	What is the problem/need the concept solves? What evidence is there for the prevalence of the problem/need?	5%
Concept description	What is the product/service/initiative? What is its core value proposition?	2%
Campaign objectives and financial needs	Financial objectives of campaign Non-financial objectives of campaign Project financial plan For investment campaigns—firm/organization financial plans	7%
Model and platform choices	Crowdfunding model choice and why? Platform choice and why?	7%
Analyses of historical campaigns	Analysis of at least 3 similar or relevant historical campaigns What are the lessons from these campaigns?	3%
Market and segment selections	Criteria for choosing segments Segment identification and definition Segment profiling and characteristics	5%
Competition and positioning	Comparison with competing concepts along critical dimensions What is the project concept's core value proposition? What is the project concept's unique positioning?	5%
Potential backer survey and analyses	What is currently used to address need by segment? (reward) Consumption preferences, capabilities, and channels (reward) Donation preferences, capabilities, and channels (donation) Investment preferences, capabilities, and channels (investment)	10%
Execution plan	Action points (what?), schedule (when?), responsibility (who?)	3%
	Value propositions = concrete rewards or investment offerings	3%

(*continued*)

Table 20.2 (continued)

Component	Content	Percentage of grade
Campaign materials	Texts and images	10%
	Video	10%
	Social media posts	5%
	PR and relevant communication channels	5%
	Relevant online communities	5%
	Relevant bloggers, journalists, and influencers	5%
Total		100%

develop their presentations and plans. The first two columns represent the content of expected presentation and written plan, while the third column represents a suggested grading scheme.

Course Evaluation

Denson et al. (2010) suggest that course evaluations are needed for improving attainment of learning outcomes. It is not the feedback about the teaching effectiveness that should matter the most, but rather the facilitation of student learning. The student evaluations from the UiA Crowdfunding Lab may provide important insights on the students' learning outcomes.

Out of the 29 master students participating in the course, 23 filled out the evaluation survey form. The results of which show how the students evaluate the way the course was taught, as well as their sense of learning. Here, students express high levels of satisfaction with 90% indicating the course was taught in an engaging way and 100% indicating the course provided them with tools for building crowdfunding campaigns. In qualitative comments students mentioned the course provided them with a sense of learning, as well as expressed appreciation of the lecturers, and the experience of working with real companies and cases. Moreover, the student's expressed appreciation of feedback along the way, which allowed them to gradually improve their project work. They also indicated appreciation for the sense of challenge that they were exposed to during the course. In this respect, 6 of the 23 respondents voiced that they experienced time pressure and a demanding workload during the course.

Areas for improvement include better use of reading list, as 65% of students indicated not to have read most of the assigned readings, and 26% indicated not to have read most of the lecture slides. There seems to be agreement that the course load is demanding in certain aspects (e.g. group project) and less demanding in other aspects (limited reading lists and no need for individual exam preparation). In any case, all activities were accumulative so that students did not stretch across different tasks, but gradually improved the same task. Dealing with critical feedback, and continuous revision of earlier work multiple times throughout the course, may expose students to demands they are not used to from most other courses they take during their university education.

Opportunities for Further Development

The course programme presented in this chapter is one of the first of its kind; hence, opportunities and directions for further development and improvement are many. In this section several selected opportunities are highlighted. The first obvious opportunity, which has also surfaced in participants' feedback, is the need for a formalized textbook that can support the course. Currently, the combination of lecture slides and article reading lists while insightful and informative nevertheless lacks the coherence afforded by a structured textbook that students can follow. Most books currently available can be characterized as light readings focused on the hype around crowdfunding, and often lack academic rigour, balanced perspective, as well as critical review of related issues. In addition, a few research-oriented academic edited volumes are also available, but like reading lists, these represent a collection of studies into various aspects of crowdfunding, rather than generic and detailed overview of its fundamental aspects. Hence, there is a need and room for a dedicated textbook oriented towards students at educational institutions.

A second opportunity is in extending the course to a longer period, where students may also manage and follow the actual real-time campaign in partnership with the case organizations. Such extension would enhance dynamism and excitement of real-time results to the process and may even further enhance student commitments to their assigned projects. However, such opportunities are limited by regulations and rules. Specifically, as is the case of UiA in Norway, it is either impossible or outright prohibited for a publicly funded education institution to engage in fundraising activities on behalf of external commercial organizations. Such practice might be possible, however, in privately owned universities and institutions.

Nevertheless, when including real-time campaigning in the course programme, it is here recommended that actual grading of students would not be based on campaign financial results, but rather on whether they have created and managed a campaign in line with guidance provided during the course. This is because students should be evaluated on their learning outcomes rather than on actual business performance, which is often influenced by a plethora of external variables outside the students' control. Furthermore, this is especially true when the very concept the students have been working with was externally provided.

Alternatively, business education has seen a growth in the usage of business simulations as one form of active learning (Clarke 2009; Levant et al. 2016). Accordingly, brought into the crowdfunding context, campaign simulation software may be developed in accordance with best practice recommendations. Such simulations will ensure satisfactory campaign outcomes in a controlled environment, when students develop and manage a campaign in accordance with the teachings. Such tools may also allow for interventions throughout the campaign process simulating real-time challenges that can be addressed in class in a new module on 'trouble shooting' common problems during the campaign. In such cases, students' grading may be linked to campaign outcomes. However, a challenge here remains when using real-life cases, as simulations may not be able to predict and include all possible relevant conditions specific to such cases that may emerge from a variety of sectors, involving novel concepts, as well as addressing a wide range of potential segments.

A different development opportunity lies in extending the course's reach. Here an opportunity may exist in converting the existing academic course into a format better suited for executive education rather than full time degree programme students. Many of the potential entrepreneurs, artists, and social activists that may benefit from training in crowdfunding are mostly busy with their ventures and projects and are not available for a series of full-day sessions. Furthermore, such audience may be more concerned with practical skill development rather than with theoretical aspects or degree awarding credits. At the same time, many of those who require these skills may also be operating under severe resource constraints that may limit their ability to invest in training. Hence, a concise, practice-oriented, and affordable adult education programme may be created based on the existing programme, while serving practitioners. Furthermore, such training may also be co-financed by dedicated governmental support agencies, incubator managers, as well industry associations.

Conclusion

While many may have heard the term 'crowdfunding', much confusion and misunderstanding about its meaning and implications abound. In order to ensure a healthy and ethical development of the crowdfunding industry, it may be important to support better informed participants. This may be achieved by the offering of crowdfunding dedicated education programmes. A need for such programmes is also based on the growing demand for equipping students with knowledge and skills that may prove useful in their future employment in an ever more digitized age, while at the same time help them understand and develop group-work, flexible problem solving, and digital skills that may be applied in a variety of different contexts. Such objectives were accommodated in the presentation of a concrete course programme based on the Crowdfunding Lab format developed at UiA in Norway. For this purpose, the course objectives, content, pedagogy, and assessment procedures have been highlighted, while presenting how they align into a coherent educational effort.

In terms of implications for practice, the illustrative case presented in detail throughout this chapter may help inform similar course design and development efforts in other higher education institutions. Furthermore, some of the opportunities for further development represent an invitation for educators to both extend and refine a wider set of tools and educational formats for crowdfunding training. These include the development of a dedicated textbook and simulation exercises, as well as the extension of course content to incorporate real-time campaigning where regulations allow for that. In addition, an opportunity towards converting existing academic course format into an adult or executive education format has been outlined and may answer a market gap currently uncovered by platforms, educational institutions, or public agencies.

Finally, in terms of implications for research, in the absence of earlier research on crowdfunding education, opportunities abound. One line of research may seek to measure course impact on participants in terms of their sense of self-efficacy as well as attitudes towards crowdfunding following such educational experience. Furthermore, studies may examine whether participants in crowdfunding education programmes are more likely to engage in either fundraising activities using crowdfunding or in contributing financially to crowdfunding campaigns than individuals who did not participate in such programmes. A different measurement of impact may relate to performance of campaigns run by individuals who have taken crowdfunding training versus campaigners who did not take such training.

An additional research direction may seek to evaluate the effectiveness of various course components in achieving its stated objectives. Here, the relative importance and impact of course materials (whether textbooks, lecture slides, or reading lists), student consultancy project experiences, actual campaign material development, and the introduction to industry stakeholders (e.g. platform representatives, successful campaigners), each may carry different influence that may align with course objectives. Such insights will be helpful for further course development and fine-tuning.

Lastly, research identifying the necessary adjustments to course content, pedagogy, and assessment tools in different contexts, as defined by their cultural, institutional, sectoral, and economic development conditions may also be helpful for effective educational experiences. Here, it is important to acknowledge that contextual conditions may vary significantly from one context to another and may require adjustments to ensure a better fit to local conditions, and hence improve students' ability to relate and engage in the course.

References

Ajzen, I. (1991). The Theory of Planned Behavior. *Organizational Behavior and Human Decision Process, 50*(2), 179–211.

Alois, J. D. (2018). UiA: Norwegian University Launches Master's Elective Crowdfunding Lab Course. Retrieved January 29, 2020, from https://www.crowdfundinsider.com/2018/10/139881-uia-norwegian-university-launches-masters-elective-crowdfunding-lab-course/.

Bandura, A. (1986). The Explanatory and Predictive Scope of Self-Efficacy Theory. *Journal of Social and Clinical Psychology, 4*(3), 359–373.

Bennett, R. (2006). Business Lecturers' Perceptions of the Nature of Entrepreneurship. *International Journal of Entrepreneurial Behavior & Research, 12*(3), 165–188.

Biggs, J. (1996). Enhancing Teaching Through Constructive Alignment. *Higher Education, 32*(3), 347–364.

Boeuf, B., Darveau, J., & Legoux, R. (2014). Financing Creativity: Crowdfunding as a New Approach for Theatre Projects. *International Journal of Arts Management, 16*(3), 33–48.

Bonwell, C., & Eison, J. (1991). *Active Learning: Creating Excitement in the Classroom (ASHE-ERIC Higher Education Report No 1)*. Washington, DC: George Washington University.

Brocato, E. D., White, N. J., Bartkus, K., et al. (2015). Social Media and Marketing Education: A Review of Current Practices in Curriculum Development. *Journal of Marketing Education, 37*(2), 76–87.

Bruton, G., Khavul, S., Siegel, D., et al. (2015). New Financial Alternatives in Seeding Entrepreneurship: Microfinance, Crowdfunding, and Peer-to-Peer Innovations. *Entrepreneurship Theory and Practice, 39*(1), 9–26.

Business.gov.au. (2019). How to Crowdfund Your Business. Australian Government. Retrieved from https://www.business.gov.au/Finance/Seeking-finance/How-to-crowdfund-your-business.

Chaney, D. (2019). A Principal–Agent Perspective on Consumer Co-production: Crowdfunding and the Redefinition of Consumer Power. *Technological Forecasting and Social Change, 141*, 74–84.

Clarke, E. (2009). Learning Outcomes from Business Simulation Exercises: Challenges for the Implementation of Learning Technologies. *Education + Training, 51*(5/6), 448–459.

Consumer.ftc.gov. (2019). Understanding Crowdfunding. US Federal Trade Commission. Retrieved from https://www.consumer.ftc.gov/articles/understanding-crowdfunding.

Crittenden, V. L., & Crittenden, W. F. (2006). The Undergraduate Capstone Marketing Course: Objectives, Content, and Pedagogy. *Journal for Advancement of Marketing Education, 8*, 79–88.

De Buysere, K., Gajda, O., Kleverlaan, R., et al. (2012). A Framework for European Crowdfunding. Retrieved from https://www.fundraisingschool.it/wp-content/uploads/2013/02/European-Crowdfunding-Framework-Oct-2012.pdf.

De Faoite, D., Henry, C., Johnston, K., et al. (2003). Education and Training for Entrepreneurs: A Consideration of Initiatives in Ireland and The Netherlands. *Education + Training, 45*(8/9), 430–438.

De Voldere, I., & Zeqo, K. (2017). *Crowdfunding: Reshaping the Crowd's Engagement in Culture*. Brussels: European Commission.

Denson, N., Loveday, T., & Dalton, H. (2010). Student Evaluation of Courses: What Predicts Satisfaction? *Higher Education Research & Development, 29*(4), 339–356.

European Commission. (n.d.). *Crowdfunding Explained*. Brussels: European Commission. Retrieved from https://ec.europa.eu/growth/tools-databases/crowdfunding-guide/what-is/explained_en.

Fox, J., Bartholomae, S., & Lee, J. (2005). Building the Case for Financial Education. *Journal of Consumer Affairs, 39*(1), 195–214.

Graeff, T. R. (1998). Writing Behavioral Learning Objectives for Marketing Courses: Meeting the Challenge of AACSB Outcomes Assessment. *Marketing Education Review, 8*(1), 13–25.

Griffin, P., & Care, E. (2014). *Assessment and Teaching of 21st Century Skills: Methods and Approach*. Dordrecht: Springer.

Haddad, C., & Hornuf, L. (2019). The Emergence of the Global Fintech Market: Economic and Technological Determinants. *Small Business Economics, 53*(1), 81–105.

Harrigan, P., & Hulbert, B. (2011). How Can Marketing Academics Serve Marketing Practice? The New Marketing DNA as a Model for Marketing Education. *Journal of Marketing Education, 33*(3), 253–272.

Heriot, K. C., Cook, R., Jones, R. C., et al. (2008). The Use of Student Consulting Projects as an Active Learning Pedagogy: A Case Study in a Production/Operations Management Course. *Decision Sciences Journal of Innovative Education, 6*(2), 463–481.

Innovation Norway. (n.d.). *Innovation Norway* [Online]. Oslo: Innovation Norway. Retrieved January 30, 2020, from https://www.innovasjonnorge.no/en/start-page/.

Jegelevičiūtė, S., & Valančienė, L. (2015). Comparative Analysis of the Ways Crowdfunding Is Promoted. *Procedia – Social and Behavioral Sciences, 213*, 268–274.

Levant, Y., Coulmont, M., & Sandu, R. (2016). Business Simulation as an Active Learning Activity for Developing Soft Skills. *Accounting Education, 25*(4), 368–395.

Michel, N., Cater Iii, J. J., & Varela, O. (2009). Active Versus Passive Teaching Styles: An Empirical Study of Student Learning Outcomes. *Human Resource Development Quarterly, 20*(4), 397–418.

Mwasalwiba, E. S. (2010). Entrepreneurship Education: A Review of Its Objectives, Teaching Methods, and Impact Indicators. *Education + Training, 52*(1), 20–47.

Piperopoulos, P., & Dimov, D. (2015). Burst Bubbles or Build Steam? Entrepreneurship Education, Entrepreneurial Self-Efficacy, and Entrepreneurial Intentions. *Journal of Small Business Management, 53*(4), 970–985.

Shneor, R., & Munim, Z. H. (2019). Reward Crowdfunding Contribution as Planned Behaviour: An Extended Framework. *Journal of Business Research, 103*, 56–70.

Simpson, T. (2013). *The Relevance of Higher Education: Exploring a Contested Notion*. Plymouth: Lexington Books.

Thomas, S., & Busby, S. (2003). Do Industry Collaborative Projects Enhance Students' Learning? *Education + Training, 45*(4), 226–235.

Wingfield, S. S., & Black, G. S. (2005). Active Versus Passive Course Designs: The Impact on Student Outcomes. *Journal of Education for Business, 81*(2), 119–123.

21

The Future of Crowdfunding Research and Practice

Rotem Shneor, Bjørn-Tore Flåten, and Liang Zhao

Introduction

As fifteen years of online crowdfunding practice, as well as a decade of crowdfunding research, draw to a close, it is high time for reflection on its future. Though thousands of platforms report operations in some 170 countries and jurisdictions (Ziegler et al. 2020), the online manifestations of crowdfunding remain relatively new phenomena. When viewed through the industry life cycle lens (Peltoniemi 2011), most national markets may be characterized as positioned at the introduction stage with few players and a lack of public awareness. However, some of the forerunners may already be positioned at the growth stage, characterized by a growing number of players as well as increasing public awareness and use. For the time being, even slowing markets enjoy strong double-digit growth and/or multibillion dollar volumes, while experiencing course adjustments rather than maturation thanks to regulatory amendments and further technological development (Ziegler et al. 2020).

R. Shneor (✉) • B.-T. Flåten • L. Zhao
School of Business and Law, University of Agder, Kristiansand, Norway
e-mail: rotem.shneor@uia.no; bjorn-tore.flaten@uia.no; liang.zhao@uia.no

R. Shneor et al. (eds.), *Advances in Crowdfunding*,
https://doi.org/10.1007/978-3-030-46309-0_21

As the crowdfunding industry evolves from an introductory stage into a growth stage, concerns are gradually shifting from proof of concept and early adoption into responsible growth, scalability, and competition. Such growth may bring new dilemmas, temptations, and opportunities that must be considered carefully by all industry stakeholders.

In this chapter, we discuss eight dilemmas and trends we expect to influence all stakeholders of the crowdfunding industry in the near future. Such discussion of practical aspects will be followed by suggestions of opportunities for future research examining related questions. Such an approach ensures research relevance in terms of both addressing issues of real concern and outlining solutions for related problems and dilemmas.

Idealism vs. Pragmatism

The first dilemma is ideological in nature and may reflect a tension between idealist objectives and pragmatist considerations. Many platforms are expected to face growing pressures regarding converting from grassroots ideologies propagating the democratization of finance and fairer re-allocation of resources in society through a crowd economy (Bruntje and Gajda 2016), towards more corporate IT and financial organizations providing professional financial intermediation services. Simply put, platform management must strike a balance between hyper-professionalism that may lead to a regression to old habits of traditional financial institutions, and hyper-idealism that may be marked by amateurism unlikely to survive intensifying competition and deep pocket investment interventions by powerful commercial entities.

In this respect, crowdfunding platforms may serve as fascinating playgrounds for developing new models of capitalism. Such models may facilitate the creation of free enterprise and capital accumulation for all while providing individuals with opportunities to reduce social inequalities and overcome certain discrimination patterns (Greenberg 2019). Here, more ventures can be established and value-creating projects executed. At the same time, more people can reap benefits from financially supporting such activities in terms of healthy interests paid on the money they have lent out, or as dividends and other income streams from equity holdings in a portfolio of start-ups (some of which are likely to succeed in the long term).

Accordingly, platform growth strategies are likely to do best when maximizing the original social objectives that brought them to fame in the first place and professionalizing their operations. Here, platform management has opportunities to create more responsible and sustainable versions of professionalism. Such efforts may imply selectively adopting best practice from traditional financial institutions and large IT companies while shedding bad practices that have led to economic crises (e.g. corporate greed, corruption), as well as information crises (e.g. fake news, violation of privacy).

Opportunities for Research

In order to better understand this dilemma and its implications, researchers are encouraged to capture platform management decision processes and the considerations that influence their decision making. Such work may reflect the extent to which ideology vs. pragmatism influences decisions, as well as the creative solutions emerging from such tensions. Finally, different configurations of relative weights assigned to different considerations, as well as the implications of the different solutions implemented, may be correlated with platform performance indicators. This will allow tracking of platform growth trajectories, as well as their long-term survivability.

Tight vs. Loose Collaboration with Traditional Financial Institutions

Closely linked to the above ideological dilemma is the strategic dilemma between tighter versus looser collaborations with traditional financial institutions. While still representing relatively small volumes and only a small fraction of the financial industry (Wales 2017), recent regulatory amendments, fast growth in the industry, and increasing public interest have attracted the attention of traditional financial institutions. For the time being, crowdfunding is far from threatening traditional finance; however, some claim that seeds of a looming threat are present (Hollas 2013). It remains to be seen whether FinTech in general, and crowdfunding in particular, may lead to similar dramatic industry reconfigurations triggered by digitalization, like those evident in the retail, entertainment, and travel industries. Nevertheless, the dynamic of disintermediation followed by reintermediation (Chircu and Kauffman 1999; Sen and King 2003) via online platforms, which often offer better terms for users, may not escape the financial industry as well.

Hence, the prevailing approach suggests that crowdfunding platforms, as part of FinTech firms, may both complement existing financing channels and fill underserved segments from which traditional institutions have either withdrawn or deemed less profitable (Haddad and Hornuf 2019). Such a non-rivalrous view opens opportunities for collaboration rather than competition between traditional and new players. Here, evidence suggests that a substantial part of what is labelled as crowdfunding actually comes from traditional financial institutions, and accounts for as much as half of recorded volumes (Ziegler et al. 2020). Furthermore, the same study shows that close to 20% of global platforms overseeing business crowd-financing (e.g. P2P business lending, balance sheet business lending, equity crowdfunding, and debt-based securities) are partially or fully owned by traditional financial institutions (ibid.). Other dominant forms of collaboration such as referral agreements and joint marketing are reported by half of all global platforms across crowdfunding models (ibid.).

Such realities reflect that the crowdfunding industry may enjoy the benefits of collaboration with traditional financial institutions in terms of enhanced legitimacy, trust-facilitation, and timely injection of badly needed funding for their operations. However, at the same time, such relations may imply increasing dependency on, as well as a heavy influence by, traditional institutions. Such interventions may be benevolent at times but may also carry risks. One risk is that traditional institutions view these collaborations as low tuition fees for them to be learning at the expense of new players' mistakes, while building own platforms in parallel which will compete with them in the future. Another risk may be that such institutions devote resources to strategically neutralize new prospective competitors by limiting industry growth from within.

Regardless of the level of benevolence behind collaborative relations, greater influence by traditional institutions is likely to be accompanied by limitations of the dynamism that characterize nimble, young, and ambitious start-ups, as well as ideological compromises that may restrain access to finance and related investment opportunities. Here, again, platform management is tasked with harvesting the good from such collaborations (e.g. public legitimacy, trust-facilitation, integration of complementary banking and payment solutions) while limiting the negative aspects of such collaborations (e.g. excessive operational limitations, restriction of innovation, risk aversion, and abuse of information for new forms of discrimination).

Opportunities for Research

This reality serves as fertile ground for new research on the extent to which crowdfunding platforms cooperate and/or compete with traditional financial institutions. It also raises questions about the influences that different collaborative modes may have on platform operations, innovation, performance, growth, and long-term survivability. In this spirit, researchers are encouraged to examine how such collaborations manifest themselves organizationally and practically, and how they facilitate information flows, as well as decision-making processes. Finally, it is interesting to explore the motivations and drivers behind such collaborative arrangements and measure the extent to which such motivations are satisfied through actual collaborative activities. These suggestions echo earlier calls for research on relations between traditional finance and crowdfunding platforms (e.g. Gomber et al. 2017; Shneor and Maehle 2020).

Financial vs. Socio-Economic Measures of Value Creation

Directly emerging from the previous dilemmas are the considerations of how to measure performance in the crowdfunding industry context. The closer the industry grows to the financial industry, the more it uses pure financial indicators to evaluate its performance and development. While these may provide important indicators about firm health, when compared to the ideological backbone that has shaped its emergence, questions arise as to whether the industry should not be evaluated on delivering socio-economic benefits as well. Here, for example, a purely financial measure will be how much money was raised, but a socio-economic measure would be how much money was raised by and for different social groups with differing financial capacities (e.g. high income vs. low income, banked vs. underbanked) and in different locations (served or underserved by existing financial institutions, urban vs. rural).

Such distinctions can be viewed through the difference between efficient and effective fundraising. While efficient implies maximum productivity with minimum waste, effective implies success in producing a desired result. When brought into the context of crowdfunding, efficient may relate to maximum funding raised in the cheapest and quickest way possible. However, effective crowdfunding may relate to raising enough funds from people who need to enter and diversify their investments, while supporting value creation activities by people who can best deliver them. In this respect, a million dollars can be raised quickly and at minimum cost from a single rich investor that invests in line with traditional investment considerations, and hence is efficient. However, the same amount can be raised more effectively from multiple less well-off small contributors that can use the opportunity to build their capital base while funding projects by capable people who may otherwise face discrimination in traditional channels, or be underestimated by experts specializing in certain industries and product categories.

Accordingly, to convey their value, platforms should indeed use financial performance indicators such as turnover, return on investment, default rates, and costs per successful campaign. However, such indicators need to come in addition to other measures of their value-creation capacities in terms of number of new ventures established, number of workplaces created, number of women and minorities entering the workforce or starting up businesses, access to finance to underserved markets provided, levels of returns on investment to retail investors vs. those gained via other investment products, and contributions to regional development where resources are more limited, to name a few.

Opportunities for Research

Interestingly, thus far most research has focused on crowdfunding performance in terms of campaign success rates (i.e. reaching minimum goal sum) and total amounts raised (Kaartemo 2017; Shneor and Vik 2020) mostly at the campaign rather than the platform level. Accordingly, future research is needed in assessing the performance of platforms, as well as the drivers of such performance, in terms of both financial and socio-economic outcomes and value creation. In addition, such studies should examine whether delivery of socio-economic value is positively associated with financial performance, or whether one comes at the expense of the other within certain ranges of scale and scope of activities.

Quantity vs. Quality as Strategic Focus

An additional dilemma intertwined with those mentioned above relates to platform strategic focus on quantity versus quality of the crowdfunding campaigns it approves for publication. Bootstrapped and resource-constrained platforms may often be tempted to approve more campaigns, aiming to raise more funds, rather than filter them based on strict quality measures. Such compromises may be necessary to an extent, but if employed excessively can lead to the tarnishing of platform image at best, and of the industry image at worst. As a result, what seems like a good strategy to get volumes going at early stages may turn into long-term reputational damage that will make it more difficult to recruit future fundraisers and backers.

A study of Canadian crowdfunding platforms including both investment and non-investment models (Cumming et al. 2019) found that platform due diligence efforts were associated with a higher percentage of successful campaigns, more fund contributors, and larger amounts of capital raised on platforms. A study by Wessel et al. (2017) based on reward crowdfunding on Kickstarter showed that increasing platform openness for third-party offerings, by relaxing platform pre-screening procedures, can destabilize a platform's ecosystem, leading to lower success rates, lower-quality information provided by campaigners, and greater uncertainty for backers. While platform income may increase in the short term, its long-term performance remains uncertain.

Furthermore, Cumming et al. (2019) found that due diligence was associated with legislation requirement, platform size, and type or complexity of crowdfunding campaigns. Such findings are also supported on a global basis (Ziegler et al. 2020), showing that onboarding rates (i.e. campaign approvals for publication by platforms) are significantly lower in investment models which are characterized by higher-legal compliance requirements and involve higher volumes on average than in non-investment models which face lighter legal compliance requirements and involve lower sums of funds raised.

Opportunities for Research

Future research should comparatively examine the long-term performance of platforms with different levels of campaign screening procedures and thresholds. Such analyses should consider minimal thresholds across campaigns, in addition to quality thresholds specific to certain crowdfunding models, sectors, and industries, as well as levels of target funding goals. Furthermore, studies classifying screening procedures and strategies may help identify the relative advantages and disadvantages of each. Additionally, it could be interesting to explore the extent to which external requirements such as national legislation and industry codes of conduct impact screening efforts, and to what extent these are driven by quality demands from the crowd.

Domestic vs. International Growth

As the number of platforms launching their operations continues to grow, so does the competition in the industry. In parallel, regulatory compliance, technological developments, and customer service costs continue to increase while quickly devouring the limited resource base of most young crowdfunding platforms. Under such conditions, platforms are pressured to achieve scale quickly for survival. And while some countries may be large enough for scaling based on domestic early adopters (e.g. the US, China, Japan, Germany, the UK), others may not have the opportunity for quick domestic growth and may need to rely on early international expansion. Such a strategy of internationalization is often referred to as the born global approach (for a recent detailed review see Øyna and Alon 2018), and when considering Internet-based companies it is referred to as Internet-enabled internationalization (Shneor and Flåten 2008), which may use online communities as drivers of international expansion (Shneor 2012).

Indeed, recent research by Ziegler et al. (2020) shows that substantial volumes of crowdfunding activities occur across borders. This study identifies P2P consumer lending as the most internationalized model with close to 50% of transactions associated with both inflows and outflows occurring across borders. This is followed by balance sheet business lending where a third of outflow volumes and a fifth of inflow volumes involve cross-border transactions. Invoice trading exhibits the opposite trend, where close to a third of inflows and a quarter of outflows originate internationally. Both equity crowdfunding and P2P business lending exhibit lower levels of cross-border transactions, accounting for around 10% of outflows and inflows. In the non-investment models, a fifth of outflows in reward crowdfunding volumes and a tenth of inflows in donation crowdfunding occur across borders. Furthermore, the study shows that while some regions depend heavily on cross-border transactions (e.g. Africa), some are dependent to a considerable degree (e.g. Europe, Canada, and Latin America), and others are less dependent on them (e.g. the US, the UK, and Asia-Pacific), or less successful in attracting them (e.g. the Middle East).

These dependencies on international scope of operations are likely to increase in the future thanks to regulatory harmonization efforts such as the European Crowdfunding Service Provider regime (European Parliament 2019), which makes international expansion of investment platforms easier, as well as by increasing domestic competition from both local and international actors entering the various European national markets (Ziegler et al. 2020).

Accordingly, while some platforms may specialize in greater localization and being recognized domestically as a local champion, such a market position may only be enjoyed by few platforms in each country and may be reserved for countries with relatively large domestic markets only. However, current modes of operation suggest a standard global approach, or limited local adjustments via glocalization efforts, as the preferred strategy for most internationally active platforms (ibid.). Heavy localization investments of international platforms in certain foreign markets remain rare and are more likely to emerge in heavily regulated markets, where legal compliance forces platforms to invest in such adjustments.

Opportunities for Research

Research into the internationalization strategies adopted by crowdfunding platforms is needed for identifying relevant patterns, drivers, and barriers by model and country of destination. In particular, unique aspects associated with Internet- and online community-enabled internationalization efforts may be of concern, as they represent new channels for international growth of firms in general, and SMEs in particular. Furthermore, understanding national market preferences and dependence on international backing and investment should be analysed in terms of policies created for supporting or inhibiting it. And, finally, the differences between attracting international backers versus fundraisers should be discussed, as the two may pose a different set of requirements and validation procedures. Such calls echo earlier suggestions for future research, highlighting the international scope and scale of crowdfunding platforms (Shneor and Maehle 2020).

Crowd Wisdom vs. Crowd Madness

Proponents of crowdfunding often refer to the value-creation potential that relies on the "wisdom of the crowd" (Schwienbacher and Larralde 2012), which to be effective requires independent, diverse, and decentralized aggregate judgement (Surowiecki 2004). Such assumption builds on the notion of "collective intelligence" (Lévy 1997), where no one knows everything, everyone knows something, and since knowledge resides in wider humanity, tapping into it via online communities provides opportunities for value creation. According to Surowiecki (2004), when averaging the opinions of many diverse, independent, and decentralized people, the errors of multiple individuals will cancel each other out, and an optimal solution will be arrived at. Others suggest that the 'wisdom of crowds' is derived not from averaging solutions but from aggregating them, and that the diversity within the crowd enhances such aggregation towards efficient problem solving (Brabham 2010). Indeed, some research finds support for these assumptions, showing significant agreement between the funding decisions of crowds and experts in the cultural sector (Mollick and Nanda 2015).

However, evidence about situations best described as the "madness of the crowd" and the "tyranny of the majority" is also abundant in human experiences. The madness of the crowd refers to situations where groups of people can be collectively misguided and even illogical and delusional (Mackay 2006). Such situations are exacerbated by herding behaviours and information cascades, where later decisions are based on earlier ones made by others (Shiller 2015). These tend to create crowd bubbles in which irrational decisions are taken by otherwise rational actors (Heminway 2014). Under such conditions, a critical mass of misinformed individuals may cause a cascade of bad decisions by a herd following them.

Furthermore, the tyranny of the majority (Guinier 1995), as adopted from political science, relates to situations where decisions made by majority groups do not account for the needs of minorities, or come at the expense of and even directly hurt minority groups. Under such conditions, a threat to being locked into an existing line of thinking coming up with the same results is more likely than massive embracing of irregular, innovative, or abnormal suggestions that overthrow the existing order. After all, innovators and early adopters are, by definition, a minority in the greater public (Rogers 1958).

Such concerns may be further exacerbated by the growth of cyberbullying, where individuals may face aggressive behaviour via online channels against which they cannot easily defend themselves (Menesini and

Nocentini 2009). Underlying such behaviour are intentional harm, power imbalance, and repetition of victimization (Grigg 2010). In the context of crowdfunding, individuals may be bullied into financially contributing to a campaign or bullied should they fail to contribute to a campaign. In other cases, fundraisers may be bullied into cancelling their campaign efforts by groups and individuals with opposing ideologies and belief systems. These situations raise concern for the well-being of affected individuals.

Crowd madness, tyranny of the majority, and cyberbullying are all phenomena to which crowdfunding platforms have dedicated limited attention thus far, outside of regulatory compliance issues that may address them. While responsibility indeed lies with regulators as well as the public, crowdfunding platforms should also develop relevant policies and practices to mitigate and address such problems when they arise. Though most platforms may be reluctant to adopt policing responsibilities of their crowds, such actions may be necessary for ensuring safe communications and transactions through their system, the well-being of their users, and by extension, the long-term well-being of the platform and the community as a whole.

Opportunities for Research

Researchers are encouraged to examine the types of harmful crowd dynamics, their extent, and the factors triggering them. In parallel, research should also investigate the strategies used by platforms and regulators to mitigate harmful dynamics in the crowdfunding market. Such work should identify the various strategies used to address the different manifestations of harmful dynamics and their relative effectiveness. Furthermore, comparative analyses of related platform policies and their associations with customer satisfaction, safety, campaign performance, and platform performance and reputation may highlight the benefits of various approaches to addressing these concerns.

Technology vs. Community Innovation

As the industry grows, competition within it intensifies, leading crowdfunding platforms to invest in innovations that may enhance the attractiveness of their services and help them achieve the scale required for survival and growth. Such efforts translate into research and development (R&D) efforts, where some are directed towards process efficiency, as in streamlining and automation of processes, and other efforts are dedicated to the improvement of service quality and customer experience with related support tools.

The recent Cambridge Centre for Alternative Finance (CCAF) global industry report (Ziegler et al. 2020) presents interesting findings in this respect concerning innovation investments of platforms in 2018. First, crowdlending platforms' R&D efforts are mostly directed towards customer verification and streamlining of processes; however, while P2P lending platforms also invest in payment systems, balance sheet lending platforms invest the most in artificial intelligence solutions. This difference can be explained by the fact that balance sheet platforms don't only intermediate but also manage the investments on behalf of investors, which are mostly institutional and involve higher sums and more frequent transactions. Interestingly, platforms offering equity model services present the most diversified R&D investments. Such efforts mostly follow R&D patterns of P2P crowdlending platforms, but unlike the latter they invest more in communications and social media promotional support tools, as well as customer relationship management. Non-investment platforms are those investing most of their R&D efforts in communications and social media promotional tools, with additional efforts towards process streamlining, customer verification, and payment solutions.

This depiction of reality may cause both comfort and distress. Achieving operational efficiencies may be critical for the viability and profitability of platforms, and by extension their survival. A focus on extensive automation and website functionalities may risk the neglect of the "community" in crowdfunding communities. In such a scenario, platforms may become a new form of e-commerce website, rather than a space for social networking, engagement, co-creation, and mutual support around projects of common interest. While platforms are unlikely to compete with or replace existing popular social and professional networking sites (e.g. Facebook, Instagram, LinkedIn), they may serve as spaces for the formation of supportive virtual communities with common interests and objectives. Neutralizing this dimension of platform roles may raise a question about their purpose and reason to exist. If platforms do not invest in developing the community and interactions within it, their campaign promotional software and external payment systems can be easily integrated into existing social networking sites, e-commerce websites, or e-finance service providers with a wider range of products (e.g. e-banking, mobile banking).

Evidence of such developments already exists. In China, for example, crowdfunding platforms are embedded and intertwined within the popular social media platforms (e.g. Tencent, WeChat, Weibo), as well as e-commerce websites (e.g. JD, Alibaba), which also serve payment processing functionalities (Huang et al. 2018). Elsewhere, Facebook has entered the donation crowdfunding market, by enabling users to launch money collections for causes they are passionate about (Campbell 2018). These developments emerge parallel to platforms either launched or owned by banks such as BNP Paribas in Belgium and France, Commerzbank in Germany, Den Norske Bank in Norway, and Triodos Bank in the UK, to name a few, including both investment and non-investment platforms.

Such developments bring the crowdfunding industry ever closer to a junction where it needs to decide what its actors want to be. Whether they will be technology providers that can be plugged into other systems as extended service channels, or a hub providing a community of users with space and services to interact and support each other, remains to be seen. Thus far, our understanding of crowdfunding assumed the criticality of community aspects in crowdfunding practice (Schwienbacher and Larralde 2012; Shneor and Flåten 2015); however, the extent to which a crowdfunding platform should be the host and facilitator of these community interactions is uncertain and will be some of the most important strategic decision platforms will have to make in the future.

Opportunities for Research

Future research should explore the roles and services offered by crowdfunding platforms, as new classifications accounting for their services, rather than types of fundraising they facilitate, will enable a better understanding of platform operations and performance. Furthermore, research should investigate the extent to which platform services and features meet user needs, be they fundraisers or backers. Furthermore, it should examine whether platforms that better meet user needs also perform better on different measures of performance. Alternatively, research could examine the efficiency and effectiveness of different organizational models of crowdfunding from independent platforms to those integrated to varying degrees with existing social media applications, and e-commerce and e-finance service providers.

Blissful Education vs. Blissful Ignorance

While many may have heard the term 'crowdfunding', it often remains poorly understood by the larger public. Due to its relative novelty, most people don't understand the complexity of its associated models and the differences between them, as well as the benefits and risks associated with each model. Accordingly, educating the public (De Buysere et al. 2012) to raise awareness and increase the development of relevant skills (De Voldere and Zeqo 2017) is becoming an important concern for healthy and responsible development of the industry.

Current educational efforts have included information provided by platforms and industry association training, which may be biased by their commercial interests. Moreover, and regardless of bias, while industry players may be motivated to develop educational materials for supporting their own business development, such efforts represent an additional burden on their limited resource base as they are likely to be young ventures. Indeed, the recent CCAF global industry report (Ziegler et al. 2020) identified e-learning support tools as the category of R&D efforts where the lowest number of platforms indicated making such investments.

Other sources of public information include that provided on some government websites, journalistic reports, and consultant reviews. Very few formal educational institutions have developed crowdfunding-specific training and education, while those that have done so report interest in such initiatives from a multitude of stakeholders.

When developing crowdfunding courses, educators are required to strike a balance between the required provision of new knowledge and the avoidance of setting narrow interpretations and boundaries too quickly and too soon. In this respect, crowdfunding represents a moving target, which evolves quickly and requires frequent refreshing of educational materials based on dynamic market developments. Here, while some fundamentals remain stable, other aspects such as business models, strategies, technologies, and regulation continuously evolve, and carry great influence on the way crowdfunding is and should be practised.

Beyond inclusion of actual developments in educational programmes, one should also consider whether, in principle, educators should at all intervene, albeit indirectly, in industry development through educational programmes. Education programmes often tend to be descriptive and prescriptive, while an evolving industry may require a more critical and open-ended presentation of facts to avoid constraining potential developments before they occur. Proponents of such a view may argue that we first need to learn more before we teach something that is still under development. However, critiques of such views counter-argue that education enables rather than constrains, and that it is through a better understanding of current possibilities, challenges, and dilemmas that one may contribute to better informed and responsible evolution of the industry.

Opportunities for Research

Since earlier research on crowdfunding education is virtually non-existent, this represents an open field with abundant opportunities for research. Some of which may include the comparison of the effects of various formats and sources of educational materials and experiences and their impact on the performance of fundraisers, as well as financial contribution behaviour of backers. Moreover, researchers may study the importance and effect of various learning units incorporated into educational programmes and measure their respective effects on cognition of participants in terms of self-efficacy, attitude, intentions, and actual behaviour. In this context, it may be valuable to consider to what extent balanced education enhances or inhibits crowdfunding practice, once participants are exposed to a more balanced review of crowdfunding's benefits and risks, as well as efforts required for successful crowdfunding. Finally, future research may explore how education on crowdfunding can potentially enhance group-work, digitalization, and twenty-first-century skills among the learners. Higher education is in dire need of finding better ways of educating students for the future of work. Research on crowdfunding education may shed important light on how this can be facilitated and applied in practice.

Conclusions

The current chapter highlighted key dilemmas and challenges that are likely to influence and shape future development and practice within the crowdfunding industry. Overall, we conclude that crowdfunding is a solution to real and substantial market gaps in access to—and distribution of—finance. However, despite its dramatic growth in recent years, we are witnessing an industry that is just scratching the surface of its real potential. This potential can be unlocked by a combination of adequate regulation, proper and balanced public education, and ethical and responsible practice by the industry's players.

The future of crowdfunding depends on the decisions that will be taken by all stakeholders involved. All of whom should resist regression to the partially dysfunctional but familiar past, and instead engage in developing a better future that is based on co-creation of value, empowerment of individuals, and the democratization of access and use of finance. This should be done by allowing a healthy degree of informed experimentation and careful risk-taking. The future will show whether and to what extent crowdfunding will deliver on these promises.

For the time being, we wish you Happy and Successful Crowdfunding!

Thank you for reading this book.

References

Brabham, D. C. (2010). Moving the Crowd at Threadless. *Information, Communication & Society, 13*(8), 1122–1145.

Bruntje, D., & Gajda, O. (2016). *Crowdfunding in Europe: State of the Art in Theory and Practice*. London: Springer International Publishing.

Campbell, J. (2018). Facebook's Changing the Nonprofit Crowdfunding Game Again: What Nonprofits Need To Know. *Social Media Today* [Online]. Retrieved February 7, 2020, from https://www.socialmediatoday.com/news/facebooks-changing-the-nonprofit-crowdfunding-game-again-what-non-profits/522479/.

Chircu, A. M., & Kauffman, R. J. (1999). Strategies for Internet Middlemen in the Intermediation/Disintermediation/Reintermediation Cycle. *Electronic Markets, 9*(1–2), 109–117.

Cumming, D. J., Johan, S. A., & Zhang, Y. (2019). The Role of Due Diligence in Crowdfunding Platforms. *Journal of Banking & Finance, 108*, 105661.

De Buysere, K., Gajda, O., Kleverlaan, R., et al. (2012). A Framework for European Crowdfunding. Retrieved from https://www.fundraisingschool.it/wp-content/uploads/2013/02/European-Crowdfunding-Framework-Oct-2012.pdf.

De Voldere, I., & Zeqo, K. (2017). *Crowdfunding: Reshaping the Crowd's Engagement in Culture*. Brussels: European Commission.

European Parliament. (2019). European Crowdfunding Service Providers (ECSP) for Business Brussels: European Parliament. Retrieved from https://oeil.secure.europarl.europa.eu/oeil/popups/ficheprocedure.do?lang=en&reference=2018/0048(COD).

Gomber, P., Koch, J.-A., & Siering, M. (2017). Digital Finance and FinTech: Current Research and Future Research Directions. *Journal of Business Economics, 87*(5), 537–580.

Greenberg, J. (2019). Inequality and Crowdfunding. In H. Landström, A. Parhankangas, & C. Mason (Eds.), *Handbook of Research on Crowdfunding*. Cheltenham: Edward Elgar.

Grigg, D. W. (2010). Cyber-Aggression: Definition and Concept of Cyberbullying. *Australian Journal of Guidance and Counselling, 20*(2), 143–156.

Guinier, L. (1995). *Tyranny of the Majority: Fundamental Fairness in Representative Democracy*. New York, NY: The Free Press.

Haddad, C., & Hornuf, L. (2019). The Emergence of the Global Fintech Market: Economic and Technological Determinants. *Small Business Economics, 53*(1), 81–105.

Heminway, J. M. (2014). Investor and Market Protection in the Crowdfunding Era: Disclosing to and for the 'Crowd'. *Vermont Law Review, 38*, 827–847.

Hollas, J. (2013). Is Crowdfunding Now a Threat to Traditional Finance? *Corporate Finance Review, 18*(1), 27–31.

Huang, Z., Chiu Candy, L., Mo, S., et al. (2018). The Nature of Crowdfunding in China: Initial Evidence. *Asia Pacific Journal of Innovation and Entrepreneurship, 12*(3), 300–322.

Kaartemo, V. (2017). The Elements of a Successful Crowdfunding Campaign: A Systematic Literature Review of Crowdfunding Performance. *International Review of Entrepreneurship, 15*(3), 291–318.

Lévy, P. (1997). *Collective Intelligence: Mankind's Emerging World in Cyberspace.* Helix Books.

Mackay, C. (2006). *Extraordinary Popular Delusions and the Madness of Crowds.* Petersfield, Hampshire: Harriman House.

Menesini, E., & Nocentini, A. (2009). Cyberbullying Definition and Measurement. *Zeitschrift für Psychologie/Journal of Psychology, 217*(4), 230–232.

Mollick, E., & Nanda, R. (2015). Wisdom or Madness? *Comparing Crowds with Expert Evaluation in Funding the Arts, 26*(8), 2015. Retrieved from http://papers.ssrn.com/sol3/papers.cfm?abstract_id=2443114.

Øyna, S., & Alon, I. (2018). A Review of Born Globals. *International Studies of Management & Organization, 48*(2), 157–180.

Peltoniemi, M. (2011). Reviewing Industry Life-Cycle Theory: Avenues for Future Research. *International Journal of Management Reviews, 13*(4), 349–375.

Rogers, E. M. (1958). Categorizing the Adopters of Agricultural Practices. *Rural Sociology, 23*, 347–354.

Schwienbacher, A., & Larralde, B. (2012). Crowdfunding of Small Entrepreneurial Ventures. In D. Cumming (Ed.), *The Oxford Handbook of Entrepreneurial Finance.* New York, NY: Oxford University Press.

Sen, R., & King, R. C. (2003). Revisit the Debate on Intermediation, Disintermediation and Reintermediation Due to E-Commerce. *Electronic Markets, 13*(2), 153–162.

Shiller, R. J. (2015). *Irrational Exuberance: Revised and Expanded* (3rd ed.). Princeton, NJ: Princeton University Press.

Shneor, R. (2012). Born Global Firms, Internet, and New Forms of Internationalization. In M. Gabrielsson & V. H. Kirpalani (Eds.), *Handbook of Research on Born Globals*. Cheltenham: Edward Elgar.

Shneor, R., & Flåten, B.-T. (2008). The Internet-Enabled Internationalization Process: A Focus on Stages and Sequences. *Journal of e-Business, 8*(1 & 2), 45–52.

Shneor, R., & Flåten, B.-T. (2015). Opportunities for Entrepreneurial Development and Growth Through Online Communities, Collaboration, and Value Creating and Co-Creating Activities. In H. R. Kaufmann & S. M. R. Shams (Eds.), *Entrepreneurial Challenges in the 21st Century*. Basingstoke: Palgrave Macmillan.

Shneor, R., & Maehle, N. (2020). Advancing Crowdfunding Research: New Insights and Future Research Agenda. *Baltic Journal of Management, 15*(2), 141–147.

Shneor, R., & Vik, A. A. (2020). Crowdfunding Success: A Systematic Literature Review 2010–2017. *Baltic Journal of Management, 15*(2), 149–182.

Surowiecki, J. (2004). *The Wisdom of Crowds: Why the Many Are Smarter Than the Few and How Collective Wisdom Shapes Business, Economies, Societies, and Nations*. New York, NY: Doubleday Books.

Wales, K. (2017). *Peer-to-Peer Lending and Equity Crowdfunding: A Guide to the New Capital Markets for Job Creators, Investors, and Entrepreneurs*. Santa Barbara, CA: Praeger.

Wessel, M., Thies, F., & Benlian, A. (2017). Opening the Floodgates: The Implications of Increasing Platform Openness in Crowdfunding. *Journal of Information Technology, 32*(4), 344–360.

Ziegler, T., Shneor, R., Wenzlaff, K., et al. (2020). *The Global Alternative Finance Market Benchmarking Report*. Cambridge, UK: Cambridge Centre for Alternative Finance.

Index[1]

[1] Note: Page numbers followed by 'n' refer to notes.

R. Shneor et al. (eds.), *Advances in Crowdfunding*,
https://doi.org/10.1007/978-3-030-46309-0

L

M

N

The manufacturer's authorised representative in the EU is Springer Nature Customer Service Centre GmbH, Europaplatz 3, 69115 Heidelberg, Germany. If you have any concerns regarding our products, please contact ProductSafety@springernature.com

Printed and bound by CPI Group (UK) Ltd, Croydon, CR0 4YY
25/09/2026
02222887-0001